Mercedes-Benz
Technical Companion™

Technical insights on service, repair, maintenance and procedures compiled from over 45 years of *The Star*, the magazine of the Mercedes-Benz Club of America

by the staff of *The Star* and the members of the Mercedes-Benz Club of America

B | **Bentley Publishers**™ .com

Mercedes-Benz Technical Companion™

Contents

1 Lubrication and Maintenance 1

Installing new power steering fluid filter. See Chapter 1, "Servicing the W126 300SD, Part I."

2 Engine, Transmission 65

Lower timing chain run in M117 V-8 engine. See Chapter 2, "Timing Is Everything."

3 Fuel, Exhaust 123

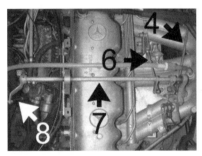

280SL throttle linkage. See Chapter 3, "How to Adjust Mechanical Fuel-Injection Systems for Maximum Power."

4 Electrical System 175

W210 E-Class headlight assembly. See Chapter 4, "Light Fantastic."

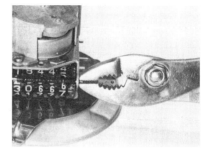

Restoring crimp on secondary shaft of odometer. See Chapter 5, "Repairing a Stalled Odometer."

Installing Bilstein lower mount into suspension arm. See Chapter 6, "Replacing W210 E-Class Front Shocks."

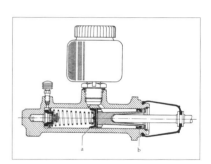

Mid-1950s brake master cylinder used with drum brakes. See Chapter 7, "Bleeding and Fluid."

Polishing with a fine cleaner to remove paint scratches. See Chapter 9, "How to Wax Your Car Like the Pros."

Bentley Publishers, a division of Robert Bentley, Inc.
1734 Massachusetts Avenue
Cambridge, MA 02138 USA
800-423-4595 / 617-547-4170

Information that makes
the difference®

BentleyPublishers™
.com

Technical Contact Information

We welcome your feedback. Please submit corrections, updates and additions to our Mercedes-Benz technical discussion forum at:

> http://www.BentleyPublishers.com

Errata information

We will evaluate submissions and post appropriate editorial changes online as text errata or tech discussion. Appropriate errata will be incorporated with the book text in future printings. Read errata information for this book before beginning work on your vehicle. See the following web address for additional information:

> http://www.BentleyPublishers.com/errata/

This book is prepared, published and distributed by Bentley Publishers, 1734 Massachusetts Avenue, Cambridge, Massachusetts 02138. Mercedes-Benz has not reviewed and does not warrant the accuracy or completeness of the technical specifications and information described in this book.

Mercedes-Benz Technical Companion™ by the staff of *The Star* and the members of the Mercedes-Benz Club of America
© 2005 Mercedes-Benz Club of America and Robert Bentley, Inc. Bentley Publishers is a trademark of Robert Bentley, Inc.

ISBN-13 978-0-8376-1033-7
Bentley Stock No. GMCC
Mfg. code: GMCC-03-1104

Library of Congress Cataloging-in-Publication Data

Mercedes-Benz technical companion : technical insights on service, repair, maintenance, and procedures compiled from over 45 years of the Star, the magazine of the Mercedes-Benz Club of America / by the staff of the Star and the members of the Mercedes-Benz Club of America.
  p. cm.
Includes index.
ISBN 0-8376-1033-8 (pbk. : alk. paper) 1. Mercedes automobile--Maintenance and repair. I. Mercedes-Benz Club of America.
TL215.M4M55 2005
629.28'722--dc22   2005000165

Many technical drawings came from Mercedes-Benz workshop manuals; for that we thank DaimlerChrysler Classic Archives and DaimlerChrysler and its predecessors and subsidiaries Daimler-Benz, Mercedes-Benz, Mercedes-Benz of North America, and Mercedes-Benz USA.

Photos on front cover, back cover (top) and spine: Stuart Dickstein and Andreas Thomas. Vehicle courtesy of Chambers Motorcars, Boston.
Artwork on back cover: Steering wheel photo by Jim Mahaffey. Suspension drawing by Daimler-Benz AG.

The paper used in this publication is acid free and meets the requirements of the National Standard for Information Sciences-Permanence of Paper for Printed Library Materials. ∞

Manufactured in the United States of America.

Foreword

by Frank Barrett,
Editor/Publisher,
The Star, 1983–2006

Since 1956, Mercedes-Benz Club of America members have been proving the experts wrong: Mercedes-Benz owners do indeed work on their own cars. During that time *The Star*, the club's magazine, has been their primary source for do-it-yourself maintenance and repair information. This book preserves the best technical information from more than 300 past issues, making it accessible to future amateur and professional mechanics.

Although it's difficult to find either a writer who can turn a wrench or a mechanic who can turn a phrase, *The Star* has been fortunate to employ several fine examples of this rare breed. Throughout this book you'll see certain names—technical editors, technical directors, authors—again and again. Two stand out: Frank King and Stu Ritter.

Frank King served the magazine from 1977 to 1999, when he died at the age of 94. One of his earliest Mercedes-Benz memories was watching "Wild Bob" Burman race the Blitzen Benz in Seattle in 1911. As an engineer with Boeing and later Curtiss-Wright, Frank never turned a wrench professionally, but his analytic approach to problem-solving worked. His technical advice in *The Star* helped thousands of Mercedes-Benz owners, for that, in 1992 he became the first American recipient of the Silver Star Award, the highest honor that Mercedes-Benz can bestow on a club member. I still miss him, but even today he's looking over my shoulder whenever I edit a technical article.

Stu Ritter has a degree in organic chemistry, but having toiled in the oil as a Mercedes-Benz mechanic for more than 30 years, he is quite different from Frank. Running his own independent Mercedes-Benz shop in Denver until 2000, he maintained and repaired most of the exotic Mercedes-Benzes in Colorado. Because he could think and write well about Mercedes-Benz technical matters and combine his knowledge with great hands-on experience, Stu was our first choice to replace Frank as our Technical Editor in 1999.

MBCA Technical Director George Murphy deserves high praise as a volunteer technical advisor. That title gets your name listed in the magazine, so 25,000 people can call you at any time with any problem. In the face of that, how George maintains his ever-sunny disposition we'll never know. MBCA and Mercedes-Benz recognized his efforts in 2002 by presenting him with the Silver Star Award, and to thousands of members he's still the "Go-To guy."

Every writer here has his special topics and special traits. Jim Mahaffey combines a respect for the past (he's a Model A owner) with a practical knowledge of the latest automotive electronics. John Lamb's broad knowledge extends from Volkswagen through Snap-on tools. Like the cars themselves, each contributor has his own unique strengths, and we thank each one for sharing his expertise with us.

Special thanks to Art Director Ken Grasman, who has designed and produced every editorial page of *The Star* since 1985, more than 10,000 of them to date!

Many technical drawings and reference information came from Mercedes-Benz service and technical publications. For that we thank DaimlerChrysler and Mercedes-Benz USA. Thanks also to Mike Mate, whose illustrations have contributed character and clarity.

Members of the Mercedes-Benz Club of America don't necessarily work on their cars because they have to. Sure they save money, but they really do it because they like the process of servicing their car and knowing the work is done properly. Most of all, they enjoy the satisfaction of a job well done. Now, thanks to MBCA, Bentley Publishers, and the writers whose work appears here, without compensation, all that experience is available to future Mercedes-Benz do-it-yourselfers.

Onward and Upward,

Frank

Editor's Introduction

by Stuart Dickstein
Editor, Bentley Publishers

This *Mercedes-Benz Technical Companion* is a selection of insights, ideas and advice from 45 years of *The Star*, the magazine of the Mercedes-Benz Club of America. The articles, written by both experienced Mercedes-Benz technicians and do-it-yourself enthusiasts, will guide you in maintaining, repairing and preserving your Mercedes-Benz, and will help you understand what's going on under the hood. As a lifelong Mercedes-Benz devotee, I find it rewarding to ensure that technical information from *The Star* archives is accessible to both current and future Mercedes-Benz enthusiasts.

The nine chapters contain articles that span a wide range of topics, from disassembling the engine to upgrading a headlight, from fixing the climate control servo to washing and waxing the car. The appendices contain guides to model, chassis and engine numbers, as well as a description of how to use the Mercedes-Benz Star TekInfo website for service, repair and parts information on the Internet. Following the appendices is a compilation of Mercedes-Benz technical information resources.

The contributors explain and illustrate repairs, service and upgrades in great detail, with practical tips often not found in factory repair information. Each chapter concludes with an ample question and answer section culled from over 2,500 queries submitted by members regarding specific issues with their Mercedes-Benz.

Whether you use this book to repair a Mercedes-Benz yourself, or have the work done at a repair shop, you'll have a clearer idea of the procedures and will be prepared with some additional tricks and tips.

Bentley Publishers is honored to have worked closely with the Mercedes-Benz Club of America to publish this book, and to make this valuable material visible to today's Mercedes-Benz owners.

As a young child, one of my first words was "Merhades," and I have been a Mercedes-Benz enthusiast ever since. I have been a member of MBCA since 1986 and an avid reader of *The Star*. I thought it would be fantastic to have every issue available at my fingertips. Having now looked more than once at every page of the almost three hundred issues, I have come to even further appreciate the passion and hard work of *The Star* staff and the MBCA members and officers.

I would like to thank the contributors who allowed us to reprint their material, Mercedes-Benz Club of America Executive Director David Cummings, past National President Donald Leap, past *Star* Committee Chair Cecil Brewer, Jr. and Legal Counsel Thomas James. I also give a special thanks to Frank Barrett, Editor/Publisher of *The Star*, for his support and contribution toward the completion of this book.

Happy Motoring,

Please read these warnings and cautions before proceeding with maintenance, repair or modification work.

WARNING—

- Some repairs may be beyond your capability. If you lack the skills, tools and equipment, or a suitable workplace for any procedure described in this book, we suggest you leave such repairs to an authorized Mercedes-Benz dealer service department, or other qualified shop.

- Before starting any major jobs or repairs to components on which passenger safety may depend, consult your authorized Mercedes-Benz dealer about technical bulletins that may have been issued since the date of the articles. Mercedes-Benz is constantly improving its cars. Sometimes these changes, both in parts and specifications, are made applicable to earlier models.

- Do not re-use any fasteners that are worn or deformed in normal use. Many fasteners are designed to be used only once and become unreliable and may fail when used a second time. This includes, but is not limited to, nuts, bolts, washers, self-locking nuts or bolts, circlips and cotter pins. Always replace these fasteners with new parts.

- Never work under a lifted car unless it is solidly supported on stands designed for the purpose. Do not support a car on cinder blocks, hollow tiles or other props that may crumble under continuous load. Never work under a car that is supported solely by a jack. Never work under the car while the engine is running.

- If you are going to work under a car on the ground, make sure that the ground is level. Block the wheels to keep the car from rolling. Disconnect the battery negative (–) cable (ground strap) to prevent others from starting the car while you are under it.

- Wear goggles when you operate machine tools or work with battery acid. Gloves or other protective clothing should be worn whenever the job requires working with harmful substances. Always observe good workshop practices.

- Do not attempt to work on your car if you do not feel well. You increase the danger of injury to yourself and others if you are tired, upset or have taken medication or any other substance that may keep you from being fully alert.

- Avoid direct skin contact with greases, lubricants and other automotive chemicals. They can contain metals and toxic substances, many of which are absorbed directly through the skin. Before use, read the manufacturer's instructions carefully. Always wear hand and eye protection.

- Avoid breathing asbestos fibers and asbestos dust. Use an aspirator when working on brake pads. Friction materials such as brake or clutch discs contain asbestos fibers or other particles which are hazardous as dust in the air. Do not create dust by grinding, sanding, or by cleaning with compressed air. Breathing asbestos can cause serious diseases such as asbestosis or cancer, and may result in death.

- Tie long hair behind your head. Do not wear a necktie, a scarf, loose clothing, or a necklace when you work near machine tools or running engines. Finger rings should be removed so that they cannot cause electrical shorts, get caught in running machinery, or be crushed by heavy parts. If your hair, clothing, or jewelry were to get caught in the machinery, severe injury could result.

- Disconnect the battery negative (–) cable (ground strap) whenever you work on the fuel system or the electrical system. Do not smoke or work near heaters or other fire hazards. Keep an approved fire extinguisher handy.

- Never run the engine unless the work area is well ventilated. Carbon monoxide kills.

- Keep sparks, lighted matches and open flame away from the top of the battery. Car batteries produce explosive hydrogen gas. If hydrogen gas escaping from the cap vents is ignited, it will ignite gas trapped in the cells and cause the battery to explode.

- Connect and disconnect battery cables, jumper cables or a battery charger only with the ignition switched off, to prevent sparks. Do not quick-charge the battery (for boost starting) for longer than one minute, and do not allow charging voltage to exceed 16.5 volts. Wait at least 1 minute before boosting the battery a second time.

- Illuminate your work area adequately but safely. Use a portable safety light for working inside or under the car. Make sure the bulb is enclosed by a wire cage. The hot filament of an accidentally broken bulb can ignite spilled fuel or oil.

- Catch draining fuel, oil, or brake fluid in suitable containers. Do not use food or beverage containers that might mislead someone into drinking from them. Store flammable fluids away from fire hazards. Wipe up spills at once, but do not store the oily rags, which can ignite and burn spontaneously.

- The A/C system should be serviced only by trained technicians using approved refrigerant recovery and recycling equipment, and trained in related safety precautions, and familiar with regulations governing the discharging and disposal of automotive chemical refrigerants. Many air conditioning systems are filled with R-12 refrigerant, which is hazardous to the earth's atmosphere.

- Do not expose any part of the A/C system to high temperatures such as open flame. Excessive heat will increase system pressure and may cause the system to burst.

- Be extremely cautious when repairing a tire that may have been inflated using an aerosol tire inflator. Some aerosol tire inflators are highly flammable. Keep sparks, open flame or other sources of ignition away from the tire repair area. Inflate and deflate the tire at least four times before breaking the bead from the rim. Remove the tire completely from the rim before attempting any repair.

- Do not touch or disconnect any high voltage cables from the coil, distributor, or spark plugs while the engine is running or being cranked by the starter. The ignition system produces high voltages that can be fatal.

- The Mercedes-Benz Supplemental Restraint System (SRS) should be serviced only by an authorized Mercedes-Benz dealer. The SRS automatically deploys an airbag in the event of a frontal impact. The airbag is inflated by an explosive device. Handled improperly or without adequate safeguards, the system can be very dangerous.

- SRS airbags that have been activated during an accident must always be replaced. Only trained personnel should work on or replace the airbag units. Improper removal or installation of the airbag unit or other SRS components may result in inadvertent activation or may render the system useless. The Mercedes-Benz authorized dealer has the proper training, specialized test equipment and repair information to service the SRS.

(continued on next page)

Please read these warnings and cautions before proceeding with maintenance, repair or modification work.

CAUTION—

- Mercedes-Benz offers extensive warranties, especially on components of fuel delivery and emission control systems. Therefore, before deciding to repair a Mercedes-Benz that may still be covered wholly or in part by any warranties issued by Mercedes-Benz USA, LLC, consult your authorized Mercedes-Benz dealer. You may find that your authorized dealer can make the repair for free, or at minimal cost.

- Mercedes-Benz part numbers listed in this book are for identification purposes only, not for ordering. Always check with your authorized Mercedes-Benz dealer to verify part numbers and availability before beginning service work that may require new parts.

- Before starting a job, make certain that you have all the necessary tools and parts on hand. Read all the instructions thoroughly and do not attempt shortcuts. Use tools appropriate to the work and use only original Mercedes-Benz replacement parts or parts that meet Mercedes-Benz specifications. Makeshift tools, parts and procedures will not make good repairs.

- Use pneumatic and electric tools only to loosen threaded parts and fasteners. Never use these tools to tighten fasteners, especially on light alloy parts. Always use a torque wrench to tighten fasteners to the tightening torque specification listed.

- Do not pour automotive fluids onto the ground, down a drain, or into a stream, pond or lake. Consult local ordinances that govern the disposal of wastes. Be mindful of the environment and ecology. Before you drain any fluids from the engine, the transmission, the power steering system, or the brake system, find out the proper way to dispose of the fluid.

- Remove all electronic control units before exposing the car to high temperature, such as from a paint-drying booth or a heat lamp. On-board control units must never be exposed to temperature in excess of 176°F (80°C).

- Before doing any electrical welding, disconnect the battery negative (–) cable (ground strap) and the ABS control unit connector. Also disconnect the airbag control module circuit at the red plug located under the floorboards on the front passenger side.

(see also previous page)

- Do not connect the battery or switch the ignition on while the airbag unit is removed from the steering wheel. Doing so will register an SRS fault and turn on the SRS warning light. See an authorized Mercedes-Benz dealer to erase the fault memory and reset the SRS.

- Always disconnect the battery cables before quick-charging the battery. Never disconnect the battery while the engine is running. When jump-starting the engine, never use a battery charger or booster battery with voltage greater than 16 volts.

- Disconnecting the battery may erase fault code(s) stored in control unit memory. Check for fault codes prior to disconnecting the battery cables. If the Check Engine light is illuminated, or any other system faults have been detected (indicated by an illuminated warning light), see an authorized Mercedes-Benz dealer.

- Disconnecting the battery will set the radio into code mode. Early radios had to be taken back to the dealer to reset. Later ones come with a code card in the car to reset.

- Do not attempt to disable the ignition system by removing the center coil wire or by removing the distributor cap (where applicable). High voltage may arc to other electrical components causing extensive damage.

- Do not disconnect the battery with the engine running. The electrical system will be damaged.

- Do not run the engine with any of the spark plug wires disconnected. Catalytic converter damage may result.

- When working on diesel fuel injectors, everything must be kept absolutely clean. Clean all pipe unions before disconnecting.

- Diesel fuel is damaging to rubber. Wipe off any fuel that spills on hoses, wiring or rubber steering and suspension parts and wash with soap and water. If coolant hoses are contaminated with diesel fuel, they must be replaced.

Chapter 1

Lubrication and Maintenance

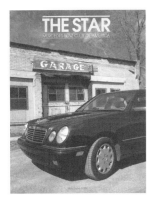

May/June 1998

September/October 1999

July/August 1998

Choosing a Shop to Repair and Maintain Your Mercedes-Benz

by Stu Ritter,
Mile-High Section

*September/October
1999*

Photo in this article
by Frank Barrett.

Moving to a new town? Just bought your first Mercedes-Benz? Having to return to your current repair shop again and again to have the same problem fixed? It's time to discuss how to pick a repair shop. I don't know if this is as difficult as picking a new doctor or dentist, but from what my customers tell me, it can be a pain in both the checkbook and the neck. As my wife likes to say, "I just married my mechanic."

Ask Around

The easiest way to find a shop is to ask your Mercedes-Benz-driving friends who they use. Ask people you know and whose opinion you trust. If you are new to the area, ask other Mercedes-Benz drivers you run across, and see which name keeps coming up again and again. Call your local MBCA section officers and ask around at MBCA events. Members tend to take good care of their cars, so their advice should always be looked into. Check recent issues of *The Star* to see if any advertised shops are located nearby, as they are usually worth checking out.

For those with Internet access, online assistance is available. For a list of mechanics who tend to be more technically oriented than usual, check www.iatn.net, where you will find the iATN shop finder. The iATN is the International Automotive Technicians Network, where 21,000 professionals from around the world gather to discuss problems. The shop finder is in the public area of the web site, while the rest is available only to registered technicians (or mechanics, as the editor likes to call them).

When choosing a repair facility, look for a combination of proper equipment, knowledge, and experience, tempered with the right attitude.

Advice is also available on several Mercedes-Benz mailing lists on the net. For customers of mine who are leaving the area, I have been able to find shops in distant cities using these lists. The list members are Mercedes-Benz owners that I communicate with almost every day, and I find their opinions valuable.

Go and See

Now that you have found a potential repair shop, it's a good idea to interview the shop manager. As a shop owner for 24 years, I always respect the car owner who stops by to chat about the possibility of my shop working on his car. After all, it's my chance to impress a potential customer. This interview works both ways: you get to know the shop, and the shop owner has the chance to understand your needs.

The first question is, "Can I deal with these people?" Can I trust my car to the man with the star? Can I talk to these people and get answers that make sense to me? Is the shop clean and well lit, or are the mechanics working in dark corners with benches piled high with junk and the flood covered with oil and kitty litter? What technical literature does the shop have available? Do they have a complete set of printed manuals and/or a complete service microfiche system? Do they have a complete set of model year *Introduction to Service* and *Technical Data Manuals*? Do they have a set of parts microfiche? Are they subscribing to an aftermarket information service such as AllData or Mitchell on Demand? (More about that later.)

From my point of view as a shop owner, you the prospective customer will be questioned in much the same way. I will try to establish a feel for whether I can trust you. I need to know that when I return your car to you when you have forgotten your checkbook, you will indeed send a check the next morning. The shop owner will also try and get a feeling for how you might react to the following situation, every repair shop's nightmare: Let's say that you have brought your clacking 560SL in for us to replace the worn right camshaft, which we had previously diagnosed. We told you the bill would be around $1,500 for the cam, new intake and exhaust rockers, new timing chain, tensioner, sprockets, and rails. I also warned you about the possible head bolt thread problem that might arise while de-installing the cam bearings. Now, as the mechanic uses a dial torque wrench so he can watch the tightening take place, bingo, the threads pull out on one bolt. I call and tell you that the bill has just increased by at least $1,000 because we now have to remove the cylinder head and helicoil the thread. I have to count on the fact that you will understand that this was not my fault; it's just the way the cars were built, and it happens all the time. That takes trust on both sides of the fence.

Dealer or Independent?

I'm often asked about the advantages and disadvantages of the three main types of repair shop.

While considering where to take your car for repair, keep this in mind. When you take it to a dealership, you can expect the latest technical information; they will use only Mercedes-Benz factory parts; they will have all of the special tools required; and the technicians will have factory training. If your car is still under warranty, it is a good idea to visit the dealership. Many provide free oil changes and services for cars under warranty, so it makes sense to take advantage of this. There may also be little updates that need to be incorporated into the electronics or the mechanicals, and this will be done when the car is brought in.

Problems that I hear about with dealerships come from having to deal with a large organization. There are layers and layers of people between you and the mechanic who will work on your car, and you understand that as a sentence is passed around a table, it changes dramatically. There are distinct advantages in being able to tell the mechanic what the problem is instead of having the symptoms relayed. Dealerships have many profit centers including new and used car sales, parts sales (wholesale and retail), leasing and financing, and more. Most independent Mercedes-Benz repair shops count on fixing cars as their only profit center, so they are usually very focused on that one job.

Independent repair shops may or may not have the latest technical information, and when choosing a shop you need to know this. These shops may use aftermarket parts and original Mercedes-Benz parts. It is up to the owner of the shop to know which parts are worth using and which are not. Parts suppliers to DaimlerChrysler sell the same parts in the German aftermarket, so the same part is often available beyond the dealer system.

Mercedes-Benz factory training is unavailable to independent repair shops. Most factory training involves repairing cars under warranty. As the cars age, they seem to have different sets of problems. New car problems are handled by dealerships, then age and wear problems come as the cars come out of warranty. Dealerships tend to specialize in the new car problems, while independents get the wear problems as the cars age. Independent repair shops tend to carry different special tools because of the different problems they see. While dealerships handle early running problems and warranty situations, independents deal with unit repair and rebuilding. I know independent shops that carry as many special tools as dealerships in the same city. Independent shops now have access to an aftermarket version of the factory's hand-held tester, and all diagnostic codes can now be read by several aftermarket scanners.

The third choice in the repair shop lineup is the "all makes, all models" shops, which work on whatever comes in the door. They will have little if any factory information, rather referring to aftermarket information sources such as AllData and Mitchell on Demand. Most questions on the iATN from techs at "all makes, all models" shops make the same statement: they have researched the aftermarket information sources, and no information is available. That's because it's really only in the factory manuals. These shops will be unfamiliar with parts sources used by Mercedes-Benz-only repair shops and will count on their American parts house to find the pieces they need. NAPA, Auto Zone, and others might work for American cars but not for Mercedes-Benz. You really don't want Chinese brake rotors on your Mercedes-Benz. This is one of the most serious drawbacks to the "all makes, all models" repair shop.

While most independent Mercedes-Benz shops are run by ex-dealership mechanics familiar with Mercedes-Benz cars, parts, and systems, the fix-it-all shops are not. You might say that they don't speak the language. I'm not saying that a fix-it-all shop can't give you good service. I'm saying that you stand a much better chance of having your car receive the care it deserves by limiting your choice to either a dealership or an independent shop that works mainly on Mercedes-Benz all day long, year in, year out.

Your Choice

Let's talk about expectations from you the customer. You brought your car in with a miss. It isn't bad, just a little skippy idle that you feel sometimes while you are driving. Here is the hypothetical situation; you make your choice:

Mechanic A says, "This is an electrical miss, so I'll replace the distributor cap, ignition rotor, and spark plug wires, and that should take care of it."

Mechanic B says, "This miss seems electrical, so I'll put it on the engine oscilloscope and see what the pattern looks like, then replace whatever I diagnose as defective."

Mechanic A decided—without looking at the car—what the miss is and wants to replace a bunch of parts. Mechanic B described what the miss seems to be and wants to diagnose it. Mechanic A wants to throw parts at the car. Mechanic B is thinking. Where you take your car and how it gets worked on are up to you. Think carefully about it, because choosing a repair shop is, in my mind, as important as choosing a doctor or a dentist.

Stu Ritter, who owns and operates an independent Mercedes-Benz shop in Denver, regularly works on models ranging from the 1950s to the 1990s. His 29-year career as a Mercedes-Benz mechanic began in a dealership service department. In conjunction with Lone Star Section member Richard Easely, Stu also operates The Mercedes List, an online technical list for Mercedes-Benz owners.

The LiteOff

by John Lamb, Contributing Editor

May/June 2000

Photos in this article by the author.

If your car has FSS, and you change your own oil, here's a handy new tool.

Readers who maintain their own recent models will be happy to know that a handheld tool is available to turn off the FSS service indicator on the instrument panel, after you have performed the service correctly and completely. The LiteOff is a plug-in device that resets the FSS service indicator on your instrument panel and can also reset the SRS-airbag light. It plugs into the 38-pin diagnostic connector in the engine compartment (photo 1). Completely modular, it comes with explicit directions. Two models are available, one for sedans, one for the M-Class. The LiteOff is powered by the vehicle's battery, and its software can be upgraded for future applications through a modular phone-style plug on the plastic barrel (photo 2). The two buttons function as follows: press button A to reset the service indicator, press button B to reset all airbag faults.

Service Indicator Light

Around 1998, Mercedes-Benz introduced the FSS service indicator light in the shape of a wrench on the instrument panel. This light alerts you when service is due. When the vehicle has been serviced according to the maintenance table (usually found in your glovebox), the technician plugs in a device like the LiteOff which resets and turns off the indicator light.

SRS-Airbag Light

The LiteOff can also shut off the SRS warning light on the instrument panel. A word of caution, though: SRS warning lights should never be shut off on a malfunctioning circuit because doing so may cause the airbag(s) to fail to deploy in an accident. The light should only be reset when a qualified service technician has verified that the entire circuit is operational. But what happens if you disconnect your battery, or the battery goes dead while you're parked at the airport? After times like these, the warning light may come on, so you may wish to reset it.

The LiteOff in Use

The device is plugged into the diagnostic connector in the engine compartment (photo 3). The directions with the unit are clear about its use—including whether the ignition key should be on or off—and which buttons to push. The unit has two buttons on top labeled "A/C" and "B/D". While testing the device, I reset the service indicator lights and the SRS light after putting a "bug" into the car, then fixing it. The device performed both jobs flawlessly. The outcome was exactly as expected, with no confusion about which buttons to push or how to do it. The service reset procedure:

1. Turn the ignition switch to the "on" position (do not start engine).

2. Plug the LiteOff into the diagnostic socket in the engine compartment.

3. Wait until the indicator stops flashing and is on steadily (about five seconds).

4. Press button "A", then release it.

5. Wait until the green light on the LiteOff flashes quickly. This indicates that the reset is complete and takes about five seconds.

6. Disconnect the LiteOff.

7. Turn the ignition to "off" then to "on."

8. Verify the service indicator light is on.

On 1996 and newer models you will be unable to reset the "check engine light," also known as the MIL (malfunction

Photo 1. Diagnostic connector on E-Class 4Matic. Locations vary but are generally near fuse panel.

Photo 2. LiteOff's port connection allows future updates.

Photo 3. LiteOff plugs into 38-pin diagnostic connector next to fuse panel. Pushing button "A" resets light.

indicator light). These vehicles have the OBD-II system, and a technician must identify the fault before the fault code or light can be reset. M-Class owners should use the model D022 LiteOff.

The unit can be ordered for $199 from DISTools online at www.distools.com or by calling 603/491-1469. The company also offers other tools and lots of Mercedes-Benz tech information and products at their website.

Mercedes-Benz 190D and 190E Oil and Oil Filter Change

by Ken Chipps,
North Texas
Section

*March/April
1985*

While the following article may seem basic, it provides an opportunity for new 190 owners to get their hands enjoyably dirty and become more familiar with their cars. We intend to publish a series of articles on 190D/190E maintenance. To insure warranty coverage, record the work done and keep parts receipts; even better would be entries in the Maintenance Booklet received with the car. Owners who intend to do their own work should buy the appropriate service manuals and read The Star.

Removing the Old Oil Filter

Filter system design requires removal of the old filter before draining to allow all the old oil to drain into the pan. Oil flows better at operating temperature, so drive the car to warm up the oil, turn off the engine and begin work immediately. The oil filter is at the top rear of the engine, partly hidden under the air cleaner housing on the 190E. On these cars the air cleaner housing must be pulled forward or removed after removing three nuts securing it with a 10-mm socket on a ratchet. Two nuts are visible from the top of the engine; the third is below the housing beside the left driver's side strut tower.

1984 190D and E, 1985 190D: 1985 190E's have different oil filters, so we'll cover them separately later. For 190D's and 1984 190E's proceed as follows. The air cleaner is still attached to the engine by several hoses. Remove the hose from the valve cover. A second hose goes toward the rear of the engine. A third hose wanders off

toward the side of the engine. Don't pull these fittings loose. Just slide the air cleaner forward slightly to give you enough room to remove the oil filter. Another way is to detach the crankcase vent hose at the bottom of the air cleaner housing. It is a bear to get back on, but this allows the housing to be removed.

Once the 190E air cleaner is out of the way, remove the bolt in the middle of the canister cap. This 13-mm head size bolt has 45 mm of thread, so there's a lot to unscrew. Withdraw the bolt and washer, then the cap. The 190D's cap is secured by two 13-mm nuts. The oil filter is a 10 by 6-cm round element. Remove it via the handle on top. A small pan helps avoid spilling oil.

Oil filter is at left rear of engine; this 190D cap is fastened by two nuts.

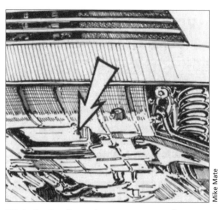

Oil drain plug (arrow); access may require removal of sound insulation cover.

1985 190E: As on the other models, hoses still hold the air cleaner housing to the engine. Remove the hose at the valve cover and pull the air cleaner off the fitting at the manifold. The 1985 190E has a spin-on oil filter under the air cleaner housing. The service manual says that the filter has check valves to prevent oil from dripping when it is removed. This is a problem because the open end of the filter faces downward. In addition, the filter fits right against the manifold. If you can't loosen the old filter by hand, use an oil filter removal wrench; various types are available at auto parts stores. The Mercedes-Benz tool appears to be basically a 74-mm socket. The part number is 103 589 00 09 00, but you can do without one. To catch dripping oil, put a rag over the open end of the filter and turn it hole-side up as you remove it.

Draining the Oil

Before draining the oil, remove the oil filler cap on the camshaft cover. To drain the oil, you must be able to reach the underside of the engine. If you do not have a cover on the bottom of the engine, the ground clearance of the 190 is sufficient for you to drain the oil without raising the car. The 190E has no cover, but to reach the 190D's drain plug, unscrew the four 8-mm head size machine screws one at each corner of the cover. With these loose, the light plastic cover may be lowered and removed.

If you raise the front of the car, the best method is to use drive-on ramps or to jack up the front end and rest the car on jack stands. Use the approved lifting points to avoid damage. Do not get under a car supported only by a jack. Follow proper safety procedures.

Place a suitable container under the drain plug, ready to catch the old oil. The location of the drain plug and the force with which the oil comes out of the hole require a rather large pan. The oil pan is the box-shaped metal part on the bottom front of the engine. The drain is on its left side. Loosen the plug with a 13-mm socket on a ratchet wrench until it can be unscrewed by hand. Then unscrew the plug with your fingers while pushing in on it. When the drain plug comes to the end of the threads in the oil pan, remove it quickly to lessen the chance of being splashed by hot oil and losing the drain plug or its washer. The plug is brass with a copper sealing washer around it. You can also remove the drain plug completely with the ratchet wrench, letting it fall into the dirty oil to be fished out later. Now is the time to catch an oil analysis sample. Follow the directions with the kit.

Installing a New Oil Filter

The year of your car determines which filter to use. Be sure to purchase the correct type. They are:

Car	M-B Part Number
190D, 1984–85	601 180 00 09
190E, 1984	102 180 01 09
190E, 1985	102 184 01 01

1984 190D or E, 1985 190D: Place the new filter in the canister, with the handle on top. The hole in the bottom of the filter element must fit over the post in the bottom of the canister. Look into the canister and you will see what I mean. Some say that filling the canister with new oil now will prevent rotating parts from being starved of

oil when the engine is re-started. The o-ring in the canister lid and the dark gray washer on the canister bolt must be replaced. These come with the oil filter. Smear new oil on the o-ring before installing it.

Re-install the lid. Tighten the fasteners by hand, then torque to the value listed below. These parts are aluminum, light and strong but soft. Over-tightening can ruin the parts, so use a torque wrench. Aluminum has a high coefficient of expansion, meaning that such parts expand and contract more than steel parts might, so it is important that they be held tightly. Your torque wrench will get considerable use, so you might as well buy it now.

1985 190E: The spin-on filter used on the 1985 190E screws onto a bolt sticking up from the engine block. Lightly lubricate the o-ring on the filter with new oil before installing it. Screw it on by hand until the o-ring touches the mounting pad, then tighten another three-quarters of a turn. Over-tightening is as likely to cause an oil leak as under-tightening.

Refilling the System

Replace the air cleaner housing, hoses, nuts, etc. Clean the drain plug and put on the new copper washer. Screw the plug into the threaded hole in the oil pan, making sure it screws straight into the hole, not at an angle. Cross-threading will destroy some threads,

and oil will leak out. Torque the bolt to the value listed below. Again, a torque wrench is essential. On the 190D re-install the bottom cover. The screws need to be tight, but there is no specific torque value.

To determine the appropriate oil, check your owner's manual and the article *Which Oil Should I Use?* in the May/ June 1984 issue of *The Star.* Put in three to four quarts, then check the level with the car on the ground. It may take another quart to fill, depending on how much old oil remains in the engine.

Checking Your Work

Start the engine. If oil pressure does not register on the gauge within a few seconds, stop it and investigate. If the pressure is OK, check underneath the car and around the filter for oil leaks. Turn the engine off. While the oil drains into the oil pan, clean up the mess you made, then recheck the level. Add oil as needed to reach the proper level.

Changing oil in the 190 sounds more difficult than it is. If you have never worked on your own car, now is the time to start. The better you know how your automobile works, the more comfortable you will be with it.

Thanks to Ryan Motor Cars of Fort Worth, Texas, (particularly Service Manager Terry LaRoux) for their assistance.

Torque Values:

Fastener	Bolt Head Size, mm	Torque, ft-lb
Oil drain plug	13	22
Oil filter canister		
190E	13	16
190D	13	16
Air cleaner nuts	10	snug
Bottom cover machine screws	8	snug

190D / 190E Tech Tips

by Ken Chipps,
North Texas
Section

*May/June
1985*

Photos in this article
by the author.

Antenna Replacement

Although it is retracted when the engine is off, there are ways that the 190's antenna can be bent or broken, but replacement is surprisingly easy.

The 190's antenna, made by Hirschmann, automatically extends and retracts, with two positions selected by a dash-mounted switch. The motor and base unit are mounted in the trunk. The antenna element is a separate part number 126 827 00 01, costing about $28, so replacement is easy even though it requires two people.

To remove the old element, set the switch so that the antenna will extend fully. Turn on the ignition just far enough to activate the radio, and turn the radio on so that the antenna extends. Loosen the retaining nut on the antenna with a 12-mm wrench. Turn off the radio for a moment, then

turn it back on. The antenna element will now pop out as it extends. While you are turning the radio back on, the second person must prevent the antenna from hitting anything.

As the element leaves the hole, note the direction of the teeth on the drive belt. The teeth on the new element must face the same way to engage the drive gear in the base unit.

Orient the new antenna element so that the teeth face the same way as the old element. Insert the drive belt into the hole in the antenna base, and be sure the belt is engaged by the gear. Now comes another part that requires two people. Turn the radio off, and the antenna element will be drawn into the base, carefully guided by the second person. If the element doesn't retract into the base when you turn off the radio, the teeth on the drive belt are facing in the wrong direction or weren't pushed in far enough.

Tighten the retaining nut on the new element, and check your work by turning the radio on and off a few times. If you tried to do the job alone, you may also have to go to the body shop to have the left rear fender repaired where the antenna element

bent it. Oh, and next time you drive into the garage, don't let the door start to come down before the car's antenna clears it, so you won't have to do this job again.

190 Body Lubrication

190D/E body parts needing periodic lubrication include the hood hinges and latch trunk hinges and latch, gas filler door hinges, the sunroof mechanism and the power antenna. Lubricants should be applied every 15,000 mi or annually. Door hinges use nylon bushings requiring no lubrication.

The purpose of lubrication is to reduce friction between moving parts, but too much lubricant is as bad as too little. Excess lubricant attracts dirt and moisture which can cause damage.

The lubricant must provide a film able to withstand the pressure between the parts, it must not interact adversely with the parts and it should protect them from dirt and water. In this case the lubricant has to be able to stick in place, so we want a grease. There are several water-dispersant lubricants available, including WD-40, but it seems to attract dirt more than some

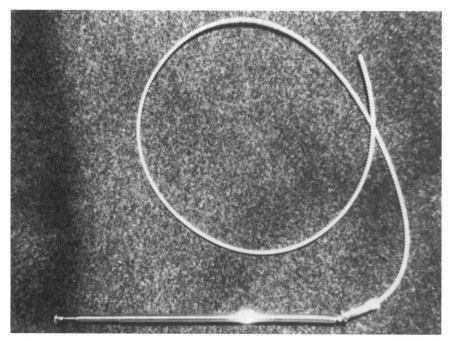

Radio antenna element

Sunroof rails (top) and hood hinges (bottom)
are easy to lubricate yourself.

others. Lubriplate makes an excellent grease, but I prefer another grease, LPS 2 (made for aircraft use).

Move the hood up and down a bit, and spray a little lubricant between the rubbing surfaces of the hinges. Lubricate the latch parts on the hood and on the body near the radiator. The trunk lid hinges are tough to get to. The determined person will climb into the trunk, lie down and use a light to see while spraying the hinges. Most of us will just lean over and spritz the general area. The trunk latch is lubricated only at the part attached to the body. The gas filler door hinges are easy to reach.

Use an old rag to clean dirt and excess lubricant from the rails and blocks of the sunroof before applying new lubricant. Lubricate the rails beneath the L-shaped piece on which the roof slides, and apply lubricant to the hinges of the wind deflector, too.

Grease attracts dirt, so a dry silicone lubricant is best for the power antenna. Extend the antenna and clean it, then cover the surrounding body and spray the antenna lightly, wiping off the excess.

190E Air Intake Clamp

The hard plastic snout on the front of the 190E air filter housing draws air from the grille area and tends to loosen at the filter housing. This is easily fixed by using a 2-1/2-in radiator clamp around the connection. Tighten the clamp snug enough to hold the two pieces together; over-tightening will crack the plastic piece.

190D / 190E Air Plenum Housekeeping

Ventilation air for the 190's passenger compartment is taken in at the base of the windshield, below the wiper. This plenum area also collects dirt, leaves and other trash, some of which finds its way into crevices in the bodywork or into the engine compartment, where it can catch and hold moisture, which could cause rust.

Make it a point to regularly check and clean this area. Open the hood to the full vertical position (be careful not to do this in a strong wind, which could damage the hood), and clean the area behind the firewall. Be especially thorough around the battery and fuse box. Keeping this area clean may save you from problems a few years down the road.

Clean an area around battery to prevent rust.

Radiator hose clamp fits air intake.

Automatic Transmission Fluid

by Frank King,
Technical Editor

*September/October
1986*

*"What transmission fluid should
I use?"*

The answer to this question has probably been shrouded in more uncertainty than any other related to service products for use in Mercedes-Benz automobiles. Even before DBAG used automatic transmissions, they recommended automatic transmission fluid (ATF) for use in their manual transmissions, but ATF has undergone a bewildering series of changes. A short review of ATF and its applications is in order.

This review will consider only automatic transmissions as we know them now, overlooking the multitude of early semiautomatics, electrics, pre-selectors and such. The fluid coupling or hydraulic torque converter combined with a three- or four-speed planetary gearbox is our subject, of which the General Motors Hydramatic is the archetype. Early automatic transmissions used engine oil as their operative fluid, but it was unsatisfactory, and GM developed a specification for an ATF that they called Type A. Around 1957 an improved fluid called Type A, Suffix A was brought out to replace plain Type A. In 1968 GM introduced a better fluid which they called Dexron, which replaced Type A, Suffix A for all automatic transmissions except Ford's. Paralleling GM's work, Ford had developed its own fluid, Type F.

One of the essential components of Dexron was oil derived from the sperm whale (see *The STAR*, March/April 1975). In 1970 the U.S. Congress declared eight species of whale, including the sperm whale, to be endangered and prohibited the importation of any products derived from these whales.

Son of Dexron

In 1971 GM discovered an additive to replace sperm oil as a friction modifier, and the new formulation was called Dexron II. Further improvements to ensure that this ATF was compatible with various materials in automatic transmissions and their cooling systems led to the current Dexron II, D-Series.

ATF is probably the most complex fluid in today's automobiles. It must transmit power through the torque converter, function as an hydraulic medium for servos and controls, provide lubrication for moving parts and act as a coolant for the transmission. ATF must fulfill most of the duties of an engine oil while dealing with additional ones. One of these is to provide precisely the right degree of friction between clutch plates, while another is to maintain a uniform viscosity despite temperature fluctuations. ATF must therefore have a high Viscosity Index (VI), an empirically derived number indicating the rate at which an oil thickens as it cools and thins as it warms.

The VI designation was instituted by making graphs of viscosity vs. temperature for two oils. One was a straight paraffin-based oil, which held its viscosity well against temperature changes. The other was a naphtha-based oil, noted for wide changes in viscosity. The slopes of the two curves were reduced to algebraic formulae, and a value of 100 was assigned to the paraffinic oil, while the naphthenic oil was given zero. Other oils could then be tested and rated against these reference values.

The index was extrapolated to accommodate oils with a VI above 100 or below zero. Today's high-quality, single-grade oils have a VI of about 100, while multi-grades run from about 130 to 140. Dexron II, D-Series has a VI of about 155 and at 0°F has about the viscosity of SAE 10W engine oil.

What to Use

Dexron is a registered trademark of GM and may be used only on products that meet the GM specifications for it. For all Mercedes-Benz automatic transmissions DBAG approves either MB ATF (part number 000 989 65 03) or the Dexron II, D-Series made by Duckhams, Exxon, Kendall, Pennzoil, Quaker State, Union Oil or Valvoline. Also approved are Esso, Gulf, Shell or Texaco. Regardless of the type of fluid recommended in previous factory literature, including that of the year your car was made, the currently preferred fluid is now Dexron II, D-Series, which has all the desirable qualities of earlier fluids plus definite improvements.

Dexron II, D-Series is also an excellent all-round lubricant for Mercedes-Benz manual transmissions and an equally good lubricant/hydraulic fluid for power steering systems up to the issuance of the latest list of DBAG-approved service products.

The latest such list, dated April 1986, specifies Fuchs Renofluid TF 10 (part number 900 989 26 03-15) for manual transmissions. For power steering, MB Power Steering Gear Oil (part number 000 989 88 03) is approved. Where these products are not available, which includes most of this country, Dexron II, D-Series may be used.

Checking ATF Level

It is important to maintain the correct level of ATF by periodically checking at least as often as halfway between changes of ATF and its filter. It's wise to check ATF level whenever engine oil is changed and before an extended trip. The ATF level is checked with the engine idling and the car on a level surface with parking brake engaged and gear selector in position P. The upper mark on the dipstick indicates the correct fluid level for a hot transmission with fluid at 80°C/176°F. Since this temperature is reached only after prolonged driving and even then can only be estimated, the fluid level check will not be accurate under most workshop conditions.

Experience has shown that actual fluid level can be determined more accurately in a cold transmission with fluid temperature between 20°C/68°F and 30°C/86°F. Proper fluid level is important in the older fluid coupling transmissions and in torque converter transmissions but is especially critical in torque converters. Overfilling of these transmissions must be avoided.

To check fluid level in a cold automatic transmission, the car should stand on a level surface with engine, transmission and all components at an ambient temperature between 68° and 86°F. With the parking brake on and the selector lever in position P, start the engine and let it idle for one to two minutes. Pull out the dipstick and wipe it clean with a lint-free cloth or a piece of leather. Insert it fully, then withdraw it and read the fluid level. The engine must be idling throughout this procedure. These instructions do not apply to the Borg-Warner torque converter transmissions used in the 1955–62 300c and 300d; for these, refer to the applicable workshop manual.

Mercedes-Benz transmissions are identified by 1) type number, 2) model number and 3) part number. For example, the 190D 2.2 uses a Type W 4 A 020, Model 722.4, part number 123 270 54 01 torque converter transmission. In the type number the W stands for *Wandler*, German for converter; the K stands for *Kupplung*, German for clutch.

Maximum Levels

Here are maximum fluid levels for specific transmissions in U.S-version Mercedes-Benz cars (refer to Fig. 1):

I. 280SE 3.5 coupe and convertible and 300SEL 3.5: maximum fluid level in a cold fluid coupling transmission of type K 4 A 040 must be 20 mm (13/16 in) below the minimum (lower) marking.

II. All models, except those in I above, started in production before the introduction of torque converters as noted in III, IV and V below: maximum fluid level in all other types of cold fluid coupling transmissions must be at the minimum (lower) marking.

III. Starting in model year 1972 with cars using the 4.5-liter engine in the W108/109 series. Cars in the 107 series using the 4.5-liter engine. Cars in the W114/115 series starting in model year 1974. All W116 series cars. All W123 series cars except the 300TD turbo starting in September 1981 and except all turbo-diesels model year 1982 and later: maximum fluid level in cold torque converter transmissions of types W3 B 050 (722.0), W 3 A 040 (722.0) and W 4 B 025 (722.1) must be 30 mm (1 3/16 in) below the minimum (lower) marking.

IV. All W201 and W124 series cars: maximum fluid level in cold torque converter transmissions of type W 4 A 020 (722.4) must be 12 mm (1/2 in) below the minimum (lower) marking.

V. All W126 series cars. All W107 series cars starting in model year 1981. All W123 series cars starting in 1982 equipped with turbo-diesel engines (300TD turbo-diesel starting in September 1981): Maximum fluid level in cold torque converter transmissions of type W 4 A 040 (722.3) must be 5 mm (3/16 in) below the minimum (lower) marking.

If the fluid level is low, add a small amount through the dipstick tube with the engine running, using a funnel. Take care that no dirt or foreign matter gets into the transmission. The distance between maximum and minimum marks on the dipstick equates to about 0.3 liter (10 oz). After adding ATF, apply the brake and move the gear selector through positions R-N-D-N-R, leaving it in each position for a few seconds, then return it to P and check the fluid level. If the fluid level is too low, the pump will draw in air, which can be heard clearly. The fluid will foam and give a false result when checking the level. Stop the engine for about two minutes until the

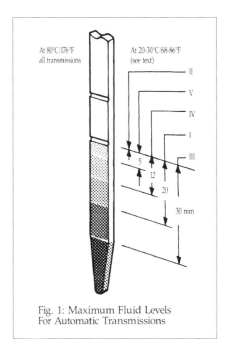

Fig. 1: Maximum Fluid Levels For Automatic Transmissions

fluid is no longer foaming, then add fluid and check the level.

Excess fluid should be drained off or drawn off with a suction device through the dipstick tube. The Vampire pump described on page 20 is particularly convenient for this. Be careful that no dirt enters the transmission. Too much fluid in the transmission will cause the gears to churn the fluid excessively, increasing the temperature of the fluid and ultimately damaging the transmission.

ATF and Filter Changes

DBAG recommends that ATF and the filter be changed at 30,000-mi intervals. If the car is subject to rigorous service (e.g., taxi service, predominantly city driving, pulling a trailer, mountainous roads) ATF should be changed at mid-interval without changing the filter. Used fluid should be examined for abnormalities. It should be a clear, bright red with no cloudiness or solids of any kind. It should be odorless or possibly smell slightly of roasted peanuts, but there should be no burnt or rotten egg smell, which indicates too long an interval between changes or operation at elevated temperatures. Cloudiness indicates that coolant or water from some other source has entered the transmission.

How to Service Your Automatic Transmission

by John Lamb,
Contributing
Editor

*November/December
2002*

Photos in this article
by the author.

Most U.S. models of Mercedes-Benz cars have automatic transmissions. Manufactured in-house, they were designed to provide superb service life with little maintenance. Except for the "sealed-for-life" 722.6 units introduced in 1996, Mercedes-Benz automatic transmissions require maintenance at regular scheduled intervals of 30,000 miles in normal use and 15,000 miles for severe use. It is possible to extend transmission life through regular service and by avoiding abuse.

Here we'll guide you through transmission service for a 1990 E-Class model, including inspection and a fluid and filter change. The work was performed on a 1990 300D 2.5 Turbo (W124 chassis).

After 250,000 miles its transmission still shifts like new. Fluid is changed every 7,500 miles, and the filter is changed every 15,000 miles. Service techniques for other models are similar.

Over the past few years, Mercedes-Benz requirements for fluid change and transmission service have changed. Newer models with the 722.6 electronically controlled transmission have no dipstick for checking fluid level, nor do they have a conventional drain plug. Service of these transmissions is best left to a qualified Mercedes-Benz dealership or service facility. (Incidentally, as the new "sealed" transmissions accumulate miles, some owners are finding that they could have benefitted by changing the fluid.) If your transmission has a dipstick, before beginning this service, use it to verify fluid level. If the transmission has no dipstick, you can buy one. The bottom line is that a change of fluid costs a lot less than a new or rebuilt transmission.

Getting Started

Start by reviewing safety precautions. Support a raised car with automotive stands designed for this purpose. Never work below a car supported by a jack, blocks, or ramps. Transmission fluid is harmful to the environment, so recycle it with your retailer or a recycling station. Avoid over or under-filling the transmission, or damage may result. Engine and transmission parts can be very hot, and transmission fluid can burn or irritate your skin, so do this job when the engine is cool, and wear eye protection and gloves.

After applying the parking brake and blocking the wheels on level ground, raise the car. It should be level when raised and high enough so you have room to move under its center. Have these tools and supplies ready:

- Mercedes-Benz-approved transmission fluid (Dexron II or AIII ATF); see your owner's manual for amount (7 or 8 quarts)
- Transmission filter kit and pan gasket (includes filter, pan seal, seal rings)
- A 27-mm socket and a 1/2-in bar or ratchet to rotate the engine (optional)
- A long 5-mm hex-head (Allen-type) socket and a 3/8-in ratchet to remove torque converter drain plugs
- An 8-mm socket, a 13-mm socket, and a 4-in extension to remove bottom covers and pan
- A torque wrench with range of 5 to 25 Nm (4 to 18 lb-ft)
- A Phillips screwdriver with #2 bit (to remove filter from valve body)
- Brake cleaner spray, 1 or 2 cans
- Drain pan and container to hold at least 8 quarts of old fluid
- Clean funnel
- Newspaper to cover work area
- Disposable work gloves, paper towels

Check Starting Level

In the back of your owner's manual (photo 1), you will find fluid specifications and capacities. The initial fill specification refers to a "dry" transmission when filled at the factory. Normally you will use the "refill" capacity, then top up the level slightly. See the chart below, from Section 2702 of the factory maintenance manual.

The fluid level must be correct, or severe transmission damage can result. The level rises as the fluid's temperature rises. Mercedes-Benz specifies that the level should be checked on 1981 to mid-1990s models at a fluid temperature of 80°C (176°F). Unless your owner's manual states otherwise, check the fluid level when the engine is fully warm and idling. The level should be between the two marks on the dipstick, preferably near the upper mark. When checking cold

Photo 1. Owner's manual lists transmission fluid capacity and type.

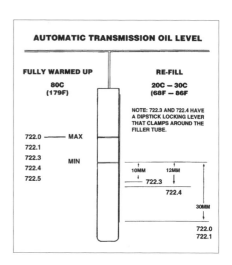

AUTOMATIC TRANSMISSION OIL LEVEL

FULLY WARMED UP	RE-FILL
80C (179F)	20C – 30C (68F – 86F)

NOTE: 722.3 AND 722.4 HAVE A DIPSTICK LOCKING LEVER THAT CLAMPS AROUND THE FILLER TUBE.

722.0 ——— MAX
722.1
722.3
722.4   MIN
722.5

10MM   12MM
722.3

722.4

30MM

722.0
722.1

fluid level, refer to the Automatic Transmission Oil Level chart from the manual.

Get Underneath

Opening the dipstick/fill tube, transmission pan, or replacing the filter and gasket requires hospital-like cleanliness. From below the car, clean the pan-mating surface with brake cleaner before removing the pan. Before removing the pan, check the new pan gasket to be sure it matches the old one (photo 2). Depending on the model, the fluid is drained from either a drain plug (722.2, 722.3, and 722.4 transmissions) or by loosening the fill/dipstick tube (722.0 and 722.1). On 126 models you must remove the crossmember to reach the torque converter drain plug. Use Loctite when replacing these bolts.

Place the transmission shifter in Neutral and apply the parking brake. If you car has the two engine encapsulation panels, remove them from below, using an 8-turn socket to remove the screws. Remove the rear panel under the transmission (photo 3); on W124 diesels, about eight screws hold this panel.

If you have help, working from below at the front of the engine, position the 27-mm socket and 1/2-in ratchet on the crankshaft pulley bolt, hidden in the center of the bottom drive belt pulley (photo 4). Be sure the ratchet is set to allow clockwise turning only. While rotating the pulley, look for the small torque converter drain plug at the bottom of the transmission housing (photo 5). When the plug is visible, stop turning the engine and remove the socket and ratchet.

If you have no one to help, find the converter drain plug by turning over the engine manually. Insert a large screwdriver between the ribs of the housing to engage the torque converter case and rotate it until the plug is aligned with the access hole. Make sure you turn the engine in its running direction, clockwise looking from the front of the car. Use care with the screwdriver; avoid taking too big

Photo 2. New filter and pan gasket

Photo 3. Noise panels removed to access transmission

Photo 4. Rotate engine by hand using ratchet and socket on front crankshaft bolt. Watch for torque converter drain plug.

Photo 5. Drain plug in transmission opening

Photo 6. Remove drain plug using 5-mm hex-head socket.

a "bite", or you'll break the aluminum torque converter cover ribs.

Unscrew the small torque converter drain plug using a 5-mm hex-head (Allen-type) socket (photo 6). Have the drain pan ready below the drain opening, and while the fluid drains out, watch its color. Healthy fluid is the color of dark cranberry juice. If it is brown or has particles in it, the fluid has been overheated, and internal wear could exist. When all the fluid has drained, replace the drain plug, using a new sealing washer. Torque the plug to 14 Nm (10 lb-ft).

Draining Work

Working at the transmission pan, clean the pan mating surface with brake cleaner to remove dirt and grease. Remove the drain plug using the 5-mm hex-head socket (photo 7) or use a suitable wrench on the dipstick tube banjo bolt. Again, observe the color of

Photo 7. Remove transmission pan drain plug using 5-mm hex-head socket.

the fluid. You can also use a Topsider Oil Changer to suck fluid out through the dipstick tube.

Remove the bolts holding the pan to the transmission (photo 8) with a 13-mm socket, the extension bar, and a ratchet. Let the remaining fluid drain, then remove the pan. Transmission fluid will continue to drip for some time, so resist the temptation to "blot" the internals with a rag; even the tiniest piece of lint can cause problems. Removing a bolt connecting one of the cooling lines or removing the dipstick tube fitting first will allow most of the old fluid to run out. Then remove the bolts that secure the pan in a sequence that allows one corner of the pan to drop first so fluid will run out in a small stream. Carefully dump out the rest of the fluid as you lower the pan by loosening the rest of the pan bolts in sequence.

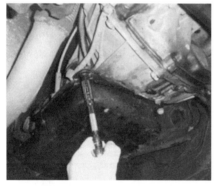

Photo 8. Remove pan bolts using 13-mm socket.

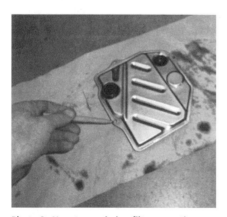

Photo 9. New transmission filter mounting holes (1 of 3). Install filter on transmission with screws.

At the bench, clean the pan thoroughly until it looks new. Install the new gasket on the pan, being sure to "clip" the rubber gasket tabs over the pan. Don't reinstall the pan yet. Near where you removed the pan, remove the three Phillips-head screws attaching the transmission filter to the bottom of the transmission (photo 9). When the filter is removed, more fluid will drain out.

Install the new filter. Start the screws by hand, then tighten them, but avoid stripping their threads. Note that the filter holes line up with the pickup tubes in the transmission. Wipe the transmission case with a clean cloth, then clean the mounting bolts. Reinstall the pan, starting the bolts by hand. Tighten all the bolts evenly in stages, then torque them to 8 Nm (6 lb-ft), starting with the center bolts. Reinstall the new drain plug and washer in the pan; torque it to 14 Nm (10 lb-ft).

Initially, refill the transmission through the dipstick/fill tube with four quarts of fluid; pour it in slowly (photo 10). Don't add all the fluid yet, or it may "leak" out onto the ground from the transmission case vent. Be sure all tools and equipment are removed from the work area, then when it's safe, start

Photo 10. Pour new fluid in slowly through clean funnel.

the engine and add the remaining new fluid. Avoid overfilling.

Final Fill

With the brakes on firmly, shift through all the transmission ranges with the engine idling. Return the shifter to Park. Check the fluid level according to your owner's manual; the usual procedure is to have the engine idling and the transmission in Park. We recommend initially filling to the lower mark on the dipstick, then driving the car and checking the level several times, using a clean, lint-free cloth to wipe the dipstick. The difference in fluid level between the dipstick marks is about one-half liter; add small amounts of fluid, rechecking the level often (see fill chart). Fluid must be at an operating temperature of 80°C (176°F) to measure the level accurately, so that means a test drive.

When done, shut off the engine. If you overfilled the transmission, you have two options to remove fluid. Either unscrew a drain plug just long enough to drain out the right amount, or suck it out using five feet of 1/4-in diameter non-bendable nylon tube (available at home centers such as Home Depot); push the hose into the dipstick tube, then siphon fluid through it. You can also use a Topsider for this purpose. If you remove a drain plug, install a new sealing washer and re-torque the plug.

The rest is the reverse of removal. Many service stations will help you to recycle the old fluid and filter. Recording the mileage and date of your service will make your car more valuable to you and prospective buyers.

Contributing Editor John Lamb is a technical trainer and lives in the Boston area.

M-Class Service for the Novice, Part I

by John Lamb, Contributing Editor

May/June 1998

Photos in this article by the author.

You can perform basic maintenance on your new ML320.

The M-Class represents a dramatic shift in service philosophy and technology for Daimler-Benz. No longer can technicians address the brand without a significant grounding in the Daimler-Benz philosophy. The newly designed 3.2-liter V-6 is engineered to meet emission levels into the next millennium. To do so, the engine incorporates new combustion technology, distributor-less ignition with dual spark plugs per cylinder, and catalytic converters that get it into closed loop air /fuel control phase very quickly. Get used to the new V-6, because you'll see this superior engine in many models.

Several basic service procedures are described below. Those that vary from normal Mercedes-Benz service are in *italic type*. For the latest service product specifications, consult your Mercedes-Benz dealer.

How to Change the Engine Oil and Filter

When changing the oil, Mercedes-Benz recommends that you allow no oil to get on any rubber bushings, so use a shield to keep oil away from those beneath the engine.

1. While the engine is warm, remove the drain plug (photo 1) using a 13-mm wrench. Allow the oil to drain into a pan, and recycle it. Replace the drain plug using a new sealing washer; tighten to 22 lb-ft (30 Nm).

2. Remove the top engine cover

Photo 1. Remove oil drain plug (arrow).

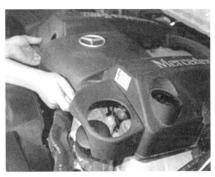

Photo 2. Engine cover being removed

Photo 3. Engine oil filter cover being removed; note tightening torque on cover.

Photo 4. Refill engine with correct specification oil; see your owner's manual.

by pulling up on both sides simultaneously (photo 2). Remove the oil filter by unscrewing the plastic cover (photo 3), then remove and discard the filter element and old o-ring.

3. Install the new filter, replace the o-ring then tighten the cover to the torque value embossed on the cover.

4. Refill the crankcase with the specified type of oil (photo 4). Oil capacity is 8.5 qt (6 liters). After the engine has run and is shut off, oil level must be between the MIN and MAX marks on the dipstick.

How to Change the Front Differential Oil

The front differential, below the engine, has a vent hose routed upward into the engine compartment.

1. Drive the vehicle to warm up the oil, then place a drain pan below the front differential housing.

2. Remove the fill/level plug, then the drain plug using a 10-mm hex-head wrench for both (photo 5).

3. After the oil is drained, replace and tighten the drain plug.

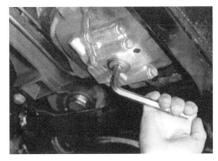

Photo 5. Front differential drain plug being removed.

Photo 6. Front differential fill/level plug being removed.

Photo 7. Fill differential as shown with SAE 90 hypoid gear oil.

4. Refill the housing through the fill /level opening with SAE 90 *hypoid* gear oil (photos 6 and 7). The quantity of oil is 1.2 qt (1.1 liters) or until oil just begins to overflow from the filler hole.

How to Change the Transfer Case Fluid

The transfer case, bolted to the back of the transmission, is lubricated by its own oil bath.

1. Drain the transfer case by removing the fill/level plug on the passenger side of the transfer case (photo 8), then the drain plug on the driver's side (photo 9), using a *3/8-in square drive ratchet* for both.

2. Replace the drain plug, then refill the transfer case. Add fluid until it just flows out of the fill opening. Torque both plugs.

3. The proper fluid is *Dexron ATF type 3 or 2E*; quantity is 1.5 qt (1.4 liters).

How to Change the Rear Differential Oil

This differential is at the rear of the vehicle in the center, underneath. A vent hose should be checked for damage or to see if it is missing.

1. Remove the fill/level plug (photo 10) then the drain plug (photo 11), using a 10-mm hex-head wrench for both.

2. Replace the drain plug.

3. Fill the housing with *SAE 90 or SAE 85W90 hypoid gear oil*; quantity is 1.6 qt (1.5 liters). Torque both plugs.

How to Change the Transmission Fluid

The transmission fill tube, accessible in the engine compartment on the passenger side, is sealed with a plug that cannot be reused.

1. Before changing the fluid, you must have a transmission dipstick and sealing plug for the vehicle. *M-Class vehicles have no transmission dipstick,*

Photo 8. Location of transfer fill plug

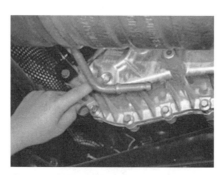

Photo 9. Location of transfer case drain plug; marking on casting above it.

and the fluid is claimed to be "filled for life." The fill tube is capped with a sealed plug.

2. Working below the vehicle with the engine off, rotate the crankshaft in its normal direction using a socket and ratchet on the front crankshaft pulley bolt.

3. Look for the torque converter drain plug to appear at the bottom of the transmission bellhousing (photo 12).

Photo 10. Rear differential fill/level plug being removed; refill with SAE 90 or 85W90 hypoid gear oil.

Photo 11. Rear differential drain plug being removed.

Photo 12. Torque converter drain plug is above cover (arrow).

4. Remove the ratchet and socket from the crankshaft bolt. Remove the drain plug from the converter using a 5-mm hex head socket, then remove the drain plug from the transmission drain pan using a 5-mm hex-head wrench (photo 13). Allow the fluid to drain.

5. Replace both drain plugs using new sealing rings; torque the plugs to 10 lb-ft (14 Nm).

6. If necessary, the transmission pan can be removed and the filter replaced; see your Mercedes-Benz dealer for details. The pan bolts are now the Torx-brand.

7. Refill the transmission slowly through the dipstick fill tube (photo 14). Use Mercedes-Benz Automatic Transmission Fluid; quantity is 7.9 qt (7.5 liters).

8. Start the engine and shift through the gears while holding the brake, then recheck the level with the shifter in Park and the engine running.

9. Remove the dipstick, then install the sealing plug. Avoid over-filling the transmission.

How to Change Spark Plugs

This engine's two spark plugs in each cylinder can be fired in sequence or simultaneously as determined by the powertrain control module.

1. Remove the spark plug boot by pulling on the boot (photo 15). Using a 5/8-in spark plug socket, remove and replace one spark plug at a time (photo 16); torque the plugs to 15-22 lb-ft (20-30 Nm).

2. Firing order is 1-4-3-6-2-5; the coils are marked to indicate proper plug wire hookup.

Photo 13. Transmission drain plug being removed.

Photo 14. Sealed plug (arrow) on transmission dipstick/fill tube.

Photo 15. Remove spark plug boot as shown.

Photo 16. Remove spark plug using 5/8-in socket.

How to Change the Air Filter

1. The air filter housing cover is held on with eight clips, six on the housing, two on the mass airflow sensor. Unclip these and remove the filter (photo 17), then look at the mass air flow meter with a flashlight. Check for oil or dirt contamination.

2. Installation is the reverse of removal.

Contributing Editor John Lamb is a technical training manager for Snap-on Tools in Boston and has participated extensively in Mercedes-Benz training on M-Class vehicles. Part II of this article will appear in the July/August 1998 issue of The Star.

Photo 17. Remove air filter clips as shown.

M-Class Service for the Novice, Part II

by John Lamb, Contributing Editor

July/August 1998

Photos in this article by the author.

Here's more on how you can perform basic maintenance on your new ML320.

As a follow-up to the article in the May/June issue, more M-Class service procedures are described below. For the latest service product specifications, consult your Mercedes-Benz dealer.

Visual Inspection

1. Working below the car, check the rubber boots on the constant-velocity joints for tearing or splitting (photo 18); if they are damaged, replace them immediately.

2. Check the several ground cables for damage and tightness. If you have any doubts, replace or clean the cable terminals and retighten them (photo 19).

3. Check the water drain holes in the doors; using a pipe cleaner, make sure they are not clogged with dirt (photo 20).

4. Check the battery electrolyte level by unscrewing one cap at a time (photo 21). The fluid should just cover the gray plates in the battery; if not, top it up with pure water. To prevent acid burns, wear eye and skin protection.

5. Engine coolant level can be checked at the expansion tank; note the marks on the side (photo 22). Top up with Mercedes-Benz coolant mixed 50/50 with water.

Photo 18. Inspect constant-velocity joint boots for damage or cracks.

Photo 20. Clean drain hole (arrow) in door using pipe cleaner.

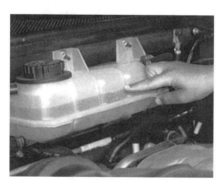

Photo 22. Check coolant level against marks on tank.

6. With the engine off, check the condition of the poly vee-belt for looseness or cracks (photo 23); if necessary, replace the belt.

7. Check the power steering fluid level (photo 24); if necessary, top up with Mercedes-Benz fluid.

Photo 19. Check all ground straps for damage, corrosion, or resistive connections. This strap (arrow) is on muffler.

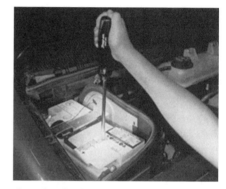

Photo 21. Check battery electrolyte; wear eye protection.

Photo 23. With engine off, check poly vee-belt; it should have no cracks and fit snugly.

Photo 24. Power steering fluid being checked.

Remote Lock System

1. Before troubleshooting the keyless locking system, be sure the batteries in the remote keypads are new and that you have gone through the reset procedure below. The battery is a lithium-type CR2025.

2. Reset the remote locking system by turning the key in the steering lock to position 2, then to position 0 and remove.

3. Within 60 seconds push both buttons simultaneously for 15 seconds.

4. Press any remote control button twice to activate the system.

MBNA has issued an update for the remote locking system; check with your dealer for details.

ML320 Specifications (1998)

Model: ML320 (163.154)

Engine: 112.942

Type: 4-stroke, gasoline, fuel-injected V-6

Bore, mm: 89.90 (3.54 in)

Stroke, mm: 84.00 (3.30 in)

Displacement, cc: 3,199 (195.2 cu in)

Compression ratio: 10:1

Power output, hp: (SAE J1349) 215 (160 kW) at 5,600 rpm

Maximum torque, lb-ft: (SAE J1349) 229 (310 Nm) at 3,000 rpm

Maximum engine speed, rpm: 6,000

Firing order: 1-4-3-6-2-5

Poly vee-belt length, mm: 2,390

Wheel rims: 8Jx16 H2

Wheel offset, mm: 61 (2.4 in)

Tires: all-season, radial ply, 255/65 R16 109T

Spare wheel: 4Jx18 H2

Spare wheel offset, mm: 30 (1.2 in)

Space-saver spare tire: T155/90 D18 113M

Electrical system alternator: 14V/115A

Starter motor: 12V/1.7kW

Battery: 12V/100 A-h

Spark plugs: Bosch F 8 DPER

Spark plug gap, mm: 0.8 (0.032 in)

Spark plug tightening torque, lb-ft: 15-22 (20-30 Nm)

Maximum roof load, lb: 220

Overall length, in: 180.6

Overall width, in: 86.2

Overall height, in: 70

Wheelbase, in: 111.1

Track, front/rear, in: 60.4

Power steering fluid capacity, qt: 1.1 (1.0 l) Mercedes-Benz Power Steering Fluid

Front wheel hub grease capacity, grams: 43 each, high temperature roller bearing grease

Accelerator control linkage lubricant: hydraulic fluid

Brake fluid capacity, qt: 0.6 (0.6 l) DOT4 Mercedes-Benz Brake Fluid

Windshield washer capacity, qt: 5.5 (5.0 l) Mercedes-Benz Windshield Washer Concentrate S and washer solvent/ antifreeze

Cooling system capacity, qt: 12.7 (12.0 l) Mercedes-Benz antifreeze

Fuel capacity, gal: 19.0 (72.0 l) including 3.2-gal (12-l) reserve

Fuel type: Premium unleaded gasoline, posted octane 91

Air-conditioning refrigerant: R134a, special PAG oil (never R12)

Contributing Editor John Lamb, a technical training manager for Snap-on Tools in Boston, has participated extensively in Mercedes-Benz training on M-Class vehicles.

The Black Death

by Frank King,
Technical Editor

*November/December
1987*

A lubrication problem is alarming Europe to the point that Germans are calling it *der schwarzer Tod*, the black death. The death afflicts gasoline engines, and the subject was dealt with in a recent issue of *auto motor und sport* magazine; much of the following is extracted from that article.

The holiday drive of a doctor from Friedrichshafen ended abruptly after 25 miles when the oil pressure warning light flashed on, followed almost immediately by loud rattling from the engine of his 1.1-liter Ford Escort. Investigation at the shop to which the car was towed showed oil starvation, causing crankshaft damage and burned-out main bearings. The cause: an oil strainer was completely blocked by tarry sludge.

This was not an isolated incident. During the previous months the central laboratory of Volkswagen at Wolfsburg had investigated over 1,000 engines whose premature demise was ascribed to the black oil sludge.

Sludge Formation

Oil sludge, the result of water, lead and carbon soot forming complex substances with parts of the oil, has always been with us. Modern oils contain additives intended to control the formation of sludge and to disperse it throughout the oil so that it is not deposited on engine parts or in oil passages. This newer phenomenon seems to involve a black, organic nitrate sludge as the engine killer. This supposition would seem to explain why gasoline but not diesel engines are affected. (Of course, the use of more highly compounded oils in diesel engines may be a reason.) The newer, high-output gasoline engines

firing lean mixtures are producers of nitrogen oxides (NO_x), while diesel engines are not. Catalytic converters to remove NO_x are only starting to come into wide use in Germany. However, the catalytic converter has no effect on NO_x while it is still in the engine. Even in a young and healthy engine about one percent of the combustion gases get by the piston rings as blow-by, introducing hot NO_x into the lubricating oil.

The technical services of both oil and automobile manufacturers are pursuing this matter and agree that the causes are not yet fully defined. It has been found that many oils classed by their makers as API service SF were exhausted of some additives before reaching the end of the normal oil change interval. The CCMC (Comité des Constructeurs d'Automobiles du Marché Commun) has introduced new specifications for oil that are more demanding than the API service designations with respect to handling higher specific power outputs and higher rpm. They have not, however, been able to address the matter of preventing the black nitrate sludge.

Sludge Causes

It is generally agreed that there are three major factors involved in the epidemic of sludge-caused engine failures:

1. Frequent short trips (causing much condensation in the oil) interspersed with high-speed driving on the autobahn (causing high oil temperatures).

2. Modern engine design, using very lean fuel mixtures, which leads to low fuel consumption but very high temperatures in the combustion chamber. Nitrogen, practically inert at ordinary temperatures, combines with oxygen at high temperatures to form NO, which goes on to combine with water in the crankcase, thus producing nitric acid, which attacks various constituents of the oil to form the nasty, black, organic nitrates.

3. Light and compact engine design, which minimizes the oil capacity of the crankcase. At the same time, the interval between oil changes is doubled or tripled while the problem is exacerbated by very tight sealing of piston rings to cylinder walls to minimize oil consumption. The idea that "she doesn't use a drop of oil between changes" indicates superior design or construction is a fallacy. The addition of a quart or two of oil between changes, to make up the oil consumed, refreshes the supply of additives. Large oil capacities, such as we find in Mercedes-Benz cars, mean that the oil runs cooler and that there is a larger reservoir of additives to neutralize acids and hold contaminants in suspension.

Another case recounted by *auto motor und sport* is that of a long-time Opel owner whose Ascona 1.8E gave up the ghost at 32,000 miles. Investigation at Opel headquarters showed that the oil strainer and the suction tube to the oil pump were totally blocked with sludge. The indignant owner insisted that he had religiously changed oil and filters every 7,500 km (4,660 miles) as recommended, using the house brand oil of one of Germany's largest supermarket chains. An unnamed Opel technician is reported to have said, "Whoever buys his motor oil there, where he also gets his margarine, should not wonder when something becomes rancid in his engine."

Is Sludge Forming?

One can readily determine whether sludge is forming in an engine by removing the oil filler cap and examining the visible surfaces. A thin film of black oil that is readily wiped off with the finger when the engine is just warm enough to touch without discomfort is normal. A tar-like layer with a gummy viscosity is a clear warning of danger ahead. If a check through the oil filler hole indicates a problem, it would be advisable to take the car to a shop where the valve cover(s) can be removed for a more thorough inspection. If any oil passages, such as the camshaft oil pipe or the oil drain hole back to the crankcase, are even partially clogged, all oil passageways, as well as the oil pump and strainer, should be positively cleaned.

While it is normal for the oil pressure to drop somewhat when the engine is idling when hot, pressure should jump up to 45 psi (or 3 bar) as soon as the engine is accelerated. Driving a car with little or no oil pressure invites engine destruction. This is so even if the dipstick shows the crankcase to be full of oil.

We don't want to invite overconfidence, but we must point out that the design and construction of Mercedes-Benz engines is such that when factory prescribed maintenance is followed and approved oil is used, they should not be susceptible to the black sludge disease. Note that all oils on the approved list (see The Oil Spot) are diesel-suitable oils and must be rated CC or CD as well as SF. While we have seen Mercedes-Benz cars with the disease in its most virulent form, they were cars which had been neglected to the point of abuse. A recently observed case was a 450SL in the shop for its 90,000-mile service. It needed new camshafts and all of the associated parts. The owner claimed that the car had always been serviced by the dealer. Records were brought out to reveal that the car had enjoyed only two oil changes in its entire 90,000-mile life. The entire area under the valve covers was covered with a layer of tarry black sludge about three sixteenths inch thick.

Many of us like to compare the mechanism of the automobile to the human body and its processes. In this vein (pun intended), one cannot avoid comparing the black nitrate sludge problem to the current concern over cholesterol in the human circulatory system. And one must again repeat the adage: the kindest thing you can do for your car is to change the oil and filter more frequently.

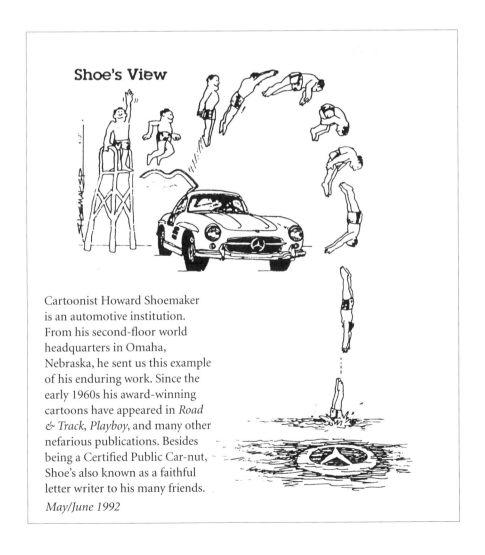

Shoe's View

Cartoonist Howard Shoemaker is an automotive institution. From his second-floor world headquarters in Omaha, Nebraska, he sent us this example of his enduring work. Since the early 1960s his award-winning cartoons have appeared in *Road & Track*, *Playboy*, and many other nefarious publications. Besides being a Certified Public Car-nut, Shoe's also known as a faithful letter writer to his many friends.

May/June 1992

Filters

by Frank King,
Technical Editor

*September/October
1994*

Filters

Next to fuel and oil, the most
frequently used service products on
our cars are filters. The dictionary
defines "filter" as any porous substance
through which a liquid or gas is
passed to remove constituents such as
suspended matter. This applies quite
nicely to our air, oil, and fuel filters.

The first automotive filters were
probably fuel filters in the form of
chamois leather or felt used in a funnel
to fill fuel tanks. Engine oil filters
came much later; early cars did not
recirculate oil, but even in the early
1950s some cars had no oil filters.
Air filters were last to become regular
equipment.

On gasoline-powered cars, a fuel
filter is needed to prevent clogging
of small passageways in carburetors,
injector pumps, or injection nozzles.
Filtering fuel as it was poured into the
tank was not good enough because
residual dirt or rust might exist in
the tank or fuel lines. Today's state of
manufacture and handling of gasoline
eliminates most problems that were
once common, and it is usual to
replace fuel filters for gasoline engines
only at 60,000-mile intervals.

Diesel fuel presents more of a
problem. While the manufacture and
handling of diesel fuel by reputable
companies is just as careful as that
of gasoline, diesel fuel itself, when
stored for any period of time, may
be a breeding ground for various
microorganisms such as algae,
bacteria, and molds. These form in
water that condenses and settles at the
bottom of a tank, either the tank of the
car or the storage tank of a supplier.
These organisms can form globs and
strings which must not be allowed to

reach the injection pump. Therefore,
in addition to a main fuel filter there is
a transparent pre-filter in the fuel line.
Regular inspection of the pre-filter
provides a warning of the presence of
such contaminating material, some of
which may get by it.

Most fuel filters for Mercedes-Benz
cars are specific to a model, and only
products of original suppliers are
generally offered in the aftermarket.

Cleaning Up the Air

Early carburetors were either updraft
or side-draft types, so they had only
coarse screens to prevent the sucking
in of leaves, paper, and similar large
scraps of debris. When down-draft
carburetors came into favor, it became
obvious that rather large fragments
could drop in and be swallowed, so
better filters became more necessary.
More important, considerable research
was being done on the causes of
engine wear and the part played by
contamination of the air consumed.
The "clean" air on a normal paved
road contains an average of one
milligram of dust per cubic meter of
air (1 Mg/M3). Air on unpaved roads
or near construction might contain 40
Mg/M3, so a small car could draw in as
much as 35 grams of dust in 100 miles.

Air-borne dust is surprisingly
abrasive, as any one who wears glasses
can attest. If the surface of the glasses
is cleaned by rubbing with a dry
tissue or cloth, scratches soon become
apparent. The effect of the same sharp
particles on cam lobes or other engine
surfaces can easily be appreciated. The
air filters on our cars present a large
surface of paper which is permeable
to air but holds solid particles above
a specified size. The area of this
paper is carefully designed so that the
resistance to air flow does not affect
engine performance. As dust builds up
on the filter, the resistance increases,
finally reaching a point where engine
power is affected.

Depending on the environment, air
filter elements usually need cleaning

or replacement at every maintenance
service. Only elements with perforated
metal reinforcements may be cleaned
with compressed air. Others should
be replaced. In replacing the element
it is important that the physical
dimensions of the replacement fit
precisely to the housing. Even tiny gaps
allow the passage of a large amount
of dust, defeating the purpose of
the filter. For this reason, only filter
elements made by original suppliers to
MBAG should be chosen.

How Dirty the Oil?

Even though our cars consume far
more air than fuel (14 ½ pounds of
air per pound of fuel), and dirt in fuel
was the motorist's earliest concern,
our great focus is on oil filters. The
oil that we put in our engines is
clean; the contaminants that we must
filter out were produced within the
engine itself except for silica, which
may have slipped in via the air filter.
The contaminants are products of
combustion and particles of metal
rubbed off by metal-to-metal friction.

For gasoline engines, Mercedes-
Benz uses full-flow filters, that is, all
oil leaving the oil pump passes
through the filter on its way to the
engine. If the buildup of particles
trapped in the filter is sufficient to
restrict the flow of oil so that oil
pressure rises beyond a certain point,
a relief valve opens, and oil continues
to flow to the engine unfiltered.

Oil filters are precisely designed so
that under normal driving conditions
the amount of contaminant collected
will not cause the relief valve to
release unfiltered oil directly to the
engine. This is the main reason why
the factory advises that oil and filter
be changed at shorter intervals under
adverse driving conditions. The filter
needs changing more than the oil.

In this context it should not be
assumed that because the oil looks
clean it is suitable for longer use. Some
relatively harmless contaminants
can cause oil to look dirty. The best

example is crankcase oil from a diesel which has been driven only two miles since oil and filter were changed.

For diesel engines, Mercedes-Benz uses an element that combines full-flow and bypass filter elements (Fig. 1). All oil going directly to the lubrication circuit of the engine passes through the full-flow section. This oil circuit is protected by a relief valve which provides an unbroken supply of oil to the engine if the filter is clogged. A bypass circuit also exists, to take oil through a finer section of the element and back to the crankcase after removing much of the soot which would rapidly clog the full-flow filter. When replacing the filter element, the oil port on the central oil tube must be checked to ensure that it is not blocked by foreign matter (Fig. 2).

Soot is a generic term for particles which are the product of combustion. These are mainly carbon and may be as large as grains of sand or as small as microscopically fine amorphous carbon. The latter in the form of lampblack is an ultra-fine polishing agent; as graphite it is a lubricant. When the carbon combines with various metallic substances, it can form a strong abrasive. The job of our filters is to remove all but the very fine, harmless soot.

The importance of proper installation of the filter element that was engineered for the job cannot be overemphasized. A cheaply manufactured or sloppily installed filter element is no better than no filter at all.

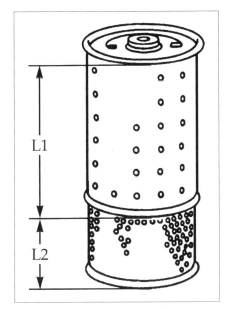

Figure 1: Oil filter element. L1 is full-flow segment. L2 is bypass segment.

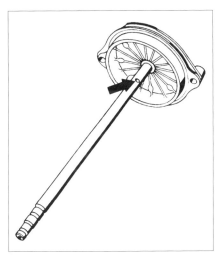

Figure 2: Central oil tube's oil port (arrow) must be kept clear.

Servicing the W126 300SD, Part I

by John Lamb, Minuteman Section

July/August 1995

Photos in this article by the author.

Mercedes-Benz turbo-diesels provide satisfying ownership if they are maintained regularly. Luckily, servicing them does not require many sophisticated tools. Here's how you can do some of the routine work on your 300SD.

Doing your own maintenance and service can extend your car's life and save money. This article supplements the *Mercedes-Benz Maintenance Manual USA* (starting model year 1981) for performing a major service on the 300SD (W126) as specified in the owner's manual at 30,000-mile intervals.

It is important that anyone doing this type of work have the proper tools and observe safe work practices. Besides the tasks below, an additional inspection should be made to check for structural damage, fluid leaks, condition of safety items (like brakes and tires) and all other mechanical items. Always begin a major service by having the engine compartment and underside degreased. Keep water and solvents away from the fuel injection pump, vacuum lines, and electronic modules. I use kitchen plastic bags to cover these components before cleaning. Keeping the engine clean has two advantages. First, you can spot leaks and know their location; second, you avoid getting dirty while working on the car, and you keep dirt out of what you are working on.

Power Steering Fluid and Filter Change

1. With the engine off, remove the power steering reservoir cover nut and cover.

2. Remove the 10-mm nut, spacer, and spring. See Photo 1.

3. Remove the power steering filter using needlenose pliers or a pick.

4. Using a Mityvac and a bleeder bottle, siphon the old fluid from the reservoir; if the car is warm, the fluid may be hot. See Photo 2.

5. Install a new filter, then install the spacer, spring, and nut. (When buying the new filter, have your chassis number, the pump brand and model number—on the pump—available for reference.) See Photo 3 and your owner's manual. Fill the container with new MB Power Steering Fluid (part number 000 989 88 03) or Dexron Mercon III fluid from a new container (opened containers of fluid deteriorate and may cause damage to the system). Replace the cover and cover nut. See your owner's manual for the correct fluid level.

6. Start the engine, then check for leaks. Shut off the engine, then recheck the fluid level.

To completely flush the power steering system, follow these steps:

1. After removing the filter in step 3 above, loosen the hose clamp on the return line to the reservoir and remove the hose. The high-pressure line usually has a threaded connector—don't disconnect it. The return line is usually clamped to the reservoir return pipe. To prevent fluid from draining out, you may have to plug the return pipe.

2. Put a drain pan under the end of the return hose, then have a helper start the engine. As old fluid is pumped out of

Photo 1. Power steering reservoir center nut being removed.

Photo 2. Use a Mityvac and bleeder bottle to siphon out old power steering fluid.

Photo 3. Install new filter as shown, then refill reservoir with new fluid.

the return hose, quickly add new fluid to the reservoir. To avoid getting air into the system during this process, keep the reservoir at least half full. To thoroughly flush the steering box, have your helper quickly turn the steering wheel full right and full left several times.

3. When fresh fluid appears from the return hose, the system is flushed. Stop the engine, reconnect the return hose, and install the new filter. Top up the reservoir, re-install the cap, then check for leaks as above.

Valve Adjustment

Valves should only be adjusted with the special tools shown in Photo 4. The engine should be cold (20°C/68°F). It is much easier to remove the valve cover after the air filter housing has been removed as described later in this section.

1. Disconnect only the throttle linkage connected to the valve cover. Remove the mounting bolts for the vacuum unit on top of the valve cover, then remove the valve cover mounting nuts and remove the cover. See Photo 5. Mark and tag all throttle linkages, vacuum hoses, and wires so you can link them back up later on. I use key identification tags.

2. Put a 27-mm deep socket on the crank hub pulley, and rotate the engine clockwise (looking from the front) until the first camshaft lobe points upward. Note whether this is an intake or exhaust valve. See Photo 6. Insert the correct thickness feeler gauge between the rocker arm and the camshaft. Avoid rotating the engine counterclockwise, or damage to the timing chain may result. Normal engine rotation can be determined by operating the starter and watching the pulleys and belts. The crank hub pulley is at the very front and bottom of the engine. The engine fan belts are driven from this pulley. Access the pulley from below the engine. If you have difficulty getting the socket onto the pulley, use a remote starter switch such as the Snap-on MT-302A instead. Connect the switch between starter terminal 50 (in the engine compartment) and the battery's positive terminal.

3. Place the valve retainer wrench on the hex valve retainer as in Photo 7.

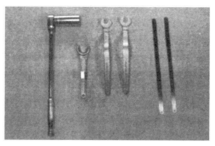

Photo 4. Tools needed to adjust valves include 27-mm socket and ratchet, valve retainer wrench, two 14-mm adjusting wrenches, feeler gauges.

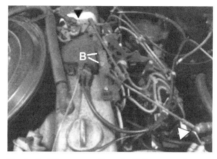

Photo 5. Disconnect throttle linkage as shown (triangles); remove mounting bolts (B), and valve cover mounting nuts (not shown), to remove valve cover.

Photo 6. Camshaft lobe (arrow) in correct position to adjust valve; feeler gauge (A).

Photo 7. Valve retainer wrench correctly inserted.

Place the two 14-mm wrenches directly above the retainer wrench, one wrench on the locknut (lower), the other on the adjuster (upper). Loosen the locknut by rotating the lower wrench

clockwise while turning the upper wrench counterclockwise. See Photo 8. The support on the retainer wrench can be moved in and out to clear obstructions.

4. Keeping the locknut loose, adjust the upper nut up or down until the correct clearance is obtained with the feeler gauge. Moderate resistance when sliding the feeler gauge between the camshaft and the rocker indicates that valve clearance is correct. Tighten the 14-mm locknut counterclockwise while holding the 14-mm adjuster nut stationary. Intake valve clearance should be 0.1 mm (0.004 in); exhaust valve clearance, 0.35 mm (0.0137 in). The valve retainer wrench is not used for adjustment and should not be turned. Because the clearance is usually reduced after the locknut is tightened, recheck the clearance after the locknut is tight.

5. Rotate the crankshaft using the 27-mm socket until the next camshaft lobe is in position. Using Figure 9, note whether it is an intake or exhaust valve, then repeat the adjustment for this valve. Continue this step until all the valves are adjusted.

6. After all valves have been adjusted, rotate the engine two complete

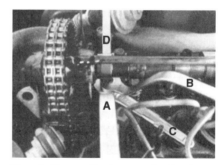

Photo 8. 14-mm adjusting wrenches (A, B) in correct position; valve retainer wrench (C) and feeler gauge (D).

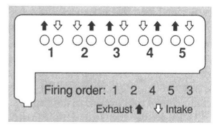

Figure 9. Layout of intake and exhaust valves.

revolutions and recheck all valves. There should be no mechanical binding from adjusting valves. If there is binding, the adjustment is incorrect. Remove the 27-mm socket from the crank hub.

7. Reinstall the valve cover using a new gasket. Torque the cover mounting nuts to 15 Nm (11 lb-ft). Reinstall all hoses, wires, and linkages.

Replacing Air Filter

Inspecting Air Cleaner Mounting Bushings

Cleaning Turbo Boost Pipe and Hollow Bolt

Grasp the air cleaner housing and move it up and down, and from side to side. If any movement exists, the rubber bushings are broken and should be replaced. If the housing is loose, unfiltered air can enter the engine, causing premature engine wear.

1. Remove the center nut and unclip the four retaining clips; remove the breather hose, the air filter cover, and the air filter.

2. To replace the rubber bushings, loosen the two hose clamps holding the plastic intake pipe between the air cleaner and the turbo; see Photo 10. Remove the pipe.

3. Remove the three 10-mm nuts and washers at the bottom of the air cleaner housing; see Photo 11. Remove the housing.

4. Inspect the mounting brackets and rubber bushings. Replace any damaged parts; see Photo 12. Use Loctite thread lock on the bushing threads.

5. Remove the hollow bolt and hose from the back of the intake manifold, as in Photo 13. Disconnect the other end of the hose at the turbo boost switch and blow clean the hose with compressed air. Clean the hollow bolt with solvent, then replace the bolt using new sealing washers. Installation is the reverse of removal.

Photo 10. Plastic intake pipe (arrow).

Photo 11. Remove 10-mm nuts (circled) to remove air cleaner housing and rubber bushings.

Photo 12. Rubber air cleaner mounting bushings (circled), turbo boost switch (1), EGR valve (2), and turbocharger (3).

Replacing Fuel Pre-Filter and Main Filter

1. Pinch off the rubber fuel supply hose going into the transparent fuel pre-filter using a fuel line clamp. This will prevent fuel spillage from the tank. Place shop rags below the filter, then loosen the hose clamps and remove the pre-filter. Install the new pre-filter. See Photo 14.

2. To replace the main fuel filter, loosen the 24-mm mounting bolt, then unscrew the filter. Replace the filter using new sealing washers. Coat the gasket of the filter with clean diesel fuel before installing.

3. Remove the fuel line clamp, then unscrew the hand pump handle and pump up the fuel pressure until the car starts. Check for leaks, then screw in the pump handle.

To prevent long-term contamination of the fuel system, use an additive such as Biobor Diesel Doctor in the fuel tank.

Photo 13. Hollow bolt (arrow) and hose to turbo boost switch; clean bolt with solvent.

Photo 14. Fuel pre-filter (A), main filter (B), main filter mounting bolt (C), hand pump (D), and supply hose (E) from tank.

Photo 15. Lubricate door hinges.

Lubrication and General Service

1. Lubricate the hood and trunk hinges and the hood release mechanism with a light oil.

2. Lubricate the accelerator rods by removing one at a time, noting its location. Clean the ball and socket, then apply a small amount of Castors DB hydraulic fluid, Mobil Aero FHA, Shell Aero Fluid 4 or ATF. Remember the base and back of the accelerator pedal.

3. Lubricate the door hinges using a needle tip grease gun such as the Snap-on YA4190 and a multipurpose grease. See Photo 15. Lubricate the door latches and the door check rods using Optimol-Optitemp TT 1 lubricant.

4. Raise the radio antenna, then clean and lubricate it using Hirschmann antenna lube or equivalent (WD-40 in a pinch) on a shop rag.

5. Lubricate the lock cylinders using a lock lubricant.

6. Check all lights for proper operation. Check air pressure in all tires, including the spare.

Servicing the W126 300SD, Part II

by John Lamb, Minuteman Section

September/October 1995

Photos in this article by the author.

Our July/August issue carried the first portion of this article, which we recommend that you read first. Although this article specifically applies to the W126 version of the 300SD, most of it can be adapted to other models.

Here we'll describe some regular fluid changes that you can do at home. As we mentioned last time, this material supplements the *Mercedes-Benz Maintenance Manual*. A reminder—always wear disposable gloves when changing or handling fluids.

Oil and Oil Filter Change

1. Place a large drain pan beneath the engine oil drain plug. Remove the 13-mm drain plug and discard the sealing washer. See Photo 16.

2. Remove the oil filler cap from the valve cover.

3. Remove the two nuts holding the oil filter cover as in Photo 17. Remove the oil filter cover and place it in a separate drain pan. Discard the large rubber o-ring in the top of the cover.

4. Remove the filter element by grasping the wire handle and pulling up as per Photo 18.

5. Clean the inside of the oil filter housing using paper towels.

6. Blow clean the hollow stem in the oil filter cover using a nozzle and compressed air as in Photo 19. Place a rag over the end of the stem to prevent oil spray. Be sure that the hole in the side of the tube is open.

Photo 16. Engine oil drain plug being removed.

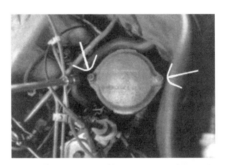

Photo 17. Remove oil filter cover nuts (arrows).

Photo 18. Oil filter element being removed.

Photo 19. Oil passage (arrow) in the cover stem being blown clean.

7. Install the new filter element until it properly seats in the filter housing. Install a new 0-ring on the oil filter cover. Coat the 0-ring with oil. Install the cover and torque the mounting nuts to 25 Nm (18 lb-ft). Working below the car, install the oil drain plug using a new sealing washer. Torque the drain plug to 40 Nm (30 lb-ft).

8. Fill the engine with seven quarts of oil. Start the engine and check for correct oil pressure; make sure there are no leaks. Shut off the engine, then recheck the oil level after two minutes. Top up the oil as necessary. Recycle the old oil.

Changing Automatic Transmission Fluid and Filter

Automatic transmissions tolerate absolutely no dirt, so be sure your funnel, wiping rags, and tools are clean.

1. With the transmission in Park and the emergency brake applied, carefully raise the front of the car and support it with vehicle stands designed for the purpose. Be sure that the car is stable and is on a flat surface. Block the rear wheels. (It is possible to drain the transmission fluid without raising the car. Always make sure the emergency brake is applied, the wheels are blocked, and the engine is off.)

2. Below the car, place a drain pan below the opening at the bottom of the transmission bellhousing. Use a remote starter switch or have a helper rotate the engine clockwise (looking from the front), using a 27-mm socket at the crankshaft hub pulley, until the torque converter drain plug (about the size of a dime) is visible in the opening of the bellhousing. Remove the drain plug using a long 5-mm hex bit such

as the Snap-on FAML5. See Photos 20 and 21. If you have a new sealing washer, discard the old one.

3. Remove the 27-mm socket from the crankshaft pulley, then remove the transmission dipstick.

4. Clean the area around the transmission pan using a spray solvent such as brake cleaner. Place a drain pan below the transmission.

5. Remove the transmission drain plug using a 5-mm hex bit. Allow the fluid to drain into a drain pan.

6. Remove the six transmission pan bolts using a 13-mm socket, then remove the pan. Working at the bench, thoroughly clean the pan, then install a new pan gasket.

7. Back under the car, remove the transmission filter by removing the

Photos 20 and 21. Torque converter drain plug (arrow) being removed; crossmember and transmission pan also shown.

three filter mounting screws. Note the location of each screw; see Photo 22.

8. Install the new filter, making sure it is properly seated against the valve body. Tighten the three mounting screws.

9. Clean the transmission-to-pan mating surface, then reinstall the transmission pan; torque the six pan bolts to 8 Nm (72 lb-in).

10. Reinstall the drain pan plug and the torque converter drain plug using new sealing washers; torque them to 14 Nm (10.5 lb-ft).

11. Through the dipstick tube, slowly pour in four quarts of Dexron Mercon III automatic transmission fluid as in Photo 23. Use a clean funnel, or rest the dipstick on the tube and slowly pour fluid onto it. Lower the car, start the engine, and move the gear lever through all ranges to circulate the fluid. Pour in the remaining two quarts. Put the lever in Park, check the fluid level, and top up as necessary. Stop the engine, then check for leaks. Dispose of the old fluid properly.

Transmission fluid level will rise as the fluid heats during running. Avoid overfilling the transmission. Since the engine and transmission will be cool, the fluid level should be at least 10 mm below the Min mark; see the May/June 1995 issue.

Replacing Engine Coolant

Use only Mercedes-Benz antifreeze (Q 1 03 0002) mixed with 50-percent drinking water or distilled water. Filling is best done with the front of the car raised. Dispose of old coolant in an environmentally friendly way.

1. With the engine cool, remove the coolant drain plug at the bottom of the radiator; see Photo 24. Drain the coolant into a pan.

Photo 22. Transmission filter being removed; undo three Phillips screws.

Photo 23. Fill transmission with engine off, using Dexron Mercon III transmission fluid.

Photo 24. Radiator drain plug (arrow).

2. Remove the expansion tank fill lap, then select the defroster button function on the climate control panel.

3. Disconnect the negative battery cable after writing down the radio code. Remove the engine block drain plug just in front of the starter motor below the air filter assembly as in Photo 25. Use an 8-in extension and a 19-mm socket. Allow the coolant to drain thoroughly, then replace the block drain plug using a new sealing washer. Be sure the battery is disconnected before attempting to remove or install the block drain plug. The starter motor has a powered terminal that can accidentally be shorted out with tools if the battery is connected.

Do not confuse the engine block heater assembly with the engine block drain plug; do not attempt to remove the engine block heater.

4. Install the radiator drain plug and tighten it using a coin. Do not overtighten.

5. Temporarily remove the radiator hose at the engine thermostat housing. Fill the engine through the thermostat housing with a 50/50 antifreeze/water solution. Reinstall the hose, and tighten the clamp. (Alternatively, fill the system through the expansion tank.)

6. Top up the cooling system through the expansion tank, then start the engine and continue to top up the level while allowing the engine to reach normal temperature. When finished, replace the tank cap, then check for leaks.

Brake Fluid Change

Mercedes-Benz calls for brake fluid changes every two years, but if you use your brakes hard and repeatedly get them hot, you may prefer annual changes. The following vacuum method is for cars without ABS; for cars with ABS, use the pressure method of brake bleeding.

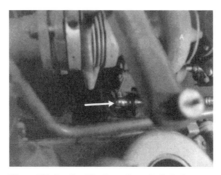

Photo 25. Engine block coolant drain being removed using ratchet and socket (arrow).

Brake fluid is poisonous and will damage bodywork, rubber, and plastic parts. If brake fluid is spilled by accident, flush the area with water. Again, wear disposable gloves when changing or handling fluids. When replacing or adding fluid to the brake system, use only DOT4 brake fluid from a new container. Brakes can be bled without removing the wheels; use a brake bleeding wrench such as the Snap-on S6186 to access the brake caliper bleeder screws.

1. With the transmission in Park and the emergency brake applied, carefully raise the car and support it with vehicle stands designed for the purpose. Check that the car is stable and is on a flat surface. Remove the wheels (loosen the lug bolts before raising the car).

2. Connect one hose from a bleeder bottle to the caliper bleed screw. Connect the other hose from the bottle to a hand vacuum such as a Mityvac. Bleeder bottle hose connections are marked on the top of the bottle.

3. Pump up the hand vacuum, then open the bleeder screw at the caliper as in Photo 26. Continue pumping the vacuum as the fluid fills the bottle. Close the bleeder screw, then check and top up the fluid in the brake master cylinder. Continue this process until clean fluid fills the bottle. Never allow the master cylinder to empty below the Min mark on the reservoir.

If fluid doesn't flow out of the caliper after pumping up a vacuum,

Photo 26. Hand vacuum pump properly connected to brake caliper. Use a 9-mm wrench to loosen brake caliper bleeder screw. Bleeder bottle not shown.

clean out the bleeder screw using a paper clip or piece of wire.

4. Repeat step 3 at the other calipers; bleed in the order right rear, left rear, right front, left front. Replace the rubber dust caps at the calipers, check and top up the fluid in the master cylinder, then check the brake pedal for firm feel. If the pedal is spongy there is still air in the brake lines. Repeat the bleeding process until the pedal is hard. Reinstall the wheels; torque the lug bolts to 110 Nm (81 lb-ft). Rather than dumping the old brake fluid, dispose of it in an environmentally friendly manner.

Replacing Final Drive (Differential) Lubricant

1. With the car on a level surface and the emergency brake on, put a drain pan below the center of the rear axle. Remove the two hex head plugs, and allow the fluid to drain completely. See Photo 27. The lower plug is the drain plug. The upper plug is a combination fill plug and level check plug. (To be sure that you can re-fill the differential,

Photo 27. Final drive drain plug being removed. Fill and level check plug at arrow. Tighten plugs to 50 Nm (37 lb-ft).

remove the fill plug first. This avoids having a stuck fill plug and a drained differential.) Also remove the vent "bolt" near the top; it looks like a bolt about an inch tall with a loose cap at the top.

2. Replace the drain (lower) plug, then fill the rear axle with approximately 1.3 liters of SAE 90 or SAE 85W/90 hypoid gear lubricant. When the level of the fluid is correct, the fluid should be right up to the opening of the fill plug. To fill the rear axle directly from the bottles that the oil is sold in, cut off part of the funnel-shaped tip and tilt the bottle up with the tip in the rear axle fill hole.

3. Soak the vent "bolt" in solvent or diesel fuel to remove caked-in dirt. To make sure it is clear, blow air through it. Re-install the vent.

Copyright 1995, John Lamb. MBCA Technical Advisor George Murphy and Technical Director Frank King also contributed to this article.

How to Build an Ignition Analyzer

by Jim Mahaffey, Contributing Editor

January/February 1999

Photos in this article by the author.

Impress your friends and tune up your vintage Mercedes-Benz with this easy-to-build accessory.

According to *Mercedes-Benz Maintenance Manual USA, Passenger Cars, Volume 1*, "If no oscillograph is available, a complete evaluation of the ignition system is impossible." After that statement come 10 pages of marvelous oscilloscope traces of signals emanating from the spark coil in a vintage Mercedes-Benz, built when distributor points were metal and tetraethyl lead was a good thing. By simply clipping a probe to the high-voltage lead on the coil, you can see the breaker contacts open and close, the ring of the capacitor and ignition coil combination, and the ramped charging of the ignition coil. The slightest problem in any cylinder will show up on the oscilloscope trace as a distinct signature, as detailed in the manual.

Scope It Out

I use an oscilloscope for radio and clock repair but lacked a means to sample the high-voltage signal, which peaks at about 6 kV. The clip-around inductive probes used in diagnostic tachometers and dwell meters are incapable of picking up the subtle inflections of the ignition trace. A bit of research revealed that the special probe for ignition analysis is a capacitor bridge. A simple, non-intrusive probe that will work with most any general-purpose oscilloscope can be built in an evening with a few simple hand tools.

I started with a miniature "chip clip" used to close potato-chip bags (in case for some reason you can't finish off a bag in one sitting). The miniature clip, for the little individual bags, is

available at grocery stores. The chip clip becomes the capacitor bridge, with the addition of:

- one alligator clip, Radio Shack #270-346
- one BNC chassis-mount jack, type 1044, Radio Shack #278-105
- one cable, 6 feet, BNC both ends, Radio Shack #278-964
- one 4.7-pf ceramic disc capacitor, Radio Shack #272-120
- three feet of 20-gauge stranded hookup wire
- one brass bar, 3/4-in wide, l/16-in thick, from hardware store

Oscilloscopes can be found for cheap at any hamfest or anywhere aged electronics are sold. I've seen them for sale in many odd places, including the Paris flea market. Mine came from a NASA auction, and it was old when Sputnik was launched. You will also need some tools:

- 3/8-in drill bit (and a drill press to drive it)
- 1/16-in drill bit
- hack saw
- vise to hold items being sawn
- file
- solder and soldering iron
- 9/16-in open-ended wrench
- sandpaper
- high-speed epoxy cement

Build It, Sparky

Begin by sawing off a piece of brass bar about 1.9-in long. Dress the end with a file, then drill a 1/16-in hole in a corner. This will be your main capacitor plate. Saw off another brass piece, 1.6-in long, round off one end of it with the file, then bore a 3/8-in hole in this end to take the BNC jack. Insert the jack and run down the 9/16-in nut tightly to hold it in place. Drill two 1/16-in holes in the bar near the 9/16-in nut.

Strip a 2-in piece of hookup wire on both ends and solder it between the center post on the BNC jack and the corner on the end of the capacitor

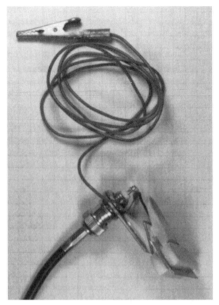

Structure of high-voltage clip.

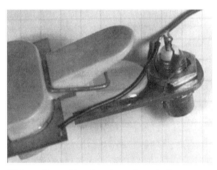

High-voltage clip, showing where holes are drilled.

plate. Solder the 47-pf bridge capacitor between the center post and one of the 1/16-in holes in the brass bar. You may want to shorten the leads on the bridge capacitor.

Strip both ends of a 3-ft length of hookup wire to make the ground wire. Solder one end into the remaining 1/16-in hole in the brass bar; solder the other end to the alligator clip.

Sand the teeth off the inside of one jaw on the chip clip. Sand off the "Chip Clip" logo. Mix up a dab of epoxy, and glue the capacitor plate to the inside of the modified jaw. The steel spring in the chip clip will hold the plate in place as the epoxy hardens. Glue the brass bar to one of the chip clip handles. You now have a capacitor-coupled high-voltage probe.

Diagnostic Methods

Connect the probe to your oscilloscope with the 6-ft BNC cable, and clip the ground wire to clean chassis metal near the engine. Set the oscilloscope horizontal deflection to 1 volt per cm, set the horizontal deflection to 1 millisecond per cm, and warm up the instrument. Clip the probe to the high-voltage line between the distributor and coil, and fire up the engine. Set the oscilloscope trigger-level to begin the trace at its most prominent feature, a high-going spike. You may need to invert the trace to make it resemble the pictures in the manual.

The high spike is called the "bias line," peaking at 6 kV, and it represents the opening of the points. It is followed by the "ignition line," ramping down slightly from a maximum of 1.5 kV. After the ignition line is a damped oscillation of the coil capacitor combination, grounding out after three oscillations. The line then jumps down and rings as the points close, and you can watch as the ignition coil takes the charge, ramping up exponentially. You are watching all four, six, or eight cylinders fire with their traces superimposed, and you notice that the ignition line dances up and down, indicating slight differences in compression ratio and fuel-air charge in individual cylinders.

Characteristic signs of trouble show clearly on the oscilloscope. A worn top bearing in your distributor shows up as a wobbling point-closure line, way before the problem shows up in engine performance. You can spot incorrect spark plug electrode gap, too rich or too lean fuel-air mixture, bad distributor rotor, bad cable, sooted plugs, or burned points. You can synchronize multiple carburetors and adjust double-contact distributors. If you would like to see the cylinders fire in sequence on one trace, build another probe and use it as an external trigger off cylinder number one. The cylinders will then appear on the trace in firing order if you increase the horizontal deflection period proportional to your number of cylinders. For example, if you have eight cylinders, decrease the horizontal deflection speed to 8 milliseconds per cm.

Tach up the engine, and watch as the ignition picture compresses. If the coil-capacitor oscillations increase heavily, it means that the fuel-air mixture is too lean, and you need to check the injection nozzle in the affected cylinder. You'll wonder how you lived without this thing.

Special thanks to Paul Springer, whose diligent research led to this design.

Oscilloscope connected to car, with ignition trace on scope.

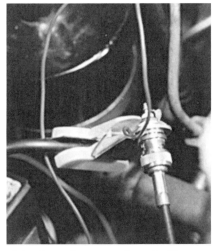

High-voltage clip connected to coil cable.

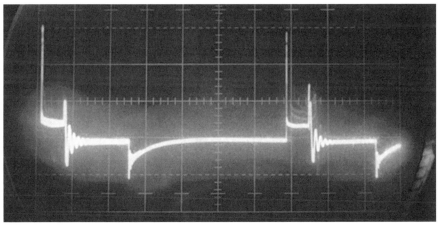

Scope-trace showing typical ignition line.

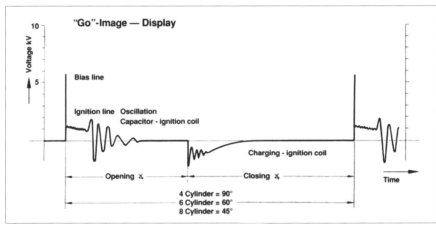

Maintenance Manual **illustrations identify diagnostic signatures.**

On-Board Diagnostics for Diesels

by John Lamb,
Contributing
Editor

*May/June
1998*

Photos in this article
by the author.

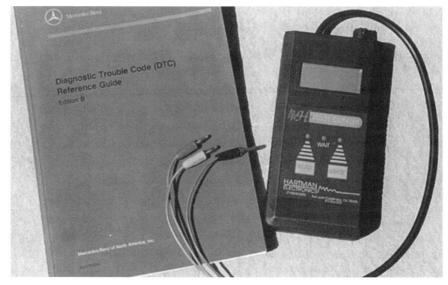

Mercedes-Benz reference guide and Hartman code reader.

*Computer-controlled diesel
performance and reliability are
conveniences that we appreciate
every day with the added bonus
of cleaner air as a result. Here's
how you can read your diesel's
computer's mind.*

Mercedes-Benz has used computer controls on its diesel engines since the late 1980s; such vehicles are equipped with a control module to enhance performance and lower tailpipe emissions. Some of the module's functions are regulation of idle speed, control of the exhaust gas recirculation (EGR), charge pressure control, and system diagnostics. The module is connected to several sensors on the engine that monitor things like engine speed, coolant temperature, air volume and others.

All recent Mercedes-Benz diesel cars sold in the U.S. incorporate the Electronic Diesel System (EDS) which uses self-diagnostics in the control module to identify operational faults within the system. When certain parameters have failed, faults set a code, and the "check engine" light in the instrument cluster alerts the driver that attention is required.

Accessing Fault Memory

Fault codes can be read by the do-it-yourselfer with a diagnostic scan tool such as the $300 Hartman diagnostic pulse counter (Mission Viejo Imports, 28701 Marguerite Pkwy., Mission Viejo, CA 92692; 800/842-1658. For a list of codes, see *Diagnostic Trouble Code Reference Guide*, published by Mercedes-Benz (part number S-2579-93A, $19.50).

The code reader is plugged into the correct terminals on a diagnostic plug in the engine compartment. After a few seconds it will display codes, if any, indicating an EDS fault. Knowing the fault code number will help a technician to pinpoint the problem. While you may not have the skill to repair the faults, the code reader allows you to access the computer and may help a professional to diagnose and repair the system. This typical list of fault codes is for a 1990 300D Turbo (124 chassis, 602 diesel engine):

Code	Possible Cause
1	No faults in system
2	Fuel rack position sensor
3	Air flow sensor
4	EDS control module or atmospheric pressure sensor (in control unit)
5	Exhaust gas recirculation valve or EGR control circuit
6	EDS control module, internal voltage supply
7	Starter ring gear speed sensor
8	Coolant temperature sensor
9	Intake air temperature sensor open/short circuit
10	not used
11	Electronic idle speed actuator or EGR valve vacuum transducer
12	not used
13	EDS control module defective, internal memory malfunction
14	EDS pressure sensor defective
15	Intake manifold air pressure control valve vacuum transducer, wastegate vacuum transducer, or malfunction in the manifold air pressure circuit.

The technician must know which system he wishes to access, such as engine controls, ABS, traction control, or climate control. Each system typically has its own computer module, its own list of fault codes, and its own socket in the diagnostic plug.

Connecting to the Vehicle

1. Make sure the key is off, then connect the code reader ground test lead (black) to socket number 1 in the diagnostic plug.

2. Connect the code reader red terminal to the battery positive (+) post.

3. Connect the code reader yellow terminal to socket number 4* in the diagnostic plug.

4. With the shifter in Park and the parking brake on, start the engine, let it warm, and make sure the automatic climate control is off.

5. Press the Read button on the code reader. If the reader displays a code, write it down.

6. Again press the Read button for possible additional codes or until the first code is displayed again.

7. Increase engine speed to 900 rpm for at least 5 seconds.

8. Repair any faults in the system, then with the code reader press the Erase button until fault codes clear.

9. Repeat step 8 to erase additional codes.

10. Shut off the engine and remove the code reader.

11. Road test the car to cause fault codes to reset. Then go back to step 1. This socket number varies with the model and the on-board module system being tested.

If the codes are read with the engine off, you will always see a code 7 displayed. This is because with the engine not turning, the starter ring gear sensor produces no signal.

Versatility

Mercedes-Benz has wired the diagnostic plug allowing you to access several systems on the car. Examples of other systems you can read are the ABS, transmission control, 4Matic, climate control, adaptive damping (suspension), anti-theft alarm, remote locking system, and others. Follow the hook-up procedures in the diagnostic manual, as the socket number in the diagnostic plug will differ.

OBD-II

Beginning in 1996, all cars sold in the U.S. had to have an on-board diagnostic system known as OBD-II that monitors engine and emission control functions. This system is an enhanced version of previous systems in that it can analyze emission control devices for correct operation and aging effects as the car is driven. Again, if a fault is detected, the "check engine" light illuminates in the instrument cluster. This system uses a new 16-pin diagnostic plug under the steering column in the passenger compartment.

Location of diagnostic plug (arrow) on 1990 300D; to access socket, pull off cover.

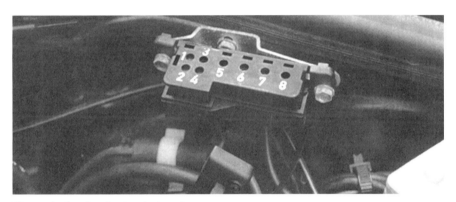

Diagnostic plug showing terminal numbers.

After pressing Read button, code 7 is displayed because engine was off, causing a "no signal" condition from the crankshaft (ring gear) sensor.

To access these systems, you must have a scan tool that is fully compatible with the OBD-II ISO standard. The pulse counter described above does not work with OBD-II systems.

John Lamb, a technical training manager for Snap-on Tools in the Boston area, has hosted several technical seminars for Minuteman Section.

Cooler Coolant

by Frank King,
Technical Editor

*September/October
1993*

After reading the "Keeping It Cool" item in our May/June 1993 issue, a member in Santa Barbara wrote to tell us about an interesting and valuable product which can increase the efficiency of your cooling system. The product is WaterWetter™, made by Red Line Synthetic Oil Corp. of Martinet, California, a company familiar to most of us for their diesel fuel additive, Red Line Diesel Fuel Catalyst.

From previous articles in *The Star*, most of you will be aware that the temperature indicated by the gauge in the instrument cluster is the temperature of coolant leaving the engine block, en route to the radiator. Coolant temperatures within the block vary widely, from a fairly tepid level where the coolant enters the block from the pump, to higher than boiling (265°F) around the exhaust valves and a few other hot spots. At these spots the coolant will be vaporizing to form bubbles which cling to the metal.

If the cooling system contains only plain water, these bubbles will be very large (Fig. 1a) because of the very high surface tension of water. If the coolant is 50:50 antifreeze and water, the bubbles will be somewhat smaller, but in either case the bubbles insulate the liquid coolant from the hot metal. Any liquid has far better heat transfer properties than the same substance in the vapor state.

This phenomenon is easily observed in the kitchen. Put some plain cold water in an aluminum or white enamel pan, and place it, without

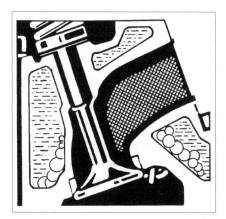

Figure 1a. Normal coolant forms large bubbles when it boils, insulating the hot metal from further coolant.

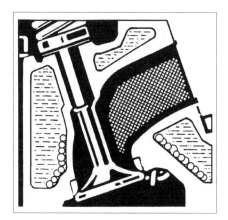

Figure 1b. With WaterWetter, smaller bubbles form, allowing better heat transfer from metal to coolant.

a cover, on a stove burner turned on high. Watch the little bubbles form at the interface between the water and the bottom of the pan. Only after enough heat has been transferred to raise the vapor pressure higher than barometric pressure will big bubbles force their way to the water surface. Boiling of the water may be hastened by breaking loose those little insulating bubbles with a wooden spoon.

Red Line WaterWetter reduces the surface tension of the coolant so that much smaller bubbles (Fig. 1b)

will be formed, and heat will transfer more quickly from the hot metal to the liquid coolant. WaterWetter consists of propylene glycol, dipropylene glycol, tripropylene glycol, and other polyglycols. It does not affect the freezing point of your 50:50 antifreeze coolant and does not affect the behavior of your cooling system until the thermostat opens. From that point on, the cooling system functions by allowing the temperature of the coolant to rise until the amount of heat received from the engine equals the amount of heat transferred to the atmosphere. By speeding up the transfer of heat to the coolant, WaterWetter allows this equilibrium to be reached at a lower average coolant temperature. This lowering of the temperature may be as much as 8°F and is most beneficial to the hottest spots in the engine.

WaterWetter will not cure a malfunctioning cooling system. It does allow a normal system to operate with less overshooting of the temperature at which the thermostat is set. This is done by reducing the surface tension of the coolant, thereby minimizing formation of insulating bubbles at hot spots in the engine.

A companion product, Red Line Cooling System Rust & Corrosion Inhibitor with WaterWetter, is unsuitable for use in Mercedes-Benz cooling systems since it contains inhibitors that are disapproved by MBAG. The product to use is plain WaterWetter.

One Shot Lubrication System Repair

by Burt Mills

May/June 1979

Photos in this article by the author.

Mounted high on the firewall of older Mercedes-Benzes, you'll find a reservoir for lubricating oil. Connected to this, there is a plunger-type pump that extends into the car, and is located above the clutch pedal. One push on this foot-operated plunger sends a measured amount of oil to those parts of the front suspension system that need lubrication. It is a simple, well designed system that has helped contribute to the long life of these fine cars.

The system was furnished by WILLY VOGEL, Berlin W-35 D.R.P., and carries the title "PUMP KURZ UND KRÄFTIG BETÄTIGEN."

These require but little attention to keep them in fine working condition. First, the strainer should be cleaned, so there are no impurities allowed into the system. The fittings should be tight to prevent oil leaks.

The second part of this system is mounted on top of the chassis just ahead of the firewall. It consists of the measuring valve. A tube brings the oil from the reservoir to the valve. There's a clean-out plug on the top of the valve. From this valve two tubes carry the oil to the transfer tubes.

On cars that have sat unused for some time, or cars that are used only infrequently, the oil in these tubes can solidify somewhat, and not respond to the pressure from the foot plunger. There's also the danger that one of the oil delivery tubes could have been damaged, though by and large they're well protected.

It's best to make a thorough check of the system to assure proper operation.

After cleaning the metering valve thoroughly in kerosene or solvent, run a medium stiff wire through the two transfer tubes. Obviously you have to disconnect both ends to do this. If the wire slips through easily, the tubes will allow the oil to move. If, however, because of engine heat (these tubes cross the firewall close to the engine) oil has solidified, you may have to work the wire back and forth a couple of times to clear the tubes.

Cleaning out the small individual tubes that carry the oil from the transfer tubes to the individual joints is more difficult. On some, you can run a thin wire through, once you've disconnected the terminal end. Others will have to be disconnected and removed to be cleaned. On those you disconnect, be sure to save the small brass washer that fits on the terminal end.

Holding the tube vertical, drip a little solvent or kerosene into it and let it set for awhile. This should work its way down the tube, loosening oil that may have thickened. A thin wire often helps loosen the oil after the solvent has had a chance to work. On a few occasions, blowing into the tube, like into a soda straw, will force the solidified oil to move.

Look for damaged places on the tubes, either by chafing where they cross through the frame, or by flattening if they've been hit by a rock thrown up by the front wheels. There can be no obstructions in the tubes if the system is to work properly.

Broken or damaged tubes can be replaced by brazing in new sections. If you don't have facilities to do this, a radiator repair shop is an excellent place to ask for help. Also, small machine shops can usually handle this sort of repair for you.

With the tubes completely cleaned, reassemble, being careful not to cross thread any of the fittings. Do not use any sort of gasket cement or shellac on any of the fittings. You should be able to get a leak-free connection if all fittings are clean, and the washer is in place.

Before you tighten the terminal end of the fittings, refill the reservoir, and push the plunger until oil drips out the terminal fittings. Then tighten each terminal fitting, wipe up the oil that dripped out at each, re-fill the reservoir, replace the cap tightly, and the system is ready to work.

I have never seen any instructions as to how often the plunger should be pushed to give the front suspension system the lubrication it requires. Information that comes with the pre-World War II Rolls Royces suggests every 200 miles while the car is operating. I presume that would be sufficient to keep the front suspension system of your Mercedes well lubricated.

Use care disconnecting oil lines from metering device. Remove unit from car and clean thoroughly with solvent or kerosene. When re-assembling, turn connections in by hand first to prevent cross threading, then tighten, using two open-end wrenches. DO NOT use gasket cement.

Tuning the Mercedes-Benz 190SL

by Edward Jahns

May/June 1959

Probably more inquiries have been made concerning the tuning of the 190SL than all of the other Mercedes-Benz motor cars combined. This, then, is a summary of the procedures involved.

Adjusting the Ignition Timing

1. Block the front left and right rear wheels to prevent the car from rolling with the handbrake released.

2. Engage the shift lever into 4th gear.

3. Jack up the rear left wheel.

4. If engine performance is considered of greater importance than motor noise in the radio—proceed to remove *all* of the spark suppressors.

I have seen engines which have had a resistor in the coil, a resistor in the center of the distributor, one for each plug in the distributor, a resistor type rotor and resistor type connectors for each plug as well as resistor type spark plugs. The currents for all plugs must pass through the coil resistor, central distributor, resistor and rotor resistor so that the spark intensity to all cylinders is reduced when these are used.

As a compromise, it is suggested to either use a resistive type rotor only—or one resistor in the central distributor cap position or four resistor type spark plug connectors *or* four resistor type spark plugs. But *not* combinations, if you wish maximum performance.

The radio ignition noise can be reduced to reasonably low levels with *no* suppressors and lower yet with one suppressor per plug *or* a resistor type rotor *or* resistor type plugs by separating the primary and secondary leads to the ignition coil and shielding the primary lead (to the distributor contact points) and grounding the shield to the distributor ground. This will not affect performance of the motor at all.

I use Champion N8B spark plugs gapped at .032 in. for maximum performance up to 4500 RPM and gapped .022 in. for maximum performance to 6000 RPM (but reduced performance from idle to 4500 RPM) since 4500 corresponds to 85 MPH in 4th, the .032 in. gap is usually most useful. Note, however, that with no suppressor, the plugs have to be gapped at least every 2500 miles (the gap will usually increase from .032 in. to .055 in. in that period). Several members have stated that they were pleased with the performance of the Lodge platinum tipped resistor type spark plugs, but not having used them, I cannot comment.

The tune-up procedure is now continued by:

5. Remove the distributor cap and rotate the rear left wheel in the direction of forward travel (counter-clockwise) until the distributor point spacing is at maximum. Remove the rotor and grasp the distributor shaft securely to check for play in the directions parallel to the distributor plate. There should be none or at worst .003 in. maximum; if in excess of .003 in. the distributor should be replaced as it will not be possible to obtain consistent point spacings for all cylinders at all speeds at all times.

6. If the points have been used for 10,000 miles or so, it would be advisable to replace them at this time, regardless of whether they are pitted or not. The contact point closing spring operates over 64 million times per 10,000 miles and because of metal fatigue loses part of its initial ability to close rapidly at highest engine RPM.

If the points are pitted and *must* be used, do not file them or otherwise attempt to alter them, but do measure and set the gap at the edges where the points are not pitted.

7. Loosen the hold down screw for the stationary point and rotate the small gap adjustment screw until the gap is .015 in. to 0.16 in.

8. Tighten the hold down screw securely and recheck the gap, which will change due to the tightening of the hold down screw.

9. Repeat as necessary until the gap is .013 in. to .015 in.

10. Apply one drop of oil to the felt on top of the distributor shaft and to the point pivot shaft. Apply a very, very light film of cam lubricant or Dow DC4 on the cam (which operates the moveable point).

Now, the timing should be set as follows: Rotate the left rear wheel until the timing marks on the starter ring gear (accessible by removing the small plate which is held by two hex head screws under the ring gear) line up with the pointer as follows:

For distributor VJUR4BR11 mk and camshaft 121-051-1401 the setting is 2° ± 1° B.T.D.C., with distributor VJUR4BR11 mk and camshaft 121-051-1501 the setting is 0° ± 1° B.T.D.C., with distributor VJ4BR11 mk the setting is 9° ± 1° B.T.D.C.

On some cars the timing mark will be found at the front of the engine on the vibration dampener, as on the 190 sedan. There appears to be no way to tell this from serial numbers.

Since the tuning-up procedure necessitates adjusting the valve tappets it is suggested that the valve cover be removed at this time to check the number on the camshaft (except, that if you have distributor VJ4BR11 mk the camshaft is the same on all engines and the valve cover can be removed later, if so desired).

Then, adjust the manual spark control to extreme counterclockwise and then clockwise about 30 degrees. Loosen the Allen screw, set horizontally below the distributor and operating a clamp to position same.

Advance the distributor from a retarded position until the points *just* barely open, *not* close. The direction of the distributor housing rotation to advance the timing is opposite to the direction in which the rotor moves when the rear wheel is turned in the direction of forward travel.

Tighten the Allen screw, making sure that the distributor is firmly pressed down into the position, examine the distributor cap for cracks and if satisfactory reinstall the distributor and make sure that all the spark plug leads are pressed firmly into same.

Adjusting the Valve Tappets

First, the engine *must* be cold. If the engine has been run in the previous 12 hours, you cannot correctly set the tappets.

To adjust a warm motor is one way to obtain excessive vibration at about 3200 RPM. The inevitable dimensional changes of one valve assembly to the next because of slightly different temperatures make it impossible to correctly set valves on a warm motor.

Proceed as follows—obtain a piece of cardboard and write:

to signify the four intake and four exhaust valves. Attach to wall or otherwise place so that the arrow points to the direction of car travel.

Rotate the left rear wheel until the heel of any cam lobe is directly on its rocker shaft, or to put it another way for clarity, the long axis of the cam lobe is at right angles to the rocker, and with the aid of the special Mercedes-Benz valve tappet adjusting wrench (available at M.B. parts departments or through your regional technical director), adjust the tappet

to .004 in. if intake (on side of engine nearest carburetors) or to .008 in. if exhaust (on left side of engine). Circle the symbol on the cardboard which corresponds to the valve whose tappet you have adjusted. Proceed by rotating the wheel and adjusting until all of the tappets have been set. Then, *repeat* and check each tappet again; this time cross out the symbols until you have checked all tappets.

For best smoothest performance all of the intakes must be set identically as must all of the exhausts. It is of minor importance if your gauges are off a few ten thousandths of an inch, but of major importance that all be set identically. You *cannot* be too careful in setting the tappets.

After the tappets are adjusted apply the handbrake and disengage the shift lever, lower car and remove blocks. Now, clean and reinstall the valve cover, etc.

Adjusting the Carburetors

The (hexagonal brass) idle jets should be removed and examined to be sure that they are not clogged and that they are marked 955. If they are not 955, replace with 955.

If the engine serial number is before 121921 5501 823 the mixing tubes (two) inside the carburetors should be changed from #42 to #43 (part #000 071 0949) and the calibrating sleeves (two) (part #000 071 0340) installed in both primary barrels.

Engines beginning with serial number 121 921 5500 709 already have these new items installed.

To install these items, disconnect the carburetor fuel lines and remove the four (4) screws that hold down the top cover on each carburetor. It would also be a good idea to clean out the bowls at this time.

The #3 supplement to the 190SL Workshop Manual shows the location of these mixing tubes and sleeves.

After they are changed (or if they are already installed) it will still be necessary to remove the tops of the carbs for accelerator pump adjustment). Check the ejection of the accelerating pumps which should be

two to three cubic centimeters per five strokes. Be sure to keep the float level up by operating the hand primer at the fuel pump, as necessary.

I use a 10 cent standard test tube which is 3-3/4 in. long and 1/2 in. O.D. 1-1/8 in. above the outside bottom checks out at 2.5 cc. This, in conjunction with a 3-1/4 in. length of 3/32 in. I.D. plastic sleeving (as used in radios under the name of spaghetti), provides a simple means for attachment to and means for measuring the quantity of fuel ejected.

To adjust the quantity, merely loosen the lock nut on the pump lever and adjust and measure until you have the correct amount, then tighten the lock nut. Of course the fuel level in the carburetor must be kept sufficiently high to be sure you are pumping fuel and you should pump slow enough to allow the pump to empty and fill each time.

After this is done, replace the covers and reconnect the fuel lines.

Hold down the carburetor linkage so that the counterweights can readily be moved and note that there is a small screw and locknut beneath same which is attached to the primary barrel shaft linkage of each carburetor. These screws, when properly set, keep the secondary barrels closed and firmly prevent movement of the counterweights when the engine is idling. For tune-up it is best to temporarily loosen these locknuts and screws so that the counterweights are free to move even at "idle". Then, tape the counterweights in the closed position. The reason for this is if the screws are not set properly, the correct idle speed of the primaries cannot be set as the counterweight screws can hold open the primary barrels.

Now proceed with the primary barrel adjustments as follows: Turn each of the primary mixture screws (on the right top of the carburetors) gently to maximum clockwise and then back off 1-3/8 turns each. Note: The secondary mixture controls, which look like the primary controls except that they are on the left top of each carburetor, should be kept at maximum clockwise at all times. Start the engine and run until it is at operating temperature.

Then, when the engine is thoroughly warm, turn it off and by prying with a screwdriver, unsnap the small vertical rod (about 6 in. long) which operates the rear carburetor linkage. Loosen the locknut on this rod so that its length can be changed, if necessary, and reinstall this rod.

Restart the engine, be sure the choke is off and that the spark control is set correctly. Turn the vertical screw on the linkage to the front carburetor so that the engine idles at 1500 RPM. Make sure that the counterweights are held securely toward the engine block.

Now, note the change in engine speed as you turn each of the primary mixture screws 1/2 turn each way. If all is well, the engine will slow up as you do this; this is ideal. However, this would be unusual and more than likely the engine will speed up as you turn one of the primary mixture controls.

This means that one of the butterflies that controls the volume of mixture to the cylinders is operating ahead of the other and must be corrected by changing the length of the 6 in. vertical rod.

If turning the primary mixture screw clockwise for the front carburetor increases the speed, this means the front carburetor is opening early and the rear carburetor is opening "late". The rod should be rotated so as to increase its length.

Conversely, if the engine speeds up when you screw in (clockwise) the primary mixture control on the rear carburetors, it means the rod is too long, so shorten it by rotation of same.

After awhile you will find that by trial and error at first, and reason later, you can set the rod length so that 1/2 turn in or out, from the 1-3/8 out position, of each primary mixture screw slows up the engine. The carburetors will then be synchronized, and if both primary mixture control screws are set identical (i.e., from 3/4 to 1-3/4 turns back from maximum clockwise but both the same) the mixture to all cylinders will be substantially the same. Now, tighten the locknut on the rod to the rear carburetor and adjust the idle speed to 1200 to 1250 RPM (800 to 900 RPM for cars with distributor VJ4BR11) by setting *both* vertical idle speed screws, on the linkages, so that a clockwise rotation of *either* one speeds up the engine.

Now, remove the tape from the counterweights and adjust the operating screws for each so that there is *no* play of the counterweights when the engine is idling and so that the idling speed is *not* increased. Lock the adjustments with the nuts provided.

To repeat, if the screws are set up too loose there will be play in the counterweights at idle, which is highly undesirable because the secondaries can partly open at will and every time you remove your foot from

the accelerator pedal it will idle at a different speed or "roll" because of excessive carburetion and if too tight the idle speed will be increased because the small screws which hold the counterweights closed will "push back" the carburetor primary barrel linkages and then you will be having these small screws do the work intended for the larger (vertical) idler speed screws and, of course, in a short time your carburetors will be out of adjustment.

Push down the carburetor linkage so that the engine runs at 3000 RPM and then hold your hand over the air intake to the air filter, maintain engine speed and the counterweights should start to rise and the secondary barrels will commence to open.

If they do not operate oil and free-up the linkages from the vacuum cells to the counterweight, check the vacuum lines to the vacuum cells for clogging and then check the tiny air filter at the rear of the cells for clogging. Do what is indicated.

It is a good idea to keep all the moving parts to the carburetors lubricated with a molybdenum disulphide oil, such as Liqui-Moly, to prevent wear in the butterfly shafts, linkages, etc., and increase the useful life of these dual carburetors. However, you will not even "place" in a "concours d' elegance" if you do use this lubricant.

Model 140 Activated Charcoal Filter Replacement

by Brian Imdieke, Desert Stars Section

January/February 2003

Photos in this article by the author.

Breathe better in your 1990-2000 S-Class sedan or coupe

The sophisticated heating, ventilation, and air-conditioning system of the 140-chassis S-Class sedans and coupes uses three separate air filters. Air entering the passenger compartment passes through a dust filter below the intake air plenum to remove dust, pollen, and soot. Re-circulated air inside the car goes through an additional dust filter under the dashboard on the passenger side. A third filter uses activated charcoal to remove odors. Standard equipment for the S500 and S600 and optional on other S-Class models, this filter is activated by a dash-mounted switch.

The maintenance booklet calls for the charcoal filter to be replaced every 75,000 miles or four years, whichever comes first (job 8382). The two dust filters are to be replaced every 45,000 miles or two years, whichever comes first (jobs 8381 and 8383). These jobs are described in the *Maintenance Manual, Vol. 2, Cars from 1981–1993* and *Vol. 3, Cars Starting in 1994*, available from Mercedes-Benz Technical Publications at 800/FOR-MERC. This procedure applies to 1990 through 2000 models.

This article will tell you how to change all three filters, which takes about three hours with only basic hand tools and a hand-type vacuum pump. If you don't have a vacuum pump, buy one; it's handy for vacuum system diagnosis (the power door locks and door-closing assist in your S-Class). These pumps can also be used for bleeding and changing brake fluid. They're inexpensive, and the money

you save on this job alone will more than pay for one.

Speaking of money, the service department at my local Mercedes-Benz dealer quoted $1,100 in parts and labor to perform this job. I ordered the parts from another dealer (who advertises in *The Star*) for $566 including shipping. A few hours of work allowed me to save $534 and enjoy the satisfaction of a job well done. That and the new filters make me breathe easier. Here's how you, too, can breathe easier.

Parts required:

- Automatic climate control dust/charcoal fresh air filter, part 140 835 0147
- Automatic climate control recirculation filter, part 140 835 02 47
- Automatic climate control active charcoal filter, part 140 830 00 18

Tools required:

- Phillips screwdrivers, #2 and #3
- Small flat-blade screwdriver
- Needle-nose pliers (two)
- Sockets: 10-, 13-, and 17-mm
- Open-end wrenches: 10- and 13-mm
- 5-mm Allen wrench
- Medium-size Channel-Lock or large pliers
- Torx driver, size 20 (T20)
- Plastic hammer
- Vacuum pump (hand-type)

Changing the Dust Filters

Remove the rubber lip seal at the top of the firewall (it contacts the hood); pull it straight upward (Fig. 1). Disconnect the vacuum line(s) on the right side of the air plenum (red and/or green) for the main air flap actuators. Older models have two lines; newer models have one. Grasp the white connector with needle-nose

pliers just behind the "ring", and press forward firmly. There may be a special tool for this, but you don't need it.

Remove the six large Phillips-head screws, five on the right (passenger's) side, one on the left, securing the air plenum (Fig. 2). Lift the left side of the plenum several inches. Remove the exterior air temperature sensor; pull it straight out. Lift out the air plenum. Lift the cover and lift out the filter. Clean the filter housing and the cover.

To replace the activated charcoal filter at the same time; remove the rubber lip seal at the base of the windshield on the left and right sides (it also contacts the hood); pull it straight upward (Fig. 3).

Remove the temperature water valve (twist, then pull down). Remove the right (passenger-side) wiper arm (Fig. 4). Pry off the trim cap at the mounting point, and remove the 17-mm nut and the wave washer. Grasping the wiper arm ahead of its pivot point, pull it upward, wiggling it to free the arm. You may have to gentle pry with a screwdriver under the arm mount or use the Channel-Lock pliers.

Remove the left wiper arm. Here you'll remove the upper half of the arm; the gear head stays in place. Turn on the ignition switch. Turn on the wipers briefly, then turn off the ignition to raise the arm from its park position. Remove the ignition key. The wiper arm can now be moved freely through most of its travel by hand. if you go too far down to the park position or all the way up to the farthest out position, do the ignition trick to get it moving freely again. Position the wiper arm for the longest extension (pointing toward the upper left of the windshield).

About halfway up the arm, below the spring-loaded pivot point, is a plastic cover; remove it by pressing it downward toward the gear head. Place a straight-blade screwdriver on the upper lip of the cover, and strike it firmly with a plastic hammer.

Remove the screw holding the arm clamp (Fig. 5), and position the arm for the shortest extension (vertical). Pull off the wiper arm. The spring at the pivot point applies pressure on the arm where it attaches to the end of the extension rod. As you pull the wiper arm off the rod, it will snap toward the windshield, likely striking it, so before pulling off the arm, put a pad (a folded hand towel works) under it at the pivot point.

Remove the plastic trim at the base of the windshield. Remove the 10-mm nut below the gear head (Fig. 6) and the nine Phillips-head screws (Fig. 7). Pull the center piece of trim from under the gear head (Fig. 8). Remove the left trim. Gently pry open the five plastic clamps at the base while pulling the trim upward to release them. Pull the lower portion of the rubber windshield seal at the bottom outside edge of the windshield upward four or five inches, and remove the trim. Repeat for the right side.

Remove the windshield wiper motor and drive assembly. Manually move the gear head down to park position. Remove the 13-mm nut and 13-mm bolt securing the L-bracket, below the motor, then remove the bracket (Fig. 9). Unplug the wiper motor wire (above the fuse box). Disengage the rubber grommet where the wire passes into the water collector, and push the wire into the wiper motor compartment. Remove the six 10-mm hex head screws (Fig. 10). Standing at the left (driver's) side of the car, slide the wiper assembly about four inches toward the right side of the car; lower the assembly, then rotate it slightly clockwise, and draw it out toward the left side. Be careful with the base of the windshield glass; it's sharp and fragile. If you hit the lower edge of the glass, you'll probably crack the windshield. Don't be afraid, just careful (Fig. 11). For now, lay the assembly on the engine.

Remove the water collector and the wiper motor mount stud. Around the stud are holes for a spanner wrench. If you don't have such a wrench, use medium-sized Channel-Lock pliers (Fig. 12). Remove the four Phillips-head screws (Figs. 13, 14), and lift the wire harness tray (behind the firewall) three or four inches. Lift the front edge of the water collector several inches, and pull it out from under the windshield (Fig. 15). Set the water collector and wiper assembly aside.

Remove the five Phillips-head screws and the stamped steel cover plate (Fig. 16). To remove the secondary heater box cover plate, fully loosen the five Torx-head screws (size 20); they are "captured", so they come out with the cover.

Remove the old filter. Attach the vacuum pump to the plastic tube in the front right corner of the filter, and apply vacuum to collapse the seal (Fig. 17). Pull the filter straight out using two needle-nose pliers to grasp the two ears, which have holes for pulling hooks (Fig. 18).

Different dust filters are used for cars equipped with activated charcoal filters and for those without. For cars with the activated charcoal filter, the filter has a layer of charcoal on its underside, acting as a pre-filter.

To install the new filter, attach the vacuum pump to the plastic tube in the front right corner of the filter, and apply vacuum to collapse the seal; insert the filter, and press it down firmly. Remove the vacuum, and install the plastic cover plate, steel cover plate, and water collector. Install the wiper motor mount stud, then the wiper assembly. Carefully re-insert the wiper motor assembly in the reverse order of disassembly. Insert all screws—including the L-bracket, screw, and nut—before tightening. Route the wiper motor wire through the water collector hole, and re-engage the rubber grommet. Connect the wiper motor wire. Turn on the ignition and wiper briefly to raise the wiper arm from its park position. Turn off the ignition, and remove the key.

Install the windshield base trim. Install the right-side trim first using the three Phillips-head screws. Tighten these screws only enough to keep the plastic from flopping around (just snug). If they are too tight, the windshield may crack. Leave the screw closest to the gear head off for now. Carefully engage the plastic snap connectors at the bottom of the trim. Install the left trim using the same procedure. Leave the Phillips-head screw closest to the gear head off for now. Slide the center trim piece under the gear head, and install the last two Phillips-head screws. Install the 10-mm hex nut below the gear head.

Install the wiper arms, left side first. Position the gear head to achieve the fullest arm extension. Slide the wiper arm onto the shaft, and insert the screw, but don't tighten it yet. Position the gear head to achieve the least arm extension (vertical). Set the gap between the wiper arm and the drive arm to 3.5 mm (0.14 in.), and tighten the screw. Position the gear head to achieve the fullest arm extension. Install the plastic trim cover. Hold the cover at an angle of about 30 degrees to the arm, push the open ends into the pivot joint, then rotate the cover down until it locks in place (Fig. 19). Turn on the ignition key. Let the wiper cycle once and park. Turn off the ignition, and remove the key. Install the right wiper arm in proper park position. Install the wave washer and the 17-mm nut, and tighten it firmly, then install the plastic trim cap.

Install the air plenum. Rest the plenum in place, lift the left side, and install the exterior air temperature sensor probe and the temperature water valve below the plenum. Lift the right side, and guide the water drain tubes into the water outlet holes. Lower the plenum into place, and secure it with the six Phillips-head screws. Attach the color-coded vacuum line(s) on the right side of the plenum. Grasp the white connector behind the "ring" with the needle-nose pliers, and press it in firmly until it locks in place.

Install the rubber lip seal at the base of the windshield on the left and right sides (it contacts the hood), and install the rubber lip seal at the firewall (it also contacts the hood).

Figure 1. Removing the lip seal at the top of the firewall.

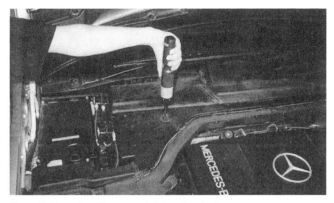

Figure 2. Removing the screws holding the air plenum.

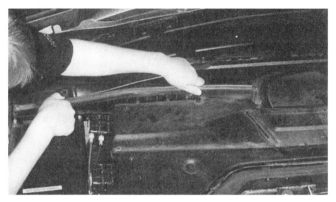

Figure 3. Removing the seal at the base of the windshield.

Figure 4. Removing the right windshield wiper arm.

Figure 5. Removing the plastic cover on the left wiper arm.

Figure 6. Removing the 10-mm nut below the gear head.

Figure 7. Removing the nine Phillips-head screws.

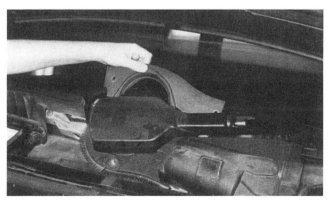

Figure 8. Pulling the trim from behind the gear head.

Figure 9. Removing the 13-mm nut securing the L-bracket.

Figure 10. Removing the six screws holding the wiper assembly.

Figure 11. Lifting out the wiper assembly.

Figure 12. Removing the wiper motor's mounting stud.

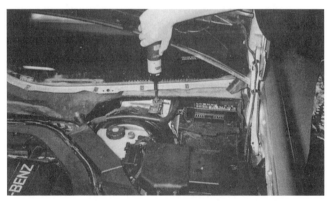

Figure 13. Removing the left screws holding the water collector.

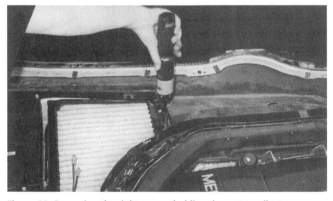

Figure 14. Removing the right screws holding the water collector.

Figure 15. Lifting the front edge of the water collector.

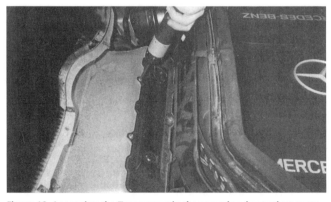

Figure 16. Loosening the Torx screws in the secondary heater box cover.

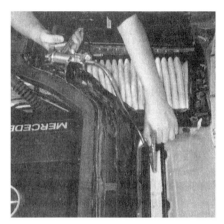

Figure 17. Applying vacuum to collapse the filter seal.

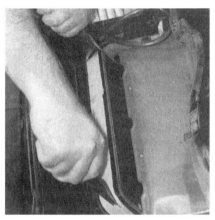

Figure 18. Lifting out the filter

Figure 19. Re-installing the plastic cover on the left wiper arm.

Changing the Re-circulation Air Filter

The air re-circulation dust filter is in the right (passenger's side) foot well. Loosen the two quarter-turn fasteners, then drop the panel down on its rear hinges. Pull the panel off its hinges and take it to your bench to change the filter media. Pull the retainer from the panel to remove the old filter material, and insert a new one. Reassemble in reverse order.

That's all there is to it. Now you can drive secure in the knowledge that you are breathing clean, odor-free air. Isn't that what luxury is all about?

Knowing When to Let Go

By Stu Ritter,
Technical Editor

May/June 2003

In the previous issue we discussed how to maintain your Mercedes-Benz for the longest possible life and to extend your enjoyment of your car. Still, you will eventually reach a point where it may not make sense to keep your older Mercedes-Benz running. Let's look at the pros and cons of paying large repair bills on older cars, which are the main factors in knowing when to let go of a car.

Finances vs. Emotions

Theoretically your decision to sell or trade any older car should he based on the cold, hard economics of ownership, but none of our arguments hold if you have an emotional attachment to your Mercedes-Benz. When emotions become a factor, economics (often called "the dismal science") goes out the window. We have seen many a Mercedes-Benz handed down from father to son, so the son's only interest became repairing the car and keeping it on the road. After all, it was his father's car. Our discussion won't deal with decisions based on emotion because that moves the discussion outside the rational envelope.

When I owned an independent Mercedes-Benz repair shop, I had to sit down with many a customer and come to a rational decision about whether it was worth pouring money into their trusty older Mercedes-Benz to keep it on the road. It's a hard thing to tell someone that "Old Paint" should be put out to pasture even though the owner wants to "make it to 500,000 miles" or hand off the car to number-seven son in a few years.

Usually a straightforward decision can be made with multi-column accounting paper and some soul searching. You know the value of the car, you learn the cost of repairs, and you work it out. Seems simple, doesn't it? Well, I can't deny that emotion creeps into the decision-making process, so it must be factored into the equation.

Occasionally, when needed repairs suddenly add up quickly, owners rush to judgment. You should always attempt to think out the process. Put emotion aside and get rational as you consider the alternatives. Try not to rush into a decision. In my 30 years in the Mercedes-Benz repair business I've seen owners make poor decisions when they heard the "bad news," and at some time in the life of every Mercedes-Benz there will be bad news.

For Example

OK, the repair shop just called, and your favorite mechanic gave you information that set off a flood of thought and emotion. That slipping between second and third gear that you thought might require a simple adjustment is actually signaling the demise of your transmission. The shop has told you that the transmission's oil pan was full of clutch material, and the slipping was a result of the loss of that material. The shop owner has spelled out various possibilities:

The transmission must come out and be disassembled for an overhaul. Minimum cost is around $1,800, with the possibility of reaching $2,400 if his shop does the work. He explains how you could also have a factory-rebuilt unit installed for around $2,800. Then you ask if he has any idea about the cause of the white smoke you talked to him about. He says, "Whoops, I forgot about that. I'll call you right back." Now you are really nervous.

The phone rings, and you grab your wallet. The news is bad: valve guides. You ask the mechanic if this is normal wear and tear, or did you do something wrong in maintaining the car. He answers that it's normal to require valve guide replacement around 150,000 miles on this model—and, incidentally, the transmissions usually go about the same mileage. Phew! What to do?

Repair Cost vs. Car Value

Let's look at this from two points of view. One owner has a 1986 300E, and the other has a 1992 300E. Both cars have covered around 150,000 miles. Both owners bought their car new, so they know how they have been maintained from day one. All services were performed on schedule, and repairs have been made as needed.

The 1992 model offers an easier decision than the 1986 model. Suppose the 1992 300E is worth about

$12,000. The cost of the transmission and cylinder head repair should be less than $4,500. When the head is removed to replace the valve guides, everything else that is worn is replaced. This may include a few rocker brackets, perhaps a hydraulic lifter or two, and a few valves. On a purely rational basis the owner would decide to proceed with the repairs. Yes, it is worth spending $4,500 on a $12,000 car. Subtract the repair cost from the car's value to determine its worth in the marketplace. It's hard to sell a used Mercedes-Benz that is puffing smoke and slipping between gears.

The owner of the 1986 300E faces a more difficult decision. The repair cost is close to the value of his car, or the numbers are so close that it makes no difference. What does he do? The car's value is minimal. Smoking, along with a slipping transmission, make the car almost impossible to sell. Repairs will cost $4,500, but the car is worth only $5,500 in good running condition. Even if this 300E is in nice shape otherwise, is it time to walk away? This is a hard spot between rocks. What should you do?

Overall Condition

First, you should appraise your car's true overall condition. Maybe it also needs suspension work, or maybe the engine is running warm, so a new radiator could be needed soon. Pull out your repair receipts, and look at the recommended repairs written on them. If repairs were always done promptly and your car is in fine mechanical shape, you may decide to keep it going. Nothing wrong with a 1986 300E in today's world.

On the other hand, if your style has been to delay repairs until the last minute and several areas need attention, you are probably facing the end of life for your car. Spending $4,500 on a mechanically correct and pristine 1986 300E may make sense, but fixing a mediocre $5,500 car does not. To the basic $4,500, add the radiator and suspension work plus whatever other work was delayed, and the car becomes impractical to fix. Even though you committed to hand it down to number-seven son, rearrange your priorities and consider a different car.

Many owners feel that if they just break even in the long run, it will be worth it. That decision is difficult to second-guess. Cars tend to go through periods where they are expensive and periods where they don't cost much to operate. Determining where you are on the curve is difficult, and we have never found a way to do it. The age-old question "Should I keep pouring money into this thing?" is tough to answer.

Will you replace your aging Mercedes-Benz with another brand or with a well-cared-for used Mercedes-Benz? Once you have driven a Mercedes-Benz for a period of time, it's difficult to leave the fold. You tend to want another. This is where the rock and hard spot really develop.

A market always exists for an older, ailing Mercedes-Benz. Someone will take it off your hands for some price, so it's not a matter of calling the junkyard to see if they are interested.

As the purchase price of a car declines, new owners are more willing to put up with problems.

Amortize Costs

Here is another way to approach long-term ownership and large repair bills: think in terms of cost per mile. Here, an older car faces a $4,500 repair bill. The average life of a set of 300E valve guides seems to be about 150,000 miles. If the car is driven in city traffic, the transmission will probably last about as long, perhaps a bit longer. So you are looking at three cents per mile for the repairs over their useful life. But you have to drive the car that distance after the repairs!

You can also spread repair costs across the expected increased life of the car to arrive at a monthly figure. Can you buy another car for the monthly cost of the repairs? Driving an average of 15,000 miles a year, it will take you 10 years to pay for these repairs. That's 120 months, and $4,500 divided by 120 is $37.50 a month. Viewed that way, it might make sense

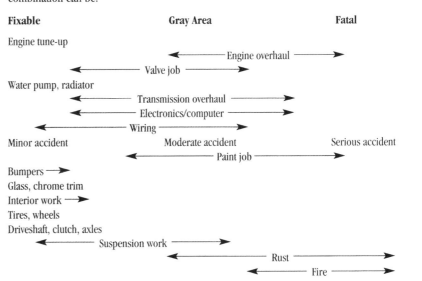

Fixable or Fatal?

Is a problem fixable, or is it fatal? This table may give you a general idea of how serious some potential repairs may be, but you should prepare a custom version to fit the specific problems you face with your own car. While any one of these problems is rarely "fatal," a combination can be.

to keep the car and put on another 150,000 miles. But when the monthly cost of repairs approaches or equals the cost of a replacement car, it is time to move on.

Repair costs of $37.50 a month make it hard to justify disposing of the car. Long-term ownership does require some expensive repairs. Most components have a finite usable life, so no matter how hard you over-maintain a car, parts only last so long. The engine in this 1986 300E could go through two or three more sets of valve guides before the bottom end requires work. The useful life of the transmission depends on where the car is driven; city living shortens its life. If you, the original owner, managed 150,000 miles on the first transmission, you can do that again several times. The life of a properly maintained transmission is probably in the million-mile range if the seals and clutch materials are replaced as they wear. The transmission's bearings and gears are very strong and well made, so replacing the seals and clutch materials will keep it going. There is no question about the quality of the original materials in our cars; they are built to go the long haul.

Upgrades

Another factor that will affect your decision is the possibility of buying a newer model. Significant differences exist between a 1986 300E (the first year for the model) and a 1995 E320 (the last year). The newer car has more power, bigger brakes, an improved interior, first-gear start, better lights, improved safety features, traction control, and more. We all know that it is smart to own the last year of a Mercedes-Benz model run.

If you decide to dispose of the 1986 car, consider a newer version of the same model or try a newer E-Class car such as the W210 chassis from 1996-onward. The newer chassis brought many improvements. Its rack and pinion steering, five-speed automatic transmission, and upgraded sound system will make your driving more enjoyable. Will traction control or ESP help your family of drivers? The same approach applies to any Mercedes-Benz model series. Over the years, both diesel and gasoline-engined models have improved immeasurably.

The major caveat about buying any newer car, of course, is to buy the best you can. Never, ever think about buying a Mercedes-Benz as a fixer-upper. Financially, that never works.

Restoration

Although restoration is beyond the scope of this technical column, we can generally say that restoring any car is almost always a money-losing proposition. Only if you sell the car can you recoup any of the costs, and even then you'll likely lose money. Unless your car is extremely rare, you are almost always money ahead to sell your tired example and find a better original car or one that someone else has lost money restoring.

While we can't tell you whether your old Mercedes-Benz is worth keeping on the road, we hope we've given you ideas on how to make a decision when the bills grow and the time approaches to say, "Goodbye, old friend."

Chart the Costs

Rate your car's condition from Excellent to Poor in each area below, then estimate the costs to bring it to excellent condition. If the total of those costs exceeds the value of the repaired car, it's probably time to move on.

Area	Condition				Repair Cost
	Excellent	Good	Fair	Poor	
Chassis					
Body/Paint					
Interior					
Engine					
Transmission					
Drivetrain					
Suspension					
Tires, wheels					
Electrical					
				Total Repair Cost:	
				Value of Repaired Car:	

Technical and Restoration Forum

Technical and Restoration Forum

Technical and Restoration Forum

Oil and Lubrication

300E Oil Change

January/February 1992

I just replaced my 1986 300E with a 1991 300E, and when I checked the oil drain access, it seems I must remove the lower shroud to get to the oil drain plug. Is there a better way? We drive the car only about 3,500 miles a year (mostly short trips), and I change the oil twice a year. Is this too often?

To drain the oil from below, you must remove the four screws holding the shroud. Before doing so, unscrew the spin-on filter using the special mm socket. Consider using a vacuum pump to draw out oil through the dipstick hole. The suction tube goes to the bottom of the crankcase and when the engine is hot, the oil will be very fluid and stirred up, so you'll get more sludge and deposits out than you would if you let it cool.

For you, twice yearly changes are necessary because your short trip driving is classed as severe use. Even if a car is simply kept on display, undriven, its oil should be changed every six months.

Oil Change Intervals

September/October 1991

I've been advised by a lubrication engineer and consultant that I can safely change oil in my 300E at 7,500–10,000 mile intervals. Mercedes-Benz recommends changing oil every 7,500 miles or six months under normal conditions. Because I drive only a few miles to and from work, I change every 3,000–3,500 miles. Can I safely extend this interval?

This point has been argued ever since the first oil was poured into the first crankcase. Experts continue to differ on it, especially if one works for an auto manufacturer, one for an oil refiner, and another owns the car. Most experts in a neutral position lean toward the car manufacturer's position or the "change twice as often" position. Given your driving habits, I'd stick with your 3,500-mile, 6-month interval. Even the best oil is relatively inexpensive, so saving 50-percent on oil is insignificant compared to the risk of shortening the life of an expensive engine.

Oil Filter Change Intervals

September/October 1991

After 115,000 miles my 1976 300D is in very good shape. I change the oil every 3,000 miles and the filter every 6,000 miles. Should I change the filter every 3,000, as well?

In all models the oil filter should be changed every time the oil is changed. Remember, compared to the cost of Mercedes-Benz engines, filters are cheap.

350SDL Oil Change

July/August 1992

I'd like to change the oil myself on my 350SDL, at least between normal services. What are the correct procedures, torques, etc.?

To do the job right, you need a torque wrench and a hex wrench for the drain plug (part number 117 589 02 07 00). Since your car has engine encapsulation panels, you may find it easier to change the oil by suction through the dipstick tube. In that case, forget the wrench and get a vacuum oil change pump from J.C. Whitney or a local auto parts store.

Torque values are 25 Nm (18 lb-ft) for the mounting nuts on the oil filter cap, 30 Nm (22 lb-ft) for a 12-mm drain plug and 25 Nm (18 lb-ft) for a 14-mm drain plug.

1. Empty the oil filter before draining or drawing off the oil. Unscrew the two nuts and remove the cover. Remove the filter element, holding a rag under it to catch dripping oil. Be sure the old rubber sealing ring is removed.

2. Suck out the oil via the dipstick tube, or remove the encapsulation panel from below, remove the drain plug and drain the oil. In either case, it's unnecessary to drain the oil cooler. Replace the drain plug, and torque it as above.

3. Put in the new filter element. Use only genuine Mercedes-Benz filters. Replace the rubber seal ring on the cover with the new one that comes with the filter.

4. Check the oil port on the central oil tube (attached to the cover). If it's blocked, remove the foreign matter. Blow through the tube with compressed air and make sure that air noticeably exits the bottom of the tube. If not, the tube and cover must be replaced.

5. Replace the cover and tighten the nuts as above. Add oil, run the engine, and check for leaks. Check oil level on the dipstick two or three minutes after stopping the engine at operating temperature.

Mixing Motor Oils

January/February 1989

Can I safely switch oil brands? Is there any difference in oils for gasoline and diesel engines?

All oils on the DBAG-approved list are compatible and can be mixed without harm to each other or the engine. Changing brands does not affect other factors such as viscosity. All oils on the list may be used for either gasoline or diesel engines. Some oils are suitable for gasoline engines but not for diesels; these oils do not have a CC or CD on the API classification label. Other oils are suitable for diesels but not for gasoline engines; these have no SE or SF on the API label, but being designed for very large engines, you're unlikely to find them in normal retail outlets or quantities.

Flexible Service System

May/June 1998

I am concerned about the new Flexible Service System on my ML320. All my life I've changed engine oil every 4–5,000 miles, and now this electronic gadget says that depending on how I drive, I can go up to 18,000 miles. Does changing oil so infrequently increase the possibility of engine wear?

The oil change interval on cars with FSS is determined by a sensor in the crankcase that measures the dielectric constant of the oil. In use, oil deteriorates mostly by contamination with wear particles, consumption or neutralization of additives, addition of foreign matter, and vaporization. Any of these—or fuel dilution—will change the dielectric constant. FSS recognizes this change instantly, faster than any other practical method, even frequent oil analysis. That ability can be a tremendous advantage to owners.

Extensive lab and field tests enabled Daimler-Benz to correlate changes in the dielectric constant with known degrees of oil deterioration. This gives a more accurate measure of the state of the oil than any estimate based on general driving habits, elapsed time, and miles driven.

FSS does not prevent you from changing oil whenever you wish. If my car had FSS, I would follow it up to a point, but I would change the oil before 10–15,000 miles. Changing even the most expensive oil is a relatively small part of the total cost of maintaining a car, so I would change at the old recommended intervals, somewhat modified depending on my actual driving conditions. Still, if FSS signaled me to change, I'd do it, and promptly.

Using oil beyond the point where it meets the minimum requirements of viscosity, additives, and freedom from contamination will certainly cause premature wear. On the other hand, today's truckers commonly go 50,000 miles or more between changes—on diesels—yet get a million miles before overhaul. Engine design and quality, combined with improvements in lubricants, allow longer change intervals than we were accustomed to even a generation ago.

Flexible Service System

Some confusion exists about the Flexible Service System (FSS) that Mercedes-Benz began using on 1998 models. The 1998 models actually have three different Maintenance Indicating Systems (MIS), two of which are called FSS. Early SLK230s (to June 1, 1997) had the first MIS, called Maintenance Reminder. A microprocessor simply watches the clock and odometer. When 7,500 miles or 365 days go by (whichever comes first, and actually 2,000 miles or 30 days beforehand), it turns on a maintenance indicator below the speedometer. The only other feature is a low oil level warning. The 7,500mi/365-day parameters can be personalized using a dealer's Hand Held Tester, so you could shorten them.

All 1998 models built as of June 1, 1997, have FSS, but there are Basic and Advanced versions. The Advanced version is in every model with the new M112 V-6 or M113 (4.3) V-8. Other models, including diesels, have the Basic version. The difference is that the Advanced FSS has the new oil sensor that measures oil level, temperature, and quality.

In Basic FSS the microprocessor records and evaluates time, distance, vehicle speed, coolant temperature, rpm, load, and low oil level. Engine type (gasoline or diesel) and oil rating (SE, SF, etc.) are coded in and used in the evaluation. The oil change interval is determined by comparing collected data against a mapping program in the microprocessor. Possible intervals in Basic FSS are 10,000 to 15,000 miles and 365 to 730 days. Basic FSS also has a low oil level warning that activates when the engine is one quart low.

Advanced FSS also records oil temperature, exact oil level, and an oil deterioration factor from the piezoelectric oil sensor and offers oil change intervals of 10,000 to 20,000 miles or 365 to 730 days. It also warns of excessively high or low oil level (by how much, to the nearest one-half qt) and of imminent oil overheating. If oil is added between oil changes, this data is recorded and will increase the miles to the next recommended oil change.

With both types of FSS, we recommend resetting the maintenance indicator every time the oil is changed. The microprocessor records the mileages of the last five oil changes and other data—such as how long you drove the car two quarts low! This data can be read by a dealer's Hand Held Tester. It's a good idea, at least while your car is under warranty, to record each oil change by resetting the maintenance indicator. Your owner's manual tells you how.

SL320 and Synthetic Oil

January/February 1995

I enjoy doing routine maintenance on my SL320. After changing the oil I prefer to pressurize the system by cranking the engine on the starter motor without having it start. Does a way exist to do so on this model? At what point will the new engine be broken-in enough to begin using synthetic oil? What change intervals do you recommend for synthetic oil? What additives, if any?

Disabling the ignition or fuel system may be possible, but it is impractical. Nowhere can a wire be unplugged, say, without affecting many other functions. Connections are through multiple plugs, and nowhere can a remote starter button be attached.

Let's back up and examine your basic premise. You evidently want to avoid running the engine without oil pressure or a supply of fresh oil at every point. This could be accomplished via one of the pre-start pumps which pump oil into the engine without even turning it over. This might be important in a freshly built engine, or an engine with a very hot turbocharger, but not so much in a normally-aspirated engine that has been used to any extent. After you change oil, a coating of it remains on

the most critical spots. Oil is designed to cling and provide lubrication during such starts. Turning over the engine without ignition will cause the same amount of wear. The cam lobes, for instance, will receive oil just as quickly—after the same number of engine revolutions—whether the engine fires or not.

You can begin using synthetic oil on the very first change, after draining the original factory fill. Change synthetic oil at 3,000-mile intervals, and never use any engine oil additive. Use of such additives could void your warranty; Mercedes-Benz is strict about this, and I agree with them 100 percent.

Canister Oil Filter

September/October 1986

My 1972 220D uses a canister type oil filter, which I would like to modify to use the simpler, cleaner spin-on filters. Can this be done?

This question comes up frequently, but unfortunately there is no way to adapt a spin-on filter. Even if an adapter could be made, the spin-on filters do not provide the full-flow and bypass filtering of the original canister type.

Wire-Coil Oil Filters

May/June 1993

Can I convert the original wire-coil oil filter of my 1956 300c to use a better modern replacement element?

This question comes up regularly with cars of that era, but as far as we know, no practical conversion exists. Does anyone out there have any more encouraging news?

M104 Oil Filter Torque

March/April 1995

What's the proper torque for the oil filter on the twin-cam six in the SL320, E320, etc.?

The official procedure for replacing the filter says, "Replace the seal ring (on the threaded cover). Insert oil filter element into threaded cover. Insert threaded cover with oil filter element and tighten to 20 Nm." That's 15 lb-ft. For other quick-change cartridges, the procedure is similar, but the instruction is to tighten by hand then turn another 90° (1/4-turn), which should give about the same torque. Incidentally, to convert metric torques, the formula is Nm x 0.7375 = lb-ft.

Oil Level Checking

January/February 2004

Be sure that the oil level in your car's engine is never above the maximum mark on the dipstick when the engine is cold. Insert the dipstick for at least three seconds before removing it to take a reading. Excess engine oil affects drivability and performance and may lead to engine damage.

Check engine oil level at operating temperature, 80°C, with the car on a level surface. Ideally, engine oil level should be about halfway between the Max and Min marks on the dipstick. Oil should not be added until the level is at or below the Min mark.

Constant topping-up with one-quarter or one-half quart does no good. Every engine has a place where it likes to keep its oil level. Some engines run close to the Min mark for long periods of time, but if oil is added, it soon disappears until the level gets back to where the engine keeps it. For approved oil classifications and correct viscosity grades, see the latest edition of *Factory Approved Service Products*, available from your dealer or from the Mercedes-Benz Customer Assistance Center, 800/FOR-MERC.

An Old Mechanics' Tale

November/December 1984

I enjoyed your article on oil in the May/June issue. I've heard mechanics from the old country say that only single-weight oil should be used in diesels because of higher combustion temperatures. The 300D (turbo) owner's manual does not mention a preference for multi-grades. Why should multi-grade oil be used in a turbo-diesel?

It is not only old country mechanics who cling to the idea that multigrade oils are not as good as single grades; many native American mechanics have also not followed the technical improvements made since multi-grades were introduced. In the 1950's, multi-grades had not proved themselves to car makers. When I bought a Porsche in 1954, the owner's manual insisted on single-grade oil. Since I lived in Montreal at the time, I had to use 10W in winter and SAE 40 in summer, with 20W-20 or SAE 30 in spring and fall. Daimler-Benz took the same position.

A multi-grade such as 20W-50 consists of a 20W base oil with viscosity improvers, which make the 20W as thick as 50-weight at 210°F. Early objections were based on a belief that viscosity improvers did not themselves lubricate, so the quality of the 20W was downgraded, and also that viscosity improvers wore out, so the higher viscosity was not maintained.

You are correct that the turbo-diesel owner's manuals do not say that only multigrade should be used, although it is implied because only 30-weight is shown as a recommended single-grade, with a note that 40-weight can be used in a suitable climate. After the 300D became a turbo, the 240D and 300D owner's manuals had a note saying that 10W should be used only in the 240D. The recommendation that only multi-grade oil should be used in a turbo-diesel is mine, not MBNA's. I base the recommendation, however, on DBAG's master list, which says: "Single-grade engine oils are recommended for all passenger car engines and for naturally-aspirated engines for commercial vehicles and industrial application." The implication is that for more severe service, single-grade should not be used in turbos. I conclude that the demands of lubricating a turbocharger while the engine is subject to higher stresses requires better lubricating quality.

More on Oil Temperatures

July/August 1985

Concerning your article "Too Cool" on page 20 of the March/April issue, I too have wondered about the operation of the oil cooler on my 1982 240D. Why does the car have such a high oil temperature? It seems to me that this imposes a severe condition on engine oil that is contaminated by piston blow-by and an oil change frequency of 5,000 mi. My 1977 240D had an oil change interval of 3,000 mi, but the 1982 model uses 5,000 mi. What improvements were made to enable the oil to go an additional 2,000 mi?

An engine's working temperature is designed as a compromise involving the fuel and lubricants available, the engine construction materials, the climatic conditions that the engine must operate under, heat exchange conditions within the engine, emission requirements and many more factors.

If engines ran cooler, internal condensation would not be evaporated so readily. If engines were designed to run at say 125°F, there would be insufficient heat for our heating systems, we would have to use lighter oil, our engines would consume more fuel per horsepower-hour, we would need larger radiators, etc. Today's engine oils, such as those on the MBNA-approved list, function very well at the temperatures encountered in today's engines. The soot that we get in our diesel crankcases does not hurt oil's lubricating qualities. Blow-by gases are harmful only when they have water to dissolve in or when the oil's additives are exhausted.

As far as I know, the principal reason for extending the oil change interval is an improvement in oil filter efficiency. I have my 1975 240D's oil analyzed regularly, and it always has plenty of TBN (total base number) left, so it can handle a lot more sulfur and acid, but the particles of metal and other abrasives keep piling up. Still, we've never heard of an engine that expired from too-frequent oil changes, and oil is cheaper than new engine parts.

190 Transmission Lube Change

September/October 1990

The manual for my 1984 190D 2.2 lists no change interval for the lubricant in the five-speed transmission. How often should it be changed?

The manuals show no change after the first, at 1,000 miles, but call for checking the level every 15,000 miles. Since there could be some water accumulation from condensation, I think it's advisable to change every 50,000 miles, perhaps more often under harsh operating conditions. The only lubricant recommended by MBAG is MB Manual Transmission Fluid, part number Q 2 09 0004, which comes only in 15-gallon containers. For automatic transmissions, a fluid change is called for every 30,000 miles.

The differential has the same instructions as the manual transmission, and I'd treat it the same. For this, Pennzoil MultiPurpose EP Gear Lubricant 4085 is recommended, as is MB Hypoid Gear Oil, part number 000 989 28 03; both are SAE 90 oils.

Transmission Fluid

March/April 1985

What type of automatic transmission fluid should I use in my 1968 280SE coupe? The service manual lists Type A for transmissions made before May 1969 and Type B thereafter. Type A doesn't seem to be available, but a Type F is also sold. I'm confused....

The system of specifying and labelling automatic transmission fluids is extremely and needlessly complex. First, never use Type F, which is only for use in transmissions made by Ford Motor Company. Use the Dexron II type, which is a Type B fluid. MBNA recommends Pennzoil brand. Service Information 0016 dated September 1982 applies.

You won't find Type A for sale in the U.S. Mercedes-Benz recommended it for use in their manual transmissions but not in automatics. Since it is no longer available here, MBNA now recommends SAE 20W-20 engine oil for their manual transmissions.

Here's a Man Who Really Enjoys His 230SL!

May/June 1994

At 520,000 miles the automatic transmission in my 1966 230SL is on its second set of seals. One mechanic says Type A fluid is mandatory; others say Dexron is OK. I've used Dexron since the first re-seal at 250,000 miles. Type A is hard to find, so is it OK to use Dexron?

When your car was built, Mercedes-Benz recommended Type A fluid, but it was already becoming obsolete. It soon became hard to find, and some people hoarded enough to last the life of the car. Mercedes-Benz now recommends Dexron II for automatic and manual transmissions. The products of reputable oil companies with Dexron license numbers D-xxxxx or E-xxxxx are OK. In addition, some may also be identified as Mercon. In other words, use the same fluid as is used in today's Mercedes-Benz automatics.

Linkage Lube

January/February 1986

I ran into a small problem while doing the 15,000-mi maintenance on my 190E. In Job No. 3022, lubricating the linkage and shafts, the manual insists on the use of one of these hydraulic oils; Castrol DB Hydraulic Fluid, Mobil Aero HFA, Shell Aero Fluid 4 or Aral 100. I can't find any of them. Is there a substitute?

Yes, most shops use automatic transmission fluid.

300E Valve Tappeta-Tappeta

March/April 1998

My 1989 300E has covered 100,000 miles, and I sometimes hear a valve tapping when starting from cold. My dealer's service manager said the hydraulic lifters never wear out but do get dirty and tap like this. He suggested that the next time I change oil, I should add a quart of automatic transmission fluid! He claimed that ATF is a highly detergent oil and will clean the lifters. He said I can leave the ATF in for the normal oil change interval without hurting anything. Do you agree?

No! Disregard that advice. Engine oils approved by Mercedes-Benz already contain the maximum dose of detergent useful to your engine. ATF is not formulated for this purpose. Some folks may not be in the snake oil business but like to think up strange uses for products designed for other purposes.

Tune-Up

280SL Plug Fouling

November/December 1989

I've had my 280SL since 1972; car and engine have done 140,000 miles. Valves and guides were replaced at about 110,000, and compression checked OK in January 1988, but the plugs foul, I only get 12–13 mpg, and oil consumption is about 1–2 quarts per 1,000 miles. Is it time for a complete overhaul, or is there something simpler that might cure the problem?

Plug fouling is uncommon in 280SL's. We suspect that your plug fouling is directly related to the high oil consumption. After 140,000 miles, you may have sticking (or even broken) piston rings, worn cylinder walls or both. If a leakdown test shows that piston rings and cylinder walls are good, remember that you have a lot of miles on the original fuel injection pump and the camshaft. We'd then suggest checking the cam for wear and rebuilding the injection pump. If that doesn't help, consider a complete engine overhaul. Money spent on a fresh pump and cam will not be wasted, as your new engine should benefit from them. A partial engine overhaul often does more harm than good because it can put added stress on already worn parts in the rest of the engine.

Platinum Plugs?

November/December 1994

You noted in past issues that Mercedes-Benz recommends against platinum spark plugs. I hadn't heard that, and when I checked my 300E, it had platinum plugs. I changed them and apparently have solved a pesky, old problem. Inconsistently the car has been reluctant to start. Hot or cold, wet or dry, the engine would—very rarely—refuse to fire. On thousands of other occasions, it was fine. The 6,000 miles since replacing the platinum plugs have been trouble-free. It could be a coincidence, but what do you think?

When Mercedes-Benz issued its October 1984 bulletin disapproving platinum plugs, it gave no explanation, which is normal in such cases. Many readers have brought up the subject. A few report better emission test results with copper plugs than with platinum plugs. Looking at the plugs, you'll notice that the platinum center electrode is flush with the insulator surface, whereas the center electrode of the copper-core plug projects into the combustion space. Whether this causes inferior performance in a Mercedes-Benz engine is unclear, but this is the most obvious difference between the types.

Platinum spark plug tip.

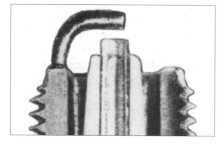

Copper-core spark plug tip.

280SL Ignition Points

September/October 2001

I can't figure out where to connect a dwell meter on my 1970 280SL to help me set point gap correctly. How often should I check the dwell or change the points?

To set the dwell on a 280SL, connect the positive lead of the dwell meter to the copper lug under the battery tray near the ignition control module. It is virtually inaccessible from the top of the engine compartment, but if you climb under the front of the car and look up under the battery, you will see the ignition module and a set of wires going to a junction block with two screws in it. One screw has a round tube extending from it; this is where you should connect the positive lead. The negative lead goes to ground. On my car, I attached an extension wire from this connection up to the coil area to facilitate checking dwell, so I didn't have to climb under the car and grope around in the dark every time I want to change the points. The breaker-controlled electronic ignition systems are easier on points, but the rubbing block still wears out, and acids from crankcase vapors still corrode the points. Changing them once a year is good insurance. Gap the points to 0.016 in; dwell should be 34 degrees.

280SE Timing

March/April 1992

Specifications for timing my 1971 280SE call for a setting of eight degrees, but the timing marks go up to only four degrees. Am I missing something?

The installation value for the ignition distributor at starter speed, without vacuum, is 10 degrees Before Top Dead Center (BTDC). The scale runs from 4 degrees BTDC to 4 degrees ATDC. I'd simply estimate the distance for 10 degrees as being a little more than twice the 4-degree distance. The 8-degree ATDC figure is the value for idle speed with vacuum.

The data book gives ignition advance values (with vacuum) of 0–5 degrees at 1,500 rpm and 25–30 degrees at 3,000 rpm. You can check these with a proper timing light. If the car runs reasonably well at these settings, you can fine tune the timing to suit the gasoline you use.

Smog Check Woes

May/June 1996

My 1972 250C is in fine condition but will no longer pass the tightening emissions tests. Various people have suggested 1) using premium gas before the test (the car originally required only regular octane); 2) adding STP to the gas before the test; 3) adding denatured alcohol to about half a tank of gas before the test. The first certainly wouldn't hurt, but I hesitate to do the second or third. The testers here never even open the hood, so I've also considered disconnecting the breather hose from the valve cover and removing the air filter element. What do you suggest?

Some states take quite a reasonable attitude to old cars, relaxing the requirements as the car ages, but other states are more restrictive. I note that you have already written to your state legislators, but you obviously need to do something more productive. I suggest a new set of spark plugs gapped to 0.8 mm (0.032 in) and driving the car hard for an hour or so before the test. Use a couple of tankfuls of the highest octane gasoline available (try Amoco or Shell). Forget the STP and denatured alcohol. Disconnecting the PCV system might be counterproductive, as it could allow a pressure buildup in the crankcase. To increase the amount of air inducted, use a new air filter element or punch holes in an old one with an ice pick; save either one for tests.

Fuel

Premium Diesel Fuel

November/December 1998

My 300D runs well or poorly, depending on where I buy fuel. Amoco's Power Blend premium diesel fuel is not sold where I live. Does Mercedes-Benz have enough clout to entice Amoco to sell it everywhere?

I try to avoid diesel fuel problems by using the same station or, if that's impossible, the same brand. I've heard of Amoco and Texaco premium diesel fuel but have yet to find it. Apparently these are being test marketed in selected cities. Since most diesel fuel is sold to truckers, there's no way that Mercedes-Benz could pressure oil companies to make a premium fuel available.

#1 and #2 Diesel Fuel

September/October 1985

What is the difference between #1 and #2? Can I use heating oil in my diesel?

The basic difference between diesel #1-D and #2-D is that #1 is made up of hydrocarbons with a lower boiling point so that it flows at much lower temperatures than #2. The cetane number of #1 is typically three to four points higher than that of #2. The higher the cetane number, the shorter the time lag between injection of the fuel and self-ignition. This means that #1 will give you better cold starts, less engine noise and smoother running. Since #2 is denser, i.e., it weighs more per gallon, you will get better fuel mileage with #2.

Do not use heating oil (burner oil) in your car. Most oil companies sell the same product as either #2-D or as burner fuel oil, #2 grade. It is illegal to use fuel oil in a vehicle used on the public roads, and most states require some form of identification to distinguish oil on which road tax has been paid from burner oil. Apart from all that, handling methods used by oil distributors and transporters are quite different for the two products. Old and dirty oil, for instance, can be disposed of by dumping it into a tank of burner oil. Burner oil is ignited by a spark, not by compression, so cetane number does not apply to it.

Diesel Fuel Additives

January/February 1985

I recently purchased my first diesel, a 1984 300D. I have heard that diesels have problems with clogged injectors and fuel tank contamination and that fuel additives do not help. A mechanic recommended adding a quart of Mobil I synthetic oil to the fuel tank every fifth or sixth fill-up. This sounded strange, so I have not used it or any other additive. What is your recommendation?

If clean, high-quality fuel is used, no additives are needed. Generally, fuel from large reputable oil companies is good, but it should be bought from a high-volume station so that it is reasonably fresh. Water condenses in storage tanks, and algae or other biological growths can occur. Also, since winter grade fuel is different from summer grade, a low-volume station may carry summer fuel over into the winter season. Clogged injectors are also the result of contaminated or low-quality fuel.

The advice regarding Mobil 1 is completely wrong. Suggestions of adding ATF (automatic transmission fluid) are likewise wrong. For a list of DBAG-approved diesel fuel additives, see page 14. Besides those listed there, Red Line Diesel Fuel Catalyst is widely used and highly thought of but has not been approved by DBAG. Since your car does not have the new trap oxidizer, you could use this product. 1985 models with the trap oxidizer should only use the three additives listed on page 14.

380 Gasoline

November/December 2002

A friend who also has a 1984 380SL claims that the 380 engine was built to run on regular gasoline and that I'm wasting my money by using 93-octane premium. Any comments?

A 1984 380SL with the M116.962 engine (8.3:1 compression ratio) requires 91 RON (Research Octane Number) or 81 MON (Motor Octane Number). In the U.S. we use the formula RON + MON /2. so this engine requires 86 octane, regular-grade gasoline. Unfortunately, our regular fuel has insufficient vapor pressure and tends to cause vapor lock at altitude. If the vapor locks occurs, use a middle-grade gasoline; otherwise, regular is fine for that engine.

Full or Empty?

January/February 1997

During the winter I drive my 190E 2.6 only once a week. Should I keep the fuel tank near empty or full?

Low fuel levels allow condensation to form and possibly corrode the tank from the inside. Keeping the tank full reduces corrosion and is safer. There's nothing worse than getting stuck in the snow on a cold night and finding that you are low on fuel.

Alcohol and Gasoline

January/February 1986

I read somewhere that oil companies are adding alcohol to their gasoline to raise the octane. What problems does this pose for rubber parts of a fuel system? How about dirt and corrosion from the water picked up by the alcohol? What does DBAG recommend, not just for new cars but for older carbureted and fuel-injected engines? By the way, about your columns: they make the club magazine!

In 1979, MBNA issued a bulletin stating that gasoline containing alcohol was approved for use in all models provided that the following conditions applied: 1) the alcohol must be ethyl alcohol (ethanol), and 2) the percentage of alcohol must not exceed 10 percent. The kind and amount of alcohol is posted on the pump (which may be Federal law).

Methyl alcohol (methanol) is a definite no-no, although it is commonly sold as a gas "dryer" or starting fluid. MBNA does not recommend any additives for gasoline, but various products sold to eliminate water from the fuel tank can be helpful if they use something other than methyl alcohol. While I have never heard of problems arising from the occasional use of methyl alcohol, ethyl alcohol is much more effective.

Thanks for the kind words.

Reach for the Sky

January/February 1987

What, if anything, needs to be done to make my1977 240D start, run and perform better when I move to high altitudes (over 4,000 feet above sea level) in Colorado?

When you move to such an altitude, your car's altitude compensator needs adjustment. Presumably it is now adjusted for sea level, which automatically handles a range of up to 3,000 feet. Any competent mechanic can do this.

Another problem will be adjusting to the colder weather. Have a block heater installed, and be sure to use oil of the proper viscosity (10W-30 or 15W-40 with an operating block heater, 5W-30 Mobil l from dead cold). Your battery should be the big 88 or 92 ampere-hour size, in good condition and fully charged. Of course, your car should have good compression and proper valve adjustment.

Regardless of adjustments, normally aspirated engines lose power with increasing altitude, and this is most noticeable in diesels such as the 240D. For this reason, non-turbocharged diesels are less popular in the high country. Anyone living above 4,000 feet should have a turbo-diesel or a gasoline-powered car with ample power–or be content to live with low performance.

High Altitude and High Octane

November/December 1987

My 1986 300E's owner's manual specifies a minimum of 91 octane (R + M/2), but in Colorado (at 5,000 or more feet above sea level) I could only buy 89 octane. I know that octane requirement decreases with altitude, but does such use of 89 octane fuel violate DBAG guidelines?

The old rule of thumb is that the octane requirement drops one point for every thousand feet, but this was for carburetor cars. Your 300E has built-in compensation for altitude, so its octane requirement will not decrease similarly. All Mercedes-Benz high altitude testing is done in Colorado using fuel available there, and the best information that we have indicates that 89-octane gasoline works well at such altitudes.

A friend in Colorado has a carbureted car with 9.5:1 compression that works fine at 5,000 feet ASL or 89-octane fuel, but at 2,500 feet ASL or lower it requires either retarded timing or bigger jets to avoid detonation. As altitude increases, mixture tends to richen, so other than possibly higher fuel consumption, you should have no problems at such high altitudes.

Approved Trap Oxidizer Additives

November/December 1989

In the past it was suggested that Heet, Chevron Techron, Biobor Diesel Doctor and LM Diesel Winter Flow were approved by MBAG/MBNA for use in trap oxidizer-equipped cars. In a recent issue only Diesel Doctor and LM Winter Flow were listed. Are Techron and Heet now disapproved?

When MBNA extended the warranty on trap oxidizers and turbochargers in cars with trap oxidizers, they probably didn't want to take even a small chance on potential damage from the use (or misuse) of combustion-directed additives such as Techron and Heet, etc. Since Diesel Doctor and LM Winter Flow are designed to eliminate algae and promote cold-weather fuel flow (i.e., they work in the tank and fuel lines, not in the combustion chamber), they continue to be approved.

Cooling System

How to Burp Your Car

September/October 1994

It is almost impossible to properly refill the cooling system of my 1970 280SE Convertible. The system gets air pockets in it, the engine overheats, then it takes a long time before this air burps out of the system. Is there a better way to fill the radiator?

When you refill the cooling system, have the car's front end at a higher level than the rear. If you have a steep driveway, park the car pointed uphill. If not, jack up the front end and support it on stands. Be sure the heater is turned on. Most mechanics lift the front end two or three feet. Otherwise, you'll just have to wait until the engine runs and pumps out the air pockets.

Coolant Change

May/June 1993

What's the best way to change coolant in my 1987 300E?

Turn the heater to high, then remove the radiator cap from the expansion tank, being careful that the coolant temperature is below 80°C (176°F), as marked on the gauge. Remove the bottom engine compartment cover, and open the drain plug at the bottom of the radiator. A piece of 1/2-inch ID rubber hose slipped over the drain opening will let you direct flow into a container. Normally this is all the draining that's done, even though it does leave some coolant in the block;

draining it requires loosening screws in the block, but that's hardly necessary and is best left to a professional.

After the coolant has drained, retighten the drain plug and slowly add one gallon of Mercedes-Benz anti-freeze to the system, then complete the filling with clean drinking water. Leave the radiator cap off, and start the engine, making sure that the heater is turned on. Watch the coolant level in the expansion tank, and add more water as the level drops. When operating temperature is reached, replace the radiator cap, let the engine idle awhile, and check for leaks. Replace the bottom engine cover, and recheck the coolant level after the engine has cooled down.

Coolant Capacity

January/February 1993

When draining the coolant from my car, I got only 8 of the 13 quarts that the cooling system is supposed to hold. Where is the rest of the old coolant, and should I worry about replacing it?

Was the cooling system full when you started? On most cars you never get all of the coolant out by draining the block and radiator because some is left in the heating system. If you change coolant every two or three years, it should stay fairly clean. If the coolant is really dirty, you could flush the system, using the system most shops have or a do-it-yourself kit from an auto parts store.

Distilled or Drinking Water?

November/December 1995

Different authorities indicate different preferences for mixing antifreeze with either drinking water or distilled water. Which type of water is preferable?

This controversy goes back a long way, but usually the choice is not critical. I believe the best coolant for Mercedes-Benz cars is a mixture of equal parts of Mercedes-Benz antifreeze and distilled water of the kind sold in supermarkets and drug stores. Here's a direct quote from 1959 Mercedes-Benz specifications: "The exclusive cooling agent for our combustion engines is water. Clean water with the smallest possible lime content should be used. If river water is to be used, this should be well filtered. Unsuitable are sea water, brackish water, brine, and industrial waste water." Current specifications call for "normal drinking water," but there's no reason not to use distilled water except convenience and cost.

Rust Inhibitors and Water Pump Lubes

March/April 1994

In a recent issue you warned of unsuitable rust inhibitors in a coolant additive. I've used other rust inhibitors and water pump lube additives for years and am concerned that one or more of these may have been a disapproved product. Can I get a list of forbidden coolant additives?

The cooling system of a Mercedes-Benz should be filled with a 50-50 mixture of clean drinking water and Mercedes-Benz Antifreeze, which contains all of the rust inhibitor/ water pump lubricant that's needed. Many rust and corrosion inhibitors contain chemicals which may harm the engine, so they should be avoided. Mercedes-Benz no longer publishes a list of approved additives. It's generally recognized that phosphates aren't acceptable in most European engines.

Maintenance and Procedure

Repair Instructions
March/April 1992

I was going to drain and replace the coolant in my 1985 300D, but the factory manual refers me to a separate Repair Instruction, #20-010, which I can't find. Can you help?

MBNA technical literature is written assuming that the user has all previous literature, so all jobs are not described in all manuals.

Job 20-010 is straightforward. To drain the system, first remove the filler cap from the expansion tank. The instructions tell you to remove the drain plugs from the radiator and cylinder block. The radiator plug is tightened with a coin or washer, and the block plug is hard to reach (probably stuck forever). Instead, you can remove the lower radiator hose. If the coolant is dirty and hasn't been changed for a few years, you can get the system reasonably clean by flushing it with plain water once or twice.

To refill it, replace the plugs (or the hose). Torque the radiator plug to 1.5-2.0 Nm and the block plug to 6-10 Nm. Slowly fill the expansion tank to the Full mark, but don't put the cap back on. Start the engine and let it warm up to 40°C. Push the Def button on the ACC panel, and set heat to Max. Run the engine intermittently until the thermostat opens. When the engine reaches about 60°C, replace the filler cap. The thermostat is self-bleeding. When coolant temperature drops below 90°C, top up the expansion tank. The important thing is to get all air out of the system by having the heating system running full blast until the coolant is above 90°C.

Hands-On Instruction
March/April 1986

I have owned a 1965 190c for years and just purchased a 1977 300D. Even after tuning up my own cars (plugs, points, valve adjustments, timing, torquing heads, etc.), I hesitate to do much work on them. Can you recommend any hands-on instruction that might be available?

I can relate the experience of two Carolinas Section members who had the same desire. Both started by taking a course at a local technical institute (vocational-technical high schools also offer good courses). One got a local independent mechanic to let her watch while he did the usual maintenance jobs. The other was able to get the vo-tech teacher to explain specific Mercedes-Benz applications. A third student even managed to get hired as an office worker by a dealer in exchange for being able to watch and gain instruction in the workshop! As an employer, the dealer (who must have been very cooperative!) did not have to worry about the usual insurance problems.

The biggest problem with do-it-yourself these days is the number of special tools and test instruments needed for newer cars. Still, the tools are available from specialists, and manuals can be obtained from MBNA.

Battery Replacement
November/December 1991

I want to replace the original batteries in my 1987 300E and 300TDT. How can I avoid scrambling the anti-theft radio when disconnecting the power?

Just maintain 12 volts at all times by connecting jumper cables from another car or by connecting a battery charger to the battery cables while you disconnect and reconnect them. Some shops keep a 12-volt motorcycle battery on hand for this purpose. Although later cars have an internal battery to prevent power loss, don't rely on it.

Super Charger
May/June 1995

Several days after I had jump-started my 1979 300D with an external charger, the battery went dead and the alternator quit. Could the jump-start have caused this problem, and would unplugging the cable at the side of the alternator have prevented it?

This kind of "What I did wrong" report is always interesting to readers, who can often learn from the misfortunes of others. It's possible that in recharging your battery you damaged the alternator. When a high-rate charger is connected, it often creates a sharp peak voltage which can damage connected components. The standard rule for using a charger is to first disconnect the negative (ground) cable. Then the charger can only affect the battery.

Valve Adjustment Tools
May/June 1985

I am trying to buy the special tools to adjust the valves on my 1974 240D. Can you tell me what I need and where I can get it?

You need three wrenches to adjust the valves on Mercedes-Benz diesels. Two are the same, 14-mm open end wrenches with two bends to offset them, part number 615 589 00 0100. The third wrench needed is an open end with serrated teeth (to keep the valve spring plate from turning) and a kind of spur on the handle. Part number is 615 589 00 03 00. The wrenches can be ordered through any Mercedes-Benz dealer.

Some mechanics adjust the valves without the holding wrench, but it is better to use it. Unless you have a device that will allow you to remotely turn the engine with the starter, you will also need a 2-mm 1/2-in drive socket for turning the crankshaft. Never turn the engine by turning the camshaft, and never turn the engine backward. If you turn the crankshaft too far for getting at a certain valve, turn it around again.

The Chase Is On

September/October 2003

I recently changed spark plugs for the first time and noticed I had to use a ratchet to turn the plugs all the way out. On other cars the plugs can be turned with my fingers after being loosened with a ratchet. The plug threads have a varnish-like substance on them. How can I clean the threads in the head without getting debris into the cylinders? I was going to try gasoline on a toothbrush, but I had second thoughts about diluting the oil, so I put the new plugs in as is.

A spark plug thread-chaser is a common tool in a professional mechanic's toolbox. We use them often to clean gummed-up threads. A thread-chaser looks like a tap. Before using it, pack the flutes with grease to capture material removed from the threads. After chasing the threads, pull the plugs on the ignition control module and crank the engine a bit to blow out anything left in the spark plug threads. To prevent this happening again, remove your spark plugs and lightly apply a little anti-seize compound to their first and second threads; it will walk back up the threads as you thread the plug into the head.

W123 Manual

January/February 1987

Could you please explain the correct way to disconnect the throttle linkage on a 1982 240D, with automatic transmission and cruise control, in preparation for valve adjustment? The Mercedes-Benz maintenance manual is very specific on valve adjustment but says nothing on disconnecting the linkage.

We assume that you have a copy of the correct maintenance manual for your car. Mercedes-Benz manuals are not designed for the do-it-yourself mechanic. They assume that you are already a reasonably trained mechanic, having conquered the basics and attended appropriate MBNA service schools.

Technicians generally try to disconnect as little as possible, just removing brackets from the cylinder head cover and moving some linkage

left, some right. Care must be taken to connect the vacuum lines properly when re-assembling.

It's easier to watch someone doing the job. If your friendly local mechanic won't let you watch (for a fee, of course), try attending (or organizing) an MBCA hands-on tech session.

Jacking Points

January/February 2003

Where is it safe to jack up a 300SD and place jackstands? I have been using a floor jack at the rubber pads on the frame directly beneath where the factory jack fits into the side. The CD-ROM manual doesn't describe recommended jacking points.

Mercedes-Benz recommends using lifting pins or lifting pads for the 126 chassis, but few mechanics use them. While they must be used on the old W100 600 models, other ways do exist. To lift the front of the car, use the crossmember just behind the oil pan. These are not factory-recommended lifting points, but almost all mechanics use them. Put a block of wood between the car and the floor jack. Using these lifting points, it is easy to place jackstands under the factory jacking points in the rocker boxes.

KPM's, Nm's and Lb-Ft

September/October 1991

How do I convert the old kpm torque figures to Nm or lb-ft?

In 1976 Mercedes-Benz changed from the old metric system, which used kilopond-meters as a unit of torque, to S.I. (Système International,), which uses Newton-meters (Nm).

Nm = kpm x 10

Lb-ft = kpm x 7.375

Lb-ft = Nm x 0.7375

Thus, for example, the old 3 kpm tightening torque for spark plugs is 30 Nm or 22 lb-ft. The 110 Nm tightening torque for lug bolts translates to 81 lb-ft.

Care and Storage

Awakening Rip Van Winkle

July/August 1988

We're going to drive a 280SEL 4.5 that has stood unstarted for 13 years with no special treatment. What do you suggest?

The main dangers are rust and sludge. I take it that you don't want to disassemble the engine, as might be normal when restoring an old car. I would begin by draining the transmission fluid and replacing it and the filter. Then squirt about an ounce of Mobil 1 5W-30 motor oil into each cylinder through the plug hole. Let it stand overnight, then try turning it over (clockwise only) by hand with a wrench on the center bolt of the crankshaft. If it's free, it should turn over without exceeding 185 lb-ft of torque; if you reach that limit, you'll probably have to disassemble it.

If it's free, drain the motor oil, drop the pan and clean the sump; replace the oil filter. Remove the valve covers and clean everything; turn the engine by hand and make sure all the valves work properly. Put in oil (Mobil 15W-30) and start the car with valve covers off. If you're lucky, oil will squirt all over and make a mess as it squirts strongly onto every cam lobe. Stop the engine, replace the valve covers and top up the engine oil.

Run the transmission through Drive and Reverse, and see if the car can be driven. Replace the coolant, flushing the system. Only time and use will tell if all seals are OK. After about an hour of normal driving, change the engine oil, transmission fluid and filters again. Check the timing chain tensioner for proper functioning. Clean and repack the front wheel bearings, and replace drive belts and hoses. Good luck!

Storage

March/April 2002

How should we store our 1995 C280? What should be done beforehand? Should the tires be off the floor? Is any special exterior care required?

You can store a car for one or two months without doing anything special. The battery may run low in that time, but otherwise there'll be no problems. If you're leaving it for three months or longer, the battery may suffer, the fuel will start to deteriorate, and dirty oil will affect the metals. For prolonged storage, over six months, leave as little fuel in the tank as you dare. Change the oil and filter before you store it, and disconnect the battery. Before you start driving again, add a few gallons of fresh fuel before starting the engine so the fresh fuel mixes with and dilutes the old fuel. Whether you drive the car or not during storage, change the engine coolant and brake fluid per factory recommendations. The worst thing you can do is to start the car weekly and let it idle. Better to let it sleep. These precautions should preserve the car's mechanical integrity.

Cars Are for Driving, Not for Storing

July/August 2002

I read your suggestions in the March/April 2002 issue regarding storage. My E320 Cabriolet is stored for five months each winter, but I've always heard that the gas tank should be filled first, and the dealer suggests keeping the battery connected.

Our recommendations were based on personal experience storing four cars over the winter and observations of cars coming into our shop that have been stored for long periods. Five months is not a long time to store a car. Gasoline lasts about six months in a tank without serious degradation. If you're parking the car for only a few

months, it doesn't matter whether the tank is full or empty; either way, the gas will be usable. If it sits for a year, would you rather have to dispose of one gallon of bad fuel or 20 gallons? Old gas won't ruin the engine, but it might make it run poorly until it has fresh gas. Leaving the battery connected almost guarantees a dead battery after five months; attaching a low-amperage trickle charger makes more sense. Everyone has their own opinion of how to store cars, and clean oil seems to be the only commonly agreed-upon procedure.

Low Mi

March/April 1993

I drive my 1988 560SL and my 1993 600SL only about 15 miles per year. Should I use MB break-in oil or Mobil 1? Should I disconnect the battery when using a trickle charger? Is there a simple way to avoid the 560SL's radio scrambling when the lithium back-up battery fails? What position should the 600SL roll bar be in to minimize pressure within the system?

Use Mobil 1 rather than break-in oil. MBAG says break-in oil is no longer required and engines can be topped off with normal oils. The break-in oil filter should be removed at the end of the break-in period.

MBAG is firm in its instruction that the negative cable be disconnected before charging the battery from an external source. The only way we know to prevent scrambling the radio when the lithium battery expires is to replace it early. A second battery can be connected while replacing it.

Pressure in the roll bar system is lowest with the bar raised.

Low-Mileage Hazards

March/April 2002

While looking for a 1984–85 380SL, I see ads for cars with less than 40,000 miles. What are the risks in buying such a car that has been stored or driven only rarely?

A lot of older SLs aren't driven very many miles each year but haven't necessarily been sitting around for years. Many of them are third or fourth cars that get driven to the golf course in the summer and sit in the garage during the winter. If properly maintained and stored, they're a pretty good deal as used cars. The interiors and paint are in good shape, and they aren't rusty. Compared to old, ratty, worn-out, high-mileage SLs, they're a steal. Most problems stem from lack of time-related maintenance and poor storage. Whether you drive the car or not, the coolant and brake fluid should be changed every two or three years. Short trips are hard on oil, so regardless of the mileage driven, the oil must be changed at least twice a year. The fuel system takes the biggest beating. Between never running more than a quart of gas through the injectors during a trip and letting the fuel sit in the system for months, rough idle and fuel system failures are the most obvious risks involved in buying a low-mileage 380SL. Still, it's cheaper to fix these deficiencies in a clean, low-mileage car than to try and revive a worn-out one. The 1984 and 1985 380SLs are the best, so if you want one, find the cleanest, best-maintained, lowest-mileage example you can afford, then enjoy it.

Operation

Reluctant Diesel

May/June 1992

My 1984 300SD has covered 84,000 miles and is in excellent condition but won't start without a block heater at temperatures of about -15°F and below. I mix Diesel No. 1 and No. 2 about 50-50. The glow plugs and battery are new, and the fuel injectors seem to work fine because the car runs well. The fuel filters are fine, and my fuel comes from a major brand truck stop. Oil is Mobil 1 5W30. What can I do when I get out somewhere with no way to plug in the block heater?

For temperatures below 10°F, I'd suggest using 100-percent Diesel No. 1. When you pre-glow, wait 40 seconds (time it by your watch) before trying to start the engine. Hold the accelerator pedal to the floor, and back off slowly after the engine starts.

If those measures don't help, the only alternative is to let the car idle. One man used to park his diesel in a New York City parking garage and leave the engine and heater running eight hours a day. At quitting time he had no starting problem and a nice warm car. When I lived in Montreal, if you couldn't plug in your block heater, the standard method was to let the car idle overnight. In Edmonton, Alberta, I've been told, on winter nights every car in a tavern's parking lot had its engine running as long as its owner was inside.

Keep 'Em Crankin'

November/December 1992

Your advice to the owner of a reluctant diesel in the May/June issue was good, and I'd like to add a tip for cold-weather starts. Most people release the starter as soon as the engine fires, which works pretty well with a gasoline engine. But with a cold diesel, keeping the starter engaged while the engine begins to fire, and holding it until the engine begins to run, will greatly increase the chances of a successful start. The starter won't be hurt; an over-running clutch protects it. Release the starter when the engine begins to rev under its own power. Not only does this technique keep the engine turning, but it keeps the glow plugs energized, too, even though the indicator light may not indicate that on some models.

You're right. And if it's cold enough that you're worried about starting, you'd better set out to start your diesel on the first try. Glow for a full minute or more, then put the accelerator pedal to the floor. Keep cranking until the engine starts because you probably won't have enough left in the battery for a second try.

Up All Night

March/April 1998

Our Minnesota winters make it hard to start a diesel unless it has a plugged-in block heater to keep it warm. When no power outlet is available, I let the car idle—even all night—with the doors locked. Will this harm the engine?

Not at all, especially compared to the stress on the battery, starter, and engine caused by cold starts in sub-zero weather. At truck stops on winter nights you'll hear dozens of 18-wheelers idling away. I used to let my locked 1978 300D idle during extreme cold weather in eastern Washington. An idling Mercedes-Benz diesel consumes very little fuel, and there's no harm to the engine. Even when running errands around town in cold weather, I used to let the car idle while locked. This saves wear on the starter motor and battery. I did a survey of my typical errands one week; I reduced the number of starts by 80 percent by letting the engine idle if I was away from the car for less than half an hour.

Oil Burner?

March/April 1998

At 130,000 miles, my 1972 450SL uses a quart of oil with every 2–3 tanks of gas. The engine doesn't leak or smoke, but this consumption seems excessive to me. The manual seems to indicate this is normal. Is it?

One quart per two or three tankfuls might be as much as 900 miles per quart, not excessive considering the car's mileage. Mercedes-Benz engines are not designed and built with the object of keeping oil consumption to a minimum, and some models expected to be driven in a sporting manner were rather loose in their consumption. To determine the cause, a mechanic can perform compression and leakdown tests. You may need new rings or a valve job, but loose engines often run well, and oil is cheaper than Mercedes-Benz engine parts.

Miscellaneous

Block Heaters for the 300CD
January/February 1985

I need advice on engine block and oil dipstick heaters. What do you recommend for my 1978 300CD?

Mercedes-Benz has block heater kits for all recent models. These are inserted directly into the side of the engine block in place of an existing water plug. The topic is covered in Service Information 20/4 and on page 52 of this issue. Although some claim good results with heaters in hose lines, I strongly advise the block heater recommended by DBAG. Dipstick heaters run a poor third to these other two types.

Windshield Wiper Maintenance 101
January/February 2002

Step one for good windshield wiper function is a clean windshield. Even the smallest pits in the glass can accumulate road grime and cause streaking, even with a new blade installed. The trick is to remove the oily residue. While Bon Ami mixed into the cleaning solution is a good idea, a much better de-greaser is lacquer thinner on a rag. The thinner gets the oily grime out of the pits and leaves nothing behind. Of course, beware the close proximity of thinner and auto paint.

My father was a picture framer, and his glass had to be very clean. He mixed water, alcohol, and a little Bon Ami powder. When you clean your windshield—using Windex or whatever—remember to clean the wiper blade, too. The rubber blade accumulates debris which needs to be wiped off. Spray a little Windex on the cleaning rag, and run it along the edge of the wiper. This gets rid of road grime so the wipers won't streak the glass when you first turn them on.

To eliminate squeaks and judders as the wiper blade moves, it must be perpendicular to the windshield glass. You can bend the wiper arm to make the blade perpendicular then test it by lifting and dropping it against the glass to make sure it stays perpendicular. Some old, thin arms take quite a bit of bending to make them square to the windshield. The new, short, stout arms are a bear to correct if they go out of alignment.

On 123-chassis and earlier cars, you can re-arch the wiper arm to re-establish the spring force that it exerts to hold the wiper against the glass. Over time, the spring under the arm pulls the arm flat, so there is insufficient tension. Just grab the arm and bend it. Put a gentle bow into it to re-establish the spring pressure. The springs in the arms wear out. If the arms are really old, replace them, and you'll get new spring pressure. It really helps.

For windshield washer mix, in my shop we used 50-percent methanol and 50-percent water with a single drop of dishwashing detergent per gallon of mix. That mix can melt ice on the glass or on the wipers and could probably even streak the wax. Oh well, better to see, anyway!

Poly Vee-Belt Life
May/June 1998

My 1991 350SD has lost its flat poly vee-belt twice in 50,000 miles, so I feel that the single belt system is worse than the old five-vee-belt system. What is your experience?

Have you ever had one of those five vee-belts break and get tangled in the others? In my contacts with shops I hear of surprisingly long life for the newer poly vee-belts. The factory maintenance schedule calls for regular inspection, which is tedious so is probably skipped more often than not. Since these belts cannot be replaced at the roadside, good maintenance people emphasize careful inspection at regular intervals.

Since two poly vee-belts have failed in your seven-year old model in 50,000 miles, it is pretty obvious that there is a defect in one or more of the pulleys or some misalignment. Unless this is corrected, you will continue to have problems. The poly-vee belt has an excellent service record and has been widely adopted in the industry.

Finding Oil Leaks
March/April 1991

I have some elusive engine oil leaks. Is there a dye that can be put into the oil and traced with a black light?

The best way to find an oil leak is to steam clean the engine and let it dry, then run it until oil appears. If the leak is down low, you may have to run it with the car on a lift. Leaking oil runs down and backward in the air stream, so you have to catch it where the leak starts. If you have several leaks, seal the top one first, then clean again and look for more. Usually, though, an experienced mechanic familiar with your model can examine your car and tell you where the leak is coming from.

Chapter 2
Engine, Transmission

March/April 1992

July/August 2000

November/December 2000

W124 Motor Mount Replacement

by George Murphy,
Technical Director

*September/October
2003*

A reader wrote, "My 1989 300E engine feels rough and noisy, especially at idle. What can I do to make it feel as smooth as these engines are noted to be?" Engine mounts in 124 models (300E/CE/D/TE/4Matics/400E/500E) and 190E models are a combination of rubber and built-in shock absorbers. A glycol-water mixture is contained in two chambers connected by a valve, much as in a shock absorber. As the engine moves up and down, the mixture moves between the two chambers and is throttled by the valve, damping the movement.

As the cars age, the mounts tend to collapse and lose the ability to absorb vibration and harshness. The solution is to replace the mounts, which should always be done in pairs to maintain correct drivetrain geometry within the chassis. Misalignment from collapsed engine mounts can cause driveshaft vibration, stressing the rubber flex disks and support bearing and causing more trouble in the future.

You can check your engine mounts for condition. Jack up the car and block it securely so that the front wheels are free to turn, as you'll need to move the steering linkage. Remove the engine compartment noise encapsulation panel, usually secured with 8-mm self-tapping screws.

Mercedes-Benz factory manuals show a 13-mm-thick special tool for measuring the gap between the engine mount and the crossmember, but you can use any 13-mm-thick object (a 13-mm bolt head, for example) to check the gap (Figure 1).

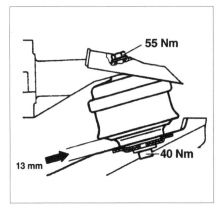

Figure 1. Motor mount to crossmember clearance must be at least 13 mm.

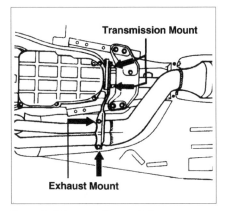

Figure 2. Exhaust and transmission mount bolt locations.

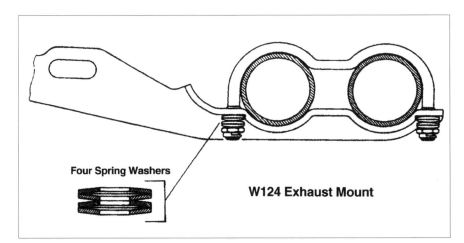

Figure 3. Spring washers on exhaust mount bolts allow pipes to expand and contract. Be careful to avoid over-tightening these bolts.

If the clearance between either motor mount and the crossmember on the side toward the engine is less than 13 mm, then you need to replace the motor mounts. If the clearance is at least 13 mm, you can still take steps to reduce tension in the engine suspension system (except models 400E and 500E). This should be done whenever the motor mounts are replaced.

First, remove the rear engine mount fastening bolt from the support. Loosen the exhaust bracket at the transmission. Loosen the U-bolt securing the exhaust pipe to the transmission. If possible, loosen the exhaust pipe from the exhaust manifold; they may be frozen together; be careful not to twist them off.

Loosen the front engine mount upper and lower fastening bolts (Figure 1). Raise the engine with a floor jack (padded with a 2x6x6 in piece of wood against the oil sump) just enough so the mounts can be rotated by hand (or replaced).

Lower the engine onto the mounts. Tighten the front engine mounts as follows: first tighten the lower fastening bolt to 40 Nm (29 lb-ft), then tighten the upper fastening bolt to 55 Nm (40 lb-ft).

Align the rear transmission mount (it's best to replace it at the same time as the front mounts). Manually lift and lower the transmission two or three times to release tension in the engine suspension and exhaust. If the threaded bores of the rear engine mount don't align with the engine support, loosen and align the support. Tighten the transmission mount bolts to 25 Nm (18 lb-ft). Tighten the engine support to 40 Nm. Tighten the

exhaust-pipe-to-manifold bolts evenly to 25 Nm.

Replace the exhaust bracket bushings and tighten the exhaust bracket bolts to transmission mounts to 25 Nm (Figure 2).

Tighten the exhaust pipe U-bolts to 7 Nm (5 lb-ft) to slightly compress the four spring washers on each U-bolt leg (Figure 3). This allows header pipe fore-and-aft movement to accommodate expansion and contraction of the exhaust system as

it changes temperature. If this U-bolt is tightened too much, it can cause binding of the header pipe(s) and possibly crack the exhaust manifold.

Finally, reinstall the engine noise encapsulation panel(s).

Your car should now feel like new. With new mounts, my 300E is so quiet at idle that I must check the tachometer to see if the engine is running. I feel no engine vibration at idle, and the car is substantially quieter at road speeds.

November/December 1959

How to Replace Your 300SD Water Pump

by John Lamb, Minuteman Section

November/December 1995

Photos in this article by the author.

This issue we'll replace the water pump on a W126 300SD turbodiesel. This fairly easy job provides a lot of satisfaction for the do-it-yourselfer, and no special tools are needed except a belt tension gauge. Replacement of the water pump is always called for if the engine is overheating because of a defective pump or if the pump is leaking coolant past its seal, down the front of the engine.

The belts should be inspected and, if necessary, replaced when the water pump is being replaced. Always observe safe work practices; let the engine cool down, carefully release the cooling system pressure cap when the engine is cool, and keep hands and other objects away from the belts and fans when the engine is running.

1. Allow the engine to cool before draining the antifreeze. Select the defroster function button, and set the temperature dial to max heat.

2. Release the coolant tank cap, then place a large drain pan below the radiator. Unscrew the plastic drain plug from the driver's side of the radiator, and allow the coolant to drain. Inspect the drain plug and O-ring and replace as necessary. See Figure 1.

3. Remove the upper radiator hose from the engine, then remove the plastic air intake bellows going to the air filter housing.

4. Remove the four 10-mm bolts that mount the fan hub to the water pump; see Figure 2. Remove the fan, and store it in an upright position.

5. Record the radio station pre-sets, then disconnect the negative battery cable. Loosen but do not remove all

Figure 1. Drain engine coolant into large pan as shown.

Figure 2. 10-mm wrench shown removing fan-to-water-pump hub bolts (black arrow).

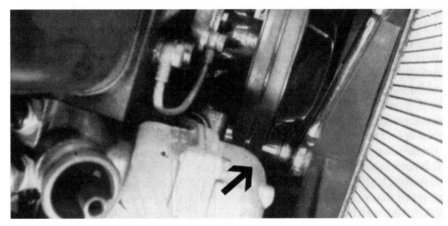

Figure 3. Ratchet and socket (arrow) shown loosening alternator mounting bolt. Be careful of radiator.

three 17-mm mounting nuts and bolts on the alternator. Always use a box wrench when loosening the mounting nuts; bolt clearance is so small that a ratchet and socket will jam against the

alternator and engine brackets as the nuts are loosened. See Figures 3 and 4.

6. Using a 13-mm socket, loosen the alternator belt adjusting bolt until the

Figure 4. Ratchet (arrow) at back of alternator, loosening mounting bolt. Ratchet is shown for illustration purposes only; use a box wrench.

Figure 5. Loosen alternator belt tensioning bolt using a 13-mm socket.

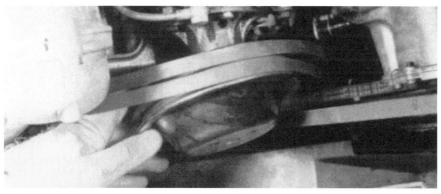

Figure 6. Remove water pump hub.

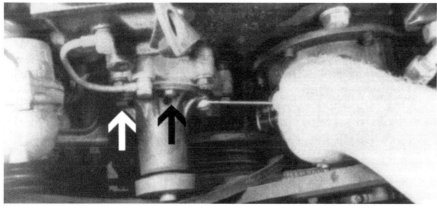

Figure 7. Remove the five water pump mounting bolts (arrows).

Figure 8. Scrape off old mounting gasket.

Figure 9. Fill engine with coolant directly into opening shown (arrow).

two drive belts are loose; see Figure 5. You may need to tap the alternator with a rubber mallet to loosen it. If the 13-mm adjusting bolt is not turning easily, make sure all the 17-mm mounting bolts are loose.

7. Remove the water pump hub, then loosen and remove the five 10-mm water pump bolts; see Figures 6 and 7. Do not remove the bolts for the water pump mounting base to engine block.

8. Remove the water pump by tapping it with a plastic or rubber hammer. Note the position of the pump cutout and vent hole so the new pump can be installed correctly.

9. Clean off all the old gasket mounting material from the mounting base. Clean the bolt holes using Q-tips. See Figure 8.

10. Working at the bench, install the new gasket on the new pump, paying attention to the cut-out position. Smear a little gasket sealer on the gasket to hold it in place, then install the new pump on the engine and tighten the bolts to 7 lb-ft (10 Nm).

11. Install the water pump hub and drive belts, then install the fan and tighten the four 10-mm fan-to-water-pump hub bolts to 18 lb-ft (25 Nm).

12. Turn the 13-mm alternator adjusting bolt clockwise until the belts are properly tensioned to 20-25 kg as measured with a belt tension gauge, such as the Krikit (part number 001 589 6921 00), or Snap-on GA424A. If new belts are being installed, tension them to 30 kg.

13. Tighten the three 17-mm alternator mounting bolts and nuts.

14. Tighten the radiator drain plug using a coin, then fill the engine block directly through the cylinder head opening with a mixture of 50-percent antifreeze and 50-percent drinking water or distilled water. See Figure 9.

15. Finish by re-installing the upper radiator hose with new clamps, fill the coolant tank with coolant up to the mark, then reinstall the air housing bellows. Start the engine, check for leaks, and top up the coolant as necessary. Reinstall the coolant tank cap.

300SD Turbo-Diesel Timing Chain Replacement

by John Lamb, Minuteman Section

September/October 1996

Photos in this article by the author.

Much has been written in these pages about the importance of engine timing chain operation. If the timing chain stretches from normal wear, valve timing and fuel injection timing will be retarded, which can cause starting problems and performance loss. If the timing chain breaks or jumps one or more teeth on the sprocket, the engine will suffer major damage from the valves hitting the pistons. Unfortunately, no warning signs tell you when the chain is about to snap or jump a tooth. Remember, a chain is only as strong as its weakest link.

Background

Owners of high-mileage engines may want to replace the chain as preventive maintenance *(the rule of thumb here is 100,000 miles. Tech Ed.)*. When replacing the chain, I strongly recommend replacing the chain tensioner, very easy during this procedure. Chain replacement is serious but not difficult work. During actual replacement, two people are needed. We assume that the car is running properly, that the chain has not jumped time, and that there is no damage from the chain having jumped time or broken.

This article only applies to W126 300SD turbo-diesel (617.95) engines. See illustration 1. Chain replacement takes about two hours. Once you begin, you must complete the job. You'll need a few special tools, including a grinding tool or cut-off tool such as a drill with a grinding wheel. A special chain tool is needed to crimp or mushroom over the new master link once the new timing chain

is installed. You need two master links: one that can be attached with two C-clips, and the master link that has to be crimped. See Photo 2. If the C-clip type of link comes with the new chain, no crimping of the master link is necessary, so the crimping tool is not needed. If you buy a chain that has to have the link crimped, get the crimping tool before starting the job. Impco rents this tool, or it can be purchased from AST (Assenmacher) through Snap-on Tools; the tool number is AST5843.

Chain replacement involves attaching the new chain to the old,

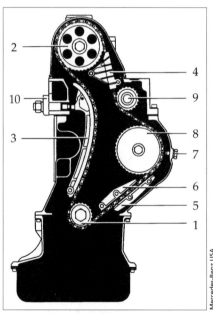

Illustration 1. timing chain: (1) crankshaft sprocket, (2) camshaft sprocket, (3) tensioner rail, (4) slide rail, (5) outer slide rail, (6) inner slide rail, (7) chain locking screw, (8) injection pump sprocket, (9) idler sprocket, (10) chain tensioner.

Mercedes-Benz USA

Photo 2. Permanent chain master link and face plate (left). Temporary master link with cutouts is at right.

then feeding the new chain around the camshaft sprocket into the engine as the crankshaft is rotated. Rotating the engine can be done only from the crankshaft pulley bolt. The new chain will emerge from the engine, and old and new chains can be temporarily joined with a master link that uses two C-clips to hold it. Afterward, the new chain is attached to itself with the crimped master link. The advantage of this procedure is that you can avoid removing drive belts or disassembling the front of the engine.

Preparing and Checking Timing Chain

To avoid disturbing the valve timing, do not use a remote starter during this procedure, and don't attempt to crank the engine over using the key starter. When rotating the engine by hand, never allow it to rotate counter-clockwise (backward).

1. Degrease the engine before starting this work.

2. Disconnect the negative battery cable.

3. Remove the air cleaner assembly and plastic intake pipe, then disconnect the throttle linkage and remove the valve cover; discard the gasket.

4. With the engine cool, remove the radiator coolant drain plug and allow approximately four quarts of coolant to drain into a pan. Remove the upper radiator hose, then remove the four fan-to-water-pump hub bolts using a 10-mm wrench. Store the fan in an upright position.

5. Using a 6-mm hex head socket, remove the bolts holding the stainless steel EGR pipe to the intake manifold. See photo 3. Loosen the two 11-mm bolts for the banjo clamps around the stainless pipe, then move the EGR pipe out of the way. Examine the EGR passages, and clean them as necessary using carburetor cleaner spray.

Photo 3. EGR valve bolts being removed.

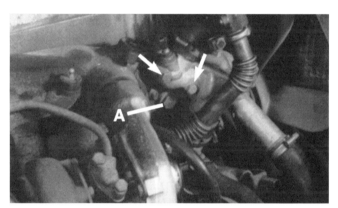

Photo 4. Thermostat housing bolts (arrows) to be removed. Chain tensioner hex plug (A) can also be seen. EGR has been moved out of way.

Photo 5. Camshaft alignment marks (arrows) must be exactly aligned.

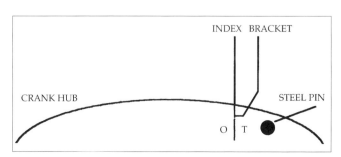

Illustration 6. TDC #1 cylinder marks on crank hub.

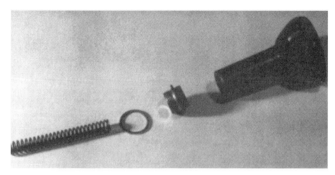

Photo 7. Chain tensioner spring, sealing washer, and hex plug; 19-mm socket and hand ratchet at right.

Photo 8. Chain tensioner opening (arrow) in the engine. The left mounting stud is shared by the tensioner and manifold.

Photo 9. Vise grips in place at 9 o'clock and 1 o'clock.

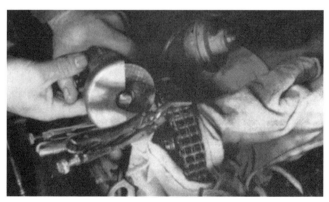

Photo 10. Rivet heads being ground off using cutoff tool. Stuff shop rags in engine openings.

6. Remove the two thermostat housing bolts using a 13-mm socket. Loosen the hose clamp at the bottom of the housing. See photo 4. Remove the thermostat housing. *Do not use a remote starter during this procedure, and don't attempt to crank the engine over using the key starter.*

7. Check for chain stretch by rotating the engine clockwise. Using a 27-mm deep socket and a 1/2-in drive ratchet on the crankshaft bolt at the front hub, set the crankshaft at 0° TDC (top dead center). For number 1 cylinder, 0° TDC on the compression stroke occurs when the vertical slash for the mark "O | T" lines up exactly with the fixed bracket flat edge. This occurs just after the steel pin on the crankshaft hub has passed the fixed bracket. At the same time, the camshaft mark must line up with the bearing cap notch. See photo 5.

The letters O | T can be seen on the hub. The vertical slash between the O and the T is the exact mark that must be aligned with the bracket. Always view the index from above the bracket to avoid parallax error. See photo 5. If the camshaft mark does not align *exactly* with its notch, chain stretch has occurred. See photo 5. Illustration 6 shows top dead center for cylinder number 1 at the crankshaft pulley and bracket.

8. Before beginning this step, make sure you have a temporary master link that uses two C-clips to join the old and new chains. Remove the chain tensioner spring from below the thermostat housing opening by removing the tensioner hex plug with a 19-mm socket. See photo 7. Remove the chain tensioner assembly by removing the mounting bolt and nut with a 17-mm socket. See photos 4 and 8. *The hex plug holds a coil spring under tension, so remove the plug slowly.*

Replacing Timing Chain

9. Using two pairs of long-nose vise grip pliers, clamp the chain to the camshaft sprocket in two places. Put pieces of protective rubber hose around the vise grip jaws. See photo 9.

Place the vise grips at about 9 o'clock and 1 o'clock on the camshaft sprocket. This immobilizes the chain and sprocket while one of the chain links is being ground off.

10. Stuff shop towels in and around the camshaft sprocket to prevent metal shavings or chain link pieces falling into the engine. Have a magnet available to trap such pieces.

11. Choose a chain link on the sprocket that is positioned between the two vise grip pliers. This link should be approximately at 11 o'clock on the sprocket. Using a cutoff tool or hand held Dremel grinder, grind off two crimped heads from the front of the link. See photos 10 and 11. *Again, do not use a remote starter during this procedure, and don't attempt to crank the engine over using the key starter.*

12. Grind the two "rivet heads" as described above. The chain link face plate can be tapped off the chain using a flat chisel and hammer. See photo 12. As you tap off the face plate, be sure it doesn't fall into the engine. See photo 13.

13. Slide the chain link slowly out of the chain toward the rear of the engine, and stop when it is about halfway out. Swivel the front two adjoining chain "wings" up out of the way. See photo 14. Remove the middle plate between the two rows of the chain, then remove the chain link entirely. The chain link is removed by sliding it toward the rear of the engine. After the link is removed, join the new timing chain to the old timing chain using the temporary master link and the two C-clips. See photo 15. Make certain the C-clips are securely fastened on the new master link.

Do not allow either chain to come off the sprocket teeth. From here, two people are needed to install the new chain. One person must keep the new chain tightly wrapped around the cam sprocket while pulling the old chain up and out of the engine. The second person must rotate the crankshaft slowly to feed the new chain into the engine.

14. After removing any metal chips, remove the shop rags from the engine. Before removing the two vise grip pliers, one person should stand on the passenger side of the engine with the new timing chain rolled out ready to install. The second person should put the 27-mm socket /ratchet on the crank bolt.

15. Carefully remove the vise grip clamped onto the old chain/sprocket at the 9 o'clock position. When the vise grip is removed, don't let the old chain fall into the engine. Hold the old chain tightly in one hand, then wrap the new chain onto as much of the sprocket's remaining teeth as possible. *Do not allow the chain to come off the sprocket teeth.*

16. The second person should remove the other vise grip pliers clamped at the 1 o'clock position of the cam sprocket only after confirming that a) the new chain is correctly linked to the old chain using the master link and C-clips, and b) the first person has tension on the old chain and has wrapped the new chain counter-clockwise over as many of the cam sprocket teeth as possible.

17. The second person should slowly rotate the crankshaft clockwise as the first person wraps the new chain onto the sprocket's teeth and also keeps pulling the old chain out of the engine. Continue until the new chain emerges from the engine. See photo 16. *Do not allow the chain to fall off the cam sprocket or to jump a tooth on the sprocket.*

18. When the new chain comes out of the engine and around the cam sprocket, the second person should stop rotating the crank when the new chain end is at 12 o'clock on the cam sprocket. Clamp the new chain to the cam sprocket as above using both pairs of vise grips, at 10 o'clock and 2 o'clock.

19. Stuff rags around the chain opening in the engine, then remove the C-clips and temporary master link. Separate the old chain from the new chain. Wrap the new chain onto the cam sprocket.

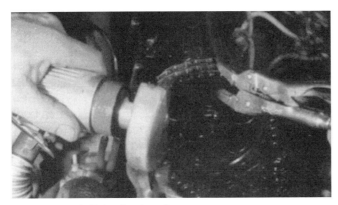

Photo 11. Grind off rivet heads as shown.

Photo 15. New shiny chain (left) attached to old chain using temporary master link.

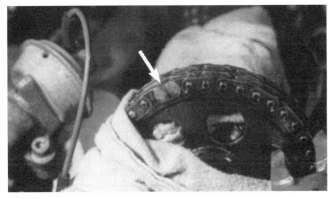

Photo 12. Face plate (arrow) ground down and ready for removal.

Photo 16. Vise grip reinstalled on new chain in preparation for chain master link crimping. New chain is emerging from engine at bottom.

Photo 13. Face plate removed from link.

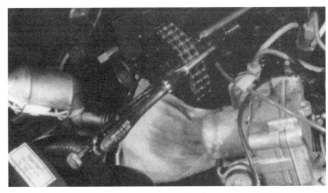

Photo 17. Chain crimping tool being installed over master link.

Photo 14. Chain "wings" swiveled out of way, middle plate being removed. Vise grips still clamped.

Photo 18. Master link being crimped using tool.

Photo 19. Shiny spots visible on spring indicate wear.

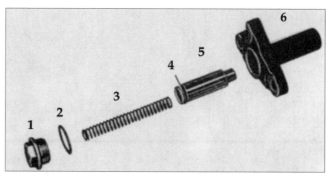

Photo 21. Exploded view of chain tensioner: (1) tensioner hex plug, (2) sealing washer, (3) tensioner spring, (4) detent spring, (5) piston, (6) tensioner housing.

Photo 20. Old spring (left) and new replacement (right). Note wear spots on old spring.

Photo 22. Pull out piston as shown and reinsert through back opening.

20. Insert the new master link to join the chain. From the rear, slide the link halfway in, then insert the new middle plate between the rows of the chain. Slide the link in completely, then install the front plate. Using the crimping tool, follow directions for crimping the new master link in place. See photos 17 and 18. The crimping tool is like a very powerful C-clamp that can mushroom the chain master link properly. The tool is tightened with a wrench until the rivet heads are crimped.

21. Remove the crimping tool, then inspect the crimp on the master link. Remove the vise grip pliers and rags. If everything is okay, rotate the engine clockwise two complete revolutions (720 degrees). There should be no mechanical locking or binding other than normal compression in the cylinders. Check engine timing as described earlier using the 0 I T hub mark and the camshaft mark and notch.

Chain Tensioner Inspection, Service and Replacement

22. The chain tensioner was removed earlier as described above. To replace it, remove the tensioner hex plug with a 19-mm socket. See photo 7 above. Remove the chain tensioner assembly by removing the mounting bolt and nut with a 17-mm socket. *The hex plug holds a coil spring under tension, so remove the plug slowly.*

23. After scraping off all the old gasket material from the engine, replace the tensioner assembly with a new one. Check that the piston is in its housing.

24. If you are going to reuse the tensioner, inspect the tensioner coil spring for signs of wear. If wear or shiny spots are visible, replace it. See photos 19 and 20. The coil spring is subject to wear and normally will have shiny wear marks on it. I recommend that you always replace the coil spring, hex plug sealing washer, and gasket.

25. Remove the oil piston from the assembly by sliding it out of the housing toward the direction of the chain. Clean all of the pieces with degreaser, and make sure that the tiny oil passage in the piston is not clogged. Reinstall the tensioner using a new mounting gasket. Tighten the mounting nut and bolt.

The tensioner works using a combination of coil spring tension and oil pressure against the piston. See photo 21. The piston inside the bore is designed to only move in the direction of the chain as the chain stretches. Do not attempt to push the piston back into the assembly. Instead, remove the piston, then reinsert it in the housing from the outside.

When I replaced the tensioner, I couldn't seat the tensioner assembly in the engine all the way to get the mounting bolt and nut started. If you encounter this, don't force the assembly in. Remove it and reset the piston by pulling it through the housing and reinserting it as described above. See photo 22.

26. Install the coil spring by placing it in the tensioner hex plug. Put the tensioner hex plug in a deep 19-mm socket with a hand ratchet, then install this entire assembly into the engine and rotate the ratchet to start the threads. The 19-mm socket and hand ratchet make it easier to start the threads of the hex plug while under tension. See photo 7 above. Torque the hex plug to 90 Nm.

Final Wrap-Up and Engine Start

27. Rotate the crankshaft two revolutions again. Double-check the engine timing using the marks described above.

28. Reinstall the thermostat housing, the EGR pipe, the valve cover, throttle linkages, vacuum hoses, and air cleaner.

29. Fill the cooling system with clean 50-percent antifreeze and water directly into the thermostat housing opening. Reinstall the fan and upper cooling hose.

30. Check the engine oil level; top up if necessary. Reconnect the battery cable, and make sure the 27-mm socket/ratchet has been removed from the crankshaft bolt.

31. Have your helper push and hold the stop lever on the fuel injection pump, then crank the engine over until oil pressure shows on the gauge. Don't preheat the glow plugs (at this point we do not want the engine to start).

32. After oil pressure is indicated, start the engine and allow it to idle for a few minutes. Check all fluid levels, and check the oil pressure and coolant temperature gauges for correct readings.

33. After the engine has fully warmed up, change the oil and filter and check for leaks.

Special thanks to Larry Croke at Auto Europa Inc. in Newton Highlands, Massachusetts, for assistance with preparation of this article. Copyright John Lamb, 1996.

Timing Is Everything

by Stu Ritter,
Technical Editor

*May/June
2000*

Photos in this article
by DaimlerChrysler
Classic Archives.

Timing Is Everything

Our Mercedes-Benz engines are either Otto-cycle or Diesel-cycle engines. Otto engines use gasoline, and diesels use oil (diesel fuel). Both are four-stroke motors, meaning that for every power stroke (when the fuel is ignited), the piston must travel up and down the bore four times. In a four-stroke engine, here's what happens:

1. **Intake Stroke:** The piston is drawn down by the crankshaft, creating a vacuum in the combustion chamber which draws in the air/fuel mixture (or just air with direct injection).

2. **Compression Stroke:** The piston is forced up and compresses the mixture.

3. **Power Stroke:** The mixture ignites, forcing the piston back down and turning the crankshaft.

4. **Exhaust Stroke:** The piston is driven upward, pushing combustion byproducts out of the combustion chamber, preparing it for stroke number one and another fresh charge.

Valves control the intake of fresh mixture and the exit of exhaust gas. The camshaft controlling the valves turns once for each power stroke, so the camshaft rotates at one-half crankshaft speed. For each revolution of the camshaft, the crankshaft rotates twice. On some engines, one camshaft controls the intake and the exhaust valves; others have an intake cam and an exhaust cam.

Now we're really accumulating things that rotate. Some V-8 and V-12 motors have two camshafts in each head, giving us four camshafts spinning in harmony with one crankshaft. We now have five shafts a-spinning at thousands of revolutions per minute.

Adding a distributor drive gear or an injection pump drive gear really adds up the things that rotate. What keeps this whole mess together and operating at the correct time? You can't have valves opening at the wrong time, or they hit the pistons, and the ignition spark must occur at precisely the correct time. The timing chain gets this job—and its name.

Chain Drive

Timing chains have served Mercedes-Benz engines with great reliability for many decades. Unlike timing belts, which must be replaced every 50,000 miles or so, timing chains show remarkable longevity if the engine oil is kept clean and fresh. Like a stronger version of a bicycle chain, a timing chain consists of a series of links. Each link is formed by two side plates connected by two pins, one at each end of the side plate. Each pin carries a roller, free to turn on the pin. A dual-row timing chain looks like two bicycle chains sharing a common center row of sideplates. Mercedes-Benz has used single-row timing chains (more on those later), but most timing chains in its current engines are of the double-row variety.

Again like a bicycle, each device that must rotate with precisely correct timing has a sprocket on one end with teeth that engage the spaces between the chain's rollers. The rollers fit into the valley between the sprocket's teeth so precisely that rotational positioning can be very accurate, allowing camshafts to be timed to within one degree of rotation. The same is true for injection pump drives and ignition spark distributor drives.

These sprockets are accurately positioned on the end of camshafts, crankshafts, and other drives by a woodruff key, a half-moon-shaped piece of mild steel. Part of the key fits into the shaft, and part sticks up and

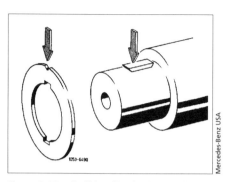

Figure 1. Woodruff key fits slot in end of camshaft (right); spacer washer (left) carries timing mark.

Mercedes-Benz USA

slides into a slot in the sprocket's hub, positively positioning the sprocket on the shaft (Figure 1).

Several devices help control the chain in its high-speed trip around all the whirring sprockets. Where the chain must change direction radically, an idler sprocket, rotating on a guide pin, just guides the chain. Flat nylon guides on one or both sides of the chain keep it on its path. One of these guides, the tensioner rail, is long with a slight curve, earning it the name "banana rail" (Figures 2 and 3).

"Wear" Equals "Stretch"

As the chain wears, it grows longer. The 1989 560SEL chain has 198 links, and each link has two pivot pins, so it has 396 pivot pins. If each pin wears one-thousandth of an inch, then the chain "stretches" four-tenths of an inch. To maintain accurate timing, this change in length must be accommodated. The tensioner rail pivots at the bottom, and a chain tensioner controls the movement of the upper end. The chain tensioner is a plunger, either spring-loaded or with engine oil pressure behind it. The tensioner pushes the tensioner rail against the chain to take up slack.

The chain is under tension from the crankshaft sprocket all the way around the run to the camshaft sprocket. If there is more than one camshaft, all are under tension. The only slack in the system occurs

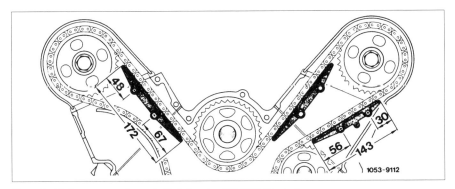

Figure 2. Chain run around camshafts in heads of M117 V-8 includes several changes of direction; dark areas are ramps to guide chain.

Figure 3. Lower chain run in M117 V-8. Large sprocket in center is an idler; right sprocket drives distributor; lower sprocket is on crankshaft.

Figure 4. Camshaft timing mark; note double-row chain.

between the final camshaft and the crankshaft, so the chain has a tension side and a slack side. The chain tensioner is on the slack side. The tensioning system can take up a certain length of chain and no more. If chain length exceeds the design parameters of the tensioning system, there is no control over the chain's slack side. Then dangerous and expensive things start to happen.

When the tensioner can no longer keep a worn chain tight, due to excessive length, the chain rides up the teeth of the sprockets. As the chain stretches and rides higher, the camshaft timing is retarded. On multi-camshaft engines, the last cam in the run is furthest away from the crankshaft, so it will be the most retarded. On single-overhead camshaft V-8s, the left cam, first in the tension run, might retard five or six degrees, but the right cam may be retarded up to 20 or 25 degrees because of the amount of chain between the left camshaft and the right camshaft. The

M117 4.5, 5.0, and 5.6-liter engines' chains are about 5-ft long.

When this happens, you will likely hear a noise on cold start. The chain is so loose that it is banging against the inside of its passages in the motor, and it is rising off the sprockets so far that it hits the valve cover. The noise, a loud slapping, diminishes in a few seconds. This sound also occurs when an oil-pressure-style chain tensioner leaks off its pressure overnight and collapses. The chain bangs against the tensioning rail. Loose timing chains are the primary cause of collapsing chain tensioners. The tensioner is designed to keep pressure against the tensioning rail, not to have the chain slapping against it.

Consequences

If a chain becomes this loose and slaps against the guide rails, there is a good chance that it will break the guide rails and jam the broken piece between the chain and the sprocket, drastically changing the cam timing. The valves hit the pistons and bend,

usually stopping the motor instantly. Often when a chain breaks a guide rail this way, it punches through the left valve cover because there just isn't room for the chain and the broken piece of rail to make it around the top of the sprocket.

It is not difficult to check a timing chain for stretch. You remove the valve cover on single cam engines; on a V-8 you remove the right-side cover. The workshop manual shows you the assembly marks. See Figure 4. One is cast into the first cam bearing; the other is a notch in a washer between the sprocket and the cam bearing. You will need a 27-mm deep socket and a ratchet handle to turn the engine over using the front crankshaft bolt. Always rotate the engine in its normal direction of rotation. It is easiest to do this with the spark plugs or glow plugs removed. Slowly rotate the engine until the assembly marks line up, then look at the crankshaft damper pulley and read the number of degrees of chain stretch directly off the pulley. With a new chain the crankshaft damper indicator would read 0/0, or top dead center. No published specifications exist for maximum allowable chain stretch. Offset woodruff keys are available to reset cam timing to accommodate 10 degrees of stretch. Since no further correction is possible, this is the maximum chain stretch acceptable to me.

Replacing a Chain

The original chain fitted at the factory is endless, without a "master link", so to replace the chain, a link must be ground apart. Replacement chains come with one of two types of master link. The easiest to install has a single clip across both pivot pins, called a "fish head" link. The fish's head always goes in the chain's direction of rotation so if it ever touches anything, it won't be knocked off. A later style of clip-type master link uses two small C clips. Another type of link, the "peen" style, requires a special tool to peen the ends of the pivot pins over onto the side plate just like all the other pins in the chain.

When a chain is replaced, sprockets should be examined for hooking of the teeth and for burrs on the side of the teeth. The tensioner rail is either replaced or re-covered, depending on the model. If the fixed guide rails show no wear, they can be left in place. If the chain was really loose and slapping all over the inside of the engine, it would be smart to replace the fixed guide rails, at least those that are visible without major disassembly. During a chain replacement, this requires a second set of hands. An aftermarket tool allows one person to wind in a chain, but I have never seen one used. To avoid the possibility of the camshaft jumping timing, I strongly recommend removing at least the rockers on the right side of a V-8. It's even easier to remove the rockers on both sides; then you can just wind in the chain without concern for timing problems.

Single-Row Chains

In 1981, for reasons known only to the factory engineers, Mercedes-Benz decided that the 3.8-liter V-8 engine for the U.S. market only would have a single-row timing chain. Throughout the rest of the world, 380s used the usual double-row chain and were trouble-free, but the single-row chains on U.S. cars wore more rapidly than normal. A single-row chain was used in 1981 to 1983 models, then the 1984 model returned to a double-row chain.

Our shop replaced single-row chains every 30,000 miles, which seemed to work until one day we had one snap at 22,000. This engine had updated sprockets, but the chain snap caused half the valves to hit the pistons and bend. We notified our customers with 1981, 1982, or 1983 380-engined cars to either convert to double-row chains or sell them. The recent four-cam V-8 and V-12 use a single-row chain, but the chain run has been nicely straightened, and these chains encounter much less trouble.

Timing chains may be old technology, but they are proven, and they work for long periods of time. Given good oil change intervals, chains have lasted 100,000 to 200,000 miles before needing replacement. Lacking frequent oil changes, timing chains have stretched beyond useful length in 75,000 miles. Inside an engine spinning at 5,000 revolutions per minute, timing is everything, and the chain is the timekeeper.

Twin-Cam Engine Valve Adjustment

by George Murphy, MBCA Technical Committee

September/October 1997

Photos in this article by the author.

A 17-mm open-end wrench and feeler gauges are used to set valve gap on the 110 engine.

The venerable 110 twin-cam, 6-cyl gasoline engine was available in 1974 through 1985 Mercedes-Benz models, though few were imported to the U.S. after 1982. The 280S/SE (116 chassis) and 280E/CE (123 chassis) are the models most often seen here. Some gray market cars also have this engine, including the 280SL (107 chassis) and the 280SE (126 chassis).

My most recent experience with this unique engine was in my daughter's 1980 280SL. The valves needed adjustment after running 600 miles following a valve job. My daughter, Kim, has a keen interest in learning how to take care of her bright red roadster, so she willingly donned her grease-spattered coveralls and rubber gloves to dive into the engine and learn about valve adjustment.

Here's How

This procedure is also shown in section 0560.10 of the *Mercedes-Benz Maintenance Manual*. It's best to do this job with a cold engine. A fully warmed-up engine is too hot, making it difficult to handle the parts. Leaning over a hot radiator is no fun, either. And, theoretically, as the engine cools during valve adjustment, the valve gaps change, making it difficult to get them just right.

First, carefully pull each spark plug wire off its spark plug; pull only on the metal shield, not on the wire. Mark each wire with the cylinder number on a piece of masking tape to make re-connecting easier. Carefully unclip the

wires from the plastic guides on the head cover. Remove the transmission throttle link that crosses the cam cover, and remove the cam cover. It is not necessary to remove the spark plugs, but if you do, first blow out the spark plug cavities with compressed air so that debris doesn't fall into the combustion chambers when the plugs are removed.

No special adjusting tool is needed, just a 17-mm open end wrench and a set of feeler gauges, one 0.10-mm (intake) and one 0.25-mm (exhaust); those are cold settings. A remote starter button makes turning over the engine easy, but two wires with alligator clips at each end work just as well. First, hook one wire to the positive post (the hot wire) on the battery. Find the large terminal strip on the right fender well; one terminal (number 30) will "jog" the engine starter when the hot wire is touched to it. Clip a second wire to this terminal, and clip its other end to a non-metallic component nearby. I use one of the

plastic tie-straps on the windshield washer bottle that secures the washer pump wire. When you want to turn the engine over slightly, momentarily touch the hot wire to this wire.

That lets you turn over the engine to get the cam lobe 180 degrees opposite the rocker as shown in Figure 1. Don't worry about getting a specific cam lobe where you want it; look and see if any cam lobe is 180 degrees opposite the rocker. If not, jog the engine to bring another lobe into position.

When you get a cam lobe where it needs to be (on the heel of the cam, opposite the top of the lobe), remove the spring clip (1 in Figure 1), using a small screwdriver to pop it off. Use the feeler gauge to measure the valve gap (arrow). Use a 17-mm wrench to rotate the valve adjusting screw (2 in Figure 1) to set the gap. Valve clearance is correct if the feeler gauge requires a tight pull (like pulling on your hair when it's squeaky clean) through the gap. Leave the spring clip off to indicate that the valve has been set. Jog the engine again

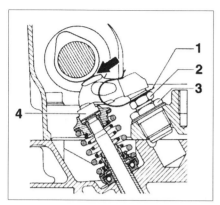

Figure 1. Valve gear includes 1) tension spring, 2) valve adjusting screw, 3) threaded bushing, 4) plunger. Cam is in proper position for adjustment, lobe away from rocker; arrow indicates where feeler gauge slips in.

until another yet-to-be-set cam lobe is aligned opposite its rocker, then remove that spring and set the valve.

As you set each valve, leave the spring clip off, so you can tell at a glance which valves have been set (no spring clip) and which haven't (spring clip still there). When all the clips are gone, all your valves should be set. If you want to make sure that all gaps are correct, re-check each valve as above and adjust them as necessary.

As you re-check each valve, install its spring clip to indicate that the valve has been checked. A plastic-faced hammer works well to tap the clip

back into place on the rocker pivot stud (see photo). Simply tap on the lower part of the clip where it snaps on to the adjustment nut. If any valve adjusting screw turns too easily less than 20 Nm (15 lb-ft) it will have to be replaced, together with its threaded bushing (3 in Figure 1).

When all the tension springs are back in place, you're finished. Look closely at each tension spring to make sure that it is seated properly. Install the cam cover, the transmission link, and the spark plug wires, and you're done.

Use a plastic-faced hammer to tap the tension spring into place.

300D Top-End Engine Work Hints

by George Murphy,
Contributing
Editor

*March/April
1992*

Photos in this article
by the author.

*How to facilitate replacing your
diesel's valve seals, cam chain and
fuel injectors and rebuilding the
vacuum pump.*

Last summer, before an extended
trip with Ol' Yeller (my 1978 Maple
Yellow 300D), I decided to do some
refurbishment on its diesel engine. The
car had gone about 120,000 miles at
the time and didn't seem to be running
very well. The valve seals leaked a
little, as evidenced by some blue
exhaust smoke. The cam chain was
stretched about 1/8-inch (indicated by
the alignment mark on the camshaft
versus the 0° mark on the crankshaft
vibration damper). There was an oil
leak from the intake manifold gasket.
The short (2-inch) coolant hose under
the thermostat housing had a slight
leak. And the vacuum pump gasket
needed changing—there was an oil
film around its housing.

This is not a step-by-step
procedure for doing each job. Based
on observations from doing this
work at home, these are simply hints
to make the work easier. So that you
have the correct torque values and
an installation guide, you'll definitely
need a Mercedes-Benz workshop
manual or at least a Haynes manual for
your model.

I acquired the parts and gaskets
needed and planned how to tackle all
these jobs at once. Think through an
involved project such as this to make
sure you have all the necessary tools.
Workshop manuals show several
complex (and expensive) tools for some
tasks, but with a little thought and
ingenuity you can do the job effectively
without a lot of expensive tools.

With rocker assembly removed, valve stems are easily accessible.
One valve here has had nuts, cap, and spring removed.

Preparation

First, take your car to a coin-operated
car wash and clean the engine.
There's nothing worse than working
on a greasy engine in a filthy engine
compartment; you get dirty from
head to toe. Before driving to the car
wash, liberally spray the engine and
adjacent areas with Gunk or other degreasing fluid. Remove the air cleaner
housing and clean those hard to reach
areas under the intake and exhaust
manifolds. Engine heat on the way to
the car wash will make the de-greaser
work better. Don't spray de-greaser
or water on electrical components or
connections. If you remove the air
cleaner housing, plug the air intake
with a big rag while cleaning to keep
water out of the intake manifold.
Don't forget to remove the rag when
you're finished.

With the engine clean, you can
start. Use disposable latex surgeons
gloves to protect your skin from
the hard-to-clean carbon present in
oil used in diesels. Used motor oil
from diesels can contain sulphur

compounds that are easily absorbed
into the skin. The gloves give you good
feel, and your hands don't dry out as
badly from frequent cleaning. A box
of 100 gloves costs only $5–$6. I buy
mine from my dentist. Be sure to use
latex gloves; vinyl seems to stretch
when exposed to fuel and oil.

Getting Started

Remove the air cleaner housing, all
drive belts, the cooling fan, and the
fan shroud. This allows better access
for a wrench (21-mm socket, the same
one that removes the fuel injectors)
to rotate the crankshaft via the center
bolt. Clean the crankshaft vibration
damper and rub chalk into the
engraved timing marks. Lightly rub the
chalk off the surface, and the engraved
marks will show up more clearly.

On models with the climate control
servo next to the air-conditioning
compressor, drain the cooling system
and remove the servo. This lets you
move the compressor away from
the engine to reach the thermostat
housing bolts and cam chain tensioner.

Don't disconnect the freon lines from the compressor, or you'll lose all the gas to the ozone layer!

It's easier to turn the engine over by hand if the injectors or glow plugs are removed, too.

Valve Seal Replacement

To make room to reach the valves, remove the fuel injector lines and the fuel injectors. So that small parts and dirt don't fall into the pre-combustion chamber, cover the injector holes in the cylinder head. After removing the injection lines, cap the fuel injection pump connections. Remove the valve rockers and shafts as an assembly; don't take it apart unless you're replacing the rockers.

Do one cylinder at a time. Move piston 1 to Top Dead Center (TDC). This can be determined by aligning the 0° mark on the crankshaft vibration dampener with the timing mark on the engine and aligning the camshaft timing mark with the notch on the front cam bearing support. TDC for other pistons can be determined by cam lobe position for the respective cylinder, i.e., when the appropriate exhaust valve cam lobe is 45° upward to the left (looking from front) and the intake valve cam lobe is horizontal to the right, that cylinder is at TDC.

The job is easier with Mercedes-Benz special valve wrenches—two 14-mm open end "bent" wrenches plus the valve spring cap wrench. Remove the top adjusting nut, then slowly unscrew the nut holding the valve spring cap until it's almost off. Check to see whether the valve hits the piston when pushed down. If it does, the piston is at TDC. If it doesn't, stop and rotate the crankshaft until the piston is at TDC. A dropped valve can ruin your whole day; you may have to remove the cylinder head to retrieve it! Again, do one cylinder at a time!

Remove the nut and the valve spring cap. Old valve seals can be pried off with the open end of a 14-mm valve adjusting wrench. Oil the valve stem before pushing the new seal on. The special Mercedes-Benz assembly

New timing chain (left) connected to old chain, ready to be cranked around; old chain will roll off at lower left.

mandrel is not necessary—use a plastic assembly sleeve (supplied with the new seal set) on top of the valve stem to allow the new seal to slide down over the threads on the valve stem. To seat the seal, press down on the metal sleeve part of the seal with your fingers. The seal should snap onto the valve guide. Check for proper seating by measuring the height from the cylinder head surface to the top of the new seal; it should be the same as an existing seal (on a cylinder at TDC).

When re-assembling, thread the valve adjusting nuts down as far as possible to allow room to install the rocker arms. Oil the camshaft and rockers, set the valve gap for a cold engine, then replace the cam cover.

Replacing the Cam Chain and Tensioner

If you're going to change the cam chain tensioner (and if you're replacing the chain, you should), you'll have to remove the thermostat housing. While it's off, replace the short coolant hose between the water pump and the thermostat housing. It's a beast to change otherwise. Fill the new cam chain tensioner with oil by submerging it in 10W oil and exercising the plunger several times.

So that the cam gear doesn't rotate and dump the chain into the engine, use bread wrapper ties or tie-wraps to hold the cam chain to the gear while you grind off the master (connector) link pins. Put rags in all holes where debris could fall into the engine.

Attach the new chain to the old chain with a new link, but don't press on the new outside link plate yet. The chain won't come apart when you're pulling it through. Have an assistant hold both chains securely as you rotate the engine with a wrench, in the normal direction (clockwise, viewed from the front) only! If you slacken either chain, the cam timing could be upset.

When the new chain emerges from the engine, position it so that the master link is at the top of the cam gear. Tie off the cam gear and chain with ties to prevent the chain from dropping into the engine.

A Mercedes-Benz chain crimping tool is convenient but expensive. After the outside link plate is securely installed, the link pins can be peened over gradually with Vise Grips. Adjusting the grip a little tighter each time, keep squeezing the pin until its end is mushroomed and looks the same as the old pins. Use a magnifying glass to inspect your work. We strongly recommend the factory crimping tool. If you don't have one, try to rent or borrow one.

Replacing Fuel Injector Tips

Remove all fuel lines and hoses. If the small rubber fuel return hoses are more than 6-8 years old, discard them and get new ones. Use the 21-mm special socket to remove the injectors. Take apart each injector and clean the threads on the steel nozzle body; make sure your work area and tools are clean! Re-assemble the new tips in clean diesel fuel, using latex gloves to protect your hands. Retorque the injectors to specification, usually 70-80 Nm (52-59 lb-ft).

Vacuum Pump Rebuild

The vacuum pump is secured to the engine with metric socket-head cap screws; use the correct metric Allen wrenches to remove it. Before starting work, thoroughly clean the outside of the pump. See Figure 1.

You don't need the special Mercedes-Benz jig to disassemble a vacuum pump. Use a 5/8-inch-thick board about 10 inches square. Lay the pump against the board and mark three equally spaced holes around the body (8 in Figure 1), then drill through the board. Use 2-3-inch screws or bolts to attach the pump body to the board. Place an object about 1-inch high—a socket works well—under the pump roller to maintain dimension "a" in Figure 1, then tighten the screws (or nuts) equally to draw the pump down onto the board. This pre-loads the strong pump spring, allowing you to change the diaphragm without damaging it.

Remove the cover screws and cover. If the cover sticks to the pump body, loosen it with a rubber hammer or a piece of wood. Remove the cylinder head screw (3 in Figure 1), but hold the disk (5 in Figure 1) to prevent twisting the diaphragm. Remove the diaphragm and its washers, and note the position of washer 7. Insert new diaphragm (6 in Figure 1) with washers 5 and 7 as shown. The boss on the diaphragm must face upward, and the washers must be positioned as shown. Use Loctite on the new center screw

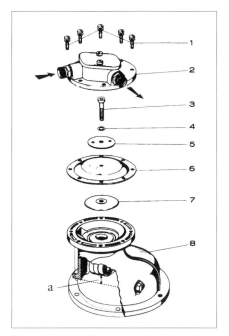

Figure 1. Exploded view of vacuum pump.

(3 in Figure 1), and install the gasket (4 in Figure 1). Tighten the screw to about 9 Nm (6 lb-ft). Hold the upper diaphragm disk (5 in Figure 1) and be careful that the holes in the diaphragm align with the threaded holes in the pump body. Install the cover, and tighten the screws evenly to 2.5-4.5 Nm (2-3 lb-ft).

When re-installing the pump, you may have to rotate the crankshaft until the vacuum pump actuating cam is at its low point so that the pump can be attached to the engine. Use a new gasket, and tighten the attachment bolts evenly to 10-15 Nm (7-11 lb-ft).

Again we suggest that you have the Mercedes-Benz workshop manual for your engine. About 500 miles after doing the job, change the oil and oil filter to remove any dirt which may have entered the engine.

Happy motoring!

Valve Job, Part I

by Stu Ritter,
Technical Editor

*July/August
2000*

*Every engine eventually needs this
simple but critical repair.*

Valve Job, Part I

After four years, you new car payments are over, and the bank has sent you the title. It was a long haul but worth it. Any little new car gremlins were repaired under warranty, and your car is running fine, so you expect many miles ahead with little more than routine maintenance. It'll be a long time before wear will affect your Mercedes-Benz. Miles of pleasant, safe motoring lie ahead.

There is nothing like buying a new Mercedes-Benz and keeping it for years. A unique feeling develops as you age with your car. As you drive, though, around the 100,000- or 150,000-mile mark you might see little puffs of blue smoke in the rear view mirror, and it will be time to pull the cylinder head(s) and refresh the valves and guides. No matter what car you drive, all engines eventually must have the upper end refreshed.

No Carbon, Just Wear

The British used to call it a "decoke." The cylinder head would be removed and the carbon (coke) removed from the intake and exhaust ports and valves. On the old cool-running, rich-burning engines, carbon formed everywhere, including atop the pistons. Removing the head and scraping this stuff out was normal maintenance. If you failed to do so, compression would increase as carbon built up. The old low-octane fuels couldn't handle the compression boost, so the engine would start detonating, possibly

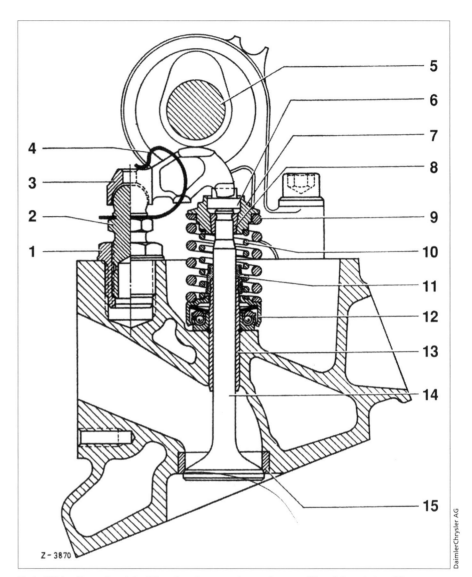

Typical Valve Gear: Cam lobe (5) pushes downward on rocker arm (3) and thrust piece (6) to depress valve (14); inner and outer valve springs (9 and 10) lift valve via retainer (7) and cone (8) to close it. Valve guide (13) is pressed into hole in cylinder head (crosshatched area) and capped by valve seal (11). Valve seat (15) seals off cylinder during combustion. Other bits include threaded bushing (1), clearance adjusting screw (2), clamping spring (4), and rotocap (12).

damaging itself. No amount of fiddling with the ignition retard lever would stop the ping, so you knew it was time to pull the head and scrape away.

Today we have no carbon build-up problems. Our engines run so hot, and our fuel injection systems control fuel flow so accurately, that there is rarely enough excess fuel to build carbon. Our primary reason for removing a cylinder head is wear—between the valve stem and the valve guide and between the valve and the valve seat.

Every valve moves up and down once for every two revolutions of the crankshaft. The valve stem is lubricated by a light film of oil that gets by the seal at its top. Guides are made of a phosphor/bronze alloy that stands up to extreme conditions quite well. In the 1960s and 1970s it was not unusual to have to replace valve guides every 75,000 to 100,000 miles. Materials have improved, so we now see mileages over 150,000 before valve guide replacement.

The amount of wear between the valve face and the valve seat depends on your driving technique. If you use large throttle openings at low rpm, the valve gets hammered into the seat from the high brake mean effective pressure (BMEP), which is the push on top of the piston from expanding combustion gases. At high rpm, BMEP is lower, so instead of hammering wear, the valve face and valve seat are blackened. At high rpm the valve spends less time on the seat, so it transfers less heat to the head and the cooling system. Valves will wear; it's just a matter of how the wear takes place.

First Steps

So after 150,000 miles your car runs well, but you notice a little blue smoke. A call to your favorite repair shop, and it's time to take it in for a look. What does the shop do?

The first diagnostic step is a pumping compression test and a cylinder leakage test, to make sure the blue smoke isn't caused by cylinder bore wear. On gasoline engines, the spark plugs may have a small clump of burnt oil residue, caused by oil leaking into the combustion chamber past worn valve guides.

If the problem looks like worn guides, the shop will use a cylinder leakage tester, which pumps the cylinder full of air with the piston at top dead center then measures how much leaks out. A mechanic will also remove one valve spring and valve stem seal and wiggle the valve in the guide to see how much free play (wear) exists; an experienced Mercedes-Benz mechanic can tell whether or not guides are worn. Sometimes we also flow a little lacquer thinner down the valve stem to remove the oil cushion between it and the guide to make the measurement more accurate.

If the guide-stem clearance is within specification, the engine needs only new valve stem seals. Installation takes about six hours on an M116 or M117 engine. It takes longer on four-cam engines but less on five-cylinder diesels. In the old days you almost

knew it was going to be the guides. These days, putting in new valve stem seals may keep an engine smoke-free for another 50,000 to 100,000 miles, depending on how you have taken care of it. This is where oil change frequency pays off. The more you invest in oil changes, the less you'll pay for engine repairs. Change the oil, and you extend the TBO (time between overhauls), as aircraft people say.

Off With Its Head

Once we decide to pull the head(s) and replace the valve guides, what goes on? Let's look in the operating room and see why mechanics earn so much money to do this.

First, the cylinder head comes off. Depending on the model, removing and re-installing the head(s) takes from six to eight hours for a simple four-cylinder engine up to 30 to 40 hours for a four-cam V-8 or V-12. That doesn't include machining of the head. During disassembly, the mechanic looks at everything carefully to find worn parts that need to be replaced.

We examine the timing chain sprockets and the timing chain rails for wear. We test the chain tensioner for wear. As we remove the cams, we examine the bearing surfaces and the lobes. Rockers, followers, and lifters get a good eyeball, too.

The entire head must be disassembled, so it costs you no more in labor to replace other worn parts. For instance, this is a good time to wind in a new timing chain, which takes only a few minutes. When I have a head off, I charge nothing to replace a timing chain; the customer pays only for the chain. All chain rails have to be removed before the head goes to the machine shop anyway, so new rails are installed during re-assembly.

In a solvent tank we use stiff brushes to get the head clean enough for the machine shop's cleaning equipment. To get it really clean, they will "hot tank" the head then use a bead blaster to clean the intake and exhaust ports and remove any accumulated carbon caused by oil that

has gotten down between the valve stem and the guide deposits. Before the bead blasting, every bolt hole will have a bolt screwed into it to keep bead media from entering the bolt hole. Having a bolt run into this media during re-assembly will jam the bolt into the threads. Then you must take it all apart to clean it out. Good machine shops are careful about this procedure.

Valve springs get washed and checked on a pressure tester, where a specified amount of pressure should move the spring a specified distance. Because Mercedes-Benz uses very good materials for valve springs, it's very rare to find weak valve springs.

All small parts are checked for wear. I like to replace most of the rubber vacuum hose at this time. This small expense pays big dividends in eliminating difficult to diagnose vacuum leaks later. For engines with adjustable valves, the valve clearance adjusting mechanism is examined closely to make sure it is still serviceable.

Machine Shop Jobs

The head arrives at the machine shop degreased and de-oiled, with the valves. My machine shop lets me bring my own parts because I always use factory valve guides. I have already measured the valve stem diameter to make sure it is within specifications. Again, in the old days, valve stems were usually worn beyond specifications, so the valves would have to be replaced. Modern guide materials seem to wear valve stems less, so now it's rare to replace a valve because of stem wear. Valve stem wear is measured in very small dimensions, demanding a good metric micrometer. If you're doing this work yourself, the machine shop can measure it for you.

There are two ways to remove and replace valve guides. The technique recommended by Mercedes-Benz is to hammer the old guides out of the head, then hammer in the new ones using a guide installation mandrel. This special tool is shaped to fit the pushing surfaces machined into the guide.

Mechanics who have worked on air-cooled engines often use a better technique. I have found that when guides are beaten out of the cylinder head, then new guides are beaten in, the valve seats take quite a bit of cutting to bring them perpendicular to the new guide. Aircraft mechanics use special drills to drill out most of the guide, leaving a paper-thin remnant. Near their tip, these drills are the same diameter as the valve stem, so they use the existing hole in the guide as a pilot. With the head clamped to the bed of a vertical milling machine, the guide is drilled out so that very little of it remains. The remaining material can then be pushed out of the head easily, almost with thumb pressure.

Rather than beating the new guides into the head, the guides go into a freezer for a day, and the head is heated to 300°F. (Tile guides may also get a shot from a carbon dioxide fire extinguisher to further chill them just before installation.) The guides are then pushed into place with a press. Chilling contracts the guide, and heat expands the guide bore in the head, allowing an easier, more accurate fit. When guides are replaced this way, very little valve seat machining is needed; the new guide is in the same

position as the old one, so the stem and seat are already perpendicular. This makes it easy to recut the valve seat, removing the least necessary amount of material.

In fact, using my hand valve seat cutters (made by NeWay) I can have complete contact on the valve seat with only two or three revolutions of the cutter. Using the beating process, you generally have to completely reshape the seat to match the new guide, removing a lot of material on one side and a little on the other because the new guide is not perpendicular to the existing seat.

Before the trip to the machine shop, the valve faces and backsides have been cleaned on a wire wheel. The carbon has been removed so the machine shop can just chuck each valve into the valve facing machine and reface it. The machine shop should be careful to maintain as much valve thickness as possible and stay within specifications. This means removing material from the valve face slowly: more time to do it right.

In the next issue we'll look at further machine work, related engine jobs that can be done now, then head re-assembly and re-installation.

Valve Job, Part II

by Stu Ritter,
Technical Editor

September/October 2000

Photos in this article by DaimlerChrysler AG.

Head Work

If the head shows signs of being warped, or slightly bent, the machine shop will lightly skimcut the head to refresh the sealing surface. If the head shows more warpage, a surfacing cut will remove more material, ensuring a flat sealing surface. When you get the head back from the machine shop, check the sealing surface carefully for burrs raised by resurfacing.

Your machinist can cut the new valve seats, or you can do it yourself if you have valve seat cutting equipment. Stick to the factory-specified minimum valve seat thickness, usually 1.5 mm for intake valves and 2 mm for exhaust valves. This ensures sufficient contact area for heat transfer, since the only time a valve face is cooled is when it contacts the valve seat in the head. Most machine shops now use modern valve seat cutting equipment that cuts all three angles of the seat at once. Such machines are expensive but quick; they do an excellent job, much better and more uniform than I can do by hand.

Re-Assembling the Head

When the head comes back from the machine shop, the valves will either be numbered to match their cylinders or taped in place. Once a valve is lapped into a particular seat, it must be re-installed there. The machine shop uses grinding paste to hand-lap each valve into its seat, ensuring a gas-tight seal. Remember, number one cylinder is always at the front of the head.

When the head is assembled with valves, springs, and keepers in place, the valve sealing should be checked. Turn the head face up, and pour a little

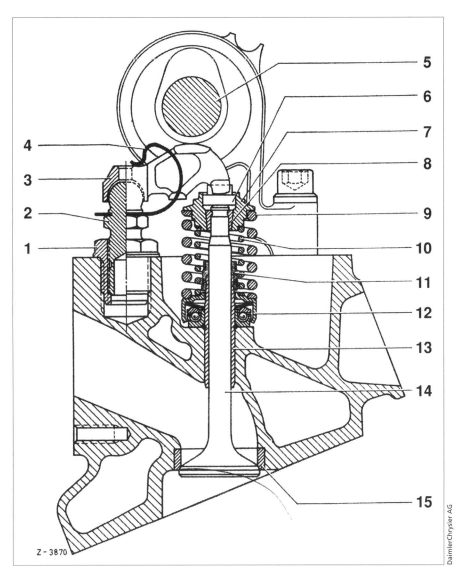

Z - 3870

Typical Valve Gear: Cam lobe (5) pushes downward on rocker arm (3) and thrust piece (6) to depress valve (14); inner and outer valve springs (9 and 10) lift valve via retainer (7) and cone (8) to close it. Valve guide (13) is pressed into hole in cylinder head (crosshatched area) and capped by valve seal (11). Valve seat (15) seals off cylinder during combustion. Other bits include threaded bushing (1), clearance adjusting screw (2), clamping spring (4), and rotocap (12).

DaimlerChrysler AG

solvent into the combustion chamber. This will eventually leak out, but it should do so very slowly. If solvent runs out rapidly, the valve is not in complete contact with the seat, which could allow combustion pressure to leak out. Take the valve out, and find out why (the valve may not be square with the seat). Better to do this on the bench than to have to remove the head again after the engine is fired up.

As the head is re-assembled, cleanliness and inspection are critical.

Everything is wiped with lacquer thinner before assembly. Rotating parts such as the camshaft, and pressure parts such as rockers or lifters, get a generous coat of assembly lubricant. Many companies make this special assembly lube, and all professional mechanics use it when assembling an engine. It's part of the technique.

On engines with manual valve clearance adjustment, we'll now set the valve clearance. The valve will move deeper into the seat after start-up,

Data	Intake	Exhaust
Valve seat width b	1.3–2.0	1.5–2.0
Valve seat angle a	45°	
Correction angle top β	15°	
Correction angle bottom γ	60°	
Permissible runout of valve seat	0.04	

1054-5910

Multiple-Angle Valve Seat Specifications: Cutting the seat at three factory-specified angles helps the valve to seal more effectively and to better transfer heat from valve to cylinder head.

Machining Valve Seat: The valve seat, a hardened metal ring around intake or exhaust port, is cut to three angles with a hand-operated cutting tool.

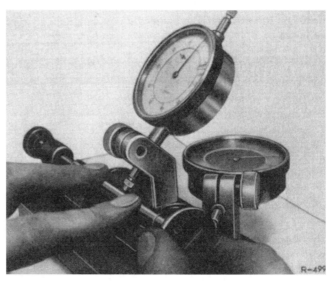

Measuring Valve Stem Run-Out: Factory measuring rig helps ensure that valve stem is straight, so it aligns properly with its seat.

decreasing the clearance, so leave a little extra. Many a new mechanic has been surprised when he first starts an engine with a just-completed valve job. If he didn't include extra clearance, the engine will start and run smoothly, but as it heats it will begin missing on a cylinder or two as the valve clearance disappears and the valve is held off its seat. Really scares the new guys! (They learn very quickly.)

If your engine has hydraulic valve lifters, you just assemble them. The lifters self-compensate for wear, and you will check the base setting later.

Avoid Abrasives

The "deck"—the top of the block— must be cleaned of old gasket material before the new head gasket is laid in place. To do this, use only razor blades. Any sort of abrasive will leave abrasive material in the bore, causing premature cylinder wear. Stay away from RotoDisks, small round pads of material that looks like ScotchBrite and fit on an air-driven grinder. ScotchBrite is carborundum encased in plastic. Ever notice that if you use ScotchBrite on a glass, it scratches the glass? It takes very hard material to scratch glass, and this is such a material. Never use these disks to

clean the deck, because you will leave abrasive residue behind.

There is no way to clean out this abrasive residue, so you will cause cylinder bore wear. I know a shop owner who had to rebuild a 6.9 engine because his mechanic used these abrasive disks to clean the decks. The bore wear was unbelievable. It meant new pistons and a rebore to the next size, an expensive experience for the shop owner, all because his mechanic tried to save a little time.

Check the Ridge

While the cylinder head is off, examine the cylinder bores. On Mercedes-Benz engines it is rare to find a ridge in the bore at the top of the cylinder. Older engines would show a little ridge, but newer ones—especially the alloy/silica-block motors—never show one. The ridge forms where the top piston ring reverses direction (combustion heat burns off the oil right where that ring stops for a millisecond). If you can feel a ridge, use a bore gauge to measure the taper and wear. The bottom ends (anything below the cylinder head) on today's Mercedes-Benz engines are so tough that you almost never see wear approaching the specified limits.

With the new head gasket laid in place, two or more mechanics carefully lay the rebuilt head atop it. The head bolts have been carefully cleaned, their threads lightly oiled to ensure accurate torque readings. When the head was removed, the engine was set to top dead center, so before the head is installed, the cam should be set to the assembly mark cast into the cam bearing or to another assembly mark provided by the factory. Engines are always taken apart and put back together at top dead center. It's the only way to set basic cam timing.

Now the cylinder head bolts are brought up to torque. Some engines use three or four tightening stages to crush the head gasket gradually and keep everything flat. Many newer engines use stretch head bolts that are brought to an even low torque then angle-torqued. This means the bolts are brought to say, 40 or 50 Nm, then they are turned 90 degrees; after a 10-minute rest, another 90 degrees of turn is applied. Stretch head bolts must be carefully measured on the narrowed portion of their shaft. If this diameter approaches the minimum specified, new head bolts are in order. In my experience, it takes three or four uses before these bolts stretch enough to require replacement.

Final Assembly

After the head is torqued and the timing chain is reinstalled, we check cam timing with a dial indicator, using the workshop manual procedure. Cam timing is not set by eyeballing the assembly marks when you put everything back together. It must be checked with a dial indicator.

Before installing the spark plugs, we usually turn over the engine on the starter motor to check oil pressure on the gauge and to be sure that oil flows out of the cam oiling device. Then we install the plugs and start the engine. Few modern engines require a cylinder head re-torque after being brought up to operating temperature, but older cars do. This varies, so read the manual carefully. Angle-torque head bolts need no re-torque. If a re-torque must be done, it is done hot, when the engine is first brought to operating temperature. While the engine reaches this temperature, check the ignition timing. When it is at operating temperature, check the fuel/air mixture. After the engine has cooled, re-check manually adjusted valves for correct clearance; hydraulically adjusted valves should have the base circle clearance checked.

Once everything is buttoned up, the car goes for a 10- or 15-mile test drive. Back in the shop, it goes onto the lift, and we look for leaks or anything loose. When it comes to major engine work, you can't be too careful. Check and re-check.

The Results

After all this work, what do you get? Of course, lack of blue smoke is the most obvious benefit. It may take a little time to burn out the residual oil that built up in the exhaust system before the guides were replaced. In the old days, when a 280SE would lose the number four exhaust guide, it would pump oil into the exhaust. When mine did that, the smokescreen was unbelievable. It took me eight quarts of oil to drive 15 miles to my shop. Then it took a few days to burn out all the oil that had been dumped into the exhaust system.

Quicker starts and smoother running are other benefits of renewing valve guides, seats, and faces. Fresh valve sealing helps the engine make more power and may regain lost fuel mileage. It also improves intake manifold vacuum because the intake valves won't leak on compression or allow combustion back into the intake manifold. Engines like good inlet tract vacuum, which sometimes solves running problems that no one could diagnose because they weren't severe enough to be real symptoms.

A valve job really freshens up a motor, bringing back a lot of that new car feel. It also means that you can look forward to another 150,000 miles of pleasant motoring. Change your engine oil frequently, and you may extend that to 200,000 and beyond. Remember: you can pay me now, or you can pay me later.

Bottom End Overhaul, Part I

by Stu Ritter, Technical Editor

November/December 2000

Photos in this article by Daimler-Benz AG.

Previous columns explained how a repair shop goes about performing a valve job, so let's go further and overhaul the bottom end.

Bottom End Overhaul

These days a bottom end overhaul is uncommon for Mercedes-Benz engines. Although combustion chamber temperatures have climbed due to emission regulations, materials quality has kept pace. Today, if the factory-suggested maintenance schedule has been properly carried out, rarely does a repair shop get to rebuild a Mercedes-Benz engine.

Modern oils are so good that we almost never see lubrication-caused problems in a Mercedes-Benz engine. Changing oil at the factory-recommended frequency practically assures maximum engine life. For conventional oils this usually means 7,500 miles between changes if the car is used almost exclusively on the highway with no short trips and in a fairly dust-free environment. For city use or in dusty country with short trips that don't bring the oil up to operating temperature, this means 3,750 miles between changes, or for synthetic oils, 7,500 miles. Short trips during the winter create some of the hardest operating conditions for an engine. It takes time for the engine to warm up to the point where the temperature sensors take the engine off a rich fuel mixture.

Boring Tasks

Once the cylinder head is off, we can examine the cylinder bores for damage. We look carefully at the

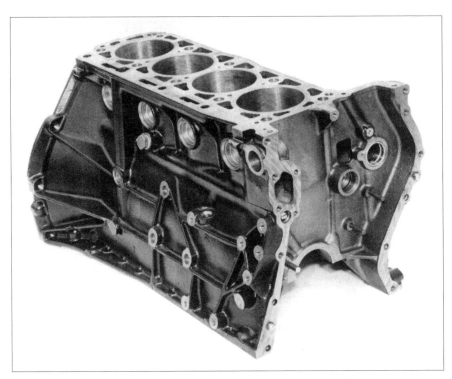

Bare four-cylinder block—without cylinder head at top, without cam drive at front, and without crankshaft and oil pan at bottom—is from a 190E 2.3-16. Inline sixes and V-engines are basically similar. Note honing pattern inside cylinders. Mercedes-Benz blocks can usually be reconditioned, rarely require replacement.

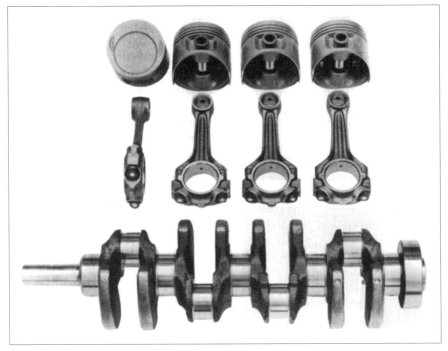

Pistons, connecting rods, and crankshaft from 190E 2.3-16. Piston pins slide through piston to attach it to small upper end of rod. At rod's larger lower end, bolt-on caps secure bearing and rod to polished crankshaft journals. Skilled machine work, precise measurement, and careful assembly are required to correctly align and fit these critical parts.

cylinder walls, trying to find scoring. If you can catch a fingernail in the cylinder wall score, the score is at least 0.0005-in (one-half a thousandth of an inch) deep and requires close examination. Many people looking at the bore of a high-mileage Mercedes-Benz engine for the first time are amazed to see cross-hatching from the original honing still present on the cylinder walls. This is normal. The honing pattern stays in the bore until the engine is very worn. We have to be careful in examining the honing to make sure that the damage we are looking at is physical, not just visual. Vertical marks on the cylinder walls may be purely optical, representing no damage to the honing. If everything else is within specifications, visual damage can be ignored.

If you can catch a fingernail in the score, it usually means a re-bore. A score in the wall forms a path for combustion gases to flow past the top-most piston ring and cause excessive crankcase pressure, also known as "blow-by". Scoring also damages the rings, weakening their seal against the cylinder wall.

The next step is to measure bore wear using a bore gauge, an inside-diameter gauge that reads off a dial indicator. In Mercedes-Benz engines, where clearances are measured in hundredths of a millimeter, you must use a metric bore gauge or a standard bore gauge that reads to ten thousandths of an inch. The bore is measured in six different locations within each cylinder, three in the direction of travel and three at 90 degrees opposite to the direction of travel. It is measured at the top of the piston travel, halfway down the bore, and at the bottom of the bore. This tells us the "out of roundness" and "taper" of the bore. The bore must be true (the same diameter) from top to bottom and round from top to bottom. Specifications for permissible out-of-roundness and taper are in Mercedes-Benz engine manuals and technical data books.

Everything south of an engine's cylinder heads is known as "the bottom end", including crankcase, crankshaft, connecting rods, pistons, oil pump, and sump.

Daimler-Benz AG

Beyond the Ridge

Next we examine the very top edge of the bore for a ridge that occurs there, where the piston reverses direction. Here, where the top ring reverses travel, combustion heat burns oil off the wall, leaving it less well-lubricated than the wall below. It is common for a high-mileage Mercedes-Benz engine that has seen good oil change frequency to show little or no ridge.

In the U.S., where wide-open throttle driving is limited, we find very little ridge. In Germany, before speed limits, you might find a substantial ridge because the cars were driven at higher throttle openings. This is one reason it is so hard to wear out a Mercedes-Benz engine in the U.S. We can't drive as long at the throttle openings used in Germany. Check the throttle pedal in your car, and you'll see that your foot is most comfortable between one-half and two-thirds throttle opening. This angle has been engineered for driver comfort at high speed. Not counting power

accessories such as air-conditioning, it takes perhaps as little as 20 or 30 hp to maintain speeds of 55 to 65 mph. At 120+ mph, power requirements are much higher, so engines must work harder, and work causes wear.

Diagnosis

In the shop, careful diagnosis must occur before working on the cylinder head. If we know that an engine's lower end needs work, we remove the engine as a complete unit. Mechanics refer to the lower end of the engine as anything below the head gasket, with the upper end being anything above the head gasket. It is much easier to remove a cylinder head with the engine out of the car and on an engine stand.

Before removing a cylinder head, we do a pumping compression test, usually followed by a cylinder leakage test to determine the motor's internal condition before disassembly. Shops that do frequent engine work will use a bore scope to look into the cylinder and examine the walls for damage before the head is removed. Bore scopes are usually fiber-optic devices with their own light source, allowing visual examination of hard-to-reach locations. This great tool lets you look around inside the motor.

As mentioned above, oil-related damage is rare in a Mercedes-Benz engine. If the oil has been changed according to schedule, we almost never see a Mercedes-Benz engine lose a rod bearing or a main bearing. One scenario that has turned up over years of examining engines taken apart for overhaul is the careless mechanic. This is a mechanic who does a routine oil change and in a rush or on a foggy morning starts the engine without oil in it. After five or ten seconds of clatter, he realizes that he forgot the oil and stops the engine. The next step is to fill the engine with oil and start it. If it is quiet, more than likely, the mechanic just forgets about it. Still, the unlubricated contact between the bearings and the crankshaft spells damage. Usually this damage will not show up for thousands of miles.

Contrary to television commercials where oil is drained from an engine and it continues to run, any engine run without oil will be damaged instantly. Oil is the only thing keeping the very soft rod and main bearing surfaces away from the very hard crankshaft surfaces. Without an adequate oil wedge between the bearing and the crankshaft journal, bearing damage occurs instantly.

Engine Disassembly

Once we determine that our engine requires attention to the cylinder walls, this means removing the engine. Engine removal and reinstallation on a Mercedes-Benz involves from 12 or 13 hours for a simple 1960s four-cylinder car to 20 or 30 hours for a late model V12. Once the engine is on a stand, we can easily rotate it and move it around the shop. The stand has a drip pan to catch oil dripping from the motor as we turn it over and start disassembly. This keeps the floor clean, and oil that hits the floor can be wiped up with a rag and lacquer thinner.

The oil pan(s) and all pulleys on the front of the motor are removed. We continue unbolting parts attached to the engine until the block is bare. When the block goes to the machine shop, it must be bare. When we are down to just the rod nuts and the main bearing cap bolts, it's time to clean up, catch a cup of coffee, relax a bit, and get ready to pay closer attention to what we are doing.

Engines are usually disassembled using hand tools so observant mechanics can look for a bolt or nut at the incorrect torque, which you don't find when using air tools. There may be a difference in an air tool's sound on a loose bolt or nut, but it is insufficient information to justify their use.

First, the rod nuts are removed. After they are measured, we throw them away. They are inexpensive, and because they are critical parts, we always use new ones when reassembling the motor. A tap on the bare rod bolt with a plastic mallet, and the rod cap is free enough to be wiggled off the connecting rod. While the rod is still against the crankshaft, the rod bolts are covered with plastic sleeves or rubber hoses so that as the rod/piston combination is removed they won't scratch the smooth bearing journal. Since you won't know if the crankshaft must be machined until it's out, you must take apart the motor carefully to avoid unnecessary expensive machine work.

Each half of each rod bearing is closely examined for damage and wear. We look at the wear pattern to make sure it is even across the bearing face, indicating that everything inside is perpendicular and parallel, as it should be. If something is out of kilter, we'll see odd wear patterns on the bearings. The rods are numbered at the factory, so there is no need to make additional marks on them. Only a real amateur takes a punch to the inside of a Mercedes-Benz engine. To make sure that the right cap goes back on the right rod, both halves of each rod are factory stamped with the rod's position in the engine and on the other side with a manufacturing number, usually three digits.

All Mercedes-Benz engines have their rods and pistons removed through the deck (top) of the block, where the head gasket lives. Use a plastic mallet to tap the rod upward into the bore, carefully guiding it around the crankshaft to avoid contact.

Crankshaft Care

With the pistons and rods out, about the only thing left inside is the crankshaft. If the engine has an external rear main seal, it is removed. To make sure the main bearing caps go back to the same location they came from, we usually number the caps with a vibrating engraving tool. The main bearing bolts are removed, and the main bearing caps are tapped off using a plastic mallet. Then the main bearings are examined for wear. If there are locating pins in the rear hub of the crankshaft, they are removed so the crankshaft can stand on end. The folks who regrind crankshafts remind mechanics to always stand crankshafts on end so they will not bend. As heavy and as strong as they are, they can still bend if stored improperly.

If you ever buy a new crankshaft from your favorite Mercedes-Benz parts department, you'll find that it comes in a box with saddles inside just like the inside of the motor supporting the crankshaft on its journals. This is the only safe way to transport a crankshaft. When we take a crankshaft to the machine shop, it goes in the corner of the pickup bed, strapped into a standing position. Just to make sure, I never even carry a crankshaft horizontally.

Now it's cleanup time. Every part is washed, dried, and lightly oiled. Internal engine parts must always be kept lightly oiled. Bright metal will rust rapidly if left unprotected. Somehow, rust never looks good inside an engine!

Next issue we'll go into cleaning, machining, and re-assembly of the engine's bottom end.

Bottom End Overhaul, Part II

by Stu Ritter, Technical Editor

January/February 2001

Photos in this article by Daimler-Benz AG.

Our previous issue discussed the early phases of rebuilding an engine's bottom end. Now we'll finish the job.

Now it's cleanup time. Every part is washed, dried, and lightly oiled. Internal engine parts must always be kept lightly oiled. Bright metal will rust rapidly if left unprotected. Rust never looks good inside an engine!

Now we'll carefully examine the parts to see which must be replaced. The pistons are removed from the connecting rods and thrown away. We would never take down an engine this far unless we knew we were going to rebore it, which requires new pistons. Simply re-ringing a Mercedes-Benz engine is inadvisable. We have had no luck at re-ringing, and in our shop we refused to do it. For rings to seat properly into the cylinder walls, the walls must be straight and round. It is impossible to hone cylinder walls and get them true without very expensive machinery, usually owned by an automotive machine shop. If you are stripping the block and taking it to the machine shop, it only makes sense to bore the engine to the next available replacement piston size.

Piston Wear

Wear usually occurs in the top ring land, the groove in the piston that carries the top ring, also called the compression ring. Many think that this ring seals because it is springy and pushes against the cylinder wall, but that's not so. The ring seals because combustion gases flow downward, around the top of the piston, and

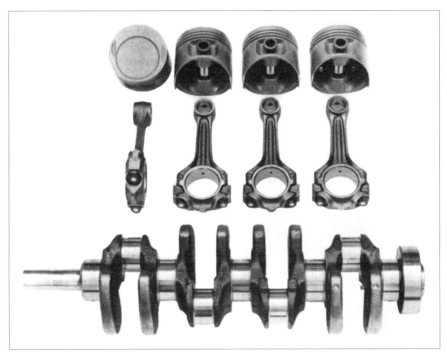

Your engine's basic moving parts—pistons (top), connecting rods (center) and crankshaft (bottom)—demand precision, care, and cleanliness during re-assembly.

through a small gap between the top of the ring and the groove. The gas then pushes the ring outward against the cylinder wall. So combustion pressure seals itself by pushing the ring into the wall. In a worn Mercedes-Benz engine the top ring land (groove) is usually worn beyond specification. If you try to re-ring this piston, it will fail to seal properly because the gap between the ring and the land is too large.

If the engine has no cylinder wall damage, we usually fit the first oversized piston. To leave as much metal as possible for future repairs, we try to machine the block as little as possible. If the cylinder walls can be trued up within the first oversize, usually half a millimeter larger in diameter, then that is what we use. Second and third oversize pistons increase in 0.25-mm increments.

If the cylinder wall is damaged, we might go directly to the second or even third oversize piston to allow enough over-bore to remove the damage. This

leaves little if any room for future repair. On rare occasions, if there is so much deep scoring in the cylinder wall that it must be bored beyond the diameter of available oversized pistons, we may buy a used replacement block or a new one with pistons fitted. If the engine is rare and valuable, we may sleeve the cylinder, though this is not recommended for anything except aluminum block V-8s.

Since diesel engines are sleeved originally, that is how they are rebuilt. Instead of boring a diesel block for an oversized piston, we remove the original liner or sleeve. The sleeve is the cylinder wall, so re-sleeving the engine completely renews the wall.

Connecting Rods

Having decided which oversized piston to use, we examine the connecting rods. The rod cap goes back on without the bearing shells in place, and the rod nuts are re-installed and brought to correct torque. The inside of the large

Piston must be oriented properly, as shown in manual.

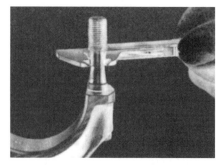

Measuring diameter determines how much connecting rod bolt has stretched, whether or not it can be re-used.

(crankshaft) end of the connecting rod is measured using a bore gauge to be sure it is within specification for size and concentricity. If it is out of spec, the big end of the rod must be reconditioned. To correct the bore, a little material is removed from the flat mating surfaces of the cap; then, to bring the bore back up to the correct size, the bore is re-machined on a connecting rod boring machine.

The rod caps are then removed and the rod bolts measured. Most rod bolts on Mercedes-Benz engines are angle-torqued; they actually stretch as they reach their optimum strength. Engine manual specifications indicate new and minimum diameters of the necked-down portion of the rod bolt. If the bolt approaches the minimum diameter, order new ones to replace them. Because the bolts must be pressed out of the bore in the rod and pressed in while the rod is well supported, this is a machine shop process.

The small (piston pin) end of the connecting rod is examined. A new piston pin is installed dry and test-wiggled. Since no specification exists for pin fit, it's a matter of feel. A good machine shop can tell you if you need to re-bush the small end of the rod. If obvious visual evidence of wear exists, the bushing is replaced. New bushings are not very expensive, and the machine shop will fit and hone them for correct sliding fit on the piston pins.

Main Bearings and Crankshaft

To measure the inside bore of the main bearing saddles, the main bearing caps are re-installed and torqued in place, and the bore gauge is set up. If an out-of-round condition is found, the main bearing saddles will be line-bored by the machine shop to make them round again. This procedure is similar to that used to correct an out-of-round condition with connecting rods. All necessary information is in the engine manual.

So now we have reconditioned rods and a cylinder bore resized for the new pistons. The block has been boiled out with the water jacket access plates removed, so the water passages will be descaled at the same time.

The crankshaft is carefully inspected for damage. It takes a lot of abuse to damage a Mercedes-Benz crankshaft. The main and rod journals are measured by micrometers to be sure they are round and within specification. If machining is necessary, find a good crankshaft shop. Mercedes-Benz gasoline engine crankshafts require no special treatment, but diesel crankshafts must be re-hardened after machining. The hardening process is called nitriding, and few shops are equipped to do it. To find a good crankshaft grinder, ask around in drag racing or road racing shops. Custom crankshaft grinders can be found in most large cities, especially those with race tracks. Our shop's machine work is done by a very experienced shop that does most of the Mercedes-Benz work in Denver. Our crankshafts are machined by another company specializing in crankshafts. Our crank grinder once made a pair of crankshafts, starting with a round billet of steel, for a Bugatti. He knows what he's doing.

When the machine shop calls, and it's all ready for pickup, go fetch your renewed parts and pay the bill. Boring a block, boiling a block, rebuilding connecting rods at both ends, and having the crankshaft done will cost about $400 to $1,000, depending on the machine shop and how much you value having the work done absolutely right the first time. The best way to find a good machinist is to ask all the Mercedes-Benz shops in town who they use. One name will usually pop up frequently, so that's the place to go.

Re-assembly Preparations

Clean the disassembly area, your tools, and the engine stand. Everything must be cleaned and put away before re-assembly. Spotless is just about clean enough. A supply of clean, lint free towels and lacquer thinner helps keep things spotless. Assembly lube is also required. We use BG assembly lube, but other good brands are available. Don't use white grease; use the specific petroleum product called assembly lube, which is designed to protect your expensive engine when you first start it.

All work done by the machine shop is now re-measured. Take nothing for granted; measure everything. If you don't, you can blame no one but yourself for assembling an engine that will soon come apart again. Building an engine properly requires a lot of measuring equipment. The assembly process is called "blueprinting" the motor. To be sure everything is exactly as it should be, measure everything and trust no one but yourself. Measure the bore, the crank, and the rods.

Now it's time to clean the block again. Fortunately for us, Mercedes-Benz has already painted the inside of the engine, so it's not like rebuilding a Chevy for the first time, when you have to paint the inside. When you get the block back from the machine shop, the bores will be oiled, but they will contain some refuse from machining. Here comes the fun part.

The block is bolted back on the clean engine stand and wheeled over the floor drain. Using hot soapy water, wash the bores out with a towel soaked in the solution. You'll see gray deposits on the towel, so wash for quite a while. We like white towels because the metal is obvious. After a while we run a clean white towel through the bore. If any gray shows at all, it's back to the hot soapy water and rub, rub, rub. Eventually the bore comes clean, leaving no residue on the towel. Solvent will not clean metal residue from the bore; only hot soapy water will do that.

As soon as the bores are clean, immediately oil them and the rest of the block where water has run. Make sure the main bearing saddles are well oiled; they are no place for rust flowers to develop because you didn't get all the water off. The connecting rods and crankshaft are also washed in hot soapy water, then rinsed in really hot water, air-blown dry, then oiled. Oil passages in the block are blown out, and a wire is passed through to make sure there are no obstructions. Rust in an oil passage is embarrassing!

Re-assembly Begins

It's ironic, but after so much time in preparation, engine re-assembly goes quickly. Read the manual several times to be sure there are no special tricks for the motor you are working on and that all torque specifications are understood. Time to get to work.

Step one is to lay in the crankshaft. Again the basic bore in the main bearing saddle is measured, the crankshaft is measured, and the main bearing thickness is measured. Subtract the diameter of the crankshaft from the basic bore, then subtract the bearing thickness, and you have the bearing clearance. To see if it is in the right range, see the specifications. Do the same with the big end of the connecting rod to be sure that bearing

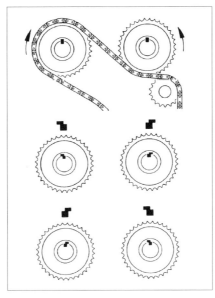

Various offset woodruff keys between cams and sprockets can be used to set cam timing.

clearance is correct. In this process of blueprinting an engine, everything is measured and compared with specifications. If anything is incorrect, final clearance will be out of tolerance, and you will need to re-measure everything to find the mistake. Correcting machining mistakes is no fun. The machine shop doesn't like to do it, and the parts folks don't like taking back the first oversize bearing set and ordering a second oversize set. Find and pay for a quality machinist who does it right the first time.

Incidentally, Plastigauge is not an engine assembly tool. We never use it when building an engine. It is used for field measurements, when you don't have everything apart.

Main Bearings

The main bearing shells are laid into each main bearing saddle, with attention paid to the position of the oiling hole. Some main bearings have an upper half different from their lower half. If you want your engine to deliver long life, pay attention to the engine manual, which tells you where everything goes. Before the bearing shells are installed, the bearing cap is wiped with a little lacquer thinner on a clean rag to make sure everything is clean. The shells are then fitted to the

main bearing caps. The cleaned and dried main bolts rest on a clean rag. We smear assembly lube on the main bearing shells and lay the crankshaft in place.

After being wiped with a smear of assembly lube, the main bearing caps are installed. You will have assembly lube dripping off everything, but don't worry about it. The main bearing caps are tapped into place with a plastic mallet, and the bolt threads get a squirt of engine oil from an oil can. A drop or two under the head of a bolt helps ensure accurate torque. The bolts are brought up to torque. A dial indicator is set up at the front of the motor, using a magnetic base on the block, and the dial is set on the end of the crankshaft to check front-to-rear crankshaft free play and be sure thrust clearance is correct.

Piston Clearance

When rebuilding an American engine, most machine shops want to have the pistons, but with Mercedes-Benz motors that isn't required. If the machine shop asks for a piston to measure, be a little skeptical. No matter the bore size, the piston-to-wall clearance is standard for every Mercedes-Benz motor. From a little 200 gas engine to a 6.9-liter M-100 V-8, piston-to-wall clearance is 0.03 millimeters. If the bore is 90 mm, piston diameter should be 89.97 mm. The bore is always sized to a round number. That 0.03-mm clearance equals about 1.2 thousandths inch (0.0012 in) which is not very much. Mercedes-Benz forges steel straps into the piston skirt to control thermal expansion, which allows this small piston-to-wall clearance, for a very quiet engine. Most American pistons demand at least one thousandth of an inch clearance per inch of bore, so with a 4-in piston you have four thousandths of clearance. Compare that to our 1.2 thousandths. Such nice sewing machines!

The connecting rods have been cleaned, and the oil passage between their big end and little end has had a wire passed through to be sure it is clear. The pistons are installed on the upper end of the connecting rod, again with assembly lube and in the right configuration according to the manual (some pistons have arrows for driving direction; others are installed based on the shape of the piston crown). Circlips lock the piston onto the rod via the wrist pin.

Installing Pistons

Some mechanics install pistons without lubricating the rings; others (self included) smear engine oil around the rings. It's one of those ongoing debates. BMW motorcycle rings are always installed dry; it's in the manual.

The ring gaps are spaced at 120-degree increments around the piston. We never have to size the ring gaps because the rings are correct as they come with the piston from Mercedes-Benz. We've pulled them off and checked end gap, but we always found it correct, so we stopped doing it. To be absolutely correct, you should pull off a compression ring and install it in the cylinder. Using a piston to push it down a bit so it is square to the bore, you can use a feeler gauge to measure end gap.

Many different styles of ring compressors can be used to install the pistons. All compress the rings into the ring lands so that they don't hit the block as they slide into the bore. We use a curly style preferred by aircraft mechanics. With the bearing shell in the bottom end of the rod, the rings are compressed, then the piston is tapped downward into position using the bottom of the wooden handle on your favorite engine assembly hammer. Light tapping and in it goes. If it hangs up, stop, remove the ring compressor, and find out what happened. Fit plastic or rubber hose on the rod bolts so they don't damage the crankshaft. Smear assembly lube on the bearing shell. Tap, tap, tap.

With the rod in place, pre-lube the bearing shell in the rod cap and install it on the rod. Be sure the lock tab for the bearing shell is correctly located. Remove the protective covers on the rod bolts, squirt engine oil on the threads, and tap the cap into place. Install the rod nuts and tighten them to the initial setting torque. Install the rest of the pistons, then bring the rod nuts to proper final torque.

Hard Part, Easy Part

Now that the rotating mass has been installed, the hard part of building the engine is over. From here, it's just a matter of reinstalling everything removed to get the block down to its bare self. While the block was bare, we removed all the chain rails in the timing chest. Before putting the rotating mass back in, we replaced every chain rail. Over time, sprockets develop a hooked shape, causing rapid chain wear. All sprockets are examined; if their teeth didn't look good, they are replaced.

Working our way upward, we re-install the cylinder head rebuilt as described in previous issues of *The Star*. We then use a dial indicator to measure cam timing, a very important step for a good engine builder. While the assembly marks get you into the ball park, cam timing is measured at 2 mm valve lift; the procedure is in the manual.

The time required to rebuild an engine this way varies. Mercedes-Benz never set times for this type of rebuild because no dealership would work this way. If the crankshaft was OK, they would order a block with fitted pistons; if the crankshaft had irreparable damage, they would order a short block. From simple to complex engines, you can expect from 40 to 80 hours of labor. This article explains some reasons why it takes so long to properly rebuild a Mercedes-Benz engine.

Technical Editor Stu Ritter has spent 30 years as a Mercedes-Benz mechanic.

Transmission Lock-Out Switch

by Paul S. Meyer,
Cincinnati Section

*January/February
1993*

Photos in this article
by the author.

Lock-out transmission switch measures about 3x3 inches; one of two
tabs on operating lever (right) broke off, disabling the switch.

You know that sinking feeling when you turn the key, expecting to hear the starter, but nothing happens? Luckily for me, it happened on a Saturday when my 1983 240D was in its garage. A second try yielded no sign of life.

The battery was in good condition, the key felt secure in the switch, and the action felt good as the key passed through its detent positions. Maybe the safety switch on the automatic transmission had failed. By allowing current to reach the starter solenoid only when the transmission is in Park or Neutral, this switch prevents starting in gear. If this switch fails, the car won't start at all.

To check this, I held the key in the spring-loaded start position while moving the shift lever through its positions (the parking brake was set, and my foot was firmly on the brake pedal). Perhaps the safety switch had just loosened and moved out of position. Still no sign of life.

Technical Director Frank King suspected the ignition switch or the safety switch. To determine whether there was any current drain, he suggested trying the key in the start position with the headlights on. No dimming of the lights would mean no current drain, confirming my suspicion that no current was reaching the starter solenoid. He also suggested that if no current were reaching the starter solenoid, the car might be started with a remote starter switch.

The headlights didn't dim, so no current was reaching the starter solenoid. I bought a remote starter switch for under $10 at an auto supply store. Hooking it up to the

two terminals on the solenoid on top of the starter was easy. After turning the key to the glow position and waiting for the indicator light to go out, one press of the remote switch immediately brought the car to life.

Monday morning, I went through the same routine and drove to my mechanic's shop, where the car was put on a lift. The safety switch was not operating but had not itself failed. A small lever with two tabs for rotating the switch had failed because the switch action had become stiff over the years (the side of the transmission gets pretty dirty). One thin tab on this lever, or bracket, had broken off. The mechanic recommended replacing not only the broken lever but also the stiff switch. If the switch were not replaced, the problem could recur.

The switch (part number 000 545 42 06, a starter lock-out switch) cost $31.38; the lever (part number 115 545 01 42) was $0.46; about 30 minutes labor was involved. The old switch

cleaned up nicely, so I kept it as an extra. The contacts inside showed very little wear. I lubricated the moving section and 0-ring gasket with silicon, and it works smoothly. It was held together with rivets, which I replaced with screws and nuts. Since the remote starter switch avoided a tow charge, I now keep it in my trunk.

Could I have avoided this problem? Maybe, because I had two warnings. The transmission safety switch also energizes the backup lights, and for some time they hadn't always come on when the shift lever was put in Reverse. This was a clue that the tabs on the lever were bending and not moving the safety switch fully.

For several months, when the shift lever was moved through its range with the engine off, I heard a squeak, rubber binding against rubber, a signal that the switch action was becoming restricted. Investigation could have led to replacement before the part failed, better than just letting it happen.

A Survey of Automatic Transmissions

by Frank King,
Technical Editor

*May/June
1992*

No component of our cars causes as much bafflement and frustration as the automatic transmission. This is an attempt to clear up some confusion and provide a reference.

First, let's explain Mercedes-Benz transmission nomenclature. The first Mercedes-Benz cars with automatic transmissions were the 300c and 300d of 1955–62. In both, you could have either the automatic or a four-speed manual transmission. Automatics, made by Borg Warner's Detroit Gear Division, offered three speeds with a torque converter and a direct drive clutch, which automatically locked up the transmission in third. Thus only first and second were geared; in third the direct drive clutch locked the torque converter to the driveshaft. This rather primitive automatic transmission did not have the type and model numbers of most true Mercedes-Benz transmissions which followed it.

By the Numbers

Introduction of the first Daimler-Benz automatic, the Type K4A-025, marked the beginning of type numbers, still used internally. The digits are all significant. The first, K, means hydraulic clutch (*Kupplung*); the second, 4, means 4 speeds; the third, A, indicates the version. The three digits after the dash indicate the designed maximum torque in kilopondmeters. Thus a K4A-025 will handle up to 25 kpm. (One kpm = 9.81 Nm = 7.23 lb-ft.)

When torque converters replaced hydraulic clutches, the K was replaced by a W (*Wandler*), but otherwise the type numbers continue as before. In 1968 a new designation for transmissions was introduced, the transmission number, three-digits followed by a decimal point and three more digits. For example, the transmission in a 1985 300D is a 722.315. The first three digits, 722, indicate a passenger car automatic. The first digit after the decimal point indicates the type (here a W4A-04) The last two digits indicate the version, i.e., the particular engine to which it is attached.

This allows us to build Table I showing all automatic transmissions used by Mercedes-Benz and the models to which they apply.

Table I: Mercedes-Benz Passenger Car Automatic Transmissions

Transmission	Application
No 722 number Detroit Gear	Used in 300c, 300d, 1955–62.
No 722 number K4A-025	First DBAG automatic. Used in 1959 220b and most subsequent models through the 280SE/SEL and 300SEL to May 1969; in 280SL to end of production.
No 722 number K4A-050, K4B-050	Used in models with 6.3-liter engine.
722.0 (W3A-040) (W3B-050)	W3A-040 used with 4.5-liter V8 engine, 1972-1980 W3B-050 used in 450SEL 6.9.
722.1 (W4B-025)	Production began in 1974. Used in W114/115 and W123 models except turbo-diesels, used in W116 300SD from start until 1981.
722.2 (K4C-025) (K4A-040)	Production began in 1968 for W114/115 models, later used in other 6-cyl models through 1973, K4A-040 used with 3.5-liter V8 engines.
722.3 (W4A-040) (W4A-055)	Production began in 1981. Used with V8 and 617 turbo-diesel engines and subsequently on most models including W140 except as noted below. W4A-055 used on V12. Over 40 variants of the 722.3 transmission exist.
722.4 (W4A-020)	Production began in 1984. Used with 4-cyl and 2.6-liter 6-cyl engines.
722.5 (W5A-030)	Used with 24-valve 6-cyl engines; basically a 722.3 with 5th speed added.

Standing and Starting

One trifling problem with automatic transmissions has never been completely solved. To be truly automatic a transmission should transmit engine power to the wheels when the driver wants and cease to do so when he wants. For the most part they do so, but when you want to stop in gear with the engine idling, the transmission insists on creeping, so you must apply the brake. Those first Detroit Gear transmissions dealt with this problem by having a solenoid valve hold braking pressure on the rear wheels as long as the throttle was at idle and the vehicle was stationary. This involved two switches in series, one on the carburetor, another on the transmission. When closed, they actuated the solenoid valve and held brake fluid under pressure in the rear brake cylinders. The carburetor switch opened when the throttle was opened. The transmission switch was held open by transmission fluid pressure from the secondary pump, which ran only when the driveshaft turned. This solution was not carried over to later cars, for reasons easily guessed. Those 300c and 300d sedans all stood in first gear and drove off in first.

Later efforts had cars standing in second and driving off in second, standing in second and driving off in first, and standing in first and starting in first, plus other variations. These all boil down to saying, "If the driver doesn't want to creep, let him keep

Table II: Automatic Transmission Standing and Starting Modes

Model	Production Dates	Gear, Standing at Idle	Gear, Drive Off
300c, 300d	1955–62	1st	1st
Most models with K4A-025, K4A-050, K4B-050	1959–69, some later	2nd	2nd
W114/115 and others, K4C-025/K4A-040	1968–73	1st	1st
190D	to 3/84	2nd	1st after slight throttle movement
190E	to 3/84	2nd	1st if more than 60% throttle given
190D and 190E, also 260E, 300E 2.6	from 3/84	2nd	1st if more than 40% throttle given
190D 2.5 Turbo	from 1987	1st	1st
Turbo-diesels 617.95, 603...all	from 1978	2nd	1st after slight throttle movement
Cars with V8 and 722.3	from 10/81	2nd	2nd in D, but 1st at kickdown D In 3, 2, or B
		1st	1st
Cars with V8 and 722.0	pre-10/81	1st	1st
Diesels (non-turbo)	pre-1980	2nd	1st via vacuum switch on linkage
Diesels (non-turbo)	pre-1980	2nd	2nd, 1st with kickdown
116 and 123 with M-110 engine	1975–80 116 1977–80 123	2nd	2nd; 1st with 123 kickdown
123 with M115 engine	1977–80	2nd	2nd; 1st with 123 kickdown
722.3 in 124, 129, 140 models	1986–on	2nd	1st upon slight throttle movement
722.5 in 129, 140 models	1990–on	2nd	1st upon slight throttle movement

his foot on the brake! If the car is on a slope, he has to keep his foot on the brake anyhow." Many people don't know which gear their car stands in nor which it drives off in. Some think their car's transmission has only three speeds because they don't know that it always stands and drives off in second!

To clear up such questions, Table II lists models with a) the gear in which they stand with the engine idling and b) the gear in which the car starts off. Those who have read this far will have already determined which transmission is in their car.

Checking the ATF

Most drivers know how to check the oil level in the engine and realize the importance of never letting it get above Max or below Min. Checking the ATF (automatic transmission fluid) level is another matter. The textbook method requires equipment placing it beyond the capabilities of all but the most rigid conformists. The problem is that the marks on the dipstick apply only when the ATF is at working temperature, 80°C (179°F), and this temperature is reached only after extensive driving. Even then, a special thermometer is needed to reach in and check the temperature. In view of these impracticalities MBNA's *Maintenance Manual* has been revised to allow checking at temperatures between 20°C and 30°C (68°F and 86°F). Table III shows dipstick levels applying at both temperature ranges. The ATF level is taken with the engine idling.

In any automatic transmission in a Mercedes-Benz, ATF level should never exceed the Max mark.

Proper transmission maintenance involves changing fluid and filter every 30,000 miles. The fluid's appearance at this time should be similar to that of fresh fluid. It may have a slight odor, as of roasted peanuts, and a slight brown tinge but nothing beyond that. At every engine oil change, ATF level should be checked and the color and odor noticed. A strong burnt odor

or blackened color warn of serious trouble inside the transmission.

The cardinal sin of transmission care is overfilling. When the level is too high, the fluid is beaten into foam which will prevent proper cooling and may be forced out the dipstick tube. The result can be damage to bearings and seals. Of course, serious underfilling can also cause problems, but slight underfilling is far less harmful than overfilling.

Manual Labor

The list of technical publications offered to owners by MBNA is notable for including no manuals on automatic transmissions except one on the K4A-025 and one on the K4B-050. Another describes operation of the 722.3 and

722.4 transmissions but includes no repair procedures. The explanation given by MBNA for the lack of manuals is that the special tools needed to disassemble and reassemble these transmissions are very expensive and would not be cost-effective to the do-it-yourself owner. Furthermore, repair and adjustment require special training.

Generally, servicing malfunctioning transmissions is confined to adjustments which can be made without opening or removing the transmission—adjusting linkages, checking for leaks through the modulator vacuum valve, and checking and adjusting the modulator pressure. Serious disassembly and repair of automatics should be left to professional specialists.

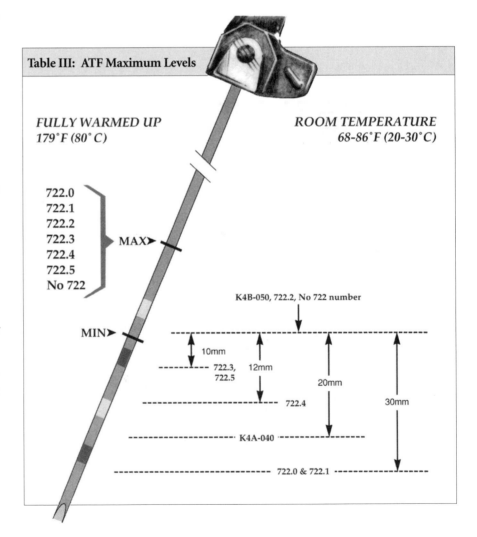

Table III: ATF Maximum Levels

FULLY WARMED UP
179˚F (80˚C)

ROOM TEMPERATURE
68-86˚F (20-30˚C)

722.0
722.1
722.2
722.3   } MAX▸
722.4
722.5
No 722

MIN▸

K4B-050, 722.2, No 722 number

10mm

722.3,   12mm
722.5

20mm

722.4

30mm

K4A-040

722.0 & 722.1

Tech Ramblings

by Frank King,
Technical Editor

*May/June
1982*

Photos in this article
by Daimler-Benz AG.

Dedicated to Quality

A new integrated engine test facility
was recently put into operation
by Daimler-Benz at Stuttgart-
Unterturkheim. Some 130 million DM
were invested to insure that Mercedes
engines would meet not only Daimler-
Benz quality standards but also the
ever more stringent clean-air standards
being imposed around the world.
Design, construction, and start-up of
this facility took three years.

The engine test facility, which
is under the control of the quality
assurance department and independent
of the production authority, has
24 preparation points and 42
dynamometer stations, arranged in
three test lines. One line handles
4-cylinder diesel engines, another
4- and 6-cylinder gasoline engines,
and the third 5-cylinder diesel and
8-cylinder gasoline engines. This is the
current set-up but all test equipment
can be readily adapted to any engine,
so complete flexibility is retained.

Upon receipt from the engine
assembly plant, engines are prepared
by being connected to fuel and coolant
supplies and other auxiliaries, and
are then allocated to their test lines
and put on one of the dynamometer
stations. The regular test cycle, applied

to every Mercedes-Benz engine, lasts
for 15 minutes during which computer
controlled and recorded tests are
conducted against 25 different criteria,
comprising the most advanced test
technology. Results are stored for
future reference, providing a basis
for evaluating reports of an engine in
service against test results. Such data
may then lead to improvements in test
techniques or in engines. From each
day's production, one percent of the
engines are picked at random for more
exhaustive testing. Also, some of the
engines are disassembled after testing
and physically checked.

Every working day, 2,200 engines
pass through the engine test facility,
corresponding to a yearly capacity
of more than a half million engines.
This capacity is needed to meet

One of the three computer-controlled lines in the new 130 million DM
engine test facility at Daimler-Benz Stuttgart-Unterturkheim.

the wide variety of engine models made by Daimler-Benz. Because of differing market requirements and the multiplicity of exhaust emission regulations around the world, Daimler-Benz must be able to offer more than 1,700 engine versions for their car and van ranges.

After the engines have been tested, they are passed through a sorting system and on to final engine assembly where transmissions, starters, and other components are fitted, including such options as air conditioning. Finally, the completed assemblies are placed in a depot from which they are distributed to the different vehicle assembly plants. Most go to the nearby car assembly plant at Sindelfingen, some to Bremen to be installed in station wagons or vans, and the remainder to other plants in Germany and Austria.

Head Bolts

This item will concern both do-it-yourself mechanics and over-the-shoulder inspectors because of the possible ruinous consequences of not being fully aware of an important change in certain Mercedes engines. From February 1979 the head bolts on all diesel engines, including the turbo, are of the 12-point Allen head type, the former Allen hex head bolts no longer being used on these engines (see illustration). A similar change was made later in 1979 to the 280 twin-cam (M110) engine.

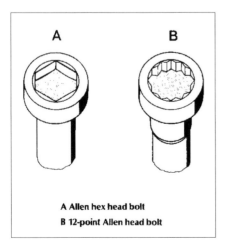

A Allen hex head bolt
B 12-point Allen head bolt

The new 12-point head bolts are somewhat longer than the previously used hex head bolts, are of a different shape, and require a different method of torquing known as "angle of rotation." This method as applied to these head bolts produces a permanent stretching of the bolt, so that a bolt that has been used even once will be longer than a new bolt. Bolts that have been lengthened more than 1 mm may not be reused.

The threaded holes in the cylinder heads designed to use the new bolts are deeper than previously, so that the head bolts cannot bottom out. Now here comes the warning: if the new type bolts are used to secure the cylinder head to a block that was made for the old type bolts, the bolts will bottom out but it will not necessarily be noticeable or recognizable that such is the case. Then either angle of rotation torquing or the earlier method of torquing will overstress the bolt without actually securing the head properly. The results could be anything from simply blowing out the head gasket to complete destruction of the engine.

To simplify the message: NEVER use 12-point Allen head bolts on an engine that was originally made for Allen hex head bolts. Further, tilting in the direction of caution tells us that 12-point head bolts should not be reused, but that new bolts be used whenever the cylinder head is being replaced after removal for any reason. Special, harder washers must be used with 12-point head bolts (olive-colored chromate).

The purpose of the change to the 12-point head bolts and the newer type head gasket used with them is to improve the preloading of the head bolts and to eliminate the need for retightening the head bolts after 300-600 miles of driving with a new gasket.

Fuel Review

More and more, owners are wondering just what they are getting from the service stations that fill their fuel tanks. If you use gasoline you have four choices, though not all at the same

station. Regular leaded (AKI below 93), premium leaded (AKI 93 and above), regular unleaded (AKI below 90), and premium unleaded (AKI 90 and above). Whether you are free to use all of these or only one depends on the year and model of your car. If you use diesel your choice is limited at best to either 1-D or 2-D, with most stations offering only 2-D. But just how much difference is there between the offerings of the different stations? If your Mercedes-Benz drinks regular leaded you need not be too concerned, for the AKI number posted on the pump tells you all you need to know. On the other hand, if your diesel is suffering from coked-up injectors and you have been told, probably correctly, that it is the result of the bad fuel you've been getting, you are almost frantic to learn where you can get clean fuel.

We can't tell you which station in your town has good fuel, but we can provide some information which may help you in your search. The API (American Petroleum Institute) and the DOE (Department of Energy) cooperate in having samples of fuel, both gasoline and diesel, gathered throughout the country, having them analyzed in various laboratories, and then having the results compiled and published by the BETC (Bartlesville Energy Technology Center) in Oklahoma.

Gasoline reports have been made twice a year since 1970 and diesel reports once a year since 1950. In the latest gasoline report, winter 1980–81, 546 samples were collected from service stations across the country. The results of the analyses have been tabulated by type of gasoline, manufacturer, and district of the country in which the sample was taken. The U.S. is divided into 17 districts for this purpose. Each manufacturer is given a code number for his gasolines, and this number is known only to him and the BETC. There is no way in which these codes can be uncovered. While 10 different analyses are made and listed, only 1 of them is of real interest to us: the octane number. The report gives RON

(Research Octane No.), MON (Motor Octane No.), and AKI (AntiKnock Index, the average of RON and MON).

Of the 546 gasoline samples taken, only 14 were below specification in AKI, of which 13 were unleaded regular and 1 was leaded regular. All premiums were above spec. Further study does not reveal anything that can be helpful. The trend of AKI over the years has been downward, as you'd suspect, but the drop has been less than one might have anticipated. Data on unleaded is available for only one year back and shows a drop of less than half a number in that time. The drop in leaded regular has been about one number over the past 10 years. In that time leaded premium has dropped three numbers, but it is hardly to be found on the market anymore.

Diesel fuel is analyzed for 13 properties and of these, 5 are significant to us as consumers: Cloud Point, Sulfur Content, Carbon Residue, Corrosion, and Cetane Number. In the survey, samples are taken from the refineries rather than service stations, as in the case of gasoline. For the current report, 192 samples were taken from 95 refineries throughout the country. Results are tabulated by type of usage, refinery, and marketing region. For the diesel report the country is broken down into five general regions: Eastern, Southern, Central, Rocky Mountain, and Western. Type of usage refers to the markets for which the refinery intends the fuel. Types of usage are: C-B (City-Bus), T-T (Truck-Tractor), R-R (Railroad), and S-M (Stationary-Marine). The fuel we use in our cars comes mainly from the T-T group or, if we are lucky, from the C-B group. Of the 63 samples taken of C-B fuel, 45 were 1-D and 18 were 2-D and none of these showed any undesirable properties. So we have our first clear clue to superior fuel: if possible, use the same fuel that the bus companies in your area use.

Turning our attention to the T-T fuels, which are the ones generally available to us, we find that of the 80 samples only 6 are 1-D. Like the 1-D fuels in the C-B group, these are almost completely satisfactory for our engines. Looking at the 74 samples of 2-D we find that with respect to Corrosion and Cloud Point none of them are below standard by either ASTM (American Society for Testing and Materials) or DIN (Deutsches Institut für Normung) specifications. The Corrosion test refers to the corrosiveness of the fuel before it is burned.

One sample was badly over both specs for Sulfur, with 31 being closer to the maximums than we would like. However, we can say that the sulfur content of our fuels is still within bounds, although it is getting worse each year. The upper limit per ASTM is 0.50%, per DIN is 0.55%, while the using industries generally regard anything above 0.40% as requiring more frequent oil changes to neutralize the effects of sulfur in the fuel. Sulfur in the fuel is converted, when burned, to gases which readily form corrosive acids. ASTM calls for a minimum Cetane Number of 40, DIN says 45. Only 2 samples fell below 40, 26 were between 40 and 45, while the average was around 45. We do not seem to be in trouble with cetane since we can live with 40 and have a better than 50:50 chance of getting over 45 when we buy our diesel.

Now we come to the black picture, Carbon Residue, with no pun intended. Carbon Residue is determined by distilling the fuel down to 10% of its original volume and then heating it until just a solid residue is left. The Carbon Residue test is the best indicator of how much coke will be left as a deposit after the fuel is burned in your engine. Here we have a sharp difference between the ASTM and DIN specs. The maximum per DIN is 0.10% for any automotive diesel fuel, while ASTM allows 0.15% in 1-D fuel but 0.35% in 2-D. In the samples of 1-D fuel collected, the average Carbon Residue was 0.069% with a maximum of 0.130%. Here again the desirability of 1-D is evident. When we examine the figures for 2-D we find an average Carbon Residue of 0.096% which is very respectable, but there were 14 cases where 2-D samples exceeded the maximum

for 1-D, and an additional 29 which exceeded the DIN spec. However, no Carbon Residue figure was given for 14 samples although all of the other tests were made and recorded. So of the 80 samples, only 23 met the DIN spec according to the report.

Fouling of the injector nozzles and other elements of the combustion chamber can be due to many factors: operation of the engine at sub-normal temperatures through short runs, stop-and-go, and excessive idling; maladjustment of the injection system; other mechanical shortcomings; but low quality fuel will cause trouble no matter how well everything else functions. This is pointed up by the discrepancy between the ASTM and DIN standards, where our U.S. refineries are permitted 3 times as much carbon residue as their European counterparts. Perhaps we should be thankful that our suppliers are not using all the latitude allowed them by the ASTM.

Unfortunately, there is no way to separate the good guys from the bad except by trial and error. There is no correlation between quality of fuel and areas in which it is sold, nor is there any indication that the big refineries are either better or worse than the smaller ones. One thing is clear: if you are having trouble due to inferior fuel, you'd better change your brand.

It should be noted that fuels were not tested for the presence of water or sediment. ASTM specifies that water and sediment should not exceed 0.05% by weight, while DIN allows 0.10%. Since the samples were all taken from the refineries we would not expect to find water present. The water found in diesel fuel gets into it during transportation and at the service station. We have advised many of our members who have been experiencing fuel problems to install a Racor water separator or similar device. This is an effective way to combat the water and sediment problem, but such devices do not remove the components which make up the carbon residue, for they are dissolved in the fuel and will pass any filter.

Factory-Approved Engine Oils

Approval applies only to the specific brand named here and does not extend to other engine oils from the same manufacturer. This information was correct as of its original publication in May/June 1982. For current information, see your Mercedes-Benz dealer or contact MBUSA's Customer Assistance Center at 800/FOR-MERC

Single-Viscosity Engine Oils
(For summer use only)

Brand	Manufacturer
CAM-2 Series	Sun Oil Co.
Castrol Heavy Duty	Burmah-Castrol
*Chevron Delo 400	Chevron Oil Co.
Kendall F-L Select	Kendall Refining Co.
Mobil Delvac 1200	Mobil Oil
*Mobil Delvac 1300 Series	Mobil Oil
*Monolec GFS (S3)	Lubrication Engineers
Pennzoil Z-7	Pennzoil Co.
Quaker State HD	Quaker State Oil
Union Heavy Duty	Union Oil Co.

Multi-Viscosity Engine Oils

Brand	Manufacturer
Castrol GTX	Burmah-Castrol
Chevron Delo 200 Multigrade	Chevron Oil Co.
*Chevron Delo 400	Chevron Oil Co.
Drydene Super V Multi-Vis	Dryden Oil Co.
Duckham's Q	Duckham, England
Mobil 1 (only below 50°F ambient)	Mobil Oil
Mobil Special	Mobil Oil
Mobil Super	Mobil Oil
Oilzum MB	White & Bagley
Pennzoil Z-7 Multi Vis	Pennzoil Co.
Quaker State Deluxe	Quaker State Oil
Quaker State Super Blend	Quaker State Oil

*Indicates an S3 quality engine oil.

Anyone who would like to make his own interpretation and analysis of the interesting data in these reports can obtain copies of them by writing to:

National Technical Information Service
U. S. Department of Commerce
Springfield, VA 22161

The gasoline report is DOE/BETC/PPS-81/3 and costs $8.00. The diesel report is DOE/BETC/PPS-80/5and costs $6.00.

Antifreeze Incompatibility

We have frequently emphasized the importance of regular maintenance of our cooling systems and the use of only factory approved antifreeze. The old days of simply keeping enough "permanent" antifreeze in the system to prevent freezing of the cooling mixture are long gone. With the advent of engine emission control systems, higher operating temperatures, pressurized cooling systems, extensive use of light-alloy engine components, and extended service intervals the subject of antifreeze for engine cooling systems is no longer simple.

Readers of the specialized automotive press, such as Diesel Car Digest, are aware that there are strong differences of opinion within the automotive industry concerning phosphate-free antifreeze versus phosphate-bearing antifreeze. Daimler-Benz firmly insists on phosphate-free antifreeze.

All Mercedes-Benz cars come from the factory with DBAG phosphate-free antifreeze installed, and this coolant will give service for two years, after which it must be drained and replaced. Now note this CAREFULLY: if it becomes necessary to top up the coolant in a Mercedes-Benz that still has the factory-installed antifreeze in its system, do NOT top up with MBNA antifreeze. The MBNA antifreeze is also phosphate-free but it is not compatible with the DBAG antifreeze. For topping up, the most suitable antifreeze is Prestone II, which is a relatively low-phosphate antifreeze. Prestone II is compatible with either DBAG antifreeze installed at the

factory, or with MBNA antifreeze available from your Mercedes-Benz dealer. The DBAG antifreeze is not available in North America.

There is an analogy here with blood typing: Type 0 blood can be transfused into persons with either Type A or Type B, but Type A cannot be transfused into Type B nor vice versa.

The use of small quantities of Prestone II (or other major domestic antifreeze based on ethylene glycol) to top up either the DBAG or MBNA solutions is acceptable. Note that "small quantities" means that not more than two quarts should accumulate in the system. Obviously, when domestic antifreeze has been used for topping up it is more important than ever that the interval between servicings of the cooling system not be extended.

If it is necessary to partially drain the cooling system of a new car, as for example to install a block heater, the drained coolant should be saved for returning to the system. After the cooling system of the new car has had its service at the two-year point and the DBAG antifreeze has been replaced by MBNA antifreeze, the wise course is to keep a spare supply of the MBNA material on hand for topping up.

To sum up: NEVER mix DBAG antifreeze, as installed in new cars, with the MBNA antifreeze used by your dealer for refilling the cooling system after it has been drained and flushed. (Reference: Service Information MBNA 20/2.)

Antifreeze is the subject of active research by all the major automobile manufacturers and chemical companies, and there will undoubtedly be major developments in coolants and cooling systems in the near future.

Exchange Parts Program

MBNA certainly never intended it to be this way, but somehow their Major Components and Exchange Parts Program has remained pretty much of a secret from most of our members. The portion of this program that is of special interest is the availability of factory-rebuilt major components on an exchange basis. Prime examples are the exchange diesel engines 220D (OM 615), 240D (OM 616), and 300D (OM 617). These remanufactured engines have been sent to Stuttgart, where they are disassembled and old worn parts are discarded. The remaining parts are thoroughly checked out and cleaned in a special seven-stage cleaning machine. Blocks, heads, crankshafts, cams, rods, pistons, and auxiliary equipment are reconditioned to exact tolerances. Along the way each part is thoroughly tested and checked for internal or external flaws. Any part that shows the slightest possibility of faltering is yanked and replaced with a new part. Once all the parts are installed and inspected, the remanufactured engine goes to the end of the assembly line where still another inspection is conducted. Each engine is put through a series of tests on a dynamometer to simulate actual operation under load. These engines, complete with alternator, starter, and fuel injection pump are then shipped to an MBNA parts depot.

These remanufactured engines carry the same warranty and provide the same performance as new ones. Many of us would actually prefer an engine remanufactured under such control and surveillance to a new one, feeling that the inspections would be conducted more critically, while the period of previous use would have uncovered any latent defects had they been present. The savings over the cost of a new engine are substantial, while the advantages over a local overhaul of the old engine must be measured in both dollars and satisfaction with the results. It has been estimated that the price of an exchange 300D engine would be 18% lower than the cost of refurbishing the various major components and parts required for a complete overhaul. The labor cost for the exchange of the complete unit is much less than that of the overhaul/repair process.

At present only the three diesel engines mentioned are available as complete exchange units. All gasoline engines are available only as new units. Short blocks and fitted blocks are likewise available only as new units.

There are a number of other components available under the exchange program, remanufactured to new standards by Daimler-Benz or by the original equipment manufacturer. Fuel injection pumps, electronic fuel injection control boxes, fuel distributors, turbochargers, alternators, starters, automatic antennas, complete automatic transmissions, and automatic transmission valve bodies are all included in the program. Regrettably, rear axles or parts thereof must be bought new.

Wheel Safety

A recent review, in cooperation with the Competition Committee, of the rules for National Events brought to the fore the need for care in the mounting of wheels, whether steel discs or light-alloys. In the same vein, MBNA has recently called the attention of dealers to this subject.

Wheel bolts (often called "lug nuts" or "lug bolts") should always be tightened with a manual torque wrench set to the upper tolerance of the specified torque. For all Mercedes wheels on all models, except the 600 (W100), the specified torque is 100 ± 10 Nm (= 73 ± 7 ft. lbs.). For the 600 the value is 170 Nm (= 125 ft. lbs.).

Wheel bolts should never be tightened to the full torque values with power impact wrenches. Such wrenches may be used to tighten bolts up to ¾ of the specified values and the final torque then applied by hand. Wheel bolts should not be torqued when the wheels are hot since the values established are for wheels at ambient temperatures; torquing to the full values when hot could result in damage to the threads of front wheel hubs or rear wheel shaft flanges.

Only wheel bolts which screw in easily should be used. Bolts which are hard to screw in or are corroded at the spherical collar should be replaced. Bolts should be clean, but not oiled or greased. Incidentally, it is a good idea to keep one or two spare bolts on hand; there is always a chance of losing one when changing a tire. If a spare tire is changed on the road with no torque wrench at hand, the bolts should be torqued at the earliest opportunity.

Care must be exercised to use the correct bolt for the wheel. The bolts for steel disc wheels are 21 mm (13/16 in.) long from the threaded end to the spherical collar, while bolts for light-alloy wheels are 29.5 mm (15/32 in.) long from end to collar. These bolts may not be interchanged under any circumstances. The light-alloy wheels referred to are, of course, the factory-supplied Mercedes-Benz wheels. If the spare wheel is of a different type from those on the car, it will be necessary to carry a set of the correct bolts for the spare.

Light-alloy wheels from sources other than Mercedes-Benz may vary widely in dimensions and quality, but the wheel bolts must be torqued to the above values. Presumably, correctly dimensioned bolts will be furnished with such wheels or they will be accompanied by a statement that Mercedes bolts for light-alloy wheels must be used. It is extremely unlikely that bolts for steel discs can be safely used with any light-alloy wheels. Common prudence dictates that light-alloy wheels should be used only when they have the official approval of some testing and inspection body such as TUV (Technische Uberwachungs Verein) or other body of similar stature. Note that the Club's rules for National Events require that any non-MB wheels must have steel inserts in the wheel bolt holes unless other evidence is furnished that safety is assured.

Technical and Restoration Forum

Engine Drivability

Engine Operation

Technical and Restoration Forum

Engine Service

Transmission Drivability

Transmission Operation

Transmission Service

Technical and Restoration Forum

Engine Drivability

Lousy Durability

March/April 1990

After 344,150 miles, my 1970 220D is beginning to have some trouble with cold weather starts. With 10W30 oil the engine turns over very freely, as though it has lost compression. After cranking for some time, it starts and runs fine. I've charged the battery, covered the engine with a thermal blanket and put a heat lamp in the engine compartment without success. Would a block heater and/or an oil dipstick heater help? All major engine components are original, and oil consumption is about three quarts per 1,000 mi.

Your engine spins freely because it has lost compression! At that mileage and oil consumption, you can expect the pistons to be a little loose in the bores, but we're inclined to suspect more. Your valve clearances may be set too close. With the entire engine at 68°F (20°C), intake clearance should be 0.10 mm (0.004 in) and exhaust clearance 0.40 mm (0.016 in). Valve clearances expand as the engine warms and contract as it cools, so if clearances are set on a warm engine, they will be too close when it cools. When cold weather is expected, intake valves should be set at 0.15 mm (0.006 in); in some parts of the U.S. and Canada it's customary to keep that clearance year 'round.

If your valve clearances are correct, check the compression. Normal values at sea level are 310–340 psi, with a minimum of 240 psi. Differences between cylinders should be no more than 40 psi. *(Darn. We sure hate to hear such embarrassing complaints about the questionable longevity of Mercedes-Benz cars, but let us face it, even after only a measly one-third of a million miles, you may just be due for an overhaul! Ed.)*

Idle Erraticism

January/February 2001

My 1988 300SEL, with 137,000 mi. runs fine for several days, then the engine will die while idling at a traffic light. It does this for a few days then returns to normal. My mechanic said it ran fine while he had it. I noticed a slight fuel leak from the fuel pump so replaced the lines, the pump, and the vacuum modulator, but that did not cure the problem. What do you suggest?

This sounds like an intermittent electrical problem. It's odd that it stalls continuously for 3 or 4 days then works fine. Have you tried taking it to the shop during the 3 days it's not working correctly? If you drive in with the car stalling in front of their eyes, they should be able to diagnose the problem.

This model has a "limp home" mode and really only needs the fuel pump and ignition system to work in order to run. It won't run perfectly and won't idle well, if at all, but it will drive down the road without an engine computer at all. The symptoms indicate an inoperative engine computer or idle speed control circuit. The most likely culprit is the overload protection relay, which powers the engine computer and is susceptible to intermittent failure due to poor solder joints. When the engine isn't idling correctly, try tapping the relay and see what happens. Opening the relay destroys the case, so it's not repairable. Otherwise, arrange to drive into the shop while the car is acting up so they can look at it immediately.

Rough Idle

January/February 2001

My 1988 380SEL, with 100,000 miles, performs well above idle but idles roughly, worst when hot. I've looked for air leaks in the manifold; could this be caused by the oxygen sensor?

Start with the basics. Apparently you've eliminated vacuum leaks as the cause by spraying carburetor cleaner around the intake manifold with the air cleaner installed. Is this a random roughness or a consistent miss? Random misses are usually caused by inaccurate fuel delivery or incorrect air-fuel mixture. If the miss is fairly consistent, isolate the offending cylinder or cylinders by loosening the fuel lines at the fuel distributor and note changes in the way the engine runs. If depriving a cylinder of fuel makes no difference, that cylinder is not producing power. Do a compression test to eliminate the possibility of a worn engine. Inspect the entire ignition system, including the spark plugs. Test the plug wires for correct resistance, eliminating a bad plug wire end. Most likely the rough idle is a result of poor fuel delivery due to bad injectors, a faulty fuel distributor, or both. Jump not to conclusions. Replacing parts is the least effective, most costly way to fix a problem. The oxygen sensor doesn't work for the first 30–60 seconds, so if it idles roughly when cold, replacing the sensor will solve nothing.

Bad Vibes

November/December 1985

We're on our fourth Mercedes-Benz, the last three being turbo-diesels. Our 1985 300SD has 12,000 mi, and when the engine drops to idle, a solid, harsh vibration occurs. A couple of hundred rpm higher, and the vibration is gone. My dealer made a vibration damper adjustment, but that did not help. He then put in two new injectors and removed the damper, which cured the problem. Is it OK to run without this damper?

This vibration is discussed in Service Information No. 07.1/9 dated November 1984. The damper should remain in place. The vibration damper must be adjusted after the engine has been broken in. In some cases there may not be enough adjustment available, so a modified adjustment screw is installed. If the damper cannot stop the vibration, the fuel injectors, compression pressure and other things should be checked. It may even be necessary to replace the injection pump.

A local mechanic reports another effective technique for stopping this vibration. The motor mounts and damper connections are slacked off, then the car is driven back and forth for a few minutes in the shop in forward and reverse gears. The mounts etc. are then tightened to normal specifications. Although this procedure is not officially called for, it evidently relieves certain stresses created during break-in and solves the problem.

Rough Diesel Idle

March/April 1990

When my 1982 300D turbo-diesel is driven on the open road for a while then stopped, the engine idles roughly. If I put my foot on the brake and increase rpm slightly, it runs smoother. I had the injectors replaced, which helped but didn't stop the problem.

The idling problem is fairly common and may be the result of having the idle speed adjusted when the engine is too hot. Coolant temperature should be between 68° and 86°F. I also suspect that the accelerator linkage may work more freely when the engine is hot, causing the quantity of fuel injected to be reduced and the idle speed thus lowered. Have the cruise control linkage checked to be sure that it isn't interfering.

300SD Idle Speed

January/February 1991

The idle speed of my 1987 300SD has drifted low, and I'd like to adjust it. How can I do so?

The diagnostic manual for your OM603 engine gives instructions for testing the idle speed control. The engine should idle at 630 plus or minus 20 rpm. Testing requires a multimeter engine analyzer such as a Bear DACE Model 40-960 or a Sun EMT-1019/Master 3, a tachometer, and special connectors. The final step, when everything else is correct, is to adjust idle speed at the trimming plug on the left side of the components compartment, close to the brake fluid reservoir. It has seven positions; the one marked "4" is supposed to give 630 rpm. Smaller numbers give lower idle speeds, and each number raises or lowers idle by 20 rpm. Obviously, you shouldn't adjust idle speed here until everything else has been checked and found OK.

280SEL 4.5 Idle

May/June 1998

I have a cherry 1972 280SEL 4.5 with 160,000 miles. Its previous owners threw dollars at it at the appropriate times, and it runs beautifully on the road. When idling cold, the engine surges; rpm go up and down for 5–10 minutes, then the idle settles down. The colder it is, the longer she chugs. The car doesn't smoke, has a clean air filter, and the injectors were all replaced 5,000 miles ago. What should I check to isolate the problem?

First have the fuel pressure tested with a cold engine. It should be 2.0 +0.1 bar; adjust it at the fuel pressure regulator and see if engine settles down. That engine was loaded with emission controls, and when they get old, they allow vacuum leakage. Check the emission devices for vacuum leaks. If the manifold pressure sensor tests bad, replace it. To do the test yourself, you should have the Mercedes-Benz factory manual for that engine; to order one, call MBNA at 800/367-6372.

300SEL 4.5 Intermittent Miss

March/April 1988

My 1973 300SEL 4.5 developed a chronic intermittent miss, especially when warmed up and idling in gear. So far we have replaced plugs, distributor cap, rotor, points, fuel injection trigger points and spark plug wires. We've also adjusted the valves, set the timing and checked the fuel injection pump and injectors. All to no avail.

In cases like this, the ignition system is the first suspect, but it is the easiest to check, which you seem to have done. Next most likely culprit is the fuel supply; even the best fuel can be contaminated by dirt or water. Another possibility is that one of the sensors that feed information to the computer is intermittently faulty. The easiest way to check is to substitute known good parts.

My ignition system and fuel checked out OK. Following your advice to check the sensors, a new throttle valve switch was installed, which solved the problem! Moreover, the car is now very much more responsive.

Starting Clicking

May/June 1999

When starting my 1987 190E 2.6 cold, the engine sometimes clicks for a few seconds until the oil pressure rises. What causes this?

The first possibility is a loose timing chain. Once oil pressure is established, the chain tensioner takes up the slack, so the chain rattling noise goes away. The second possibility is a hydraulic valve compensator (aka a lifter or tappet) that is bleeding down while the engine is off. When oil pressure builds, the excessive valve clearance is eliminated, and the tapping goes away. A mechanic can reproduce the noise while listening to the engine and determine where it comes from. If it's the chain, install a new timing chain and tensioner. If it's the valve compensators, I'd just live with it unless the noise persists after oil pressure is established.

Slow Starting

May/June 1990

My 1985 190E 2.3 is slow to start. When it was newer it started in 1–2 seconds, but after 34,000 miles the engine takes 4–7 seconds to fire. If I restart it within up to five hours, it's fine. Replacing the fuel distributor helped for a short while, but it's doing it again.

MBAG considers 4–5 seconds a normal starting time for the 190, 260 and 300 gasoline engines. A *Service Information* bulletin was recently issued to this effect.

Noisy 240D Starter

July/August 1988

When starting my 240D after it has stood outside in temperatures around 0°F, its starter sometimes makes a grating noise for three or four seconds.

The noise is probably a slight interference between the starter drive gear and the ring gear on the flywheel caused by thick grease slowing down disengagement of the starter. The remedy is removal of the starter motor and cleaning of the gears and the shaft of the starter drive. See the article on starter motors under Technical Topics in this issue.

Diesel Run-On

September/October 1994

After I switch off my 1981 300D, the engine keeps running, and I have to press the stop lever in the engine compartment to stop it. What causes this?

The diesel engine is stopped by turning off the fuel supply via a vacuum-operated switch on the injection pump which receives vacuum from the switch on your dash. Vacuum comes from a pump at the front of the engine through a tube to the dash. If a defect exists in this system, the stop lever under the hood can be used to turn off the fuel supply.

The most frequent cause of failure is loss of vacuum, either through a leak in one of the plastic tubes or in another vacuum-operated mechanism such as the door locks, or failure of the vacuum pump itself. When this pump starts leaking, it may suck oil from the crankcase which will eventually flow to the ignition switch, making it inoperative. Because the switch is expensive, it is important to have this problem fixed quickly.

Engine Operation

Filthy McNasty

March/April 1997

I recently bought a 1982 240D, and after having the dirty-looking coolant changed, took it on a 750-mile trip. On return, the coolant was again dark brown to black. I was told that the head gasket might be leaking or the head might be cracked. Any opinion?

Your description indicates that combustion gases, engine oil, or both are getting into the coolant. If you're lucky, the cause is a blown head gasket. If not, it could be a cracked head or block. In any case, find the cause now and correct it. If you continue to drive the car, the coolant passages in the head will become coated with gummy carbon residue that will prevent heat transfer and cause overheating. A bad head gasket will only get worse and may leak coolant into the cylinders, with possible serious damage.

If a leakdown test does not pinpoint the cause, the head should be removed and the gasket checked. If the gasket appears defective, replace it, reassemble the engine, and see what happens. If the old gasket was not the cause, the head and block will have to be further checked by a competent mechanic, and replacement may be necessary.

Oil Filler Cap Seepage

May/June 1993

My 1985 500SEL, with 175,000 miles on it, leaks oil from the right side valve cover oil filler cap. A new cap and gasket were no help. Two gaskets were no help. Compression is normal, and the spark plugs are clean. Do I have a crankcase venting problem, or is this something I must live with?

Your oil filler cap problem is common and is caused by blow-by. Even in new cars, slight leakage between cylinder wall, piston, and rings causes compression to slightly pressurize the crankcase. The Positive Crankcase

Ventilation (PCV) valve usually accommodates this.

Try bending the lugs which hold on the cap so that they apply more pressure. If this doesn't work, about all you can do is wipe off the valve cover each time you open the hood. The seat on the valve cover neck is probably not making perfect contact all around, but it would be expensive to try to true up this area. I have the same problem on my diesel, and I just wipe up every time I have the chance.

110 Engine Oil Leak

May/June 1996

My European 1978 280SLC (110.982/6 engine) has covered 124,000 miles since it was overhauled and has an oil leak that no one wants to tackle. Its air filter is up front next to the radiator. A plastic duct connects the filter to the engine air intake. This duct has a hose connected to it coming from the cam cover. Oil seems to get from the cam cover through this hose and into the engine's intake system. Oil consumption is about 500 miles per quart, but the oil pressure gauge stays "pegged" at speed.

The PCV (positive crankcase ventilation) system on the 110 fuel-injected engine is similar to that of other Mercedes-Benz engines in that blowby fumes are sucked into either the intake manifold or the air cleaner housing. In the 110 engine (due to the intake manifold vacuum in the low and partial load range) in addition to blowby, clean air from the filter is drawn into the engine via a hose line connected to the cam cover. If any part of this system (particularly the part that supplies fresh air to lower the vacuum on the blowby gases) is clogged with oil sludge or dirt, the system will inhale too much blowby and oil vapor. This may be the cause, so check every hose, nozzle, and valve for cleanliness. Another alternative is that after 124,000 miles your engine is worn and thus allowing excessive blowby; a leakdown test can determine that.

300E Oil Leak

January/February 1996

Despite my mechanic's efforts, my 1987 300E continues to leak oil from the front cam cover seal. Is there a solution?

MBNA addresses the problem on *Diagnostic Directory Sheet 2*, in position K1, which all dealers have. The special sealant used is Omni Visc 1050, part number 002 989 45 20; directions for use are on the package.

6.3 Oil Leaks from Heads

September/October 1992

Both heads on my 1970 300SEL 6.3 leak oil at the rear. Compression is normal, there's no water in the oil, and the oil lines and injection pump do not leak. What do you think?

The answer is simple but unpleasant. You probably need new head gaskets. Before installing them, the heads should be checked for flatness and machined to correct any irregularity. Maximum permissible unevenness lengthwise is 0.08 mm (0.003 in); maximum permissible unevenness crosswise is zero. Permissible height of roughness is 0.006 to 0.014 mm (0.0002 to 0.0006 in). Oil pressure passages run from the block through the head gasket to the valve gear. It is not uncommon for the first breakdown of the gasket to be at the oil hole, particularly on the right-hand head.

Leaky 300SD Valve Cover

July/August 1988

The valve cover on my 1983 300SD leaks. It appears that the nuts are too tight— and bottomed out on the studs. Should I put a washer under the nuts or replace the gasket? What about gasket sealant?

Correct torque for the valve cover nuts is 11 lb-ft (15 Nm); tightening beyond this value may warp the cover or distort the gasket. Make sure that the cover is not warped, then clean it thoroughly and carefully replace the gasket. No sealant should be used. Make sure the cover and gasket fit securely, then finger-tighten the nuts. Torque them to 8 lb-ft, then to 11.

M103 Engine Oil Leak

July/August 1997

The top front cover on the engine of my 1989 300E is leaking again. I plan to repair it myself (job number 01-212) but am having trouble finding the specified front cover to cylinder head sealant (002 989 00 20 10) and the sealant (001 989 61 20 10) for the sides of the oil-free groove of the timing case cover. What gasket sealant works best?

It is not unknown for cars with only 20,000 miles to leak here. The Mercedes-Benz silicone sealant (001 989 61 20 10) is special, and I doubt that a Permatex or Loctite equivalent exists (if so, we'd like to hear of it). My mechanic uses this sealant to attach and seal the front cover to the head. It is rather expensive, but one tube does many jobs. Be aware that this difficult and frustrating job, requiring a special guide sleeve tool, may be best left to a professional.

Leaky 280SL Front Seal

March/April 1990

Any suggestions on how to keep a 280SL's front crankshaft seal from leaking oil? I've replaced it twice, but it leaks more than ever.

After removing the old seal, the edge of the receiving bore for the sealing ring should be de-burred then smoothed with fine emery paper. Any roughness will cause rapid seal wear. Before inserting the sealing ring, moisten the lip of the seal with oil. The ring should be inserted with an installation bushing, part number 111 589 17 61 00. If it isn't seated perfectly, it will leak.

Oil Pan Gasket Leak

July/August 1992

I've replaced the oil pan gasket of my 1983 300D twice, but it still leaks. What kind of sealer should I use?

Assuming that the pan is straight and uncracked, try M-B Silikon Sealant, part number 001 989 61 20 10. This comes in a one-ounce tube and is probably much the same as 3M Super Silicone Sealer or other domestic sealers made by Permatex, General Electric, et al. Tighten the bolts evenly and don't over-tighten them. Proper torque for the M6 bolts is 10 Nm (7 lb-ft) and for M8 bolts, 25 Nm (18 lb-ft).

Hot Time in Philly

May/June 1998

I don't drive this car much, but during the summer the thermostatic fan seems to run virtually all the time. This is a big V8, and things are crowded under the hood, but is this normal? Summer is hot in Philly, but not that hot. This fan runs whether or not the air-conditioning is on.

The fan relay could be stuck closed. The fan should run only when coolant temperature exceeds 97°C or Freon temperature exceeds 62 °C. Either condition actuates the fan relay, and the fan runs.

Hot E500

September/October 1998

I'm at my wit's end. My 1994 E500 overheats in ambient temperatures over 80°F with the air-conditioning on. If I turn off the air-conditioning and get some clear air, it cools down. My dealer replaced the thermostat, fan assembly, and radiator, and I switched to Red Line synthetic oil and Water Wetter, all to no avail. The MBNA zone service rep drove the car and told me it was normal for the temperature to rise above 100°C, but other Mercedes-Benz cars I have owned would stay at around 88°C. I recently had a larger radiator and an oil cooler installed with no effect. Any suggestions would be appreciated.

The MBNA rep is right. The normal operating temperature of your car is 100°C. My own car runs at about the 100°C line whether the air-conditioning is on or not and regardless of speed or mountain roads. Higher operating temperatures are all part of the ongoing effort to produce more efficient engines. The old days of engines that chugged along at 80°C are gone.

380SL Cooling

March/April 1990

When started after standing overnight, my 1982 380SL's engine temperature slowly rises to about 100°C then drops abruptly to above 80°C. My mechanic says this is common with that engine and can be corrected by replacing the thermostat after removing the metering pin that operates in the thermostat seal orifice. I bought a thermostat and modified it before installation, which corrected the initial temperature rise. What does the metering pin do and could this modification be harmful?

This temperature rise is not unusual in the 380SL. MBAG gives two corrective measures. One is to install a new thermostat and gasket, using extreme care to ensure that the gasket hole and metering pin are perfectly centered in the control bore. The second fix is to cut off the holder and pin which have been binding in the control bore or the guide groove of the inlet connection. Apparently binding is due to inexact positioning of the thermostat when it is installed. Cutting off the pin is probably most likely to avoid recurrence of the trouble. The control bore ensures that, independent of coolant temperature, there will always be flow to the coolant pump, but the amount is metered by the pin. Without the pin there will be constant flow through the 4.3-mm-diameter control bore. We see no likelihood of cooling problems as a result of this repair.

380SE Viscous Fan Coupling

September/October 1991

My 1980 380SE seems to run hot (about 210–220°F). How can I tell whether the viscous fan clutch is working properly?

I wouldn't be concerned if the engine runs at 220°F or even higher in hot weather when driving hard with the air-conditioning on. Efficiency of cooling systems drops with age as deposits form in the block and radiator. With the engine hot, stop it and feel the radiator core with your hand. It should be hot all over. Cool spots indicate that coolant flow is partially blocked there.

With the engine off, it's possible to turn the fan by hand against the resistance of the viscous fluid, but there's no test for the amount of resistance. With the engine running, the fan turns at about 75 percent of engine rpm and should change speed as rpm's change. As the engine reaches 4,000 rpm, the fan should slow to about 400 rpm, as the car will then be travelling fast enough to cool the engine without the fan.

560SEC Coolant Temperature

May/June 1989

My 1989 560SEC seems to run too hot, with coolant temperatures around 92°C (198°F). Should I have a lower-temperature thermostat installed? Should I let the engine idle a bit to cool off before I shut it down?

Your car has a three-phase cooling system. During warm-up, up to a coolant temperature of 80°C, only the bypass valve is open, and no coolant circulates through the radiator. In the mid-phase, in which the car operates most of the time, both the bypass and the main valve are partially open, depending upon ambient temperature and engine load; coolant temperature will be between 80° and 95°C. In the third phase, near full-load operation in high ambient temperatures, the bypass and main valves will open fully, and coolant temperature will be above 95°C. Your 92°C temperature seems perfectly normal, so don't even think of changing thermostats; that concept is outmoded in today's cars.

A coolant mixture that gives a freezing point of -30°C (-22°F) will have a boiling point of 130°C (269°F) in a system with a No. 140 closing cap, which is what your system should have. A short idling period before turning off the engine would only apply if the coolant temperature were above 110°C (230°F) or so. The latest engine designs are intended to run at higher temperatures than we used to consider normal. A coolant temperature of 190°–210°F is normal for cars of the late 1980's.

Hot 420SEL

March/April 1992

On hot days the coolant temperature gauge in my 1986 420SEL can reach the red line (120°C, 248°F). The coolant is 50-50 water-antifreeze, and there appears to be no corrosion in the coolant. What do you suggest?

Assuming that the gauge is correct (and that's worth checking), a simple test can tell whether the radiator is doing its job. After driving to bring the engine to full operating temperature, stop the car, and turn off the engine. With the palm of your hand, feel the radiator on the engine side, checking for areas that are cooler than others. A cool spot indicates a flow blockage.

A cool spot in the center of the radiator can affect fan operation. Until coolant temperature reaches about 105°C (221°F), the fan will run at only 600 rpm. When air heated by hot coolant hits a bimetallic strip in the fan, a valve is opened, allowing viscous fluid to circulate through the fan hub, causing the fan to rotate in concert with the engine. A centrifugal device releases the fan at rpm levels associated with normal highway speeds, when the fan is no longer needed.

If air coming through the center of the radiator is not heated, the fan won't lock on. There could also be a defect in the visco-fan. To check fan operation, start the engine and note that the fan runs rather slowly, only because of drag in the hub. As coolant temperature rises above 100°C (212°F), the fan should speed up. Fan rpm should rise and fall with engine rpm.

If the radiator and the fan are OK, the cooling system may have lost its efficiency through corrosion and deposits, even if the cooling system has been properly serviced. Even normal water contains suspended solids; to see what they do, look inside a kettle.

MBNA specifies a special flushing process under job No. 20-015. Basically a citric acid flush, this should be done only with proper equipment.

The water pump should also be checked. Solid particles in the coolant may have worn the pump's impeller, making it less effective. Impellers are a press fit on their shaft and have been known to loosen. Pump effectiveness can be felt with a hand on the outlet hose to the radiator. With the thermostat wide open, pulsations should be clearly felt.

Valve Stem Seals

March/April 1992

In three recent engines (my 190E 2.3-16, a family member's 1987 260E, and my 1990 300E) with which I am acquainted, high oil consumption (over one quart per thousand miles) has been blamed on worn valve stem seals. At mileages under 30,000 we have been told that new valve stem seals are needed and that this is a fairly common problem. Is there a new seal to supersede the old type?

In April 1989, MBNA issued a *Service Information* publication on oil consumption. Valve stem seals of a new plastic material, viton, were to be installed in all cars that did not already have them. Applicable *Service Information* numbers are 05/3a and 18/7a. If your car has already had viton seals installed, a white dot should have been painted on the valve cover. Except for early 190E 2.3-16 models, we haven't had a lot of complaints about oil consumption, but it has been known to increase then decrease on its own. Some engines are designed to use more oil than others, so we wouldn't worry until consumption was consistently in the range of one quart per 500–700 miles.

190E Oil Consumption

May/June 2001

My 1986 190E 2.3 has excessive blowby—oil accumulates in the air cleaner—and consumption is one quart per 700 miles. The engine has 84,000 miles, compression is good, the plugs don't foul, and there is no smoke from the exhaust. Is this oil consumption normal?

Not for your engine. You say it has excessive blow-by, which indicates worn piston rings, but have you watched the PCV outlet from the valve cover to see how much smoke comes out? Assuming that the air filter element is not soaked with oil, it's not abnormal to have some oil residue in the air filter housing. Check that the orifice to the PCV hose going back into the intake manifold is not clogged. One quart per 700 miles is a lot. I'll bet if you follow the car as it drives away cold, you'll see blue smoke from the exhaust. The bottom end of these engines is pretty tough. At 84,000 miles, there should be no problem with the pistons. I suspect that the valve stem seals are hard as a rock and the valve guides are worn. Start by replacing the valve stem seals and rechecking oil consumption.

Oil Pressure Rise Time

May/June 1987

My 1974 240D has 74,000 miles on it. Since new, the oil pressure takes several seconds to build up from a cold start. Once the car starts, pressure quickly goes to 45 psi. Is this normal?

When the engine is started on a very cold day, actual oil pressure at the engine can jump to over 100 psi, so the oil pressure gauge has a restrictor in the line from the engine to protect the gauge from damage. The delay you see is mostly a result of this restrictor. Remember, too, that for practical reasons the gauge's sensor is not located at the most critical point for oil pressure.

Oil Consumption

May/June 2000

My 1985 380SE was using a quart of oil per tank of gas, so I switched to higher viscosity oil. Now it uses a quart every two tankfuls. Gas mileage has also decreased. I can find no oil leaks, there's no smoke from the exhaust, and oil pressure seems normal. The engine has 210,000 miles on it. What do you suspect?

Worn valve guides and seals. If oil isn't leaking out, it must be burning in the combustion process or pouring into the exhaust system. If there is little or no smoke, oil is not coming into the cylinder via the intake valve guides. When exhaust guides leak, oil gets sucked into the exhaust manifold without being burned. This can cause smoke as the oil burns in the exhaust but not as much smoke as oil that goes in the combustion chamber. I assume that the spark plugs have been inspected for oil burning. Lower fuel economy could be a result of the exhaust system and catalytic converter getting plugged with oil deposits. Given the high oil consumption, one or more exhaust valve guides may have loosened in the head, allowing oil to pour down the annulus between guide and head. This can be confirmed by inspecting the guides one at a time with the valve springs removed and compressed air holding up the valve. You may find guides that can be wiggled by hand in the head. Removing the heads and doing a valve job with new guides is the only repair, and after 210,000 miles, it should be no surprise.

Smoking Coupe

March/April 1996

My 1970 250C emits a cloud of smoke when started cold but not when the engine is warm. The engine had a valve job about 4,000 miles ago, and the transmission modulator has been replaced. Oil pressure is OK, and only occasionally does the car smoke oil on the road. Before we take it apart, can you offer any suggestions?

You seem to have eliminated the transmission modulator. If the smoke is blue, valve seals would be the first guess, but a proper valve job would have replaced these. If the smoke is white, you may have a blown head gasket, which allows a bit of coolant to enter a cylinder. With the engine cold, pressurize the cooling system to 20 psi; if it holds for 20 minutes, the system is OK. You could also have the engine oil analyzed for the presence of ethylene glycol (antifreeze).

Reading Between the Lines

March/April 1996

How does the crankcase ventilation system on the 280SL (M130 engine) work? I'm interested in knowing how it keeps oil out of the intake manifold. The shop manuals are vague on this.

The system is fairly crude by today's standards. Blowby gases and crankcase emissions pass through the pipe connection into the top of the cylinder head (valve) cover to the venturi control unit in front of the throttle valve. From there they are carried with intake air to the combustion chamber. To prevent freezing of the condensate and sticking of the throttle valve, the venturi control unit is heated by coolant. The only way to check the system is to be sure that all passages are open.

We sense that you may really be asking another question: Why is my 280SL smoking? On both gasoline and diesel engines, blowby increases with engine wear, so if you haven't already done so, run a leakdown test to check for worn piston rings, cylinder bores, valve seats, and valve guides. As rings and bores wear, the compression and combustion pressures can more easily enter the crankcase and force oil through the vent system and into the intake system.

Tappet Racket

November/December 1997

During cold starts my 1988 300SEL's engine occasionally makes a loud metallic tapping noise for a few seconds then quiets as oil pressure builds. I currently use conventional 20W50 oil, changed every 3,000 miles, and the car has covered 101,000 miles. Any ideas?

The most likely source of the noise is one or more leaky hydraulic valve tappets. Normally oil cannot leak out of a tappet's chamber, but wear, dirt, or deposits can interfere with correct operation. Special tools are needed to verify the proper working of these tappets.

400E Valve Tapping

March/April 1997

My 1993 400E makes a lot of tapping noise at idle. When the dealer sprayed solvent into the intake manifold per the factory information, the noise disappeared, but it returned after a few thousand miles. The dealer recommended using Chevron gasoline, but that's inconvenient. What else can I do?

The carbon buildup that can cause loud valve tapping and rough idle takes the form of gummy or varnish-like deposits on the intake valve stems. These don't initially cause leakage, but they do slow the last bit of closing motion. This may not explain the noise, but if the solvent alleviated the problem, it seems logical. I suggest trying Amoco, Shell, or Texaco gasoline.

Helicopter Noise

July/August 1996

My 1984 300CD runs well but makes a non-metallic "whap-whap-whap" noise that sounds like a helicopter flying overhead, possibly one whap per engine revolution. As the engine warms up, the noise diminishes, and at normal operating temperatures the engine noise drowns it out. The frequency of the noise is directly related to engine rpm, not with car speed. All of the drive belts seem to be OK.

Diagnosing engine noises by mail isn't easy, but check for softened or disintegrating engine mounts. If the normal rocking of the engine increases, a part such as a hose or even the mount itself can make noise in harmony with the engine. As the engine warms, it vibrates less, so the noise diminishes. *(Editor's Note: An exhaust leak? As the exhaust manifold, pipe, or joint heats up, the leak seals itself. With the engine cold, block the exhaust outlet to see if you can locate the noise.)*

Engine Service

Worn Alternator Mounting

September/October 1986

My 1972 220D is approaching 400,000 mi, and one consistent problem involves the alternator mount. The alternator pivot bolt hole continually elongates, even when fitted with a metal bushing. I've consumed numerous alternator pivot bolts, at least three adjusting rods, an equal number of the studs that attach the rod to the block and many sets of the four rubber bushings, even a new alternator mount. Later models have a different design which doesn't seem adaptable to my car. What can be done?

I recently persuaded Ken Marino, Tampa Bay Section, to join the Technical Committee with special emphasis on parts for older cars. He advises that you should be sure the rubber mounting bushings at the block (part number 121 150 00 49) are good and that the pivot bolt is tightened at every oil change. The original 8-mm pivot bolt can be replaced by a 10-mm bolt such as that used on the later 300D (part number 000 931 010 244) by drilling out the holes in the mounting bracket and alternator.

Dwelling On It

July/August 1985

What is the best way to rotate the engine of my 1968 280S to get the breaker arm on the peak of the cam lobe? The manual specifies a dwell angle of 40° plus or minus 1°. How sensitive is this setting? Which direction should the setting favor so that wear on the rubbing block will keep the dwell within specifications?

The best way to rotate the engine is also the easiest. Remove all spark plugs and turn the crankshaft with a socket or box wrench on one of the bolts holding the harmonic balancer on the crankshaft. Turn only in the direction of engine rotation. If you turn too far, go around again. Never rotate the camshaft directly. It is too difficult to be precise if you rotate the engine by means of the fan belt or starter motor.

The factory tolerance of plus or minus one degree is a good indication of the sensitivity of the dwell angle. Earlier six-cyl engines had a wider tolerance, but all later cars have the same one-degree figure. Engine performance would not be adversely affected within this range. Reasonable care and good tools should make it possible to get within one-half degree of the desired setting.

Since normal wear on the rubbing block increases the dwell angle, it would appear to be good practice to favor the lower end of the permissible dwell range, but DBAG probably allowed for this in establishing the 40° midpoint setting. Still, I would err on the downside, but by as little as possible.

Oily 250 Points

January/February 1994

Every 1,000 miles I must replace or clean the distributor points on my 1971 250 because they are continually being coated with oil. The distributor has new bushings and a new felt seal. Oil seems to be attracted to the points, not the rest of the distributor. How can I stop this problem?

This was a problem right from the start with this model. The points carry very low current so do not burn away the oil film as do the points in older, conventional ignition systems. The problem was eliminated in later models by better sealing the distributor from crankcase fumes and by changing the means of breaking the primary current. Many owners carried ordinary business cards to clean the points periodically. The alternative is to install an aftermarket ignition system with a different type of breaker.

Valve Volumes

November/December 1985

Recently a mechanic adjusted the noisy valves of my 1974 280C (90,000 mi) and returned the car with the engine purring and quiet. Soon, however, I realized that gas mileage was down 30 percent, and the car struggled on hills. I referred the problem to another shop, which returned the car with valves noisy as hell but with improved mileage and plenty of power. Which setting is correct, and will noisy valves hurt anything?

The valves on your 1974 280C should be set (with the engine cold) as follows: intakes, 0.10 mm (0.004 in) and exhausts, 0.25 mm (0.10 in). Cold is defined as approximately 68°F. With a warm engine, say 115° to 170°F, clearances should be 50-percent larger, but no competent mechanic would set the valves on a warm engine. To allow your car to cool down, take it to the shop the night before adjustment or early in the morning for a late afternoon adjustment. Every point on the engine should feel cool to the touch.

When the valves are properly adjusted on any Mercedes-Benz without hydraulic valve adjusters, the valves should make a quite audible clicking noise. It's really a pleasant sound when all the clicks are equally loud. Overhead cam engines (such as yours) in correct adjustment always have quite noticeable valve noise unless they have hydraulic tappets.

The mechanic who set your valves too close probably did so on a warm engine. Setting the valves too close will damage the engine more quickly and more seriously than setting them too loosely. Valves set too loosely can damage the engine but not as seriously. In Mercedes-Benz engines, valve clearances increase as the engine gets warmer. In fact, if the car is to be operated with outside temperatures below 0°F prevailing for long periods, intake valve clearance should be increased to 0.15 mm (0.006 in), or it may be hard to start the engine in the cold, as the intake valve may be held open.

A small dwell angle (i.e., a larger gap) is good for starting and performance at low speeds and causes less arcing between the points, which will thus last longer. A larger dwell angle (i.e., a smaller gap) is good for high-speed performance, but more energy is stored in the coil and discharged at the plugs, so there will be increased arcing and more wear at the points. Factory specifications are, of course, a compromise to give optimum performance in normal use. If the entire ignition system is in good condition, a large variation in dwell angle will be tolerated under favorable conditions.

(Editor's Note: Older cars may experience wear causing an unwanted variation in dwell angle during normal operation, so it is wise to occasionally check the dwell throughout the rpm range with a dwell meter rather than simply relying on static or low rpm settings.)

Cam Angle

March/April 1986

One manual says to adjust my 230SL valves with the cam positioned at a right angle (90°) from vertical and facing the adjustment nut, while a mechanic tells me that the cam should point straight up (180°). Which is correct?

The 180° position is preferable, but the 90° position is not wrong. Just remember that you want the cam base circle against the rocker arm, which is easiest to ensure when the cam lobe points straight up. At the 90° position it is somewhat more likely that the cam could be positioned slightly off the base circle. Most mechanics I know set it at the 180° position, but it isn't necessary to be too fussy about a few degrees one way or another.

Folding Hose

March/April 1996

Because the top radiator hose on my 1990 300D 2.5 Turbo collapsed after the engine cooled, I replaced it. The new hose continued to collapse, so I replaced the radiator cap, but it still does so occasionally. What could be causing this?

Have the radiator cap checked according to Job No. 20-430. A vacuum valve in the center of the cap is supposed to release at 0.1 bar (1.5 psi). The valve must rest against the rubber seal; it must be possible to easily raise it, and when released, it must spring back. Be sure that the system contains a 50-50 mixture of water and Mercedes-Benz antifreeze. If you see any corrosion around the radiator cap or cooling system, remove it.

Plastic Radiator Tank Fixes

May/June 1995

Water seeps out of the top of the radiator of my 1990 300D 2.5 Turbo from the joint where the plastic top tank meets the metal radiator. I've been told that the only sure fix is to replace the radiator. Is there a less expensive alternative?

The radiator's maker, Behr, bonds the plastic part to the aluminum radiator using special machinery, and the official line has always been that repairs away from their factory were impractical. Still, several members found local shops that could make the repair; I have no history on how these lasted. Two radiator shops now advertising in *The Star* do this type of repair. I believe they have repaired radiators ready to ship, with a core charge refunded after you send them your old radiator.

Torquing Heads

May/June 1987

After having an intake manifold gasket replaced, my 1972 350SL with 39,000 miles on it developed a coolant leak. We subsequently found two broken head bolts on the right side, which were replaced. Checking the other head for good measure, we found two more, which were also fixed. The engine had previously never been opened. The coolant leak stopped, but now I have a slight oil leak from the right head area. The valve cover gasket has been replaced and the head re-torqued, but the leak still makes a small spot if the car stands for any time. Where do you think the leak could be coming from, and why do you think the head bolts broke?

It is possible for oil to leak out of the head gasket at the rear of the engine because there's an oil passage there between block and head. Make sure that the oil isn't coming from the valve cover gasket, as these sometimes leak. If that isn't the cause, it's likely the head gasket.

The broken head bolts were probably over-torqued. When these engines were new, there was a strict procedure for torquing and re-torquing the head bolts, but it was later found that this did more harm than good. The latest head gaskets do not require that the heads be retorqued.

Head Switch

May/June 1989

The 3.5-liter EFI V8 (M116) has a short stroke and a 9.5:1 compression ratio. The 4.5-liter EFI V8 (M117) has a longer stroke and various compression ratios up to 8.8:1, producing up to 250 hp in European form. Can I improve the power output of my 4.5-liter engine by switching to the high-compression 3.5-liter heads?

A 116 head will probably fit a 117 engine, but this doesn't mean that you will get the compression boost. Compression is determined by the pistons, too, so it might seem more logical to try fitting 116 pistons. Then you'd have to be concerned about valve-to-piston clearance and many other factors (deck height, etc.), so you'd have to essentially rebuild the engine rather than simply switch heads. We know of no one who has tried this, but careful exploration in the great American spirit of individual innovation seems admirable. Good luck!

Thread Cleaning

September/October 1998

The threads for one spark plug in my 1956 180's cylinder head are severely damaged. Is there a way to repair the head, or should I look for a new one?

If only the threads are bad, you can buy and use a re-threading tool that looks like a double-ended tap; one end of the tap fits small spark plug threads, the other fits the larger size. I keep one around because almost every Mercedes-Benz I have owned has had at least one plug hole stripped by the previous owner or a bad mechanic.

Grease the tap liberally to catch metal particles. Thread it into the spark plug hole, using a 3/4- or 7/8-in deep socket to drive it. Thread it all the way in, then back it out. The plug hole threads should be good as new. To prevent seizing the next time you change plugs, lubricate the cleaned threads with silicone spray. I've rescued several plug holes this way; it beats replacing the head.

190E 2.3 Engine Swap

July/August 1996

My 1987 190E 2.3 uses a quart of oil every 200 miles and has some blow-by. I bought a 1991 190E 2.3 engine with automatic transmission and all the computer bits. Will it interchange, and can I use the 1991's EZL ignition system?

Both engines are 102.985 units, so they will interchange, but you may have problems with different placement of some ancillary units. If the 1987 car has a manual transmission, you'll have problems changing it to an automatic, so swap just the engine. It's not practical to use the EZL system with the 1987 engine because some sensors are built into the engine.

Break-In Procedure

November/December 1998

I'm rebuilding my 190E 2.3 engine. Is there a factory-recommended assembly lubricant? What is the correct break-in procedure?

Use any good assembly lube; check with local automotive machine shops for recommendations. With the engine back in the car, crank it with the ignition disconnected to build oil pressure. Avoid heavy loading of the engine for the first 500 miles or so. Don't let the engine labor in a high gear, and avoid long periods at constant rpm. Keep the engine below 3,500 rpm, and don't exceed 1,500 rpm without a load on it. After 500 miles, change the oil and filter and gradually increase the operating conditions to normal.

RPM in Old Engines

May/June 1987

I'm nearing completion of an extensive engine rebuild on a 1963 220SEb coupe, which will leave the car virtually new mechanically. What's the right way to drive this car? It has the old 4-speed automatic that seems to give a choice of either very low or very high rpm. Leaving the automatic to choose the gear results in engine rpm below 2,000, while manually down-shifting pops you up to 3,500–4,000. If you know these old cars, you know what I mean. Which causes more engine wear, continual low rpm or frequent high revving?

There's little dispute about relative wear at very low speeds vs. higher speeds. Low-rpm operation under heavy loads can reach the point where oil is squeezed out from between the metal surfaces, then you have direct contact and extreme wear. Keep engine rpm over 1,500 if you have any significant load on it. After a reasonable break-in period of perhaps 2,000 miles, gradually run the rpm up in short bursts to 4,000 and watch the coolant temperature and oil pressure. After the engine is loosened up, you should be able to run it to 5,000 rpm, but remember that although everything is restored to new dimensions, the process of metal fatigue has been going on for many years. It's best not to tempt fate too much.

A friend comments that when he first bought a wildly expensive ($4,000 in 1968) sports car, he shifted up at no more than 3,500 rpm. After about a day of that, he got fed up and started going higher, frequently to redline. His engines have lasted much better than average, and he's had a lot of fun since then! He claims that blowing the carbon out is good for the driver as well as the car. Of course, all this assumes regular oil changes and maintenance. Don't be afraid to rev your engine as long as the needles stay out of the red.

Tensioner Replacement

May/June 2000

If I change the timing chain and guides on my 1981 300D after 180,000 miles, should I change the tensioner, too?

You can replace the chain and rails without replacing the tensioner, but with that mileage it would be a good idea to replace the tensioner, too, since it's already off.

Timing Chain Streeeetch

January/February 2002

I've read that when a timing chain is checked for wear that three to five degrees is acceptable but more than seven requires replacement. How is the stretch measured?

Mercedes-Benz measures the difference in camshaft timing vs. crankshaft timing, which indicates chain stretch. They publish specifications for correct camshaft timing, which can be measured but is a fairly time-consuming process. A V-8 requires temporarily installing a solid compensating element for the number one intake valve (when measuring the right bank), installing a dial indicator to indicate two mm of valve lift, hand-cranking the engine to two-mm valve lift, then comparing the crankshaft reading to the specification. If the specification is 12° ATDC (for example), and you have two mm lift at 18° ATDC, the chain has stretched enough to retard timing by 6°.

Since there is no official limit on how far off your cams can be and no specified timing chain replacement interval, collective experience indicates recommended intervals for replacement. Replacing a chain at 100,000 mi is conservative from a failure perspective but reasonable from a performance viewpoint. At 150,000 mi it's a good idea, something to schedule for the near future. By 200,000 mi, performance starts to suffer, and chain failure is possible, though remote with a well-maintained car. If you have a 380 with a single-roller chain, convert it to double-roller tomorrow, then follow the above recommendations.

Transmission Drivability

Reversed Gears

July/August 1986

Our 1976 300D has 140,000 mi behind it. Sometimes when backing out of the garage, the car jerks to a stop. If we then put it in drive, then reverse again, it works fine. More rarely, when we shift to reverse, the car goes forwards! The problem seems to happen only when the weather and the car are cold. Our dealer has been unable to cure the problem.

From what you write, we can't diagnose the exact problem, but it sounds as if it could be a worn transmission linkage, especially in view of the car's age and mileage. We suggest a second opinion, which is a good idea whenever a problem persists. Most mechanics deserve two chances at a problem, but if that's not enough, go elsewhere.

If you are working with a Mercedes-Benz dealer, ask him to make an appointment for you to meet with the MBNA Field Service Rep from the zone office. Service reps see unusual problems and can likely help you and the dealer's service personnel. If you are working with an independent shop, simply try another. You'll soon find an experienced mechanic who can diagnose the problem.

Shift Delay

September/October 1990

Our 1990 300SE stays in low gear for a long time before upshifting, much different from our 1987 560SEL. No one can tell me why. Can you?

We suspect that you're experiencing a delayed shift, not from first to second but from second to third. To hasten heating of the catalytic converter for emissions purposes, the second-third shift is now delayed until a specific coolant temperature, engine load and elapsed time is attained; after that, it shifts normally. Maximum elapsed time between start-up and shift is 80 seconds. Maximum car speed, above which the shift occurs regardless of the delay process, is 30 mph. Above 86°F (30°C) the delay doesn't occur.

Harsh 190 Shifting

March/April 1986

My 190E jerks when shifted from park into reverse. The car has been in for service three times, but the problem persists.

There is a reference to this problem in the Diagnostic Reference: Sudden, Harsh Engagement in gear lever position R. The remedy is to install an additional restrictor, part number 123 277 01 39, in the oil supply bore, a simple operation. The fact that the problem is mentioned means only that it has occurred before, not that it is frequent or persistent. We have had no similar complaints.

Slow Cold Upshift

November/December 1998

When starting cold and accelerating slowly, my 1990 300E's transmission won't upshift from second to third gear until above 3,000 rpm then almost immediately shifts into fourth gear. After that, the transmission shifts normally. I changed the transmission fluid and filter, and everything looked normal. What is your diagnosis?

To warm up the catalytic converter quickly, your 1990 300E's transmission has a built-in upshift delay from second to third gear. After the first shift and some warming, the delay is not repeated. You'll get used to this; if the delay device malfunctions, you'll need only minor repairs.

Reverse Shift Delay

September/October 1992

After shifting to reverse, my 500SEC takes a few seconds to actually move. No one seems able to offer a solution. What can I do to reduce this annoying delay?

A longer delay when engaging reverse compared to the delay in engaging forward gears is inherent in the transmission design. Based on my experience, at normal temperatures it should only be a second or so. Reverse engagement requires one more element to be actuated (a multiple-disc brake) than for forward gears and requires locking the freewheeling unit. Further, the accumulator which assists shifting between forward gears is not used when engaging reverse from a standstill. The delay could be eliminated by a design change but is thought desirable for safety. Since Reverse is usually engaged from Park, the delay prevents jerking the driveline when shifting from Park to Drive or another forward gear.

A longer than normal delay may be caused by sludge or gum in the valves inside the transmission, which can only be corrected by opening it and checking the parts. I'm frequently asked about this delay, but no standard is specified for it.

Don't Try This at Home

January/February 2001

The automatic transmission in my 1982 300SD hesitates and lurches when shifting gears. This may be a common problem because I encountered it in a similar car. A friend told me about an adjustment on the transmission, but I can find no details in my shop manuals.

I think what you're describing is a transmission slip on upshift, probably most noticeable on the 2-3 shift. This is a common problem for the 722.3 transmission with the 617.95 engine in the 300SD. The 123-chassis turbodiesels have the same problem, but it's less common. The usual scenario is a 1-2 shift that snaps your neck, a 2-3 shift that slips and takes a long time to complete, and a 3-4 shift that you don't even feel. The primary culprit is excessive wear in the valve body. If you disassemble the valve body (don't try this at home), you'd find all the holes in the steel plates hammered by the check balls, so they don't seal properly, causing incorrect band and clutch engagement timing. A new valve body will make an expensive but effective improvement in shift quality.

Your friend is talking about the modulator adjustment. This affects shift harshness, but if all shifts are soft, increasing modulator pressure will stiffen all three shifts. If 1-2 is hard already, tightening the 2-3 shift will make 2-3 unbearable. If the transmission is not too far gone, a combination of vacuum valve, modulator, and control pressure cable adjustments can dramatically improve all the shifts, but this is a tricky operation.

Transmission Operation

Summerfall/Winterspring

November/December 1997

Regarding the S/W mode switch on the transmission of the new E320, I prefer the W mode because it has a hill-holder capability. It also starts in second gear, which I don't mind, but I'm told that using the W mode except in slippery conditions can damage the transmission. Is that true?

You've been badly misinformed. With the switch in the W position, the transmission starts in second gear, and shifts—up or down—are softer and occur at lower speeds than in the S mode. This means less wear and more gentle application of forces, and fuel efficiency may be slightly improved. The S mode starts in first gear and offers better performance. Check the driver's manual, and you'll see that you can use either mode anytime you want with no concern.

Manual Transmission Leak

July/August 1997

The manual transmission in my 1968 250 leaks where the shift rods enter the side of the case. Is there any way to stop this without disassembly? What lubricant should I use in it?

Sorry, but eliminating the leak requires transmission removal for replacement of the bushings and seals. Resist the temptation to try any additive aimed at stopping the leak. Currently Mercedes-Benz recommends Mercedes-Benz Transmission Fluid, part number 000 989 26 03. Because of the many lubricant formulation changes since 1968, I hesitate to suggest another lubricant.

Lifetime Transmission Fluid

January/February 1999

My 1998 E300 Turbodiesel's owner's manual indicates that the transmission has a permanent fill of automatic transmission fluid, and the cap on the automatic transmission dipstick reads, "Workshop Only." What if the transmission leaks?

You are correct about the dipstick of the 722.6 automatic transmission, which comes from the factory with a lifetime fill of special fluid used only in this transmission. According to DBAG, no other ATF should be used, and the dipstick should only be removed by a factory-trained mechanic. There is no provision for topping up the fluid except via a special funnel. In case of a leak, one or more sensors would warn the electronic control system, which would then switch to the limp-home mode. The factory's thinking is that more harm can be done by over-solicitous owners and untrained "foreign car" mechanics than can result from preventing amateur intervention. This is a bit like the elimination of oil pressure gauges.

Auto Transmission Modulation Pressure

May/June 1991

The manual for my 1981 280CE's automatic transmission (type K4C 025) calls for a modulating pressure of 9.3 psi when the car is idling and 54 psi when the accelerator is depressed. The pressure on my car doesn't drop from 54 psi when the throttle is released. The control pressure linkage is correct. Can you suggest a cause?

When checking the modulating pressure, first disconnect the vacuum hose and plug it. This will give you the actual pressure, unaffected by manifold vacuum. When checking the car on the road, you should have the vacuum connected and get the full pressure at about 35 mph with the engine at full load, that is, accelerating hard or on a hill or dragging the brakes.

Pressure should drop to 9.3 psi at idle. If your car has a steel vacuum line from the intake manifold to the modulator valve, it may be full of rust and unable to induce the necessary vacuum at the valve, a common problem as the cars age. The cure is simply a new vacuum line; if that doesn't fix things, you probably need a new modulator valve.

Transmission Service

Transmission Adjustment

November/December 1991 (Startech 1991)

My 1971 280SL's automatic transmission was recently replaced with a factory unit, but it shifts very hard from first to second and from second to third. Can it be adjusted?

These fluid coupling transmissions are very sensitive to correct linkage set-up, and it is incorrect to just reduce the modulator pressure to soften the shifts, as many unfamiliar mechanics may attempt. A specific sequence of adjustments must be closely followed prior to modulator pressure adjustment. To adjust linkage and pressures on the K4A 025 automatic transmission:

1. Connect a pressure gauge to the transmission modulator test connection.

2. Turn on the ignition. Check voltage at the throttle switch; at idle position both contacts should have voltage. Off idle, only one contact should have voltage. If necessary, adjust the throttle switch.

3. Observe the double-lift solenoid and linkage through the inspection plate on the right side of the transmission tunnel. Off idle, ensure that the solenoid goes to mid-position. If necessary, remove, disassemble, and free up the solenoid, or check the electrical circuit.

4. With the ignition on but the engine off, depress the kickdown switch with the accelerator pedal. The solenoid should move upward.

5. Start the engine and let it idle. Observe the pressure gauge. Shorten the linkage rod to the solenoid until the pressure rises, then lengthen the rod until the pressure drops. Repeat as necessary to get the linkage rod just at the pressure transition point. Important: do not lengthen the rod more than necessary.

6. For the full throttle check, disconnect and plug the vacuum line to the modulator. Start the engine, raise rpm to about 1,500 to open the idle contact. If the modulator pressure value deviates from specifications (in the technical literature), adjust it to specifications now.

7. For the kickdown check, do as above except actuate the kickdown switch with your other foot. The pressure gauge value should be higher.

Transmission Tool

November/December 1995

Your article on automatic transmissions in the May/June issue was very informative. What is the diameter of the roller used to check the VCV pressure? And where on my 1982 300SD do I connect the 10-bar gauge to check modulator pressure?

The roller is a self-made tool. It should be a disk 20 mm in diameter, 5 mm thick, with a 3.1-mm hole in the center. The gauge for checking modulator pressure is connected to the left (driver's) side of the transmission, about halfway back. Don't confuse it with the connection for governor pressure, near the front. The plug for modulating pressure is easy to see on photographs of the transmission out of the car, but in the car it is hard to see and awkward to reach.

Sticky Shift Knob

May/June 1999

I want to replace the gear shift gate insert in my 1970 280SE, but the shift knob won't come off. Is there a trick to removing it?

The shift knob on a floor-shift 108 chassis does indeed just press on. A slick way to remove it is to wrap a crescent wrench in a rag and adjust it closely around the shift lever shaft. Hit the wrench with a hammer, and the knob will pop off. If it breaks or is harmed, I believe they're available separately. A spot of Super Glue may be needed during reinstallation.

Chain failure is often caused by old chain rails breaking and getting sucked into the gears. When a new chain is installed, have the upper three rails, the tensioning rail, and the tensioner replaced, too.

Chapter 3
Fuel, Exhaust

September/October 1997

May/June 2001

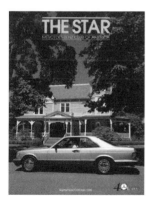

September/October 1996

Solving Hot-Start Problems

by Frank King,
Technical Editor

September/October 1997

You may have thought that hot-start problems were long ago wiped out, like smallpox, but cases involving older models still come up regularly in the mail and via telephone calls.

A hot-start problem can arise when an attempt is made to restart a gasoline engine that is at or around its normal operating temperature on a hot day and has been shut off for a short period. It goes back to the days when all cars had carburetors, and it gave rise to an urban legend, The Ice Cream Story. This tale, which bears signs of being true, was first printed in a service manual of the Holley Carburetor Co.

The Ice Cream Story involves a lady who had a custom of taking drives in the summer and stopping at the neighborhood drug store for a quart of ice cream as she neared home. She complained to her automobile dealer that sometimes the car would not restart after she bought her ice cream unless she bought vanilla. Her story made its way upward until a Holley technical representative called and asked for a demonstration.

The first drive involved a stop for vanilla. The lady went into the drug store and returned five minutes later. The car started perfectly. On the next drive the store had a special on butter pecan ice cream, which the lady bought, returning to the car 20 minutes later. The car would not start. The tech rep recognized a classic case of carburetor percolation and showed the lady the standard way of dealing with it. He also checked the store and found that since vanilla was by far

On mechanically fuel-injected 108, 109, 111, and 113-bodied cars, a hot start relay can be added to the relay rack on the left side of the engine compartment. *See Technical Reprint No. 2.*

Mike Mate

the most popular flavor, the druggist pre-packed quarts of vanilla but packed quarts of all other flavors only as customers requested them. Thus vanilla customers were served quickly, while those wanting other flavors had to let their cars soak in the sun.

The problem goes back to the nature of gasoline. Water is a simple compound that boils at 212°F at sea level. Gasoline is a blend of more than 200 individual hydrocarbons ranging from butane to methyl naphthalene. The lightest fractions of gasoline will boil at about 100°F, the heaviest at 437°F. Fifty percent of the gasoline will boil at temperatures between 170°F and 240°F.

When a car is driven long enough to reach full operating temperature on a hot day, the underhood temperatures remain reasonable because of the strong stream of air blowing through,

but when the car is stopped and the engine is turned off, underhood temperature rises rapidly, peaking in about 20 minutes. The gasoline in containers or pipes under the hood will start to boil gradually, and the pressure in the lines in a carbureted car will force the gasoline out of the carburetor jets, with the effect of flooding the carburetor. This is not true flooding, but percolation in the terminology of the carburetion industry. Techniques for dealing with this problem were developed and are now widely understood. Our interest in the problem centers around cars using fuel injection.

Mercedes-Benz gasoline injection systems require a constant supply of fuel to the engine at a certain pressure. Unlike the diesel systems, in which the supply pump is integral with the injection pump, this is provided by an electric pump or pumps at the fuel tank. As long as the engine is running, a stream of fuel is pumped from the tank to the engine; the portion not consumed by the engine is pumped back to the fuel tank. Thus the entire fuel supply is constantly circulated from the tank to the engine compartment and back.

Starting in 1968 with legislation and regulation of emissions and continuing into the 1970s with the oil embargo, gasoline refining became almost chaotic. New techniques to allow a greater amount of gasoline to be refined, combined with the switch to unleaded gasoline, caused shifts in the form of the distillation curve of gasoline at service station pumps.

The effect was most noticeable in the models with closely cowled engine compartments such as the 450SL, 450SLC, and 280SL. Underhood temperatures rose higher and more quickly. Drivers were left trying to start engines which had only foam and gasoline vapor in the fuel injection lines in the engine compartment. A multitude of remedies was suggested, most of which had no effect. The designers at the factory did come up with a real cure in 1980 and subsequent models. This was a fuel cooler which consisted of a heat exchanger that used refrigerant from the air-conditioning system to cool the fuel that was returning to the tank, thus maintaining a cool supply.

One way to trick the system was to turn the ignition key to position 2 (run) but not on to Start. The electric fuel pump can be heard running, but it turns off after about nine seconds. The key is turned to Off then back to position 2, which causes the pump to pump fresh fuel up to the engine. This procedure is repeated three or four times, then a start is attempted, usually with success.

One modification that worked well involved installing a switch to be used for just a few seconds. This switch actuated the cold start valve, which would then give a rich injection into the intake manifold. Once the engine starts firing, the fuel pump sends up a fresh supply of liquid gasoline. Mercedes-Benz made specific parts to do this on mechanically injected cars (see our *Technical Reprint No. 2*).

Any member considering buying a fuel-injected car of 1979 or earlier model year should inquire about the previous owner's experience with hot starting. The syndrome is often referred to as "vapor lock", a term created back in the days when most cars relied on vacuum devices to bring fuel from the tank to the engine. If a loop in a fuel line allowed a bubble of vapor to lodge at its top, vacuum could only stretch the bubble, not move fuel. As now used, vapor lock means the formation of excess vapor which leans the air-fuel ratio.

Lambda and Oxygen

by Frank King,
Technical Editor

*November/December
1987*

Photo in this article
by the author.

Most of us picked up our first smidgeon of Greek in school when we learned that the ratio between the circumference of a circle and its diameter is π, pronounced "pi," and that π is 3.14 or 22/7. A little later we learned that it was closer to 3.1416 but that it was a transcendental number which could never be calculated exactly. The symbol π goes back to medieval Greek being the first letter of the word "perimeter". Centuries of use have made it sacrosanct. No other Greek letter has been accorded the unique usage of π, but let's look at λ, called lambda. If you are into automobiles of the 1980's, you're bound to encounter lambda.

In automotive engineering, lambda has a single, important meaning. Gasoline powered internal combustion engines must take in a mixture of air and gasoline fuel in a ratio that can vary over only a narrow range. The air-fuel ratio is always expressed in terms of weight. The ratio at which the amount of oxygen in the air is just sufficient to burn all the fuel is called the stoichiometric ratio. Our gasoline engines can just barely run on an air-fuel ratio as lean as 18:1, called the lean misfire limit, or they can run on a mixture as rich as 6:1. Rich mixtures consume more fuel per hp per hour but give more power down to a ratio of about 12.4:1. Below this point performance declines rapidly and fuel is wasted to no positive effect. Thus for practical purposes the usable range is from 17:1 to 12:1 (Fig. 1). The stoichiometric ratio varies only slightly with different gasolines. In its technical literature, Daimler-Benz uses 14.5 as an average rule.

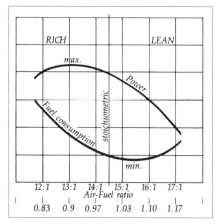

Figure 1. Air-fuel ratio vs. power and fuel consumption.

The Lambda Ratio

As the art of carburetion developed into a science, the Greek letter λ, lambda, was selected to symbolize the ratio of the quantity of air actually supplied to the engine to the quantity of air required to exactly meet the stoichiometric air-fuel ratio. In other words:

$$\lambda = \frac{\text{amount of air supplied}}{\text{theoretical air requirement}}$$

When lambda equals 1.00 the theoretically correct mixture is being supplied. When lambda is less than 1.00 (say 0.9) there is a deficiency of air, a rich mixture. When lambda is more than 1.00 (say 1.10) there is an excess of air, a lean mixture. As government regulations controlling emissions became stricter, the lambda factor and precise control of it became predominant.

Early catalytic converters were quite effective in oxidizing hydrocarbons (HC) and carbon monoxide (CO) into harmless carbon dioxide and water vapor, but they did nothing to reduce nitrogen oxide (NOx) emissions. In model year 1980, Mercedes-Benz started using a three-way catalyst that was able to greatly reduce the emissions of HC, CO and NOx. However, the successful functioning of the catalyst was absolutely

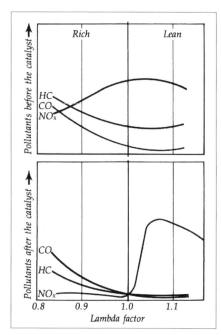

Figure 2. Lambda factor vs. pollutant emissions.

dependent on maintaining the lambda factor very close to 1.00 (Fig. 2). With a rich mixture (deficiency of air) there is more unburned HC and CO in the exhaust gas, but since rich mixtures burn cooler, there is less NOx. With a lean mixture (excess of air) there is less HC and CO in the exhaust gases, but since lean mixtures burn hotter, more NOx is formed.

The O₂ Sensor

Development of an effective lambda control unit was made possible by an ingenious device, the O₂ sensor (Fig. 3.). (O₂, the chemical symbol

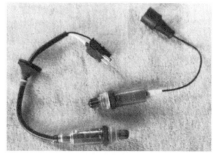

Oxygen sensors include the heated type (left, with two conductors) and unheated type (right, one conductor).

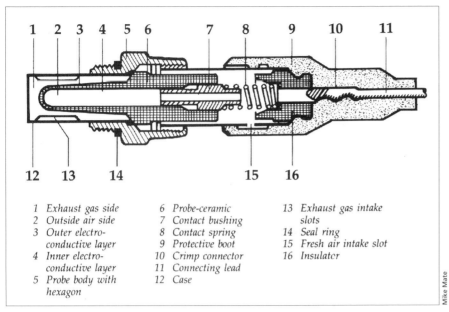

Figure 3. Typical oxygen sensor.

1 Exhaust gas side	6 Probe-ceramic	13 Exhaust gas intake slots
2 Outside air side	7 Contact bushing	14 Seal ring
3 Outer electro-conductive layer	8 Contact spring	15 Fresh air intake slot
4 Inner electro-conductive layer	9 Protective boot	16 Insulator
5 Probe body with hexagon	10 Crimp connector	
	11 Connecting lead	
	12 Case	

Mike Mate

for molecular oxygen, is used as shorthand to distinguish normal atmospheric oxygen from negatively charged oxygen ions O⁻.) The O_2 sensor consists of a thin, hollow probe of zirconium oxide ceramic in a metal case. Both inner and outer ceramic surfaces are coated with a thin layer of gas-permeable platinum. In addition the platinum on the exhaust side is protected by a porous layer of ceramic from fouling by combustion products.

This ceramic probe, though appearing rather like the ceramic insulator of a spark plug, is of an entirely different substance, which at a temperature of approximately 300°C/580°F becomes conductive to oxygen ions. The ceramic probe is housed in a metal tube to protect it from physical damage and allow it to be mounted in the exhaust pipe. Slots in the tube allow exhaust gas to circulate around the outer platinum coating. Through the metal housing the outer platinum coating is in electrical contact with ground (−) while the inner coating is connected through a bushing and spring to an outside lead (+). At operating temperatures negatively charged oxygen ions will flow from the inner to the outer coating as long as there is an excess of oxygen in the ambient air as compared to the exhaust gas.

The essential characteristic of the O_2 sensor is that when the air-fuel ratio of the mixture being consumed in the engine is stoichiometric, i.e., when lambda equals 1.00, the voltage generated by the flow of oxygen ions stabilizes at a point between 0.3 and 0.7 volts. If the mixture becomes rich, the voltage rises to almost 1.0 volts because the lack of oxygen in the exhaust speeds up the flow of ions from the inner to the outer coating. Similarly, if the mixture becomes lean, the voltage drops nearly to zero because of the increased oxygen present in the exhaust gas (Fig. 4). The O_2 sensor is very stable in the critical range in which lambda equals 1.00 but becomes extremely sensitive when

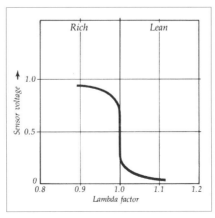

Figure 4. Lamda factor vs. sensor voltage.

any divergence from that value occurs. It gives what is, in effect, virtually a digital signal—a sharp on or off—when the mixture diverges from a lambda of 1.00, and such signals are highly intelligible to computers.

O_2 Sensor Characteristics

Before describing how the lambda control unit uses the information furnished by the O_2 sensor, let's look at a few of the unit's salient characteristics. On Mercedes-Benz cars the O_2 sensor is in the exhaust pipe just downstream of the primary catalyst or in the primary catalyst itself. It requires no routine maintenance but it does wear out. In 1980 to 1985 models a warning light, activated by a counter on the odometer, indicates that the sensor needs replacing. At 30,000 miles the light comes on and remains on until the sensor is replaced and the counter is disconnected. Starting with model year 1986, a logic circuit detects any malfunction of the sensor, and the warning light is turned on.

The sensor is easily damaged by a blow, so care must be exercised in working near it. It should never be sprayed with undercoating, rustproofing or solvents which could block the flow of outside air to it. Leaking engine oil, brake fluid or other fluids can upset its calibration. Severe damage can be caused by using the wrong gasoline. Any fuel containing lead or silicon will destroy the sensor by coating the platinum layer. If only a little lead gets into the gasoline, the damage may be limited to reducing the effectiveness of the sensor. Further driving with pure unleaded gasoline will gradually burn off the deposit if it hasn't been thoroughly baked on.

There should be no silicon in gasoline, but it may get there accidentally. A more likely source is the silicon-based gasket material sometimes used to seal valve covers, oil pans, intake manifolds and similar joints. Silicon is the principal element in glass, and when it is deposited on the surface of the sensor, it can form a glaze that destroys the sensor. Since they may be drawn into the intake and passed on to the sensor, the use of silicone sprays around the engine should be avoided.

Testing the O_2 sensor on a Mercedes-Benz is not a job for the do-it-yourselfer. In particular, no voltage should ever be applied to the sensor, either by attempting to check continuity or resistance with an ohmmeter or multi-meter or by any other means. The result will be the destruction of the sensor. It may be checked only with a special tester, following factory prescribed test procedures or by replacement with a unit known to be good.

Lambda Control and Mercedes-Benz

Lambda control was first applied to Mercedes-Benz cars in model year 1980, the same blessed year that brought the fuel cooler. These improvements were applied to both the M110 engines (280E/CE/SE) and M117 engines (450SL/SLC/SEL). The lambda control system consists of the O_2 sensor, frequency valve, throttle valve switch, oil temperature switch, voltage supply relay and excess voltage protection unit. When the O_2 sensor reaches an operating temperature of 300°C/580°F, it signals the electronic control unit if the fuel mixture is either richer or leaner than the ideal lambda value of 1.00. The electronic control unit conveys signals received from the O_2 sensor to the frequency valve in the form of electrical impulses.

The frequency valve is a solenoid valve which, depending on the impulses received from the electronic control unit, varies the differential pressure at the metering slots in the fuel distributor and thereby alters the amount of fuel injected at any given position of the metering slots. The frequency valve operates at a constant on-off frequency to control the differential pressure, but the impulses from the electronic control unit regulate the ratio of time on and off during each cycle. In normal running the ratio will be around 50-percent

on; a 60-percent on-off ratio indicates a rich mixture. Put more simply, the frequency valve makes the mixture richer or leaner. During operation the electronic control unit monitors the function of the O_2 sensor. If a malfunction occurs, the frequency valve is sent impulses at a fixed on-off ratio which allows the engine to continue to run, although not at its optimum efficiency.

Since driving conditions sometimes require the engine to operate temporarily above or below a lambda of 1.00, i.e., leaner or richer than the ideal, a throttle valve switch is installed in the throttle valve housing to handle either of two conditions: idle or full throttle. At idle the throttle valve switch has the effect of limiting the operating range of the O_2 sensor through the electronic control unit, thus eliminating fluctuation of engine speed when idling. At full throttle a contact causes the electronic control unit to function at a constant 60-percent on-off ratio, i.e., a rich mixture.

Screwed into the oil filter housing is the oil temperature switch. At engine oil temperatures below approximately 16°C/60°F this switch connects the electronic control unit to ground, producing a fixed 60-percent on-off ratio. Above 16°C/60°F, the oil temperature switch opens, and the electronic control unit resumes its normal cycling.

The lambda control system receives voltage from the voltage supply relay, behind the glove box. To prevent damage to components of the lambda control system in the event of overloading the electrical system of the vehicle (e.g., fast charging of the battery, loose battery connection, etc.), an excess voltage protection unit is connected ahead of the voltage supply relay.

Model by Model

In model year 1981 the lambda control system was continued unchanged on the M110 engine. In this year the M116 engine was reintroduced in the

380SL, 380SLC and 380SEL. The latter was the first of the 126-series cars, the 116-series having been dropped. The M116 engine also used the lambda control system. On the 380SL and 380SLC the O_2 sensor was still placed downstream of the primary catalyst, but on the 380SEL it was in the primary catalyst. The M116 engine had a new idle speed control which required an input from the lambda control unit.

For model year 1982 the M110 engine was dropped from the U.S. line of cars and the 380SLC was replaced by the newly developed 380SEC. There were no changes from the lambda control system used in 1981 nor to any systems that received outputs from it.

For model year 1983 there was no change in the U.S. line of cars and no change in the lambda control system. However, the electronic idle speed control, which depends in part on output from the lambda control system, was modified. The changes enabled it to stabilize idle speed in response to engagement of the air-conditioning compressor, movement of the gear shift lever from P or N to a driving position, or a partial load (fast idle) throttle movement.

The M117 engine returned to the U.S. line in model year 1984 in the 500SEL and 500SEC, having grown to displace five liters. The M116 engine remained available in the 380SE and 380SL. These cars all used the same lambda control system as in 1983. The new 1984 190E 2.3 and its M102 engine brought new emphasis on lambda control. The M102's fuel injection system, designated CIS-E, is a further development of the CIS (Continuous Injection System) used by DBAG since model year 1976. The system of mechanical injection remained unchanged, but the correction functions were now electronically controlled, with idle speed control and lambda control being integrated into the new electronic control unit. The frequency valve was eliminated and its function taken over by the electrohydraulic actuator. This unit, flanged onto the fuel distributor, operates as a solenoid-actuated plate valve to regulate the differential pressure. Naturally, the O_2 sensor becomes even more important. In the 190E 2.3 it is immediately downstream of the intersection of the two exhaust pipes and is now electrically heated to ensure virtually immediate effectiveness of the O_2 sensor after the engine is started.

Model year 1985 brought only minor changes to lambda-related functions. For M116 and M117 engines an acceleration enrichment switch was added. This vacuum-operated switch grounds the lambda control unit when acceleration is demanded by the driver's foot (or the cruise control), causing a change to a 60-percent on-off ratio (rich mixture) until the vacuums within the switch equalize through an orifice. For the M102 engine, internal changes were made in the electronic control unit which altered the method of limiting maximum engine speed and the cold-start system.

Four new gasoline engines were introduced in model year 1986, and the M102 was carried over. New were the 16-valve M102, the M103 in the 300E, the 4.2-liter M116 and a 5.6-liter M117. The 3.8 and 5.0-liter engines were dropped from the U.S. line. All the new engines used CIS-E fuel injection with lambda control similar to that on the M102 engine, with electrically heated O_2 sensors. A warning light indicated malfunctioning of the O_2 sensor, replacing the previously used mileage counter on all models except the 190E 2.3.

Model year 1987 saw the introduction of another new gasoline engine, the 2.6-liter version of the M103, sold in either the 201 or 124-series cars. Its CIS-E and lambda control systems were almost identical with those used in the 300E. All other engines retained CIS-E and lambda control unchanged from 1986, except that the 190E 2.3 also got the malfunction warning light for the O_2 sensor.

How to Adjust Mechanical Fuel-Injection Systems for Maximum Power

by Stu Ritter, Technical Editor

November/December 2003

Photos in this article by the author.

Proper adjustments can make your mechanically fuel-injected engine run much better.

A question on my Mercedes-Benz e-mail list (mercedes@mercedeslist. com) asked how to tune the fuel-injection pump of a 1971 280SL for maximum power. Few mechanics who were around during that era and knew the procedure are still working. The information below consolidates Mercedes-Benz technical schooling, the technical literature, and 30 years of experience.

The car's owner asked how the injection pump should be adjusted to get the best performance. We'll start at the beginning and describe all adjustments, to both the linkage and the injection pump. Without correctly adjusted linkage, you are wasting your time fiddling with the pump. A properly set 280SL runs strongly; here's how you can make it do so.

Basic Tune-Up

Before starting, be sure the engine is tuned exactly to specs. Check the timing advance—mechanical and vacuum—to be sure they are exactly right. As you rev the engine, make sure the mechanical advance reads the correct number of degrees for the rpm shown. Make sure the distributor vacuum unit starts advancing when it should and that the total vacuum advance is correct. For later cars with vacuum retard, make sure the amount of retard is correct and that the plumbing is correctly installed so that retard is lost as soon as the accelerator is depressed. Be sure the electronic switching gear that controls

the vacuum retard works correctly and that the retard cancels under the right conditions. In our shop we would pull the distributor, chuck it up in the distributor machine, and make sure all the numbers were on spec. If you don't test, you don't know.

Valve clearance should be set to exactly 0.003-in intake and 0.008-in exhaust. This means a very tight pull on the feeler gauge with the cam lobe absolutely perpendicular to the rocker arm. When the valves are properly adjusted, the engine has a distinct sewing machine note. If valve clearance is loose, the sound is different, much more metallic and clattery. To make sure you use the correct pull-through force on your feeler gauge, set a micrometer to the thickness of the feeler gauge and try to pull the gauge through. Most do-it-yourselfers set the clearance too loose. Accuracy demands a very tight feel, and a feeler gauge is capable of accuracy to one ten-thousandth of an inch.

Cam timing should be set with a dial indicator, right on spec. Instructions are in the 108-109-111-113 service manual. Dialing-in the cam timing is mandatory for maximum performance. The procedure may seem daunting the first time, but you'll be surprised how easy it is. Mercedes-Benz cam timing specifications are measured at 2-mm lift. The dial indicator simply tells you when you have arrived at the 2-mm lift point. Compare your timing with the specs in the *Technical Data Manual*, and adjust the camshaft using offset keys to zero-in on the proper spec. If you really want to blueprint the system, measure all the timing specs.

Re-torque the intake manifold nuts. Besides making sure there are no intake or exhaust leaks, this tightens one of the main injection pump linkage pivot supports.

The Linkage

Now for the fun stuff. First things first. Examine the throttle linkage

(Photo 1) carefully. All adjustments should be checked, and the linkage should be lubricated using automatic transmission fluid (ATF). Greases other than thin synthetics get sticky when ambient temperatures plummet. The linkage is adjusted from the top down.

The linkage must be mechanically tight and free from play everywhere, so any balls or sockets showing play must be replaced. All throttle linkage parts are available. Most of the balls and sockets screw in, but some must be ground off to replace them. The replacement ball has a screw thread on the back side that uses a nut to hold it in place of the ground-off rivet.

The fit of the pivot bearing in the support bracket on the spark plug side and in the bracket on the intake manifold is very important, which is one reason you re-torque the intake manifold. The brass pivot balls wear because many mechanics don't clean and grease them when they take off

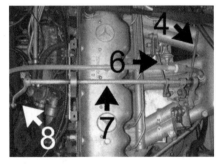

Photo 1. 280SL throttle linkage: 4) air regulating rod; 6) throttle linkage pull rod; 7) regulating shaft (cross shaft); 8) injection pump regulating rod.

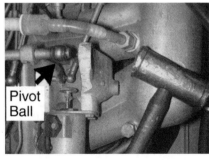

Photo 2. Use brass hammer to remove cross shaft.

the linkage to remove the valve cover. To remove the cross shaft, use a brass hammer to tap the end of it where it butts out of the bracket (toward the driver's side), and it will pop out of the manifold pivot point. (See Photo 2.)

Next, unbolt the bracket on the spark plug side. Make sure you don't lose the two centering nuts, which help keep the bracket rigid and in the proper position. The pivot bearing is held in place by a circlip. Remove the circlip, and slide the pivot bearing off the cross shaft. If previous mechanics used a steel hammer instead of a brass one, the end of the shaft may have to be filed to remove "divots" from the steel hammer to let the pivot ball come off. This pivot is very easy to replace.

The pivot bearing in the bracket on the spark plug side is a bit different. It doesn't look as if you can replace it, but you can. Once you pull the cross shaft out of it, just pop out the bearing. To remove the cross shaft from the bracket, drive out the roll pin on the injection pump rod arm (#8 in the illustration 07-14/8 in the manual, Photo 1 in this article). Pull the arm off the shaft, and the shaft will come out of the body of the bracket. (See Photo 3.)

Scribe a mark on the arm and shaft so you reassemble them in the right position. Then fit a large tapered punch into the hole in the brass pivot bushing and pop it out. Notice that it can only go in one direction. Pop the new one in. Pivot balls are cheap, and keeping the linkage free of play makes a huge difference in how the engine runs. (See Photo 4.)

Throttle Stop Screw

Make sure the injection pump lever operates smoothly, without glitches. Sometimes the lever doesn't hit the stop on the pump until you engage the starter (the start enrichment solenoid pulls it back). Make sure the throttle plate stop screw is set correctly. (See Photo 5). That screw's only job is to make sure the throttle plate isn't grabbed by the throttle housing during cool-down; it has nothing to do with idle speed. Loosen the lock nut, and back out the screw until it no

longer contacts the throttle plate arm. Slowly advance the screw until it just touches the arm, then perhaps one-tenth turn more. With the linkage rod disconnected, push the throttle plate arm toward the closed position, and it should almost get tight in the bore of the throttle body.

Throttle-Closing Damper

If the engine has a throttle-closing damper, make sure the stroke of the damper is 4 to 5 mm; the stroke is adjusted with the double nuts on the end. (See Photo 6.)

With all upper linkages (air, fuel, and regulating) rebuilt and removed, a special tool fits through the hole in the bearing bracket on the intake manifold (Figure 07-14/7 in the manual). If you

Photo 3. Roll pin holds arm on shaft.

Photo 4. Pivot ball and bushing.

Photo 5. Throttle stop screw setting.

don't have the tool, you can make one out of a small piece of tubing. This sets the zero position for the linkage. If this zero hole is not in the bracket, set the injection pump rod to 233 mm, and we'll go from there. (See Photo 7.)

Set the linkages to fit tension-free, then remove the locating tool and let the linkage move to its stop. While moving the linkage, watch it carefully; make sure both the air (throttle plate) and fuel (injection pump) activating levers move at the same time when you pull rod 6 (Figure 07-14/8 in the manual, Photo 1 in this article). If one leads the other, adjust the rod lengths so both activating levers (air, fuel) move at the same time. Then pull rod 6 all the way to full throttle, and make sure both air and fuel levers rest on the full-load stops, except that the air venturi lever should have about 1-mm play.

The next step depends on which transmission your car has. The instructions in the manual are clear about how to adjust each of the throttle pedal linkages. The adjustments take care of free-play and pre-load for the automatic transmission linkage.

Photo 6. Throttle-closing damper.

Photo 7. Hole in bearing bracket.

Every time the valves are adjusted, perform this linkage procedure when the valve cover is reinstalled. Clean, lube, and check everything for play. The E service covers this work. We kept all linkage parts in stock, as they do get used. Replace any bent linkage pieces. Precise control of the injection pump demands absolutely straight linkage. If your linkage pieces are bent, you can use a set of protractors to test and adjust the correlation between the air and fuel rods, but it is far easier to replace the bent linkage. A chart in the workshop manual gives throttle plate openings vs. injection pump lever movement in degrees. Before doing anything else, be sure the linkage is correct. Make no assumptions. If you don't correlate bent linkage, nothing else you do will make sense.

The Injection Pump

Adjusting the injection pump requires a portable exhaust gas analyzer, a vacuum gauge, and an electronic tachometer for the road test procedure; there can be no substitutions. Portable CO (carbon monoxide) analyzers can be found used; many garages have them lying around because they are no longer used very often. Inexpensive versions are available from the sports car racing community.

We made a bracket to hang below the dash in the middle of the car to hold the three instruments so driver and passenger could both see them. While driving, you use the throttle and the brake pedal to hold a certain vacuum level (engine load) at a certain rpm. The passenger can record the exhaust gas reading. Make sure the brakes do not overheat during this road test.

The road test procedure in the *Technical Data Manual* sets idle, lower partial-load, upper partial-load, and full-load specs. Idle CO, set with the idle mixture screw, is measured with engine in neutral at 800 rpm with the engine oil at 80°C. Don't adjust the engine until the oil is at operating temperature. Remove the air filter on the warm-up device (Photo 8), and make no adjustments until there is

absolutely zero air flow through the warm-up device. This insures that the warm-up thermostat has indeed closed the added air valve, taking the engine off choke. Make no adjustments until the added air is stopped.

Use the throttle and brake during the road test to balance engine load (vacuum) against rpm, then take the exhaust gas readings. Back streets work well, as the required road speeds are not high except for the full-load test.

Full-load is adjusted by removing the 5-mm Allen bolt from the upper inner corner of the rear of the governor body at the back of the injection pump. Stick a long, thin screwdriver into the pump and try

Photo 8. Wrench on added air filter at rear of injection pump.

Photo 9. 5-mm Allen bolt covering access to main rack adjusting screw on injection pump.

Photo 10. Governor with idle screw in center, lower and upper partial-load screws around it.

to find the full-load stop screw in the middle of the rack (extremely hard the first time), and turn it in the direction shown in the manual. (See Photo 9.)

The full-load stop screw affects the pump's entire range. One or two clicks at a time is the maximum adjustment. Record every adjustment on paper. Keeping the adjustments in your head won't work. An accurate record of where you came from and where you went prevents you from getting lost in a very expensive place. Correcting a misadjusted fuel-injection pump requires a lot of road testing by a professional.

The Governor

To adjust the lower and upper partial-load screws, in the middle of the governor spring set (Photo 10), you will probably need to remove the back of the injection pump. Except on the M100 pump, these screws can't be reached by removing the idle mixture adjustment screw. The silver screws are the upper partial-load screws, and the black ones adjust the lower partial-load. The screws are opposite each other. All adjustments are made with the engine stopped.

The idle-adjusting screwdriver is a built-in spring-loaded tool that is normally disengaged. You must push it into the idle screw and rotate it until it clicks into place. Adjustments are made with the engine stopped. As the engine runs, the governor and the idle mixture screw both spin, so if you try to engage the idle mixture screw with the screwdriver while the engine is running, it will instantly back out until it hits the rear cover of the injection pump. Then you will have to remove the rear cover of the injection pump to reinstall the screw (Photo 11).

Take readings in all four operating ranges and compare them to the specs in the *Technical Data Manual*. The table below covers the 230SL, 250SL, 250SE, 300SE/C, 300SEb, and 300SEL along with the 280SE/8, 280SL/8, and 300SEL/8.

Many pumps that we adjusted over the years were found to be correct at idle and at full load but lean in the

For Six-Cylinder Models:

Engine condition for test	Model years 1968–69	Model years 1970–72
Full load 3,000 rpm, 3rd gear	2.0 to 4.0 %	2.0 to 5.0 %
Lower partial load 1,500 rpm, 3rd gear, 300-mm mercury	1.5 to 3.0 %	0.2 to 1.0 %
Upper partial load 3,000 rpm, 3rd gear, 300-mm mercury	0.2 to 1.5 %	0.1 to 1.0 %
Idle speed	3.5 to 4.5 %	2.0 to 5.0 %

For 300SEL 6.3 and 600:

Engine condition for test	Model years 1968–69	Model years 1970–72
Full load 2,000 rpm, 4th gear	2.5 to 4.0 %	2.0 to 4.0 %
Lower partial load, 1,500 rpm, 3rd gear, 400-mm mercury	0.5 to 2.0 %	0.1 to 1.0 %
Upper partial load, 2,500 rpm, 3rd gear, 400-mm mercury	0.2 to 1.0 %	0.1 to 0.6 %
Idle speed	3.5 to 5.5 %	3.5 to 5.5 %

lower and upper partial-load ranges, causing strange running problems. If the middle ranges were even slightly out of spec, the engine would run fine but wouldn't make full power through the midrange. Proper adjustment takes time, especially if you must remove the back of the pump to make the midrange adjustments.

After the road test, compare your numbers to the charts above. Think about which screws require movement. Realize that moving the full-load stop screw affects the mixture across the entire range. It takes time to guess how many clicks of each screw move the mixture in each range because the

adjustment varies for each injection pump; there is no set number. Play with both the idle and full-load screws, the easiest to get to, and see what the reaction to adjustment is.

Cold-Start Valve

If the mixture doesn't react correctly and seems slightly erratic, check for leaks at the cold-start valve, which will cause higher and perhaps erratic CO readings. To check for leaks, remove the 7-mm-headed bolt in the middle of the valve, then, with the ignition on and the fuel pump running, touch the hole to see if fuel is present. Any

fuel there indicates a leaking cold-start valve. (See Photo 12.)

Book time for this procedure is 2 to 4 hours, depending on how much has to be adjusted. Using the specifications from the exhaust gas/roller stand/dyno chart in the *Technical Data Manual* and the data from road test, you can set the injection pump exactly where it needs to be for maximum power in all speed ranges. This procedure cannot be done on a fuel-injection pump stand, only on the engine that the pump is mated to. This takes into account variances within the engine, the injection pump, and the injection nozzles. Setting the system's CO specs is the ultimate tune-up.

To set the warm-up mixture (rich/lean) and warm-up engine speed, see the manual; use a portable gas analyzer to bring the warm-up device into line. There are shims for both the cut-out temperature and the mixture while warming up.

Taking the time to set a fuel-injection pump this way makes an amazing difference in the feel of an engine; really hard pulls through the entire gear range are possible in a 280SL. All transitions—from idle to lower partial, to upper partial, and to full load—are strong. A car set up this way will usually chirp the rear tires on second to third gear shifts.

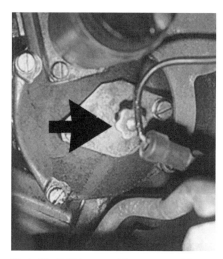

Photo 11. Built-in screwdriver engages idle mixture adjustment screw in governor.

Photo 12. Remove this bolt to test cold-start valve for leaks.

Diagnosing Pre-Glow Systems, Part I

by Frank King,
Technical Editor

*July/August
1996*

One great virtue of the passenger car diesel engine is that the fuel is ignited by the heat of compression rather than electrically—without spark plugs, ignition coils, high-tension cables, capacitors, distributors, contact breakers, or trigger points. One disadvantage of compression ignition is that it does not work in a cold engine, requiring help to overcome the dissipation of heat to the cold engine. In our engines this assistance takes the form of an electrical pre-heating system.

The diesel pre-heating system is relatively simple and trouble-free, requiring no regular maintenance. Still, sometimes a diesel engine does not start or starts only with difficulty. Assuming that the battery can supply sufficient energy and that the engine oil is of suitable viscosity, suspicion will fall on the pre-heating system. This article describes diagnosis of pre-heating system complaints in engines with the glow plugs connected in series, i.e., model years 1958 through 1979. An article to follow will cover engines with glow plugs in parallel.

First Group: Pre-heat / Starting Switch-Operated

This group includes the 190D, 200D, 220D, and 240D with engines 621, 615, and 616, model years 1958 through 1976. The wiring diagram for these pre-heating systems is in Figure 1. Complaints to be dealt with are no start even though the engine turns over at a reasonable starting speed, or hard starting. The only instrument

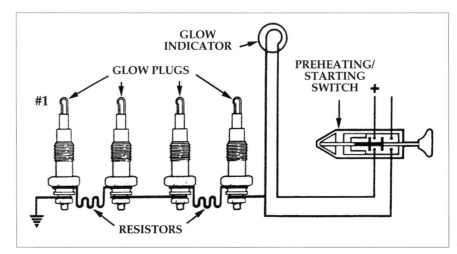

Fig. 1. 1958 through 1976 190D, 200D, 220D, and 240D; engines 621, 615, 616.

needed is a simple voltmeter with a range of 0 to 15 volts. Test procedure is 1) pull the pre-heating/starting switch to the Pre-Glow position, and 2) measure the voltage at the input (+) position of the rear (#4) glow plug.

If the voltmeter indicates approximately 8.5 volts, the glow system is OK; check the fuel system, pump timing, and engine compression. If the voltmeter indicates approximately 12 volts, an open circuit exists between the rear glow plug and the ground at the front of the engine. Connect the negative lead of the voltmeter to ground, and check voltage at input and output connections of each glow plug. When the voltmeter reads zero, the open is at that point.

Diagnosing Pre-Glow Systems

If the voltmeter indicates zero volts, an open circuit exists between the rear glow plug and the input from battery + (positive). Pull the pre-heating/starting switch out fully (engaging the starter), and measure voltage at the input of the rear glow plug. If the result is approximately 8 to 10 volts, you have an open glow indicator, open pre-heating/starting switch, or open

wire. If voltage is zero, you have either a defective pre-heating/starting switch or an open wire.

If the voltmeter indicates other than 8.5, 12, or zero volts, the circuit resistance is incorrect. Check all connections for looseness or corrosion. Remove the glow plugs, and check their condition. Clean carbon from glow plug holes with special reamer, part number 617 589 00 53 00.

Second Group: Key-Operated, First Version

This group of cars includes the 1975 and 1976 300D, with engine 617.91. These cars had the first version of the key-operated, series-connected glow plugs, identified by the grounding of the first cylinder glow plug through the thermo-time switch. The wiring diagram for this system is in Figure 2. If the complaints are no start or hard starting, proceed as follows:

1) turn the ignition switch to Pre-Glow position, and 2) measure voltage at the input (+) connection of the rear glow plug.

If the voltmeter indicates approximately 10.5 volts, the glow plug circuit is OK; check the fuel

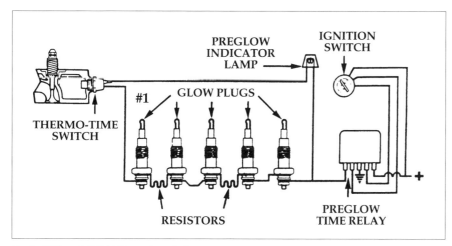

Fig. 2. 1975 and 1976 300D; engine 617.91.

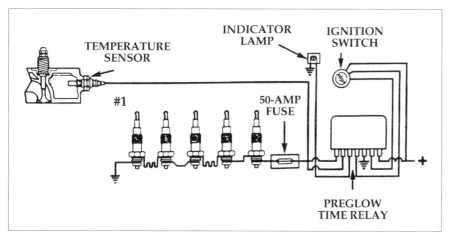

Fig. 3. 1977–79 240D (engine 616.912) and 300D/CD/TD (engine 617.912).

Third Group: Key-Operated, Second Version

This group of cars includes the 240D, with engine 616.912, and the 300D/CD/TD, with engine 617.912, all from model years 1977 to 1979. These cars had the second version of the key-operated, series-connected glow plugs, identified by the separate 50-amp fuse on the rear wall of the engine compartment. The wiring diagram for this system is in Figure 3. If the complaints are no start or hard starting, proceed as follows: 1) turn the ignition switch to Pre-Glow position, then 2) measure voltage at the input of the 50-amp fuse.

If the voltmeter indicates approximately 10.5 volts, the glow plug circuit is OK; check the fuel system, pump timing, and engine compression. If the voltmeter indicates approximately 12 volts, an open circuit exists between the rear glow plug and the ground at the front of the engine, #1 glow plug. Connect the negative lead of the voltmeter to ground, and check voltage as for the first version above.

If the voltmeter indicates zero volts, there is an open circuit between the rear glow plug and the input from battery positive (+). Check the 50-amp fuse. If it is OK, install a new pre-glow time relay and re-test. If the reading is still zero, check for an open wire. If the voltmeter indicates other than 10.5, 12, or zero volts, the circuit resistance is incorrect; check as advised for the first group.

Diagnosing Pre-Glow Systems

If the engine starts, but the indicator lamp does not light, 1) unplug the wire from the temperature sensor, and connect the wire to ground, then 2) turn ignition switch to the Pre-Glow position. If the indicator lamp lights, the temperature sensor is defective. If not, either the bulb or the pre-glow time relay is defective, or there is an open wire.

system, pump timing, and engine compression. If the voltmeter indicates approximately 12 volts, an open circuit exists between the rear glow plug and the ground at the front of the engine, #1 glow plug. Connect the negative lead of the voltmeter to ground, and check voltage at the input and output of each glow plug. When the voltmeter reads zero, the open is at that point. A 12-volt reading at the output of the front glow plug indicates a defective thermo-time switch.

If the voltmeter indicates zero, there is an open circuit between the rear glow plug and the input from battery positive (+). Install a new

pre-glow time relay, and re-test. If the reading is still zero volts, check for an open wire.

Diagnosing Pre-Glow Systems

If the voltmeter indicates other than 10.5, 12, or zero volts, the circuit resistance is incorrect; check as advised for the first group.

If the engine starts, but the indicator lamp does not light, proceed as follows: 1) unplug and ground the lamp wire at the thermo-time switch, then 2) turn the ignition switch to Pre-Glow position. If the indicator lamp lights, the thermo-time switch is defective. If the indicator lamp doesn't light, the bulb is defective or there is an open wire.

Tune-Up, Anyone?

Before the transistor was invented (1948) and found its way into every phase of civilized existence, there was a ritual known as "taking the car in for a tune-up." Tune-up is defined in the dictionary as "...adjustment of a motor or engine to put it in efficient working order."

In those good old days it was understood that a tune-up included installing new ignition contact points, condenser (capacitors were for radio buffs), and spark plugs, although spark plugs that seemed in good condition might just be cleaned and re-gapped. Also included was adjustment of the carburetor and idle speed. If the customer complained about low power or pinging of the engine under load, the spark timing would be checked and adjusted.

No routine maintenance jobs — checking the battery, fluid levels in the transmission and rear end, coolant, or belt (note that that is singular)— were included. A tune-up definitely did not include an oil change, chassis lubrication, or brake adjustment.

Today we hear people say that they had the car in for a tune-up, but what does that mean? The standard Mercedes-Benz lubrication service includes no adjustments. The maintenance service, recommended at 15,000-mile intervals, includes at least 50 inspections. (We refer here to Mercedes-Benz service applicable to model years 1986 and onward.) If you watch this job being done by a competent, conscientious technician, you will be satisfied that his work is worth the price. All fluid level checks include corrections as required.

For the modern equivalent of a tune-up, you need to take the car to your service facility and complain that it is just not running right. This requires specifics such as: the idle is rough, pick-up is poor, cannot exceed X miles per hour, fuel economy is falling, engine is running hot, engine pings, engine stumbles or stalls. You are now inviting diagnosis and should expect to pay for anything beyond an offhand opinion.

Suppose your 1991 300E has covered 73,000 miles, and you experience rough idling and stumbling when the engine is not fully warmed. At your service facility the car will be checked by several diagnostic devices. There is no way to guess what the machines may say. Maybe they'll call for new spark plugs, but they may also indicate other things not up to spec. No longer can you just replace everything that might be below standard. Unless your car has a simple coil/points/plugs ignition and a single carburetor, the old tune-up is a thing of the past.

Diagnosing Pre-Glow Systems, Part II

by Frank King,
Technical Editor

*September/October
1996*

In the previous issue we described the procedure for diagnosing diesel pre-glow systems in which the glow plugs are connected in series. This article carries on with systems in which the glow plugs are connected in parallel.

When Mercedes-Benz introduced diesel-powered passenger cars, the state of development of glow plugs limited the voltage and current that could be applied to an individual plug. Consequently, not only did the plugs have to be connected in series, but heavy iron wire resistors had to be included in the series circuit. These resistors produced substantial heat which was wasted on the outside air. A further disadvantage was that if one plug was bad, the whole circuit was broken, just like the old Christmas tree lights in which the whole string went out if any single bulb burned out.

Development of the sheathed-element glow plug, also known as the pin-type or pencil-type, significantly improved diesel engine starting qualities. This plug heats more quickly to a higher temperature and is much more resistant to combustion chamber conditions. Procedures for diagnosing and solving problems with these systems follow.

First Group: 1978–80

This group includes the 1978–80 300SD with engine 617.950, the 1980 240D with engine 616.912, and the 1980 300D/CD/TD with engine 617.912. The wiring diagram for these pre-heating systems is in Figure 1. The first complaint to be dealt with is no start, indicator lamp blinks for 30

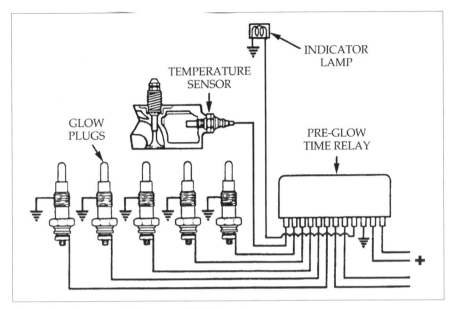

Fig. 1. Glow plug system in first group, 1978–80 models.

seconds with key in pre-glow position. The test procedure is 1) turn ignition switch to the Pre-Glow position, and 2) measure voltage at input of the 80-amp fuse inside the cover of the pre-glow time relay.

If the voltmeter indicates zero volts, an open circuit exists between the fuse and input from battery positive; you will have to trace the circuit back to the battery. If the voltmeter indicates approximately 12 volts, measure the voltage at the output of the fuse. Zero volts means the fuse is open; battery voltage (11.5-12 volts) means the pre-glow time relay is defective.

If the complaint is engine starts, indicator lamp blinks for 30 seconds after engine starts, you will need either an inductive pick-up ammeter (preferred) or an ohmmeter. The preferred procedure is 1) clamp inductive ammeter pick-up around the lead of a glow plug, 2) turn ignition key to Pre-Glow position 2, and 3) read the ammeter after 10–20 seconds. If the indication is more than 15 amps, the glow plug is defective. If the indication is less than 8 amps, check the glow plug lead; if it is OK, replace the glow plug.

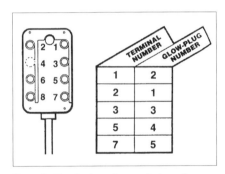

Figure 2. Terminal numbers and glow plug numbers, 1978–80 models.

The alternate test procedure using an ohmmeter will not determine actual heat output of the glow plugs, which if low may cause hard starting at cold temperatures. First, disconnect the large connector at the pre-glow time relay, then measure the resistance between ground and terminals 1-2-3-5 (and 7 if it is a 5-cylinder engine). See Figure 2. If the indication is infinity (∞), the glow plug or wiring is defective. If the indication is one ohm or less at all terminals, the pre-glow time relay is defective.

If the complaint is engine starts, indicator lamp does not light, the

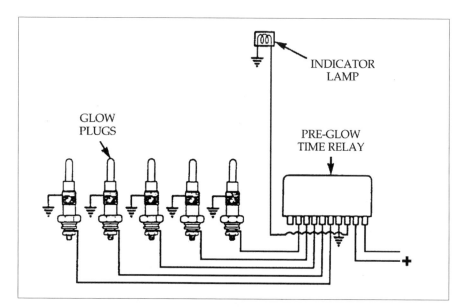

Fig. 3. Glow plug system in second group, 1981–88 models.

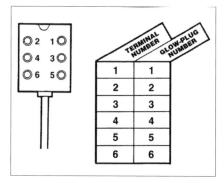

Figure 4. Terminal numbers and glow plug numbers, 1981–88 models.

test procedure is 1) turn the ignition switch to Pre-Glow position, then 2) disconnect the lamp wire at the temperature sensor and connect it to ground. If the lamp comes on, the temperature sensor is defective. If the lamp stays off, remove the small connector from the pre-glow time relay. Measure the resistance between terminal 1 of the small connector and ground. If the indication is infinity (∞), check the indicator bulb and check for an open wire. If the indication is 100 ohms or less, the pre-glow time relay is defective.

Second Group, 1981–88

This group includes the 1981–83 240D (engine 616), the 1981–85 300D/CD/TD /SD (engine 617), and 1984–88 cars with engines 601, 602, 603, and 606 (190D 2.2, 190D 2.5, 190D 2.5 Turbo, 300D 2.5 Turbo, E300 Diesel, 300D Turbo, 300TD Turbo, 300SDL Turbo, 350SD Turbo, 350SDL Turbo, 300SD, S350 Turbo, and E300 Diesel). Figure 3 is the wiring diagram for these pre-heating systems.

The first complaint to be dealt with is no start, lamp does not light. The test procedure is 1) turn ignition switch to Pre-Glow position, and 2) measure voltage at the input of the 80-amp fuse inside the cover of the pre-glow time relay. If the voltmeter indicates zero volts, an open circuit exists between the fuse and input from battery positive; trace the wiring back through the connector on the right-hand wheelwell to the battery. If the voltmeter indicates approximately 12 volts, measure voltage at the output of the 80-amp fuse. A reading of zero volts indicates a defective 80-amp fuse. A reading of approximately 12 volts indicates a defective pre-glow time relay.

If the complaint is hard starting, lamp on or off, the preferred test procedure is 1) clamp the inductive ammeter pick-up around the lead of a glow plug, 2) turn the ignition key to Pre-Glow position 2, and 3) read the ammeter after 10–20 seconds. If the reading is more than 15 amps, the glow plug is defective. If the reading is less than 8 amps, check the glow plug lead; if it is OK, replace the glow plug.

An alternate test procedure using an ohmmeter does not determine actual heat output of the glow plugs, which if low may cause hard starting at cold temperatures. First, remove the large connector from the pre-glow time relay, then measure resistance between ground and terminals 1-2-3-4 (and 5 on 5-cylinder engines, 6 on 6-cylinder engines). See Figure 4. If the reading is infinity (∞), the glow plug or wiring to it is defective. If the reading is one ohm or less at all terminals, the pre-glow time relay is defective.

If the complaint is engine starts, indicator lamp does not light, the test procedure is 1) remove the small connector from the pre-glow time relay, and 2) measure resistance between ground and terminal 3 of the small connector. If the reading is infinity (∞), the bulb is defective or the wire to it is open. If the reading is less than 100 ohms, the pre-glow time relay is defective.

Third Group, 1989 and Later

Basic diagnostic procedures for pre-heating systems in this group are the same as for the preceding group, with certain changes. The pre-glow system provides up to 30 seconds of pre-glow time if needed and also provides an after-glow time of up to 180 seconds. Actual times are determined by engine coolant temperature as sensed by the ECT sensor. The heating portion of the pre-glow plugs is reduced to 23 mm from the previous 27 mm.

Each glow plug is monitored by a microprocessor in the pre-glow time relay. In addition, with the engine running, the glow plugs are continuously monitored by a low test current. The pre-glow indicator lamp will light for approximately a minute if one or more glow plugs fails (engine running).

The pre-glow circuit is protected from short circuits, but instead of the 80-amp fuse, an electronic pre-

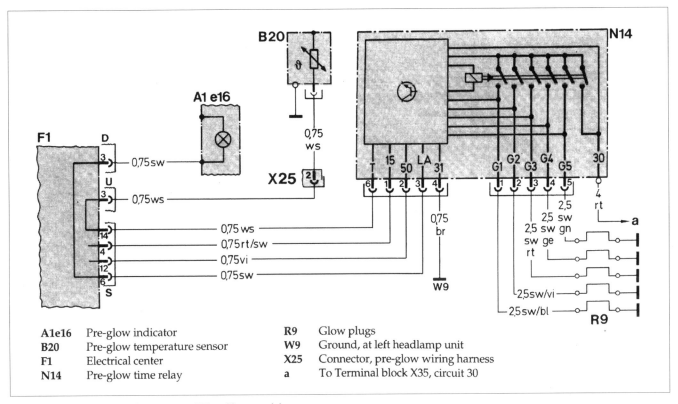

Fig. 5. Wiring diagram, pre-glow system, 1989 and later models.

A1e16	Pre-glow indicator	**R9**	Glow plugs
B20	Pre-glow temperature sensor	**W9**	Ground, at left headlamp unit
F1	Electrical center	**X25**	Connector, pre-glow wiring harness
N14	Pre-glow time relay	**a**	To Terminal block X35, circuit 30

glow system is used; see Figure 5. If a short circuit occurs, the circuit is interrupted. After the short circuit is repaired, the relay is operational again. To reset it, the key in the steering lock must be turned back to position 0.

The pre-glow indicator malfunction procedure is:

1. Lamp is off during pre-glow time or comes on for approximately a minute with engine running. Possible causes: one or several glow plugs or the pre-glow time relay may be defective. Remedy: check current draw of each glow plug (must be more than 8 but less than 15 amps) or replace the pre-glow time relay.

2. Lamp is off during pre-glow time or with engine running. Possible causes: bulb defective, open circuit to lamp, or defective pre-glow time relay. Remedy: Check the bulb and wiring for continuity; replace the pre-glow time relay.

3. Lamp is on continuously, engine starts normally. Possible cause: sticking of pre-glow time relay. Remedy: replace the pre-glow time relay.

4. Lamp is off continuously, engine does not start or is hard to start, engine hesitates, may emit blue smoke. Possible causes: Short circuit at one or more glow plugs, open circuit to lamp, or defective bulb; defective pre-glow time relay. Remedy: check current draw of individual glow plugs, check the bulb and wiring for continuity, replace the pre-glow time relay.

Turbocharger Repair

James A. Mahaffey, Contributing Editor

March/April 1996

Photos in this article by the author.

The turbocharger is probably the best innovation in diesel engines since powdered coal was dropped from the fuels list back in 1893. Efforts to double the power of a diesel by supercharging the intake air using an exhaust-gas turbine began early this century, but the concept proved impractical until high-temperature alloys were developed during World War II. In the 1950s, heavy equipment, truck, and stationary diesels were successfully equipped with turbochargers. In 1975, Mercedes-Benz modified the OM617 three-liter, five-cylinder diesel engine by installing a Garrett AiResearch T-04B turbo and promptly broke three world speed records using it. In 1977 the 300SD was introduced with the OM617A turbocharged engine, and passenger diesels have not been the same since.

The turbocharger in your 300D or 300SD, with "AiResearch" cast into the aluminum compressor housing, was built by the Allied Signal Turbocharger Group in Torrance, California; European 300Ds may have a similar unit built by KKK Turbolader. Figure 1 shows a typical unit, model TA-0301. The exhaust turbine is in a cast iron housing bolted to the short exhaust manifold on the right side of the engine. Exhaust gas at up to 1,000°F spins a small, light nickel-alloy turbine, then exits rearward through a stainless steel bellows connected to the exhaust pipe. The turbine is shafted directly to an aluminum-alloy centrifugal volute compressor, which takes filtered air at the spin axis and blows it into the intake manifold. Boost pressure is controlled by a simple mechanical servo mechanism consisting of a spring-loaded exhaust bypass valve,

Figure 1. Garrett AiResearch TA0301 turbocharger from 1983 300SD leaks oil, a common problem in older turbos.

or waste-gate, controlled by a rubber diaphragm connected to the blower output by a hose.

Bearings and Seals

At full boost the turbo shaft turns at up to 140,000 rpm. At this speed, familiar mechanisms such as ball bearings and conventional oil seals simply do not work. The two extreme-speed bearings are perforated bronze sleeves, fitting loosely in the cast iron bearing housing, or core, and loosely on the precision-ground shaft. Try to move the end of the compressor shaft with a fingertip, and it will wiggle disquietingly on a perfectly set up turbocharger. If it will not wiggle, something is jammed.

As the turbine spins, oil pours from a dedicated pipe onto the top of the bearings, and the spinning shaft generates a tremendous localized oil pressure. Spinning metal never touches metal. The shaft rides the oil film between it and the inside diameter of each bearing, and the bearings ride the peripheral films of oil forced through the radial perforations, turning at about one-third shaft speed.

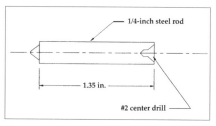

Figure 2. A shop-built adaptor lets you pull the compressor all the way off with a conventional gear pulley. This steel piece should be polished 0.003- to 0.005-in undersize so it will fit easily in the compressor axis.

There are no oil seals, but outside the sleeve bearings, in grooves at both ends of the shaft, are tiny cast iron piston rings meant to remain stationary as the shaft turns. These are gas seals, to prevent high-pressure exhaust or compressed air from blowing away the oil. After lubricating and cooling the bearings, oil falls out the bottom of the bearing housing by gravity and is recirculated by the engine oil pump. Oil is slung into drain slots at either end of the shaft before it has a chance to leak out the ends into the intake structure or the exhaust.

Step 1. Clean the turbocharger with nonreactive solvent or detergent, clamp the exhaust inlet in the bench vise, and make scribe lines between components so you can reassemble it with plates aligned at proper angles. These versatile units are designed to be usable with a variety of engine layouts, so each plate in the stack can be rotated 360 degrees with respect to other plates.

Step 2. Unbolt the bellows clamp using a 1/2-in open-end wrench.

Step 3. Remove the waste-gate hose using pliers, and discard it. These hoses suffer a lot of stress and generally need replacement.

Step 4. Unbolt the compressor housing from the seal plate using a 1/2-in wrench. Turbocharger data are stamped on tag shown. The vestige of an important gasket baked onto the rim of the seal plate must be scraped off carefully so as not to modify the seat on the plate, unless you're doing a complete overhaul with the kit, which includes a new seal plate.

Step 5. Remove the exhaust nozzle at the end of the turbine housing. These nuts are extremely tight, so expand its inside diameter by heating it with a torch. Technically these are 1/2-in nuts, but once they are expanded under heat, a 13-mm wrench fits much better than a 1/2-in. These special high-temperature alloy nuts are not sold by AiResearch as spare parts. Actually there's no reason to remove this nozzle unless it is damaged or closer access to the turbine throat is needed to remove soot.

Step 6. Remove the six Grade 8 bolts holding the bearing housing to the turbine housing, then carefully separate the two castings by tapping the bearing housing with a shop hammer behind a wood block. These bolts are screwed in very tightly, and access is limited on two of them; loosen them, partially separate the castings, then loosen some more. Heat the holes in the turbine housing, not the bolt heads, with a torch to make removal possible. Use the 13-mm wrench; a 13-mm flange wrench can be useful for breaking loose the more difficult access cases without rounding the bolt heads.

Step 7. Evaluating the bearing's condition is tricky. Measuring at the end of the shaft gives an unpredictably high reading; a usable approximation is to measure at the middle of the shaft, barely accessible through the oil drain opening. Clamp the bearing housing to something stable, and feed the dial indicator to the shaft at an angle as shown, then move both ends of the shaft up and down. This unit indicates 0.007 inches, on the edge of tolerance; maximum runout is 0.0065. Further evaluation will come from measuring the bearings up close.

Problem Diagnosis

The AiResearch turbo is a thoroughly engineered component built to high standards of precision and balance. It will last as long as the engine, given that 1) lubricating oil is plentiful, perfectly clean, and the correct weight, 2) intake air is pure and free of particulate matter, and 3) the combustion process is correctly timed and metered to prevent carbon buildup in the turbine.

The most interesting turbocharger failure modes are the most rare. (Our favorite is "inhalation of threaded fasteners." Avoid storing screws in the air cleaner while working on the engine.) Anything other than air at the intake will erode the compressor wheel, and this will lead to unbalance, which will lead to bearing failure. Something as soft as salt spray can damage the compressor. A grain of sand in the intake hits the rim of the wheel at a linear speed of about 1,800 feet per second, and it will always nick the aluminum. Anything larger than sand can destroy the compressor wheel in one quick, loud incident. (Examine a few compressors, and any residual stinginess about buying air filters will disappear.)

The exhaust turbine is made of a high-temperature nickel alloy with thin, delicate-looking blades fastened to the wheel by spin-welding; the wheel is similarly welded to the steel shaft. Possible trouble at this end comes from bits of carbon building up in the exhaust ports, then breaking loose and hitting the turbine blades. Drop a valve seat or a prechamber tip into the exhaust stream (an admittedly rare occurrence), and the turbine destructs.

Beware of a "hot shutdown," in which the engine is stopped with the turbine running at full boost. This could occur in the unlikely event of running out of fuel while traveling at highway speed. Here the turbine loses its necessary oil supply from the engine oil pump while still spinning at top revs. This can melt the bearings or score the journals and bores. Even a more moderate hot shutdown, possibly caused by pulling into a parking space

Step 8. Unbolt the seal plate from the turbine housing using a 10-mm combination wrench.

Step 9. Fix your 14-mm 6-point socket vertically in the vise and use it to hold the turbocharger by the fixed nut on the turbine end of the shaft.

right off the expressway and killing the engine, can cause overheating in the bearing housing, and chronic hot shutdowns eventually cause bearing troubles. Before turning off the engine, always let it idle long enough for the turbine to spin down. Overheated conditions can cause coking in the oil passages or soot buildup in the turbine housing. Restricted oil passages cause premature bearing wear and make overheating worse.

More common and moderate turbocharger problems can result in an unusual amount of exhaust smoke from oil leaking from the bearings into the exhaust or the compressor end, or unusual noise. You should never be aware that the turbine is running by hearing it over the diesel clatter. If you can hear it whine, the bearings could be worn out, but before unbolting the turbocharger, eliminate other symptom sources. Turbo noise can be caused by a dust/oil mixture caked on the compressor wheel, an obstructed air intake, an air leak anywhere from the air filter to the engine, or an exhaust gas leak or obstruction anywhere from the tailpipe to the engine. Blue exhaust

Step 10. The compressor wheel is removed in two stages. First, move the wheel up to the end of the shaft by pulling on the seal plate with a three-jaw gear puller centered on the shaft end.

Step 11. Second, back off the puller and insert the specially built adaptor, designed to allow force to be applied to the shaft after the puller screw has bottomed out on top of the compressor wheel. Continue to pull, removing the compressor wheel and seal plate. Examine the seal plate bore for scoring. If the piston ring has moved in the bore and caused wear, the shaft has run unbalanced, and the seal plate will leak oil.

smoke can be caused by engine problems and by failed bearings or gas seals in the turbo.

Bearing problems are most likely caused by oil supply problems. (Once you've taken apart a few turbochargers, no one will have to remind you to change oil on schedule.) The turbo runs 35 times faster than the engine, and the problem of small, gritty particles in the oil is proportionately magnified. It is important to change the oil after any work that disturbs the oil space, even as slight as removing the valve cover.

Teardown

Allied Signal prefers that any turbocharger problem be resolved by sending the unit to the factory for

Step 12. Clean the compressor wheel and examine it for any modification that would lead to unbalance. This one looks perfect. If it didn't, this unit would be buttoned up and sent to the factory, as a bad compressor wheel would lead to a cascade of problems in the bearing housing.

Step 13. Remove the flinger sleeve and bronze thrust bearing. These are loose on the shaft and should lift off easily. New units are provided in the kit. If you re-use the original pieces, clean them thoroughly with an oil solvent such as Gumout. Pry out the square-sectioned rubber seal for replacement. The compressor-side piston ring is on the flinger sleeve.

Step 14. Use snap-ring pliers to compress the ring holding the bearing, and pull it out. Snap-ring pins on pliers had to be ground down slightly to fit small ring-holes.

Step 15. Pull out the bearing, or turn the housing over, and it should fall out. Turn the housing over and remove the snap-ring and bearing from the other side.

Step 16. Evaluate the condition of the bearings by measuring OD with a micrometer and ID with a telescope gauge and a micrometer. This one seems perfect. Tin is worn off, but under an eye loupe, bearing surfaces show no scratches. Check the bearing bores in the bearing housing and the shaft, particularly if there is damage to the bearings. Shaft diameter should be 0.4000 in.

Step 17. Here's what caused this turbo's oil leak—a broken piston ring on the turbine side.

Step 18. Clean and flush the bearing housing, then install parts from the kit by reversing disassembly procedure, and hopefully the turbo will run another 12 years.

Thanks to Ken Redmond of The Benz Store in Chamblee, Georgia, for providing examples of AiResearch turbines, and to Joel at Diesel Injection for his patience.

a rebuild; they discard everything but the end castings and return an essentially new turbocharger. This is the most practical way to repair a damaged compressor, turbine wheel, shaft, or bearing housing. Still, the company does sell individual parts through distributors and even a parts kit containing everything needed to rejuvenate a turbocharger having the normal wear of 20 years of service. For the hard-core home mechanic who needs adventure, we offer this detailed, illustrated procedure for disassembly and analysis of the AiResearch turbocharger. The kit of essential gaskets, bearings, clips, fasteners, and a new seal plate costs $80. Ours, part number 468400-0000, came from Diesel Injection & Electric Co., 231 Main St., Forest Park, GA 30050; 404/361-2222; find your local distributor by calling Allied Signal in Tucson, Arizona, at 602/469-1000.

Individual bearings cost less than $7 each and can be bought in standard-standard (ID-OD) or any combination of 5 and 10 thousands oversized. Normal bearing tolerances are in Table 1. New piston rings cost less than a dollar each. Shafts can be reground, bores can be trued, and cylinders can be restored by built-up welding for less than $50 per operation from the parts distributors.

One part unavailable at any price is the waste-gate actuator, a cast-metal chamber containing a spring-loaded rubber diaphragm to open the waste-gate. The turbo shown here suffered an air leak in the actuator, which would definitely affect its performance. The actuator disassembles easily by prying loose an internal ring using a small-bladed screwdriver.

The diaphragm in this case, a robust white rubber-coated fabric, was innocent of holes or cracks. The problem was a particle blown under the rim by the compressor; simple cleaning solved it. These units can be sensitive to raw diesel fuel somehow finding its way into the intake, impacting on the diaphragm, and causing it to rot; otherwise they seem tough. The waste-gate should open at 10 psi, or 7.5 psi on some early models.

Back Together

If you buy individual parts or dismantle the turbocharger just for analysis, you must at least buy a compressor gasket for reassembly. Fasteners in excellent condition can be reused. Always replace the waste-gate hose with a new, foot-long piece of 5/8-inch black rubber hose.

The piston rings are small enough that no tools are needed to install them. Expand a ring slightly with your fingers, slip it over the shaft end, and maneuver it into the slot. No need for a ring compressor; the bores are chamfered to automatically compress the rings as the turbine housing and seal plate are screwed down.

Reassembly parameters are in Table 2. Of particular importance is the compressor nut tightening. To prevent bending the shaft, use equal pressure on either side of a T-bar holding the socket, or a torque wrench with two U-joint swivels in series. Put a drop of oil on the threads before screwing on the nut. Correct torque on this nut is essential to center the nut on the threads and maintain balance. The compressor wheel is not keyed.

No lock nuts are used, although the compressor clamp plates should be turned over to the unscarred side when you put it back together. Use one drop of Loctite on each of the four seal plate screws.

The minimum tool list is:

- a bench vise
- a pointed scribe
- a three-jaw gear puller plus a wrench to turn it
- a built gear-puller extension (see Figure 2)
- common pliers
- inside snap-ring pliers
- a 10-mm combination wrench
- a 1/2-in combination wrench
- a 3/8-in 12-point socket
- a 14-mm 6-point deep socket
- a wood block
- a shop hammer
- a T-bar
- a plumber's torch (MAPP or propane).

Helpful extras are a 13-mm combination wrench and a 13-mm flange wrench. To evaluate the bearings you need a zero- to 1-inch micrometer, a 1/2-in telescope gauge, a 5/8-in telescope gauge (or an inside micrometer), and a dial indicator with a 2-inch reach.

For correct assembly of the compressor nut, a torque wrench is strongly recommended. A 1/2-in, open-end torque wrench, technically needed to tighten the turbine housing screws, is a special tool rarely found in home toolboxes. Bolts are aircraft Grade 8, with a dry torque rating of 1,428 in-lb, so there is no chance of breaking them with an open-end wrench of a size that will fit in the confined spaces separating the turbocharger castings.

Good luck, and please resist the temptation to spin up the turbine on compressed air. Remember, while running it must be aggressively lubricated by the engine's oil pump.

Table 1. *Bearing Specifications, inches*

Bearing ID: 0.4010 to 0.4014

Bearing OD: 0.6182 to 0.6187

Bore: 0.6220 to 0.6223

Radial Bearing Clearance:
0.0030 to 0.0065

Table 2. *Reassembly Parameters*

Torque, compressor housing bolts:
110 to 130 in-lb

Torque, seal plate bolts:
75 to 90 in-lb

Torque, turbine housing bolts:
100 to 130 in-lb

Torque, shaft nut:
18 to 20 in-lb plus 110 degrees

Shaft stretch: 0.007 to 0.008 in

How to Put Zip in Your Zeniths

by Stu Ritter,
Technical Editor

*May/June
2001*

Photos in this article
by Daimler-Benz AG.

For a pair of Zeniths to work correctly, certain prerequisites must be met. You must have a good distributor without much shaft wobble, a properly working vacuum advance/retard unit, good spark plugs and wires, and a good distributor cap and rotor. All tune-up specs must be set on the money. The valves must have been adjusted, and the cam timing should be in the ballpark. On 1970 and later models with emission advance/retard electronics, they must work correctly, and the timing must stay where it belongs according to the manual.

Check Your Jets

That was step one. Zeniths have a reputation for warping the top plate, the carburetor cover. When the cover warps, a break occurs in the idle air circuit as the engine gets up to operating temperature, so the idle speed starts to drop, then the engine will die. If this symptom fits your carburetors, first make sure that the idle shut-off jets are functioning.

If your car has the electric idle shut-off jets, and they malfunction, you will lose the idle on that carb. To test the idle fuel shut-off valve, follow the electrical feed line from the carburetor until you come to a connector. The connectors are clipped onto a plate on the passenger-side fender which contains the advance/retard emission control relays on the 250/8, or they are mounted with two clips on the frame rail on the 280S/8. (Remember, the /8 means "start of production 1968".) Just

Figure 07-3/2. Locking ring (circlip, part 123) holds starter connecting rod in place.

pull the plug on the connector, and you should lose the idle on that car, and the engine should begin running rough. Plug the connection together again, and the engine should resume its normal idle. Quoting Mercedes-Benz service training literature: "Note: Shut-Off valve malfunction produces the same characteristics as a 'Plugged' Carburetor Idle Jet." So, this is the first test. If there is no reaction from either electric jet and the engine won't run, check the connectors for power using a test light.

Warped Covers

If the electric idle valves are working correctly, the next step is to remove the car cover and check it for warpage. With a cold engine, to remove the top cover, first remove the cover on the choke connecting rod on the side of the carb. Then loosen the Allen-head or cheese-head screw until the connecting rod is loose. On early

versions of the carb, this part is out in the open, right above the choke assembly. The workshop manual calls for removing the circlip that holds the arm onto the choke rod, but that usually means a lost circlip upon reassembly, so try to avoid doing that. (It just means a little more fiddling when reassembling the carb.) See Figure 07-3/2 in the service manual. (Note: References and figures throughout this article are from *Service Manual, Passenger Cars Starting 1968, Series 108, 109, 111, 113, Maintenance, Tuning, Unit Replacement.*)

Unscrew the nine cheese-head screws holding down the cover and remove them. Remember the screw in the middle of the cover, down in the well where the air cleaner screw goes into the carb cover. Right next to the choke linkage, between the linkage and the first top cover screw, you will find a little place where you can place a screwdriver blade and pry off the

Figure 07-3/4. Black arrows indicate cheese-head screws securing carburetor cover. White arrow indicates idle air bleed hole.

Figure 07-3/5. Prying off carburetor cover with screwdriver.

top cover. The gaskets tend to bake in place, so you have to pry them off. Try not to damage the cover when prying (Figure 07-3/5).

You did remember to have a pair of new gaskets on hand, didn't you? With the cover in hand, remove the old gasket. It may fall off, or you may have to spend time with a single-edged razor blade scraping off all the old gasket material. Once the surface is clean, check the cover for flatness

using a straight-edge. It's easy for the cover to be flat in one plane and not in another, so check it every 30 degrees around the circumference.

If the cover is warped—and if you have been losing idle, there is a good chance it will be—you can either flat-file it or put it on a wide belt sander with a gentle grit belt to flatten it. Remove as little metal as possible, just enough to get it flat. You don't need a perfect surface because the cover is

flexible and mates to the gasket. If this were a metal to metal junction, that would be another story.

Heat-Risers

Trying to repair the top cover of the carb is not worth the time and effort unless you determine the cause of the warping. It doesn't make sense to repair the symptom and not treat the problem. We'll almost lay odds that you will find your exhaust manifold heat-riser flaps jammed in the exhaust manifold and jammed in the partially "heat-on" mode.

When we worked in dealerships in the early 1970s, when these models were current, the shop foreman would always check the heat-risers to make sure they were free and could move according to the heat requirements of the carbs. For the mechanics this could mean 15 minutes of swearing and applying penetrating oils and brute force to get the heat-risers to move. We would squirt the heat-riser shafts with penetrating oil, take our largest pair of channel-lock pliers, clamp them on the heat-riser weight, and try to move it. We would wrench it back and forth until it finally broke free; if it didn't, we had to tell the shop foreman so he could call the customer to get an OK for a rebuild. Every E Service required checking the heat-risers to make sure they were free. These days nobody bothers to make sure the heat-risers are free.

The heat-risers are thermostatically operating flaps that sit directly in the exhaust stream and divert hot exhaust gas to the underside of the carb to heat it during the warm-up cycle. A bi-metallic spring and a counterweight operate the flap. Since these flaps live in the very harsh environment of the exhaust stream, they are prone to jam. They tend to jam in the heat-on position, so hot exhaust gas is directed to the bottom of the carb all the time. Heat-risers can be rebuilt, but it is a swine of a job, requiring removing the intake/exhaust manifolds and taking everything apart.

The carbs just cannot stand to be heated by exhaust gas all the time. The heat-risers are exhaust-heat activated, so heat is directed at the base only when the carbs are cold. When the carbs are baked in exhaust heat all the time, things go awry.

The bushings supporting the heat-riser shaft are replaceable. As amazing as it may be, all of the parts are available from your local Mercedes-Benz dealer. The shafts will have to come from Germany, but they are available.

- Small Parts Kit, 123 140 00 27

- Shaft Kit, 130 143 00 05

- Shaft kit extra parts, 130 990 03 40, 000 991 18 61

- Flaps, 114 143 00 06

The shop manual doesn't describe this procedure. It's simple, though; if you can take off the manifolds, you can repair the heat-risers. It will test your knowledge of heating and beating, as we used to say. Without repairing the heat risers, it makes no sense to repair the carburetors because they will warp again. You can't subject the carbs to full exhaust heat all the time; it just causes warping.

Base Gaskets

Another problem that develops from jammed heat-risers is pulled-in base gaskets. It's easy to tell if this has happened; just open the throttle all the way and look into the carburetor throat. If you see gasket material intruding into the bore at the base of the carb, the gasket material is intruding into the fuel/air flow and disturbing it. You must replace the base gaskets, which is a simple matter of removing the carbs and replacing the gasket material, which is supplied glued to the insulating flanges (Figure 07-2/1).

Once all of the tune-up specs are correctly adjusted, and the heat-risers are working as designed, you can adjust the Zeniths to run properly, knowing that they will hold their adjustment. For a set of Zeniths to

Figure 07-2/1. Installation sequence of insulating flanges and heat shield.

function the way they were originally meant to function, all adjustments must be made at least once to be sure they are correct. If you don't do all adjustments at the same time, you can't be sure of how everything will work together. This set of adjustments, called Basic Adjustments, appears in the shop manual, and the book time is 2.2 hours for both carbs. That's 2.2 hours for an experienced mechanic in a dealership environment with all required tools at hand. So plan accordingly. See the service manual, sections 07-3/3 to 07-3/6.

Adjustment Procedure

This list from Mercedes-Benz service training documents may differ slightly from the manual, but this order makes more sense and has a logical progression.

1. Venting Valve

This valve vents pressure in the float chamber to the atmosphere, which avoids fuel percolation in the float chamber.

  a) Remove the carburetor interconnecting linkage.

  b) Remove the vacuum throttle controller (take it off).

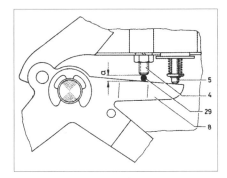

Figure 07-4/15. Adjusting float housing venting valves.

If the carb has a stop screw, adjust the screw to provide 2.5-2.8 mm of vent pin lift.

On earlier carbs, without the adjusting screw, and after all other carb adjustments have been made, bend the arm at the notch to provide 2.5-3.0 mm of vent pin lift (Figure 07-4/15).

2. Accelerator Pump

To check the accelerator pump for proper function, the top cover and the pre-atomizer in the primary stage must be removed.

  a) Check the start of injection. Immediately on opening the throttle, a powerful jet of fuel should emerge.

b) Check the injection quantity using a graduated container pump for one full stroke. The correct volume is 0.7–1.0 cc. If the injected quantity needs to be adjusted, bend the activating lever.

c) Check the direction of injection. For cars with automatic transmissions, the fuel jet should hit the bore 10–15 mm below the upper edge of the bore. For cars with manual transmissions, the fuel jet should hit the throttle plate where it touches the bore of the carb. See Figure 07-4/14.

3. Float Level

To check the float level, the next section (plate block) of the carb must be removed. Again, you do have new gaskets for this section, don't you? With the new gasket in place, measure the distance from the bottom of the plate block to the bottom of the float. This is usually right on the numbers; all /8 models measure 21–23 mm, while the 220Sb is 18–20 mm. Both carbs must be set to the same float height. If the float must be adjusted, shims are available with these part numbers and thicknesses:

0.5 mm	000 997 81 40
1.0 mm	000 997 28 40
1.5 mm	000 997 82 40
2.0 mm	000 997 83 40

4. Second-Stage Diaphragm

With the plate block section removed, lift the second stage diaphragm, and put your finger over the vacuum holes inside the venturi. Release the diaphragm, and if there are no leaks, vacuum will hold the diaphragm.

5. Idle-Speed and Mixture

Complete instructions in the manual cover this procedure. Sections 07-4/1 through 07-4/7 detail the adjustments discussed here, including the usual factory diagrams. This shows you how to bring the carbs to the same rpm using the idle-speed adjustment links and adjust the fuel-air mixture using a tachometer. Before attempting to

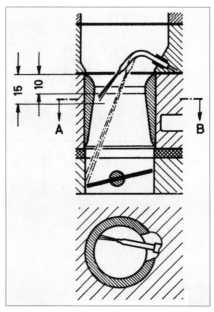

Figure 07-4/14. Proper direction of accelerator pump injection.

adjust the idle, remove the mixture adjustment screws and check for ridges on the taper of the needle. If the needle had been forced into the carb, which puts a ridge on the taper, the idle will never be smooth. When replacing the screws after inspection, screw them in lightly until they just touch, then back them out 2–2.5 turns as a starting point, which will vary depending on the carb version.

6. Linkage

Adjust the long rod between the two carbs so it fits tension-free.

a) Short rod with free-play from bellcrank: with the free-travel fully extended, the link should fit tension-free. If it needs to be adjusted, loosen the clamp bolt on the bellcrank and adjust.

b) Short rod without free-play with adjuster: adjust the rod so that the bellcrank is lifted from its rest position by 2 mm.

7. Choke Cover Tension

For 1970 and later models, the chokes are adjusted 5 mm in the rich direction; experience has shown that up to 20 mm rich can assist cold starting by increasing tension on the

choke covers—and therefore on the chokes. For all cars before 1970, set the choke covers on the marks.

8. Choke Fast-Idle Speed

Although the shop manual is silent on this, service training literature recommends removing the fast-idle speed adjusting screw and spring from the rear carburetor, with all adjustments made to the front carb. The procedure is fairly involved and varies depending on the carburetor version you own. Follow the procedure in the manual for your version.

9. Choke Gap

Set the carbs at fast idle by actuating the choke step cam (open throttle and close, with a warm engine); hold pressure against the choke flaps to move them into the on position. Depending on which car you have, the gap varies from 2.0 up to 2.6 mm. Again, check the manual.

Start the engine without touching the throttle. Lightly push against the choke flaps to try to close them until a stop is felt. Do not force them beyond this point. Using a rod, measure the gap between the choke flap and the carb body. This gap must exist to allow sufficient airflow during cold starts and warm-ups. The gap is adjusted with the adjusting screw on the dashpot behind the choke cover. If the correct gap can't be set, it may be necessary to relocate the choke-connecting lever on the choke rod. If you adjust the lever height, make sure the choke flap still opens and shuts fully afterward.

10. Vacuum Dashpot

Reinstall the dashpot, and follow the instructions in the manual for the version you are working with. The dashpot is adjusted with the engine at full operating temperature.

11. Fuel Return Valve

At operating temperature, slowly open the throttle while watching the return valve pin. At 2,000 rpm the pin should be fully lifted. Adjust at the spring tension adjusting screw.

12. Idle-Lifting Switch

On cars with automatic transmissions, a switch for idle-speed control is located on the front carb. Attach a test light to the ground side of the switch, and open the throttle slowly while watching the light. The switch should turn out the test light at 1,400 to 1,600 rpm (switch opens). It is adjusted by loosening the switch mounting screws and pivoting the switch.

More Tips

A quick note about adjusting the mixture screws. While the factory manuals recommend using a tachometer to monitor engine speed and an exhaust gas analyzer to monitor tailpipe emissions of CO, the best technique is to find and set the best idle speed. Learn to listen to the tone, note, or hum of the engine. With a tachometer hooked up, set each mixture adjustment screw for maximum idle speed. You will probably have to go back and forth between the idle speed links and the mixture screws, using the Syncro Test Device to keep idle speed and mixture equal on both carbs. If your state has smog requirements for older cars, you must have the mixture set using an exhaust gas analyzer.

You can check the accuracy of your adjustments by momentarily blocking the idle air bleed in the top cover with a ball-point pen and noting the rpm drop on the tachometer. The drop should be the same for each carb. The idle air bleed, shown in Figure 07-3/4, is right below the choke shaft, opposite the linkage side. If you suspect that dirt has gotten into the idle circuit because of a dirty fuel filter, a really quick fix is to use an air nozzle to blow back through the idle circuit via that bore with the engine running while moving the linkage toward full throttle. This is an old mechanic's trick to save time. Sometimes it works, sometimes it doesn't, but it's so easy that it's worth a try. If blowing through the idle air bore doesn't clear the idle, remove the idle mixture adjusting screws, and blow through that passage. Fuel will shoot out of the carb. Always wear safety glasses when working on carbs; gasoline in the eye is no fun.

Worn linkage is a real problem with Zenith carbs because not all of the pieces are still available from Mercedes-Benz. It helps to scour junkyards for carbs and linkage pieces and collect them against future need. These are hard parts to find, so it makes sense to stockpile them if you want to keep a Zenith-carbureted engine running for a long time.

If the central hold-down screw for the top cover (under the air filter hold-down screw) ends up with stripped threads, you can repair it by drilling and tapping the hole to 6 mm and using an Allen-head bolt with the outside diameter of the head ground down to fit the hole.

Some Zenith parts are still available from Mercedes-Benz, some from the aftermarket. These cars are approaching 30 years old, and parts are hard to find, which is a shame, because a set of properly set Zeniths can make an M130 engine run as well as—if not better than—fuel injection.

Photographs appearing here are from the pertinent Mercedes-Benz factory workshop manuals.

Zenith to Weber Carburetor Conversion

by Frank Barrett,
Editor/Publisher

*May/June
1985*

Photos in this article
by the author.

*If your old 220, 230 or 250 has Zenith
carburetors, you may have already
considered changing to Weber
carburetors to improve carburetor
operation and fuel mileage. We
recently converted a 1966 230S.
Here's how.*

Zenith carburetors were used on most
six-cyl 220Sb, 230, 230S, 250 and 250S
models from about 1963 to 1972.
Some cars, as miles accrue, develop
symptoms of carburetor problems:
worsening gas mileage, poor idling,
backfiring, etc. My friend Joe's 80,000-
mi 1966 230S, otherwise like new, had
these problems. Joe had already tried
to fix the air leaks in the Zeniths and
had spent money with mechanics who
tried to do likewise. Rebuild kits are
available for about $60, but they do
not cure the air leak problem caused
by warping of the carburetor bodies.
Used carburetors are tough to find and
offer no guarantee of improvement.
New replacement Zenith 35/40 INAT
carburetors cost $631 each, so when
we heard of a kit to convert to Weber

carburetors, we thought it might offer
a completely fresh alternative.

The Weber kits are designed and
assembled by JAM Engineering,
tailored to each model, and come
with a good set of instructions. The
kit for Joe's 230S, which has a fender-
mounted air cleaner, consisted of
two Weber 32/36 DGEV downdraft
dual-throat carburetors, complete with
all hardware, linkage, fuel line, gaskets
and fasteners needed for proper
installation. Other kits are custom
tailored for other models.

Installation

We set aside a day to install the carbs,
but the work actually took only about
three hours. The first step was to
unpack the kit and review the parts
list and instructions. We laid out all
the parts on the workbench, where
they looked a little daunting to Joe,
who wondered aloud if we could do
the job properly.

Following the instructions, we
disconnected the battery (to avoid
sparks) and set to removing the old
carburetors. Off came the air cleaner.

Disconnecting the idle jet solenoid
wiring, the vacuum line to the front
carb, the fuel supply and return lines,
the throttle linkage and the electric
choke wiring was simple. We had a
slight problem reaching two or three
of the carb-to-manifold bolts next
to the valve cover. Removing the
valve cover made it much easier to
get wrenches on them. Off came the
Zeniths, along with their heat shields
and gaskets. Right away we covered the
holes in the manifold so that nothing
could fall into the engine.

These Weber carburetors are used
on several different cars, so the kit
provides a few minor parts to adapt
them to specific models. Joe's 230S had
idle jet solenoids (to prevent run-on
when the ignition is switched off),
so the regular idle jets were removed
from the Webers and replaced by the
new solenoid-controlled jets provided
with the kit. The throttle linkage arms
were also replaced with kit-supplied
arms designed specifically for the
model. The four air cleaner mounting
studs were removed from the top of
the carburetor casting, and the kit-
supplied air cleaner adaptor plates
were installed with a gasket between
them and the carbs. Air cleaner hold-
down bridge plates had already been
attached using Loctite to prevent the
screws loosening.

Now the carburetors were ready
to mount to the manifold, but first
we had to slightly modify the heat

**Original Zenith 35/40 INAT (below) dwarfs
new Weber carburetor (below right).**

shields to allow clearance for the idle adjusting screw. This simply consists of flattening a short piece of the lip along one edge of the heat shield; instructions say to flatten the whole lip, but only about an inch needs to be bent flat to clear the idle adjusting screw, so we cut the lip with a hacksaw and simply bent down the short section of it in a vise.

The kit came with four phenolic spacers and eight gaskets to fit between manifold, heat shield and carburetor. It's not specifically spelled out in the kit, but the proper sequence is to sandwich each spacer between two gaskets. One sandwich then goes between manifold and heat shield; the other goes between heat shield and carburetor. The two intake holes in the gaskets and spacers are asymmetrical, and the pieces must be installed to match the similar holes in the intake manifold. The carbs are then easily bolted into place, along with the bellcranks for the throttle linkage (after which we replaced the valve cover). Those two shiny new carburetors look great!

Vital Connections

We next made the various connections needed to bring the Webers to life. The throttle linkage is simple, using the old connecting link between the carbs plus a new front link and one short link to each carburetor. Instructions for exact linkage lengths are provided. We put a dab of grease in each snap-on linkage joint, then checked to make sure that throttle travel was OK by pressing down the accelerator and watching to see that the carburetor throttles opened fully. No adjustment was necessary.

Next came the fuel line. The fuel return line is no longer used, so it can

Gasket, phenolic spacer and modified steel heat shield.

be removed to a point beneath the battery tray, where it is plugged with a plastic plug and screw clamp provided in the kit. The new fuel lines consist of three pre-cut pieces of hose, a tee and enough hose clamps for installation. The old fuel line is shortened with a hacksaw. After trimming the fiber covering back about an inch, the new lines are connected to the old line near the front of the valve cover. Assembling the tee and lines on the bench before installation in the car makes it easier to tighten the clamps.

The old vacuum line from the distributor is connected to the front carburetor vacuum fitting. The rear carb's vacuum fitting is plugged, using a plastic plug supplied. Electrical connections to the idle jet solenoids and the electric chokes take just a few minutes. All necessary terminals are supplied with the kit, which even includes a few plastic tie-wraps to help keep the wiring tidy. After you connect the wiring, be sure to check that power is actually reaching the jets and chokes.

3, 2, 1, Ignition!

Now it's time to reconnect the battery and start the engine, which takes a few seconds extra cranking because the carburetors have no fuel in them, of course. Joe's 230S started up and ran smoothly immediately. It settled down to an even idle, and as the engine warmed up, the electric chokes opened.

The electric chokes may need adjustment, which is simple. With the engine cold, the chokes should be closed. As the engine warms up, the choke plates should swivel open until they are vertical. Each choke can be adjusted by loosening three screws on the choke clamp, turning the plastic choke spring housing until the plates are properly oriented, then tightening the clamp. Duck soup.

Instructions are provided for fine tuning the Webers. Our set ran so well right out of the box that we put off playing with the idle mixture and linkage until our next trip to our favorite mechanic. We did slow the idle a tad, using the idle speed and mixture adjustment screws. If your car has an

automatic transmission, idle speed will be determined by the need to keep the car running while it idles in gear, even with the stock carbs.

After installing the air cleaner (using the old o-rings between the carbs and the old metal housing), we went for a road test. The car started immediately and ran without a fault. Since Joe's car has an automatic transmission, we checked to be sure the electric kickdown switch worked, which it did (if you have to adjust the throttle linkage, you may also have to adjust the kickdown linkage, but instructions are provided in the kit). Because the Webers have their own throttle return springs, we had removed the stock spring, and throttle response was excellent.

Here it was, only a few hours after starting, and we were finished. The car runs smoothly again, and gas mileage is improved over that of the old carburetors.

The Bottom Line

Total cost was $716, including $356 for the adaptor kit, $140 for each of the two Webers and $40 each for the two idle jet solenoids (needed only on cars so originally equipped). JAM provides a one-year warranty (limited to the cost of the kit), as well as a technical assistance number. In certain states, alteration of induction systems of some vehicles used on public roads may be illegal. In California, for instance, these kits are regrettably not legal for other than off-road use on any pollution controlled (post 1967) vehicle. JAM is presently in the application stage for an exemption for their Weber kits.

If you install one of these kits, you might wonder about replacing the entire stock air cleaner assembly with two small Filtron units, thereby eliminating the need for the adaptor plates. But JAM's adaptors allow you to 1) retain stock appearance, 2) keep the stock valve cover vent line routing, 3) have the stock air cleaner serviced at any Mercedes-Benz dealer or specialist shop and 4) draw cooler air from the grille area rather than hot underhood air.

190SL Carburetion: Solex vs. Weber

by Frank King,
Technical Editor

*March/April
1984*

Photos in this article
by Frank Barrett.

*Among 190SL enthusiasts, one
enduring controversy is that of
which carburetors to use. The
190SL was originally equipped with
Solexes, but these are frequently
replaced with Webers. Proponents
of each are frequently seen locked
in debate in parking lots next to
a 190SL with hood raised, and the
discussion usually is continued over a
cold one in the nearest bar. MBCA's
Technical Director, Frank King, has
never published his views on this
topic until now....*

This question is one in which both
sides are right in part, but both go
astray when prejudices cause acrimony
and disparagement. To face the central
issue, the overwhelming weight of
informed opinion is that, even when
both are working properly, the Weber
40 DCOE is a better carburetor
for the 190SL than the Solex 44
PHH. By "better", we mean not only

performing the intended functions
more precisely, but also continuing to
do so for an extended period without
frequent service. Because the 190SL's
two carburetors must be precisely
synchronized, servicing and adjustment
problems increase geometrically. The
Solex does not continue to work well
for long, so the decision is clearly in
favor of the Weber.

The Solex, when working properly,
is a beautiful device. The second
barrel of each carburetor is opened
by a membrane actuated by engine
vacuum which works against a poised
weight and a coil spring which hold
it closed or return it to the closed
position when no longer needed. The
forces of the weight and spring are
fairly constant, but the vacuum varies
with the velocity of air drawn in by the
engine, as well as with temperature,
humidity and barometric pressure.
Since the membrane is subject to
deterioration and the linkage suffers
from wear and dirt, the system's
functioning is impaired with time
and use. Even in proper adjustment,
Solexes do not stay that way for long.

While Solexes are right, they give
somewhat smoother results than
Webers, assuming that the Webers are
set up for smoothest performance.

Webers can, of course, be set up for
best power, and the car will be quicker
than with Solexes. The M121 engine
of the 190SL is, however, close to
the limit of reliability (with its three
main bearings), and extracting more
performance than the Solexes can offer
can lead to rapid wear. The Solex wears
around the throttle shaft, resulting in
idling and adjustment problems. Some
necessary parts are often discarded by
careless mechanics. The overflow pipes
designed to carry off the fuel that
percolates from the Solexes whenever
the engine is stopped are an example.
Without these pipes, gas drips onto
the exhaust manifold. The 190SL is
burdened with a large intake plenum
chamber which, with the Solexes, is
cantilevered out from the engine.
A diagonal brace below is usually
removed to allow access and never
replaced. Thus weight extending out is
supported only by the attaching bolts,
and normal vibration loosens the
gaskets between the intake manifold
and the engine, etc., permitting air to
leak in.

The Weber installation is much
more compact, with little, dryfoam
air filters and no plenum chamber. As
the darlings of the better "foreign car
specialists", Webers are easier to service;

Stock 190SL Solex carburetion system.

Weber carburetion system on a 190SL.

parts are readily available and cheaper than Solex parts. Webers are not perfect, but they are well designed and finely built. They cannot, however, be simply taken out of the box and installed with the instructions from the factory in Bologna. The proper combination of venturis, jets and settings for U.S. fuel and conditions, including linkage modifications, has been worked out, and the excellent results can be seen at club driving events. The use of Webers on 190SLs in MBCA driving events was approved in 1982; on the other hand, for those interested in concours, where value is placed on originality, Webers would be a liability.

A little history may be in order, too.

The Solex (*Editor's note: the name Solex has no meaning, being created solely–no pun intended–for the carburetors.*) was invented by two Frenchmen in 1910; the French Solex company still owns all rights to it and manufactures it in France. Solex also owns the Zenith carburetor, another French invention, and Stromberg, an American invention. Before World War II, the *Deutsche Vergaser Gesellschaft* in Neuss, across the Rhine from Düsseldorf, acquired rights to manufacture Solex, Zenith and Stromberg carburetors and to develop carburetors using any of the patents involved. Daimler-Benz began using Solex carburetors as early as 1928. After WWII, DBAG used only Solexes from *Deutsche Vergaser* until 1965, when Zeniths were used on some models, and 1968, when Strombergs were also used on some models. *Deutsche Vergaser* has probably the finest carburetion research and development laboratory in the world, so thirty years ago it was natural for DBAG to look to them to develop carburetors for the 190SLs M121 engine. This same engine was used in the 190 sedan with one Solex 32 PAITA downdraft carburetor, giving 24 percent less horsepower.

Weber was founded in 1923 in Italy by Eduardo Weber. In 1941 Fiat bought half of the company stock and in 1951 the remainder, so Weber is now owned 100 percent by Fiat. In 1955 Weber was not the widely known success it is today, and one would hardly expect DBAG to go to Italy, England or another foreign country for development of a new carburetor for a new engine.

Even when the 190SL was new more than twenty years ago, really competent technicians with training and experience on the 190SL were rare. In those days, dealers usually had two labor rates: one for sedans and another, about 35 percent higher, for sports cars such as the 190SL and 300SL. Many dealers preferred not to see a 190SL come in, for it usually meant repeated returns for corrections and an unhappy customer.

The principle that "the factory knows best" is a pretty sound one, even though the factory may be wrong once in a while. There can be few people more convinced than I that DBAG has always been truly committed to *"Das Beste oder Nichts"* ("The best or nothing"), as Gottlieb Daimler put it, but he was realistic enough not to say *"Die Vollendung* [perfection] *oder Nichts"*. What is best today may not be so good tomorrow….

Considering price, a kit of two new Webers can be had for under $500, while new Solexes would cost at least three times as much. Perhaps I should mention a third alternative. By 1967 *Deutsche Vergaser* had got it right with the side-draft Stromberg 175 CDT. Two of these constant-venturi carburetors were used on the 4-cyl M115 engine that powered the 220 and 230 of 1967–1976. Some manifold modifications allow these to be used on the 190SL with, I am told, superior results.

So much for the Solex vs. Weber affair. My judgment of their relative merits is based on discussions over the years with drivers in club competition, with technicians (both independent and at dealers), with my friend Frank Mallory of Silver Spring, Maryland, and, most conclusively, with a small group of experts who prefer to remain unquoted.

Replacing Your 300D or 300E Exhaust System

by John Lamb, Contributing Editor

November/December 1997

Photos in this article by the author.

Sooner or later the muffler, exhaust pipe, or connections on your 124-chassis 300D or 300E will probably rust through or break. Still, the exhaust system can be replaced by a do-it-yourselfer with a standard array of metric hand tools, a safe sturdy jack, and vehicle stands.

At a leisurely pace, removal and installation take about two hours. When you shop for a new system, consider how long the original system served before you choose to replace it with inferior parts. There are differences in material quality. Mercedes-Benz parts have stronger, thicker metal, more rigidity, and better rustproofing, so go for original parts (Photo 1).

Safety First

Before starting work, review these safety precautions. Do not work alone. Do not support a car using only a jack; use proper jackstands. Work on a flat hard surface, block the wheels, put the transmission in Park, and firmly apply the parking brake. Let the car cool down before working on it; exhaust parts can stay hot for hours. Wear safety glasses plus ear and skin protection. Have an assistant help you remove and install heavy parts. Replace self-locking nuts, bolts, and other items subject to wear with original Mercedes-Benz parts.

Let's Begin

Begin by spraying all mounting bolts and nuts with a bolt-loosener such as Würth Rost Off, WD-40, or PB Blaster. To prevent a flare-up, the exhaust system must be cold. Let the spray soak overnight if possible. Inspect the exhaust system to determine which

pieces need replacement. Pay attention to the rear muffler welded seam, which develops rust pinholes. If the car has high mileage, I recommend replacing the entire system. It is false economy to replace a second part soon after replacing another part of the system. Disassemble the exhaust system only after you have removed the entire system from the car. Specialty tools—muffler chisels and air cutoff tools—will make the work easier (Photos 2, 3, 4).

You will discover one of the joys of working on a Mercedes-Benz–the outstanding hardware quality. These parts are designed to last decades, not just years. I've removed manifold nuts from a 14-year-old car with a single twist of a ratchet.

1. Raise the car using a jack. Support it on jackstands. (If you can drive the right, passenger-side, wheels up onto a curb or sidewalk, you can work on the exhaust system without raising the car; be sure the wheels are blocked, the parking brake is on, and there are stands underneath as a backup.)

2. To prevent anyone starting the engine, remove the ignition key. Open the hood to its highest position.

3. If necessary, remove the two plastic noise panels from below, using an 8-mm socket; 6 to 12 screws must be removed.

4. On gasoline cars, remove the oxygen sensor from the front pipe using an oxygen sensor wrench or open-end wrench. Working from below, slowly unscrew the sensor without damaging its wiring harness. Put the sensor aside where it will not get hit or damaged, as it will be installed in the new front pipe.

5. Remove the mounting nuts attaching the front downpipe to the exhaust manifold or turbo connector (Photo 5). A 300D requires a 12-mm flexible (universal) socket and a long extension bar to reach the nuts from below. On some cars, such as a 300E,

these nuts may be accessible from the engine compartment.

6. Remove the U-shaped clamp holding the front pipe to the transmission.

7. With a helper supporting the weight of the exhaust system, remove the rubber donuts attaching the system to the floor pan. The exhaust system is heavy and may drop suddenly, so be careful. Always replace the rubber donuts; cut off the old ones with shears or a knife.

8. Slide the entire system out from under the car, and inspect it for salvageable parts.

Installing the New System

1. Wipe a little anti-seize compound on the threads of the studs where the front pipe mounts to the engine.

2. On gasoline cars, put a little anti-seize on the threads of the oxygen sensor, then install the sensor in the front pipe. Torque to 40 Nm (30 lb-ft). Since anti-seize compound will rapidly damage an oxygen sensor if allowed to contact the sensor tip, don't let it get inside the exhaust pipe or on the sensor tip on gasoline cars.

3. Mount the front pipe loosely to the engine, and install the nuts finger-tight.

4. Using new self-locking nuts, and being sure the curved washers are properly oriented, install and tighten the U-shaped clamp at the transmission to 7 Nm (5 lb-ft). The washers are designed to accommodate expansion and contraction. Tech Advisor George Murphy suggests leaving these bolts finger-tight until the car has warmed up once, then applying final torque.

5. Tighten the front pipe nuts evenly to the engine; torque them to 30 Nm (22 lb-ft).

6. Working at the outlet end of the front pipe, coat the flange connection, metal spacer, and bolts with anti-seize compound (Photo 6). Install the

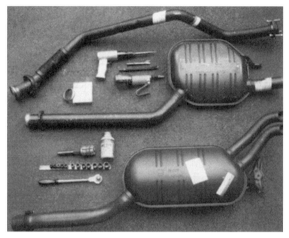

Photo 1. Entire 300D exhaust; top to bottom: front header pipe, middle resonator, rear muffler.

Photo 2. Air cutoff tool for cutting old bolts and pipes.

Photo 3. Muffler chisels can separate rusted connections.

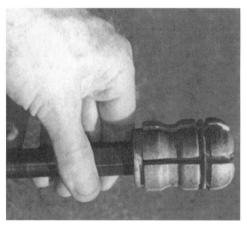

Photo 4. Muffler expander opens sleeve connections.

Photo 5. Front header pipe with flange connection to engine.

Photo 6. Metal spacer between front pipe and middle resonator (300D shown).

Photo 7. (Left) Middle resonator donut hanger (arrow).

Photo 8. (Right) Rear muffler should have rubber bumper (not shown) installed at arrow; muffler is supported by rubber donuts at outer hooks.

middle resonator to the front pipe, then support the resonator using a new rubber donut (Photo 7). Tighten the flange bolts to 20 Nm (15 lb-ft).

7. Check the old rear muffler for a rubber bumper, and install this bumper on the new muffler (Photo 8).

8. Coat the sleeve connection for the middle resonator to rear muffler with anti-seize compound. Install the rear muffler so that the sleeve connection is tight. Install the rubber donuts to support the rear muffler. Tighten the sleeve clamp to 20 Nm (15 lb-ft).

9. Reinstall the noise panels, then safely lower the car to the ground.

10. Run the engine for 15–20 seconds to check for loose fittings or leaks. A large rag can be stuffed into the rear of the system to test for leaks.

11. Test drive the car to check for rattles.

Water and Diesel Fuel Don't Mix

by John Lamb, Contributing Editor

November/December 1999

Photos in this article by the author.

Diesel owners are such fanatics about the reliability and economy of their cars that when problems strike they may feel they have been unfairly dealt a bad hand. I recently experienced this sensation with my 1990 300D 2.5 Turbo. Troubling symptoms came on suddenly and occurred whether the engine was cold or warm–and despite my having performed service and filter changes just a month before (I had dutifully logged the date and mileage in my service logbook).

Water Won't Burn

On start-up, the engine would run on less than its full five cylinders, and it lacked the usual power. The tailpipe would spew some blue and black smoke. With the engine turned off, I lifted the hood and looked for hoses that may have fallen off or other things that might be out of order. Nothing was amiss. Next I inspected the primary fuel filter, the clear plastic one on the driver's side of the engine compartment (photo 1). There I noticed what appeared to be water in the fuel.

As a pre-emptive strike, I went to my favorite auto parts store and bought a can of "dry-gas" suitable for diesel engines. I also called my Mercedes-Benz dealer and asked Charlie, my parts contact, to have two fuel filters waiting for me.

Rusty Filter

Now the details. Having changed both fuel filters about 3,000 miles ago, I was puzzled how water in the fuel could be the culprit. I changed the secondary fuel filter, which is done by loosening the two bracket hold-down bolts and

Photo 1. Primary plastic filter (arrow).

Photo 2. New fuel filter (left); rusty filter (right).

Photo 3. Diesel fuel supplement.

removing the center-filter stem bolt (you'll need 19- and 13-mm sockets). Spinning the filter off the bolt, I was shocked by what I saw. The entire top of the filter was rusty (photo 2).

Immediately I knew that my problem was water in the fuel. I cleaned the center bolt and carefully recycled the old fuel filter without spilling fuel. When installing the new secondary filter, I filled it with a diesel fuel supplement before mounting it (photo 3). This would allow the engine to start immediately without having to crank over to purge any air, and it

would force a concentrated solution of the fuel supplement through the injection pump and the injectors. I also changed the primary see-through fuel filter. Then I poured the "dry-gas" supplement into the tank and filled it with diesel fuel.

Ounces of Prevention

To prevent water damage to your Mercedes-Benz diesel engine, remember:

• Diesel fuel is lighter in weight than water, so theoretically water should settle to the bottom of the fuel filter canister.

• When pouring off old fuel from the filter, look for water as the canister empties. Water damage to the injection pump is very expensive to cure. In harsh climates, change the fuel filters often; I recommend every 7,500 miles.

• Although Mercedes-Benz doesn't endorse fuel-drying additives, those who want to use them should make sure that the additives they choose are suitable for diesel fuel systems and engines, then use them occasionally throughout the year.

• If you change the fuel filters yourself, wear disposable gloves and be sure to prevent any dirt from entering the fuel system.

• Changing the clear plastic fuel filter is easy. Just loosen the two hose clamps and remove it. The arrow on the filter should point in the direction of fuel flow, toward the injection pump.

• Finally, make sure that the fuel tank cap is always in place and that you keep the tank full of fuel in the winter or whenever temperature extremes or other climatic conditions may cause condensation in the tank.

John Lamb, Minuteman Section, is a technical training manager for Snap-on Tools in the Boston area.

Idling in Fuel-Injected Engines

by Frank King,
Technical Editor

*March/April
1988*

More on Idling

In the January/February issue we discussed the necessity for an idling mode of operation of any automotive internal combustion engine. While idling, the engine maintains power to operate such auxiliaries as the alternator and air-conditioning, is ready for a smooth transition to the operating mode and keeps fuel consumption to a minimum. The process of adjusting the idle speed on carbureted engines was described, and a table of factory-specified idle speeds was presented. Now we'll look at idling in fuel-injected engines.

Why Injection?

The last model year in which a carburetor-equipped car was sold by MBNA was 1978. All carburetors, from the simple carburetors of the first cars to the most complicated and ingenious devices of the present day, share one inherent obstacle. All face the problem of metering and distributing a mixture of a gas (air) and a liquid (gasoline) which have widely different densities and viscosities. Changes in the rate of flow of air do not simultaneously produce the same change in the flow of fuel, so various compensating devices and auxiliaries must be incorporated.

The development of mechanical fuel injection ensured the success of the diesel engine—and provided inspiration for work on the development of gasoline injection. The problems inherent in the carburetor were intensified in aircraft applications, so it is not surprising that Daimler-Benz adopted gasoline injection for its World War II aircraft engines. The superiority of these over American and British engines of the period was primarily due to the effectiveness of fuel injection over carburetion.

Gasoline injection requires more precise execution of the design than does diesel injection. The diesel engine runs with an excess of air, so fuel metering can be less exact. Also, the higher viscosity of diesel fuel provides lubrication to the plungers and enables them to seal with less tight clearances. Gasoline must be precisely metered to match within narrow limits the amount of air, while gasoline's lower viscosity requires minute clearances. In a gasoline injection pump the clearance between the plungers and cylinder wall is just a few microns (thousandths of a millimeter).

One feature that gasoline injection systems have in common with carburetors is the throttle valve, usually referred to simply as the throttle, which controls air flow to the engine. The type of throttle valve almost universally used on automobiles, sometimes called a butterfly valve, consists of a flat metal disc with a shaft running diametrically across it. The shaft is mounted diametrically in a narrowed portion of the passage for intake air (or, in the case of a carbureted engine, the air-fuel mixture). Because of its characteristic shape, this throttle passage is often called the venturi. By nature, when a butterfly throttle valve is large enough to pass the air volume needed by the engine at full power, it is incapable of being adjusted precisely to the small flow needed for idling. Therefore, an air passage capable of fine adjustment is required with injection systems as well as with carburetors.

General Adjustment Requirements

Before describing idle adjustment for the various injection systems, let's outline a few general directions:

1. The engine must be warmed up but not overheated as might be the case after a long hard drive. The oil should be at 104–176°F (60-80°C); for cars made after 1976 this should be checked with an oil telethermometer.

2. The control linkage must operate freely from accelerator pedal to throttle. All linkages must be correctly adjusted and must return to the idle stops cleanly.

3. There must be no air leaks in the intake system. Leaks of air between the air cleaner and the intake valves are the commonest cause of poor idling and adjustment difficulty.

Early Mechanical Systems

The 300SL of 1954 was the first production car to use gasoline injection. The same system was used on the 300Sc of 1955 to 1958 and was continued on the 300SL coupe and roadster until the Tatter's discontinuation in 1963. It consisted of a six-plunger pump injecting directly into the cylinders during the intake stroke. The quantity of fuel injected was regulated by a vacuum system which sensed air flow through the throttle valve tube and sent directions to the control rack in the injection pump.

When the engine idles, the throttle is completely closed, and idle air is admitted through a bypass. Idle speed is regulated by a screw which controls the effective size of this idle air passage. Idle mixture richness is regulated by an idle fuel jet in the throttle valve tube. Once the proper size idle fuel jet is found, it remains in place. There were at least four different designs of throttle valve tube used, with different placement of adjustments and connections. Undoubtedly, owners of 300SL's or 300Sc's have long since become intimately familiar with these engines, so this general description is provided only for completeness of the record.

The next Mercedes-Benz to get gasoline injection was the 300d in

1957. Direct injection of gasoline into the cylinders caused oil dilution in the frequent warm-up phases of a car used for daily transportation, so DBAG changed to port-type injection for the production cars. This system injected fuel into the intake pipes rather than directly into the cylinders. Injection pressure was around 250 psi compared with the 575 psi of direct injection. Fuel quantity was controlled by the same vacuum system actuated by airflow in the throttle valve tube, and idle speed is adjusted in the same basic manner. This system was a transitional stage between direct injection and true port injection.

Early Port Injection

In 1958 the 220SE was introduced with a two-plunger injection pump, port injection and control of fuel quantity by precise mechanical linkage of the throttle valve to the adjusting lever on the injection pump. A centrifugal governor moves the control rod of the injection pump in accordance with engine speed and the position of the fuel adjustment lever. The injection pump turns at one-half engine speed but has double-lobed cams, so fuel is injected at every turn of the crankshaft. Each plunger supplies three cylinders through distributor fittings, so the fuel for each cylinder is injected as two separate shots for each power stroke. Injection lines lead to injection valves in the intake pipes, where atomized fuel is squirted at the intake port. The same system was used on the 220SEb of 1959–65 and the 300SE of 1961–63.

Idle speed is adjusted by the idle air throttle screw (Fig. 1) located on the venturi control unit (throttle valve tube) to control air flow through the bypass. Mixture control is effected by the idle control knob at the rear end of the injection pump. This adjustment has become familiar to many owners and is often abused. It is found in two forms: 1) as used on the earlier 220SE (Fig. 2) with the R1 injection pump and 2) as used on all subsequent pumps on cars equipped with mechanical gasoline injection

(Fig. 3). The idle stop screw on the throttle should be set so that the throttle is completely closed, but not binding, while the adjusting lever on the injection pump just touches the idle stop screw on the pump. The idle stop screw on the injection pump must not be changed or adjusted, since this would change the basic setting of the injection pump. If this coordination of the two idle stops doesn't exist, the linkage must be corrected, a job beyond the scope of this article.

Idle speed is set to the specified value by adjusting the idle air throttle screw. If the engine then idles smoothly, no further adjustment is needed. If the engine speed fluctuates with a rhythmic beat, indicating too rich a mixture—or if the engine vibrates, running unsteadily, indicating too lean a mixture—the engine should be stopped and the mixture adjusted via the spring-loaded idle control knob at the rear end of the injection pump.

If idle speed has moved out of the proper range, it should be corrected with the idle air throttle screw; if this produces uneven running, readjust the idle control knob. This process is repeated as necessary. When the engine runs smoothly at the correct speed, the idle will increase about 40–60 rpm if the idle air screw is turned out a few turns. If idle speed increases by more than 60 rpm, the mixture is too rich. If the idle speed remains constant or the engine begins to vibrate, the mixture is too lean.

The idle control knob must not be operated with the engine running because it rotates as soon as it engages the slot of the adjusting screw on the governor. Also, the idle control knob must not be turned more than one notch at a time, nor more than a total of three notches in either direction. An engine that has endured the adjustments of a series of owners and mechanics may have lost the original pre-set primary position of the idle control screw so that you can't determine whether the idle control screw has already been turned too many notches in either direction. There is no way in which the original primary position can be recovered by

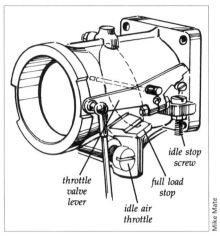

Figure 1. Typical throttle valve, as used on 220SE.

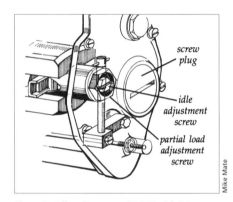

Figure 2. Idle adjustment, 220SE with R1 pump.

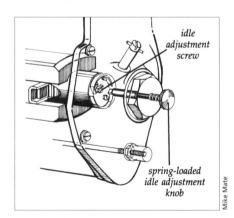

Figure 3. Idle adjustment, 220SE.

manipulation on the car. The primary position must be set on the test bench of a qualified service facility.

R1 Injection Pump

A minor variation of the foregoing procedure occurs on early 220SE cars equipped with the R1 injection pump, which does not have the spring-loaded idle control knob (used to engage the adjustment screw on the governor). Before the idle adjustment screw can be adjusted on this pump, the screw plug (Fig. 2) must be turned out to gain access to the adjustment screw. Originally a lead seal secured this plug, and it must be detached. The idle adjustment screw is turned notch by notch, as in the preceding process, but care must be taken not to turn the partial load adjustment screw at the same time. The partial load adjustment screw should be held steady with a socket while the idle adjustment screw is being adjusted. After the idle adjustment screw has been adjusted, the partial load adjustment screw should be moved to the right against the alignment lock.

Since oil runs out of the housing when the idle adjustment screw is turned out, the oil must be topped up and oil level checked after idle adjustment. After each setting of the idle adjustment screw, the screw plug must be re-installed; otherwise the oil in the injection pump housing will be thrown out.

230SL, Etc.

In 1963, when the 230SL was introduced, it used the definitive form of pure mechanical gasoline injection—with a separate plunger in the injection pump for each cylinder, injection valves at the intake ports and control of fuel quantity through linkage between the throttle valve and the adjusting lever on the injection pump. Thus, all injection pumps had either six or eight plungers. Idle adjustment is the same as for the two-plunger system. All subsequent models with pure mechanical injection used the same system as the 230SL.

In this article we're dealing with the idling stage only as it relates to keeping the engine in readiness to go to work. In 1968 the U.S. government initiated emission control regulations. Compliance required precise engine control while idling as well as while running, because idling occurs in circumstances which promote high concentrations of pollutants.

Idle Speeds

The following idle speeds are specified by MBNA for USA cars with gasoline injection, 1954 to 1987.

Model	Engine	Injection Type	Idle Speed, rpm
300SL, 1954–63	M198 w/std. cam	A	700–800
300SL, 1954–63	M198 w/race cam	A	1,000–1,100
300Sc, 1955–58	M199	A	500–600
300d, 1957–62	M189	B	600–650
220SE, 1958–60	M127 III	C	700–800
220SEb, 1959–65	M127 III	C	750–800
300SE, 1961–63	M189	C	650–700
230SL, 1963–67	M127 II	D	750–800
600, 1963–72	M100	D	560–600
300SE, 1964–67	M189	D	650–700
250SE, 1965–68	M129	D	750–800
300SE/SEL, 1965–67	M189	D	750–800
250SL, 1966–68	M129 III	D	750–800
280SL, 1967–71	M130	D	750–800
280SE /SEL, 1967–72	M130	D	750–800
300SEL, 1967–70	M130	D	750–800
300SEL 6.3, 1968–72	M100	D	560–600
300SEL 3.5, 1969–72	M116	E	700–750
280SE/SEL 3.5, 1970/72	M116	E	700–750
350SL/SLC, 1970–71	M116	E	700–750
280SE/SEL 4.5, 1971–72	M117	E	700–800
300SEL 4.5, 1971–72	M117	E	700–800
450SL/SLC/SE/SEL, 1972–75	M117	E	700–800
450SL/SLC/SE/SEL, 1976–80	M117	CIS	700–750
450SEL 6.9, 1975–79	M100	CIS	580–620
280E/SE, 1977–81	M110	CIS	750 ±50
380SE/SEL/SEC, 1981–82	M116	CIS	500 ±50
380SE/SEL/SEC, 1983–85	M116	CIS	650 ±50
500SL/SEL/SEC, 1984–85	M117	CIS	650 +100/−50
190E 2.3, 1984–86	M102	CIS-E	720 ±50
190E 2.3, 1987	M102	CIS-E	750 ±50
190E 2.3-16, 1986–87	M102	CIS-E	890 ±50
300E, 1986	M103	CIS-E	650 ±50
420SEL, 1986	M116	CIS-E	650 +100/−50
560SL/SEL/SEC, 1986	M117	CIS-E	650 +100/−50
190E 2.6, 1987–	M103	CIS-E	700 ±50
260E, 1987–	M103	CIS-E	700 ±50

Injection types: A = six-plunger mechanical, direct into cylinder; B = six-plunger mechanical, into intake pipe; C = two-plunger mechanical, into intake port; D = six- or eight-plunger mechanical, into intake port; E = electronically controlled injection; CIS = continuous injection system; CIS-E = continuous injection system with electronic control.

Consequently, adjustment of the idle speed on 1968 and later cars should be done with instruments that measure compliance with applicable emission control regulations.

Electronic Fuel Injection

In September 1969, the 280SE 3.5 coupe and convertible and the 300SE 3.5 were introduced, becoming available in the United States in 1970. These cars' most significant technical advance was their electronically controlled fuel injection, the Bosch D-Jetronic system, familiarly known as EFL. This system meters the correct amount of fuel through electronically controlled electromagnetic injection valves. Each cylinder has an injection valve in the intake port of the cylinder head, directly before the inlet valve. Fuel is injected intermittently, once per working stroke. The amount injected is determined by the duration of the valve opening, which is dictated by the electronic control unit. Injection pressure is provided by the main fuel pump at 28.4 psi (1.96 bar).

The electronic control unit (ECU), familiarly called the black box or brain, receives signals from seven or eight sources and sends out orders to the fuel pump and injection valves. There is the usual throttle valve, which must be snugly closed when idling, and the idle air bypass, familiar from the old mechanical systems. An idle speed air screw controls the amount of air that can pass through and is used to adjust idle speed in the same way as those on mechanical systems. This should not be confused with another component which bypasses air around the throttle, the auxiliary air valve, which is thermostatically controlled and handles engine warm-up. The idle speed air screw is generally just left of the auxiliary air valve, which is directly behind the ignition distributor.

Idle speed mixture control is a function of the electronic control unit but can be varied by ±10 percent with an adjustment screw on the ECU box, the only manual control on the box.

Since the ECU is at different points on different models, it should be located at leisure in good light. On models 107 (350SL, 450SL, 450SLC), the ECU is accessible after loosening the inner lining under the glove box. On Models 116 (450SE/SEL), it is in the right front footwell. The adjusting screw is accessible upon removal of ornamental molding.

CIS Injection

A completely new injection system was introduced for model year 1976, a mechanical system with control of the quantity of fuel through an airflow sensor. Fuel is injected continuously while the engine is running, so the system is referred to as the CIS (Continuous Injection System) or the Bosch K-Jetronic system. All air for the combustion process is drawn past the airflow sensor. There is the usual throttle of the butterfly valve type, but it is downstream from the airflow sensor. There are also the usual throttle bypasses: one for idle air, one for auxiliary air. These passages, however, bypass only the throttle, taking air that has passed the airflow sensor and leading it around the throttle. When the engine idles, the throttle must be completely closed.

Idle speed is controlled by the idle air adjusting screw, about four inches

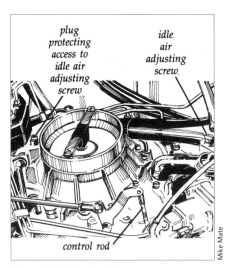

Figure 4. CIS Injection System.

forward and slightly left of the airflow sensor. Idle mixture adjustment should not be attempted without such tools as an oil telethermometer, tachometer and CO measuring instrument; the following provides an understanding of the process and is not a work instruction.

Between the airflow sensor and the fuel distributor is a protective plug which is removed for access to the idle mixture adjusting screw. This may be turned with a three-mm Allen wrench for a hex socket screw. The screw is turned clockwise for a richer mixture, counterclockwise for leaner. This adjustment alters the relationship between airflow sensor and mixture control plunger. The protective plug must be re-installed after adjustment.

With succeeding model years the protection of this idle mixture adjusting screw against tampering or untrained access has become more secure. It started in model year 1976 with a screw plug and progressed to a tower sealed with a steel plug which is inserted at the factory with a special tool after the idle mixture is set.

As of model year 1981, government regulations require that the idle mixture adjustment be inaccessible in order to prevent unauthorized adjustment. The idle mixture may be checked and adjusted only in cases of replacement of fuel injection/emission control parts or engine repair. In doing so, the adjustment tower is destroyed by drilling, and a new tower must be installed with break-away bolts.

In 1980, Daimler-Benz began phasing lambda closed-loop control into their cars, and adjustment of the idle mixture became virtually impossible except to well-equipped and authorized facilities. By 1984, electronic control of idle speed was added, and idle speed and idle mixture both became factory-set functions. Either the idle is correct in all respects, or there is a malfunction in the system, and that is not a subject for twiddling screws and replacing jets.

Technical and Restoration Forum

Technical and Restoration Forum

Exhaust

Turbocharger

Technical and Restoration Forum

Starting and Idling

230SL Starting Surge

January/February 1992

When I try to start my 1964 230SL, the engine revs high then dies. It does so up to 10 times before it idles smoothly. At idle I can hear air being drawn into the injection pump; as the engine warms up, the noise stops. If you can solve this for me, I'll put you in my will.

Your injection pump has probably been readjusted so often that it is hopelessly out of adjusting range. It probably needs overhaul and calibration. There may be other good shops for this, but we understand that Pacific Fuel Injection in Burlingame, California (418/342-5536) does an excellent job.

As a temporary fix, disconnect the air line from the injection pump to the intake manifold, and plug both connections, which eliminates air being drawn through the pump into the manifold. It'll be better, but fixing the pump is the ultimate solution.

Slow Fire

November/December 1997

My 1969 280SL has an entirely new fuel injection system, but when starting from cold or if hot after 30 minutes or so, the engine stumbles for a few seconds then runs fine. Fuel pressure is good.

A unit called the fuel pressure regulator or fuel accumulator—in the fuel line after the fuel pump and filter—maintains a constant pressure in the fuel supply system for a fairly long period. If the system is in good condition, that could be up to several weeks. If for any reason the fuel leaks back into the tank, this regulator or accumulator must be refilled and

brought up to pressure by the pump before the engine will run smoothly. A technician will normally check fuel pressure with the engine running or shortly after it has been shut off, which does not reveal the leakdown condition. Since you have eliminated other likely causes, you may find that the problem is caused by fuel leaking back into the tank. This is not a Mercedes-Benz idiosyncracy. I would expect to find it on any car with Bosch fuel injection, usually in older cars.

Rough Idling 450SL

July/August 1996

My 1976 450SL sometimes idles roughly and may stall when I accelerate from a stop. If I ease up on the throttle, it gets to cruising speed, where the problem disappears. The fuel pump no longer buzzes when I start the engine, which now takes more turns to fire. I know that a switch on the fuel distributor stops the pump if the engine is not running; could this cause the problem?

Replacing the fuel pump may help. A check valve inside the pump maintains residual pressure in the fuel line when the engine is not running. The fuel pump runs only if the starter motor is actuated or the engine is running. You can check the safety switch as follows: with the ignition turned off, remove the air filter; disconnect the plug from the safety switch; connect a voltmeter to the positive (+) of the battery and alternately to the two terminals of the switch. With the sensor plate of the airflow sensor *not* depressed, the voltmeter should read 11 volts on both contacts. If the meter shows 11 volts on only one contact, the mixture regulator must be removed, and the contacts of the safety switch must be cleaned.

560SEL Rough Hot Start

May/June 2001

My 1986 560SEL has had excellent care and has only 38,000 miles, yet during warm starts it stumbles for a few seconds before running smoothly. The fuel pump was replaced, I use 93-octane gasoline, and I put in Techron occasionally to keep the injectors clean, but that hasn't helped. How can I fix this problem?

Start by testing fuel pressures to make sure the rest pressure is maintained. If the system fails to maintain 2–3 bar for over half an hour, the problem is the injectors leaking off. Techron or other additives can prevent fuel injection system clogging but are less effective after the problem has developed. The solution is to replace all of the injectors. CIS fuel-injection systems do not like sitting unused for long periods of time. Moisture and fuel evaporation leave deposits that are not easily dislodged, so low mileage and meticulous care are no guarantee that you'll avoid fuel-injection problems.

230SL Hot Start Problem

January/February 1991

My 1966 230SL runs well but is tough to start when hot except when left for only a few minutes. When the engine cools, it starts fine. I checked the solenoid on the intake plenum, and it is activated during starting.

Assuming that the usual tune-up procedure hasn't helped, you may recall that today's gasoline vaporizes at lower temperatures, causing vapor lock, which prevents fuel from flowing to the engine. With the engine running, cooler fuel from the tank doesn't have time to boil, so this doesn't occur.

The remedy is to activate the cold-start device for a few seconds when starting a hot engine. This can be done by installing a one-second time switch to give a short squirt of fuel when starting. Part number for the switch is 001 545 16 24; part number for the cable harness to connect it is 108 540 10 09. An alternate is installation of a momentary switch that the driver can use while starting the engine, but this isn't exactly original equipment.

Leaky Injectors

May/June 2000

With 85,000 miles on it, my 1983 380SL is driven less than 3,000 miles a year, but it starts hard when warm. Started cold, it runs perfectly, but when warmed up, it starts then stalls then requires excessive cranking to re-start. My mechanic, who can't duplicate the problem in his shop, is puzzled.

It sounds as if the fuel injectors are leaking off pressure when the car is stopped hot. As the injectors leak, the lines empty, leaving no fuel in them. When you restart the car, depending on temperature, it may start—on the cold start valve or on the fuel that has leaked down onto the intake valves— then die. As the lines fill again while you're cranking, the engine starts on a couple of cylinders and eventually runs on all eight as all lines are purged of vapor. To rule out the loss of system pressure when the engine is shut down, have the fuel pressures checked, especially the rest pressure. If that pressure stays above 2 bar for 30 minutes or more, replacing the injectors should solve your problem.

Rough Idling Diesel

November/December 1995

At 105,000 miles, my 1982 300D turbo-diesel has had a rough idle for some time. After an earlier algae problem I used Biobor Diesel Doctor, which helped a bit, but the condition persists. What can you suggest? Could it be the injectors?

From your description, it seems likely that the injector nozzles are fouled with deposits. I suggest trying Chevron Techron, following the instructions on the bottle. If the first treatment doesn't help, try a second but no more. You could then try Lubro Moly Diesel Purge. Both additives are available from advertisers in *The Star*. If neither helps, the injectors should be removed and checked by a properly trained and equipped mechanic. It is more effective to replace injectors with rebuilt ones than to clean and adjust them locally. Injection timing should also be checked, but it is unlikely that it will have changed. It would also be prudent to replace the timing chain and tensioner at your present mileage, although chain wear is probably not the cause of the rough idle.

Drivability

Hesitant 450SL

March/April 1998

My 1979 450SL runs roughly when I try to accelerate with a cold engine, almost as if the fuel is being cut off intermittently. After standing for a while, it runs fine. I thought it might be bad gas, a faulty fuel pump, or a clogged fuel filter, but it's not. How can I isolate the problem?

The cold-start problem is probably a malfunction of the warm-up/ enrichment phase of the fuel injection system. This senses engine temperature and increases the control pressure, which enriches the air/fuel mixture. As the engine warms up, enrichment is reduced. If the cause is not found, the car will probably continue to run poorly. The cold start device is separate from the warm-up, so you will be able to start the engine, but it will not continue to run in very cold conditions. The warm-up also provides full-load enrichment, so even the warm engine will accelerate poorly.

450SLC Hesitation

May/June 1999

My 1980 450SLC lacks power and hesitates when I apply the throttle. I have replaced the fuel pump, accumulator, filter, injectors, distributor cap, rotor, plug wires, and spark plugs with new parts. I have "scoped" the engine, and the electrical system looks good. Compression is between 178 and 185 psi. The problem persists. I am at my wits' end. The only thing I can think of is the fuel distributor. Are there any adjustments I can make to it, can it be rebuilt, or should I buy a new one?

How have you diagnosed the problem so far? Have you connected a set of CIS pressure gauges and examined the warm-up regulator, which controls the fuel quantity injected through the fuel distributor? It seems you have thrown a bunch of parts against the problem without taking the time to have the problem properly diagnosed. Hesitation is usually caused by lack of on-throttle enrichment, which is managed by the warm-up regulator. When the regulator notices a drop in engine vacuum (as you step on the accelerator), it enriches the mixture for acceleration. This can only be tested with the CIS pressure gauges. No individual fuel distributor parts are available; rebuilt units are available from Bosch.

Cool Your Jets

January/February 1997

My 1975 450SL runs beautifully all winter and when first started on summer days, but on hot Texas days, when started after being driven for an hour then standing 10–15 minutes, it has less power and runs roughly. I've replaced the fuel pump, fuel filter, coil, plugs, and points to no effect. I solved problems with vapor lock on an antique car by running a return fuel line back to the tank; could the return line on my 450SL be blocked? The electric fuel pump stops after a few seconds, which means that hot fuel is not being returned to the tank.

The 450SL's tight engine compartment causes fuel to overheat as it passes through the lines, and the problem is compounded by heat from the 1975 model's nearby catalytic converters. When you stop, fuel in the lines near the engine vaporizes, and the injection system pumps foam instead of liquid fuel to the cylinders; the pump works less effectively doing so. On fuel-injected models, gasoline circulates back to the tank whenever the engine is running; this keeps cooler fuel coming on the supply side, but eventually the fuel in the tank becomes warmer, thus easier to vaporize.

When you switch on the ignition, the fuel pump runs for only 10 seconds unless the engine starts. The best way to flush out the hot fuel is to switch on the ignition, then as soon as the pump stops, turn it off and on again to re-start the pump. Repeat this until you get cooler fuel from the tank. When starting under these conditions, hold the throttle pedal to the floor. Since a larger quantity of fuel can absorb more heat without vaporizing, keeping the fuel tank as full as possible will also help.

The 1980 models solved this problem with a fuel cooler integrated into the air-conditioning system. We know of no one who has retrofitted this system or found another convenient cure (hood louvers?), and today's gasolines don't help. If anyone has a simple, cost-effective cure, we'd like to hear about it.

Slow Warm-Up
July/August 1995

My 1971 280SE recently had a complete tune-up but continues to have the same problem; it runs roughly or stalls while reaching operating temperature. It starts well and runs well cold or fully warmed, but if I come to a stop after three or four minutes of driving, the engine runs roughly and sometimes stalls. It always starts again, but it may do this several times before reaching normal temperature. I have experience as a professional mechanic and have the workshop manuals, but I can't locate the trouble. Can you help?

In the manual's chapter on fuel injection is a section called Warming Up Mechanism with a drawing of the corrector assembly of the fuel injection pump. This assembly contains a cooling water thermostat, and hoses carry coolant to and from the corrector assembly. This device provides more fuel and air during warm-up.

Your symptoms indicate a malfunction in this warm-up system. The thermostat may be defective, or the settings may be such that the device is inoperative. Deposits may have formed around the thermostat or in the coolant lines; hoses can deteriorate and swell inside, restricting flow. The warm-up mechanism is supposed to operate with gradually decreasing effect until the coolant temperature reaches 60–68°C (140-155°F), when it no longer functions.

The warm-up mechanism, best identified by the coolant hose running to and from it, should not be confused with the cold-starting mechanism.

Slow Diesel!
July/August 1995

My 1979 300SD has covered about 85,000 miles and has recently slowed down even by diesel standards. My mechanic and I replaced a faulty turbocharger and had the injection pump rebuilt, but the car is only slightly faster. Top speed is only about 65 mph, and acceleration is poor. The fuel injection system has been checked; the turbocharger is operating; the fuel system and filters are fine. The fuel tank is clean, and the engine compression is good. The transmission checks out, and the vacuum system operates properly. Any ideas?

The aneroid compensator on the injection pump may not be working properly. This device reacts to increasing turbocharger boost pressure and moves the main rack in the pump to supply additional fuel. An even more common cause might be an interruption in the line to the switch-over valve, part of the engine overload protection. If the line is plugged, or if it slips off the switchover valve, it signals the injection pump that fuel should be reduced to the amount supplied to a naturally aspirated engine. This makes the car behave as if it were not a turbo but a plain 300D.

Operation and Fuel

Fuel Pump Failure
November/December 1990

My 1978 280CE ran out of gas 50 ft from the pump. I tried to restart it and failed, so I pushed it to the pump and put gas in, but it still wouldn't start. My mechanic told me I needed a new fuel pump, that the bearings in the pump are lubricated by fuel and can burn out if one runs out of gas. Is this right?

Normal life for a fuel pump is 100,000 miles; many last longer, but anything over 100,000 is exceptionally long service. These pumps run either 1) when the key is turned to the start position or 2) when the engine is running. If the engine stops, the fuel pump relay turns off the pump. What probably happened in your case is that a well-worn pump inhaled sludge and water from the bottom of your tank as it ran dry. This, or running the pump dry, could finish off an old pump. On the other hand, your car may not have actually run out of gas. The fuel pump may have failed just as you reached the gas station, causing the engine to stop even though a little fuel remained in the tank.

Fuel Injection Pump Oil Level
January/February 1991

My 250SL's fuel injection pump overflows with oil. After the excess is sucked out, it overflows again after a few hours of driving. Will this damage the pump, and how can I fix it?

There are two possible causes. First, there should be a restrictor in the oil line to the fuel injection pump. If the pump was removed, this restrictor may have been lost and not reinstalled. Second, if the pump was removed and reinstalled, excessive sealant may have squeezed out to form a bead, reducing the size of the opening into the crankcase. This hole may also be blocked by sludge, restricting oil return to the engine.

Reg'lar or Ethel?

September/October 2003

I bought my 1972 280SE 4.5 from the original owner, who always used premium fuel. The owner's manual suggests an octane of at least 91. Some say I can use regular gas, others say premium. I don't want to compromise the car's health or performance, but I don't want to pay $45 to fill the tank unless I need to.

To determine which fuel to use, you must dig through much misunderstanding. First, the octane requirement in the 1972 owner's manual is Research Octane Number (RON). Today's pumps show octane numbers that are RON + MON divided by 2, MON being Motor Octane Number. The old 91 RON is regular gasoline today, with an octane number between 85 and 87, depending on altitude. This is more than ample for an engine with as low a compression ratio (8:1) as yours. Regular gas will compromise neither health nor performance. Increasing octane above that required to avoid pre-ignition (knock) gains nothing in power. Power is measured by the BTU's in the fuel, not its anti-knock rating. The anti-knock rating tells you whether or not the fuel has sufficient protection against pre-ignition for your engine's compression ratio. The higher the compression ratio, the more anti-knock protection is needed.

We don't rely on knock sensors in modem engines to retard the timing when we use lower-grade fuel on a permanent basis. The problem with regular gasoline is that the refining process allows it to be too volatile, so it vaporizes rather easily, causing vapor lock if the fuel system doesn't hold pressure long enough. We suggest a mid-grade fuel, as its vapor pressure specs are much better than those for regular. If you hear pinging under load, especially in hot weather, have your Mercedes-Benz mechanic check your ignition timing and the advance mechanism in the distributor. The 280SE 4.5 uses vacuum retard at idle, so when you step on the throttle, the timing jumps 15 to 20 degrees immediately, so timing must be set correctly.

220S Carburetors

May/June 2002

The engine in my 1962 220S, with twin Solex 32 PAIATA carburetors, was rebuilt three years ago, but after standing unused it is getting harder and harder to start when cold. It has spark, and will start and run beautifully when warm. The mechanic who rebuilt the engine can't seem to help. What do you suggest?

If the engine always runs fine when warm but is hard to start cold and runs roughly then, the problem is probably in the carburetors. If you have a fuel delivery problem—a clogged tank strainer or faulty fuel pump—it would show up warm as well as cold. These carburetors have manual chokes and accelerator pumps. By pumping the throttle while looking into the primary venturi, you can check to see that the accelerator pumps are squirting fuel into the venturi. If they aren't, it can be very hard to get enough fuel into a cold engine to get it to start. The chokes tend to be fairly trouble-free, but the fuel passages could be plugged. (If the float valves are stuck closed, no fuel can get into the float chambers.) Old carbureted cars don't like to sit for long. Even using fuel preservative, in less than a year their internal passages can get plugged with deposits from evaporated fuel. if you are not comfortable disassembling the carburetors and cleaning the jets and passages, have a professional do it. Ask other section members about nearby independent shops. (*Two local shops were suggested to this member. Ed.*)

Fuel Supply Snag

January/February 1993

While restoring a 1969 300SEL 6.3 that had not been run for years, I had trouble getting a steady supply of fuel to the engine. I cleaned or replaced the fuel filters, flushed the tank, rebuilt the fuel level sender assembly, and cleaned the fuel pump. While draining the tank, fuel flowed out for a few seconds then slowed to a trickle.

You'll probably find that the problem is caused by a clogged fuel tank vent line. This line goes to a valve box that opens at two different pressures. At the lower pressure, 12–18 millibar, gas vapors flow to the crankcase. If pressure rises to 35–50 millibar, vapors are vented to outside air (this was changed in 1970). If pressure becomes negative, as when fuel is sucked off to the engine or the temperature drops, a third valve opens at 12–16 millibar to allow outside air into the tank. If that third valve or the vent line is clogged, fuel flow from the tank will slow. In some diesels, which have a different kind of pump, we have seen fuel tanks collapse as the vacuum inside increased.

You can easily check to see if this is the problem. So that air can enter the tank, leave the filler cap loose. Some have cured this problem with a vented filler cap, but that's illegal and bad practice. If the tank was thoroughly flushed, and all scale or deposits removed, the vent should be the culprit.

Ponton Octane

November/December 2003

In the September/October issue you discussed gasoline octane ratings based on RON (Research Octane Number) and MON (Motor Octane Number). You said the old 91 RON is equal to today's regular gasoline with an octane between 85 and 87 (RON+MON divided by 2): "This is more than ample for an engine with as low a compression ratio (8:1) as [a 1972 280SE 4.5]." What does this mean for 1950s 220S/SE engines with 8.7:1 compression? The 220S manual specifies 93- to 95-octane fuel according to the Research Method (ROZ). How does that ROZ figure relate to today's octane ratings? Do these engines require today's premium gasoline?

ROZ is the German equivalent of RON, and 93 to 95 RON (ROZ) fuel was fairly low octane in its day, when fuels of up to 104 and 106 octane were available at the pump. An 8.7:1 compression ratio is considered low and would not need premium fuel. Early 1960's American engines had compression ratios as high as 10:1 or 10.5:1 for street use, without knock sensors. While the cylinder head of the ponton engine is a fairly old design and may cause pre-ignition from hot spots, modern fuels have excellent knock prevention. If I owned a ponton, I would probably run it on middle-grade fuel. At altitude, as here in Denver, I would even think about running it on regular. An 8.7:1 ratio should not cause detonation.

240D Idle Adjusting Knob

May/June 1988

I'd like to know more about the idle adjusting knob on my 1982 240D. Is there any other use than during cold weather starting?

The basic purpose of the idle speed adjustment is to provide extra fuel for a fast idle after cold starts, as cold oil is more viscous, requiring more power to overcome internal friction. As the engine warms, the idle speed is returned to normal.

Other uses may not have been thought of when the car was being designed. Starting diesels can be difficult at very low temperatures, and it can finally become so cold that they won't start without help. I lived in Montreal for 26 years, and the common wisdom there was that if you got caught overnight where you couldn't run your block heater, you should let the engine run all night at fast idle. The idle speed adjustment makes this possible.

Some drivers also find that the engine vibrates annoyingly when idling with the air conditioning on, so they use the adjustment to speed up the idle.

Diesel Fuel Tank Capacity

March/April 1993

The fuel tank on my 1982 240D is supposed to hold 17.2 gallons, including 2.5 gallons in reserve. Even after running completely out, the most fuel that I've ever been able to put into it is 15 gallons.

A friend, curious about the actual capacity of his 240D's tank, deliberately ran out of fuel. He was then able to put in only 14 gallons. Investigating, he found that the lower 2 or 3 inches of the screen in the tank which surrounds the outlet to the pump was covered with tar-like residue, blocking the flow when about three gallons remained in the tank.

Removing and cleaning the screen cured the problem. Drain your tank and check the strainer. Fill the tank only up to the point where the filler hose kicks off. Overfilling can cause spillage in the trunk and diesel fumes in the car. After the tank is drained then filled this way, drive until the reserve light comes on, then fill the tank again. You will then know if the light comes on too soon and how much fuel you have in reserve.

Knowing of the difficulty in starting a diesel that has run out of fuel, I never let mine run out. Only once in 13 years have I had the reserve light come on. On trips, I stop for fuel when I need 8 or 9 gallons.

Diesel Fuel Inlet Clogging

September/October 1990

My 1981 300SD idles roughly when the tank gets below one-quarter full. I've changed the fuel filters to no avail, but before I tear into the fuel tank or the fuel pump, can you suggest any other cure?

It sounds as though the fuel filter in the tank is clogged part way up. The filter, a cylindrical screen around the outlet pipe, can clog from the bottom up so that you can't use the fuel below the clogged level. As the fuel level approaches the clogged section, fuel supply becomes erratic, so the engine idles roughly. There's probably also some sludge in the tank bottom that should be cleaned out. There's no easy way out. We know of no cleaner that will eliminate the tarry sludge. You'll have to clean the tank.

WassaWasserSeprater?

November/December 1998

What is a water separator, and do I need one on my diesel?

My diesel period included plenty of trouble caused by water in the fuel supply. I bought most fuel from high-volume pumps with near-new tanks, where the station owner tested for water. Nevertheless, water always seemed to be present in the fuel tank due to condensation, which cannot be eliminated, plus condensation in the station's underground tanks and the delivery tanker.

Even minute amounts of water are the enemy of injectors and injection pumps. Because tiny droplets of incompressible water are larger than the holes in the injector tips, when the injection pump forces the water/fuel mixture through the injectors, the carefully sized holes, which determine the spray pattern, become enlarged. This alters the pattern needed for quiet operation and good fuel economy. In my 1978 300D, purchased new and driven 120,000 miles, fuel economy dropped about 10 percent, and idle rattle increased. Instead of an even clatter, combustion noises became uneven: "taptaptap TAPtaptap TAPTAP taptap."

Since Mercedes-Benz diesel models had no water separators in the fuel system, my factory warranty replaced 13 injectors or injector tips. Dealers were rebuilding injectors and resetting the pressures then, but now, because of labor costs, they simply install new or factory-rebuilt injectors. That does not mean that the injectors are calibrated properly, so they should be checked before installation.

Other diesel car manufacturers provided water traps, some with warning systems, to try to solve the problem and reduce warranty claims. Anyone owning a boat with a diesel engine will probably find a water separator in the fuel line ahead of all filters and the injection pump.

Racor-brand water separators, used in marine and diesel truck applications, look like an old-fashioned fuel filter with a removable transparent Lexan bowl comprising the bottom half. A brass valve on the bottom of the bowl drains it. In the upper housing is a removable four-micron paper filter. I changed it every 4,000 miles, probably overkill, but after installation, injector troubles vanished for 70,000 miles until I sold the car. To show how little water it takes to destroy injectors, I never found more than a teaspoon of water in the bottom of the bowl.

The Racor unit is about the size of a large grapefruit. I made a bracket and mounted it on the wheelwell by the main filter. It was plumbed into the fuel line before the pre-filter using diesel fuel hose and high-quality clamps. All connections must be absolutely airtight because fuel is being drawn, not pushed, through it, so a leak will pull in air, and the engine won't run. Normal change intervals on the main filter and pre-filter were overkill but I wanted no further grief, which would be costly.

Diesel Knock

September/October 1988

What makes diesel cars knock? Some are very noisy, while others aren't. Why?

Typical diesel knock is almost always caused by late or incomplete combustion. A very cold engine always knocks because the cold engine delays the burning of the fuel; as the engine warms, the knock should disappear. If not, the cause may be poor fuel (low cetane number), a bad injector spray pattern or late injection. If the spray pattern is incorrect, some fuel does not start to burn when it should; then, as it is heated by the burning of the rest of the fuel, it suddenly explodes, causing the knock. A poor spray pattern can be caused by deposits on the injector nozzles or by faulty adjustment of the nozzles.

It's uncommon for an injection pump to get out of time and inject too late (or too early, even more rare), but it can happen. Injection pump timing is checked by determining the point at which injection starts.

Diesel knock should not be confused with the louder noise of a diesel engine compared with a gasoline engine. The much higher compression pressures in a diesel make it inherently noisier than a gasoline engine of similar capacity. This is one reason for encapsulating diesel engines as DBAG has done, which also makes some seem quieter than others.

Service

High Tension Mixture

September/October 1991

When adjusting the fuel mixture of my 1984 190E 2.3 via the mixture control screw, in the mixture controller, the factory manual states, "Turning to left = tension higher," and, "Turning to right = tension lower." What does this mean? Which way is leaner, and which way is richer?

Left is leaner, right is richer.

Zenith's Nadir

July/August 1996

The Zenith carburetors on my 1966 230S have float bowl vent valves. When idle speed drops, a lever pushes up on the vent valve shaft and raises the rubber diaphragm against spring pressure. When the valve is so opened, the space above the fuel in the float bowl is connected to the outside atmosphere. Because this transition coincided with a stumble or hesitation, I bent the lever to the side so that it could not open the valve, and the engine ran better. The idle mixture could be set leaner, and the engine was less likely to stall. When another mechanic re-activated the valves, the engine began to stall again, and the inside of the tailpipe turned black instead of the usual healthy gray-brown. Should I disable the float valves again, and will this do any harm?

The float bowl vent valves are intended to prevent carburetor flooding when the throttle is closed, which causes high vacuum in the intake manifold. An expert on these carburetors suggested that you had already answered your own question. Disable the vent valves and enjoy the best running your engine is capable of.

E300 Diesel Fuel Filter Replacement

March/April 1996

Changing the fuel filter on my 1995 E300 Diesel is different from the old diesels. Can you verify the proper replacement procedure?

Changing the filter on your 606.910 engine is similar to the same job in previous diesels with two exceptions. First, your car has only one fuel filter; the old familiar plastic in-line filter is not present. Second, the injection system bleeds itself automatically, like the 601, 602, and 603 engines, so there's no need for the old hand pump bleeding. Still, it's wise to fill the new filter element as full as possible with fresh diesel fuel so that less cranking will be needed to start. When the engine starts, run it at about 1,500 rpm, and keep it running for a few minutes. If you stop the engine before the automatic bleeding is complete, restarting it will be difficult. Check for leaks with the engine running, as usual.

Capital Problem

November/December 1985

I've owned three diesels (two 240D's and a 300D turbo-diesel), and on each the small rubber cap on the rearmost injector fuel leak-off fitting has split and caused leakage of fuel into the engine compartment. I now carry an extra cap in the glove compartment. What can be done to prevent the problem?

Most diesel owners carry a couple of spare rubber caps to replace the one on the fuel leak-off fitting of the rearmost injector nozzle when it starts to leak. Such leakage will be noticed quickly because of the strong smell of diesel fuel when the engine is stopped after a drive. When the engine has cooled down enough to permit touching the cap, replacing it is easy. If the old cap is stuck, a pointed knife blade may be used to remove it.

Starting with November 1984 production, a modified cap was installed which should have a much longer service life than the old all-rubber cap. This new cap can be identified by the metal plug in the end. Its part number is 403 070 00 55 or 403 070 03 55; cost is about $1.50. If you've never had to replace the cap, thank your thoughtful mechanic, who probably replaced it during routine service.

Air in Fuel Lines

January/February 2000

I just changed both fuel filters on my 1984 240D: I bled the fuel line, but it won't start. What am I doing wrong?

After replacing fuel filters, pump the hand pump to fill up the main filter and injection pump. Pump it until you hear a buzz from the return line check valve on the engine side of the injection pump. The engine should then start with a minimum of cranking.

Exhaust

E420 Oxygen Sensor, Low Coolant Warning
March/April 2002

My 1994 E420's engine stumbles on cold starts, and in cold weather it surges when idling until it's warmed up. Is the oxygen sensor heated? Would a new oxygen sensor prevent this, or is it an engine management computer problem? Another problem is that the low coolant light comes on every few months, even when the level is normal The light may stay on for a few days then go out. Any ideas?

The oxygen sensor on your car is heated. If the heater fails, the sensor will still work, but it will take much longer to reach operating temperature (about 600°F). If the sensor generates no signal, the check engine light will eventually come on. A good sensor starts generating a signal within one or two minutes. If your cold running problem occurs only before the sensor kicks in, the oxygen sensor is not faulty. When the engine is operating in "open-loop", before the oxygen sensor is hot, the fuel mixture is controlled by the computer based on inputs from various sensors. If any of these sensors is faulty, or if a mechanical problem exists that the sensors can't recognize, the engine may run oddly.

There are no "vacuum leak sensors" or "clogged fuel injector sensors," so the possibilities are almost endless as to what is causing the car to run poorly in open loop. Since it runs fine when warm, the oxygen sensor is probably working but compensating for the problem by trimming the fuel mixture. This engine's electronic throttle actuator may be causing erratic idle and balky acceleration. If the symptoms are reproducible, take it to a reputable repair shop and have them diagnose the problem.

If the low coolant level light comes on when the level is correct, the sensor is faulty. I've found with another German car that if the antifreeze concentration is too weak, such as pure water, the sensor indicates a low level even when the reservoir is full. I haven't experimented with Mercedes-Benz sensors, but they may do the same thing. Either way, the sensor is cheap, so replace it.

Oxygen Sensor Indicator Light
November/December 1989

The oxygen sensor light in my 1984 190E 2.3 came on at about 31,200 miles. In the section covering oxygen sensor replacement, the factory manual tells you to remove the warning light bulb. Why should the indicator light be thus disabled?

The EPA once required that all new cars have the 30,000-mile warning light and that oxygen sensors be replaced then. The light comes on only after the first 30,000 miles, and it was found that oxygen sensors usually lasted much longer than expected. The 1986 and later cars don't have the light. At the 30,000-mile service, remove the bulb and forget the light. Any competent mechanic can check the oxygen sensor. When it fails, the fuel injection goes to the full-rich mode. The car will run, and performance may not be diminished, but fuel mileage and emissions will suffer.

Fried Spark Plug Wires
November/December 1988

My 1975 450SL, which has the catalytic converter right under the exhaust manifolds, has been frying spark plug wires. The number one spark plug wire lasts only a couple of weeks. Is there a fix, such as a shield?

This common problem is usually caused by the removal of the heat shield over the exhaust manifold. If the shields are still in place on your car, the next most likely cause is an exhausted and overheating catalytic converter. Because performance will be affected and the heat could contribute to vapor lock and even fire danger, replacement of the catalytic converters is essential. The catalytic converters were moved from this area on later SL's.

Cracked Exhaust Manifold
July/August 1992

My 1972 350SL's right exhaust manifold is cracked between the two rear cylinders. The manifold has expansion joints, but parts catalogs show it available only as a complete assembly, at more than $700. Can I buy just the rear half, or is there another way to repair it?

You could have the crack welded up with nickel by a good machine shop. This form of brazing uses nickel as the bonding metal instead of brass. After welding, check the mating surfaces and, if necessary, grind them to restore the proper geometry at the mating surfaces. You could also buy a used replacement. Either alternative is far less expensive than buying even half of a new unit.

OM603 Trap Oxidizers Are OK

May/June 1989

My 1987 300D Turbo has a trap oxidizer and has covered 20,000 miles. I've heard conflicting reports about the possibility and consequences of trouble with the trap oxidizer. What symptoms should I watch for? Is failure likely to damage other engine components, including the turbocharger? What can I do to make the trap oxidizer last longer and operate correctly?

The probability of trap oxidizer failure is not clear. There are two forms of failure: a simple clogging with solid particles or a release of abrasive particles which may cause rapid turbocharger wear. Clogging is the most common problem; it shows up as a gradual loss of power, particularly at higher speeds. The car can still be driven.

Clogging should have no harmful effect on the turbocharger—it simply slows the flow of exhaust gas to the turbine. We've never heard of secondary engine damage as a result of oxidizer or turbocharger damage. Clogging is associated with slow driving, frequent starts and stops and inferior fuel quality. The use of any fuel additives except Chevron Techron (to clean injectors), Biobor Diesel Doctor (for algae fighting) and LM Diesel Winter Flow (for cold-weather operation) is strictly forbidden. Damage caused by use of unauthorized additives is not covered under warranty.

Fuel characteristics and driving habits are important factors in trap oxidizer performance. If you drive your car as above, take it out on the highway once a week and run it at the speed limit long enough to thoroughly warm up the engine.

Trap oxidizer problems showed up on the OM617A engine used in 1985 California turbo-diesels. DBAG made special extended warranty arrangements for these cars, including free replacement of the trap oxidizer at 30,000-mile intervals. Your car, which has the OM603 engine, is not affected, but if you experience power loss, the dealer must perform certain specific tests and inspections. The concern of owners of 603-engined cars is natural, but we believe there is no need to worry.

Turbocharger

Hose Hackers

September/October 1998

My 1985 300SD has 197,000 miles on it. A prior owner or a sneaky mechanic cut a hole in the bottom of the 90-degree rubber hose connecting the turbo waste-gate diaphragm and attaching to the rigid plastic hose to the vacuum regulating devices on the fenderwell. This causes the turbocharger diaphragm and the regulating devices to "see" atmospheric pressure at all times. When I fixed the hole, the engine seemed to make less power. What was the perpetrator trying to accomplish by venting this vacuum line? Should I expect any damage or wear from driving the car with this vent in place?

Skullduggery is afoot! A previous owner or his mechanic-accomplice may have defeated the waste-gate to maximize engine performance. So why did Mercedes-Benz deprive us of this neck-jerking power there for the taking? Should we all go to the garage at once and cut this offending hose? Put that knife away. The problem is not that simple.

A great deal of thought went into the waste-gate boost control valve. Its purpose is not to protect the turbocharger. The turbine, which normally runs at 100,000 rpm, can easily turn at 153,000 rpm, beyond the engine's needs. The waste-gate is also not there to prevent engine damage. A separate safety switch cuts fuel delivery to the fuel injection pump if overboost is detected at the intake manifold. The waste-gate's purpose is to make boost pressure available at the lowest possible engine speed and to minimize turbocharger response time.

During full-load acceleration from idle, a 300SD makes 40 mph in about eight seconds. The turbocharger reaches full boost, about 1.63 bar (9 psi), in three seconds then levels out. So after three seconds the turbo is running full boost, and there is zero spool-up time from there on. From a steady 55 mph, there should be no turbo-lag to accelerate.

Turbochargers were used in stationary diesel engines before being applied to cars. A stationary diesel usually runs at only one speed, so the turbine was built to give maximum boost at that speed. But automobile engines must make power over a wide rpm range, so their turbochargers are designed to give maximum performance at low speed and maintain that performance over the remaining performance range. You have far more blower than you need to run at cruising speed.

Why is boost pressure limited to 1.63 bar? Wouldn't more boost mean more performance? While your 300SD's turbocharger can deliver over 3 bar, the engine does not seem to operate over about 1.7 bar, just outside the limit imposed by the waste-gate. So defeating the waste-gate gains a little power increase but not enough to make it worthwhile.

Why doesn't a diesel engine give more performance at 2 bar than at 1.7 bar? The engine is probably generating more indicated horsepower at 2 bar but no more net horsepower. Anything gained by the increased oxygen supply to the cylinders is lost by the increased force necessary on the piston upstrokes to compress this overheated, hypercharged gas. This is why intercooling is necessary to cool the intake charge (making it more dense) and extract the best performance from a turbocharged engine. Instead of intercooling, where the air-charge is pre-cooled at the intake, Mercedes-Benz diesels cool the pistons using oil spray from below. (Diesel's first successful engine, in the late 19th century, was supercharged, and its piston was cooled by water conducted through a hollow connecting rod.)

For performance tweaking it makes as much sense to increase oil cooler airflow as it does to tune the waste-gate valve.

Increasing boost pressure puts tremendous mechanical and thermal loads on the engine. The engine is working against itself and producing into increased heat. Connecting rods, pistons, rings, crankshaft, and valves—all designed for the increased demands of turbocharging—are stressed beyond their design envelope, which causes early engine death. So your pressure safety switch is working, preventing engine destruction by throttling back fuel delivery. But a much better way to manage boost, leading to good performance, economy and long life, is to let the waste-gate function.

This and other aspects of the OM617A engine design are covered in SAE Technical Paper No. 780633, The Turbocharged Five-Cylinder Diesel Engine for the Mercedes-Benz 300SD, by Kurt Oblaender, Manfred Fortnagel, Hans-Jürgen Feucht, and Ulrich Conrad. It is available from the Society of Automotive Engineers, 400 Commonwealth Dr., Warrendale, PA 15096.

Fore and Aft Play
November/December 1986

My 1982 300SD has covered 125,000 miles, and while checking an oil leak, my mechanic noticed quite a bit of lateral play in the turbocharger shaft. He didn't seem concerned. Is there a way to determine when the turbo should he replaced?

Turbochargers on Mercedes-Benz diesels are noted for their longevity, and your mechanic is rightly unconcerned. There are no lateral loads on the shaft, which floats on a cushion of oil. End thrust from the driven turbine is balanced by the opposing end thrust from the compressor impeller. If there were anything wrong with your turbo, it would be evident through noise, vibration or clouds of smoke from an oil seal failure.

More on Turbo Surge, Heater Problems
May/June 1989

In the March/April issue we answered a question on turbocharger surge with cruise control engaged in a 1987 300D Turbo (Cruise Blues, page 18). We have since received more information that helps to explain and solve the problem:

A Mercedes-Benz dealer's service manager writes: "On 1986 and 1987 turbo-diesels, turbo boost can cause cruise surge. MBNA issued *Service Information 07.1/15, 54/15*, dated January 1988, to rectify the problem. When cruising at certain speeds, boost pressure can quickly rise from near zero to its full value and hence cause a significant power increase without any movement of the throttle linkage. The cruise amp responds by decelerating, thus letting the boost pressure collapse and beginning a power-on, power-off cycle. The modification outlined in the *Service Information* dampens the injection pump's response to boost pressure changes and smooths the power curve."

Another Mercedes-Benz dealer's service manager wrote that the cure described in the above *Service Information* involves "installing a vacuum damper in the EGR/transmission vacuum circuits. The job is quite involved. We have had good results with this retrofit."

The same reader provides valuable input on several questions regarding 1981–82 300D heaters in the same issue (*It's Wintertime Again…* on page 18). "All likely have the same problem. From experience we've found that the weakest link in the second-generation climate control is still the water valve. Luckily it is less expensive than the old servos. The new heater 'mono valves' are also about the only part, other than the fuses, that can be visually checked. The valve can easily be checked by removing the four screws on top of the valve and lifting the valve element from the housing. Inspect the rubber diaphragm on the bottom of the solenoid valve, and you will usually find a torn diaphragm. These 'mono valves' are supposed to have been changed in production to be stronger."

An independent shop owner commented on our response to the same questions. "On the 1972 350SL the problem is most likely loosening of the nuts holding the flap shafts to the lever assembly. They are easily accessible by dropping the under-dash panels. If the nuts are retightened and the flaps are jammed, the lever will not move, and the repair as mentioned in [the November/December 1988] issue will have to be performed." He adds, "Regarding problems with the later climate control, it has been our experience that the fault lies in the mono water valve. A quick check is to loosen the radiator cap, remove the plug from the valve, undo the four screws on top of the valve, remove the center unit and check for a torn diaphragm. Repair kit number 000 845 06 44 will usually cure the problem."

Thank you, gentlemen, for your excellent input and assistance! One of the most valuable aspects of this column is that it often generates input from experienced mechanics who have faced and solved similar problems. We welcome their input.

Why the Mercedes-Benz 250SL costs $6,897

From hand-fitted body panels to final hand-sprayed enamel coat, the 250SL is meticulously assembled on one of the world's least frantic automobile production lines.

Exquisitely well built as it is, the 250SL is no brittle showpiece. It is a highly virile machine: "This combination of absolute security, complete stability, and plain old hell-raising fun must be driven to be believed," states *Car and Driver*.

Not a 300SL

The 250SL's road-holding abilities are almost inexhaustible. This smaller, lower car even eclipses the legendary 300SL in sheer handling prowess.

Some clues: the 250SL stands a mere 4 feet, 4 inches high—yet overall width is almost 6 feet. Its track is so wide-stanced that those chubby, 14-inch *radial ply tires* seem to bulge out from the body sides to straddle the pavement. You ride on a fully independent, low-pivot rear swing-axle suspension—a design proved on the world-champion 300SLR.

The 250SL's 4-wheel *disc* brakes stop you squarely, smoothly, without pulling or fading, even in repeated hard panic stops.

Mit Einspritzer

The 250SL is only stretched to its peak when the speedometer needle nudges 124 mph. You could level off at 100 mph and stay there until it became boring or illegal.

A 6-cylinder, single overhead camshaft engine turns the trick (while turning 6500 rpm). There are few stronger or more potent 2.5 liter engines known, and one secret is an *Einspritzer*—fuel injection

system. Another secret: a high-speed bench test before it leaves the factory.

Exotic but solid

At 3000 lbs., the 250SL is one of the world's most *solid* two-seaters. The body is welded up, not bolted together. It is also hand-filed, sanded and buffed before painting. Slathered with 20 lbs. of undercoating. Coated with two primer layers. Painted, then painted again—by hand-spraying.

Hardly Spartan

The 250SL may never qualify as a pure sports car, simply because it is too comfortable. You're cradled in a contoured, thickly padded driver's seat that resembles an armchair more than a typical sports car "bucket."

"They grip, support, relax and ventilate your body supremely well," reports Britain's *Motor* magazine of these seats. They also recline. Thousands of tiny holes in the upholstery material keep air circulating. Two slots on the rear of both backrests allow pent-up heat to escape from *inside* the seat structure.

Visibility in the 250SL is so airy it's almost eerie. You sit high. The car's waist is low. Side windows arch up over 15 inches. You watch the road ahead, not a vast expanse of hood. The psychological edge alone is worth an extra 5 mph.

You can actually pack luggage in this car. There is room for 7 cu. ft. of duffle in the trunk. You can stow another 5 cu. ft. in the carpeted area behind the seats.

Options

The world's best power-assisted steering and a remarkable, *4-speed* automatic transmission are two of the few optional extras you may feel you need.

There are 3 models to choose from: the Roadster, with convertible top; the Coupe, with an all-weather removable metal hardtop that neither feels nor looks removable; and the Coupe/Roadster, which offers both and is illustrated here.

Your authorized Mercedes-Benz dealer will be glad to furnish a 250SL for a thorough test run.

Advertisement from November/December 1967 issue.

Chapter 4

Electrical System

November/December 1998

May/June 1990

January/February 2004

Repairing the E-Class Seat-Control Switch

by Jim Mahaffey, Contributing Editor

May/June 2004

Photos in this article by the author.

Invest a little time, and save yourself $130.

It's often appropriate to toss a failed automotive part into the recycling bin, but that can be a waste. One such case is the seat control switch assembly in the inside door panel of 1996–2003 E-Class cars. These switches, particularly the forward-back switch, are used often, so they eventually break. A replacement costs about $130. After a failed seat-control on our E320, we decided to try a repair before buying a new unit.

For instructions on removing the inner door panel, which contains the seat control, see "Working on E-Class Doors" in our May/June 2003 issue. Once you have the door panel off, flip it over and find the black plastic seat-control module. You had to unplug the seat-control cable from it to remove the panel from the door. The module is held in the panel by four spring catches near its four corners and sticking above the flat terrain (Figure 1). Pulling upward on the module, actuate the catches individually, using a thumbnail to push them inward; on the fourth actuation the module will spring free of the panel.

Figure 2 is a front-view of a left-side unit; the right-side is a mirror image. This collection of five seat-control switches is a fine example of good ergonomic engineering. It's shaped like a side-view of the seat, and to move the seat you simply move this effigy as you want the seat to move. It is simple, direct, requiring no written instructions or legends on the switches. The three memory push buttons, in a vertical column behind the seat-effigy, are lit by yellow LED's integral with the switches and are unlikely to need replacement.

To reach the inner workings of the module, individually actuate 10 spring-catches around its periphery (early examples use three small Phillips screws). These catches, unlike those holding the module in the door, are not obviously placed but are visible, deeply recessed behind small slots in the four sides of the module. Using a small-bladed screwdriver, press each catch inward while exerting upward force on the lid. The back of the module, which must be so removed, is shown in Figure 3.

Eventually the lid will break free, and you will see the back of the circuit board (Figure 4). To remove the board from the module and see the switches, just pry off the headrest button. Using two small-bladed screwdrivers, one under the top and one under the bottom of the headrest effigy, pry it off gently. The circuit then falls out of the shell, and you can see the workings of this engineering marvel. At first it's disappointing—just five double-pole/double-throw momentary toggle switches and four push-buttons. There are no active electronics here (Figure 5).

The question is, what broke? Why does the forward-back switch, the middle one in the lineup at the bottom of the circuit, no longer actuate the seat motor? Turns out this same failure-mode affects many circuit boards in Mercedes-Benz cars—a solder-joint is cracked. One of the four pins on the forward-back switch no longer makes perfect contact with the circuit, as the solder bonding it to the board has succumbed to metal fatigue. A quick touch with a soldering iron, using a tiny amount of lead solder, and the seat-control switch assembly is repaired. You can find these failures and confirm repair using an ohmmeter. Measure the resistance between each pin and another node in the circuit connected to the pin by printed wiring. If you see a difference in resistance between the pin and the solder holding it, you have found the failure.

It's usually possible to see the crack in the solder, but in this case the fault was extremely subtle, so we used a microscope (Figure 6). The failure is just below the number 2 on the circuit board in Figure 4. In the microscope you can see that the solder stratified when it cooled during manufacture, becoming a weak point. Look closely, and you may see a hairline crack on the lower side of the solder blob. This was not an obvious failure; a brief, naked-eye examination would not have found it.

The module reassembles easily. Just drop the circuit back into the shell, snap the lid back on, and push on the head-restraint knob. The module then snaps back into the door panel.

This was an easy fix, but eventually one of the toggle switches may fail. In that case, you can use another failed unit to make one operational unit. Find a good toggle switch on a junked module, de-solder it from the circuit board, and solder it into the unit to be repaired. When a new one is $130, anything is possible!

Figure 1. Freshly removed from the door, the switch module is visible, clipped into the back of the panel. It comes out easily by pressing four latches.

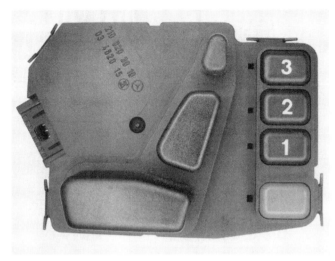

Figure 2. The module is a marvel of ergonomic, if not electrical, engineering.

Figure 3. The back of the module. Removing the lid on the back is not as straightforward as taking the module out of the door panel; you must release 10 hidden latches.

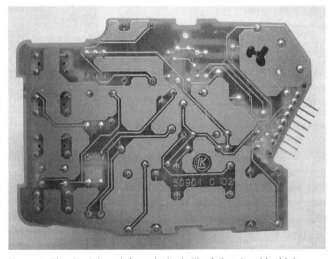

Figure 4. The circuit board, from the back. The failure is solder blob, right under the number 2 on the circuit board part number.

Figure 5. The circuit board front, showing the switches. All toggles are the same type of switch and, if necessary, could be interchanged with toggles from another board.

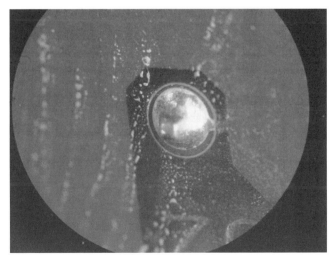

Figure 6. The failure-point, seen through a 20x stereo microscope.

Five-Minute Shift Indicator Light Fix

by John Lamb, Contributing Editor

November/December 1998

Photos in this article by the author.

How many do-it-yourselfers does it take to change a light bulb?

One annoying repair that any car needs is replacing burned-out light bulbs. It's more hassle to take the car to a shop than to replace bulbs yourself, but given today's complicated cars, how do you do it without getting in over your head or breaking something? Well, follow along as we change a light bulb that illuminates the gear selector position indicator. Although I call this a five-minute fix, it might take eight minutes or more if you look around under the console or clean parts before reassembly.

This repair was made to a 1990 300D, but all W124 300E and related models should be similar, except those with the extra console compartment. The gear selector light is in a holder below the wood trim panel. Have a replacement bulb handy, then follow these steps:

Removing Trim

Using an old credit card that won't scratch the wood, carefully pry under the plastic trim around the gearshift (photo 1). Pull up evenly around its circumference. Pull back the carpet trim in the center console using a sewing awl or needle (photo 2). Remove the Phillips-head screw holding the wood trim to the console (photo 3). Carefully lift the rear of the wooden console trim (photo 4). Some switches are part of the wood trim assembly. Avoid bending the wood, or it will crack. Never force the wood trim.

When there's room to get your hand under the wood trim, lift under the console and guide it out. Plastic

hooks at the front of the wood fit under the radio; be careful not to break them during removal.

Replacing Bulb

At the left front of the shifting mechanism, look for the small bulb assembly with two wires to it (photo 5). Pull it down and out of its socket. Replace the bulb, then test the circuit with the lights on (photo 6).

Photo 1. Use a credit card to pry up the trim piece carefully.

Photo 2. Pull back the carpet trim to reach the screw.

Photo 3. Remove the screw as shown.

Installation is the reverse of removal. Clean and polish the wood trim, and look down into the switch assemblies for signs of spilled coffee or other liquids. If necessary, clean it with electronic contact spray.

Photo 4. Working at the back of the wood trim, slowly pull it upward.

Photo 5. Bulb located as shown. Chassis up to end number 920983 use bulb 000 825 00 94; later cars (with brake interlock) use 072601 012230.

Photo 6. Test bulb with lights on.

Advanced Radio Repair:
The Becker Grand Prix Electronic

by James A. Mahaffey, Contributing Editor

January/February 1994

Photos in this article by the author.

With some care and these instructions you can repair most Becker Grand Prix Electronic radios.

During the 1970s the Becker transistorized AM/FM radio underwent constant change and improvement. Field-effect transistors and integrated circuits were added, the push-button tuning mechanism was flattened to fit in the same chassis with a cassette deck, and the cassette transport was redesigned to automatically play both sides of a tape without removing it and flipping it over.

With the turn of the decade the entire concept of the Becker radio changed. The old reliable induction tuned receiver with a twist-knob volume control was replaced by a completely new design, the Grand Prix Electronic, featuring a digital synthetic tuner with a digital volume control, digital station-selector, and digital clock, all controlled by a special built-in microcomputer. Many esoteric features were now possible, including AM stereo, automatic volume compensation for road speed, and a clock alarm to turn on the radio.

Inside, these new-wave Grand Prix radios look very intimidating (the service schematic is a six-page foldout). On the other hand, having autopsied dozens of them, I find that the problem in a failed Grand Prix is most often mechanical, not electronic. With patience, a set of small tools, and a magnifying glass, you can probably fix your Grand Prix Electronic.

Figure 1. A typical Grand Prix Electronic. Earlier models had buttons instead of levers for volume control and tuning; later models have a wider display window in the center.

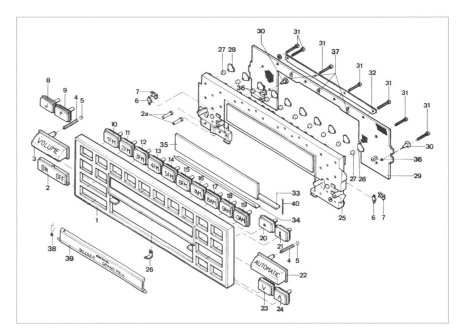

Figure 2. Grand Prix Electronic (model 754) front panel, exploded view. The typical front panel tears down into 96 pieces plus a circuit-board subassembly. Reassembly can be challenging.

Small Problems

A common failure is volume control lever breakage. (The earliest Grand Prix had buttons instead of levers for volume and tuning.) In Figure 2, an exploded view of a front panel, item 25 is a piece of molded styrene plastic with pivots for the volume and tuning levers protruding forward. Under hard use these pieces can break off, leaving the control lever hanging in space.

Replace item 25 by first removing the front panel from the chassis, as shown in the first steps of the illustrated cassette-deck repair. Before dismantling, wait until you have a

replacement unit from Becker (part number 533.734-254 for model 754) or a scrounged one from a junked radio. A fresh memory of where things go is important. Place the front panel face-down on the bench, and use a jeweler's screwdriver to remove the seven long screws (items 31) that hold the circuit board to the escutcheon (item 1). Earlier radios also have two short screws holding the LCD display panel; remove these, too. Carefully lift the circuit assembly away from the escutcheon plate. Now remove the remaining two short screws (items 30). In some cases these are slotted screws, in some cases Phillips-head.

The circuit board will now peel away from the clear plastic frame, revealing many small, critical pieces.

Each push-button on the front has associated with it a copper force-conducting pin (integral with the button in later models), a rubber buffer (item 27), and a triangular, dished piece of hardened metal (item 28). As you press on a button, the convex metal blister will collapse suddenly against a set of gold-plated contacts, giving a positive, bounce-free switch contact and a reassuring click sensation through your fingertip. When you reassemble the unit, make sure that each button on the front is followed by a pin through the plastic frame, a rubber piece, then a triangular switch-piece, concavity toward the circuit board, convexity toward the button. The pins (items 2a) for the coupled On/Off buttons are clear plastic, to conduct light.

Carefully remove the control levers (items 3, 22), broken unit first. Each has four moving pieces (items 4, 5, 6, 7), including a tiny steel ball destined to roll away and hide. Then pry cautiously at the end of the unbroken unit with a screwdriver blade, and the lever will snap free of its two pivots.

Reassemble on a new plastic frame starting with the two control levers. Make sure that each has its coil spring (item 4) inserted, and snap them onto the pivots with finger pressure. Using chassis grease as an adhesive, glue a steel ball (item 5) onto the end of a spring sticking through the frame toward the circuit-board side. Now glue the contact (item 6) and the contact bearing (item 7) together using grease, and hold the assembly glued to the end of your finger. With the radio in the normal, horizontal position, the contact (item 6) should be vertical, concave side facing the ball, or the front of the radio. The bearing (item 7) should be horizontal, concave side against the contact, or facing front.

Push together the spring, ball, contact, and bearing, finishing with the back of the bearing (item 7) flush with its rectangular socket in the back of the plastic frame. Expect to make several attempts. Nothing but gravity and the grease adhesion keep these tiny pieces together once they are placed correctly, and you don't want to do it twice, so be careful as you insert the second set of toggle pieces. Confirm correct assembly by holding the bearing hard against the frame with an index finger while toggling the lever up and down. It should feel correct, snapping up, snapping down, and returning to neutral automatically.

If you have noticed any lights out on the front of the radio at night, now would be a good time to replace the socketless bulbs (part number 475.221-392) on the circuit board. Place all the switch components correctly in the plastic frame (item 25), always keeping it face down, and screw on the circuit board using the two short screws (items 30). Be sure that all buttons are oriented properly in their appropriate holes in the escutcheon (item 1) and that the cassette door (item 39) and its spring (item 38) are properly positioned, and fasten the frame to the escutcheon using the seven long screws (items 31). The clear plastic gasket (item 32) must be positioned under the top middle screws.

Another common failure is to have segments of numbers on the display panel disappear. It's probably impractical to repair this yourself, as the electronic components are surface mounted on flexible mylar, but Becker has an exchange program; they will exchange your failed front panel for a rebuilt unit for about $85.

Cassette Problems

In the Grand Prix Electronic everything changed—except the auto-reversing cassette drive, lifted from the previous-generation Becker Europa Cassette radio. To reverse a cassette or play the other side, the deck must reverse the motion of the tape, invert the head, swap the feed/take-up functions, unload a capstan, and load the other capstan. To fast-forward, both capstans are unloaded, and full voltage is applied to the transport motor. To rewind, the cassette is reversed, fast-forwarded, then reversed again to restore the original tape direction.

A large solenoid mounted transversely across the back of the cassette deck executes all five reversing functions simultaneously. A trapezoid shaped plastic pivot called the "switch balance" translates and distributes the impulse stroke of the solenoid core to the various functions and toggles the state of motion between "side 1" and "side 2." This pivot takes a beating and may break during a switch maneuver, with the cassette deck stuck going in one direction and possibly jammed.

To help you replace the switch balance, a 25-step illustrated procedure follows. Before ordering the new part from Becker, you must determine which type of switch balance you have. The cassette deck underwent many internal design changes not obvious from looking at the radio. Figures 3a and 3b show the two types of head switch, and Figure 4 shows the corresponding switch balances. The early type requires a mechanical linkage from the head to the switch balance, with an extra pin on the balance to make the connection. The improved model deletes this function from the balance by switching the head electronically.

Wow!

If your cassette player's clarity and volume have deteriorated, examine the head where it touches the tape. It should be clean, polished chrome. A slight buildup of brown residue from tapes will noticeably affect performance. Clean it regularly with a cotton swab and tape-head cleaner or with the special swabs provided by Becker in sealed packages. Severe head contamination can occur if the car is parked on a hot day with a cassette left in the player. (With no automatic eject on power-off, the Grand Prix allows this.) The tape will bake onto the head, and the player will act as if it's dead. Flake the thick residue off with your thumbnail (too soft to harm the head), and clean the remainder in the usual way.

A common tape-player problem is an audibly noticeable variation in tape speed, called "wow". Several possible causes exist. Examine the capstans closely. They should be spotless, mirror-finished chrome. Any hint of lubricant on the capstans, possibly introduced by detailing the console, can cause slippage and wild wowing. The capstans could be covered with residue or have strings of broken tape, threads, or even hair wrapped around them. Examine the serpentine drive-belt and idler pulley. I've seen cases in which an idler pulley seized and melted the belt. Otherwise, belts seem to last forever and should require no adjustment.

If the transport is free and clean, but a high-frequency wow exists, try to wiggle the motor-pulley. If it moves at all from side to side, then the motor bearing is worn, and the motor must be replaced. Check the voltage across the motor. It should be 7.0 volts DC, dead steady.

Both spindles in the cassette deck have electronic tachometers. If the supply spindle stalls while playing a tape, the deck interprets it as an end-of-tape and executes an auto-reverse. If both spindles stall, the deck considers it an error and kicks out the tape. If your Grand Prix won't hold a tape and play it, check to see that the spindles turn, at least momentarily, when you push in a tape. The belt may have slipped off, the motor may not be getting power, a bearing may be seized, or the cassette itself could be jammed internally. Make sure that both cassette spools turn freely.

Early units had mechanical tachometer pickups with two gold plated whiskers per spindle acting as make-and-break switches. These can wear out, or they may need cleaning. Later units have a permanent magnet disc on each spindle driving Hall-effect pickups on the transport frame, and these should last forever.

Caution

If your radio has a display window as wide as the cassette slot, it probably has the anti-theft circuit (European Becker

Figure 3a. Early cassette units inverted the head with a rotary switch connected directly to the back of the head. It couples through a lever back to the switch balance.

Figure 3b. The improved head switch uses an analog-switch array in an integrated circuit, with no mechanical connection to the switch balance.

Figure 4. The switch balance on the right (part number 278.424-241) goes with the early, mechanical head switch. The one on the left (part number 377.864-241) goes with the improved electronic head switch.

Mexico Electronics have the anti-theft feature regardless of window width). A special socket on the back of the radio plugs into the car separately from the main power, speakers, antenna, and antenna control. The anti-theft plug is set so that as you remove the radio, the plug will always disconnect before the fixed power is unplugged.

If the radio detects that the plug is out while the car's alarm system is on, the system will disable the microprocessor, scrambling the radio. Providing that you can prove that a particular radio is yours, Becker can reprogram it for a price. Later radios could be de-scrambled by a dealer or via a code number provided to the owner. To avoid scrambling, be sure the alarm system is off before removing the radio.

The alarm automatically activates whenever the car battery is reconnected, so if you re-connect the battery just before removing the radio, switch off the alarm first. To avoid scrambling, always disconnect the car battery first, to kill fixed power to the radio, and leave it disconnected until the radio is out of the car. When re-installing the radio, disconnect the battery first; re-connect it only after the radio is fully installed.

The following is an illustrated cassette deck repair procedure.

Step 1. With a screwdriver, turn the front-panel latch counterclockwise to the "O" position.

Step 2. Pull off the front panel.

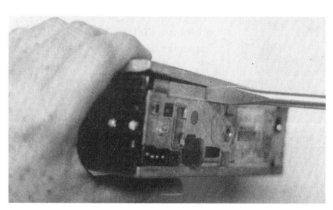

Step 3. Pry off the top and bottom covers.

Step 4. Remove the two screws holding the front of the bottom circuit board.

Step 5. Remove the accessory plug in back.

Step 6. Pry up the bottom circuit board carefully. Strips of gold-plated contact fingers, bridging the top and bottom circuit boards and the cassette deck, will disconnect.

Step 7. The circuit board swings out of the way on hinges, revealing the internal workings.

Step 8. Remove the two short screws holding the cassette deck to the steel frame of the radio.

Step 9. The cassette deck lifts out as a unit. A single red wire disconnects from a pin on the top circuit board, and the bridge board unplugs from a strip of holes in the top board. The red wire carries main positive power to the deck; ground is through the frame. The ribbon cable connecting the bridge board to the deck is fragile. It will unplug from the deck, but avoid doing so.

Step 10. Unbolt the solenoid using a 5-mm, open-end wrench.

Step 11. Unlock the coil spring between the solenoid clapper and the frame.

Step 12. Slide out the tiny E-clip on the switch balance pivot.

Step 13. Rotate the solenoid, moving the clapper out of the cutout in the switch balance and out of the way.

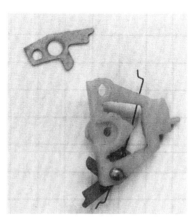

Step 14. Lift out the switch balance. This wrecked unit has an almost invisible crack in the plastic at the now empty pin socket, and the spring-rod is dislocated. Notice that the pin holding one of the levers has disappeared, and the lever was set free to rattle around in the circuit. These metal pieces often crash in to the motor-control board, shorting out circuits and making things appear worse than they really are.

Step 15. Guide the new switch balance in over the pivot. Important: the levers on each side of the switch balance must straddle the two fixed pins sticking up out of the frame. First locate the balance over the pivot, then hook the back lever over its pin, then force the front lever outside its pin, against the spring-rod tension, and push the balance down over the pivot. The picture shows the "front lever" being held by a pair of tweezers, with the lever barely hooked over its corresponding pin.

Step 16. Rotate the clapper back into the cutout, and slip the E-clip back on.

Step 17. Replace the two cap screws holding the solenoid.

Step 18. Re-connect the coil spring. You can now test the installation by applying +12 volts DC to the red wire and -12 volts DC to the frame. Plug in a cassette. The "1 2", fast-forward, rewind, and eject keys should work.

Step 19. Guide the cassette deck in from the back. When installing the deck, observe three points shown in Steps 20, 21, and 22.

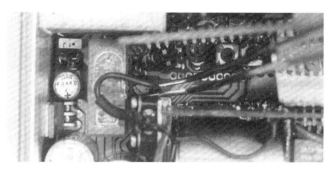

Step 20. Push power connector down over its pin on top circuit board.

Step 21. Be sure that this red wire goes in the slot in the bridge board.

Step 22. Be sure that the pin on the side of the cassette deck frame mates with the slot in the guide bar on the radio frame.

Step 23. (No photo). Now replace the two screws holding the cassette deck to the radio frame.

Step 24. Swing down the bottom circuit board and reconnect it to the strip of contact fingers. Find the rectangular pilot (a tab on the bridge board), and use it to guide the fingers into the holes. Replace the two screws holding the circuit board to the front of the radio frame. Plug in the front panel and the accessory plug.

Step 25. You may want to take this opportunity to adjust the motor speed. Apply 12 volts to the radio, plug and speaker, and insert a cassette. Turn the motor-control potentiometer using a jeweler's screwdriver until it sounds right. Press the covers back on, and the job is finished.

How to Refurbish Your Cruise Control Actuator

by Farrell Wiser,
Mile-High Section

January/February 1998

Photos in this article by Kent Spencer.

When I bought my 1985 300D, the previous owner pointed out several problems it had, which was fine with me, since it swung the price in my favor. Most of these just required simple parts replacement, but the faulty cruise control was more subtle. He said, "It engages when you hold up the lever, but when you let go, it disengages. As long as you hold the lever up, you can feel it accelerate."

I knew from experience that if both brake light bulbs were burned out, the cruise control would not engage. Since mine would engage but not hold the selected speed, at least one bulb had to be OK. I checked them anyway. No luck. They were fine, with functioning Osram bulbs in both units. Next I pulled the amplifier from under the dash and checked it for cold solder joints on the circuit board. No luck; they were OK.

Now it was time to buy a re-manufactured amplifier. Sure enough, with the new amplifier, the cruise control lever would cause it to engage and hold the selected speed. Great, but sometimes after the cruise control was holding a selected speed, a slight surge was detectable. This could be eliminated by putting my foot on the accelerator just enough to damp the throttle movement (which could barely be felt in the pedal).

"Now it's getting ugly," I thought. MBCA Technical Advisor George Murphy confirmed that the VDO cruise control actuator can cause this problem if the feedback potentiometer is dirty or defective. Time to remove the actuator and check it (or fix it, if it's just a dirty pot). Here's how:

Figure 1. Cruise control actuator is connected to throttle mechanism via rod (arrow).

Figure 2. Brace actuator arm with Vise-Grips (we forget the generic name) as you remove 13-mm nut.

1. Find the actuator. On five-cylinder diesels, it's the metal box above the spin-on fuel filter, with the rod going to the throttle controls on top of the valve cover (see Figure 1). Mine, on a 1985 300D, is part number 000 545 86 32. Disconnect the rod between the actuator and the throttle controls; if you'll be driving the car without the actuator, disconnect both ends; otherwise you need disconnect only the actuator end.

2. Disconnect the electrical connector to the actuator; the cable is probably secured with nylon ties, which can be removed and re-used.

3. With a 10 mm wrench, remove the three bolts holding the actuator to its mounting bracket. Note the position of the washers and spacers involved (Figure 1). Remove the actuator, and take it to a comfortable work surface.

4. Mark the position of the arm in relation to the shaft and housing, then bend back the locking washer and remove the 13-mm nut holding the actuator arm onto the output shaft. Brace the arm with a Vise-Grip-type wrench while loosening the nut because the parts inside are plastic and can break if you apply too much force (Figure 2). Remove the arm.

5. Remove the four Phillips-head screws securing the cover that the shaft protrudes through. The cover is positioned by a locating pin with a peened-over head, which must be ground off level with the surface of the cover (Figure 3). Use a Dremel tool grinder or a small file.

6. Carefully remove the cover, keeping 'inward' pressure on the end of the shaft so that the shaft and the mechanism behind it stay in the housing and only the cover comes off (Figure 3).

7. Remove the output shaft and gear. Be careful to note how the spring, shaft, and gear interact (Figure 4).

8. Examine the circuit board that the little "wipers" rub across, that is, the feedback potentiometer that tells the amplifier where the arm is. A working unit may be dirty or caked with grease, etc. (Figure 5). A failed unit will have worn wipers, pits in the contact surface, and bent or broken parts. It may also have broken gear teeth, broken springs, or other non-obvious defects. These parts are unavailable individually, so you'll have to replace the whole unit.

9. If everything looks OK, just dry or dirty, clean it by carefully wiping off the grease; use spray-type contact

Figure 3. Actuator cover is positioned by nub (top arrow) which must be ground off before it can be removed. Shaft protrudes through hole (lower arrow).

Figure 4. Pay attention to how the spring, shafts, and gears fit together.

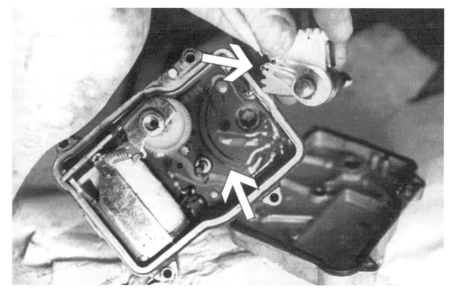

Figure 5. To ensure proper electrical contact, clean grease and dirt from "wiper" (top arrow) and contact surface (bottom arrow).

cleaner on a Q-tip. Clean the wipers that contact the circuit board, then lubricate the circuit board strips with a thin film of conducting grease. A crack in the feedback "pot" can be repaired using a rear window defroster wire repair kit. Carefully paint conductive fluid over the crack, then let it dry; repeat for good contact. Burnish the repair with a pencil eraser, clean it with contact cleaner, then check for continuity across the repair using an ohmmeter.

10. Reassemble the actuator in reverse order—be sure to assemble the spring and sector gear correctly—and reinstall it. Clean and lubricate the rod-ends as you re-connect them. Re-install the electrical cable and connector (clean the connector pins with contact cleaner), and install the cable ties.

September/October 1959

Pete Janzen

Horn Rings

by Frank King,
Technical Editor

*May/June
1980*

This section contains things you can do easily at home to repair and restore your car. We welcome any suggestions from readers.

Horn Ring Problems

Minor, annoying problems with the horn ring tend to plague the W108, W114 and W115 series cars. On some, the horn ring seems to sag closer and closer to the steering wheel, until the horn can only be sounded if the ring is pressed at the top or bottom center. On other models, the ring loosens until a ringing rattle is produced every time the front wheels go over a surface irregularity.

These problems are both caused by the sagging and loosening of a set of springs inside the steering wheel hub. Happily, it is a relatively easy thing to get to them and beef them up.

Pull off the center pad from the steering wheel. This will expose five nuts recessed into the hub. Use a 13-mm wrench and remove them. Remove the spring washers under them, and the wheel will lift off the hub. Use a Phillips screwdriver to remove the horn wires.

With the wheel upside down, you will see three Phillips screws. Remove them, and the component parts will separate. They consist of the wheel, the horn ring, the horn contact unit, and the plate that holds the whole thing together.

The problem comes because the three springs in the contact unit have weakened, allowing the ring to settle and rattle. Three thin rubber grommets set on top of the contact unit, between it and the retaining plate, will restore the springiness and solidity to the

system. We found three grommets in a parts drawer in the garage. A couple of dabs of foam-backed tape would probably do as well. If the material you use is too thick, contact will be continuous and the horn will blow all the time. The right amount is easy to feel out, however, so do not despair. Reassemble the unit by reversing the above steps, and enjoy a rattle-free horn ring that sounds the horn whenever and wherever you press on it.

Installing a Third Brake Light

THE STAR

by Harry J. Goos,
Northeastern
Pennsylvania
Section

*September/October
1986*

Photos in this article
by the author.

*The government has legislated a
third brake light on all new cars sold
in this country. If you'd like to install
one in your pre-1986 Mercedes-Benz,
here's how to do it for most late
models, and in particular, the 300D.*

If your car's chassis is still in
production (W107, W126, W201),
you're fortunate. Factory center brake
lights used on current versions of these
bodies are available from your dealer
in colors to match most late-model
interiors; the W107 unit is exterior and
requires painting.

If your car's chassis is no longer in
production, you'll need an aftermarket
brake light unit, offered via dealers,
independent garages, mail order or
auto parts stores. Find the one that fits
best and looks right. The unit should
fit snug against the rear window so
reflections don't bother you at night.
The unit I installed in my 1980 300D
is a Tetley Model T1666, which fits
perfectly against the glass and leaves
room to open the first-aid box.

Before you begin installation, buy,
borrow or rent a right-angle electric
drill. A regular electric drill won't allow
you to drill straight down through the
rear shelf; using one at an angle will
result in a misplaced hole because the
mounting metal is well below the rear
parcel tray. A straight drill could also
damage the rear window defroster wires.

Get the vacuum tank out of harm's
way. If you drill through the parcel

Third brake light unit mounts at center of
rear shelf, flush against glass.

tray without moving the vacuum
tank, you'll drill right into it. Remove
the back vertical trunk panel by
unscrewing the four screws holding it.
You can then reach the vacuum tank
below the rear window. Remove the
plastic rivet holding the tank, which
can then be lowered several inches so
that it's clear of the drill bit.

Mounting

The brake light should be positioned
in the exact center of the rear parcel
shelf. Put masking tape in the
approximate center, then measure
and mark the exact center on the tape
with a pencil. Check and re-check
measurements before drilling. Center
the base on the pencil mark and put
tape on both sides of the base.

Assemble the light unit and
position it with the head at the proper
angle and tight against the glass. Place
strips of tape in front of and behind
the base. Remove the light and check
that the tape markings position the
base square with the rear window.

My light unit came with a template
for drilling the mounting and wiring
holes. If yours doesn't, you can easily
make one by putting paper over the
base of the unit and tracing the holes.
Put the template in the taped area and
drill through the holes in the template.
As you drill, the thick sound-deadening
material will wrap around the bit, so
start with a sharp bit. The center hole
is for the wiring, and the smaller side
holes are for the mounting fasteners.
You can use sheet-metal screws or small

Before mounting the new light, remove the vertical trunk panel fasteners
indicated by arrows and move the vacuum tank to prevent damage.

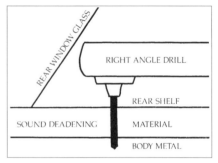

REAR WINDOW GLASS

RIGHT ANGLE DRILL

REAR SHELF

SOUND DEADENING   MATERIAL

BODY METAL

A right-angle drill may be necessary to drill
the mounting holes.

black Allen-head bolts to mount the
unit. Make sure the screws or bolts are
short enough to clear the vacuum tank
when it is reinstalled. Install a rubber
grommet in the center hole, push the
wires through it, then mount the unit.

Wiring

Run the hot wire to the left brake light.
On the Tetley unit the hot wire was
yellow. Disconnect the plug at the back
of the tail light in the trunk and slit
the plastic cover of the wiring harness
about an inch back from the plug.
Locate the brake light wire, black with
a red stripe on my 300D. Connect the
new hot wire to the brake light wire
using the appropriate connector.

Put a washer-type ground
connector on the end of the unit's
ground wire and connect it to the
existing ground above the left rear
wheel well. Test the light before you
button things up. After testing, wrap
the connections with electrical tape,
re-assemble the trunk and check again
to see that all lights work properly.

The Alternator

by Frank King,
Technical Editor

*May/June
1990*

The era of the automobile started in 1886 with two quite different cars, the three-wheeled Benz and the four-wheeled Daimler. One of the fundamental differences between their engines was the method of igniting the compressed air-fuel charge. The Benz used an electric spark inside the combustion chamber. The Daimler relied on a hot tube, rather like a thimble, with the open end in the combustion chamber and the closed outer end heated by a gas flame.

During the 19th century, internal combustion engines were invented and developed like dandelions sprouting in the spring. Hot tube ignition was popular in the early stages, but electric ignition, which relied on batteries and buzzers and primitive low-tension magnetos, had taken over in the automobile field by the end of the century. Even the conservative Gottlieb Daimler, who had a patent on the most effective hot tube system, changed over to electric ignition by 1898.

Until around 1910 the only consumers of electricity on automobiles were the ignition systems. These required very little current, and a well-charged battery could supply a car's needs for several days without recharging. Batteries were charged by the rather crude generators of the day, either in the garage or on the car.

In 1819, Hans C. Oersted discovered the effect that an electric current flowing through a wire had on a magnet near the wire. This led to Michael Faraday's discovery in 1831 that an electric current was generated in a copper disc rotated between the poles of a magnet. In 1832, one Hippolyte Pixii constructed a generator using permanent magnets and wire armature windings (Fig. 1). This generated

alternating current, useless then, so he contrived the first commutator. This used contacts to reverse the connections from the armature coils at the moment the voltage was reversing so that the output was direct current (Fig. 2). In 1845, Charles Wheatstone replaced permanent magnets with electromagnets excited with direct current from a battery. In 1857 he added self-excitation, whereby the magnet windings received current from the armature windings. From then on, developments in generators came rapidly.

Two developments around the period from 1912 to 1915 had a drastic effect on the electrical system of the automobile. One was the tungsten-filament light bulb, which made electric lights feasible on automobiles. The earlier carbon filament bulbs could not withstand the car's vibration and the road shocks involved in driving. The second was the invention of a practical electric starter by Charles F. Kettering. These two current consumers made it imperative that cars be equipped with a generator that

could always provide as much or more electrical energy than was being demanded.

How Generators Work

In the basic generator, copper wire windings of an armature are rotated so that they cut the magnetic flux (lines of force) flowing between the iron poles of field magnets. Voltage generated varies directly as the speed with which the windings cut across the magnetic flux and with the density of the magnetic flux. A slowly rotating armature or a weak flux means lower voltage; increasing speed of rotation or a denser flux means higher voltage. Since a generator in an automobile is expected to function automatically, some system of regulation must be provided so that the generator is not connected to the battery until it is generating enough voltage to charge the battery. If the battery were connected to a generator producing less than battery voltage, the battery would try to drive the generator and would be quickly discharged.

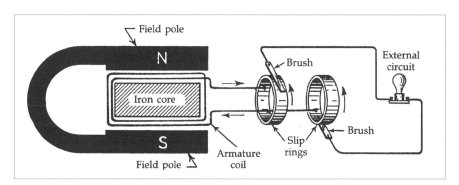

Figure 1. The alternating current generator.

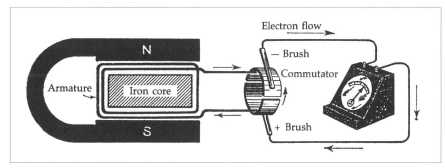

Figure 2. The direct current generator.

At the other end of the scale, if the speed of the car were increased, the voltage would continue to rise, resulting in an overcharged battery, burned out lamps and an overheated generator. Quite a number of complex and convoluted systems of voltage regulation were invented and applied. When the writer was first getting his fingers into the innards of automobiles, in the 1920's and 1930's, the common system of regulation was the third brush system. In addition to the essential "cutout" (the relay that broke the connection between generator and battery at low voltage), a third brush was located between the two output brushes. It could be moved and fixed in place to control the self-exciting field coil voltage which produced the magnetic flux. This adjustment merely set a maximum output for the generator, but one could readily reduce the maximum output for long, fast trips, avoiding the need to use the headlights in the daytime to avoid overcharging the battery. This system was crude by today's standards, and home battery chargers, often of the trickle type, were in common use. Also, every service station offered battery charging as a regular service.

As automobiles took on more electrically operated devices, the need for more generator capacity and better regulation increased. Generators of more refined design, with regulators which controlled voltage according to the state of battery charge and the immediate electric load, were in use from World War II until, in the case of Mercedes-Benz, alternators started to come into use in 1963.

Generators in post-World War II Mercedes-Benz cars (Fig. 3) have electromechanical vibrating-type regulators and provide an adequate supply of electric power while maintaining the battery charge. But the increasing use of electric powered ancillary equipment, coupled with changes in driving habits that involved more time idling in traffic, spurred development of still better generating equipment. This took the form of the alternator.

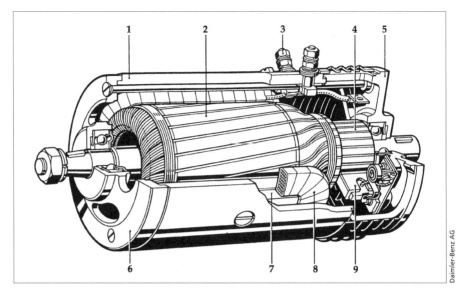

Figure 3. DC Generator: 1) stator frame, 2) armature, 3) terminal, 4) commutator, 5) commutator end shield, 6) drive end shield, 7) pole shoe, 8) excitation winder, 9) brush holder and carbon brush.

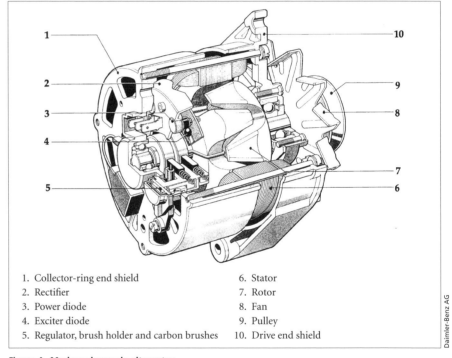

1. Collector-ring end shield	6.	Stator
2. Rectifier	7.	Rotor
3. Power diode	8.	Fan
4. Exciter diode	9.	Pulley
5. Regulator, brush holder and carbon brushes	10.	Drive end shield

Figure 4. Modern claw-pole alternator.

How Alternators Work

There are two basic differences between the DC generator and the alternator (Fig. 4). First, the construction. The rotor of the alternator is the field magnet, consisting of two discs each having six intermeshing claws. The exciter winding, which is fed direct current through two slip rings, lies between the clawed discs. The exciter current is low, and the windings are small and compact. This construction allows the rotor to resist the centrifugal force of high speeds, allowing the alternator to operate over a wide speed range. Alternators on modern Mercedes-Benz cars turn from around 2 to 3 times as fast as the engine.

As the second difference between generators and alternators, in the latter the stator carries the field windings on laminated cores. These are at three points, 120 degrees apart, and in them three-phase current is generated. Outputs of the three field windings are fed to three positive diodes and three negative diodes. A direct current with only a slight ripple is thus produced. By comparison, a DC generator's field windings are wound on the rotor (armature) axially, making a long, heavy body subject to centrifugal force. The generated current is taken to the multiple segments of the commutator where it is mechanically rectified into direct current.

Alternator Advantages

The alternator's usefulness on automobiles depended on the development of the transistor for rectification and regulation. Earlier devices would have been too heavy and cumbersome to handle the higher output of the alternator. A brief review of the essential features of the alternator tells why it has replaced the generator on modern automobiles:

1. The alternator delivers power even when the engine is idling, thus guaranteeing an adequate supply of current for all loads.

2. Rectification of the three-phase current is done electronically through stationary diodes, therefore avoiding the problems which are common with mechanical rectification through the commutator and its brushes.

3. The diodes perform the function of a cutout relay.

4. Alternators are considerably lighter than DC generators because of their greater mechanical efficiency.

5. The alternator has a long service life, limited only by the bearings, brushes and collector rings.

6. Alternators have a higher resistance to external influences such as high temperatures, dampness, dirt and vibration.

Getting Excited

In an alternator there are three circuits: 1) the pre-excitation circuit-excitation by battery current; 2) the excitation circuit—self-excitation; and 3) the main, generation circuit.

Pre-excitation is necessary because the residual magnetism in the iron core of the excitation winding is insufficient during starting or at very low engine speeds to cause the self-excitation required for building up the magnetic field and thus to generate the desired voltage. In the excitation circuit are a power diode (negative) and an exciter diode in series for each phase.

Self-excitation can't start until the alternator has at least overcome the voltage drop (2 x 0.7 volt = 1.4 volts) of these two diodes. So pre-excitation current—with sufficient current consumption of the generator warning lamp, which is in series in the circuit—causes a large enough magnetic field to help get self-excitation going.

The generator warning lamp is in the pre-excitation circuit and acts as a resistor when the ignition switch is turned on. As a result of the voltage difference between the alternator and the battery, the pre-excitation current flows from the positive pole of the battery via the generator warning lamp to the positive pole of the alternator. When the lamp is lit, the alternator is not yet delivering current. As soon as self-excitation is initiated and the alternator is feeding the vehicle electrical system, the lamp goes out.

The excitation circuit's function is to produce a magnetic field in the excitation winding of the rotor and thus induce the desired voltage in the three-phase winding of the stator. Some of the rectified current of the phase windings is supplied as excitation current via the carbon brushes and collector rings to the excitation winding and the regulator.

The main, generator circuit takes alternating current induced in the three phases through the power diodes in the bridge circuit, which combines and rectifies the three phases into direct current, which is then delivered to the battery and the current consuming loads.

Rectifying and Regulating

The alternator system comprises three components: generator, rectifier and voltage regulator. The rectifier consists of six power diodes and three exciter diodes (Fig. 4) and is not repairable in the regular service facility, being buried inside the alternator. It converts three-phase alternating current into smooth direct current, and by the nature of the diodes also serves as a cutout.

The voltage regulator has the task of keeping the generated voltage constant over the entire engine speed range, irrespective of electrical load on the alternator or its rotational speed. Automatic voltage regulation is difficult because of variations in engine speed and fluctuation of the connected loads. At high engine speeds and low electrical loading, voltage must be limited to a set value to protect the loads against over-voltage and the battery against overcharging. In addition, the electrochemical properties of the battery must be allowed for when it is being charged. The charging voltage must be higher in cold weather than in summer (Fig. 5).

The voltage generated in an alternator is directly proportional to its speed of rotation and to the strength of the excitation current. If an alternator were run with constant

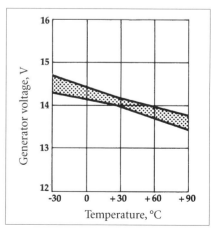

Figure 5. Regulator Tolerance: for 14-volt generator voltage, regulator allows voltage variation related to air temperature.

full excitation, no loads and no battery, voltage would rise with the speed of rotation. At 10,000 rpm (3,500 engine rpm) it would be 140 volts. The principle of voltage regulation consists in regulating the excitation current as a function of the voltage generated by the alternator. Automobile electrical systems with a 12-volt battery are regulated in the 14-volt range. Mercedes-Benz specifies that voltage at the battery with the engine running at 3,000 rpm and only ignition load shall be 13.0–14.5 volts.

As long as the voltage generated by the alternator remains below the set voltage, the regulator doesn't operate. When the voltage exceeds the tolerance range, the regulator reduces it by interrupting the excitation current. The voltage then decreases. When it drops below the set value, excitation is increased, and voltage rises until the set value is again exceeded. This cycle takes place in milliseconds so that the voltage is regulated to the desired mean value. At low engine speeds the excitation current is allowed to flow for a relatively long time and is reduced only briefly. Conversely, at high engine speed the excitation current flows only briefly and is reduced for a comparatively long time.

This switching on and off does not cause abrupt increases and decreases in the excitation current because of the nature of the excitation winding, which represents a high inductive load. When switched on, current increases gradually (in terms of the electronic world) during on-time, along with the buildup of the magnetic field. When switched off, current decays during off-time, along with the decay of the magnetic field.

With voltage control, current limitation is unnecessary because the armature reaction limits the maximum current permissible for full load. At full load the majority of the excitation ampere-turns is compensated by the armature reaction, so only a small proportion of the ampere-turns is effective.

When alternators were introduced on Mercedes-Benz cars, starting with the 230SL in 1963 and continuing until the fall of 1974, electromagnetic vibrating-type regulators were used. These regulators control the voltage by electromechanical means. Excitation current is varied by the opening and closing of a moving contact pressed by a spring against a fixed contact. When the rated voltage is exceeded, the contact is lifted off by an electromagnet. This switches a resistor into the excitation circuit, reducing the excitation current and thus dropping alternator voltage. When voltage drops below the set value, the magnetic force decreases, and the spring's force closes the contact again. This cycle is repeated continuously. Regulators of this type are not mounted on the alternator. Their size and characteristics require them to be mounted on the vehicle's chassis.

Transistor Regulators

The transistor regulator's advantages are so significant that it has become standard equipment with the alternator. These advantages must be credited to the transistors and Zener diodes installed in the form of single or integrated components on a small printed-circuit board, forming a simple, reliable unit. The chief advantages of the breakerless transistor regulator are:

1. shorter switching times permit closer regulation tolerances;

2. no wear and thus freedom from maintenance;

3. spark-free switching preventing radio interference;

4. insensitivity to shock, vibration and climatic effects, therefore high reliability and low failure rate;

5. electronic temperature compensation; and

6. compact construction permitting mounting on the alternator, making connecting cables unnecessary.

Transistor regulators are compact units mounted on the alternator. They are readily removable and replaceable.

They are not repairable or adjustable. Their design and operating principles are entirely electronic and beyond the scope of this article.

Faults and Fixes

If the alternator could have its own way, it would be installed on the car so as to meet these conditions: 1) good accessibility for re-adjusting the tension of the V-belt and performing any maintenance work; 2) adequate cooling both for the heat from the alternator and for the heat from the engine; and 3) protection against dirt, moisture, shock, impact and leakage of fuel, coolant, battery fluid and engine oil.

Obviously other components competed for space in the crowded engine compartment, but the alternator has done pretty well except for accessibility in some models. In spite of any difficulty, however, it is important to maintain proper tension on the drive belt. If a belt is too tight, it will shorten the life of the bearings; too loose, and it will slip and shorten the life of the belt while failing to drive the alternator smoothly. The only other maintenance required is to see that the alternator is kept free of the fluids mentioned above. It isn't harmed by rainwater or road splashes.

The alternator must be the paragon of components of the modern automobile, at least as it is installed in Mercedes-Benz cars. It can be expected to perform flawlessly without maintenance for 100,000 miles or more if not abused. By far the most common failure is a broken V-belt, not really the alternator's fault. Nevertheless, there are occasions when it does not generate or generates too much. The alarm in nearly all such cases is given by the generator warning lamp (charge indicator lamp/charging control lamp, etc.) which, if all is in order, must light when the ignition is turned on and must go out as soon as the engine starts. The warning lamp is thus a means of checking whether the alternator is operating satisfactorily and whether it is supplying power to the connected loads.

But the warning lamp does not indicate whether, or at what engine speed, the battery is actually being charged. If there is a heavy load on the system, it is quite possible that, despite the warning lamp having gone out, the battery is not being charged but is discharging. The lamp therefore provides no information on the state of charge of the battery, although it is often referred to as "charge indicator lamp" (as in your Mercedes-Benz owner's manual).

The generator warning lamp is an essential element of the alternator circuitry and the best single indicator of the state of the electrical system. If the lamp lights while the engine is running, it may indicate a broken belt. In this case the belt must be replaced before the vehicle is operated. Otherwise the water pump cannot operate, and serious engine damage may result. If the lamp fails to light before starting, with the key in position 2, it indicates a condition which must be repaired as soon as possible.

Current Notes

The Mercedes-Benz owner with more than a casual technical interest can't help wishing that the factory would provide both an ammeter and a voltmeter on a car so thoroughly engineered. The voltmeter would reveal battery condition to some degree and would warn of any faults in regulation before damage was done. The ammeter would alert the driver to overloading or discharge of the battery.

Of course, one can always take the car in to the shop and have the system checked out with elaborate instruments that will even show the rippled shape of the generated current.

The alternator must only be operated with the regulator and battery properly connected. Operation without the battery results in high voltage peaks that will probably damage the rectifier and regulator. If, with the engine either stopped or running, the battery is connected to the electrical system with the poles reversed, the diodes in the rectifier will be destroyed immediately, and the regulator may also be damaged.

Throughout the life of the car, the vast majority of Mercedes-Benz owners will scarcely be aware of the existence of the alternator as long as regular inspections are made and the belts replaced as needed. For the unlucky few or the technically minded, a list of possible faults, causes and corrective actions is in Table I. Investigative or corrective action should always take account of the complex electronic systems in later model cars.

The cooperation and assistance of the Robert Bosch Corporation in supplying information and illustrative material for this article is gratefully acknowledged.

Table I: Alternator Troubleshooting Guide

Fault:	Cause:	Corrective Action:
Battery not being charged or being insufficiently charged	1) Open circuit or contact resistance in charging circuit 2) Battery defective 3) Alternator defective 4) Regulator defective 5) V-belt loose	1) Eliminate open circuit or contact resistance 2) Replace battery 3) Replace alternator 4) Replace regulator 5) Adjust V-belt
Generator warning lamp not lit when engine not running with ignition switch in on-position	1) Generator warning lamp bulb blown 2) Battery discharged 3) Battery defective 4) Leads loose or defective 5) Regulator defective 6) Short circuit of positive diode in alternator 7) Carbon brushes worn 8) Oxide layer on collector rings, open circuit in excitation winding	1) Fit new bulb 2) Recharge battery 3) Replace battery 4) Replace leads, clean and tighten connections 5) Replace regulator 6) Replace alternator 7) Replace carbon brushes 8) Replace alternator
Generator warning lamp still lit brightly at high engine speed	1) Lead D +/61 has short circuit to ground 2) Regulator defective 3) Rectifier defective, collector rings fouled, short circuit in lead DF or rotor winding 4) V-belt slipping or broken	1) Replace lead or eliminate short circuit 2) Replace regulator 3) Replace alternator 4) Adjust or replace V-belt
With engine not running, generator warning lamp lights brightly but still lights less brightly or glows when engine is running	1) Contact resistances in charging circuit or in lead to generator warning lamp 2) Regulator defective 3) Alternator defective	1) Eliminate contact resistances 2) Replace regulator 3) Replace alternator

Replacing the Antenna on a W126 Chassis

John Lamb,
Technical
Committee

*July/August
1997*

Photos in this article
by the author.

Many owners have experienced a power antenna mast that doesn't go all the way up or down (Figure 1). The usual cause is the antenna's nylon winder wearing out. Repairing the power antenna is easy for the do-it-yourselfer; here's how.

When ordering a new antenna mast, you must know the nylon winder's length and whether it is a toothed or toothless type. To determine whether the antenna has a toothed winder, remove it from the motor housing. Toothed winders have distinctive teeth. Non-toothed winders have serration that look like

teeth. If you are unsure, remove the old antenna and take it along to match it to the new part.

To begin, put the antenna switch in the Max position, then turn on the radio. You should hear the antenna motor run for about 15 seconds. If not, your problem is the motor or the control wire to it; replacing the antenna will not solve these problems. To replace the antenna:

1. Turn on the radio, and make sure the antenna switch is at Max. Listen for the antenna motor to run as above.

2. Hold the chrome antenna base with a pair of lock-joint pliers while loosening the 12-mm hold-down nut; see Figure 2. To avoid scratching the chrome, wrap the plier jaws with tape.

3. Remove the antenna mast by pulling the entire mast and nylon winder from the chrome base. You should feel some resistance while pulling the nylon winder out of the motor. Note whether the winder teeth face the front or rear of the car.

4. Pull back the trunk carpeting, and find the antenna motor. Remove the cover screws and motor cover. Make sure the winder mechanism is clean and that there are no broken nylon pieces or nylon shavings in the housing. Check the tube between the motor assembly and the fender, and clean it as necessary. A little white grease can be applied to the motor gear sectors. Note the large

hex clutch adjuster on the winder mechanism (see step 8).

5. Compare the new antenna with the old one. Both should have the same length nylon winder and should have teeth or not, depending on antenna style. Begin feeding the new replacement antenna winder into the opening at the chrome base. Be sure the teeth face correctly as noted during removal. See Figure 3.

6. As the nylon winder begins to engage the mechanism, some resistance will be felt. Stop here. Have an assistant turn off the radio. At the very same time as the antenna motor "retracts" the mast, begin feeding the winder and mast into the opening. Toward the end of the "down" cycle, before the antenna motor stops, begin hand-threading the 12-mm hold-down nut into the chrome base.

7. Finish by tightening the hold-down nut while holding the chrome base with the pliers; avoid over-tightening. Turn on the radio and see if the new antenna works properly. Lubricate the mast with antenna wipes or WD-40.

8. If the new antenna doesn't extend or retract properly but the motor runs for the proper time, check the winder clutch for proper tension. The clutch is the large nut under the motor cover described above. Bend the lock tabs away from the hex flats, put a socket on the hex, and hand tighten without a ratchet or bar. Bend the locking tabs back down and check for proper operation.

Figure 1. Power antenna mast extending only part way, failing to retract fully.

Figure 2. Loosen antenna nut with 12-mm wrench while holding chrome base with pliers.

Figure 3. Begin inserting new antenna nylon winder; note which way the teeth face.

Upgrading Early W124 Headlights

by Max Scheinwerfer, Mile-High Section

July/August 2000

Photos in this article by the author.

The 1986 through 1994 300E, 300CE, and 300TE were never noted for their great headlights; here's how to improve them.

The stock headlights on our 1988 300TE were less than amazing. Then, to avoid stone chips, we had installed stick-on plastic headlight protection, but as the plastic aged, it diffused the light. Our night vision is also not what it used to be, so when Technical Editor Stu Ritter showed us the European 500E lights he'd put on his 400E (with a European dash-mounted height adjuster), we quickly said, "Let's do it!"

What You Need

- Left headlight assembly, Hella part 1EJ 004 440-111 (for 1986–89 models)
- Right headlight assembly, Hella part 1EJ 004 440-121
- Two 12v H4 halogen 100/80-watt high/low-beam lamps, Osram 64194
- Two 12v H3 halogen 80-watt fog light lamps, Osram 64153
- Two starter booster relays, Volkswagen 431 951 253H
- Two relay holders, Hella 87123
- Eight Hella female spade connectors that clip into the relay holder sockets, Hella 87272
- Two six-pin electrical connectors, Mercedes-Benz part 006 545 80 28 (socket) and 009 545 30 28 (cover)
- Six feet of 14-gauge insulated wire, push-on terminals, butt-type wire connectors, heat-shrink tubing, grommet

W124 upgraded with European headlights.

- Six feet of 10-gauge insulated wire, from battery to relays
- Inline fuse holder, 40-amp fuse
- Ten feet of vacuum tubing, two Y- or T-fittings
- European headlight switch panel, Mercedes-Benz part 124 60 03 65
- European headlight level control vacuum switch, Mercedes-Benz part 000 800 04 73

Besides normal hand tools, you'll also need a soldering iron and homemade wire hooks to pull out the instrument cluster.

Undoing Things

After disconnecting the battery, remove the old headlights. Behind each side marker assembly, unplug the power socket, release the tab, and push out the assembly. New side markers come with the headlights, but you must switch the old three-pin U.S. socket onto the Euro units, which come with two-prong sockets.

If your car has headlight wipers/washers, this conversion will cost you both, but that's a small price for more light. (You can have wipers, but it'll cost you another $600 for the necessary parts and labor.) Fold down the wiper arms, undo the 8-mm nut, and wiggle the arms off the

shafts. Unbolt the two 8-mm nuts holding the metal trim below the headlights, disconnect the washer hose, and remove the trim. Undo the black plastic headlight unit fastener on the sheet metal panel above each headlight. Undo the four 8-mm bolts holding each headlight unit in place. To reach the inside bolt on the left unit, first remove the air intake tube and snorkel. Remove the headlight units and unplug the headlight and wiper motor power cable sockets.

If your car has headlight wipers, the horizontal painted metal trim panels below the lights have holes in them. You can order new, primed panels without holes, part numbers 124 889 05 63 and 124 889 06 63. Have them painted to match or order a spray can of paint in factory color from Tower Paint (800/779-6520) and do it yourself. (The spray can paint is more susceptible to rock chips than properly applied body shop paint, which costs little more.)

Before installing the new bulbs in the headlight assemblies, cut off the small rounded tab on their mounting flange. Keep your fingers off the glass parts of the bulbs, and clean them with alcohol solution before installation. Keep the lower-power bulbs that come with the new headlights as spares. Notice that the new headlight assemblies have a circular vacuum servo to move the headlight reflectors.

Wiring Tips

We wired the new headlights so that when the low beam is on, the fog lights can be switched on or off; for maximum high-beam output, when the highs are on, the lows and fog lights are on, too. The VW relays, which handle up to 40 amps, are required for the high-amperage bulbs we're using. Working as remote switches to turn on the low beams and fog lights when high beams are selected, they can be mounted on the left headlight assembly. The relays reduce voltage drop by keeping the power wiring as short as possible.

Check the circuit diagram and terminal numbers on the headlight assembly; terminal numbers are also in the *Bosch Automotive Handbook* (page 790, 4th edition). Before you cut and solder, understand how the power flows. Solder all wiring connections; as Stu says, "A crimped connection is a mechanical connection; a soldered connection is an electrical connection." With high power in a critical circuit, this is no place for quick and dirty.

Pop the cover off the stock female headlight power sockets, and you'll see that the gray wire goes to the fog light pin; the yellow goes to the low beam pin, the white to high beams, brown to ground. Identify each of the new headlight unit's six male pins, and wire the new six-pin female socket accordingly (trim back the shrink tubing). Terminal 58 is unused; it's for the small round European running light above the main headlight bulb; disconnect that gray wire, and tape up the terminal. (In the U.S., the side marker light serves this purpose; that's why it has three pins instead of two on European cars.)

High-beam power will control the low-beam and fog light relays, so cut the white wire and, using a soldered-on butt connector, add 8–10 in of 14-ga wire with a 2-in jumper on the end to go from terminal 86 on one relay to the same terminal on the other. Before installing the terminals, slip heat

Step 1. Before upgrading.

Step 2. Headlight relays are necessary to handle additional power.

Step 3. Remove existing headlight units.

Step 4. Disconnect power to headlight washer motor.

Step 5. Clip off rounded tab on flange of new bulbs.

Step 6. Rear of new light unit as delivered; circular actuator adjusts headlight level.

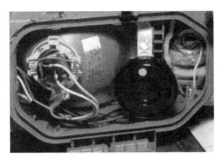

Step 7. Rewired headlight unit; power socket snaps onto back of bulb.

Step 8. Remove female headlight socket from end of existing cable.

shrink tubing onto the wires; heat it with a heat gun or a match held some distance away.

Slot the two relay holders together; mount them on the back lid of the left headlight unit so they face upward

with the terminals down (to keep out water and crud). Work out the best spot and check clearance; the air-conditioner receiver/drier is close, as is the self-leveling hydraulic reservoir on wagons. Drill two mounting holes in the cover, and bolt on the relay holders. To keep out water, drill and grommet a third hole, for the wires, on a downward-facing surface of the headlight cover

To power the whole shebang, run a new 10-ga wire from the battery's positive terminal to the left headlight. Route it under the cowl air intake, and install the 40-amp inline fuse holder next to the battery. The ground wire from the left headlight can be connected to the existing ground connection behind the unit or to any other convenient ground.

Installation

Remove the black outer gaskets from the stock headlight units; avoid yanking off their mounting tabs. Install the gaskets on the new headlight units. Transfer the three nut clips from the old units to the new. Attach the ground wire, then slide in the new left headlight unit. Be sure the hood release cable doesn't bind, and see that clearance exists behind the relays. As you tighten the three mounting bolts, line up the headlight face with the fender. Replace the air intake snorkel and flex pipe.

Slide in the new side marker units; plug in their power sockets and the six-pin headlight power sockets. The windshield wiper power socket remains unplugged, as do the headlight washer hoses; to avoid wasting washer fluid, disconnect the power socket of the headlight washer pump on the fluid reservoir behind the right headlight.

Headlight Level Control

Now we'll install the tubing and dash switch for the vacuum-powered headlight-leveling system. First, use a short piece of rubber hose to connect the vacuum line to the plug on the back of the right headlight. Run the hard vacuum tubing under the fender joint back to the battery, then beneath the cowl air intake over to the brake booster area. Run a similar line from the back of the left headlight to the brake booster area; join them with a Y- or T-fitting. Now to get the vacuum

Step 9. Rewired power connections; spliced dark wire is to relays.

Step 11. New 10-ga power supply wires from battery.

Step 13. New unit in place (old trim panels were used temporarily).

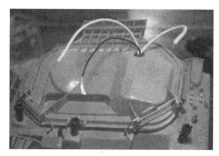

Step 10. Back of new headlight unit with new wiring.

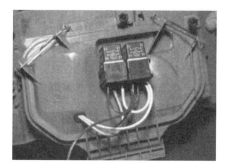

Step 12. Relays mounted on rear cover of left headlight unit.

Step 14. Vacuum lines join up behind brake booster then go through firewall grommet.

line through the firewall. Under the cowl, on the firewall just right of the brake booster, is a rubber grommet with several lines through it. Using needle-nose pliers, carefully pull out one of the unused nipples, then feed a length of vacuum tubing from the Y through the nipple.

Inside the car, pull the headlight knob off its shaft, and undo the 24-mm nut holding the panel; wiggle out the panel, left side first. The vacuum lines will run behind the instrument cluster, so you need to get in there. Pull up the floor mat behind the brake pedal, and unclip the speedometer cable clamp so it can move. Slip the wire hooks in on each side of the cluster, and ease it part

Step 15. New switch and level control panel in place; knob pushes onto shaft.

way out, right side first. Unscrew the speedometer cable connection, and unplug everything else. Remove the cluster entirely, then reach in (right of the speedo cable) with long pliers to pull through the new vacuum line. This line must be long enough to reach the new level control switch near the headlight switch.

Your vacuum source will be the economy gauge line, which you pulled off the back of the instrument cluster. Install a tee in that line and run the new line to the level control switch, with a check valve to allow the vacuum to work but to prevent backflow; the black side of the check valve must be toward the vacuum source (suck it and see). If your car has no economy gauge, use another convenient vacuum source.

The "light-out" warning lamp is part of the price of this improvement; the more powerful bulbs confuse the system enough to light that lamp, so you need to disable it. Looking at the instrument cluster face, determine which lamp this is, then go to the numbered sockets at the back (number 5 on ours) and remove the bulb.

Reinstall the connectors and the speedometer cable behind the instrument cluster, and slide it back into place. Push the level control into the switch panel, and install the vacuum source hose to the top connector (number 1) and the line to the headlights on the bottom connector (number 2). Reinstall the switch panel, the 24-mm nut, and the headlight switch knob

Fire 'Em Up

Reconnect the battery, start the engine, and turn on the lights! If things don't work, recheck your wiring. Aim the headlights using the three black 13-mm aiming screws behind each unit. The outside screw controls left/right aim, the center one controls height, and the inner one controls fog light height. Setting the headlight level switch to 1 as normal allows 0 as a high position and 2 and 3 as low positions to accommodate heavy loads. If your car has self-leveling rear suspension, you might use the 2 slot as normal. If the level control switch doesn't work, you may have reversed the vacuum connections to it, or you may have a vacuum leak in the new tubing.

You'll find the light output amazing. Our light meter measured high-beam output four times the stock level! The low beams have better spread and output. The high beams may not look as powerful as they actually are; the fog lights come on with the high beams, and their lenses splash light downward, close to the car, masking long-range improvement. That can be solved by switching lenses. The 300E/400E fog light lens aims light downward. The 500E used a driving light lens to direct light farther ahead. Both can be ordered from U.S. sources. We started with the fog light set-up but switched to the driving light lens.

This $900 conversion was worth it. Doing it yourself can save on labor but requires about a day. You can also offset the cost by flogging your stock lights via a Trading Post ad. Let there be light!

The usual disclaimer applies about violating various local, state, and federal laws, most of which were written back in the "dark ages."

Installing European Headlights on W116 300SDs

by Mike Roth,
Los Angeles Section

January/February 1982

Photos in this article by the author.

As with all other Mercedes-Benz models, the W116 looks best with European headlights.

A recent factory service bulletin pointed out a severe problem when an owner attempts to install the factory Bosch headlights on a 1978–1980 300SD Turbodiesel with the W116 body. The problem arises because the car was developed solely for the U.S. market, and was never intended to have anything but sealed beam lights. The problem is that the air intake for the engine is fitted to the back of the right-hand sealed beam unit, and uses air coming through the unit to feed the engine. When the unit is replaced with the Bosch type, airflow through it is reduced drastically because of tighter clearances.

Two things happen when the lights are simply installed without taking into account the design differences in the 300SD from a 450. First, the engine may be starved for air, and have a severe lack of power. Second, if the back cover of the light unit is removed to allow the engine proper breathing, the reflector is soon tarnished and the right-hand light becomes less and less efficient.

A relatively simple fix not only allows the engine to take air from the area between the radiator shell and the light unit, but also provides a "four fog light" operation with the underbumper lights in addition to the ones built into the Bosch units. (If desired, you can set up driving lights under the bumper and work them from the secondary position of the light switch. See the Driveway Mechanic article in the November/December 1981 *Star*.) The project requires the following parts:

- One set European headlight assemblies
- Twelve 1½-in. Phillips sheet metal screws with washers
- Two H4 European headlight bulbs
- Two H3 European fog light bulbs
- Six feet hookup wire
- One tube liquid rubber
- One piece aluminum at least 14cm x 21cm x 1.5mm or 2mm
- One flattened aluminum soft drink can
- About two–three hours of time

Tools required are as follows:

- Soldering iron and rosin core electrical solder
- Wire cutters and electrical tape
- Electric drill with assorted bits

Procedure

1. Remove the sheet metal valence below the headlight assembly. Remove the windshield washer reservoir by lifting it straight up and place it aside. On the right side, remove the upper bumper unit and the battery.

2. Remove the side marker lights by unscrewing the white knurled knobs.

3. Remove the light bulb from the lens assembly. Put the assembly aside to re-use later.

4. Working on the left side first, remove the six screws that hold the sealed beam unit in place. Note: Standard terminology refers to the left and right sides of the car as seen from the driver's position.

5. Remove the electrical connector from the rear of the unit.

6. Remove the left side unit from the car.

7. Remove the 3-pin plug and 2 bulb plugs from the American assembly and install in the European assembly to allow the American side marker lights and turn signal lights to work.

8. European headlight units have an integral fog light. To activate them, solder a wire to the brown ground wire at the plug in the headlight assembly and run it to the ground on the fog light terminal. Remove the white (fog-hot) wire from the European light and move it to the American receptacle in the European assembly.

9. Remove the cable clamp and the remaining European wiring from the headlight assembly. Insert the new (old) wiring plus the fog light hot lead under the seal. Use liquid rubber to re-seal the rubber lip to the headlight frame.

10. Run the fog light hot lead to the fog light cable area below the bumper.

11. Slit the fog light cable insulation to get to the two cables within.

12. Brown is ground—don't touch it. The other is the hot lead. Splice the cable from the headlight assembly to the fog light cable, then carefully tape up the connections.

13. Replace the new European headlight in position. Run the fog light cable under the headlight assembly fog hot lead.

14. Use the new (longer) screws to secure the headlight assembly.

15. Replace the side marker bulb in its original position with the cable clamp.

16. Replace the side marker light assembly, using the white knurled knobs. Insert the bulbs in the proper positions, H4 in the headlight and H3 in the fog light. Connect the 3-terminal plug to the H4 bulb.

17. Replace the lower valence panel. The following steps are the differences between the left side and the right side. Wiring is the same as the right side.

18. Remove the black plastic cover from the rear of the right side headlight mount.

19. Remove the air hose from the air cleaner to the air horn on the headlight mount.

20. Remove the air horn from the headlight mount.

21. Using the aluminum from the soft drink can, cut a piece to size and seal up the rear of the mount with it. Use plastic rubber around the edges so that it will be airtight. For a finishing touch, use a spray can of your car's body color and spray the aluminum plate.

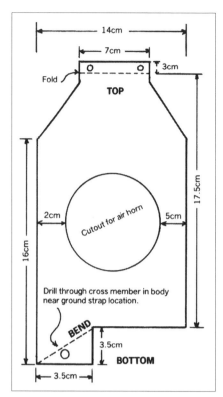

Drawing of new air horn bracket. Fabricate from sheet aluminum or steel. Not drawn to scale. Position holes in top to match factory holes in bodywork.

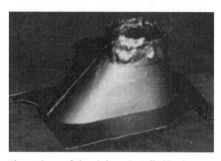

Three views of the air horn installed in the fabricated bracket.

22. Fabricate an air horn holder according to the drawing. This fits between the top support brace and the brace below and behind the headlight assembly.

23. Insert the air horn into the new bracket with the horn pointing up.

24. Drill two holes in the bracket to match the two existing holes in the top brace. Drill a third hole in the bracket and the car where the bracket touches the lower cross member next to the ground strap connection.

25. Insert the bracket into the car, bending the lower tab so that it touches the lower cross member. Use three bolts and bolt it into place.

26. For a more "factory" look, paint the horn and bracket, as well as the point where you drilled the cross member, to reduce the possibility of rust.

The air horn/bracket assembly installed in the new location.

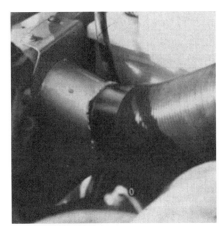

The original hose fits perfectly, and the 300SD can breathe as well as before.

27. Reconnect the stock air hose from the air cleaner to the relocated air horn.

28. Reassemble and reinstall the valence panel, bumper unit, washer reservoir battery, etc.

29. Aim new lights. A future Driveway Mechanic article will deal with the proper aiming of European headlights.

300SD Headlight / Air Flow

May/June 1988

My 1979 300SD has European headlights, but apparently due to changing to these lights, the air cleaner system doesn't work properly. The air duct is supposed to connect to the back of the headlight assembly, but then the headlight glass yellows. Will disconnecting the duct hurt the air cleaner system?

The original 300SD was built only for the U.S. market, using sealed beam headlights. The air intake was designed around the headlight housing for these lights. When the original lights were replaced with European lights, drivers complained of a serious power loss. (Included among them was the then-president of MBCA.) Various ducts were cobbled up to obtain a free flow to the air cleaner. I know of no kit made to cure this, but try using today's halogen headlights (Bosch, GE, Sylvania, etc.), which are the same size as the old U.S. sealed-beam units.

More On 300SD Euro Lights

July/August 1988

In the May/June issue we addressed a problem with mounting European headlights on a 116-body 300SD. Dave Girgen, Houston Section, writes with the following suggestion:

The problem of restricted air flow to the air cleaner when mounting European lights on a 116-body 300SD can be cured using the following parts, which look neat and original:

- One #117 094 03 82 hose MBNA retail price $4.04

- One #117 094 00 11 air duct MBNA retail price $7.01

- Two pan-head sheet metal screws

Use the hose to extend the original hose far enough to reach the duct, which can be mounted on the frame rail under the battery tray. Trim the duct slightly so that it can be moved forward and mounted just behind the louvered panel under the headlight.

Light Fantastic

THE STAR

by Frank King,
Technical Editor

*November/December
1995*

Photos in this article
by Daimler-Benz AG.

*Mercedes-Benz brings you closer to
the ultimate headlight system.*

Forgive us for beginning an article on headlights by looking backward instead of forward. It is historically almost impossible to find an automobile intended for public roads that does not have some sort of lights. We know from her own account of the first long-distance drive in 1888 that Berta Benz had no lights on the three-wheeler, but all later pictures show some kind of lights. These carryovers from lamps used on horse-drawn carriages of the day usually had a wick and burned kerosene, like railroad lamps.

The earliest lights that attempted to light the road ahead were acetylene lamps, which mixed calcium carbide and water to produce a gas flame. It is said that the best of these lamps, large in diameter and with bright silver reflectors, evoked protests because they dazzled pedestrians and other drivers. So started a long, unending controversy.

Electric lighting with an incandescent bulb was invented by Edison in 1879, but small, low-voltage bulbs with sufficiently sturdy filaments to endure the jolts and vibration of an automobile were not made until after 1910. By World War I, practically all cars had electric headlights. There were dozens of different ways of providing combinations of high driving beams and dipped, no-glare beams. Europe was ahead in the development of effective road lights, particularly with the large Bosch and Marchal units that graced Mercedes or Hispano-Suiza or Rolls-Royce cars.

Sealed Beams

The great problem with these technically advanced lights and their humble cousins was that the reflectors tarnished and lost their effectiveness. A few of us are old enough to remember polishing reflectors with lamp black and olive oil. Any harsher abrasive would quickly remove the silver.

A real breakthrough was the sealed beam unit invented in England in 1937 and developed in the U.S. by General Electric. The light was not as good as the best European lights in new condition, but they stayed as good as new until they burned out. The reflecting surface was molded into a glass bowl which had the filament molded in. The covering glass lens was sealed to the bowl, and the resulting chamber was filled with a mixture of nitrogen and argon. U.S. regulating bodies established the sealed beam as the only legal headlight in the U.S.

Tungsten, long used for light bulb filaments, melts at 3,370°C under normal conditions, but in the vacuum of early bulbs it started to vaporize at 2,300°C, leading to early failure; as the tungsten wire vaporized, the molecules were deposited on the cooler glass bulb. It was discovered that by filling the bulb with an argon/nitrogen mixture, filament temperature could be higher, since the vaporizing point rises under pressure and the gas conducts heat away from the filament.

Halogen Bulbs

General Electric discovered in 1959 that if bulbs were filled with a halogen (bromine, chlorine, fluorine, or iodine), the vaporizing tungsten formed a halide compound which then split and deposited tungsten back on the filament. This allowed the temperature of the filament to be raised and the output of light per watt of electricity to be doubled. Because of the high temperature, it was necessary to make the envelope of quartz. This

led to the early name "quartz-iodide" for these bulbs, now simply called halogens. The principle was later applied to sealed beam lights.

The demand for better road lights continued, and development proceeded, particularly in Germany. Headlight design conflicted with the effort to reduce air resistance. Larger diameter headlights are more efficient, and their effect is improved when they are higher above the road. Various elaborations of paraboloid and ellipsoid reflectors were tried with some success but no real breakthrough.

In Germany in 1991 there were five different types of headlights of more or less experimental nature offered. The Audi S4 and the BMW 750i tried lamps with DE (three-axis ellipsoid) reflectors. The BMW 750i and the Volkswagen Golf also tried an early form of gas-discharge bulb, while the Mercedes-Benz 600SE (Germany only) tried a multi-focus reflector. None of these was really satisfactory.

New E-Class Lights

The new E-Class (W210) offers two headlight systems developed in a joint project of Hella and Mercedes-Benz. Standard equipment lights use H7 55-watt halogen bulbs for both high and dipped beams. This bulb emits 1,500 lumens, whereas the H4 60/55 double-filament bulb with which we are familiar emits 1,000 lumens from the low beam side. (The lumen is the SI unit for light emission; a household 100-watt bulb emits about 1,700 lumens.) The H4 bulb uses a metal shield under the low-beam filament to prevent light from hitting the lower half of the reflector. Such light is reflected upward and cannot be used in the ordinary dipped beam.

One outstanding feature of the new headlights is the use of "free-form" reflectors. Distinct from previous reflectors based on adaptations of

Standard E-Class lights use free-form reflectors, H7 bulbs; turn signal light is above low-beam unit (left).

Optional xenon lights use D2R gas-discharge bulbs with a clear cover lens and a patterned inner lens. High beams still use H7 bulbs.

Low Beam Comparison

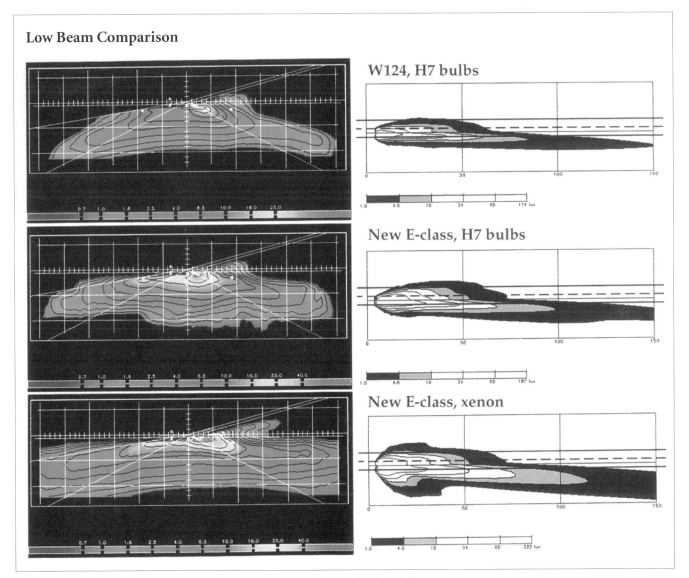

W124, H7 bulbs

New E-class, H7 bulbs

New E-class, xenon

Headlight output comparison includes W124 with H7 bulbs, new E-Class (W210) with H7 bulbs and with xenon lights. Shading indicates light intensity; distances are in meters.

geometric forms, free-form reflectors are generated through computer simulation and repeated tests. The objective is to use every particle of light emitted by the bulb and direct them in the desired direction. In effect, the computer simulation treats the reflector as if it were composed of thousands of tiny mirrors, each aimed for maximum efficiency. This design works so well that no corrective lens is really needed in front of the bulb. In practice, the covering outside lens is used to fine tune the light pattern.

The high beam headlight also has its own free-form reflector and uses an H7 bulb. When the high beam is switched on, the dipped beam remains on. Even discounting the benefits of the free-form reflectors, this system more than doubles the light put on the road as compared to 1995 systems.

Optional Xenon Light Bulbs

While the Hella/Mercedes-Benz team worked on improved lighting, it considered the possibilities of the latest generation of gas-discharge bulbs as a light source. The lighting efficiency of gas-discharge devices has long been known. We are familiar with the bluish mercury-vapor and sodium-vapor lamps used for lighting highways and public areas. Electric discharges in tubes filled with one of the "inert" gases are well known as neon tubes. (Because helium, neon, argon, krypton, xenon, and radon were thought to be incapable of forming compounds with other elements, they were once called "inert gases." Since 1962, when xenon was forced to combine with platinum fluoride, they are called "noble gases.")

When an electric current is passed through xenon, a brilliant white light is emitted. Research and development in the electrical industry brought forth the D2R-35W gas-discharge bulb (Figure 1) used in the dipped beam section of the optional headlight system of the new E-Class. This bulb consumes only 35 watts but emits 2,800 lumens, an efficiency

of 80 lumens per watt. The H7 bulb consumes 55 watts for 1,500 lumens, an efficiency of 27 lumens per watt; an H4 bulb in dipped mode consumes 55 watts to give 1,000 lumens, 18 lumens per watt.

The D2R-35W bulb consists of a micro high-pressure bulb inside a protective ultraviolet (UV) filtering bulb. The actual light source is an electric arc between two electrodes 4.2 mm apart. The arc burns continuously at 85 volts but must be started at 25,000 volts by an electronic starter and ballast system. Starting time from cold is 1.5 seconds, and the bulb's service life exceeds 2,000 hours. As with all electrical light-producing devices, there is a slow drop in light emission. By half-life, approximately 1,000 hours, light emission of the bulb drops by about 25 percent. These bulbs do not burn out suddenly as incandescent bulbs do but gradually fall off in brightness. Bulbs are readily replaceable.

Light from these xenon headlights is a brilliant white, leaving normal headlights looking relatively yellow. More precisely, the color temperature is 3,860°K. Only about three percent of light emitted by the D2R-35W bulb with its UV filter is in the UV range. Still, safety UV glasses should always be worn when adjusting the lamp or in case of direct eye contact with the open lamp. Pressure inside the lamp in the cold state is 7 bar (102 psi) and in the hot operating state, 100 bar (1,450 psi). During operation the protective

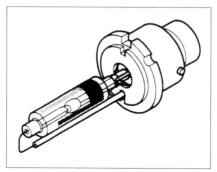

Figure 1. Xenon D2R-35W bulb uses protective ultraviolet filter, shielding, and plug base; it draws 35 watts and lasts 2,000 hours.

bulb will be at a temperature of 700°C (1,292°F), and the lamp base will be at 180°C (356°F). Protective gloves should always be worn when working on the lamps, and bulbs should never be touched with bare hands, even when cold and out of the car.

To Aim and Protect

One objective of the Hella/Mercedes-Benz team, besides better illumination, was to make one system which would comply with all lighting regulations of all industrial nations. Hella had already been given approval, under the latest European regulations, for polycarbonate lenses, and this material was adopted for the new E-Class headlights. Compared with glass cover lenses, these new lenses reduce vehicle weight by 3.3 pounds. Polycarbonate is the only plastic permitting sufficient production accuracy for the four-headlight system to fit the car with equal gap measurements. The lens cover is easily replaceable. The gap between it and the bodywork is covered by an elastic seal that prevents dirt from entering or wind noise from developing.

The cover lens of the dipped beam portion of the standard H7 lamp differs from the clear cover lens of the xenon lamp by having refractive ribs molded in to fine tune the output. The xenon version has a structured inner lens for optimal light distribution. The high beam lamps are the same in both versions.

The xenon lamp is so bright that it could not secure approval in many countries if it were not accompanied by some method of assuring correct aiming at all times and under all vehicle loads. The new, dynamic headlight leveling system developed for the W210 uses magneto-resistive axle sensors, a microprocessor-controller, and fast servo motors to sense and correct headlight aim for all changes in the vehicle's center of gravity. Not only changes in passenger and trunk loading are compensated, but also dynamic changes—acceleration or braking. As the car accelerates, the front end rises, and traffic coming in the opposite direction would be dazzled. When braking, the nose dips, and the lighted field of vision is shortened and diminished.

The convex plastic cover lenses required a new method of cleaning them while the car is moving. The result is a jet cleaning system. On each side a telescopic rod carries a nozzle from which a spray of water is projected onto the lenses. The rod is drawn back into the bodywork, where it is protected from damage when not in use; when activated, it extends about 4-1/2 inches.

The W210's lighting system results from teamwork between Hella and Mercedes-Benz which started with the F100 research vehicle in 1989. The new system involved building many test reflectors based on computer simulations and testing them in Hella's 460-ft light tunnel. The cleaning system and weather resistance were tested at the Hella rain test track, while the usual

Telescopic headlight-cleaning wand projects 4.4 inches, squirts cover lenses, then recedes.

Mercedes-Benz test teams carried out extreme summer and winter tests. In more ways than one, the headlights are among the most outstanding features of the new E-Class cars.

The prompt, responsive help of Hella KG Hueck & Co. in furnishing technical information and illustrations is appreciated.

1996–2003 E-Class Combination Switch Replacement

by Jim Mahaffey,
Contributing
Editor

January/February 2004

Photos in this article by the author.

How to replace your E320's turn signal and headlight switch

The combination (turn signal, headlight) switch on your 1996 to 2003 (W210) E-Class car will eventually break. Two of mine did within seven years of service. The tiny plastic pillow-blocks which allow forward/backward motion—to control the headlights—failed, giving me an excuse to go into the steering column and learn more. Steering column work involves safety considerations, because you must disconnect and remove the driver's airbag. The new combination switch retails for about $140. There is no practical way to repair the bearing when it breaks, but you can at least save the replacement labor cost.

For this job you'll need a 13-mm combination wrench, a medium-sized (#2) Phillips-head screwdriver, a 10-mm Allen wrench (deep, with a long arm), and a T27 Torx driver. The Torx driver must be short enough to fit between the steering wheel and the dash; a socket-based Torx tool will not fit in the recess through which the fastener must be removed. Special tool 128 589 00 10 00 is available from Mercedes-Benz, but I used a folding Torx driver from the hardware store.

Step by Step

First, remove the ignition key and disconnect the battery. Lift out the back seat, using the latches and handholds at the two corners, and set it aside. Disconnect the ground strap on the battery using the 13-mm wrench, and set it out of reach of the battery post (Photo 1).

Photo 1. Disconnect the battery at the negative (ground) end.

Photo 2. Use a short T27 Torx driver to release the airbag; this is the left-side access tunnel.

Photo 3. Use the same tool on the right-side access tunnel.

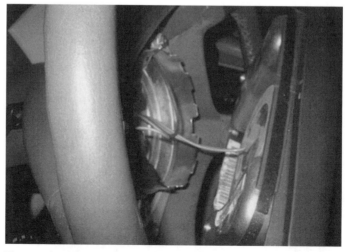

Photo 4. The airbag removes outward and is now held only by its connector.

Photo 5. The connector snaps off. Carefully set aside the airbag, metal side down.

Photo 6. Disconnecting the rest of the airbag wiring harness, here the gray wire, connected to ground.

Photo 7. Disconnect the yellow wire, also connected to steering wheel ground.

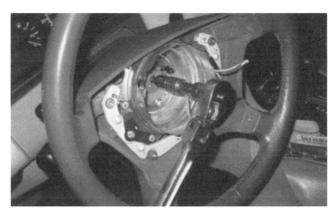

Photo 8. Lean into your socket handle to undo the steering-wheel fastener.

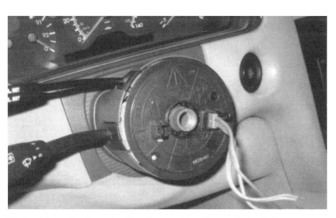

Photo 9. The steering wheel is off, revealing the contact spiral.

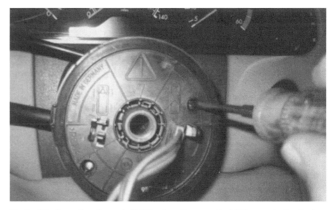

Photo 10. Two deeply sunk Phillips-head screws hold the contact spiral.

Disconnect the airbag from the steering wheel center. Two holes on the back of the steering wheel (Photos 2 and 3) give access to the two T27 fasteners, which may remain in the steering wheel after the airbag is released.

Disconnect the gas-generator squib from the wiring harness. A green wire, going into a red connector, terminates at the center of the back of the airbag (Photo 4). Pull it off (Photo 5). When you restore this connection, it should connect with a distinct click. Set aside the airbag, metal side down. A static electric spark could set off the airbag, so suppress any urge to touch the contact point with your finger.

Disconnect the rest of the airbag wiring harness. On the right is a gray wire, connected to a ground point with a spade connector. Unlock this connector by pressing its base with your thumbnail (Photo 6). On the left is a yellow wire, which is not locked on, also connected to steering wheel ground; disconnect it (Photo 7).

Remove the steering wheel using a 10-mm Allen socket on a long breaker bar (Photo 8). On some cars the screw

Photo 11. Pull out the wiring

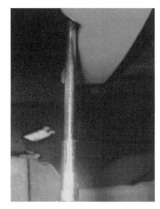

Photo 12. One screw holds the hood release, which is under the crook in the lever, as shown.

Photo 13. One more screw holds the left under-dash, at the corner.

Photo 14. One more screw holds the cruise-control lever.

Photo 15. The cruise control has been laid aside, showing the two remaining screws holding the combination-switch chassis to the steering column.

Photo 16. One screw is at six o'clock.

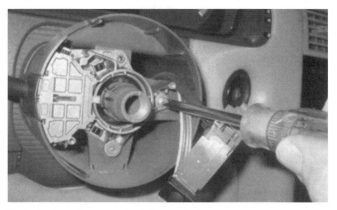

Photo 17. The other screw is at three o'clock.

backs out easily, but on others the thing is screwed in with vengence. The bolt is coated with Loctite. If you have a tough one, have someone strong hold the steering wheel. The meanest brute cannot keep that steering wheel from turning until it stops against the steering lock. I assure you, from experience and conversations

with pros, that you cannot break a Mercedes-Benz steering lock with hand tools. Use a premium-quality Allen socket and a long-handled breaker bar, and lean into it hard. It will yield. Set aside the wheel.

You will now see a black plastic thing at the end of the steering column (Photo 9). This spiral contact replaces

the former rotating double-circle of brass and two spring-loaded brushes, which got dirty and worn. A piece of copper-on-mylar circuitry, wound into a spiral, now connects the airbag to the firing circuit. It should last forever under normal use, but treat it gently. It is held by two counter-sunk Phillips screws at two and eight o'clock. Remove

Photo 18. Pull out the combination switch; jerk the cable to help identify it under the dash.

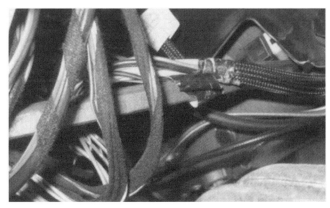

Photo 19. The cable is taped to a steel member under the dash. It is too crowded to show you where the connector is stuffed; you'll have to find it by feel.

Photo 20. The connector being released from the body wiring.

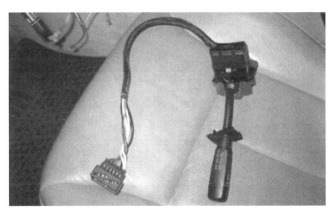

Photo 21. Here's what the little monster looks like, freed of its bondage to the car.

the two screws (Photo 10), pull the spiral off the steering shaft, and let it hang by its wiring harness (Photo 11).

Under the Dash

You must get under the dash to disconnect the combination switch. Instead of removing the entire under-dash, you can reach the connector by pulling down the left side of the under-dash (the right side is held by a vexing hidden fastener). Remove the hood release via a single Phillips-head screw below the left corner of the red lever (Photo 12).

Remove the Phillips-head screw at the left forward corner of the under-dash (Photo 13). The under-dash can now be snapped loose from the dashboard by pulling down, and you can snake an arm into the vast, unknown region behind it.

Meanwhile, back at the column, remove the cruise-control lever. A

single Phillips-head screw atop the steering shaft holds it (Photo 14). Let it hang by its wiring harness (Photo 15).

Release the combination switch by removing two Phillips-head screws at three and six o'clock (Photos 16 and 17). The unit will then pull free of the steering column and will be connected to the car only by its cable (Photo 18).

Release the combination switch connector block. The cable is tied to the car by a single wrap of electrical tape. Unwrap it (Photo 19). Find the connector block by feel, and pull on the cable to identify it. The connector's elaborate locking mechanism is released by pushing a sliding block to the side (Photo 20). If you can't feel the sliding block move, you haven't released the connector.

The connector may or may not withdraw through the steering column end. In one of two cases I found that the connector's progress was blocked by a plastic bracket, clipped

to a metal member below the steering shaft. I managed to unclip it using a thumbnail, and upon reassembly it easily clipped back into position. This work is in such a cramped position that I couldn't photograph it. The factory procedure suggests removing the casing tube around the steering column, but this does nothing to relieve the connector.

As you reassemble, using the new combination switch, the steering column and underdash will seem to jump back together. The under-dash snaps smartly back into place with a push from your palm. Reconnect the battery ground, and re-install the back seat. Convince your radio that it has not been stolen by resetting its code, and reset the clock.

That's it. if you've installed the steering wheel crooked—usually one spline counterclockwise—and can't get used to it, repeat the first five steps.

Technical and Restoration Forum

Technical and Restoration Forum

WARNING—

Please exercise care and safety by reviewing the following Warnings and Cautions before attempting any of the service procedures described in this section.

- Some repairs may be beyond your capability. If you lack the skills, tools and equipment, or a suitable workplace for any procedure described in this book, we suggest you leave such repairs to an authorized Mercedes-Benz dealer service department, or other qualified shop.

- Before starting any major jobs or repairs to components on which passenger safety may depend, consult your authorized Mercedes-Benz dealer about technical bulletins that may have been issued since the date of the articles. Mercedes-Benz is constantly improving its cars. Sometimes these changes, both in parts and specifications, are made applicable to earlier models.

- Disconnect the battery negative (−) cable (ground strap) whenever you work on the fuel system or the electrical system. Do not smoke or work near heaters or other fire hazards. Keep an approved fire extinguisher handy.

- Keep sparks, lighted matches and open flame away from the top of the battery. Car batteries produce explosive hydrogen gas. If hydrogen gas escaping from the cap vents is ignited, it will ignite gas trapped in the cells and cause the battery to explode.

- Please see pages vii and viii at the front of this book for a thorough list of Warnings and Cautions.

Battery, Starter, Alternator

Battery Plugs

November/December 1994

The battery in my 450SL has small plugs in each filler hole. To check the electrolyte level, these plugs must be removed, which is a pain in the neck. What is their function, and are they really necessary?

The plugs prevent electrolyte spillage and promote recombination of the hydrogen and oxygen freed during normal operation of the battery. They must be removed to add water. If it has these plugs, your battery must be a low-maintenance type.

Reluctant Starters

May/June 1987

After 25 years of working professionally on Mercedes-Benz cars, a problem has stumped me. A 1969 300SEL 6.3's starter would not function at times, particularly when the car was hot. The starter, neutral safety switch, some wiring and the ignition switch were replaced to no avail. Finally, a separate pushbutton switch was installed under the dash, which cured the problem. Since then, I've run into the same problem on a 1974 280, which responded likewise.

We've heard of this problem on other models, too. I think that you'll find the problem to be low voltage at the starter solenoid, most likely due to a defective air-conditioner/starter relay (assuming that the other parts you mentioned are in good shape). When starting, the current goes from the ignition switch (terminal 50VI/WT) to the AC/start relay. After long use, the contact points in this relay become burned and pitted, offering more and more

resistance to the flow of current to the starter solenoid. One indication of this fault will be heating of this relay when you try to start the car with the regular starter switch; the relay will become very hot if you continue to try to start the car this way.

Check this with a voltmeter at the 87 terminal of the relay (a VI wire 2.5 sq mm). You're probably only getting four or five volts here. This big violet wire (about #12 US gauge) goes to a connector which connects to the starter. If replacement of the AC/start relay doesn't correct the problem, I'd suggest using a voltmeter to trace the current from the starter solenoid back to the ignition switch. Somewhere along the line, the current flow is impeded or—less likely—drained off.

Alternator Boost

March/April 1996

I've added 80/100-watt H4 headlights and an in-line fuel heater to my 1984 300D, which has a 55-amp alternator. Because I live in a cold climate, I'm concerned that heavy use of the heater and rear-window defroster could weaken the battery charge at low speeds. Can I replace my 55-amp alternator with a 65-amp unit from a 1981 280CE, which looks just the same?

You can bolt in any Bosch alternator as long as they belong to the same size series. For example, the Bosch nameplate on your 55-amp has the line K1->14V55A20. If the 65-amp alternator has a nameplate with K1->14V65A21 in the same position, you can interchange them. The important points are the initial K, which indicates size, and the arrow ->, which indicates clockwise rotation. During the same period Mercedes-Benz used 70-amp alternators on the 380SL and 380SLC with K1->14V70A20 on the plate.

Body and Interior

Hot Mirrors

November/December 2002

Are heated rear-view mirrors temperature-activated? Mine are hot almost all the time during the winter. During the summer they are completely cool. I thought they were broken until the temperature suddenly dropped into the 50s last night; then they were hot again.

Electrically-heated outside rear-view mirrors have been available since September 1985. The heating element on the back of the mirror glass is controlled by a thermostat, also on the rear of the glass, which turns the heater on and off depending on ambient air temperature.

Weeping Washers

January/February 1994

The windshield washer nozzles on my 1979 450SL leak, and I've noticed the same thing on other SLs. What causes the leak, and how can I cure it?

Dribbling from the washer nozzles is caused by expansion of the fluid and water vapor in the reservoir. Because the 450SL hood fits low over the engine, temperatures are higher than in sedans. A check valve in the line to the nozzles holds a supply of fluid at the nozzles. When the reservoir heats up, the vapor expands, and some fluid is forced out.

Keep the reservoir less than full, and be sure that its cover has a vent hole or that the cover is loose enough so that pressure can't build up in the reservoir.

Seat Belt Warning Light

January/February 1992

When the belt is buckled, the seat belt warning light comes on randomly in my 240D, even when driving. It seems to come on when some other electrical device (AC, fan, cruise control, etc.) is used.

The switch in the seat belt buckle is closed when the belt is unbuckled. Buckling up opens the switch, so foreign matter in the buckle could have the effect of closing the switch. Several electrical circuits use the same ground, G102, behind the center of the instrument panel. It's possible that this ground connection is loose, but otherwise, check and clean the contacts in the buckle.

Alarming Driving

July/August 1992

Because of your excellent, informative articles, I continue to enjoy my membership. I would love to see even more of each issue devoted to technical issues. Meanwhile, the anti-theft alarm on my 560SEL triggers erroneously, sometimes when driving. The anti-tow sensor has been disconnected. Any suggestions?

As with most electronics, alarm problems are often caused by defective soldering or dirty connections. In the diagnostic manual for alarms, the first instructions are:

1. Check fuse #15 and fuses in the auxiliary fuse holder (F14).

2. Disconnect 8-pin and 14-pin connectors from anti-theft alarm control unit.

3. Check sockets in connectors for good solder connections and tight fit on pins of anti-theft alarm control unit. Check sockets with gauge; they must not be spread apart.

In the case of the alarm system becoming activated while driving, it is especially important to check the tightness of socket no. 2 of the 14-pole connector.

Becker Grand Prix

May/June 1986

AM reception of my Becker Grand Prix Electronic radio in my 1985 300D is affected by bumps in the road. First, one bump reduces volume to a point that adjusting the volume will not compensate, then another bump restores reception. The radio and antenna have been replaced with no improvement.

Since both radio and antenna have been replaced without improvement, a poor ground or other electrical or antenna connection is one possibility. Complaints about the Grand Prix radio have been more frequent since 1984, and although they are different from yours, they seem to have one thing in common: when a new radio is installed, the trouble often seems to remain.

I suggest that you ask your dealer to arrange a meeting with the MBNA Zone Technical Representative to resolve the problem. Since the radios work well in most cars and MBNA is very cooperative in settling problems, your radio should be able to be fixed.

Cruise Control

Cruise Control and Brake Light Bulbs

March/April 1994

The cruise control in my 1979 300SD has gradually failed, and my mechanic tells me that it might be due to a replacement brake light bulb. He says that some replacement bulbs can cause such a slow failure. This is too bizarre for me to comprehend. Can you explain?

That story about certain brands of brake light bulbs causing malfunctions in the cruise control has been around for a long time, and I thought it had died away. There is no truth at all to it.

For the cruise control to be engaged, terminal 8 of the amplifier must sense ground through the brake lights. When the brakes are applied, the brake switch closes, electrically removing the ground. Your problem may be in the wiring and contacts, but all elements of the system should be checked to locate the real source of the problem.

The linkage from the accelerator pedal to the injection pump must operate smoothly and freely. The cruise control system has four elements: 1) the switch on the steering column, 2) the speed sensor, 3) the control unit (amplifier), and 4) the actuator. Few problems are found in the switch or the speed sensor. The control unit compares the speed of the car as read by the sensor with the desired speed set by the driver via the switch. It then sends a signal to the actuator to hold the throttle steady, open it (for more speed), or close it (to slow down). The actuator is powered by vacuum and must be checked for response to signals from the amplifier. If it is OK, and if vacuum is available, the amplifier must be at fault. New or rebuilt units are available.

If *both* stop light bulbs are burned out or loose, the cruise control will not work at all. If at least one bulb is good, no matter who made it, the fault lies somewhere else.

Hunting License

May/June 1998

When I engage the cruise control in my 1983 300D Turbodiesel, the car stays close to the speed selected but "hunts", at any speed, especially after cresting a hill. This constant acceleration and deceleration is annoying. How can I make the cruise control operate smoothly?

The unpleasant sensation that the cruise control is "hunting" too much is usually caused by friction in the throttle linkage. As dirt collects on the linkage's joints and lubricant dries up, your throttle foot grows unconscious of the increasing friction because it occurs gradually. When the cruise control actuator tries to move the linkage, its first effort does not work because of the friction. Effort increases until the friction is overcome, then the linkage moves with a jerk.

The remedy is to disassemble the entire throttle linkage, joint by joint, and clean it thoroughly. In re-assembly, use no grease or solid lubricant. Hydraulic oil as used in aircraft is best, but since it's hard to find, you can use automatic transmission fluid to lubricate the joints. Once the throttle linkage moves freely, the cruise control should hold a set speed without disturbance.

Headlights

450SE Headlights

March/April 2004

What would be the least expensive way to improve the headlights on my 1973 450SE without going to the expense of European headlights?

The best, least expensive modification for the U.S. four-headlight setup is a set of replacement round headlights with a European pattern (E-code) that take halogen bulbs; then you can install 100W/135W bulbs in the high/low and 100W bulbs in the fog lights. Relay everything and use 12-gauge wire so there is no voltage drop at the bulbs, allowing them to draw all the current they can. You can also relay the fog lights to come on when you go to high beam, which would give you 470 watts of carefully aligned light on the front of the car. This setup will draw 40 amperes at 12 volts, and you have a 55-ampere alternator. I wouldn't plan on running on high beam for an entire night, as eventually you will start to draw down the battery. You could also switch the relay controlling the fogs so you could turn them off when not needed.

Set 'Em and See

November/December 2003

How can I align my European headlights. Can it be done in a home garage?

For European asymmetrical beams, the instructions are in the 116 manual, under chassis electrical, 82.2-040/1. Position the car 10 meters (33 ft) from a wall. Draw a line on the wall at the same height as the center of the headlight. Set the upper portion of the low beam to this height.

For U.S.-spec headlights, the *Bosch Automotive Handbook* says that headlights are aligned using mechanical aiming devices. They give no specs for U.S. headlight alignment, but there are pages of specs for Euro lights. We prefer to adjust lights on a dark road and just set them where we like them. Have someone else block one headlight while you align the other. One great advantage of the adjustable European headlights is that you can adjust them while you drive. To us, that feature alone is worth the price of the headlights.

Headlight Flashing

May/June 1992

Although the multifunction stalk on my 1967 250SE has a position for it, the headlight flasher switch has never worked. How can it be connected?

At one time headlight flashing was illegal in the U.S., so American models had the system disabled. In our March/April 1982 issue, Harley Juth, Northern New Jersey Section, described how to make the flasher work. Since it may be useful to you and others, here's an edited version, with a letter from the May/June 1982 issue on the same topic.

Hooking Up the Headlight Flasher

These instructions apply to the 200, 200D, 220, 220D, 230, 250, and 250C (W114 and W115) and may apply to the larger-bodied 250S, 280S, 280SE, and 300SE (W108) cars.

1. Remove the fuse block cover and locate the #1 fuse. With a test lamp, determine which side of the fuse wiring is fuse protected. To do so, remove the fuse. The unprotected side will light the test lamp. The fuse-protected side will not. Note which side this is.

2. Disconnect the battery's negative (ground) terminal.

3. Locate the wiring harness from the lighting stalk on the steering column to the first sleeve union (plug-in connector). Slit open the plastic harness covering about four inches from the connector.

4. In the slit, locate the red wire with a blue-white stripe and the white wire with a violet stripe.

5. Splice new wires into them (preferably of the same colors), long enough to reach the fuse block.

6. Remove the two mounting screws holding the block to the inner fender. Invert the block to expose the wiring on its bottom side.

7. Crimp or solder a terminal lug to the red-blue/white wire and fasten it to the #1 fuse terminal on the fuse-protected side.

8. Locate the fuse-protected side of the #10 terminal of the fuse block; install a terminal lug on the white-violet wire and connect it there.

9. Re-install the fuses, fuse block, and cover, re-connect the battery cable, and the headlight flashers should work.

In a letter in the May/June 1982 issue, William Wild, Mile-High Section, commented: "On my 1971 300SEL 6.3, it was not necessary to splice any wires. The red-white/blue wire connecting the flasher switch to fuse #1 had been snipped off at the terminal on the fuse block. The wire was bent double and taped close to the fuse block. It was simply a matter of crimping on a new terminal connector and attaching it to the fuse block where the snipped-off wire would have gone."

Chapter 5

Body, Interior

March/April 1991

July/August 1990

January/February 1997

How to Fix Your Vacuum Door Locks

by George Murphy, Technical Committee

March/April 1991

Photos in this article by the author.

Typical diaphragm failure.

Figure 1. 1) retaining ring, 3) actuating rod, 43) circlip (don't remove).

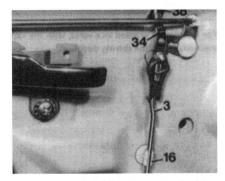

Figure 2. 3) control rod, 16) clip, 34) safety clip, 38) locking bar.

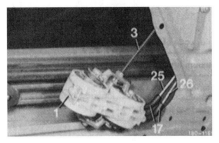

Figure 3. 1) vacuum element, 3) control rod, 17) connections, 25) and 26) vacuum lines.

Vacuum-operated door, trunk, and fuel door locks on 1973–84 W123 models are operated by a simple device consisting of two chambers connected to a vacuum source, each with a rubber diaphragm (Fig. 1). When vacuum is applied to one chamber, its diaphragm pulls inward; the other chamber is vented, so a link moves it outward. This movement is transmitted through a linkage to the lock, causing it to release or lock.

The rubber diaphragms crack with age, and resulting vacuum leaks prevent the mechanism from working. The system allows manual override, so you can still lock/unlock the doors, but if the fuel door unit fails locked, you may have to dismantle it from inside the trunk. Replacing the diaphragms is simple. You need a small and a large Phillips-head screwdriver, a flat-blade screwdriver, and pliers.

Lower the window all the way. To remove the door panel, remove the chrome door latch trim plate and the plastic cover behind the inside door handle. Remove the screw holding the chrome interior handle trim to allow removal of the armrest screw. Remove the lower armrest screws through holes below the armrest. Check for other trim to be removed, especially around the window. Unscrew the door lock button. Pry the panel's plastic retaining pins out of the door; place a thin-blade screwdriver between panel and door next to the pin, and carefully pry the panel outward.

Lift the panel to release the clips along the window channel. Leave these clips attached to the door; it's easier to refit the panel with them on the door, not the panel. Note whether more hooks must be engaged when the panel is re-installed. Unplug the power window switch. Your door is probably lined with a plastic sheet. To access the lock and vacuum actuator, carefully pull off the plastic, starting at the bottom. Leave it attached at the top, and tape it out of your way.

The vacuum actuator is in the bottom of the door. Remove the two screws holding it to the door. Disconnect the actuating rod from the lock button mechanism near the top of the door (clip #34 in Fig. 2). Twist the vacuum hoses off the unit (note which goes where, or you may have one door that unlocks when all others lock!), and remove the actuator and actuating rod from the door (Fig. 3). Remove the actuating rod link from the diaphragms; they can be pushed out of the grooves in the diaphragm connectors. Don't remove the tiny circlip on the rod; it's easy to lose, and nothing is gained.

Carefully pry off the four plastic retaining rings (#1 in Fig. 1) and remove all four diaphragms; no sense doing all this work for only one, so change all four now! Be sure the actuator body is clean inside. If there's engine oil in it, you probably have a leaky vacuum pump (on

diesels); get it repaired immediately, or you'll experience the joy of replacing all rubber parts in all of the vacuum systems!

Fit the new diaphragms onto the actuator body; make sure the edge of the diaphragm fits smoothly into the groove around the edge of each chamber. Replace the plastic retaining rings, noting where the hook is

New diaphragm (right) is held in place by clip (center).

engaged to the body of the actuator. Reassemble the actuator rod link to the diaphragm connector, and re-install the unit in the door. Connect the vacuum hoses and test it. If all is OK, reassemble the door. Re-install the plastic sheet; use GE RTV Silicon to cement it if necessary. (Before that, tighten all nuts, bolts, and screws in the door; you'll be surprised how quietly it closes when you're finished.) Re-install the door panel and trim.

Diaphragms can be obtained from Performance Analysis, Oak Ridge, Tennessee, or from Auto-Lux, Santa Ana, California. They are not sold by Mercedes-Benz dealers.

The contented Mercedes Owner   *November/December 1959*

Seat Belt Updates

**by Frank King,
Technical Editor**

*January/February
1989*

Replacement, updated seat belts for series 108 and 109 cars are now available from your Mercedes-Benz dealer, per *Service Instruction 91/10.* The original two-piece shoulder/lap seat belts are no longer available. To replace worn-out equipment or to upgrade the car's safety features, an automatic locking retractor seat belt system for 108- or 109-series cars has been developed and is offered in kit form for retrofitting by dealers or do-it-yourselfers. Even if the car wasn't originally equipped with seat belts, the new system can be installed.

The automatic locking retractor system requires four anchorage points–one at the tunnel for the lock and three at the B-pillar (between front and rear doors) for the reel. On vehicles with an existing two-piece shoulder/lap belt system, only three anchorage points were used, all with SAE threads, but the fourth anchorage point needed for the automatic inertia reel already exists in the B-pillar, approximately 255 mm from the base. This anchorage will accept an SAE 7/16"-14 UNC threaded fastener. Remove the B-pillar cover to verify the exact location of the fourth anchorage before piercing a hole in the cover for access.

Factory records indicate that the following vehicles have a threaded fourth anchorage point, but to ensure accuracy the B-pillar cover should be removed and the existence of the fourth anchorage visually confirmed:

Designation	Model	Chassis End #
280S	108.016	004915
280SE	108.018	004190
280SEL	108.019	004323
280SE 4.5	108.067	start of production
280SEL 4.5	108.068	start of production
300SEL	109.016	000226
300SEL 6.3	109.018	start of production
300SEL 3.5	109.056	start of production
300SEL 4.5	109.057	start of production

Vehicles not originally equipped with seat belts have three factory-installed anchorage points. The fourth anchorage point needed for the automatic locking retractor system must be located and installed in the B-pillar as described in *Work Instruction No. 215, Group 91*; you can consult this at your dealer's or send a stamped self-addressed envelope to the Tech Editor for a photocopy.

The following vehicles may have either an unthreaded fourth anchorage point or no fourth anchorage point at all. Remove the B-pillar cover and check:

Designation	Model	Chassis End #
250S	108.012	end of production
250SE	108.014	end of production
280S	108.016	004914
280SE	108.018	004989
280SEL	108.019	004322
300SEL	109.105	end of production
300SEL	109.016	000225

There are two versions of the retrofit seat belt kit. The first, part no. 114 860 16 85, for cars originally equipped with seat belts, consists of one retractor assembly, one buckle assembly and four trim caps. The second, part no. 115 860 42 85, includes the above parts plus one threaded plate and two Phillips-head screws and is for cars not originally equipped with belts. The retractor and buckle assemblies include bolts.

Working on W210 E-Class Doors

by Jim Mahaffey, Contributing Editor

May/June 2003

Photos in this article by the author.

For years I have enjoyed working on my Mercedes-Benzes, puttering in the comfort of my own garage. Still, each new model generation brings a period of adjustment in which I must come to grips with more complexity, but eventually I develop enough skill to at least avoid bothering professional mechanics with light-bulb replacement.

My latest car, a 1996 E-Class with stylish W210 body, seems a giant leap forward in technology from anything I've yet worked on. In the past I'd been intimidated by the seeming rocket science of a turbocharged diesel and the complexity of mechanical fuel injection, but these technologies softened with a couple of decades of study, so I now work confidently on them. Coming to grips with this more advanced W210 E-Class may take a little longer, but I've got to start.

On first study, the E-Class seems to be one large, self-propelled data-processing system. It dares me to touch it with a screwdriver, lest I break something. With that in mind, I started my exploration with the doors. Even they are more complex than ever before, stuffed with speakers, seat-controller modules, airbags, and infrared receivers. As it happens, the first part on my E320 to need replacement was the driver's inside door pull. Touched every time I enter or leave the car, it had developed a dingy, worn look. My procedure, adapted from the Mercedes-Benz service publication *Body Assembly*

Jobs II, Model 210, includes a few important additional steps, making it possible to remove the door panel without breaking it, which is our goal.

Opening the Door

Inside the door lies much mechanical mischief, with many parts that can fail and require replacement. To work on the door, you will need a medium-sized Phillips-head screwdriver, a T25 Torx driver, a 13-mm box-end wrench, and, most important, the "installation wedge." This curved plastic wedge, Mercedes-Benz part 110 589 03 59 00, is built specifically to remove interior panels without scratching the delicate polished wood or plastic surfaces; you will need it for any future interior work.

Step 1. *(See photographs matching step numbers.)* Disconnect the battery. Technically, this is unnecessary. Although you will be working near an explosive device, the side airbag, you won't actually touch its wiring or mounting screws. Still, the instructions for work involving airbags are similar to those for disarming a torpedo. They give me pause, so I advise extreme caution. With the battery disconnected, there's no way you can accidentally set off the airbag, and you need not worry about accidentally erasing the seat memory or sending something expensive up in smoke.

First, make certain that you have the radio reset code. As soon as the battery is disconnected, the radio considers itself stolen, and you will re-code it as a last step. The code is on a wallet-sized card, and instructions for re-coding are in the radio manual in your document case.

Remove the back seat cushion by reaching under the corners, one at a time, and pulling upward on the hidden plastic levers. Lift out the cushion; this is an excellent time to remove the detritus left by passengers in the crease of the seat. Mine seemed full of metallic glitter and cookie crumbs.

The battery is on the right side, under the seat. Use the 13-mm box-end wrench to loosen the negative terminal, and lay it aside. When loosening or tightening this terminal, avoid applying excessive force to the post; it is easy to crack the plates in these high-density batteries. Behind the battery is one of three fuse panels, and it's good to know where this is. Most non-essential functions, such as the sound system, telephone, and GPS system, are fused at this panel.

Detail Work

Step 2. Unscrew the door lock button by turning it counterclockwise with your fingers; this step was left out of the service document.

Figure 1. The battery is under the back seat, in front of one of three fuse panels.

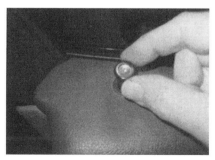

Figure 2. Unscrew the lock button using nothing harder than your fingers.

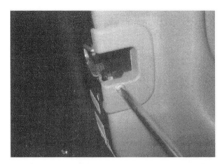

Figure 3. The lock-plate is held on by just one Phillips-head screw.

Figure 4. Use the correct tool, and the handle recess pops out easily.

Figure 5. The screw is directly behind the recess.

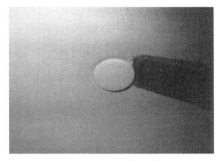

Figure 6. The cover comes off easily using the installation lever; a steel tool would break plastic covers such as this.

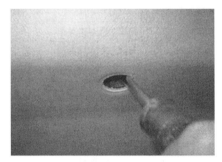

Figure 7. Behind the cover lies another screw.

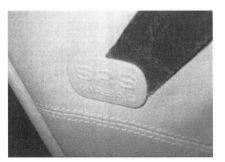

Figure 8. The undocumented SRS cover is retained by a hidden cord tied to the door panel.

Figure 9. The last of the big screws, behind the SRS cover.

Figure 10. The foot-light is easily removed using a thumbnail. Unclip both connectors; there is no polarity, so it doesn't matter which connector goes back on which spade-lug.

Figure 11. A typical panel-popping stance, using the wedge to gently force the door panel off the door.

Figure 12. Unhook the cable from the door lever, using your index finger. The multi-pin connector for the seat controller is a few inches forward of this position.

Figure 13. A T25 Torx driver will remove the three fasteners holding the door pull; here the lower fastener is being unscrewed.

Figure 14. The upper fasteners are backed by a steel plate that must be installed on the new door pull.

Step 3. Remove the lock-plate; a small Phillips-head screw holds it on.

Step 4. Remove the handle recess using the installation wedge. Using anything else will damage the panel. Just press it into the edges, using the your palm, and the recess pops out in one piece.

Step 5. Remove the large Phillips-head screw behind the handle recess.

Step 6. Remove the cover-plate below the pull handle, using the installation wedge.

Step 7. Remove the large Phillips-head screw behind the cover plate.

Step 8. Pop out the SRS plate. The installation wedge accomplishes this without leaving a mark. (Steps 8 and 9 were left out of the official manual, which led to many broken hearts, according to the man behind the parts counter at the dealership.)

Step 9. Remove the large Phillips-head screw behind the SRS plate.

Step 10. Remove the foot-light. (This was left out, too.) You need nothing more than your thumbnail. Pull off the two spade-connectors, one of which is locked on by a spring.

Step 11. Pop off the door liner. Insert the installation wedge all around the door, starting at the top. With the pointed end inserted between the steel door and the wood-composite panel, hit the end of the wedge with your palm, and the panel will pop away in increments. After doing the top, do the left side, then the bottom, and finally the right side.

Step 12. Unhook the control cable for the inside door lever. It literally hooks into the top of the lever mechanism.

Step 13. (No photo). Unplug the seat controller, which is a small, multi-pin connector with no locking mechanism.

Step 14. (Figures 13 and 14). You have now removed the door panel without breaking anything. Subsystems and components in the door may now be accessed for work. To replace the door pull, remove the three Torx screws holding it.

A T25 Torx driver will remove the three fasteners holding the door pull. Figure 13 shows the lower fastener being unscrewed. The upper fasteners are backed up by a steel plate that must be installed on the door pull (Figure 14). Before you complain about the $40 cost of a replacement door pull, consider that it is assembled from five pieces, including a steel thread-plate, a brass screw-bushing, and a hand-fitted MB-tex covering.

Together Again

Step 15. (No photo). To re-assemble the door, reverse the steps. Your palm exerts sufficient force to pop the door panel back into place.

Step 16. (No photo). After you've reconnected the battery, reset your clock. All stored memory functions, such as seat and mirror positions, will have been preserved.

Step 17. (No photo). Re-code your radio; it will have remembered your station presets.

There it is. You've successfully worked on the E-Class. It's a long way from rebuilding the air-conditioner, but this is at least a step.

Vintage Trip Odometers

by Jim Mahaffey, Contributing Editor

January/February 1997

Photos in this article by the author.

The concept of the resettable trip odometer predates the automobile by a solid century and even predates the totalizing odometer. Thomas Jefferson had a trip odometer on his carriage, installed on a rear hub in a square wooden box. Soon after automobiles became available, cable-driven instruments combining a speedometer, a trip odometer, and a totalizing or "season" odometer became useful accessories. Mileage readouts came in many forms, including rotating disks, clock hands, and a horizontal row of numbered drums. The numbered drums quickly became the technology of choice.

The numbered-drum readout was invented in 1623 by Wilhelm Schickard, an obscure professor of Oriental languages at the University of Tübingen. The key to Schickard's mechanism, originally used in an adding machine, was his use of an incomplete sprocket wheel with only one tooth, driving a complete sprocket wheel having ten teeth. Every full revolution of the one-tooth wheel would kick the complete wheel ahead by only one-tenth of a revolution. This mechanically simulated a carry operation in base ten arithmetic. The device was easily expanded to several decimal places by cascading multiple gear-sets together, with a vertically mounted drum on each gear-set used to display the numbers.

A modern trip odometer based on Schickard's mechanism consists of four rotating drums on a common shaft, running horizontally, with each drum having the numbers 0 to 9 printed on its edge with a spacing of 36 degrees

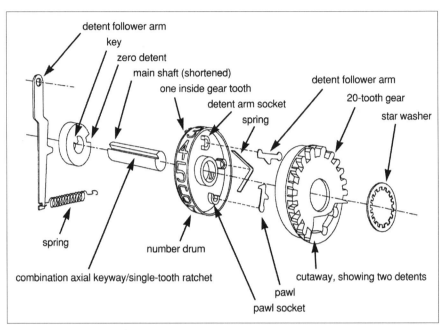

Twist-Knob Odometer Number Drum.

per numeral. The right face of each drum is incised with 20 gear teeth. The left face is cut to a similar pitch with only two connected gear teeth, or one complete inside gear tooth.

The rightmost drum, indicating tenths of a mile, rotates continuously as your car rolls, driven by a takeoff from the main odometer through a reversing pinion. With every complete rotation, or each full mile, the two teeth on the left face of this drum momentarily engage a pinion on a secondary shaft parallel to the main shaft. This pinion is in constant engagement with the drum to the left, indicating miles, and the brief movement of the pinion rotates this drum by 36 degrees. With every complete rotation of the tenths-mile drum, the miles drum surges ahead by one mile. Similarly, a complete rotation of the miles drum is relayed as one-tenth of a rotation to the ten-mile drum through a pinion on the secondary shaft, and each full turn of the ten-mile drum results in a click ahead on the hundred-mile drum. The trip odometer is simple, reliable,

mechanically rugged, and will not lose its mileage accumulation if the power fails. The trick is resetting it.

The Hard Way

There are two ways to reset the trip odometer on a VDO speedometer head. Vintage cars usually have the twist knob reset; newer cars have the push button, introduced around 1977.

Avoid resetting a push-button trip odometer while the car is moving. Pushing the button may cause the trip odometer to jam, which may or may not correct itself in time.

Resetting by twisting a knob is the complex scheme. The knob, usually on the left side of the speedometer on sedans, is turned clockwise. On the right side on SLs, it is turned counter-clockwise. As you turn the knob, the four drums roll up and begin to align with one another, such that all are registering the same number. Keep turning, and eventually all the drums will line up, and the mechanism will fall into a straight line of zeros with a distinct click. The click is so positive

A vintage trip odometer with twist-knob reset, stripped down to its essentials. Part of right-angle reset shaft is at far left; secondary shaft with three pinions runs across bottom; zero-detent follower runs vertically across left side of mechanism, with a coil spring connecting back to the secondary shaft. White tenths-mile drum on right is wide enough to accommodate spring-loaded clutch.

All-metal trip odometer from early 230SL, from below. Note cast metal pinions on secondary shaft across bottom of number drums, with attached square cams, and associated one-piece flat spring screwed to frame. Ratchet clutch on tenths-mile drum is clearly visible.

Two types of right-angle reset drive. On left is the common type, with steel crown-gear on brass pinion, both press fitted. Older, more elegant design uses matched bevel gears fitted with set screws.

Newer trip odometer, still used in digital electronic speedometer heads. Reset lever is at bottom left, its pivot shaft running across bottom of mechanism. Secondary shaft with four plastic pinions is mounted below number drums; three flat-spring fingers hold them in place.

that you could reset it with your eyes closed or on a dark rainy night at a gas station.

The knob turns the main trip odometer shaft backward, through a right-angle gear drive. An asymmetric channel cut along the shaft's length acts as a single ratchet tooth. The drums are normally free to turn vertically on the shaft and register miles, but force it backward, and the channel catches a spring-loaded pawl inside each drum. With only one ratchet tooth, all drums eventually

catch at the same point on the shaft as it turns through 360 degrees.

Each drum is assembled from two halves, the left half having the partial Schickard gear, the right half having the complete gear. The right half remains bound by its associated secondary-shaft pinion and is not free to move. The left half, imprinted with numerals, contains the pawl and is free to move backward. The right half has ten semi-circular detents spaced around the inside, and these are influenced by a spring-loaded detent

follower in the left half. These detents make the drums line up evenly in the trip window as they are reset and make the right and left halves stick together during normal mileage counting.

The rightmost drum (white with red numerals) has no built-in detents, but it does have a coil-spring clutch between the incomplete and the complete gear halves.

The zero click is provided by a fixed detent wheel on the main shaft at the far left end, using the ratchet channel as a keyway. A follower arm bears against it, and this preferentially stops the main shaft with all drums set to zero. There is no reason for the shaft to turn as miles are counted, as it is simply used as an axis.

The drums and pinions are plastic castings, with each drum consisting of five moving parts plus a fastener. The trip odometer is normally subjected to very low stress levels, but the reset operation is a bit more traumatic, and opportunity exists for mechanical mischief inside the drums.

The Old Way

An interesting variation of the twist-knob reset appears on early 230SLs. Some early 1960s speedometer mechanisms were made completely of metal. These units are exceptionally well built and give an impression of precision clockwork. They are easily spotted in a car, as the tenths-mile drum is dull metal-colored instead of the usual white.

The drums are metal castings, with the outer edge machined on a lathe then anodized, dyed black, and filled with white lacquer in the numeral indentations. The reset ratchet for each drum is a one-piece circular bronze spring keyed to a slot along the main shaft axis and bearing against a ramped tooth in the hollowed drum. Both the incomplete and the complete gears are cast into the one-piece drum. The problem of detenting the drums into a straight line behind the odometer window is handled by the counter-shaft pinions, which are encouraged to move in one-quarter turn increments by built-in square cams. The cams are followed by flat spring-fingers of blued steel. The tenths-mile drum is equipped with a ten-tooth ratchet clutch, which allows it to be turned backward.

These older speedometers are also distinguished by being sealed in steel cans, which give a good water barrier, as long as the two illuminator bulbs are tightly in place, and prevents corrosion of the moving metal parts.

Also distinctive is the input shaft angle, which is coaxial with the speedometer needle shaft. This was changed to a 45-degree downward-pointing input shaft to reduce the bend angle of the speedometer cable in the 230SL. These features were carryovers from the 300SL and 190SL instrument designs.

The right-angle reset drive uses brass bevel gears secured to the shafts by set screws. The reset knob is also held by a slotted set screw. In the later units used in the 1960s and 1970s, the knob is suspended independent of the shaft. When you pull the speedometer mechanism from its case or from the dash, the knob stays with the lens; a flat key surface on the shaft will re-engage the knob upon reassembly.

The Easy Way

The reset scheme in newer trip odometers is completely different and involves fewer moving parts. The three mileage drums are driven with conventional pinions on a secondary shaft, and the tenths-mile drum is driven directly, a fine-pitched pinion coupling the right and left halves of this drum. The right half connects back to the odometer drive, and the left half is the tenths-mile display.

Each plastic drum has a heart or "cardioid" cam cast into its left side. A flat cam-leader is poised behind each drum, pivoting on a common shaft. Pushing the reset button on the instrument unloads the secondary shaft, levering it forward against a flat-spring array riveted to the speedometer frame. This releases the number drums of normal constraints and allows them to be positioned at will. Simultaneously the cam-leaders are pushed forward against the heart cams, which snaps them all into position with zero forward. Release the button, and the secondary shaft springs back into engagement with the drums, ready to count miles.

This same method, called a "flyback," has been used for a century in mechanical stopwatches to reset

the seconds hand with a push-button. Failures are few on these units, but if anything does break, it can be repaired.

Repair and Restoration

The worst thing you can do to a trip odometer is to lubricate it. Light machine oils (particularly penetrating oils) soak into the plastic parts, causing them to expand, soften, and jam. Parts in the odometer move so slowly that the usual action of oil, in which a moving part is lifted off a bearing surface by a shock-wave effect in the lubricant, does not apply. It is usually sufficient to thoroughly clean and polish the parts, particularly the shafts.

A possible exception is the all-metal trip odometer, in which some clock oil could restore the action in a heavily worn unit. Here, oil acts as a filler, taking the place of worn or pitted metal. A lubricated unit must be periodically cleaned with solvent and relubricated, as oil collects abrasive dust and eventually becomes a grinding compound.

A problem unique to the metal trip odometers is that the lacquer in the numerals hardens with age. Extreme heat and cold cause the drums to expand and contract, cracking the lacquer and flaking it off. This problem can be fixed by painstakingly repainting the numerals with a single-bristle brush. Another possibility is to work paint into the engraved numerals with a lacquer stick (used in camera repair shops to restore markings on lens barrels), then wipe away the excess with a cloth.

An odd problem with later trip odometers is that soot accumulates on the tenths-mile drum. The source is unknown, but it may come from rubber or plastic pieces slowly oxidizing and evaporating in close contact with indicator bulbs. Use a Q-tip to polish it off the drum by rotating the drum with your thumb while holding the secondary shaft forward.

A cased speedometer, as used in an SL or some SELs, may be dismantled for access to the trip odometer by grinding off the crimped edge of the chromed bezel. Polish the bezel first with red rouge on a cloth wheel. Press the back edge of the bezel against a vertical grinder (belt sander) as you slowly turn the unit in your hands. Use a fine belt. The soft brass rim will quickly grind away in a place that is normally out of sight to the driver, pressed against the dash. When you have confirmed that the entire crimp is gone, tap the rim from the back with a mallet, and it will spring off. The glass lens and internal trim ring will fall out, and the mechanism can be removed from the front after the two fastening screws are removed from the back. Use this opportunity to clean the inside of the glass. Reassemble the bezel by just pressing it back on. If it does not snap on positively, you can improve its grip with a little epoxy cement. This method allows access to the speedometer internals without stressing the fragile brass bezel.

The only source of repair parts for your trip odometer is a similar trip odometer. Find a unit as similar as possible at a recycling yard, and practice by first dismantling the junked unit. Dozens of different speedometers have been used in Mercedes-Benz cars. The button-reset units use different angular positions of the heart cams, which are not interchangeable. For the twist-knob units, the width of the number drums varies. The odometer drive shafts, worms, and gears seem different in every model.

Here I often acknowledge my recycler, Ken Redmond of the Benz Store. In this case it is more appropriate than usual, for without the huge variety of oddball speedometer problems he brings to my attention, I would be unable to analyze this subject adequately.

Repairing a Stalled Odometer

by James Mahaffey, Peachtree Section

November/December 1990

Photos in this article by the author.

Here's a step-by-step, do-it-yourself guide to mending balky mileage counters.

If your VDO odometer has stopped indicating the distance you have traveled, you're not alone. The weakness in this otherwise robust mechanism seems to be the friction fit of a pot metal driving gear on the main odometer shaft. Fortunately, it's easy to fix.

The ideal set of tools for odometer repair includes a set of pin punches, a 2-ounce ball peen hammer, a 7-ounce ball peen hammer, tweezers, a blade-type screwdriver, a jeweler's flat file, slip-joint pliers, a cold chisel, and a bench vise. Still, there's room for considerable improvisation in tools for this job.

Disassembly

Disassembling the VDO speedometer head from the front will spoil the calibration, so go in from the back. Start by removing the two screws holding the back plate with a screwdriver (Figure 1). With the back plate off, the ends of the main odometer shaft, holding five numbered drums, and the smaller secondary shaft, holding five small sprockets, are visible. On some VDO speedometers it may be necessary to remove the cast metal speedometer drive housing, fastened to the odometer frame with two slotted screws.

Remove the crimp on the end of the steel secondary shaft by filing it away with the jeweler's file (Figure 2); remove only enough metal to round the shaft end. Gently punch out the secondary shaft using the light hammer and a 1/16-inch pin punch

(Figure 3). Punch it only far enough to clear the frame.

Next, carefully punch out the main shaft, using the light hammer and a 3/32-inch pin punch, so that the pot metal gear on the end is free to be removed. The tin shield near the other end of the shaft will have to be temporarily bent away from the brass pinion on the main shaft for clearance. Note the exact position of the pinion, after the main shaft has been punched, in Figure 4. Now, remove the pot metal gear using tweezers; be careful not to disturb the arrangement of the number drums and secondary sprockets (Figure 5).

Shrinking the Hub

You were able to remove the gear so easily because it was spinning freely on the mainshaft. The goal is to slightly shrink the hub so that it will press-fit tightly onto the shaft. Set up a special anvil by mounting a cold chisel vertically in a bench vise, blunt

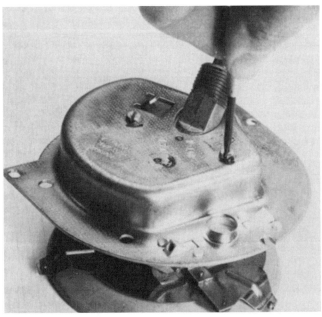

Figure 1. Removing backplate.

Figure 2. Filing secondary shaft.

end up. Place the gear flat on the cold chisel top (Figure 6), put a 5/16-inch pin punch on top of it, and strike it smartly with the heavier hammer.

Re-insert the gear into the odometer mechanism with the fully toothed side facing the frame, and tap the main shaft back through it, using the heavier hammer and a 3/32-inch pin punch (Figure 7). Do this in two steps. First tap the end of the shaft until it bottoms out in the pot metal gear, then put the end of the shaft through

the bearing hole in the frame. The gear should fit tightly on the main shaft.

Be sure that the numbers are lined up straight in the dial, then re-insert the secondary shaft in the frame. The sprockets will fit between the number drums. Recheck the numbers in the dial window. It is possible to install a drum with the numbers half-submerged in the window. Restore the crimp on the end of the secondary shaft by squeezing it with pliers (Figure 8). Replace back plate.

If the speedometer head has been howling, especially when cold, remove the thick, yellow grease on the gears and replace it with white lithium grease before the back is remounted. The odometer mechanism, trip odometer, and speedometer are not lubricated. Only the drive gears and worm are greased. Also, drip some 30-weight oil into the end of the speedometer cable.

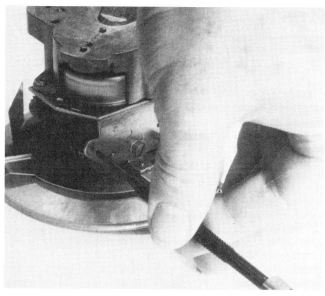

Figure 3. Punching out secondary shaft.

Figure 4. Position of main shaft after punching.

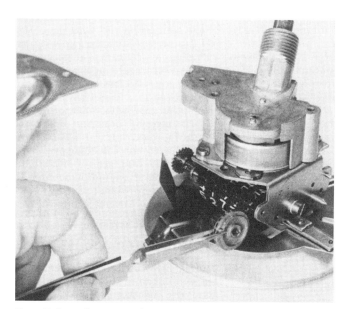

Figure 5. Removing pot metal gear.

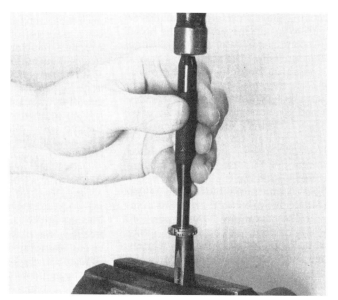

Figure 6. Shrinking the hub.

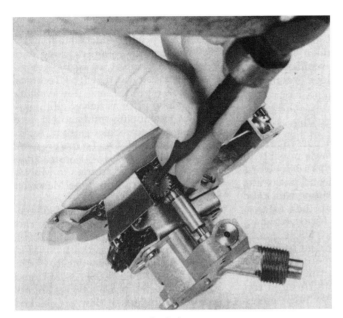

Figure 7. Mounting gear on main shaft.

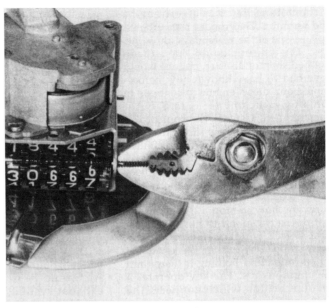

Figure 8. Restoring crimp on secondary shaft.

Servicing the VDO Mechanical Clock

by James Mahaffey, Peachtree Section

July/August 1990

Photos in this article by the author.

From the mid-1950's through the mid-1970's, each Mercedes-Benz car was equipped with an electrically wound VDO mechanical clock. These clocks, marked "VDO KIENZLE", are exceptionally well-made and long lived, some having run for decades without service. The Kienzle was replaced by the VDO Quartz-Zeit, with a quartz oscillator movement, and factory replacement clocks for Kienzle-equipped cars are likely to have this newer movement fitted into the old-style case. Although the accuracy and stability of the VDO Quartz-Zeit are superior to those of the Kienzle, for the sake of authenticity a failed mechanical clock can usually be restored to like-new condition.

The Kienzle mechanism is basically a 19th-century pocket-watch movement with a modified Borg-type winder that rewinds the clock spring every two minutes using an electromagnet. There are two movable electrical contacts. The upper contact is on a short-throw lever above the electromagnet; the lower contact is on a spring-loaded flywheel. In the unwound condition the two electrical contacts come together, completing a circuit through the electromagnet. The magnet pulls down sharply on the upper contact lever, throwing the other contact piece out of the way, breaking the circuit and winding against the spring. The spring's force is imparted to the escapement through a ratchet pawl attached to the flywheel. When the spring runs down, the contacts touch, and the process repeats.

In the original Borg design, the most fragile part was the flat helical mainspring. In the VDO variation, the flat spring was replaced by an indestructible coil spring, in tension, wrapped around a drum coaxial with the flywheel. The mainspring will not break, but the VDO clock has three usual failure modes: burned electrical contacts, a blown internal fuse and lubrication failure. Detectable wear on bearings or gear teeth is rare.

Disassembly

The clock can be fully serviced with minimal disassembly. After removing the clock from the car, remove the three nuts holding the plastic dust cap in place with a 5-mm socket wrench; see Figure 1. The cap is extremely fragile. Wipe out any soot that may have accumulated in the cap with a tissue and set it aside. If a plastic ring surrounds one nut, this is the warranty seal, indicating that the clock has had no previous service. Chip away the ring, using miniature diagonal cutters.

Locate the electrical contacts. They are probably touching, but if not, start the balance wheel manually, and let the movement run until the contacts come together. Insert the tip of a relay-contact cleaning tool between the contacts and stroke them until they appear clean under magnification. Figure 2 shows the contact cleaning process.

Cleaning and degreasing the clock present a problem. The usual clock and watch cleaning solutions will not work

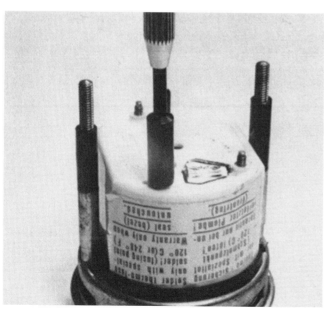

Figure 1. Removing the dust cap.

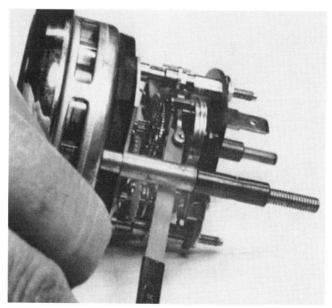

Figure 2. Cleaning the electrical contacts.

in this case because the clock contains various perishable components, including lacquered magnet wire, plastic, rubber, phenolic and carbon steel. The clock mechanisms are usually contaminated with curious black particles, presumably the product of lubricant and rubber products burned in the spark between the electrical contacts—and vaporized portions of the contacts themselves. The best way to clean the works is to suspend the clock in a soap-and-water solution for a few minutes, rinse under running water, drain and blow dry gently with a heat gun. Figure 3 shows the clock being cleaned in dishwashing detergent.

As soon as the works have cooled from drying, lubricate them with a fine grade of clock oil. Transfer the oil to the bearings in very small droplets, using a needle or a piece of wire as shown in Figure 4. Apply very slight amounts of oil to the gear teeth. Do not oil the jewelled balance-wheel bearings.

Suggested Modification

The internal fuse consists of a solder bridge between two bronze lugs at the base of the electromagnet. Normally the bronze piece that acts as the positive power conductor is bent away from the phenolic back plate so that it contacts the bronze lug at the magnet base, with the two soldered together. The spring action of the power-conducting strip puts the fuse in tension, and if it blows, the strip will spring back against the phenolic plate. Solder with a melting

Figure 3. Cleaning the works in soapy water.

Figure 4. Lubricating the rear escape-wheel bearing.

Figure 5. Silicone diode (002) soldered to fuse lugs.

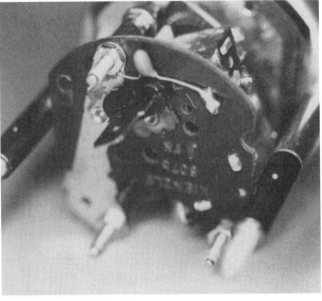

Figure 6. Capacitor, between magnet frame and case.

point of 248°F is specified by VDO to restore a blown fuse.

An alternative to restoring the fuse is to install a circuit modification consisting of a silicon diode and a capacitor. This will suppress the high-voltage spark that occurs at the gap between the contacts as they fly apart. (This is self inductance. When current in the magnet dies because the contacts part, the magnetic field collapses, inducing a reverse current which makes a destructive spark across the contacts.) Solder a 1N4002 diode or equivalent across the fuse lugs with the cathode (striped end) toward the coil; see Figure 5 for the exact position of the diode. Solder the positive side of a 1-microfarad 35-volt tantalum capacitor to the magnet frame on the back plate of the clock, and connect the negative side to ground, under the nearest 5-mm nut, as shown in Figure 6.

Connect the clock to a 12-volt DC power source to test it before replacing the dust cover. If the movement is sluggish, some bearings may be dry, but it should loosen up as oil works into the bearings. Use a jeweler's screwdriver to turn the adjusting shaft protruding through the back plate—clockwise to slow the movement, counterclockwise to make it run faster. Check and adjust running speed for a day or two before reinstalling the clock. The two access holes in the back

of the dust cover are normally covered with white plastic tape.

Buff the chrome bezel with white rouge before reinstalling the clock. Scratches in the transparent plastic crystal may be reduced with a moderate polishing compound, as in automobile wax or toothpaste. If the clock is mounted in the instrument cluster, it is rim-lit at night by the instrument lighting, but if it is mounted separately, it has an on-board bulb, which may need replacement. The only bulb that will fit is a special bayonet-base unit with an 8.5-mm envelope, now available as the Thorn 37R, part no. 0022T4W.

Sources

The relay-contact cleaning tool is available from Jensen Tools in Phoenix, Arizona. Clock oil is available from S. LaRose, Greensboro, North Carolina. The 255°F solder has been impossible to find in an alloy without indium, which will exchange with the bronze in the soldering lugs with time, causing the melting temperature to drift. A 255°F bismuth-lead solder is made by Arconium Specialty Alloys in Providence, RI, but the minimum order is $325. Thanks to Bernie Tekippe of Classic Clocks in Atlanta, Georgia, for his advice.

How to Fix a Wipered-Out SL

by Michael Egan and
Raymond Schlicht,
Greater Washington
Section

*September/October
1998*

Photos in this article
by Michael Egan.

*How to remove and replace the
windshield wiper mechanism in your
1963–1971 230/250/280SL.*

Windshield wipers elicit little interest
until they quit, which happens only
when it's raining and you need them.
Since the newest W113 pagoda SL is 27
years old, sluggish or immobile wipers
happen with increasing frequency.
After years of operating at a healthy
gait, my wipers began operating
sporadically, then intermittently, and
finally needed manual assistance just
to move. Then they stopped entirely,
parked vertically on the windshield.

The first question was whether
the problem was with the wiper
motor or the transmission assembly.
Disconnecting the transmission from
the motor revealed that the motor
ran well, but the wiper arms barely
moved when forced by hand. The
transmission was the culprit. This is
a mixed blessing: the motor is easy to
replace but expensive; the transmission
is cheaper but a bear to replace.

The illustrations show where
the problem develops. Due to
poor drainage from the two body
depressions where the wiper shafts
project through the cowl, common
to the W113, water fills these wells
and seeps down the shafts of the
wiper mechanism, causing corrosion
and seizing of the shaft. There are
provisions for drainage of the wiper
arm shaft wells in the W113 but
not the well-defined holes at each
recess that exist on other models of
this era. The W113 uses a somewhat
camouflaged horizontal drain created
by the gaps between the ends of the air
scoop panel and the cowl sheet metal
(Photo 1). If water puddles in these
recesses, the drains can clog, and water
is probably seeping down the wiper
shaft. Rust stains below the dash at the
shaft holes confirm this.

To prevent this, be sure that the cap
seal (part 111 824 00 72) is intact. On
230 / 250SLs, the original stainless steel
cap seals (no longer available) should
be replaced by the newer plastic/rubber
type (Photo 2). It may also help to
periodically lubricate the wiper shafts
with a light penetrating/lubricating
oil after removing the wiper blade,
cap, related hardware, and seal ring
(Photo 3). Still, once shaft corrosion
has started, all the oil in the world won't
cure the problem, as owners testify.
The only solution is replacement of the
transmission assembly.

Although many SL gurus have
replaced the wiper transmission, no one
told me exactly what should be done
or in what order. This replacement

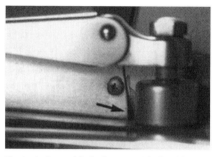

Photo 1. Assembled wiper arm/shaft with
drain (arrow).

Photo 2. Wiper arm with metal and later
plastic cap seals.

Photo 3. Wiper shaft with arm removed;
arrow indicates lubrication point.

W113 wiper arms.

took 16 hours, but barring any other repairs, it could be done in 10. The transmission costs approximately $160, with $20–$30 more for miscellaneous grommets, bolts, etc.

If you lie on the floor of the car and look up under the dash, you will discover that the wiper mechanism must have been the first part installed when the car was assembled, with everything else built around it. This is especially evident looking from the driver's side, with your head pillowed by the clutch and brake pedals. To replace this mechanism, you must first remove all components between the dash and the firewall. You might think optimistically that this could not possibly be right and search for a better plan. Unfortunately, though, with few exceptions, the facts can be expressed simply:

1. Remove all dash components in reverse order of factory assembly.

2. Replace wiper transmission assembly.

3. Reassemble dash in factory assembly order.

The following sequence was developed by doing the job on an early 280SL. Moving through the sequence, it may appear that certain steps can be omitted, but that's an illusion. On the bright side, since so much has to be removed, you can fix all those dash problems that have nagged you for years (lights out, heater cables stuck, tachometer broken, etc.). If your car is fitted with air-conditioning, give up now.

The Sequence

1. Disconnect the battery.

2. Remove the three under-dash cardboard covers.

3. Remove the radio or the center dash radio-delete plate; unplug all attached wires and cables, and remove the unit completely, which gives access to the clock.

4. Remove the clock; make notes on the terminal/wire connections for reassembly.

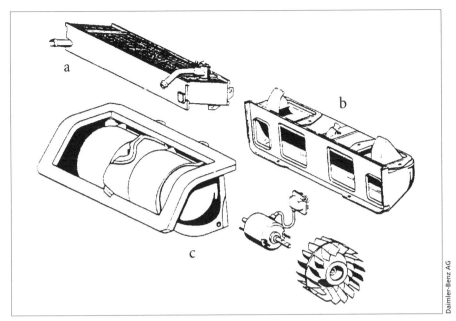

Figure 1. Heater details: a) heater core, b) air distribution box, c) fan, blower motor, and case.

5. Disconnect the light wire and remove the glove box. With the clock out of the way, the double fork and spring device for the glove box door can be carefully removed, facilitating glove box removal.

6. Remove the center dash radio speaker.

7. Remove the tachometer and speedometer, noting the brackets and wiring arrangement.

8. Remove the bracket and move the center instrument cluster out of the dash to the limits of its attached tubes and cables; don't stretch them. Support the cluster.

9. Unplug the wiring harness from the back of the ignition switch and move it out of the way; no need to remove the switch.

10. Remove the heater air distribution box (Figure 1) by unbolting the two defroster ducts (two bolts each on top of the distribution box) and the small wiring junction. Two bolts (bottom) and two clips (top) hold the box to the fan assembly. Disconnect the flapper cable to move the box out of the way (helpful but unnecessary).

11. Remove the heater blower motor and case (Figure 1). The bottom mounting bracket must be unbolted

Figure 2. Cardboard defroster ducts.

from the blower case and the transmission tunnel floor (one bolt each) before the blower case can be removed. To remove the bolt securing the bottom mount to the floor, peel back the transmission tunnel carpet and remove the access plate from the passenger side of the tunnel (the access plate on top of the tunnel is for the shift linkage). This is a good time to check the heater core (Figure 1) for leaks and replace it if necessary. No need to remove the heater core for the job at hand.

12. Carefully remove the right and left cardboard defroster ducts (Figure 2) and vent hoses, held to the upper

dash openings by horseshoe-shaped rubber grommets. The driver's side is the tightest fit.

13. Disconnect the operating cable for the fresh air cowl vent flapper and move it out of the way (this cable goes through the wiper transmission assembly).

14. The wiper transmission assembly (Figure 3) is now exposed. From outside, remove the wiper arms, covers, and seals, then unscrew the shaft nuts. From under the dash, remove the four wiper transmission-to-firewall attaching screws. Disconnect the crank arm from the wiper motor shaft. Withdraw the wiper transmission to the passenger side and out.

15. Reassemble in reverse order. Install the new wiper shaft body grommets in the body before installing the new transmission. Before reconnecting the transmission crank arm to the motor shaft, be sure that the motor and the transmission assembly are each in the "park" position. Before installing the wiper arms, test run the mechanism.

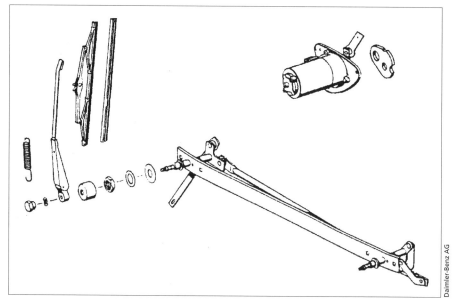

Figure 3. Windshield wiper assembly with motor.

Daimler-Benz AG

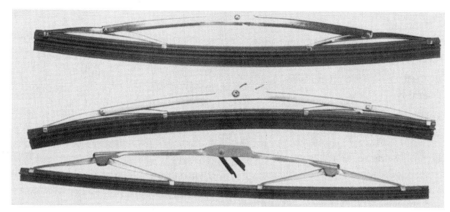

Correct wiper blades for the W113 series are 12.1-in (305-mm) long. Top to bottom: blades for the 230SL and 1967 250SL and early 280SL (painted); and late 280SL (skeleton).

Curing SLC Window Condensation

by Dieter Arnold, International Stars Section

November/December 1988

The louvered rear quarter windows of the SLC models sometimes have moisture condense between the glass. Replacing the windows does not always help, so here's an alternative.

This is not a simple job, but it makes a good weekend project. The windows are two pieces of glass with the plastic louver frame between them. The assembly is vacuum sealed, but as the car ages, the seals dry out and leak, allowing air to enter. Moisture in the air then condenses in the assembly. Here's a way to use engine vacuum to keep the windows tight and remove moisture between the glass.

You'll need two one-way vacuum check valves, two rubber vacuum T-connectors, three feet of rubber vacuum hose, six inches of plastic vacuum tube (about 3/16-in diam.) and some two-part epoxy cement. Carefully inspect the windows. If they are badly discolored, or if the louvers are flaking, you might as well start with two new windows.

Remove the rear seats and interior side panels. Note the button in the panel for the seatback release; you'll be tapping into the blue vacuum line. Start the engine and check whether, with the appropriate door closed, you have

vacuum at the blue line. If not, check the vacuum system before continuing.

Locate and mark a spot near the front bottom corner of the window where you can drill a 3/16-in diam. hole in the plastic frame, and insert a piece of vacuum tubing. There will be an area where the hose won't show inside the window. Remove the chrome molding on the outside of the window, then carefully remove the window assembly from inside the car. Several screws hold the window from the inside.

Drill a 3/16-in diam. hole at the spot you marked in the bottom section of the plastic frame. Prepare a two-in piece of vacuum line, and rough up one end with sandpaper. Epoxy the line into the hole drilled in the frame, allowing 1½ in to protrude. After the epoxy sets, test the window with a vacuum tester; there should be no leaks. If you find a leak, inspect the circumference of the windows on both sides, and seal any leaks with epoxy or sealant. Install the window in the car, taking care to tighten the screws evenly, not overly tight—the frame is only plastic. After installation, recheck the window for leaks.

Install the vacuum T-fitting in the blue vacuum line at the seatback release button. Install a check valve in the third leg of the T-fitting so that air can pass through the valve, thus holding a vacuum in the window. Connect the window tube to the check valve with a length of vacuum line. Reinstall the side trim panels and the rear seat. You're done.

Gray Market

**by Stu Ritter,
Technical Editor**

*November/December
2001*

*That bargain early-1980s model
may not be what you think it is.*

Remember the Gray Market?

If you're shopping for a used 1980s Mercedes-Benz, especially a W126 S-Class sedan or an SL, the car that you see may not be exactly what you might think it is. During the early to mid-1980s, Mercedes-Benz of North America was the sole official US importer, but many Mercedes-Benz cars came to this country via the gray market, whereby individuals or businesses could import individual cars. These included models not officially imported. Today some of these "special import" models may be

fine cars, and they may be offered to you at low prices, but often they carry significant risks in the areas of:

Service Availability: Many US Mercedes-Benz dealers refuse to work on gray market cars; today, few US mechanics—in dealerships or elsewhere—have much experience on them.

Parts Availability: US Mercedes-Benz dealers probably do not stock (or even want to special order) parts that are unique to European models.

Service Information Availability: Finding owner's manuals, workshop manuals, or other technical data for gray market cars in the US is virtually impossible. Manuals for equivalent US models cover most but not all systems. Mercedes-Benz USA does not sell manuals for gray market cars.

Reliability: Poorly converted European models can suffer from electrical, driveability, maintenance, or even safety problems.

Insurance: Not all auto insurance companies will write policies on gray market cars.

Resale Value: Gray market cars are usually worth much less than US models as used cars, and some dealers (Mercedes-Benz and otherwise) will not accept such cars as trade-ins.

For these reasons, even two decades later, you need to know how to recognize a gray market car.

Background

In the early 1980s a vacuum developed in the US as dollars became worth quite a few German marks, and too few Mercedes-Benz cars were available to satisfy the demand. Americans also wanted models that were not officially imported. So the gray market was born. Americans went to Germany and cleaned out the used car market.

Unlike the US, where new Mercedes-Benzes are usually in stock and available for immediate delivery, buying a car in Germany was different

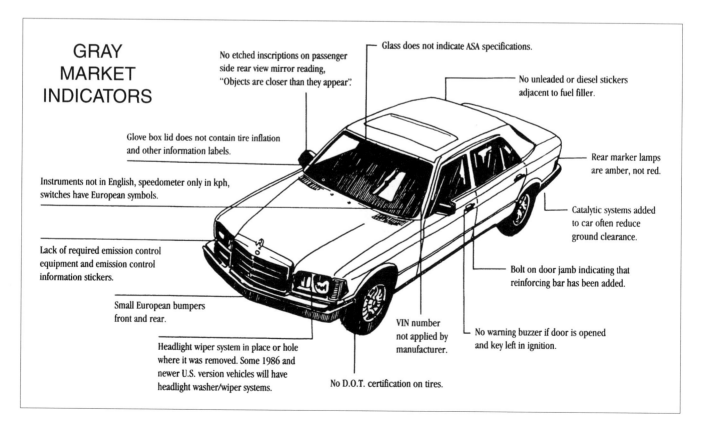

GRAY MARKET INDICATORS

No etched inscriptions on passenger side rear view mirror reading, "Objects are closer than they appear".

Glass does not indicate ASA specifications.

No unleaded or diesel stickers adjacent to fuel filler.

Glove box lid does not contain tire inflation and other information labels.

Instruments not in English, speedometer only in kph, switches have European symbols.

Lack of required emission control equipment and emission control information stickers.

Small European bumpers front and rear.

Headlight wiper system in place or hole where it was removed. Some 1986 and newer U.S. version vehicles will have headlight washer/wiper systems.

No D.O.T. certification on tires.

VIN number not applied by manufacturer.

No warning buzzer if door is opened and key left in ignition.

Bolt on door jamb indicating that reinforcing bar has been added.

Catalytic systems added to car often reduce ground clearance.

Rear marker lamps are amber, not red.

in the early 1980s. You would place your order, then wait for your car to be built. There was no German distributor to place advance orders with the factory for inventory. Cars were ordered by dealers, then you waited.

Personal Experience

In 1986 I went to the factory with a friend to pick up his new 230E. He had ordered it after the Frankfurt auto show in fall 1984, and it took about 15 months for him to receive his car. For the herds of Americans who suddenly showed up in Germany with lots of money, there were few new cars to buy. The first wave of gray marketers cleaned out the best used cars, those under two years old with low mileage and minimum exposure to German winter salt. Many beautiful cars came to the US.

At first, the gray market was a way to buy models that were never officially imported to the US. You might also bring in a higher horsepower car without being required to modify the engine or the exhaust by taking a once in a lifetime (per individual) exemption from EPA requirements on a car that was at least five years old. I took advantage of that exemption and imported a 1980 500SE in 1985.

Because Europeans ordered their cars individually, and almost everything was an option, many cars were not as well equipped as those brought in by Mercedes-Benz of North America. My 500SE had cloth seats, wind-up windows, and manual climate control with individual temperature controls for driver and passenger. It did have a sunroof, cruise control, and a fire extinguisher. Other cars had power front windows and manual rear windows. Equipment varied widely depending on the options specified by the original purchaser. Sometimes the price of the options would almost equal that of the base car. Many options that Americans took for granted were rarely ordered in Germany because of their cost.

By the late 1980s the dollar had lost some of its strength, and used cars were harder to find in Germany. Americans had cleaned out the German used car market. There was always one good source of nice, one-year old cars. Daimler-Benz factory workers were allowed to buy new cars at a discount. If you were interested in a basic model such as a 200D (124) or a 200 or 230E, hundreds were available in the Stuttgart newspaper every day, but most Americans weren't interested in these plain Jane cars.

My gray market buying trip was my first trip to Germany since my Army days in the 1960s. I managed to hook up with some old friends, one of whom was the sales manager for a Mercedes-Benz dealer. I also established connections with one of the multi-line auto handlers and arranged to take his trade-in late-model Mercedes-Benz cars. I had the same arrangement with the dealership sales manager. Over a two-year period I imported 11 cars and remained a registered importer for several years afterward.

Paperwork

Importing the cars to the US was not difficult. First they were transported to a port for ocean shipping or to Frankfurt for air shipment. In 1984 the mark was around 3.5 per dollar, so it cost only $1,400 to air-freight a car from Frankfurt to Chicago. This is how I sent my 500SE over.

The undercarriage had to be steam-cleaned for the US Department of Agriculture. With the shipping documents, you would arrange for a customs broker to have the required paperwork prepared for the car's arrival. Any car less than five years old had to be converted to EPA and DOT standards. About $250 per entry covered having the broker obtain the Environmental Protection Agency (EPA) and Department of Transportation (DOT) releases and post a bond required by the US government to ensure that after being imported the car would be brought into compliance with the applicable regulations.

If a car was imported by an individual, that person was allowed a once in a lifetime EPA exemption allowing one car to be brought in just as it had been—engine and exhaust-wise—in Germany. This wonderful exemption was soon taken advantage of. Many gray marketers imported cars under the names of friends and family, then sold them immediately. That was not the intent of the exemption and was one reason the government stepped in to control the gray market.

Government Approvals

The DOT standards included converting the headlights to US standard sealed-beam units, certifying the safety glass, changing the speedometer to English (mph) from metric (kph), installing seat belt buzzers, and so on. The DOT also required that door bars be installed that would at least equal the factory-installed door bars in cars made for the US market. We developed a DOT-approved system using 4130, schedule 40, chrome moly steel tubing that was far stronger than the factory's sheet metal bars.

The Vehicle Identification Number (VIN) had to be displayed on the driver's side windshield pillar so it could be read from outside, just like American versions. This is one of the easiest ways to identify a gray market car because none of the conversion tags looked anything like a factory tag.

DOT standards were not hard to meet, so on the whole they were well met. Pre-engineered kits were available from large importers that could be installed by a really proficient do-it-yourselfer. To clear the car through DOT, you had to supply a complete set of photographs showing the conversion and identifying the car by VIN on each photograph; this and a pile of documentation would earn you a DOT release, which would be shown to the bonding company, which would then clear the bond that you had purchased.

EPA conversions were a horse of another color. The only way a car could pass EPA standards and have its EPA bond released was by being fitted with a smog kit pre-engineered for its specific year and model. The usual changes included adding air injection to the exhaust system using an air pump and thermovalves for the control circuits. The exhaust system would be changed to include catalytic converters that had been approved for that engine class. The entire engineered kit had to be photographed as it was installed, then the documentation went to the EPA, which would clear the car as being smog-legal by conversion and issue paperwork to that effect. In most states this paperwork had to be kept with the car for smog testing and registration. The EPA release would then clear the EPA bond, and the car was home.

Many EPA conversion kits were poorly engineered. I saw many conversions with exhaust catalytic converters mounted right next to the transmission with no heat shielding. Not only did this cook the transmission from radiant heat, it also made such simple operations as transmission fluid changes nearly impossible without removing the exhaust system. Fuel system connections were often made with less than Mercedes-Benz-quality couplings and hoses. Quite a few engine fires occurred on gray market cars. The quality of the electronics in many engine management systems were at best "Mickey Mouse." A year or two after the conversion, we often had to take apart the dash and console to try to diagnose electrical problems stemming from poor conversion work. Many conversion shops did not employ mechanics to install the modifications, so the wiring was a nightmare, with wires twisted and taped instead of being soldered and shrink-wrapped.

High-performance models such as 5-liter V8s were popular gray-market imports, but very few diesels were brought in. Making a diesel engine meet EPA requirements involved changing the injection pump to match the US version of the pump. This was

expensive, so few importers saw a market with great profit potential for diesel-powered cars. I serviced one 1984 300TD (non-turbo) with a five-speed transmission for several years. The car was quick, even at Denver's 5,200-ft altitude. It was a delight to drive, but I never figured out how they had managed to get it to pass smog tests with the injection pump that was on the car.

Identity Cards

It is usually easy to identify a gray market car. You just need a little information about the conversion process. Some of the most obvious differences between gray market and officially imported US cars are:

Window Glass: A European car's glass does not carry ASA specifications on the lower left-hand corner of the windshield. A US windshield could read, "AS 1 M 83-3 DOT 25." European models did not have these markings.

Fuel Decals: Occasionally the converter would forget to install the unleaded fuel decal or the diesel fuel decal on the dash.

Catalytic Converters: Looking carefully at the catalytic converters on a gray-market car, it is easy to see that they were added-on, not original equipment. Often the catalytic converters would hang very low and reduce ground clearance because of the way they were installed.

Door Bar Bolts: One big give-away of a Euro model are the bolts in the door jambs that held the door bars installed by the converter. US models, which had "bars" installed at the factory, had no such bolts.

DOT Tires: Back in the 1980s, when the cars were brought in, their European tires bore no DOT ratings on the sidewalls. Although the tires usually had a high speed rating, say "V" for S-Class models, the US DOT rating did not appear. Of course, by now the original tires have probably been replaced.

Headlight Wipers: If 1985 and earlier European models were originally equipped with headlight wipers (not yet available on US models), the wipers were sometimes removed, but the panels under the headlights were not replaced, so you could see a hole in the panel.

Bumpers: The small European bumpers are an immediate give-away. True, during conversion they would be reinforced with chrome moly tubing, but nevertheless, they were the small bumpers, while all US models had the extended "crash" bumpers from 1974 onward.

Emission Decals: Not all of the emission control equipment stickers were always put on a converted car. During the gray market period, as Mercedes-Benz of North America caught on to the tricks of the trade of the converters, those particular decals became very hard to get.

Metric Instruments: While proper conversion required a replacement speedometer reading in mph rather than kph, other gauges might not be changed. There could be temperature gauges reading in Celsius and oil pressure gauges reading in bar, though this was so even in many 1980s US models.

Glove Box Decals: Few converters went to the trouble of getting and installing all the glove box decals covering tire pressures and other information.

Rear View Mirror: One easy give-away on a converted car is that the passenger's side mirror probably does not have "Objects are closer than they appear" etched into the glass. Few converters went to the expense of changing that mirror.

SL Rear Spoiler: Many gray market SLs have a black rubber rear spoiler on the trunk lid, a European option. Most were left in place.

Vehicle Identification Number: Mercedes-Benz VINs begin with WDB, but US cars had letters in positions 4 and 5, while European cars had the chassis designation—107, 126, etc.—in positions 4 through 6. For example:

| US | WDBBA45A9EA000059 |
| European | WDB1070451A000059 |

Good or Bad?

Fifteen years after the height of the gray market era, quite a few of these cars are still around. Many models never intended for the American market were modified to make them work here. Many interesting models were available, such as the early 500SL and 500SE. At the time, these cars were not imported by Mercedes-Benz of North America (now Mercedes-Benz USA), but there was and is a market for them. I've known many happy owners of gray market cars, though in the first few years it took quite a bit of work to straighten out hamfisted conversions done on the cheap. Once the cars were right, they were wonderful. One basic S-Class model, the 280SE, was fitted with a six-cylinder engine for Europe, but the US did not get that model after 1977. Many 280SEs were "specially imported" in both the 116 and the 126 chassis. They were delightful to drive, without the nose-heaviness of the V-8 S-Class models, and returned good fuel mileage.

My 1980 500SE, an early version, had 240 DIN hp and a 2.87:1 rear axle ratio. It was fast off the line and accelerated very well. The eventual US version of the 500SE had 184 hp buckled to a lackadaisical 2.24:1 rear end. The German version got better than 20 mpg due to its 8.8:1 compression ratio and free flowing exhaust. The 500SLs were even faster than the sedans.

The gray market offered models not imported by MBNA and engines that were not "smogged" if the new American owner was taking his once in a lifetime exemption. Great cars abound, but let the buyer beware. Many had their odometers rolled back when the speedometers were changed. I saw examples in my shop when a car would come in showing 45,000 miles yet needing a new timing chain. That didn't compute, and when we looked at the car more closely, it showed signs of 145,000 miles. Gray market cars are absolutely "Caveat Emptor."

Technical and Restoration Forum

Technical and Restoration Forum

Doors

300SD Door Panel Removal
March/April 1990

The driver's power window of my 1983 300SD has failed, but I can't get the door panel off to fix it. How is this done?

You need a factory service manual. The chassis/body manual for 126-chassis cars is $50 plus $5 postage from Technical Publications, MBNA, One Mercedes Dr., Montvale, NJ 07645. (A complete catalog of manuals for all models can be obtained from MBNA at this address.)

To remove your door panel, first remove the hand grip/armrest. Remove the metal inlay around the door latch by prying it loose, then removing the screw in the recess. Pry off the cover at the upper end of the hand grip. Undo the screw beneath it, then remove the two screws further down the hand grip/armrest and remove it. Remove the screw on the upper part of the door, and pull off the reveal molding upward. Next, remove the enclosure around the door lock. Undo the screw down below on the door lining, and pull the lining upward. The lining is hung on, not clipped on. Of course, this will be much clearer when looking at the illustrations in the manual.

Nervous Noises
March/April 1986

My 1982 300SD is perfect except for a constant metallic rattling which seems to be in the rear door on the passenger side. It has been in the shop twice for this with no cure. Do you have any suggestions? Enclosed is a self-addressed stamped envelope, or you may call me collect. I love the car, but this constant noise is getting on my nerves....

It is extremely difficult, as you have discovered, to isolate a noise such as this. It reminds me of the apocryphal Detroit tale of the Coke bottle hung on a string inside a sealed inner panel of the car by a disgruntled assembly line worker. My 240D had a noise of this kind. Three different mechanics thought it came from three different places. It was finally found by a mechanic who discovered a shiny spot where a bolt head had rubbed on the chassis. The wrong motor mount had been installed on one side.

The door panel can be removed easily. If that doesn't locate the noise, remove everything loose from the car, including the jack, spare tire and tools from the trunk, and drive it to see if there's any change. I would also suspect the shock absorber on that side. Drive the car while someone in the back seat listens with a stethoscope. Get the car up on a chassis lift, put it in gear and "drive" it while someone watches and listens beneath it. The only way to find the noise may be to systematically eliminate various areas one by one.

Glass and Seals

Synthetic Bag Balm?

September/October 1996

Ever since we bought our SL320, it has suffered from squeaks caused by the side window glass rubbing against the hardtop seals. Our dealer has been cooperative in trying to solve this, and has adjusted the windows outward, but the problem persists. Is there a factory fix, or has your experience generated a solution?

No factory fix exists, but I suggest that you try applying a light coat of ordinary hand lotion. Apply it to your hands, then wipe your finger along the edge of the glass. Another possibility is a light coat of lip balm. Avoid the kind containing petroleum or Vaseline, and get the "all natural" kind sold in health food stores. This kind usually lists beeswax, candelilla wax, and coconut oil as ingredients. A thin coat should stop the squeaks. We trust that the glass has not been adjusted so far outward that it leaks.

280SL Window Guides

May/June 2001

The passenger-side window of my 1969 280SL is loose, so I took off the door panel to have a look. The glass is in a rectangular channel with no inserts or brackets to steady it. The driver's side window has rubber strips inside the channel, but I can't find any of this material. The 280SL uses plastic brackets glued to the glass, but where can I find this rubber stuff?

What you found in the driver's side window tracks was "window run" found in many old Mercedes-Benz models, such as the 280SEL. It is available by the meter from Mercedes-Benz. Originally, 113-chassis SLs had pot-metal guides with nylon inserts glued to the glass that ran up and

down the window track. Over time these can come unglued from the glass and fall into the bottom of the door. As you found in the "repaired" driver's door, a previous owner found it quicker (and less expensive) to install a strip of window run in the track for the glass to slide in than to remove the glass and re-glue the blocks. I don't think the pot-metal brackets are available separately, so if they aren't in the bottom of the door, you'll have to buy new glass or do a quick fix with 108-chassis window run.

SL Windshield Scratching

March/April 1993

After only 22,000 miles I've had my 500SL (R129) windshield replaced once, and now it needs another. The wipers scratch the surface. How can I prevent this? All four tires needed replacing at 13,000 miles and will soon need to be replaced again. The tires develop flat spots which thump in cold weather. Is there a better choice of tire for wear and ride?

Regarding the windshield scratching, MBNA suggests turning on the windshield washers immediately whenever you first activate the wipers. The lubricating effect of the washer fluid may mitigate the scratching, caused by dust particles.

Tires with high speed ratings (VR and ZR) have shorter tread lives. Tires develop flat spots, especially after being driven hard, then allowed to cool in one spot. This has occurred most in the new S-class cars, and MBNA has replaced some tires with Pirellis (see your dealer). Other tire makers are working on the problem, but for now, Pirelli seems the best bet.

Dusty Trunk

September/October 1988

I drive a 1987 300D in severe dust conditions, and it sucks dust into the trunk. I've tried various combinations of air-conditioning, window and sunroof with no improvement; blocking the air-conditioning exhaust ports in the trunk helps. Under the same conditions my 240D, 280SE and 450SE had no problems.

Air flows from the passenger compartment into the trunk, where it is exhausted through two openings, one on each side of the car, concealed by the bumper. Flaps on these ports are intended to form a one-way valve. If they are stuck in the open position, air (and dust) could enter. To find the source of the dust, remove the plastic trunk liner and check these ports, the trunk lid seal, the seals around the taillights and any other body openings in the trunk.

In dusty conditions, keep the windows and sunroof closed and the air-conditioning on, with re-circulation. This will slightly pressurize the passenger compartment and trunk.

SL Hardtop Seals

May/June 1995

When I drive my 450SL fast, air whistles through the hardtop seals, and when I drive over bumps, the hardtop rattles. Are these inherent problems, or do I just need new seals?

Wind noise is not inherent. Since your car is at least 15 years old, the seals have probably hardened with age, so we suggest replacing them, which could also reduce the rattling. When you install the hardtop, be sure to follow the proper sequence. First, with both doors open, insert the rear bow locking pin into the latch hole. When the rear bow lock is engaged, align the front and side locks with their attachment points, and lower the top gently. Apply gentle downward force on the top to engage the front bow locks, then insert the locking handles into the slots on the inner side of the locks. Rotate the handles to the outer positions and remove them. To engage the side locks, insert a locking handle into the slot from the rear of each lock. Rotate each handle to its forward stop, then remove the handles. If the cap on a side lock pops off while the lock is being engaged, realign it, and push it down until it snaps into place. Turn the locking lever clockwise to position B. Either that, or slow down and stick to smooth roads.

Elusive Trunk Leak

May/June 1990

When it rains or when the car is washed, the right spare tire well of my 1979 300SD gathers water. The rubber gasket seems sound, and there are no leaks at the tail light.

Try to determine where the water is not coming from. The drain hole in the bottom of the tire well has a rubber plug that lets water out but not in. Tape over the hole, and see if that helps. If you still get water in the trunk, remove the trunk mat and paint a border around the upper edge of the tire well with white poster paint, the kind that's water soluble and easily wiped off. Incoming water will leave a trail. The rear window is also a suspect. Tape over the glass/seal/trim joints and see whether this helps.

First, Remove Doors

March/April 1997

The hoses protecting the wiring and vacuum hoses between the body and doors on my 1973 450SE are cracked and broken. I'd like to replace them, but I'm told that I'll have to take the doors off to do so. Is there any other way?

The only way to install the new rubber hose is to remove the doors and door linings, disconnect the wires and vacuum line, insert the new protective hoses with wires and vacuum line through them, and reinstall the doors and liners. This problem is much the same as that encountered with rubber boots over rear axle joints. Someone should invent split protective hoses. Cutting a new hose lengthwise then gluing it after installation may be an option.

280SE Fender Removal

March/April 1985

My 1972 280SE needs a new front crossmember, and to replace it, the front fenders have to come off. A body shop told me that they would have to be torched off and welded back on because the sealant between fender and body cannot be loosened. I'd like to find a less drastic way to remove them, and I need to know what sealant I should use when I reinstall them.

The sealant glue used on your car holds so well that any attempt to remove the fender by force after removing the bolts will damage the metal. Removal with a torch is quick and cheap, but not the best way. With care and patience, you can remove the fenders yourself.

Remove all the bolts. Using a linoleum knife or a single-edge razor blade held vertically, cut through the glue. Having the car in a warm place will help, as the glue becomes more plastic with warmth. You can warm it gently with a propane torch, being careful not to overheat and warp the metal. It will be a long, tedious job and hard on the hands, but it can be done. Do not try to remove the glue from the body or fender—just slice through it. When you re-install the fender, instead of glue or sealant, use 3M Rubberized Undercoat, which comes in a pressurized can with a long nozzle to allow it to be injected into the right spots.

Instruments

SL Instrument Glitches

May/June 2001

My 1990 500SL has an erratic instrument cluster problem. When I activate the turn signals, the dashboard warning lights flash once in unison and the seatbelt warning light blinks. Sometimes the gauges go to zero for a moment; they may remain at zero until the engine is shut off and re-started. My dealer suggests replacing the instrument panel ($1,000 plus) to see if that fixes it. Are there more economical options?

A power distribution or grounding problem is creating a sneak path in the instrument cluster. It can be caused by an oxidized contact on a fuse or connector, or a cracked printed circuit trace on the panel's circuit board. Check, clean, and rotate all fuses that feed the instrument cluster. If that doesn't help, remove the cluster and clean and burnish all connectors and sockets feeding it. A relay contact burnishing tool and a pencil eraser are good for this, but sometimes just removing and re-inserting the plugs a few times will do the trick. Carefully inspect ground connection W1 (page 54-3.00 ETM) behind the instrument panel. If that doesn't cure it, look for a cracked trace or solder joint on the instrument cluster circuit board on one of the power or ground traces. Pay particular attention around the connector sockets, as this is where the most mechanical stress occurs. A jeweler's loupe is helpful for this kind of mechanical inspection, as the crack can be nearly invisible.

Airbag Age

March/April 2004

A sticker on my 1986 190E 2.3-16 calls for airbag replacement by March 1996. The owner's manual calls for replacement in 10 years. What's the wisdom on replacing airbags?

Mercedes-Benz extended the airbag exchange time to 15 years from the installed date. It's very possible that the 15-year period will be further extended as longer-term testing and field research become available. The company has always been conservative when it comes to safety matters; in today's litigious society they make careful decisions about safety equipment.

Speedometer Conversion

July/August 1984

Is it possible to convert the 85-mph speedometer in my 1980 450SLC to a 160-mph speedometer, standard on current models?

Your 1980 450SLC has a mechanical speedometer, the last year that Mercedes-Benz used them. For 1981 they changed to electronic speedometers, still limited to 85 mph. When the 85-mph restriction on speedometer readings was lifted in 1983, a bulletin was issued to dealers cautioning that if a new 160-mph speedometer was installed in a 1981–82 car, a warning label had to be applied to the instrument cluster to caution the driver that scale markings were changed.

I don't know if a conversion is possible, but you could replace the instrument with a 1979 (non-85) version. Palo-Alto Speedometer, an advertiser in *The Star*, may also be able to help; their address is 718 Emerson St., Palo Alto, CA 94301, telephone (415) 323-0243. VDO, the manufacturer of Mercedes-Benz speedometers, has a service branch at 980 Brooke Road, Winchester, VA 22601.

Speedometer Change Halves Fuel Consumption

January/February 2000

Road Star Section member Marvin Findling wrote, "For months the fuel consumption of our 1983 380SL increased. Technicians evaluated several causes, replaced parts, and made adjustments, but there was no decrease in consumption: eight to nine miles per gallon, highway driving!"

Marvin's service advisor suggested checking the odometer. After several trips over a measured mile, the main odometer and trip odometer were both found to register about half the actual distance, even though the speedometer was accurate. A certified new speedometer corrected the situation, and highway mileage is now 16 to 18 mpg with all accessories on.

This experience is not unique. Odometers in aging VDO speedometer units can be inaccurate when the odometer number wheels lose their grip on the shaft that drives them. The solution is to disassemble the speedometer and repair the odometer. If this is beyond your ability, one economical solution is to send it to an expert for repair. I have used Overseas Speedometer & Clock Repair in Austin, Texas, and found that owner Rick Borth provides prompt, economical service. If you call for instructions, he can also help you to check your speedometer calibration. Other advertisers in *The Star* can also help.

Balky 280SL Speedometer

May/June 2001

The speedometer in my 1970 280SL (manual transmission) is accurate in the three lower gears, but in fourth it can lag by about 50 percent. The needle is steady. What might be wrong?

The transmission output flange nut may be loose. The speedometer drive at the back of the transmission has no keyway, so if the nut is loose, the drive gear can slip on the output shaft, causing erratic speed indication. The speedometer may also be faulty. If you have an electric drill that can run at high speed in reverse, remove the speedometer and test it with the drill (counterclockwise rotation).

Worn Turn Signal Switch

July/August 1996

I've had four 115-body cars, and every one has had a problem with the turn signal switch. When I move the handle to signal a turn, the handle won't stay set, and I have to hold the handle in place, then let go when I've completed the turn. How can I get it to stay?

The turn signal switch can be modified by deepening the notch in the switch with a small toolmaker's file. Remove the switch as far as the wires permit, and file the notch where the spring detent fits. Too much deepening, and the switch won't cancel after the turn. Most experienced Mercedes-Benz mechanics can show you how to do this.

Locking System

Locking System All Wet

January/February 1994

The central locking system on my 1984 300SD only works when it's raining or very humid. The cruise control is similarly affected.

Your problem is probably caused by a poor ground connection at G103, the ground in the left-hand rear wheel well inside the trunk. This ground serves the vacuum pump (central locking) and the brake light (cruise control). Malfunction of other components served by this ground—the left rear light, trunk light, antenna motor, and fuel gauge sender—might not be noticed so easily.

Frozen 123 Door Locks

May/June 2001

The door locks on our 1983 and 1984 W123 models often freeze after a cold damp night. Graphite lubricant doesn't help much. What's the definitive solution?

The solution is to remove the handle assembly, disassemble the lock tumblers, clean out the dirt, and pack the tumbler assembly with Mercedes-Benz sliding roof paste (similar to petroleum jelly). If the little metal flap covering the key slot is missing, this solution will be short-lived. Keep high-pressure water from blasting into the key hole, as it can wash out the lubricant. Spray lubricants offer a short-term solution; water can still enter and freeze if there's no grease to keep it out.

To remove the handle: 1) open the door and remove the two Phillips-head screws near the door seal, 2) pull the handle and give it a whack with your hand toward the front of the car (disengaging the forward screw from

its slot in the door at the front of the handle), and 3) put the key in the tumblers and rotate it to disengage the lock shaft from the latch, then pull the handle assembly out of the door. Once it's on the bench, you can figure out how to disassemble the tumblers and clean and lube them.

Finding Vacuum Leaks

November/December 1994

The central locking system on my 1979 300D has a leak that I can't find. The locks work when the engine is running, but not after it is shut off for a minute or so. The vacuum lines and check valves show some engine oil. How can I find the vacuum leak?

The easiest way to describe the method of finding a vacuum leak is to compare the vacuum system to a direct-current electrical circuit. Think of the leak as a short circuit to ground. To diagnose the electrical circuit you would use a volt-ohm meter. For the vacuum system you need a vacuum tester such as the one sold by Impco or other suppliers of automotive test equipment. The tester is a combination vacuum pump and vacuum gauge.

With this tester you can apply vacuum to each section (or circuit) of the vacuum system. With a certain vacuum applied, usually about 0.5 bar, watch the gauge to see how quickly it leaks down. If a line loses more than 2 mbar in a minute, you have a leak. First apply the tester to the line from the vacuum pump to the brake booster, on the booster side of the check valve. The procedure for the entire car rates four or five pages of description in the *Service Manual*. You can work it out for yourself, but the job can be time-consuming, as you must disassemble some items to test some lines and units. The engine oil in the lines makes us suspect that your vacuum pump may be leaking.

Sunroof

Balky W124 Sunroof

May/June 2001

Last time I tried to open the sunroof on my 1987 300D, it made a loud pop as the two plastic slides connecting the sunroof to the metal "bridge" (where the sunroof cable is attached) broke. The first repair step in the factory manual is to close the sunroof, but how do I do this without more damage or removing the headliner?

It sounds as if one of the track mechanisms attached to the metal panel broke. If the sunroof is still closed, to remove the metal panel for repair, you need to slide the sunroof headliner back to access the retaining nuts. Get your fingers under the front of the headliner, and pull straight down to unclip the four clips at the front. Slide the headliner toward the rear, and you will see the 8-mm nut holding the panel to the track mechanisms. The 1986 Model Year Introduction Manual includes procedures for removing and adjusting the sliding/pop-up sunroof.

Sunroof Cable Breakage

January/February 1996

My 300SDL is on its third sunroof drive cable, and I hardly ever use the darn thing. Maybe that's the problem. How can I prevent it from breaking?

Broken sunroof cables are common and might be caused by dirty or unlubricated sunroof rails. Cleaning and lubricating these rails (Job No. 7730) is supposed to be done every two years. When a cable breaks, it often kinks first, damaging the sheet metal channel, which can lead to wear and breakage of subsequent cables. More frequent cleaning and lubrication of the sliding rails may help to prevent more breakage.

Chapter 6

Suspension, Steering, Tires, Wheels

W201 and W124 Front Suspension Repair Tips

by George Murphy

September/October 2000

Based on experience with two cars, a 190E 2.6 and a 300E, both with more than 170,000 miles, here are some thoughts on front suspension work.

Changing the front struts is straightforward, but first get a Mercedes-Benz chassis manual. To order one, call the Mercedes-Benz USA Client Assistance Center, 800/367-6372. The manual assumes that you will remove the steering knuckle for other work, hence a spring compressor is specified. They can be rented from Performance Products, 800/789-1963.

Disassembly

Loosen the appropriate lug bolts, then using the jack point behind the front wheel, raise the left or right front of the car until the tire is just off the ground. Block up the front suspension by placing a jack stand under the lower control arm so it is supported just as it would be if the car were on its wheels. This support must be at the outer end of the control arm (4). Remove the wheel, and be sure the car is supported securely, as it would be with the wheel on the ground.

Install the spring compressor, and tighten it until the spring's coils are slightly compressed and the spring is loose in its mount. To change the strut, undo the upper strut mount nut (11a), using a metric hex driver to hold the shaft. Remove the three lower strut mounting nuts. So that it

doesn't swing downward and stretch or damage the brake hose, support the steering knuckle on a block of wood. Remove the old strut.

Before ordering new parts, inspect the rubber parts at the top of the suspension strut. Raise the rubber dust boot (11f) to inspect the detent stop (11h); to get a good look at it, pull the stop downward on the shaft. If the stop and the boot are in bad shape, get new ones. Replace the upper rubber mount (11c) at the same time.

Reinstallation

Install the new detent stop (11h) on the strut shaft, oriented as shown in the drawing. Attach the dust boot (11f) to the flange on the new rubber mount (11c), and install the mount. Install the new strut into the upper bushing, but don't tighten anything

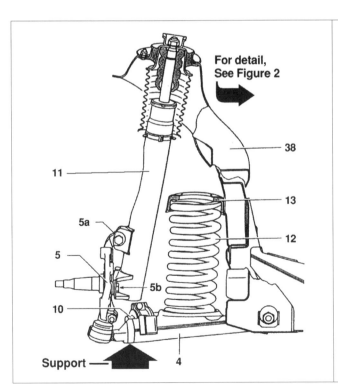

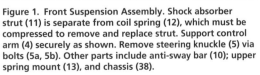

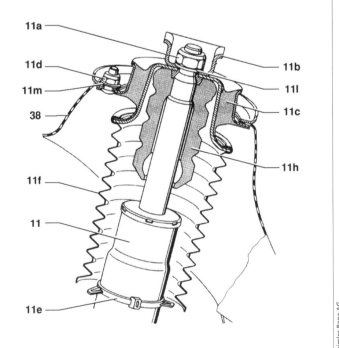

Figure 1. Front Suspension Assembly. Shock absorber strut (11) is separate from coil spring (12), which must be compressed to remove and replace strut. Support control arm (4) securely as shown. Remove steering knuckle (5) via bolts (5a, 5b). Other parts include anti-sway bar (10); upper spring mount (13), and chassis (38).

Figure 2. Upper Strut Attachment. Shock absorber strut (11); upper strut mount nut (11a); extension stop (11b); rubber mount (11c); hex nuts (11d); retaining strap (11e); rubber dust boot (11f); detent stop (11h); washers (11l, 11m).

yet. Clean the surfaces in the steering knuckle with a wire brush. Clean the mounting bolt threads, apply Loctite, then install them. First, torque the two lower bolts to 110 Nm (82 lb-ft), then torque the bolt and nut at the lower end to the same value. Torque the upper mount to 60 Nm (45 lb-ft), again holding the shaft with a metric hex driver.

Slowly release the spring compressor, making sure the spring is seated correctly. Replace the wheel, jack up the car, remove the jack stand, and lower the car to the ground. Repeat all this for the other side, then have the front end aligned by a good Mercedes-Benz front end mechanic. If necessary, take along your own alignment specs, as the specs supplied with the wheel alignment equipment may be incorrect.

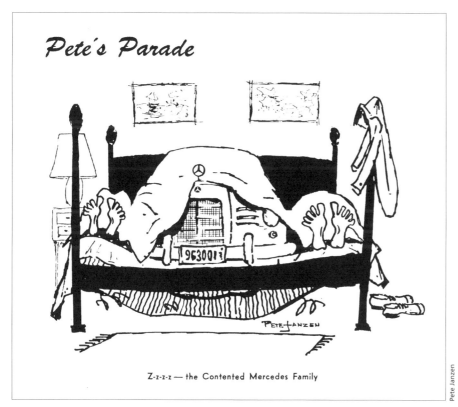

Pete's Parade

Z-z-z-z — the Contented Mercedes Family

Pete Janzen

November/December 1959

Self-Leveling Suspension Care

by George Murphy,
MBCA Technical
Advisor

*September/October
1998*

Self-leveling rear suspension, standard on U.S. W123 and W124 station wagons, keeps them level under load. The W126 S-Class gasoline sedans were equipped with the same system starting in 1981. (Some gray market S-Class cars have hydropneumatic suspension at the front and rear, like the 450SEL 6.9, using the hydraulic system for full suspension of the car without the traditional springs.)

Figures 1 and 2 show the typical wagon self-leveling system; S-Class sedans are similar. Major components include: 1) engine-driven pump, 2) the oil supply tank, 3) the level controller, 4) the pressure reservoir, and 5) a spring strut for each wheel plus connecting lines.

The level controller at the rear of the car senses rear suspension position through a lever (6) connected to the torsion bar (10). When a load is applied, the rear suspension deflects, moving the lever on the level controller; this routes high-pressure fluid to the spring struts to raise the car back to level. When the load is removed, the level controller bleeds pressure from the struts to let the car return to level. In the pressure reservoirs (4), a flexible diaphragm separates high-pressure nitrogen gas (b) from hydraulic fluid (a). Acting as the rear shock absorbers, the compressible nitrogen absorbs road shock transmitted by the fluid. The spring struts simply move in response to fluid pressure to keep the car level. Traditional coil springs (18) carry the weight of the car.

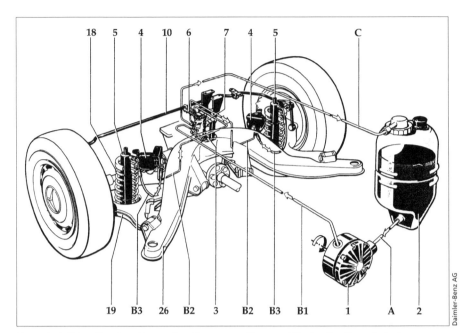

Figure 1. Self-Leveling Rear Suspension. 1) pressure oil pump, 2) hydraulic oil supply tank, 3) level controller, 4) pressure reservoir, 5) spring strut, 6) lever on torsion bar, 7) connecting rod, 10) torsion bar, 18) rear spring, 19) semi-trailing arm, 26) rear axle carrier. Lines: A) suction line, oil supply tank to pressure oil pump; B1) pressure line, pressure oil pump to level controller; B2) pressure line, level controller to pressure reservoir; B3) pressure line, pressure reservoir to spring strut; C) return line, level controller to oil supply tank.

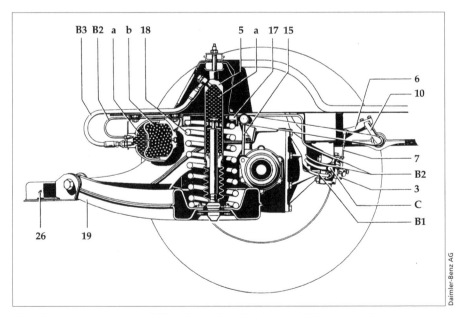

Figure 2. Rear Suspension Detail. 3) level controller, 5) spring strut, 6) lever on torsion bar, 7) connecting rod, 10) torsion bar, 15) torsion bar connecting rod, 17) rubber mount, 18) rear spring, 19) semi-trailing arm, 26) rear axle carrier. Chambers, lines: a) oil chamber, b) gas chamber, B1) pressure line, pressure oil pump to level controller, B2) pressure line, level controller to pressure reservoir, B3) pressure line, pressure reservoir to spring strut, C) return line, level controller to oil supply tank.

Self-Leveling Maintenance

Being a mechanical engineer in nuclear power plants, I worked on steam turbine hydraulic controls. To keep the huge turbines on-line and generating electricity, these hydraulic systems had rigorous maintenance requirements, so I was surprised to find no reference in Mercedes-Benz maintenance booklets for the care of self-leveling suspension. The principles, fluids, and components are similar, and wear and contamination are more severe than power plant systems.

Experience with this system on Mercedes-Benz cars shows neglect as the prime cause of failures and leaks. A car receiving "dealer maintenance" all its life would receive little attention to the hydraulic system other than topping up the reservoir. These systems need periodic fluid and filter replacement. I recommend that the fluid and filter be changed at 30,000-mile intervals, the same as the transmission and power steering (other oft-neglected systems).

Maintaining the System

To replace the filter and fluid you'll need a new filter (part 002 18 55 01) and four liters of Mercedes-Benz hydraulic fluid (part 000 989 91 03), a one-gal container and a few feet of hose to catch old fluid, and two helpers. Put the heaviest helper at the rear of the car, the other in the driver's seat.

1. Disconnect the fluid return line from the cap at the fluid reservoir and remove the cap. Connect a piece of scrap hose to the return line to route dirty oil to a one-gal container under the car to catch the fluid as it comes out.

2. The filter (2h in Figure 3) is under the fill cap. Remove the old filter, and leave the cap off the reservoir. Remove the reservoir from the car, and dump out the old fluid. If the reservoir is dirty, clean it thoroughly with soap and water, dry it, and re-install it.

Be sure to re-connect the oil pump suction line (A).

3. Pour clean hydraulic fluid into the reservoir up to the full mark. Have the other bottles of fluid ready to pour in. Take off each cap, and remove the foil seal; you must be quick about this.

4. Have one helper start the engine; have the heavier one sit on the rear of car to exercise the suspension while you pour new fluid into the reservoir. As fluid is pumped through the system and into the catch bucket under the car—this is called "feed and bleed"—keep feeding in new fluid. Don't let air be drawn into the pump. When clean fluid emerges from the return hose, stop the engine (and stop bouncing the rear of car—it's annoying!).

5. At the rear, find the level controller (3), attach a hose to its bleed screw (like a brake bleed screw), and open the screw to let the lines drain. Start the engine, and have your helper

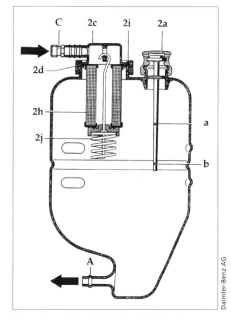

Figure 3. Oil Supply Tank, Plastic Version. 2a) closing cap with oil dipstick, 2c) cover with connection, 2d) rubber sealing ring, 2h) filter element, 2i) closing nut, 2j) closing spring, a) maximum mark, b) minimum mark, A) suction oil supply, tank to pressure oil pump, C) return line, level controller to oil supply tank.

bounce the rear of the car to force fluid from the struts until clean fluid is expelled. Close the bleed screw, and tighten any loosened lines.

6. Fill the reservoir to the full mark, install a new filter, and reconnect the return line to the cap. Start the engine, check for leaks, and top-up the fluid level if necessary.

What Goes Wrong

Aging pressure reservoirs generally show up as a harsh, bumpy ride. These parts usually last about 100,000 miles. As the reservoirs age, the pressurized nitrogen gas inside diffuses through the internal diaphragm, and the reservoir eventually loses its ability to act as a shock absorber.

If the spring struts are leaking, it's time for replacement. They are not repairable. The engine-driven hydraulic oil pump is reliable and rarely fails unless metal particles get inside. If the pump is leaking, there are two sources of leakage—the shaft seal at the rear of the pump or the front cap o-ring. Leaky pumps can be repaired; these parts are available from Mercedes-Benz: shaft seal, part 004 997 01 47; body gasket, part 114 236 00 80; and the cap o-ring, part 010 997 43 45. The two internal o-rings, not available from MB, can be obtained from Performance Analysis Co., Oakridge, Tennessee.

Don't try to adjust the level controller connecting rod (7). The original factory setting must be maintained. Adjusting the rod can cause continuous pressurization of the spring struts, causing rough ride and knocking. If the car rides too high or too low, refer to the Mercedes-Benz Chassis Manual, Section 32, Chassis Suspension System, to correct the problem. Your car was right at one time with the present setting, and no amount of adjustment can compensate for worn or leaky struts or depleted reservoirs.

Changing Rear Air Suspension Bellows

by Frank Barrett, Editor/Publisher, & Charles Herrmann, Mile-High Section

March/April 1995

Photos in this article by Frank Barrett.

Does your car have airbags? Not in its steering wheel, in its suspension. If so, here's how you can replace two of them.

When (not if) your air-suspended 300SEL (3.5, 4.5, 6.3, etc.) drops to its knees, the cause could be leaking air lines or fittings, worn air valves, or leaking airbags (bellows). Depending on load, the system operates at 5.5 to 8 atmospheres (80 to 116 psi). Finding a leak usually involves searching the pressurized system with soapy water in a spray bottle, but a rubber bellows that looks old and seriously cracked is a natural suspect. Mercedes-Benz recommends changing them every 100,000 km (62,000 mi), but actual life varies. Changing the rear bellows is easier than changing the front ones, so let's start there.

Disassembly

First, to reveal the nuts holding the metal air chamber beneath the car, open the rear doors and the trunk lid, and remove the back seat. Just lift the lower cushion; the seat back is held by two bolts with nuts high on the front wall of the trunk.

Having a lift to raise the car helps, but you can use a floor jack and jackstands. Take the usual safety precautions, and position the jack clear of the rear trailing arm. Remove the wheel and tire. Using 17mm and 14mm open-end wrenches, loosen the air line on the inner side of the air chamber above the bellows. (The left side has two lines; the right, one.) Let air pressure bleed down, then detach the line(s) from the air chamber.

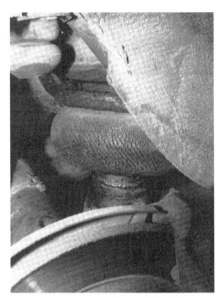

Old airbag looked terrible but only recently began leaking.

Good airbag shows only minor cracks after 10 years.

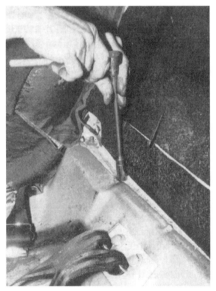

Bolts under seat (and under trunk) hold air chambers beneath car

Front end of rear trailing arm must be detached.

Lower the car, and undo the two 13mm nuts at the rear of the lower seat area. Lift the front corner of the trunk mat (in front of the shock tower), and undo the 13mm nut there. The top of the air chamber is now free.

Raise the car and loosen the three 13mm nuts holding the bracket at the front end of the trailing arm. After

undoing the 22mm nut holding the front of the trailing arm to the body and bracket, you can lower the arm enough to wriggle out the bellows and chamber.

If the conical metal air piston above the trailing arm sticks to the bellows, undo the 17mm bolt beneath it, remove the piston along with the bellows, and separate them on the bench using a pry bar. Pick all the dirt out of the six Phillips-head screws securing the retaining ring to the chamber. If rusty, these screws may be difficult to remove; soak them with penetrating oil a day or two beforehand. A simple impact tool helps, too. Remove the six screws, three retainer strips, six nuts, and the locking clips that hold each nut in place.

As you separate the bellows and ring from the chamber, note how they fit together, then pry the old bellows out of the ring. Clean the ring and the nuts, etc. Use a wire brush to remove dirt from the upper piston where it sticks into the bellows. Dirt here can wear the rubber.

Re-Assembly

Now you're ready to start re-assembly. Squeeze the new bellows into the retaining ring. Start it without lubricant, but spray on a bit to slide the last tough part into the ring. After cleaning the rim of the chamber, re-attach the bellows using the Phillips-head screws, retainer strips, nuts, and clips. To prevent each clip from twisting as you snug down its screw, use a metal pick or a screwdriver to hold the clip in position. Tighten the six screws to a torque of 14 ft-lb.

Replace the o-ring seal inside the chamber's air line fitting(s). Now you can position the bellows/chamber assembly on the car, first attaching it to the chassis. Loosely connect the air line(s) while things can still be moved. Re-install the piston above the trailing arm, aiming it into the bellows. The bellows assembly should stay in place while you lower the car to re-install the two nuts in the rear seat area plus the one in the trunk.

Raise the car and tighten the air line fittings (11 ft-lb) and the bolt under the piston. Clean the front attachment bracket, raise the front of the trailing arm, and re-attach it and the bracket to the chassis. You might find it easiest to attach the 22mm nut loosely to hold the arm and bracket, install the three nuts holding the bracket to the chassis, then

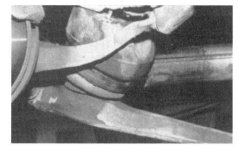

With trailing arm lowered, bag and air chamber above it come out.

Hammer and impact driver loosen recalcitrant screws.

Inserting new bag into retaining ring.

Ring and bag, foreground, removed from air chamber.

Conical piston above trailing arm must be centered in bag.

Re-attaching bag and ring to air chamber.

Disconnecting linkage allows use of leveling valve to control air flow into bag.

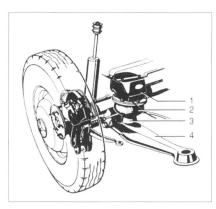

Rear air suspension includes 1) air chamber, 2) bellows, 3) air piston, and 4) trailing arm.

255

tighten the big nut to 72 ft-lb. While doing this, the piston will move up into the bellows; be sure that it is centered.

Now you'll re-pressurize the air system to push the bellows down over the piston. You can control air flow to the unit by using the rear leveling valve in front of the fuel tank. Undo the nut holding the lower end of the vertical link to the valve (avoid un-snapping the ball joint; doing so might break the insert, and the ball can be hard to re-attach). Slowly raise the rear of the trailing arm a few inches with a jack, until the axle is about horizontal, and pressurize the system from your air hose via the filling valve on the side of the tank in the left front fender (or by starting the engine). Raise the arm on the rear leveling valve to let air flow into the bellows, watching it as it fills and settles around the piston. Be sure

the piston is centered in the bag. Re-attach the valve control arm.

With the system pressurized, check for air leaks with your soapy water spray. Replace the wheel, lower the car to the ground, clean your hands, re-install the seat, and you're done. Start the engine, and the car will level off. Because you haven't disturbed them, there's no need to worry about alignment or level settings.

Front bellows are tougher to replace because the work must be done on the car, not on the bench. As soon as ours leak enough to demand replacement, we'll describe that job!

Thanks to German Motors in Lakewood, Colorado, for their kind and skillful cooperation in the preparation of this article.

190SL Rear Suspension Repair

by Matt Joseph

March/April 1989

Photos in this article by the author.

A while back we repaired the rear suspension of a 1958 190SL; both fault and repair were interesting enough to cause us to photograph them.

Instead of the tube frame of the 300SL, the 190SL used an early version of hybrid unit construction with a vestigial stiffening perimeter sub-frame. DBAG favored the 190SL with a swing-axle independent rear suspension located fore-and-aft by trailing arms bolted to cups welded to the unit's perimeter stiffening member. The design of the cups didn't allow for corrosion, so the attaching structures tended to disintegrate. As bad as the problem is, the repair that DBAG soon devised for it is terrific.

Unit Construction

Unit-bodies go back almost to the beginning of cars. In the 1930's, companies like Citroën, Renault and Lancia were well into unit construction, and there were several pre-WWII U.S. attempts to manufacture cars with unit substructures. The real blossoming of unit construction came after the war. Fiat, Rover, Dyna-Panhard and others were well into this format before 1950, and in this country Hudson and others used hybrid forms of unit construction that combined unit bodies with integral perimeter frames. In 1957 Chrysler began designing all their models with unit construction, with a stamped sheet metal platform and front chassis stubs carrying the driveline. Other American companies gradually followed this lead, and today few if any frames are put under passenger cars.

Unit construction is generally lighter and more rigid than separate body/frame assemblies, but unit-boded cars can pose immense restoration problems. Most or all of their chassis strength is supplied by stamped sheet metal, but one area that required design evolution over the years was the attachment of suspension components to the chassis. While a frame is endlessly adaptable to welding, bolting and riveting components to it, unit bodies don't share this ease. Frames represent concentrated strength in concentrated space. Unit bodies spread loads over wider dimensions and provide no neat attachment points that can withstand great torsional and longitudinal forces. Attaching suspensions to unit-constructed cars requires considerable engineering. One reason for the popularity of McPherson strut designs is the relative ease with which they can be attached to a sheet metal chassis.

Unfortunately, early unit-constructed cars were sometimes not highly evolved in suspension attachment. Combined with a general lack of knowledge regarding corrosion protection, this led to problems as the cars aged. The attachment of the 190SL's trailing arms' stationary ends to the unit-perimeter strengthener was an example, and this junction failed on many cars over the years.

Great Factory Repair Part

Not long after the first cute little 190SL hit the roads in the mid-1950's, folks began having problems with the rear suspension attachments. By the early 1960's I saw all manner of odd and crude repairs to attach the rear trailing arms. The 190SL's rear axle housing is fastened to the chassis; swing axles and universal joints allow the outer ends of the axles to move up and down. The axles support the body via coil springs and are primarily located by massive stamped trailing arms secured to a stiffening perimeter member

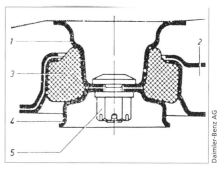

Factory sketch shows arm socket with parts in place; 1 = new mount; 2 = trailing arm; 3 = rubber bushing (donut); 4 = lower cup, and 5 = nut. Look carefully, and you'll see that as drawn, arm would move between rubber donut and chassis. Actually, the arm socket has a small rim under donut. When donut is compressed by nut and lower cup, it is held in place by this rim.

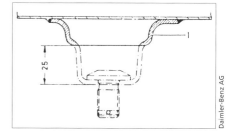

Factory sketch shows what should secure trailing arm. Horizontal line halfway through cup shows where it is supposed to be cut for repair with factory part, but this car required its complete removal.

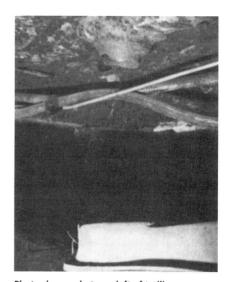

Photo shows what was left of trailing arm after ravages of corrosion. Remains of mount's base are at top of photo, front end of trailing arm below. Damage resulted from water collecting in chassis member and running into cup. Trapped, it rusted cup from inside.

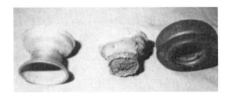

Old and new parts, from both sides. New upper cup repair piece and lower cup are at left; rubber bushing (donut) that goes between cup halves is at right. Replacement cup is made of much sterner stuff than original. Note completely deteriorated condition of old parts (center).

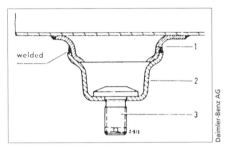

Factory sketch shows detail of repaired structure: 1 = old base; 2 = new cup, and 3 = new mounting stud. Chassis metal that mount is welded to is open, allowing moisture to collect in cup. We rustproofed the inside and outside of new cup and drilled two small weepholes to let out moisture that collects inside it. Mount will have to be checked periodically to make sure it doesn't succumb to corrosion again.

First, remains of the original securing cap must be leveled to correct dimension, and then area has to be cleaned (photo). A small electric-drive wire brush is ideal for this kind of cleaning before welding and doesn't make the mess that sandblasting does.

around the sheet metal chassis. This connection includes a plate welded to the unit stiffening member and a cup welded to the plate. The cup has a bolt extending down from the center of its lower surface. A large rubber donut fits against the cup, and the trailing arm socket fits against the donut. A shallow inverted cup goes under the donut and trailing arm, and the assembly is secured with a nut that clamps the two cups and arm together, compressing the donut. This damps vibration and allows the trailing arm to move as the axle, secured to it at the rear, moves up and down. The trailing arm also secures the axle and wheel laterally. More sophisticated versions of the layout are used by DBAG to this day.

Attaching a rear swing-axle suspension to a unit chassis (where trailing arms could no longer be bolted to a rigid frame) was successfully accomplished, but the attachment corroded quickly in service. I grew up in the Northeast and moved to the corrosive Midwest, and after about 1965 I never saw one of these cars that had not required repair in this area. Some of the repairs were bizarre. I remember one where threaded rod and torch-cut plates came through the floor behind the driver's seat. In addition to securing the trailing arms below the floor, the rods formed the basis of a rather nasty-looking roll bar!

By the time I got the job of repairing the 190SL, I had lost touch with the trailing arm attachment problems of these cars. Reviewing the situation, I decided to fabricate something out of washers, discarded shock absorber mounting parts or the like. Before committing to such a cobbled approach, it occurred to me that since most 190SL's would have by now required this repair, it was possible that someone had fabricated the necessary parts and sold them as a kit—in this work you always hope for the best. My first call revealed that DBAG had long ago issued parts and instructions for this repair. Sure enough, in the shop manual in the back of the car was a description with diagrams of the steps necessary to make the repair. The part, called "new

Replacement repair piece and bottom cup, assembled, being held in place. Actual position for welding is supposed to be determined by factory jig, but this wasn't available, so we determined position by comparison to other side of car. Small variations in orientation of parts will not affect car's handling.

We checked position of cup to make sure it would allow bolting on trailing arm. It did, and here arm is supported by jack while two tack welds maintain correct position of parts.

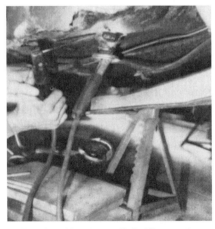

With tack welds temporarily holding repair part in position, the trailing arm was lowered and welding completed. During welding, a sheet of aluminum was used to shield fuel line near welded area.

Competed repair; position matches other side of car.

Welding completed, arm was bolted up to check position then lowered and welding area cleaned and coated to prevent corrosion. Welding burned protective plating off repair part and, of course, cup stub that we welded on had no protection.

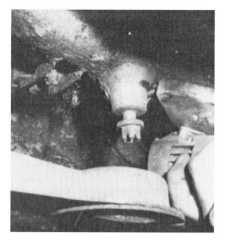

Because mounting was so deteriorated on left side of car, right side was suspect. When right trailing arm was lowered, its chassis mounting cup appeared sound from outside. Unfortunately, corrosion can attack from inside, so to be sure of the cup's integrity, cut it open and look. Drilling inspection holes and welding them shut won't work here because you can't see enough. Right-side cup is being cut off with small electric grinder. Naturally, this cup was perfect, with factory primer still on its inside. When you have to do such destructive inspection, you almost wish the results would indicate that repair is necessary, but that wasn't the case here.

lower section of step bearing" and numbered 120 350 06 33, was ordered and arrived.

Even the smallest gun for our wire-feed welder was too bulky to easily reach the area to be welded. Access is limited, and lack of headroom makes it difficult to see what you are doing. Stick welding with a bent stick turned out to be best. We used a 7011 rod, and tried both DCEP (direct current, electrode positive) and AC. Surprisingly, the AC worked best because it required us to fuse a lot of material off the edge of the new piece. Usually our welder's DC feature produces a better arc for out-of-position welding than the AC option.

The repair part, well thought-out as a permanent repair, is relatively easy to install and substantial enough that it

is doubtful that the problem will recur. Corrosion-proofing the repair, with periodic inspection and maintenance, should guarantee the repair's integrity for as long as humans are inclined to collect and nurture obsolete vehicles.

This neat repair part saves fumbling around with ad hoc kitchen table hardware that probably wouldn't work very well—or last very long even if it did work. If you encounter a problem on a car that seems likely to be common, see how others have dealt with it earlier. You will often find solutions far better than anything you could devise on your own. This saves your creative energy for problems requiring real inventiveness and avoids wasting it on problems solved long ago by others. Of course, there are bad aftermarket solutions to automotive problems, so when you

find repair parts and technology, you may not have found something usable or desirable. Look at after-the-fact solutions individually and evaluate them on their own merits.

Matt Joseph is a contributing editor to Skinned Knuckles *magazine, from which this article was adapted. To subscribe, contact Skinned Knuckles Publications in Monrovia, CA.*

Restorer John Grm, Jr., Comments

An alternative repair method is to weld the new cups to a new section of floor panel, as the old floor may also be weakened by rust. To do so, you'll fabricate a new floor panel section, weld the new cup to it, then fit it to the old floor using a simple jig plate. First, establish the position of the old cups by measuring between them and finding the center point; according to factory dimensions, the center of the new mount should be 21-7/8 inches (555 mm) from the center of the chassis. Measure from the front axle to the old cup to establish the proper front/rear position; the center

of the mount should be 19-7/8 inches (505 mm) forward of the center of the rear wheel (measuring horizontally). After establishing these dimensions, remove the old cup and sandblast the area to get it as clean as possible.

As a jig, attach a plate to the old floor panel with two small bolts, then determine the correct position for the cup and drill a 1/4-in hole through the plate and floor at that point. Then remove as much of the old floor as is necessary (without disturbing the jig, of course). After the cup is welded onto the new floor panel, use the hole in

the jig plate to locate the new cup and floor panel properly, then shape and weld the new panel into position and remove the jig plate.

For rust-proofing, apply a chromate primer. Use a spring compressor to compress the rear springs when loosening the trailing arms. Remove the interior near the welds, and take off the fuel lines and the fuel tank. There have been cases where tanks were left on and fumes from the tank's overflow line were ignited by welding. Removing the tank and lines takes longer than just blocking the overflow, but it is much safer.

Front End

by Frank King,
Technical Editor

*May/June
1986*

Your car's front suspension and steering mechanism are critical to proper control, comfort and roadholding. Here's a basic primer on a frequently mysterious subject.

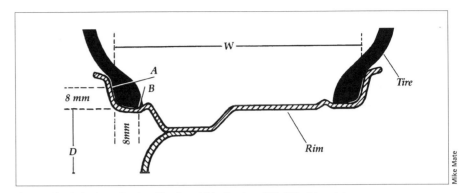

Fig. 1. Wheel Rim Cross Section: Tire fits within the rim width (W); A is point for measuring width and lateral runout; B is point for measuring diameter and vertical runout; D is wheel diameter.

Front End

In automotive parlance, "front end" is understood to include the front wheels, front suspension and steering mechanism. Front-drive cars include drive mechanism, too, but for now we won't concern ourselves with that. Most drivers' interest in the front end stops at turning the steering wheel left to go left, right to go right. If the wheel is released, the car should go straight, but in the contrary way of things, it seldom does. The average driver takes an interest in the front end when the car wants to go either left or right on its own whim, when a rhythmic bouncing or vibration sets in, or when his front tires wear strangely.

To the casual eye the front end of today's car seems little changed from that of a 1901 Mercedes. Tires are fatter, wheels smaller, and the assembly is pretty well covered by bodywork. But the simple rigid axle with wheels mounted on each end has disappeared, replaced by independent suspension at each wheel. Independent suspension improves ride quality, control and roadholding but has brought its own problems. Front end design has been the subject of continual evolutionary change since the days of "knee action" and the need to periodically lubricate 30 or 40 points.

The term "front end" is usually thought to include everything from road surface to steering box. This article addresses the components involved in "front end alignment"; tires will be covered in a future article.

Wheels

Traditionally a wheel consists of a hub, a rim and the disk or spokes connecting them. Since the demise of quick demountable rims and wood-spoked artillery wheels, the rim and disk have usually been a single unit or fixed assembly on the car. Today we loosely use the terms wheel and rim interchangeably to designate the part on which the tire is mounted and which is attached to the hub by the lug bolts. The brake disk is bolted to the hub, and the assembly is mounted on the steering knuckle by means of two tapered roller bearings and a clamping nut.

The front wheel assembly's design provides for proportional distribution of the car's weight on the bearings, i.e., the centerline of the tire and wheel passes through that point between the bearings where the load-carrying capacity of the two bearings is balanced.

The location of the centerline of the tire and wheel with respect to the bearings is described as wheel offset, the distance between the centerline of the wheel and the contact surface of the hub (Fig 2). When the car moves in a straight line, bearing loads are balanced. On curves or rough roads there will be brief periods of imbalance, but these can be tolerated. If wheels of the wrong offset are used, there will be a constant imbalance

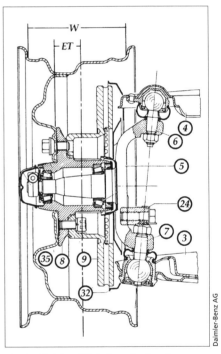

Fig. 2. Wheel and Hub Cross Section: Lower control arm (3); upper control arm (4); steering knuckle (5); guide joint (6); supporting joint (7); front wheel hub (8); brake disc (9); steering knuckle arm (24); cover plate (32); wheel (35). ET indicates wheel offset.

of load on the bearings, which can shorten their life. Wheels with the wrong offset have other harmful effects on front wheel alignment, which could be beyond the range of correction by normal adjustments.

All Mercedes-Benz 14-inch wheels since 1963 had the same 30-mm offset until the introduction of the 1984 190D 2.2 and 190E 2.3, which use a 50-

mm offset. Starting with January 1985 production, the 190D 2.2 and 190E 2.3 had 15-in wheels with a 49-mm offset. These 15-in wheels are interchangeable with the 14-in wheels of these models only. Having a 44-mm offset, 190E 2.3-16 wheels are different from all others in the 190 series and are not interchangeable with any other car.

Wheels for the 1986 W107 (560SL) and W126 (300SDL, 420SEL, 560SEL, 560SEC), with a 25-mm offset, are different from any others and non-interchangeable. Wheels of the W124 (300E and new 300D) cars have a 49-mm offset and are not interchangeable with other series. (Note: While some interchanges may be physically possible, and there is no doubt some design tolerance, the interchange information above is based upon DBAG/MBNA recommendations. If you replace your wheels with either Mercedes-Benz or aftermarket wheels, offset can be checked as per Fig 2).

Wheels must be round and true, but their nature dictates greater tolerances than we expect in engine parts. DBAG specifies that steel or alloy wheels have no more than 1.0-mm vertical (radial) runout and no more than 1.5-mm lateral (axial) runout. Forged wheels must be within 0.6 mm vertically and 1.0 mm laterally. In plain words, vertical runout is "out of round," and lateral runout is "wobble." Except for steel wheels, where lateral runout can be measured at the edge of the rim, wheel runout should be measured without a tire mounted. Alloy wheels are machined on the inside so should not be measured on the outside. DBAG also specifies that runout of mounted tires should not exceed 1.2 mm vertically and 2.0 mm laterally.

Front wheels each mount to a steering knuckle, which is fastened at the bottom to the lower control arm (A-arm or wishbone) and at the top to either an upper control arm or a damper strut (shock absorber strut). The axis around which the steering knuckle rotates is the kingpin, a word carried over from the days when the steering knuckle actually turned on a steel bar or pin. Since the introduction of ball joints, which offer more degrees of freedom, the kingpin is purely a geometric concept—the straight line extending from the lower ball joint to the upper ball joint or the upper support of the damper strut —and is often called the steering axis.

Your car's steering behavior depends on the proper interaction of these front end elements. Let's consider the adjustments and variables in a sequence of checking and correction.

Chassis Leveling

During a front end check, it is usually assumed that the remainder of its structure is literally in good shape. When the car is relatively new and has not been in a collision, this is reasonable. Proper front end alignment requires that the chassis be in correct relation to the road. If you follow the alignment procedure and it is impossible to adjust to normal values, or if the car misbehaves after the specified values are reached, check the chassis measurements. If they are out of tolerance, the chassis may have to be straightened or other adjustments may have to be made.

Proper loading of your car is essential preparation for front end alignment. The fuel tank should be full, the spare tire and all normally carried tools in the trunk and the tires inflated properly.

The following description of front wheel alignment includes reasons for the adjustments. This is not a do-it-yourself guide but rather a help in understanding the process.

Toe-In

Toe-in, the condition in which the front wheels turn in toward each other, is measured in two ways, 1) as the angle formed by projection of the wheel centerline in degrees and minutes and 2) as the difference in distances between the forward and rear edges of the rims at hub level in mm. The measurement is properly made with a 20- to 25-lb force applied to spread the wheels in front. The force is necessary because rubber bushings and plastic ball joints in a modern front end are somewhat flexible. Steering gear must be in the straight-ahead position, precisely achieved by inserting the center position control screw in the closing plug hole of the steering gear housing to locate the power piston. Toe-in is adjusted by shortening or lengthening the track rods (tie-rods).

Because of various bending and friction forces when the car is moving, toe-in goes to zero. On Mercedes-Benz cars, static toe-in ranges from 2 to 3 mm ±1 mm or 0° 20' to 0° 30' ±10', depending on the model. Nominal values should be the goal. Too much or too little toe-in results in excessive wear of the inner or outer edge of tire tread, with edges of tread blocks appearing ragged or feathery.

Camber

Camber is the angle that the centerline of the wheel makes with the vertical when viewed from directly in front of the wheel. In the days of solid front axles, a marked degree of positive camber was used, the tops of the front wheels leaning outward. The word camber originally meant "arched," describing roads that are higher in the center than at the edges. The original reasons for tilting the wheels outward are obscure but may have been an attempt to keep the wheels perpendicular to the road surface (which assumes that everyone drove in the middle of the road...). Another theory is that positive camber placed more of the car's weight on the inside wheel bearing, which was stronger and mounted on the thicker and stronger part of the spindle of the steering knuckle.

Straight-line stability is also affected by camber. As a demonstration of the effect of camber, lay a styrofoam cup on its side and roll it. The cup rolls in an arc, of course. Given enough camber, your tires will have a smaller diameter on one side than the other, with similar results. Whatever the reason for positive camber, it is no longer applicable. Mercedes-Benz models of the 1950's and 1960's use a positive camber of no more than 0° 30'. Models of the 1970's and 1980's use zero camber or no more than 0° 20' positive. The 190E 2.3-16 uses 0° 20' negative camber.

Caster

Caster is the angle that the kingpin leans from the vertical as viewed from the side of the car. When the kingpin leans toward the rear of the car, caster is positive. A familiar example of positive caster is the front wheel of a bicycle. Positive caster gives a trailing effect to the wheel, as the kingpin axis (steering axis) intersects the road ahead of the center of the tire-road contact patch.

Positive caster is one of the most important factors contributing to stable, straight-ahead driving, but since positive caster makes the wheels harder to turn, a compromise must be made. Although it would be possible to increase the assistance of power steering to decrease your steering effort, road feel would be lost under such conditions.

On some models an additional caster effect called caster offset is used, locating the spindle ahead of the kingpin, which reduces the amount of trail. Caster offset is built into the design and is not adjustable.

It's important to note that in Mercedes-Benz front ends, any adjustment to caster affects camber, and vice-versa. Before the W116 series in 1974, Mercedes-Benz front ends used caster in the range of 2° 15' to 3° 40' with no caster offset. In the W116 and subsequent series, the caster ranges from 8° 45' to 10° 30' positive with some negative caster offset.

Kingpin Inclination

Kingpin inclination is the inward leaning of the kingpin across the car, measured as the angle the kingpin axis makes with the vertical when viewed from in front of the car. It is built into the design. Kingpin inclination positions the point where the kingpin axis meets the road in relation to the centerline of the tire-road contact patch. The distance between this point and this line is called kingpin offset (or steering offset or scrub radius).

Designed into the front end, kingpin offset is the result of kingpin inclination, hub dimensions, spindle dimensions and wheel offset. Kingpin offset is positive when the centerline of the wheel is outboard of the kingpin axis, negative when it is inboard and zero when they coincide. See Figs. 3 to 5.

Mercedes-Benz cars had positive kingpin offset until introduction of the W 116 series in 1974. Zero-offset steering was introduced on those cars and used on the W123 and W126 cars. On the W201 and W124's, a slight negative kingpin offset is used. It is important to differentiate between kingpin inclination (the relation between the kingpin and the wheel) and camber (the relation of wheel to frame and hence to road). Both refer to leaning across the car, but only camber can be adjusted.

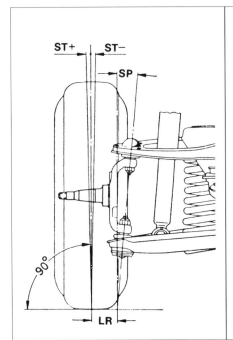 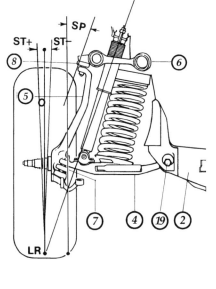 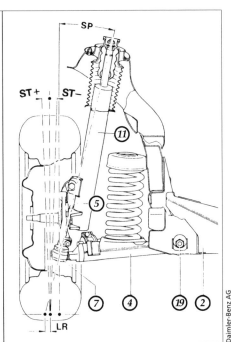

Fig. 3. W107, W114 and W115 Front Suspension: camber (ST); kingpin inclination (SP); kingpin offset (LR). To match workshop manuals, German abbreviations and corresponding numbers are used here.

Fig. 4. W116 and W126 Front Suspension: camber, etc. designated as in Fig. 3. Frame cross member (2); lower control arm (4); steering knuckle (5); upper control arm (6); supporting joint (7); guide joint (8); camber adjustment bolt (19).

Fig. 5. W201 and W124 Front Suspension: camber, etc. designated as in Fig. 3. Frame cross member (2); wishbone (4); steering knuckle (5); supporting ball joint (7); damper strut (11); camber adjustment bolt (19).

Caster has the effect of causing the car to run straight because the tire contact patch trails behind the intersection of the steering axis and the road. Kingpin inclination also tends to keep the wheels pointed straight and causes them to return to straight after being turned to steer. This is the result of the kingpin axis. When the wheels are straight, the front end is closest to the road. Turning the steering wheel actually raises the front end slightly. When you release the steering wheel, gravity pulls the front end down, which straightens the wheels.

Comfort and Roadholding

Roadholding is the ability of a car to go where you intend, along the path you choose, under reasonable circumstances. In our cars, used for all types of driving, these circumstances include comfort. Every Mercedes-Benz is designed to provide a balance of roadholding and comfort consistent with its perceived purpose. Front end design is one of the most important elements in the total concept. To obtain the widest enjoyment of your car, maintain the front end to factory specifications. These specifications have been established after careful analysis and extended trials, with the basic mission of the car the constant objective.

The front end should be aligned to the factory's nominal values. Tolerances, plus or minus, are only for checking to determine the need for re-alignment. Given anything resembling normal use, it is a mistake to deliberately stray from factory values to try to improve certain characteristics. Since all elements interact, the result will harm overall performance.

When should front end alignment be checked? A new car is assumed to be in proper adjustment. At about 800–1,000 mi, front wheel bearings must be adjusted for correct end play, but no other adjustments should be necessary unless there is unusual tire wear or abnormal steering behavior. At each 15,000-mile service the steering, tires and all maintenance-free joints of the front end should be checked for looseness, damage or excessive wear. At 30,000-mi intervals toe-in should be checked and front wheel bearing hub caps repacked with roller bearing grease.

A full-scale front end alignment is required only in cases of accidental damage, aberrant steering behavior or excessive wear. It is comforting, though, to check alignment after 50,000 to 60,000 miles to confirm that all is well.

Need New Shocks?

by Frank King,
Technical Editor

*September/October
1993*

When you drive into a tire store for new tires, or if you complain to your regular service shop that the car doesn't ride as well as it used to, you may be told that you need new shocks. How reliable is such an off-the-cuff diagnosis?

Shock absorbers are actually energy converters which convert kinetic energy to thermal energy. The kinetic energy is generated by movement of the mass of the unsprung weight of tires, wheels, and running gear relative to the mass of the rest of the vehicle and its load. The thermal energy takes the form of heat in the oil inside the shock. This heat is transferred to air blowing by the shock.

When the car is driven over a bump, the impact is taken by the tires and springs and the shocks. The springs deliver some of this energy back in the form of rebounding, which is also absorbed by the shocks. If the shocks are unable to handle their job, safety and comfort are impaired.

All Mercedes-Benz cars since 1946 have been equipped with gas-pressure shock absorbers (Figure 1). In these shocks the working tube is exposed to the air. The piston rod is shielded from dirt by a plastic protective tube.

With this type of shock it is normal for a little oil to be carried past the seal by the piston rod. This oil then seeps down the working tube and collects dust. Oil on the outside of the tube may be mistakenly thought to be a sign of excessive wear in the shock. Only if the amount of oil is sufficient to run down to the end of the tube or other signs of trouble exist should the shocks be suspected of being defective.

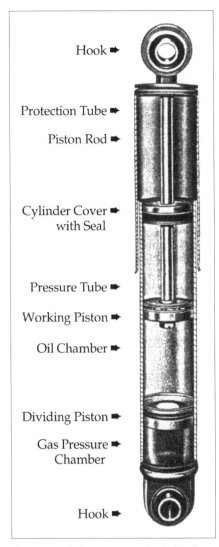

Hook ➡

Protection Tube ➡

Piston Rod ➡

Cylinder Cover ➡
with Seal

Pressure Tube ➡

Working Piston ➡

Oil Chamber ➡

Dividing Piston ➡

Gas Pressure ➡
Chamber

Hook ➡

Figure 1. Typical gas-pressure shock absorber actually uses oil and gas.

The number of miles driven with the shocks is of little value in evaluating their condition. Climate, road conditions, and driving habits vary so widely that no arbitrary figure can be assigned as a minimum or maximum mileage to be expected. If driving is confined to paved roads and no excessively corrosive conditions are encountered, 100,000 miles for original equipment shocks would not be unusual.

A reliable diagnosis of the condition of the shocks can be made only by checking the following six points (see Figure 2):

1. **The rocking-horse effect.** Upon hard braking, the nose of the car dives, and the rear rises rather alarmingly. If the car has been brought to a standstill, it will seesaw like a rocking-horse as it comes to rest. The seesawing is a strong indication that new shocks are needed. This condition leads to longer braking distances.

2. **Swaying body and/or bottoming of springs.** With increasing wear of the shocks, the car body will sway from side to side, producing a very uncomfortable ride in spite of the increasing softness of the springing. Such wear also leads to bottoming of the springs, especially when the rear of the car is more heavily loaded than usual.

3. **Oil on the shock or physical damage to it.** This can only be seen from under the car or with the wheels dismounted. Oil on the shock indicates trouble only when it is sufficient to run down the outside of the working tube. The working tube should also be examined for dents which might have been caused by a rock or other road obstacle. Of course, deep or extensive rusting must be taken seriously.

4. **Uneven tire wear.** Particularly on the driven wheels, this may be due to undamped wheel vibrations, the result of defective shocks. Flat spots are formed on the tires which even an untrained eye can recognize as out-of-round.

5. **Bouncing wheels and vibrating steering.** Bouncing is most readily noticed from a following car. Even on a slightly rough road, the wheels will momentarily lose contact with the road, producing a steering vibration which can be felt in the steering wheel.

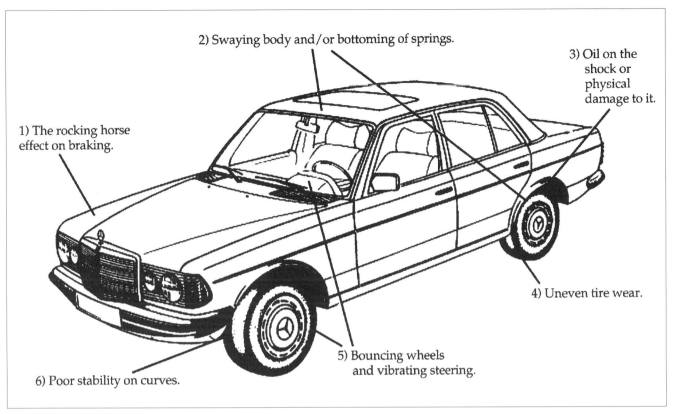

2) Swaying body and/or bottoming of springs.

3) Oil on the shock or physical damage to it.

1) The rocking horse effect on braking.

4) Uneven tire wear.

5) Bouncing wheels and vibrating steering.

6) Poor stability on curves.

Fig. 2. Check these six points for reliable diagnosis of the condition of the shocks on your car.

6. Poor stability in curves. Particularly on rougher roads, the car fails to follow the direction of the wheels and bounces toward the outside of the curve. The condition worsens if the brakes are applied in the curve. The car will also lean outward abnormally.

All of these conditions must be judged in relation to a similar vehicle in first-class condition. For example, all cars dive at the front to some degree but will recover without the rocking-horse effect. An excess of any of these conditions warns that the shocks are worn. Incidentally, the old test in which each corner of the car is given a hard jounce by hands on the bumper in an attempt to simulate the natural spring-rate frequency is of extremely limited value.

Of course, precise tests can be run on testing machines, but the shocks must be removed, and the equipment is found in very few shops. Replacement is more certain and probably least costly in the long run.

Replacing W210 E-Class Front Shocks

by Jim Mahaffey, Contributing Editor

March/April 2004

Photos in this article by the author.

It's easy—if you've got the right tool.

Front shocks don't live forever. My W210-bodied E300 Diesel's shocks required attention. The W210's shock mountings—and those of the W170, W202, and W208—differ from those of earlier bodies. To remove the top (piston-end) of the shock in the engine compartment, we can no longer use two wrenches, one holding the piston-rod and one turning the nut. There is no room to swing a wrench, and the narrow, vertical space above the shock is surrounded by fragile systems, such as the cruise control linkage on the left and heater valves on the right.

Mercedes-Benz solves the clearance problem by offering a special tool: socket wrench, part 202 589 00 09 00, built specifically for this task and priced as jewelry. Examining one, I was delighted to find that it is built using a tool found in the trunk of every new Mercedes-Benz—the spark plug wrench in the tool-roll.

The tool in Photo 1, part 123 581 00 67, is not very inspiring as a spark plug wrench. It's a piece of steel pipe, formed hexagonally at the ends, with holes punched into the sides, through which you insert a screwdriver to turn it. The shock-absorber wrench is the same but has a lug welded to the side for connecting a torque-handle. A special socket down the center of the pipe connects to the end of the piston-rod and holds it still while you turn the wrench on the holding nut. The special tool still has the screwdriver holes, uselessly punched in the sides.

It's easy to build your own special shock absorber wrench to make

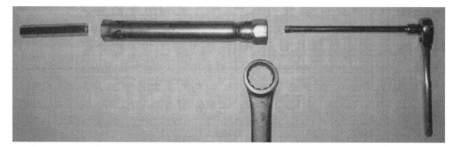

Photo 1. Exploded view of shock-absorber tool shows Lisle stem-socket, spark plug tool, 5-in extension, 1/4-in ratchet handle, and 25-mm box-end wrench.

Photo 2. Built-up tool in position over front shock absorber for removal or installation.

changing shocks an easy, 10-minute exercise. Buy a Lisle Shock Absorber Tool, no. 20400, made by the Lisle Corp. in Clarinda, Iowa, and available at most Pep Boys stores for about $11. The tool consists of one "shock nut socket" and two "stem-sockets." The intent is to drive the nut holding the stem with the nut-socket, and hold the stem still with the stem-socket, but the tool is far too short to fit the crowded corridor in a recent Mercedes-Benz, and the nut-socket size is incorrect.

Get the stem-socket with a 5-mm socket on one end and a 1/4-in socket on the other. Feed a 5-in socket-wrench extension (1/4-in drive) through the

big end (21 mm) of the pipe, and snap on the 1/4-in end of the stem-socket through the small end (17 mm). Snap the other end of the extension onto a 1/4-in socket handle. Grip the big end with a 25-mm box-end wrench, and you've got the tool. The 5-mm end of the stem-socket slips over the piston rod, and you hold it still with the 1/4-in socket handle while you turn the box-end wrench. The 17-mm end fits the nut to be removed.

The socket sizes of the plug wrench (Photo 2) in the tool-roll can vary. Some have a 16-mm, and you need the 17-mm socket. If you lack the 17-mm socket on the pipe, buy one at

Photo 3. When installing Bilstein lower hub into suspension arm, use alignment tool to center hole for bolt.

a hardware store. Once you have the tool, follow these steps to replace a shock absorber:

Step 1. Open the hood, and position the tool over the shock-absorber end that sticks through the fender skirt. Hold the piston rod still with the socket handle while turning the box-end wrench counterclockwise, removing the 17-mm self-locking nut. (Some installations use two 17-mm plain nuts, jammed together. In this case, remove both nuts individually.)

Step 2. Remove the steel washer, then the rubber donut. You may have to pry out the donut with a bladed screwdriver, as they can stick to the steel after long use. Install the skirted rubber donut, as supplied, over the piston rod on the new shock absorber.

Step 3. Jack up the car and remove the wheel. Turn the hub outward slightly.

Step 4. With a 17-mm box-end on one side and a 17-mm socket on the other side, remove the bolt holding the end of the shock absorber in the wishbone. Pull the shock absorber out toward the front of the car.

Step 5. Feed the top of the new shock absorber through the hole in the fender skirt, then guide the bottom of it into position on the wishbone. The hub fits snugly because it has new rubber, so you may need help lining up the holes for the bolt. Use a conical alignment tool or "tapered punch," also available at the hardware store.

Step 6. Replace the bolt and self-locking nut holding the end of the shock absorber in the wishbone (see Photo 3), using the new hardware provided. Specified torque is 55 Nm. Replace the wheel, and lower the jack.

Step 7. Feed the new rubber and washer over the piston-rod end, and start the nut. Run the nut down using the special tool, with the top socket-wrench ratchet reversed. Specified torque is 19 Nm, but you are compressing a new piece of rubber, and the force on the wrench is hardly smooth.

That's it. You have replaced a shock absorber, and you've made good use of a tool.

Replacing Sub-Frame Mounts

by Fred Vetter,
Vintage
Committee

*January/February
1991*

Sub-frame mounts work with engine mounts to isolate the chassis from shock and vibration. Here's how you can diagnose and fix failed mounts.

As my buddy Clarence slid the floor jack under the front of my 1966 250SE Coupe, he muttered, "You put the jack right under the oil pan, right?" "Try the hump a little further back," I replied. We were still funning, with nothing more in mind than changing a tie rod end. But when the jack went down, the garage got awfully quiet.

As Clarence released the jack and the front wheels hit the floor, the entire engine suddenly rose as if coming up out of a hole in the floor! It rose so far that I thought it'd keep on going! How in blazes had we managed to unhinge the whole damn engine? Well, we hadn't unhinged anything. We'd witnessed a classic symptom of massive (both sides) failure of the sub-frame mounts. Since such failures have major engine damage and safety implications, here's how to determine whether you have the problem and how to change the mounts.

Background

The magnificent six-cylinder engines of 1960–71 (108, 111, 113 etc.) cars are supported by two main rubber-sandwiched-between-steel engine mounts low on the left and right, midway back on the engine. The mounts are fastened not to the chassis but to the sub-frame carrying the front suspension. A third drivetrain mount attaches to the chassis behind the transmission.

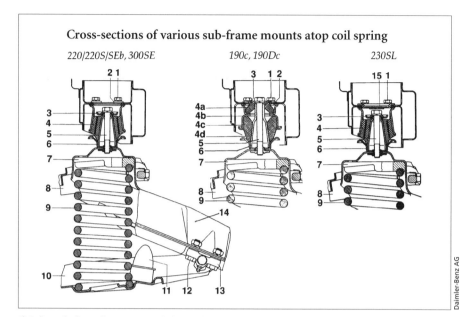

Cross-sections of various sub-frame mounts atop coil spring

220/220S/SEb, 300SE   190c, 190Dc   230SL

Daimler-Benz AG

1) Bolts w/lock washers secure sub-frame mounts, 2) washers, 3) stop plate, 4) sub-frame mount, 4a) top rubber mount, 4b) step bearing, 4c) bottom rubber mount, 4d) support tube, 5) center bolt fastens sub-frame to mount, 6) cup for mount, 7) rubber spring mount, 8) upper control arm, 9) spring, 10) lower control arm, 11) rubber buffer, 12) control arm mounting bolts, 13) pivot for control arm, 14) sub-frame, 15) stop.

The mounts, between chassis and sub-frame, help to hold the sub-frame in place. The engine and sub-frame mounts prevent road shock and engine vibration from reaching passengers. If sub-frame mounts fail, and many cars of this vintage could have at least a partial failure, the engine could move, stressing the whole drivetrain. Such failures account for torn-loose radiator hoses, fan blade collisions with the radiator, suspension noise, vibration, etc.

Have Mine Failed?

Failed sub-frame mounts are a frequent reason for a loose-feeling front end on older cars—or why they often droop a couple of inches in front. Subtly, the usual failure leaves the mount looking OK, comfortably squeezed between the chassis and sub-frames. You can't see the separated metal and rubber when the car sets normally on its wheels. Unless

seriously failed, the mounts do their job—until your front wheels abruptly drop into a pothole, or a hump in the road makes the front end momentarily lift, then come down hard.

If you hear a heavy thunk under such conditions, or a metal-to-metal clang on a good bump or on a washboard road that bounces your front end rapidly, the rubber has collapsed enough to allow the sub-frame to hit the chassis, and you badly need new sub-frame mounts. Engine mount failure is also caused by the force of an engine wanting to drop with the sub-frame yet being held up by hoses, wires, and rods that give only so much.

Checking the Mounts

The mounts are in a recess under the chassis, on top of the sub-frame; their tops can be seen about halfway back in the engine compartment's left and right sides. On the left, take

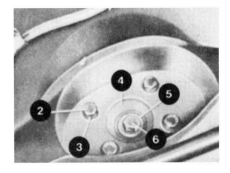

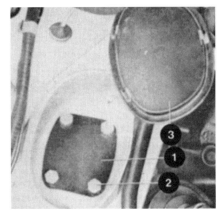

Top view of sub-frame mounts and cover. Top photo: 2) bolts w/lock washers, 3) washers, 4) rubber mount, 5) stop plate, 6) center bolt w/lock washer. Bottom photo: 1) stop, 2) mounting bolts w/lock washers, 3) cover.

Sub-frame mount failed unit at left shows separated rubber and metal; normal unit at right

out the battery case to see the top of the mount in its cozy pocket. On the right, you'll likely find a black plastic oval cap over four bolts at the top flange and the main (center) sub-frame suspension bolt. It's just below and outboard of the intake manifold and cold-start valve on fuel-injected models, outboard of the carburetors on others.

Now comes the jack test. Put your floor jack under the curved crossmember of the sub-frame behind the oil pan. Chock the rear wheels, put the car in gear, and get that parking brake full on. Raise the car and install jackstands under the chassis just behind the front wheel wells. The front wheels must be 4–6 inches off the ground. With the stands in place, lower the jack 3–4 inches so that it partially supports the car. Check the car's stability. You can't do this on an ordinary drive-on lift, but a chassis lift that lets the wheels drop is great.

Access in the wheel wells is easier if you remove the wheels, but it's not

essential. Find the lower part of the sub-frame mounts. If it looks like the right photo, there's no separation. If you can see the metal tube, as in the left photo, the rubber/metal bond is broken. If the mount is no longer cone-shaped, it has collapsed. I've had a new pair separate in 2,000 miles although I recall no incident that may have caused it.

Replacing the Mounts

The part number for a sub-frame mount kit for my 1966 250SE Coupe was 108 586 00 33; other models differ. You'll need a friendly hand at one point, but the rest is easy. You don't have to drop the whole front end

or change the alignment. Clarence and I began by scratching our heads and making clucking noises for five minutes. I clucked loudest 'cause it was my car. Neither of us had done this job before but have now done it often enough to lead you through it.

Support the sub-frame with light jack pressure on the crossmember as mentioned earlier. Before serious jacking, remove the battery, its base and the cover over the mount (easier with the car lower). Remove the four top corner bolts and the main bolt running through the mount and into the top recess of the spring (new bolts come with the kit). This frees the mounts for removal, which may seem

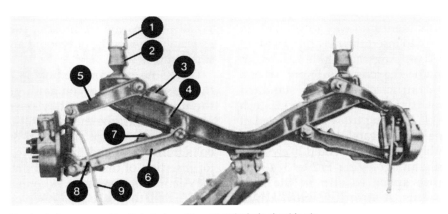

Front sub-frame assembly: Note jack position. Parts include 1) guide pin, 2) sub-frame mount, 3) engine mount, 4) front axle support, 5) upper control arm, 6) lower control arm, 7) rubber buffer, 8) steering knuckle, 9) brake hose.

a puzzle; it looks as if there's no way, but there is.

Remove the wheels, and get the front of the car up and steady. You'll need rags, a can, and two brake line caps (the round rubber caps on the bleed valves of the brake calipers are perfect). Disconnect both front brake hoses (the flex lines) at the top end, and cap the metal brake line with the rubber caps. You'll have to add fluid to the master cylinder and bleed the brakes later, but you'll tear the hoses if you don't disconnect them.

Move each upper and lower control arm downward as far as possible. Installing new mounts takes more room than removing the old ones, which have probably broken into two pieces. To make room, disconnect the bottom of both shocks (two bolts) and disconnect the engine torque damper; it looks like a skinny shock at the extreme front, right of center on the sub-frame. Take the nut off the bottom and pop it loose.

If you can't lower the control arms and tilt the sub-frame enough to get the new mounts in, you may have to remove the tie rod end. Sometimes tie rod ends drop easily. Remove the cotter pin, run the nut out flush with the end of the tapered bolt, and with a piece of hard wood and a heavy hammer, swat the tie rod bolt downward. It will help (and save replacing the rubber boot usually damaged by a removal fork), if you make a notched 2x4 the right length to support the steering arm (from the wheel), to which the tie rod is attached. The support reduces the shock when hitting the tie rod bolt.

Here's the gimmick. You may think there's no way to get enough space to insert the new mounts short of dropping the whole front end. You need a long, sturdy pry bar or a hydraulic spreader; a standard crowbar won't cut it. I use a 1.25-inch thick, 5-ft long truck axle, pointed at one end. Be careful, you don't want to bend the Benz!

You'll likely need only an agonizing 1/2- to 3/4-inch more space to slip in the new mounts. A strong downward pry near the sub-frame pocket does it. While you provide the muscle, your assistant removes the old mount and slips in the new.

There's no plate on the bottom of the new mounts, so you can't get them in wrong. Once they're in, remove the bar; the mounts will be loose enough to turn and insert the bolts from above and line up things for insertion of the center bolt once the A-arm comes up a bit. Reconnect things, refill the brake fluid reservoir, bleed the brakes, and hang on the wheels. Notice how differently the engine moves as you lower the jack. Check your engine mounts, including the one at the rear of the transmission; it's easy while you're there.

That's it. You've solved the sub-frame mount mystery. If you keep the ol' doll for any substantial time, you may get to do this job again. When those sub-frame mounts have had the cure, your Mercedes-Benz will show you exactly how it's supposed to look and feel.

Oversteer and Understeer in Normal Driving

by Frank King,
Technical Editor

*May/June
1991*

You'll encounter the words "oversteer" and "understeer" in almost every automotive magazine road test. Usually a car is said to show moderate understeer until near the limit in curves, where it changes to oversteer. The impression is that these terms are relevant only at speeds far above normal, but this isn't necessarily so. Here our purpose is to explain oversteer and understeer, the factors that determine when they occur, and their effects on normal driving. Competition driving is another topic altogether, although anyone interested in such can pick up some hints from the following!

We frequently hear that ABS brakes don't "repeal the laws of physics," and this is equally true of everything in our natural experience. The particular laws referred to are those known as Newton's laws of motion. Part of Newton's genius lay in reducing concepts to words; simply stated, his three laws of motion are:

1. A body acted upon by no net force continues in its state of rest or of uniform motion in a straight line.

2. Change of motion is proportional to the applied force and takes place in the direction of the straight line in which that force is applied.

3. Every action (force) is accompanied by an equal and opposite reaction (force).

Cornering Force

Oversteer and understeer are types of behavior exhibited by an automobile when it travels a curve or is subjected to side forces. Your car is controlled by friction with the road. It accelerates, brakes, turns, and maintains a straight course through the friction of its tires with the road. The tire is the dominant factor, so we will examine how a tire is able to turn a car by exerting a side force on the wheel, turning the car onto the desired curving course, and holding it there.

Consider a car traveling in a straight line on a flat road with each front wheel toeing inward at an angle of one degree (no modern Mercedes-Benz in proper adjustment would have so much toe-in; this is just for illustration). Each wheel exerts an inward thrust of a magnitude depending on the load on the tire, its inflation pressure, its design characteristics, the width of the wheel rim, the camber of the wheel, and the speed of travel. A wheel running with its center plane at an angle (however slight) to the direction of travel produces a force called its cornering force. The angle between the center plane of the wheel and the path actually traveled by the wheel is called its slip angle.

Up to a point, the slip angle can be accommodated by the tire, but as that point is exceeded, the tire tread can no longer maintain contact with

the road, and the tire skids. Driving on ice or snow, you may have had graphic but fearful experience with slip angles. If you turned the front wheels in one direction, but they slid straight on in another, their slip angles were extremely large. If the rear wheels skidded outward in a curve, their slip angles were also extreme.

These are the classical definitions of oversteer and understeer. Oversteer occurs when the slip angles of the rear wheels are larger than the slip angles of the front wheels. Conversely, understeer occurs when the front wheel slip angles are greater than the rear slip angles. When front and rear slip angles are equal, neutral steer occurs.

How Does It Feel?

The sensation that you feel in a car that understeers is one of stability under normal highway driving. Driving harder on a curving road, you feel that the steering wheel must be turned more into the curve than seems appropriate for the degree of curvature. If a curve is taken at too high a speed, the front wheels tend to plow, and the car continues almost straight ahead, eventually sliding off the road at a tangent.

The sensation that you feel in an oversteering car is one of instability and constant need for correction under normal highway driving. On a curving road you feel that the car turns with less movement of the steering

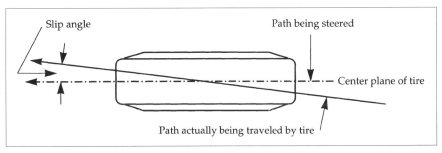

Figure I. Slip angle.

wheel than would be appropriate for the curve. At too high a speed, the rear wheels lose adhesion first, the rear end skids outward, and the car spins.

The usual reaction of a driver who feels his car begin to slide in a corner is to back off the throttle and steer into the corner, and he is safest doing this in an understeering car. Releasing the throttle can lighten the rear of the car and thus provoke oversteer at the limit, so passenger cars intended for normal highway use are designed to understeer slightly. Just how much understeer is chosen depends on safety considerations and the car manufacturer's perception of customer demand and skill.

Tires Are the Key

In meeting design criteria, tires are highly significant. For practical reasons a car must have virtually the same tires on all four wheels. Further, a car must be capable of operating with a considerable variation in weight distribution between front and rear wheels. Choices of tire size, inflation pressure, and rim width are influenced by certain oddities of tire behavior.

The relationship between wheel load, slip angle, and cornering force for a typical tire at a given inflation pressure is shown in Figure II. At any given slip angle the cornering force, or side thrust, rises with increasing load until a maximum is reached, after which it declines. Of course there is a different set of curves for each size of tire and inflation pressure, but in all cases the shape of the curves is similar. The effect of this tire characteristic is that size and pressure must be chosen so that under extreme cornering conditions, where there is a substantial dynamic transfer of load from inside to outside wheels, the load on the outside wheel will not fall far beyond the peak of the curve.

For example, in Figure II a load of 1,000 lb at a slip angle of five degrees (point A) gives a side thrust of 560 lbs. With no dynamic weight transfer this would give a total side thrust for two

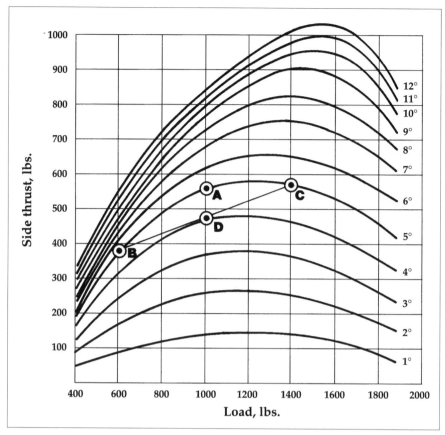

Figure II. Cornering force vs. tire load at various angles.

front wheels of 1,160 lbs. However, there will always be dynamic weight transfer as a car negotiates a curve. Assuming a transfer of 400 lbs from the inside to outside wheel, we get side thrusts of 380 lbs (point B) and 580 lbs (point C) for a total of 960 lbs, an average of 480 lbs per wheel (point D). Thus, to maintain the desired cornering force, the driver must increase his slip angle as speed (and weight transfer) increase. In this example, the slip angle would have to be increased to about six and one-half degrees.

The curves in Figure II apply to one particular tire at a certain inflation pressure. For different tires or inflation pressures the load and side thrust values will differ, but the shape of the curves will be similar in all cases. Because exceeding the optimum traction point means that traction will then decrease, it is always desirable to have tire and pressure be such that the tire operates on the rising portion

of the curve. The effect of inflation pressure on cornering power of a typical tire is shown in Figure III.

While it might appear that all that is necessary to attain any desired cornering power is to increase inflation pressure, there are other limiting factors. The contact area of the tire will decrease, ride will become intolerably hard, and the wheels will bounce so that road contact is lost for a considerable part of the time.

Other Factors

Many other factors affect cornering power and hence oversteer or understeer. A wheel leaning toward the center of curvature has higher cornering power than one that is vertical or leans away. Mercedes-Benz front wheels are usually designed to lean in by from -0°50' in the case of 129 models (wheels leaning in at the top are considered to have negative camber) to 0° on 126 models, with

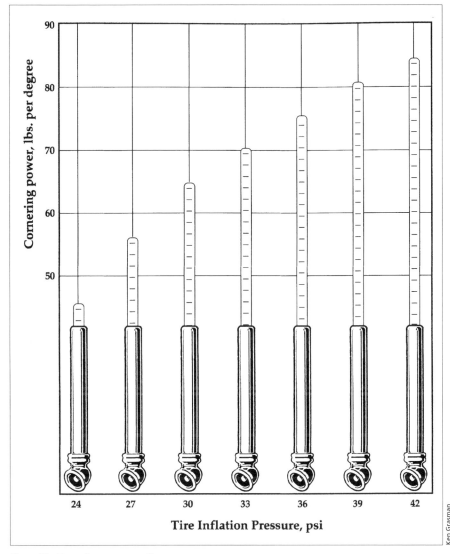

Figure III. Cornering power vs. tire pressure.

the car feels on the road? It all goes back to Newton's laws of motion. There is a term which is in wide popular use, usually with incomplete understanding, which should be cleared up here. It is "centrifugal force". Centrifugal force is a pseudo-outward force on an object rotating about an axis. The inward force required to keep an object moving in a circular path is called centripetal force. From Newton's first law we know that a body in uniform motion in a straight line continues that motion unless acted upon by a force. From his second and third laws we see that a body which follows a curved path does so only because of the centripetal force which pushes it from a straight line, and that the curve will be followed only as long as the centripetal force acts. Once the centripetal force ceases to act, the body will move in a straight line, tangent to the curve and not outwardly from the curve (think of the slingshot that David used against Goliath). It is the reaction to the centripetal force that the passengers in the car feel as their bodies try to move in a straight line but are constrained by the car.

Now let's look at what happens when a car that understeers enters a curve (Figure IV). You steer in the desired direction, producing a side thrust at the front wheels, turning the car onto a curved path. The car takes an attitude in which it points more sharply into the curve than would appear necessary, so that the rear wheels can take up a slip angle sufficient to provide the side thrust needed to hold the car on a curved path. Since this is an understeering car, the slip angle will be larger at the front wheels than at the rear, and you will feel that you are steering into the curve and the rear end is following. In Figure IV the line A-B is the centerline of the car, and C-D is the curved path which the car is following. E-F is the direction in which the car is traveling at a given instant (the tangent to the curve), and is the straight line which the car would travel if friction between tires and road were instantly removed.

other models having negative cambers between these values.

Rim width affects cornering power. The wider the rim on which a given tire is mounted, within reason, the greater its cornering power. Tire manufacturers specify a range of suitable rim widths for each tire size. For example, Pirelli recommends that a 205/70VR14 be mounted on 5-, 5.5-, 6-, 6.5-, or 7-inch rim. Mercedes-Benz uses 6.5-inch rims for these tires. Pirelli lists 5.5-, 6-, 6.5-, 7-, or 7.5-inch rims for 205/65VR15 tires, and Mercedes-Benz uses 7-inch rims. As always, there is a trade-off. Wider rims give a stiffer ride. It is interesting that in 1988 Mercedes-Benz

changed the 560SEL/SEC rims from 7- to 6.5-inch to get a more comfortable ride on US-version cars.

Other factors affecting cornering power are pretty much built into the car and not as readily accessible to change by the owner. They include suspension geometry, spring rates, anti-roll bars, and height of the car's center of gravity. Note that all of these factors affect the transfer of weight during cornering, which in turn affects tire behavior.

Centripetal Force

Just how does all of this translate into oversteer, understeer, and how

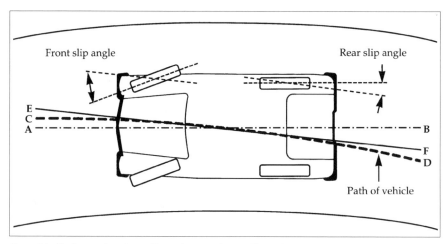

Figure IV. Understeering; front slip angle exceeds rear slip angle.

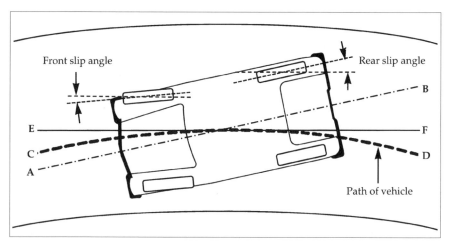

Figure V. Oversteering; rear slip angle exceeds front slip angle.

Now let's look at the oversteering car (Figure V). You steer in the desired direction, producing side thrust at the front wheels and turning the car onto a curved path. Since this is an oversteering car, the front wheels need less slip angle than the rear, but the attitude of the car must be brought farther into the curve so that the rear wheels can take up the necessary slip angle. The front wheels must be turned too far and then brought back to their proper slip angle at the exact moment the rear wheels reach their proper slip angle. When stability in the curve is reached, the front wheels will be at a smaller slip angle than the rear wheels. In this simple maneuver you feel that the rear end of the car wants to come around on the outside,

and, quite correctly, that this must be counteracted by steering toward the outside of the curve. This is how dirt-track racers drive, with tails hanging out and front wheels pointed outward.

On the Straight

The effects of oversteer and understeer are not limited to cornering, or following winding roads. An understeering car traveling a straight road will respond to a disturbing side force such as a gust of wind or a change in road camber by moving away from the force as shown in Figure VI. Since the car understeers, the front wheels have less cornering power than the rear, so the car turns away from the disturbing (centripetal) force into a curving path. Even before the driver

can respond, centrifugal force will partly counteract the disturbing force so that less corrective steering by the driver is needed. The driver senses only a need to turn the steering wheel toward the disturbing force. Most roads have some camber to the right, which drivers correct for without noticing that they do so. (In fact, many drivers—and even operators of wheel alignment shops—believe erroneously that Mercedes-Benz cars have a designed-in bias which causes a slight tendency to turn to the left to neutralize normal road camber.)

Now watch an oversteering car traveling the same straight road. It responds to a disturbing force by turning toward that force in a curving path while the car, as a whole, moves away from it. This is because the rear wheels have less cornering power than the front. The centrifugal force will be in the same direction as the disturbing force, thus increasing it and forcing the car to turn still further into the curve. The driver corrects by steering away from the force until the correct slip angles are established, and the car proceeds down the road with the rear end hanging out away from the disturbing force. The sensation of driving an oversteering car is one of continual instability.

If your car feels this way, check the tire pressures! As noted earlier, almost all cars are designed to understeer. With tires of the same size, front and rear, it is essential that the correct difference in inflation pressures be maintained. Since all current Mercedes-Benz cars use rear-wheel drive and front engines, their front tires are the more heavily loaded and thus develop the same slip angle at lower pressures than the rears. To obtain the desired understeer they are usually inflated two to four psi less than the rear tires. The exact difference depends on the model. On the 450SEL 6.9, with its large engine, the same pressure is used front and rear. For cars carrying a full load of passengers and luggage, the difference may be increased to five or six psi (as specified

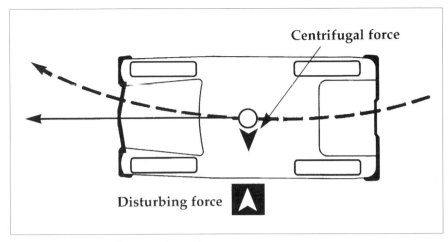

Figure VI. Side force's effect on understeering car.

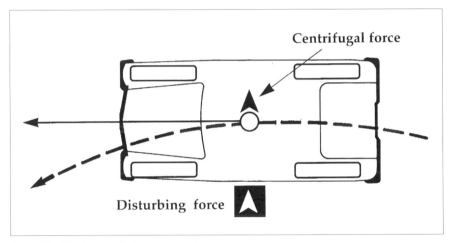

Figure VII. Side force's effect on oversteering car.

in your owner's manual or on the car). The factory specified difference should be maintained, even if tires of a different size from original equipment are installed.

Weight Transfer

A typical comment in road test in popular car magazines might go something like this: "The car shows mild understeer in normal driving, shifting to neutral steering as the limit is approached in curves." This should apply to any well-designed car. In a curve there is always weight transfer from the inside to the outside wheels. In hard driving this transfer can be large, in some cases reaching 100-percent. Recall those pictures of cars

cornering at speed with the inside wheel off the ground. The laws of gravity haven't been repealed; all of the weight has been transferred to the outside wheel.

Figure II shows that extreme weight transfer can mean severe loss of cornering power. If the loss is greater at the rear wheels, behavior will shift from understeer to neutral steer and may continue on to oversteer.

Adjustments

What can you do to increase or decrease the understeer (or oversteer) characteristics of your car? Its characteristics are the result of a series of design compromises. If understeer is good, will more understeer be

better? What are the negatives of the various steps?

First let's consider briefly the steps involving major modifications. Lowering the car's center of gravity reduces weight transfer in curves. Smaller diameter wheels are usually impractical. Installing shorter, stiffer springs lowers the car but at some cost in ride comfort and durability of the running gear. There may also be problems of interference, but a lower center of gravity does improve cornering power.

Increasing negative camber of the wheels (within reason) improves cornering power. This is more effective at the rear wheels and alters the car's behavior toward understeer. Up front, increasing negative camber adds cornering power, but front wheel geometry generally results in some reduction of negative camber of the outside wheel as the car rolls in a curve, in addition to the loss through weight transfer. However, the net effect of increasing negative camber in front is to increase oversteer.

Anti-roll bars, called stabilizer bars in current Mercedes-Benz technical publications and torsion bars in older factory literature (also known as sway bars or even anti-sway bars), may be applied to either front or rear axles when the wheels at that end are independently suspended. They would have no function on a solid axle. The advantages of independent wheel suspension over solid axles are conclusive, but there is one disadvantage that is significant here.

As a car rounds a corner, independent suspension permits a greater degree of roll. Thus, to reduce roll, stabilizer bars are installed. As a car corners, the bars resist the simultaneous compression of the springs on one side and extension on the other. Since Mercedes-Benz cars have independent suspension at both front and rear, stabilizer bars are fitted at both ends, but with stiffer (i.e., larger diameter) bars in front. Increasing roll resistance at the front increases understeer.

Roll resistance is a complex subject, being determined by suspension geometry, spring rates, dampers, tire characteristics, and weight distribution. The ultimate effect of changes in stabilizer bar stiffness on modern cars can only be predicted by elaborate computer simulation and finally determined by actual tests. As an example, the new 300SL uses bars of 30 mm in front and 10 mm in the rear, whereas the 500SL uses 29 mm in front and 13 mm in the rear.

Now we come to the factors which affect cornering power and therefore influence understeer or oversteer without modification of the car itself. Wider rims increase cornering power, but as noted earlier, the factory specified rims are usually within one-half inch of the maximum recommended for the tire specified. A wider tire will also increase cornering power, but the amount of change will not usually be appreciable unless wider rims are also used. The combination of wider tires and wider rims gives more cornering power and also tends to decrease either understeer or oversteer since there is less change at the end with the smaller slip angle.

The greater cornering power of wider tires applies only to dry road surfaces; on wet pavements the advantage, for other reasons, is with narrower tires, all else being equal.

The easiest way to alter understeer is by changing tire inflation pressure (see Figure III). A pressure increase of two psi in the rear tires will increase understeer to a degree quite noticeable to most drivers. A common demonstration may occur when tire pressures are "checked" by an uninformed or careless service man who provides 36 to 40 psi all around. Nervous or unstable handling will be very apparent.

Think About It

Understanding and contemplation of the cornering process and Newton's laws can add to your driving pleasure. The importance of proper tire inflation and having identical tires on all four wheels becomes apparent when reviewing the car's behavior under extreme conditions. When the limit of tire adhesion is reached in a curve, the understeering car plows straight ahead toward the outside of the curve, scrubbing off speed. The oversteering car will spin, with the rear end whipping around toward the outside.

The degree of understeer provided by the factory is close to optimum for most of us in highway driving. Too much understeer gives the impression that turning force is lacking, and that the car wants to plow ahead despite your efforts to control it. For anything approaching normal driving, nothing good can be said for oversteering. Even absolutely neutral steering, with equal weight distribution front and rear, doesn't make for relaxed driving, as it lacks the countering reaction to side winds of understeering. So change oversteer and understeer characteristics deliberately and make irrevocable modifications with caution.

For high performance use, especially competitive events, the normal settings described above are often successfully deviated from. Although that's a topic for another time, everything above still applies.

Suspension Tuning

To Increase Oversteer
(or Decrease Understeer)

- Lower rear of car
- Stiffer rear springs
- Larger rear stabilizer bar
- Stiffer rear shock absorbers
- Lower rear tire pressure
- Decrease rear toe-in
- Decrease rear camber
- Increase front camber
- Increase front toe-in
- Wider front track
- Wider front tires
- Wider front wheel rims

To Increase Understeer
(or Decrease Oversteer)

- Lower front of car
- Stiffer front springs
- Larger front stabilizer bar
- Stiffer front shock absorbers
- Lower front tire pressure
- Increase rear camber
- Increase rear toe-in
- Wider rear track
- Wider rear tires
- Wider rear wheel rims

Fixing Squeaky Steering on 123 Chassis

**by George Murphy,
Technical
Committee**

*January/February
1991*

Photo in this article
by Daimler-Benz AG.

When the steering wheel was turned, my aging 1978 300D squeaked and groaned, and its steering effort had increased. First I thought the power steering pump was failing, but investigation found the noise at the intermediate steering arm bearing. The arm attaches to a journal on the right side of the sub-frame below the engine. The arm pivots on a bolt held in the journal by bushings (Figure 1). With the wheels off the ground, the steering arm should move easily by hand; in my case, the pivot bolt was bound tightly, preventing free movement.

A kit is available for 123 models to replace the necessary parts, part number 124 460 00 19; dealer price is about $70. The kit contains a new bolt, nut, bushings, and washers to replace all moving parts in the mechanism. The workshop manual shows several special tools used for the job, but it can be done by substituting a little imagination.

The first part is easy. Undo the nut (9) from bolt (1) and remove the bolt. Note whether your car has washer (3) installed; it maintains proper steering geometry on models so equipped. Next, remove the dust cap (8) and pull out the steel slide bushings (5a) from rubber mount (5d). You may need a drift to drive out the slide bushings. The rubber mounts can be driven out with a brass or steel pin; I used the old bolt for a driver. You can drive out the top mount from below, but up above. there's no room to swing a hammer to drive out the lower rubber mount.

I used a 5/8-inch steel rod about 2 feet long to reach down beside the engine from above. A few blows with a hammer, and the old rubber mount was out.

Installation is not exactly the reverse of disassembly. Be careful with the new rubber mounts. Clean the bore of the journal bearing with solvent, then apply a light coat of white grease or graphite to help the new rubber mount slide in. Push both upper and lower mounts into the journal as far as possible by hand. Then, using the new bolt, nut, and some washers, tighten the nut until the mounts are seated in the journal. Remove nut, bolt, and washers.

The rest is easy. Lightly grease and press in the slide bushings (5a) and reassemble according to Figure 1. Be sure the rubber lip on the rubber bushings encloses the steel slide bushings. If your car had it, be sure to reinstall washer (3). Torque the nut to 87 lb-ft (120 Nm). When I finished, the steering felt and sounded like new. The noise was gone, and steering effort was noticeably lighter

Intermediate steering arm bushing assembly
is found under car, connects with tie rod.

Figure 1. Intermediate steering arm bushing;
1) hex bolt, 2) intermediate steering arm,
3) washer, 4) sealing washer, 5) rubber slide
bearing assembly, 5a) slide bushing (metal),
5b, c, d) rubber bushing, 6) journal bearing,
8) dust cap) 9) self-locking hex nut.

Technical Topics

by Frank King,
Technical Editor

*May/June
1989*

Vibration and Resonance

As a glance at any dictionary will show, there are few broader terms than vibration and resonance, but here we'll deal with how they affect our control of, and comfort in, our cars.

Vibration is a rhythmic throbbing or pulsation as a mass moves to and from a position of equilibrium. Figure 1 shows a simple example; a mass is suspended by a spring, and when a disturbing force is applied, the mass moves up and down at regular intervals. These oscillations gradually diminish because of resisting forces that are always present. These damping forces may be air or fluid resistance, the internal friction of the vibrating body or friction between sliding surfaces. In any vibrating system a certain number of oscillations will occur in a fixed period of time; this is called the natural frequency of the system.

Resonance is the response of a system to the periodic driving force transmitted to it by another vibrating system. When the driving frequency equals the natural frequency of the resonant system, the response is greatly enhanced. We've all heard of wine glasses being shattered as a soprano hits the resonant note, though most of us have seen it only in television commercials.

Vibration and resonance at the natural frequency are normal, but much more common are forced vibrations. If you bounce the front end of a stationary car (preferably without shock absorbers) at the right frequency (not too quickly, not too slowly), it will continue bouncing at its natural frequency, which be low enough so that nothing is disturbed. If you now drive the car (with shock absorbers attached) down a road with washboard bumps, the wheels will be forced to vibrate up and down at a rate determined by the distance between the bumps and the speed of the car. These forced vibrations travel through the car, and somewhere they may find a system, perhaps a muffler, that resonates to them.

In the modern automobile's interlocking systems we have a galaxy of parts that may vibrate or resonate at either natural or forced frequencies. Any vibration in a car is uncomfortable to some degree, and as cars become ever more refined, our tolerance for vibration decreases. When the running gear vibrates, it conveys an insecure feeling, adding to our discomfort. To the driver, such vibrations threaten his ability to control the vehicle.

Automobile design progress has led to lighter and more refined cars capable of higher speeds. Unfortunately the components of such cars are much more prone to vibration than were the 5,000-lb, 40-mph monsters of yesteryear. Modern cars must be smoother, and smoothness means absence of vibration. This is attained by decreasing tolerances in the basic design, combined with increased damping and more effective insulation.

Table 1: Runout Tolerances

Wheels		Mounted Tires	
Permissible radial runout, mm	Permissible lateral runout, mm	Permissible radial runout, mm	Permissible lateral runout, mm
Steel wheels		Steel wheels	
0.8 (1.0)	0.8 (1.0)	1.0 (1.2)	1.5 (2.0)
Light alloy wheels		Light alloy wheels	
0.6	0.6 (1.0)	1.0 (1.2)	1.5 (2.0)

(Values in brackets valid before model year 1987)

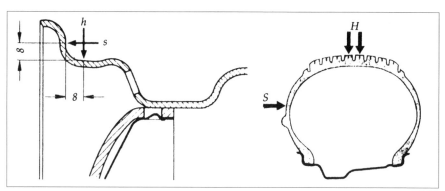

h = measuring point for radial runout runout
s = measuring point for lateral runout runout

H = measuring point for radial runout
S = measuring point for lateral runout

Figure 3. All dimensions are in millimeters. Steel wheels can be measured for runout on the outside of the rims. Light alloy rims can be measured only on the inside of the rims since they are machined only there. Runout of tire and wheel assemblies can be measured only when tires are warm from running. When cooled off, they will have temporary flat spots.

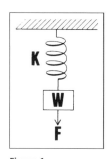

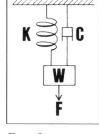

Figure 1

Figure 2

Damping refers to forces which absorb and diminish vibration. Some damping is inherent in all mechanical systems, and devices may be added to a system to increase damping. Figure 2 shows a damper (shock absorber) added to the system shown in Figure 1. Insulation is a specialized form of damping intended to absorb vibrations that would otherwise be transmitted to other parts of the machine.

Wheel Vibration

The most common vibration problem in automobiles is wheel vibration, which is more annoying if it is in the front wheels. Vibration or a similarly disturbing failure to run straight and true may be caused by misalignment of the wheels—usually the front wheels but not uncommonly the rears.

In proper adjustment your Mercedes-Benz should run at any speed with no wheel vibration. It should go in the direction you point it without wandering and should respond with a minimum of effort as you correct for road conditions. When the car no longer does so, because of wear, accident or replacement of some part, it's necessary to balance or align the wheels.

Wheel Balancing

Wheel balancing is one of the most widely offered services in the land. Sometimes the most casual job of balancing will suffice, but we frequently hear from members who have had their wheels balanced at three or four different shops yet still have vibration problems. A similar situation exists for wheel alignment. Let's look at the procedures and equipment recommended by DBAG to ensure that your car is in the condition intended by its designers.

First, wheels must be round and straight, i.e., runout must be within the range in Table 1. The correct runout measurement points are shown in Figure 3. Wheel and tire assemblies that are out of round can be balanced but will still cause vibration. Mercedes-Benz steel wheels have a green spot on the outside of the rim, and alloy wheels

Table 2: Common Causes of Vehicle Vibrations

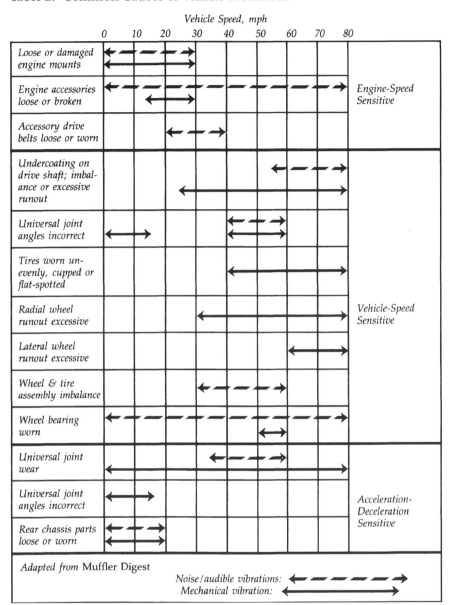

have a countersunk spot on the inside of the rim. Manufacturers of HR- and VR-rated tires mark the softest spot (which becomes the high spot when rolling) on their tires with a green dot, to be aligned as closely as possible with the rim mark during mounting.

Under favorable conditions wheels can be balanced on old, even obsolete, equipment, but the complex nature of proper wheel balancing requires modern equipment and a skilled operator. Wheels should first be balanced statically and dynamically, off the car. Ideally, the wheel should be horizontal, on a vertical spindle and

held by a centering cone. One system capable of meeting the latest, most stringent requirements for off-car balancing is the Hunter System 700 Computerized Wheel Balancer; there are other brands of similar equipment. Less sophisticated equipment may produce satisfactory balance, but when difficulties occur, the most advanced technique should be used.

After the wheel is properly balanced, the job should be checked by rotating the wheel by two mounting holes (144 degrees) and re-testing it. If balance is still correct, the wheels should be mounted on the car for a test drive. If vibration still exists, the wheels must be rebalanced on the car; this should never be done until runout has been checked and the wheels have been dynamically balanced.

Effective rebalancing on the car requires that it be on solid ground with doors firmly closed; to avoid damage to the differential, the rear wheels must be driven only by the engine. Weights placed on the outside of the rim must be increased or decreased by no more than 20 grams; otherwise, overall balance will be disturbed, and off-car dynamic balancing must be repeated. DBAG recommends the Hofmann IPK Finish Balancer for on-car balancing.

Wheel Centering Clearance

Before rebalancing on the car, the wheel centering clearance should be used to minimize the effect of any residual imbalance. Modern Mercedes-Benz wheels are located by the center hole, not by the lug bolts. For easy wheel changing there is some clearance between the wheel's centering hole and the car's hub. The diameter of the hole may be 66.50 to 66.57 mm, and the hub diameter may be 66.35 to 66.40 mm, so the clearance may be as little as 0.10 mm or as much as 0.22 mm.

To minimize residual imbalance, rotate the wheel so that the lightest point is at the bottom, loosen all lug bolts while holding the wheel in that position, then retighten them to the proper torque in proper sequence.

With the wheels balanced so that they can be spun on the car without vibration, and with runout verified on the car as being within permissible limits, a road test may (rarely) still show annoying vibrations. Vibrations may be felt, heard or both. Vibrations sensitive to vehicle speed may be blamed on the wheels even though they actually arise in some other part. Table 2 lists frequent causes of in-motion vibration. Table 3 lists some sounds which demand immediate attention when heard in a moving car. Both tables list only general indicators, not precise diagnostic clues.

Table 3: Sounds to Investigate

If you hear...	While...	Check...
Rumbling	Driving straight	• Tires for overinflation when they are cool • Front and rear wheel bearings for damage
	Turning	• Front wheel bearings for wear or looseness
Clunking	Accelerating/Decelerating	• Engine mounts for breakage or looseness
Squealing from under hood	Turning	• V-belt or power steering for looseness
Tire squeal	Turning	• Tires for underinflation • Wheel alignment • Tie-rod ends for looseness • Tires rubbing against car body, suspension, or brake line
Tire squeal	Driving straight	• Severe wheel misalignment • Brakes dragging • Tires rubbing against body or suspension
Clunking or rattling	Driving over bumps	• Stabilizer bar for looseness • Loose suspension bolts • Control arm bushings, tie-rod ends, or ball joints for wear • Exhaust pipe, muffler, or catalyzer hitting chassis or rear axles • Trunk for loose bowling balls
Rattle or tinkle from wheel	Driving slowly	• Wheel covers for loose gravel, loose lug bolts, loose wheel covers
Squeaks	Driving over bumps	• Ball joints, tie-rod ends, and control arm bushings for wear or lubrication • Shock absorbers for damage

Wheel Alignment

This service is offered almost as widely as wheel balancing. As you might expect, the difference between a This Week's Special wheel alignment and a really up-to-date job is about as great as the difference between Civil War battlefield surgery and today's reconstructive surgery in a modern hospital.

The purpose of wheel alignment is to position the wheels relative to the chassis and road precisely as your car's designers intended. Usually alignment is thought of as involving only the front wheels. This assumes that the rear wheels thrust straight ahead along the centerline of the car and that the front wheels need only be set to the correct camber, caster and toe-in to allow the car to drive straight ahead without wandering and to turn and return to straight-ahead driving in response to your steering input.

Misalignment Symptoms

Among the most frequent symptoms that you need wheel alignment for are:

1. vibration felt in the steering wheel

2. unusual tire wear patterns or abnormal wear rates

3. pulling of the car to one side or the other

4. wandering from the path the driver wishes to follow

5. failure of the steering to return to straight ahead after turns

6. observation of the car while it stands on level pavement

7. observation of the car from behind while being driven

8. improper reactions to sudden forces such as side winds, bump steer, brake dive and evasive maneuvers

9. lack of feedback from the road, a dead feeling

10. steering wheel not centered

Many of these symptoms may have causes other than misalignment of the wheels, but if the cause is not readily apparent, or if the problem isn't corrected by the obvious solution, wheel alignment is needed. Often a casual alignment with relatively primitive equipment may correct the fault. Wheel balancing, for instance, may cure front end vibration or some forms of abnormal tire wear. Simple toe-in adjustment might correct excessive tire wear on inner or outer edges. But we're concerned here with a complete, thorough job which will handle the most intractable cases.

The Alignment Process

Wheel alignment should start with a visual check of the chassis height at all four corners to ensure that the chassis has the correct relationship to the level road. If, for example, the car is too low in front because of sagging springs or too low in back because of excess weight there, it may be impossible to align it to specifications because the caster adjustment range may be insufficient.

Wheel alignment traditionally gives front wheels the toe-in or toe-out specified by the designer and measured with reference to the vehicle's geometric centerline, which runs longitudinally through the center of the car. Toe-in or toe-out is designed into the stationary vehicle so that the wheels become parallel to the vehicle centerline and each other as they are subjected to driving forces and rolling resistance when the car moves.

Traditional centerline alignment may work if the rear wheels are square with the geometric centerline. But if the rear wheels create a thrust line different from the geometric centerline, the front end geometry will be off center, and the steering wheel will be cocked as the car moves straight ahead. See Figure 3a. The thrust line is the direction of the combined thrust of the two rear wheels, reflecting their location and direction with respect to the centerline.

Alignment to the vehicle's thrust line gives much better results than aligning to the geometric centerline. In the thrust line method, individual rear wheel toe-in is measured (but not adjusted), and the thrust line thus created is used as a reference for front wheel alignment. See Figure 3b. Thus the steering wheel will be straight when the car goes straight. Still, although the car will behave well, it will "dog track" as though the chassis were bent by collision at one front corner.

Four-Wheel Alignment

The ultimate wheel alignment is a total four-wheel alignment. The rear wheels are first brought to the car manufacturer's specifications, then the front wheels are aligned to the centerline, which coincides exactly with the thrust line. See Figure 3c. This makes all four wheels parallel, rears tracking fronts, with steering centered as the car moves in a straight line.

With complete DBAG specifications and information on the interaction of adjustments, it is possible to align the wheels of a Mercedes-Benz using only primitive measuring devices. It is also, if serious maladjustment exists, about as difficult as putting Humpty Dumpty together again. Because the rear wheels are independently suspended, there's no rigid axle to be spotted as out of alignment and producing a deviated thrust line.

Although there are several machines to align wheels, DBAG and other car manufacturers recommend the Hunter System D111 digital wheel aligner, which provides accurate read-outs so

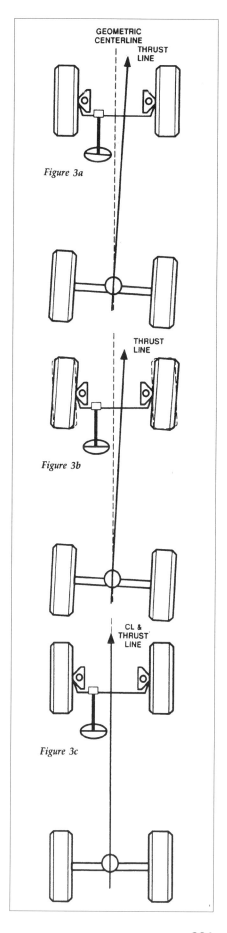

Figure 3a

Figure 3b

Figure 3c

that the mechanic knows the effects of his adjustments and their relation to specifications.

A complete wheel alignment includes a check of chassis height and verification of the thrust line. Tire inflation pressure will be checked and the steering wheel centered. If the thrust line is off-center, rear wheel alignment will be adjusted.

Toe-in will be set, both for total toe-in and for toe-in at each wheel. Too much toe-in causes tire scuffing at the outer edge; too little, or toe-out, causes scuffing at the inner edge. Unequal toe-in may cause the front end to pull to one side.

Camber, the tilting of the top of the wheel from vertical, is positive when the wheel leans out from the centerline of the car and negative when it leans in. If not specified, camber figures are positive. Each front wheel should have the same camber; uneven camber causes the car to pull to the side with the most positive camber.

Caster, the tilting of the top of the steering axis from the vertical, is positive when the axis leans backward, negative when the axis leans forward. Caster figures are positive if not otherwise designated. Mercedes-Benz cars are not designed with negative caster, but it may be found in damaged cars or when the front sags and the rear is high on non-original tires or springs. Negative camber, or insufficient positive camber, makes the car wander and may cause front wheel shimmy, even with balanced wheels. Too much positive camber makes the car hard to steer and intensifies road shocks. A difference in caster from side to side makes the car pull toward the side with the least positive caster.

The track difference angle (turning angle) will be checked. This involves steering to the left so that the left front wheel is 20 degrees from straight ahead, then measuring the angle of the right wheel. It must be less, by an amount which differs with different models. (The inside wheel on a turn must always turn more sharply than the outside wheel.) The turn is then repeated to the right, and the same difference must be found. Incorrect track difference angle causes tire scuffing in turns and tire squeal.

With a sophisticated alignment machine, steering axis inclination may also be checked. Before ball-joint suspensions were common, steering axis inclination was called king pin inclination. (The May/June 1986 issue of *The Star* has a detailed description of front end terms.) King pins on Mercedes-Benz cars went out in the early 1970's when production of the 108 and 109 chassis ended, but there's still an imaginary line where the king pin used to be. The inclination of this line from the vertical toward the center of the vehicle is the steering axis inclination. Steering axis inclination is built into the car and isn't adjustable. An accident may alter it, making correct alignment impossible, so it should be checked.

Road Test

The final judgement on the state of the running gear comes in a road test. Ideally such a test should include a stretch of smooth pavement with no more than a slight tilt to the right for drainage. On a road with a tilt to the right, a car with perfect alignment will drift off to the right, pulled in

that direction by gravity. The driver will then have to steer slightly to the left to counteract this force. Similarly, a side wind will cause the car to turn away from the force of the wind, and a steering correction must be made. A fair road test thus requires a road with no tilt and no cross wind.

Road surface irregularities are transmitted to the car body through tires, wheels, springs, shock absorbers and rubber mounts, all of which absorb forced vibrations and cancel them out as they are produced in a vast range of frequencies.

One situation can provoke a resonance that is annoying and difficult to eliminate. Pavement, particularly asphalt, tends to take on a waviness. Slight humps and hollows cross the road at regular intervals, and driving over these waves can induce rhythmic motion. If the distance between waves is such that the front wheels are in a trough while the rears are on a peak, the car tends to canter or gallop at certain speeds. This is freeway hop, or as the Germans call it, the Bonanza Effect. It is independent of wheel balance or alignment and can be dealt with only by the manufacturer's selection of spring rates and damping rates. We all meet this effect to some degree when we drive certain roads that somehow produce unpleasant noises and an undertone of vibration.

Sound wheel balancing and alignment by a proficient operator on modern equipment can ensure that your car gives you all the comfort and control of which it is capable.

Wheel and Tire Guide

by Stu Ritter,
Technical Editor

*March/April
2002*

*How to choose high-performance
wheels and tires for your
Mercedes-Benz*

Mercedes-Benz has always felt that
the wheels and tires on its cars
should be kept at original equipment
sizes. According to the company,
modifications should be done by
it—or at least with its authorization—
so that all of its engineering knowledge
can be applied. U.S. Mercedes-Benz
dealers sell Mercedes-Benz and AMG
accessory wheels that have been tested
at the factory and meet all applicable
technical requirements. If you plan to
change the wheels on your car, keep
this in mind, though other excellent
options certainly exist.

Many wheel manufacturers
produce excellent wheels equaling
Mercedes-Benz quality, but the
question always comes down to
fitment. Will the desired wheel and
tire combination fit the car? Will it
clear the suspension? Will it clear the
brakes? Will it interfere with brake
cooling? How will it affect handling,
comfort, safety, steering response,
braking, and cornering ability?

Translating Dimensions

When upgrading your car's wheels,
picking a sexy-looking wheel design
might be your first thought, but it's
more critical to first consider fit,
particularly the offset dimension of
the mounting face, where the wheel
mounts to the hub, to the centerline
of the rim. This dimension sets the
horizontal position of the wheel/tire
in relation to the suspension. In
Germany, offset is referred to as ET,
and on Mercedes-Benz cars it is always
positive. The offset is given last in the

Pirelli & C. S.p.A.

wheel designation, as in 7Jx15 H2 25,
which translates to:

7 = Rim width, inches

J = A code for the height and
contour of the rim flange

x = Code letter for a one-piece,
low-bed rim

15 = Rim/tire diameter, inches

H2 = Rim profile on the outside and
inside of tire bead area

25 = ET, offset, mm

These figures have always been
available for all Mercedes-Benz steel

and alloy wheels. In fact, along with
date of manufacture, they are stamped
into the factory's steel wheels and cast
into their alloy wheels. Interchanging
factory wheels is usually simple; just
make sure everything matches. When
changing to a larger-diameter wheel
and a lower-profile tire (say, replacing
65-series, 15-inch tires and wheels
with 50- or 55-series, 16-inch) it is
important to work with someone
experienced at changing wheel sizes.
While the new wheel itself may fit
and clear all suspension and brake
components, a tire mounted on it may
rub on the suspension or the body.

Mercedes-Benz factory wheels are hub-centric, meaning that they are centered on the suspension hub and that the lug bolts only serve to hold the wheel onto the hub, without performing any centering function. Although the factory lug bolts have a spherical collar, they do not center the wheel on the hub. Thus it is important that wheels be balanced on a hub-centric wheel balancer, not the type that mounts the wheel on lug bolts. Hub-centric balancers (as most modern units are) have tapered plates that hold the wheel on the balancer using the center hub of the wheel.

Why Upgrade?

The rubber meets the road at a relatively small contact patch at each tire. Increasing the size of that contact patch has always been a rewarding way of improving cornering speeds and steering response. Lower-profile

tires have much quicker turn-in and usually feel more precise-steering. When choosing a new tire/wheel combination, make sure it will work for you. To be sure that your new lower-profile wheels and tires fit and work well, deal only with known, reputable tire and wheel dealers who have done plenty of successful Mercedes-Benz interchanges.

With a plethora of wheels available in the aftermarket, where do you start and where do you stop? Wheels are now available that let you install 17-, 18-, or 19-inch tires on certain models. According to the Plus-1, Plus-2 concept, as wheel diameter increases, overall tire diameter should stay the same, maintaining overall gear ratios and speedometer accuracy. To maintain overall tire diameter, a wider tire's aspect ratio (profile) must decrease. Hence a 195/70/14 tire might be switched to a 205/60/15, which then

might migrate to a 215 or 225/50/16, then to a 245/40/17, more or less, give or take.

To help you choose a replacement tire with the proper overall diameter, tire manufacturers publish the number of revolutions per mile for each tire size. You can try to match these figures for the new size to your original size, but the numbers often vary. You can also sit and figure out the nominal overall diameter of your present tires and wider replacements, but actual sizes rarely match nominal sizes. So, apart from experience, the only reliable way to judge tire/wheel fit is to, as the British say, "offer it up."

To see how the new wheel/tire combo fits, mount it on the car. Preliminarily there's no need to mount all four; try one wheel/tire at each position. Often a local wheel and tire dealer will have a used wheel and tire to let you do so before committing your dollars to an entire new set. With the new wheel and tire on the car, make sure they turn freely throughout the entire suspension travel and steering arc. See that they avoid rubbing on the shock absorber, suspension arms, brake calipers, brake lines, fender lips, or internal body panels.

No Free Ride

As a tire's width is increased, its aspect ratio goes lower, and its sidewall is shortened, so the tire becomes stiffer, and so does your ride. Consider how much of that Mercedes-Benz comfort you want to exchange for more traction or precise handling. Think carefully because as you reduce tire profile, ride gets harsher unless the suspension was originally designed for that aspect ratio.

Recent sporty Mercedes-Benz suspensions are designed for 40- and 45-series tires, yet—much to our amazement—the ride is usually very compliant. Having recently driven a C32 AMG with its original 17-in wheels and 40- and 45-series tires, we found the ride amazingly comfortable. Firm but comfortable. We have also driven cars with 40- and 45-series tires where the ride was appallingly,

DaimlerChrysler AG

teeth-jarring stiff, never a Mercedes-Benz trademark. The difference is that the C32 AMG's suspension—spring rates, shock absorber damping, and suspension geometry—is designed specifically for low-profile tires. But if you just throw a set of 40-series tires on your 10- or 20-year old car, you'll be in for a rude surprise. Its suspension was designed for stock tire sizes, so a low-profile tire alone will make it ride like a truck.

On its newest models, Mercedes-Benz fits larger wheels and lower-profile tires to clear larger and larger brake disks, but they simultaneously engineer the suspension systems to match the tire's low profile. Jumping from 14-in to 17-in wheels on a car never designed for such may not make sense. Before changing you car's wheels and tires, think about what will happen to ride quality. Yes, there are handling and traction advantages to wider, lower-profile tires, but there are also drawbacks: harshness, tramlining, aquaplaning. Moderation is a good thing.

Reading Tires

Reading a tire's sidewall has never been easy, and current federal standards require the sidewall to read like a miniature encyclopedia. Let's look at a modern tire sidewall and review some of the information it carries. Parts of the encyclopedia are self explanatory and of little interest.

As an example of earlier radial tires, here's what the nominal size tells you:

P185/70HR15

P = Passenger car tire

185 = Cross-section width of the tire, mm (to convert to inches, divide by 25.4)

70 = Aspect ratio of width to height; 185 x 0.70 = 129.5 mm; the tire is 185-mm wide and 129.5-mm tall. If it were 60-series instead of 70-series, the tire would be 111-mm tall.

H = Speed rating of 130 mph

R = Radial (B = Bias, D = Diagonal, rarely used)

15 = Wheel rim diameter, inches

A more modern radial tire would carry the following information:

P225/50 R 16 92V

P = P-Metric passenger car tire

225 = Cross-section width of the tire, mm (to convert to inches, divide by 25.4)

50 = Aspect ratio of width to height; 225 x 0.50 = 112.5

R = Radial tire

16 = Wheel rim diameter, inches

92 = Load rating

V = Speed rating

The tire's size is obviously important, but it's easy to overlook several other vital factors: load rating, maximum pressure,

temperature capability, and wear rate. This information is included in the tire's "service description." The service description's load and speed ratings give you two facts. The number provides the load index, and the letter indicates the speed rating. The service description appears right after the tire size. In our P225/50 R 16 92V example, we have a tire that can carry up to 1,389 lb and can be driven at speeds up to 149 mph.

Load Ratings

The load rating, or maximum load information, tells you the heaviest allowable load per tire according to the inflation pressure. Four tires must support the static weight of your car; to determine that overall weight, see your owner's manual or weigh the car at a commercial scale, adding the weights of fuel, passengers, and other cargo. Make sure the car's total weight doesn't exceed four times (for four tires) the tire's load rating.

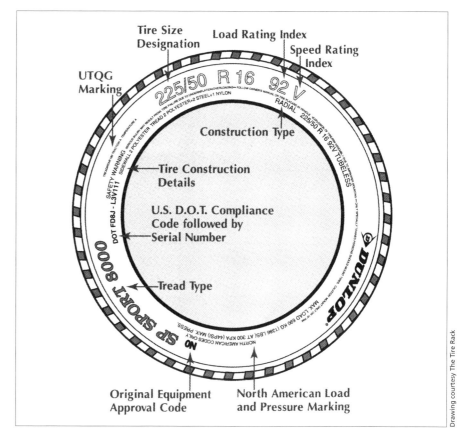

Figure 1. Tire sidewall information.

Drawing courtesy The Tire Rack

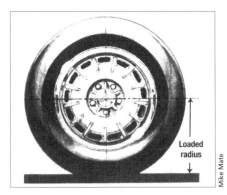

Loaded radius differs from unloaded radius, so check it with wheel and tire installed on car.

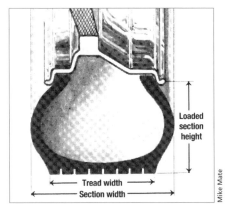

Tire/rim cross-section illustrates difference between section width and tread width. Profile equals section height divided by section width.

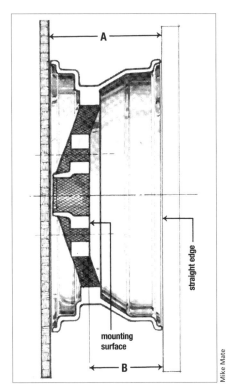

Wheel offset is the distance from the center of the wheel's width to its mounting flange.

$$\text{Offset} = \text{Backspacing, B} - \frac{\text{Wheel width, A}}{2}$$

Load Ratings	
Rating	*Capacity, lbs*
90	1,323
91	1,356
92	1,389
93	1,433
94	1,477
95	1,521
96	1,565
97	1,609
98	1,653
99	1,709
100	1,764

Speed Ratings		
Rating	*Maximum Speed, mph*	*Maximum Speed, kph*
Q	99	160
R	106	170
S	112	180
T	118	190
U	124	200
H	130	210
V	130	210
VR	149	240
W-ZR	168	270
Y-ZR	186	300

The tire's service description provides both the load rating and the speed rating of the P-Metric tire. Euro-Metric tires—which do not have the P prefix in the tire size—have slightly higher load ratings, by approximately 30 pounds per tire

While load ratings range from 70 through 110, most Mercedes-Benz cars require tires rated between 90 and 100. Load and speed ratings for specific models are in the Mercedes-Benz Technical Data Manuals, in section 40, Survey of Rims and Tires. These manuals are available from Mercedes-Benz USA's Customer Assistance Center at 800/FOR-MERC.

Maximum pressure is either 35 psi for P-Metric tires or 36 psi for Euro-Metric tires. Some high speed-rated tires show a maximum inflation pressure of 44 psi, which has been established for handling purposes. This figure is purely the tire's maximum design pressure. It is not used to set actual operating tire pressures.

Speed Ratings

Speed ratings are established in a tire laboratory, where the tire is mounted on a wheel and pressed against a rotating drum at a pressure that matches the tire's rated load. Speed is increased in 10-kph (6.2-mph) increments every 10 minutes until the tire meets its rated speed, then the

tire is run at that speed for another 10 minutes. The service designation of VR 92 tells you that the tire has met the 149-mph standard at a load of 1,389 pounds for 10 minutes after being brought up to that speed as described above.

Speed ratings apply only to tires that are undamaged, properly inflated, and within their load capacity. Most tire manufacturers maintain that a tire that has been damaged by a cut or a puncture—even though it has been properly repaired—no longer matches the manufacturer's original speed rating. This also applies to plugs used to repair punctures.

Older V-rated tires indicated a maximum allowable speed in excess of 130 mph, while the new VR rating allows a top speed of 149 mph. The ZR rating—once thought to be the highest speed rating that tires would ever require—has been superceded by the new W and Y rated tires. A ZR in the tire size and a W in the speed rating, P245/45ZR17 96W for instance, indicates that the tire is W-rated, capable of safe operation at speeds up to 168 mph. Both W and Y speed ratings carry a ZR in the tire size.

Tread Wear

The Uniform Tire Quality Grade (UTQG) system establishes ratings for tread wear, wet braking traction, and temperature handling abilities. These tests are conducted by the tire manufacturer, not the federal government. Tire manufacturers follow a set of guidelines in determining UTQG numbers. The numbers represent a comparison between the test tire and a reference control tire. Traction and temperature ratings are specific performance numbers, but the tread wear indicator is established through field testing by tire manufacturers. The tread wear ratings are best used when comparing tires of the same brand.

A tire's tread wear rating shows how it wears in field testing, following a specific course designed by the Department of Transportation. A tire with a wear rating of 150 should last 1.5 times as long as a tire with a rating of 100. The wear rating indicates nothing about the performance of a tire; it just gives you a general indication of how the tire will wear compared to other tires made by the same manufacturer. It should not be used to compare, say, Brand X and Brand Y, even tires with the same wear index number. As with all tire index numbers, the wear index assumes correct rotation and tire pressure.

Traction Ratings

The traction indicator gives you an idea of the straight-ahead wet braking ability of the tire, shown by a grade of AA, A, B, or C. The AA-rated tires have the best wet braking ability. The best score used to be A, but as tires improved, the manufacturers introduced a grade of AA in 1997. This indicator is for straight-line braking only and says nothing about wet cornering ability. Every tire on the Mercedes-Benz approved list carries at least an A traction rating.

Temperature Ratings

Temperature resistance is also shown as A, B, and C, indicating the tire's resistance to heat generated by high-speed driving. For passenger car tires, C is the minimum accepted standard. Federal Motor Vehicle Safety Standards establish the test parameters. All tires that we use on our Mercedes-Benz cars carry an A temperature rating.

Tire construction details show the tread composition of the tire. The tire's labeling shows how many belts are in the tread and the sidewall and their materials. Belts are usually steel, nylon, or polyester.

Though the above covers most of the information on the sidewall that is of interest to a Mercedes-Benz driver, other safety warnings apply to tire installers.

Frequent Wheel and Tire Questions

It's been years since we explored the mysteries of wheels, tires, and Mercedes-Benz. Earlier articles by previous technical editor Frank King went into great detail on tire sizes, and they remain current and applicable. See Technical Topics in our November/December 1995 issue and "Which Tire?" in the March/April 1987 issue (for a reprint of both, send your name, address, and $10 to Tire Reprints, *The Star*, 1235 Pierce St., Lakewood, CO 80214, or call us at 303/235-0116.)

To update that information, we posed common car-owner questions to tire engineers at Mercedes-Benz, Pirelli, Continental, and Nokian. While a few of their answers indicate careful adherence to the "factory line" due to possible liability issues in our litigious society, the engineers were most helpful. A cautious Mercedes-Benz owner should heed this expert input.

How has the factory developed the "approved tire list"?

The Mercedes-Benz tire engineering department, which is entirely dedicated to testing and approving tires for Mercedes-Benz cars, develops the list. Tires are selected via testing and their ability to meet the original equipment specifications established by Mercedes-Benz.

Tires get onto the list based on their performance characteristics. The approved list has been developed to ensure that the proper tires are chosen for the car in terms of load capacity, speed capacity, and comfort and handling characteristics. Vehicle dynamics and accident avoidance performance are also tested.

Why does the approved list exist in the first place?

It's a guide for Mercedes-Benz owners in choosing replacement tires that have been thoroughly tested and which meet all factory criteria for satisfactory performance under adverse conditions. If a Mercedes-Benz driver uses a tire from the approved list for their specific model, we can be sure that our car performs as we intended it to.

How are recommended tire pressures determined?

Recommended pressures for our cars are mainly derived from the European Tire and Rim Technical Organization (ETRTO). In conjunction with tire manufacturers, international organizations, and legislative bodies, ETRTO has produced industry-accepted standards for tire sizes, load ratings, and speed ratings, all relative to inflation pressures.

Why do inflation pressures for the U.S. seem lower than in Europe for certain chassis?

Recommended pressures are determined by extensive testing between Mercedes-Benz and the specific tire manufacturer, taking into account the tire load (car weight), carrying capacity, ride, and handling characteristics. Various countries [i.e., markets] have different tire pressures for the same chassis because different value weights are assigned to the tire and vehicle characteristics. For instance, U.S. drivers value comfort more than handling, so they may use a slightly lower pressure to enhance ride comfort

Recommended tire pressures on the gas filler flap door are the absolute minimum inflation pressures. Never use less than this pressure. Pressure is increased for heavy load and sporty driving. Ideally, tire pressure should be measured cold because the air temperature increases as the tire rolls and flexes, and this increase in temperature increases air pressure. Warm tire pressures should never be adjusted below the pressures on the fuel filler flap.

Tire pressures can also be adjusted to alter steering characteristics. At recommended pressures, if you find the car ploughs in turns, increase front tire pressure by three to four psi to decrease understeer. If you live where the roads are rough and full of potholes, check your tire pressure weekly. Air gets beaten out of tires when they hit holes in the road, leading to dangerous under-inflation. The factory maintains that the higher load pressures can be used all the time with some sacrifice in comfort but an improvement in handling.

Some members report signs of under-inflation when using the gas flap inflation pressures.

So many factors contribute to tire wear that we really can't conclude anything without specific data. Generalizations cannot be made because the scenario is likely to vary from car to car.

In Europe and other countries with no effective speed limits speed ratings are critical, but how do they apply to U.S driving? Some members question the need for V-rated tires when all they do is drive to the store at 40 mph.

Mercedes-Benz: Our approved tire list is our recommendation for tires that give known results on our vehicles. If a person wants to put a lesser tire on their vehicle, they can compromise vehicle safety. Speed ratings are not only about the maximum speed a tire can safely operate at but rather part of an entire engineered package that includes inflation pressures, load ratings, and speed ratings. Anyone who makes ill-informed changes in these areas can seriously compromise safety and performance.

Tire Company: If a car is originally equipped with V-rated tires, use V-rated tires as replacements. In addition to the speed ratings being related to the maximum tire and car speed, they also are related to internal tire construction, which directly affects handling capabilities at all speeds. If an owner downgrades from the original equipment manufacturer's specified speed rating, maneuvers at all speeds are compromised, and the vehicle will not handle according to the original design specifications of the auto manufacturer. Also, for the U.S., potential legal liabilities are associated with downgrading tires based on speed rating; most vehicle and tire manufacturers specifically warn against this practice.

Editor's Note: Putting lower-speed-rated tires on a car is akin to wearing a lighter, cheaper bulletproof vest. You may never drive over the rated speed, but the speed rating offers a general indication of the quality of a tire's construction, and high-speed-rated tires tend to be built better and thus resist heat, load, and road hazards better. Your Mercedes-Benz was designed to protect you from injury, but lower-rated tires compromise its ability to do so. Fit the right tire. Doing otherwise may be hazardous to your health or that of someone you love.

How is the UTQG wear rating determined?

This rating is determined by comparing the subject tires' wear performance to that of the industry-accepted control tire. The test takes place over a distance of 7,200 miles, normally with one control vehicle and two to four test vehicles fitted with the subject tires. All testing takes place with the tires operating at 85 percent of maximum load.

Where can MBCA members find proper inflation pressures for modern tires on older collector cars?

We assume you are referring to the installation of radial tires on cars originally equipped with bias-ply tires. We can't make definitive statements since we haven't tested older cars with newer tires. Still, we may be able to provide an approximate rule of thumb from our Classic Center technical staff. Stay tuned.

Why must all four tires on a car be the same, even snow tires?

Mercedes-Benz: Different tires have different characteristics, and you would not want to unbalance the car's dynamic performance. We strongly recommend using tires of the same size, speed rating, and load rating. Even within that framework, different tread compounds, belt packages, and so forth give different tires unique personalities.

Tire Company: Tires of different ratings and internal constructions have different slip angle characteristics, which means that the tires react differently to the same steering input. Mixing tires with different performance characteristics can cause a handling problem when you need it least, such as during an evasive safety maneuver.

Are there differences between P-Metric tire ratings and Euro-Metric tire ratings (speed, load, etc.)?

Mercedes-Benz: We don't use P-Metric tires, only Euro-Metric.

Editor's Note: Staff experience with P-Metric and Euro-Metric tires reveals that within a given brand and size, Euro-Metrics are more stiffly constructed than P-Metrics and are generally preferable.

Tire Size Equivalents

by Frank King,
Technical Editor

*November/December
1995*

*Here's how to determine what
tire sizes will best substitute for
the original tires on your older
Mercedes-Benz.*

The most frequent questions that we
receive deal with replacement of tires,
sometimes due to dissatisfaction, more
often because the original size is no
longer available. This article may help
you to make your decision when faced
with non-availability of the desired size.

Non-availability may be due
to obsolescence or because the
manufacturer of a certain tire may not
choose to make it in your car's size.
Newer tire designs may be made only
for wheels of larger diameter than
those on your car. Then, the only fix
may be new, larger diameter wheels.
Some owners when shopping for,
say, 205/60R15 tires, may be offered
205/65R15 tires as a substitute. Are
these similar enough to be satisfactory?
Some owners like the appearance and
handling advantages of wider tires
and want to know which wider sizes
may be satisfactory substitutes for
the original equipment. Owners of
certain older cars or cars which had
special, unique original tires may find
that they cannot find duplicates of the
original equipment.

This article describes how to find a
useful substitute tire size. Table I lists
all 13-, 15-, and 16-inch tire sizes used
on Mercedes-Benz cars offered to the
North American market from 1947
until 1968 (the 9.00x15 continued
beyond). Table II lists all 14-inch sizes
used from 1963 onward, both 80-series
and 70-series. Except for the wheels
on the 190 models of 1984–85, wheels

used for these 14-inch tires had an
offset of 30 mm. Table III lists all sizes
used from the 14-inch era through
1995. Table IV is a list of load indexes
and equivalent loads in pounds per
tire at the inflation pressure noted on
the sidewall.

Load Index

To select a substitute size, first note the
load index of the original equipment
(O.E.) tire. The substitute must not
have a lower index; a higher index is
quite suitable. Next look at the number
of revolutions per mile. You will want
the substitute to be as close to the O.E.
tire as possible.

Revs Per Mile

A note of caution. Different
manufacturers calculate revolutions
per mile differently. In some cases it
is found by driving along a level road
and actually counting the revolutions.
The figure will vary depending on
the car's speed. The loaded radius is
lengthened by centrifugal force, but
the amount differs from one model of
tire to another. Of course the actual
unloaded diameter of the tire could be
used to calculate a theoretical number
of revolutions per mile or could even
be used directly for tire measurement.

However, revolutions per mile is
a regular dimension in the reference
guides of tire manufacturers, and
the figures given here are taken from
the guides of Dunlop, Michelin, and
Pirelli. Not all are the same for each
size, and not all manufacturers make
every size, and not all models by a
given manufacturer are the same.
For example, the figure in Table III
for a 195/65R15 tire is 834, but for
the Dunlop D60 A2 it is 847, for the
Michelin MXV4 it's 841, and for the
Pirelli P4000, 836. Most important, each
manufacturer cautions that revolutions
per mile dimensions are subject to a
deviation of three or four percent.

Speed Ratings

Most drivers are aware of the
significance of tire speed ratings,
identified by the letters S, T, H, V, or Z
as either part of the size designation
(HR) or part of the service description
(94H). Original equipment speed
rated tires should be replaced with
tires of the same or higher speed
rating; failure to do so compromises
the car's safety / speed capability.
Maximum speeds corresponding to
these letters are: S=112 mph, T=118,
H=130, V=149, and Z=over 149. These
speeds can be held for relatively short
periods with properly inflated, fairly
new tires which are not overloaded.
Any driver who intends or expects to
drive in the 130+ mph region should
investigate with the tire manufacturer
the limitations of any replacement tire.

Having matched or closely
approximated the O.E. tires, you can
check the offerings of your tire dealer
with reasonable assurance that the
replacements will work well.

If wider tires are to be fitted to the
same wheels, the matter of section
width must be considered. In general,
O.E. Mercedes-Benz wheels and tires
allow extra space for fitment of snow
chains, so you can try tires that are
up to one inch wider than O.E. with
probable success. Still, no guarantees
exist that wider tires will not interfere
with part of the vehicle's structure.

Certain models have restrictions
on replacement tires, notably the
300SEL 6.3 of 1968–1972. The O.E.
tires for this car were 195VR14, Type
70. Mercedes-Benz Technical Data
books give this note regarding tires for
this car: "Special version of standard
size 215/70VR14 with restricted
dimensions. Do not confuse with 80-
series tire 195VR14 or tire 195/70VR14.
Never use tire 205/70VR14 for vehicle
type 109.018 (the 6.3), since it is
smaller and weaker when compared
with the 195VR14 Type 70." Since

no other car used that particular tire, the manufacturers allowed it to become obsolete. The owner of a 6.3 should consult with other owners regarding replacement tires such as the 215/70VR14 and interference problems. [As we've mentioned before, Coker Tire has 215/70VR14 Michelin XWX tires, and they fit properly. Ed.]

New Wheels?

Replacement of O.E. wheels with Mercedes-Benz wheels of a different size requires careful checking. Replacement of 13-inch Mercedes-Benz wheels with 14-inch Mercedes-Benz wheels is common and sensible; both have the same offset and same lug screw pattern. Other switches of Mercedes-Benz wheels can be fraught with danger. Substituting a wider wheel with a different offset risks interference. Since the 14-inch, 30-mm offset wheels were dropped, a wide variety of offsets has been used, varying from the 21.5 mm of the 6-1/2Jx15 wheels of 1988–91 to the 51 mm of some of the latest models.

Wheel offset (ET in German) is the distance from the mounting surface of the wheel (where it contacts the hub) to the center line of the wheel. On all Mercedes-Benz cars the offset is positive, i.e., the centerline of the wheel is closer to the center of the car than the mounting surface of the hub is. In other words, the mounting surfaces are farther out from the car than the centerline of the tire is. A wheel with a smaller offset moves the centerline of the tire outward. A larger offset moves the centerline of the tire inward, toward the car.

When choosing aftermarket wheels, their offset should be very close to the original offset. The other item of great importance is that the aftermarket wheels should be centered by the hub of the car. All O.E. Mercedes-Benz wheels are hub-centered. The hub and the wheel center hole are an accurate fit. The lug bolts do not center the wheel; they simply hold it onto the hub. Only the most expensive aftermarket wheels are hub-centered;

Table I: 13-, 15-, 16-inch Tires, 1947–68 U.S. Models

Tire Size	Load Index	Aspect Ratio	Revs per Mile	Section Width	Alternative Tire Size
6.40x13	78	95	855	6.40	185/70R13
6.70x13	82	95	835	6.70	195/70R13
7.00x13	80	88	840	7.00	205/70R13
7.25x13	83	88	820	7.25	205/70R13
7.50x13	86	88	815	7.50	——
6.40x15	80	95	790	6.40	185/70R15
6.50x15	87	95	770	6.50	195/75R15
6.70x15	87	95	770	6.70	195/75R15
7.00x15	88	95	749	7.00	195/75R15
7.60x15	90	95	745	7.60	195/75R15
9.00x15	103	80	730	9.00	235/75R15
5.50x16	80	95	785	5.50	——
6.00x16	88	95	757	6.00	——

Table II: 14-inch Tires for Wheels of 30-mm Offset

Tire Size	Load Index	Aspect Ratio	Revs per Mile	Section Width
80-series:				
6.95R14	88	80	853	6.95
175R14	88	80	853	6.90
185R14	91	80	836	7.28
7.35R14	91	80	832	7.35
7.75R14	95	80	794	8.07
205VR14	96	80	794	8.07
70-series:				
175/70R14	84	70	870	6.90
195/70R14	91	70	834	7.68
205/70R14	93	70	828	8.07
215/70R14	96	70	802	8.46

others are lug-centered. It may be extremely difficult to balance lug-centered wheels.

When tire-shopping, remember that you are the customer, and the customer is always right. Some tire retailers may want to sell what is in stock, so they may be less than wholly committed to seeing that you get exactly the tire you want. Thankfully, other tire dealers are much more helpful.

Table III: Later Tires

Tire Size	Load Index	Aspect Ratio	Revs per Mile	Section Width
185/65R15	87	65	851	7.3
195/65R15	91	65	834	7.7
205/55R15	91	55	872	7.9
205/60R15	91	60	840	8.0
205/65R15	94	65	813	8.0
205/55R16	88	55	837	8.0
225/50R16	92	50	812	9.2
225/55R16	95	55	802	8.9
225/60R16	97	60	784	8.9
235/60R16	100	60	770	9.1
225/45R17	90	45	836	8.7
235/45R17	93	45	821	9.4
245/45R17	95	45	806	9.8
255/45R18	99	45	773	10.0

Table IV: Load Index and Equivalent Loads

Load Index	Max Load, lbs	Load Index	Max Load, lbs
77	908	91	1,356
78	937	92	1,389
79	963	93	1,433
80	992	94	1,477
81	1,019	95	1,521
82	1,047	96	1,565
83	1,074	97	1,609
84	1,102	98	1,653
85	1,135	99	1,709
86	1,168	100	1,764
87	1,201	101	1,819
88	1,235	102	1,874
89	1,279	103	1,929
90	1,323	104	1,984

Wheeling Right Along …

by Frank King, Technical Editor

January/February 1991

Wheels and Lugs

Lately we've heard of a number of problems associated with replacement wheels—some aftermarket wheels, others Mercedes-Benz factory wheels installed on models for which they were not intended.

In the July/August 1989 issue we covered wheel sizes and types, with emphasis on maintaining the originally designed wheel offset when installing wheels of a different size or design. We failed to emphasize the importance of using the correct lug screws to attach the wheel. Damage to hubs as a result of trying to use lug screws with the wrong threads or wrong length has been reported. Such damage can be expensive and may require new hubs.

Lug Screws

All lug screws used on Mercedes-Benz cars since 1963, except for the 600, have had an M12x1.5 thread. The M signifies that the thread is metric. The 12 is the diameter of the screw in mm. The 1.5 is the pitch of the thread in mm, i.e., the distance from one groove to the next, not coincidentally the distance the screw travels per turn. Note that M12x1.5 does not indicate length of the screw. When given, length is added thus: M12x1.5x13. For coarse-thread screws with pitch not shown, the length is added thus: M6x25.

For 12-mm threads, the standard pitch is 1.75 mm, and usually the screw is simply called an M12, omitting the pitch figure. The M12x1.5 is a metric fine, 12-mm screw; there is also an extra-fine M12x1. None of these

threads may be substituted for another. Forcing a coarser or finer thread into a bore will strip the threads—naturally in the more expensive hub. Lug screws are made of high-strength steel.

Applications

Lug screws vary in length according to the wheel for which they are designed. Regardless of length, each screw has 14 threads which take up 21 mm at the end of the screw. There are three different shank lengths, i.e., length from the end of the bolt to the start of the spherical collar: 21 mm, 29.5 mm, and 40 mm. The 21-mm-long screws are used with steel sheet wheels or light-alloy sheet wheels (similar in appearance to steel wheels). The 29.5-mm-long screws are used only with 14-inch forged light alloy wheels, either the older style or the new style on the 1984–85 190E 2.3 and 190D 2.5. Additional length is necessary because of the thickness of an alloy wheel.

The 40-mm-long lug screws differ by the height of the head and, for those with heads 10.5-mm high, in finish. The 40-mm-long screws with 43.5-mm heads are used on 107-, 126-, and 129-series cars. The 40-mm long screws with 22.5-mm heads are used only on the 190E 2.3-16. The 40-mm-long screws with heads 10.5-mm high are used on 124-series cars; those with a dull finish (Dacromet-coated) may be used only on alloy wheels with steel bushings. Those with a bright finish (high polish galvanized) may be used on alloy wheels with or without steel bushings.

Lug screws should be installed absolutely clean, with no lubrication. Dirty screws or bore holes should be cleaned with a toothbrush and gasoline or brake cleaner and dried before using. Screws should turn easily with the fingers until the tightening torque stage is reached. If there's resistance, the bore should be cleaned up with an M11x1.5 tap. All Mercedes-

Benz M11x1.5 lug screws should be tightened with a torque wrench to 81 lb-ft (110 Nm).

Screw Length Important

Where do problems arise? In the case of aftermarket wheels, the screws furnished may be of the wrong pitch. Screws that are too short do not get enough grip. Screws that are too long interfere with the parking brake mechanism at the rear wheels. If aftermarket wheels are installed with Mercedes-Benz screws, the wheel thickness may not match the screw length. If fewer than six threads are firmly engaged, the threads are likely to strip when proper torque is applied. This can happen when either a screw is too short—or too long so that the unthreaded shank of the screw damages the threads in the hub when torque is applied.

Wheel Offset

Problems with damaged threads often arise when original wheels are replaced by aftermarket wheels or wheels from a later model, usually for appearance or to enhance performance. The article referred to above emphasized the importance of maintaining the original factory-designed wheel offset when using other than original wheels. That article stated: "Since 15-inch new style wheels cannot be used on other models originally equipped with 14-inch wheels…" The word "cannot" ought to have been "should not", for it is possible to mount some 15-inch Mercedes-Benz wheels in place of older 14-inch wheels, but it is unwise to do so. We have heard particularly of mounting 15-inch wheels from 1986–89 560SL's on 1985 or earlier 380SL's and on 450SL's. Those 15-inch wheels have an offset of 25 mm with 7-inch-wide rims, while the 14-inch wheels have an offset of 30 mm and 6.5-inch-wide rims.

The argument has been put forth that the greater width of a 7-inch rim balances the decrease in wheel offset. This is nonsense. The effective point at which the wheel load is applied to bearings, hub, spindle, and suspension depends on the location of the center line of the wheel and tire. The location of the centerline of the wheel with respect to the bearings and hub varies from model to model. The size and strength of bearings, hub, and spindle are all designed for the stresses applied with that particular geometry.

Steering geometry and relative location of brake discs are likewise affected by changes in wheel offset.

In the case of aftermarket wheels with wider than original rims, there may be a tendency to use less negative offset than that specified by the factory to avoid interference at the inner side of the wheel. All Mercedes-Benz wheels have negative offset, i.e., the center plane of the wheel is inboard of the mounting surface of the hub. The German word for wheel offset is *Einpresstiefe*, abbreviated ET. These letters are often stamped on the inside of wheels, followed by the offset in millimeters.

Never attempt to use 14-inch wheels on a car designed for 15-inch wheels; there is insufficient room inside the smaller wheels for the brake components. This applies even to the 190E and 190D of 1984 and 1985, which can use 15-inch wheels of later 190E and 190D models but not 190E 2.3-16 wheels.

Learn and write down the part number of your wheels and their offset. Since the 1986 change to 15-inch wheels, assume nothing about wheel interchangeability. For example, the 1988–89 300CE used 6.5x15 wheels, offset 49 mm, part number 124 400 18 02, the same as the 300E sedan's. For 1990 the 300CE got the 24-valve engine and new wheels, 6.5x15, offset 48 mm, part number 124 401 08 02. This is a cast light-alloy wheel without steel bushings and without fins on the inside of the wheel. The old wheels can't be used on the new car because of the space required for new brakes.

Before buying that beautiful new set of wheels offered as an unrepeatable bargain, check the offset and fit carefully. Above all, be careful with new lug screws.

Technical and Restoration Forum

Technical and Restoration Forum

Drivability

Higher Differential Ratios
March/April 1984

I am rebuilding my 1974 450SL engine and am interested in lower cruising rpm and better fuel mileage. If I lose some acceleration, I won't be disappointed. Is there a set of higher differential gears that I can substitute for my stock ring and pinion?

Your present rear axle ratio is 3.06:1, the same as the 450SE and 450SEL. Other Mercedes-Benz U.S. models use lower ratios (higher numerically), except the 6.9 at 2.65:1. The older 6.3 used 2.82:1 or 2.85:1 ratio, but these axles are completely different from yours.

It might be possible to use the 6.9 axle but you would probably have to use the entire assembly, from one outer universal joint to the other. The 6.9 has a limited slip differential as standard equipment. The 6.9's ring and pinion might fit in place of your present gears, but correct assembly is so difficult that MBNA may not sell just the gears. The best bet would be to find an entire axle from a used parts supplier.

Such a change would reduce engine rpm by 13 percent at a given road speed. Overdrive transmissions usually give about a 20 percent reduction, but I know of none available for the 450SL. You might find one in Germany but at great expense. A 6.9 rear axle would also be expensive; you would likely find that the results do not justify the expense.

350SL Vibration
March/April 1985

My 1972 350SL vibrates only at 30–40 mph, but as weight is added (full fuel, more passengers, etc.), the vibration becomes more pronounced. What might be causing it?

It is difficult to analyze a vibration through the mail, but I assume you have already checked tire balance and wheel alignment. You can check engine vibration by putting the transmission in the lowest gear and driving at 30–40 mph. If the vibration still occurs at that speed, it is not the engine, but is somewhere in the drivetrain. Next, drive the car 40 mph, then slip the transmission into neutral so that the car is coasting and the engine is idling. If the vibration still occurs, the rear axle and driveshaft are the most likely sources.

Your car is now over 12 years old, so the original rubber mounts for the engine and drivetrain may have deteriorated. Also, check the driveshaft bearing, driveshaft mounting flanges and all universal joints. The alignment of the driveshaft and axles is affected by loading of the car. If work has been done on the driveshaft, it is possible that it was re-assembled incorrectly, so that it is out of balance.

Differential Oil Change
September/October 2003

At 70,000 miles, should I change the rear differential oil in my 1989 560SL, and which synthetic oil is best?

Yes, change the oil, but no synthetic gear lubes are approved by Mercedes-Benz for their passenger car differentials. *Specification for Service Products, Sheet 235.0* lists many manufacturers of GL-5 hypoid gear oil in SAE 90 or SAE 85W/90 that are suitable. Virtually any well known brand of hypoid gear oil will work well. We suggest changing it every 30,000 miles.

Steering at Play

July/August 1997

The steering of my 1988 300E has 1 to 1½ inches of play; after checking the steering linkage and installing new tires, my mechanic feels the problem is steering box wear. Could the problem be anything other than this expensive part?

Steering play is usually due to gradual wear in all of the parts of the front end linkage. The steering box is subject to wear, but the joints in the linkage usually have to be replaced once before replacing the steering box. Besides the ball joints and tie rod ends, the mounting of the idler arm in its rubber bushing should be checked with a dial indicator. If play exceeds 0.5 mm, the rubber bushing should be replaced.

The three steering gear mounting bolts should be re-tightened to a torque of 80 Nm (59 lb-ft); they should not be loosened to check the torque. Check for play in the flexible steering coupling, too. Mercedes-Benz specifies maximum steering play of 25 mm (1 in) at the steering wheel rim. An old rule of thumb is that two fingers is OK, but three fingers is too much (excuse the pun). Before replacing the box, have the system checked by a more experienced Mercedes-Benz mechanic. If the fault is in the box, Mercedes-Benz requires that it be replaced, not repaired.

Turbo Trailering

May/June 1985

I have been told I should not tow a trailer with my 1984 300D. Is this true? Are there restrictions on towing a trailer with a turbo-diesel? Is there a suspension package available to maintain a level attitude?

I have never heard of any unusual restriction on towing with any Mercedes-Benz. When towing a trailer with any model, the maintenance program should be based on severe conditions so that oil and other lubricants are changed more frequently and wear on such parts as brake pads is checked more often.

Caster, Camber and Cornering

January/February 1985

My 1981 240D has 185/70-14 Michelin XVS tires. Which combination of caster and camber settings (maximum or minimum) will provide optimum cornering capability?

Theoretically, increasing the caster will make the steering more stable on straights but slightly harder to turn; when in a turn, the wheels will have more tendency to straighten themselves. Changing caster within factory settings is not likely to have much effect on pure cornering power.

An outside, loaded wheel has greater cornering power if it leans toward the center of curvature, i.e., has negative camber. Good suspension design controls the change in camber as the suspension is loaded and unloaded. To maximize cornering power, set the camber towards the most negative specified setting. For your car, camber is specified as 0° + 10' or -20'.

Whatever the settings, the differences would be miniscule in comparison to what wheel and tire improvements would do. I suggest 6-in alloy wheels with more performance-oriented tires. In 185/70-14, tire choices would be limited, but an experienced autocrosser suggests the Yokohama A008, Michelin MXL, Pirelli CN36 or the old Phoenix Stahlflex 3011 if you can still find them; Semperit's replacement for the Phoenix doesn't seem to be as good. In 195/70x14, a slightly wider but taller size, you could use the BFG Comp T/A, Michelin XWX, etc., but these would gear the car slightly higher, not always desirable. Then, of course, there are even wider wheels and lower profile tires. …

300E Front End Vibes

May/June 1988

Ever since I bought my 300E, it has had a front end vibration. At low speeds these vibrations can be felt only in the steering, but at high speeds (80 mph) the whole car vibrates. I've changed tires and shock absorbers and made other front end adjustments to no avail. Any suggestions?

Some early 300E's had a vibration problem, usually around 65 mph and particularly when braking. In January 1987, modified wishbone bushings were phased into production to correct steering wheel and vehicle vibrations. Repair kits were made available to dealers to allow retrofits to earlier cars. Both the W124 (300-series) and W201 (190-series) cars are very sensitive to out-of-balance and/or out-of-round wheels. Before 1985 the tolerances for tire and rim runout were 1.2 mm vertical and 2.0 mm lateral, but these have been reduced for all models. Vertical runout should not exceed 0.8 mm for the tire and wheel assembly on any model.

Weighty Problem

March/April 1987

I love my 1985 380SE, but I'm disappointed in its behavior on snowy and icy roads, where it skids and slides on hills and in corners. Why?

There are two reasons for the behavior you note, which is not limited to Mercedes-Benz. One is the weight distribution, whereby 55 percent of the weight is on the front wheels, 45 percent on the rear. Second is the rear suspension design, which allows a change in rear wheel track as the rear wheels move up and down. When the tires move sideways, they lose some traction.

Before 1978 I lived and drove four Mercedes-Benzes in Montreal. We always put extra weight in the trunk for the winter, usually from 120 to 200 lbs of dry sand; over 200 lbs is too much. Sacks of lead shot also work, and the editor (in Colorado) says he's seen boxes of sand sold specifically for this purpose. I assume you're using snow tires on all four wheels.

Suspension

Oingo-Boingo

July/August 1996

The former owner of my 1972 280SE 4.5 replaced the rear axle hydraulic compensator with a coil spring. My mechanic says this works fine and saved money and that all I lose is the self-leveling feature. What is your advice?

For cost reasons, it has been common practice to replace the hydropneumatic compensating spring with a steel spring. If you're happy with the handling and ride and don't miss the self-leveling, leave it as is.

Bag It

September/October 1994

To avoid the cost of replacing the airbags in my 1972 300SEL 4.5's suspension, I'm considering converting to coil springs. A previous owner said that he had to replace the bags every couple of years. Which way should I go?

If you could find someone to do it correctly, changing to coil springs would probably cost more than replacing the airbags. Actually, these bags are usually long lasting. Those on one staff member's car are at least 14 years old yet still work fine. A lot depends on climate and road conditions, but don't let air suspension scare you off; it's quite simple.

6.3 Gunk

November/December 2003

When I purge the suspension air tank on my 1971 300SEL 6.3, "oil" also comes out! Is this normal?

When you drain the reservoir of any air compressor, you get a mixture of oil and air. It is normal for an air compressor tank to deliver a gunky-looking mixture as it is emptied. As air is compressed, moisture in the air ends up in the reservoir. No matter how good the factory air-drying system is, there will still be water in the suspension system. Whenever the alcohol bottle is allowed to empty, the air suspension takes in water vapor. That vapor mixes with oil vapor from the compressor, and the residue remains in the tank to show up as oily water when you bleed the system.

Stiffer 400E Springs

January/February 1999

The suspension of my 1992 400E is too soft. Does the list of 300E Sportline parts in the September/October 1997 issue also apply to the 400E?

The list of parts for converting a W124 sedan to the Sportline version applies to your 400E but with special attention to the notes about front springs. A good parts person at a dealership should be helpful in selecting the right front springs and rubber mountings. Before going this route, you might try increasing tire pressures or switching to different tires.

Stiff Riding 6.9

November/December 1995

After 53,000 miles, my 450SEL 6.9 rides harshly. We replaced two pressure tanks, but it still rides like a truck. What is the likely cause?

Your car's hydropneumatic suspension uses compressed nitrogen as the springing element. Sealed in reservoirs at pressures up to 1,100 psi (75 bar), the nitrogen can slowly leak out. With a lower volume of nitrogen, springing becomes stiffer. To restore the normal ride, you'll probably have to replace all four pressure reservoirs.

Leaky 300TD Pressure Reservoirs

May/June 1991

My 1980 300TD has covered 177,000 miles. Because the rear struts were leaking, the rear of the car sagged, and it rode hard, I recently replaced the struts, but the ride is still hard. Could the air cells be bad, and how can I tell?

The pressure reservoirs (air cells) can be checked for proper gas pressure. When new, they contain gas at 333 ± 15 psi (23 ± 1 bar); the minimum pressure is 220 psi (15 bar). As pressure decreases, ride gets harder because there is less gas to act as a spring, and the reservoir fills with oil. The reservoirs aren't field repairable and must be replaced. Their usual life of about 10 years varies from car to car.

Lower 190E

May/June 1988

I would like to lower my 1987 190E 2.6. Can I use parts from the 190E 2.3-16 to do so?

Practically speaking, no. The 16-valve car's rear suspension is quite different, incorporating a hydraulic self-leveling system, and parts are expensive. If you want to lower your car, several aftermarket suspension kits are available to do so. Write to Bilstein of America at 11760 Sorrento Valley Rd., San Diego CA, 92121 or to Sebring Automotive Enterprises (who sell Koni products) at 127-11 94th Ave., Richmond Hill, NY 11419.

Rubber Baby Buggy Bushings

January/February 2003

I read about replacing rubber suspension bushings. How many pieces are there in my 500SEL, and how expensive are they to replace? How do I know if they need replacement?

Suspension components are connected to each other via rubber bushings. Every component has at least one bushing, and some (lower control arms) have two or three. Over years of use, especially in dry climates, rubber bushings dry out and start to collapse. When bushings collapse, they no longer locate the suspension parts correctly, so the suspension can become misaligned. With the car on a lift, you can usually see if the bushings and the bolts that go through them are not concentric. You can

also spot bushings that are cracked and falling apart in the last stages of decay. Collapsed bushings can also be felt while driving, through a vague feeling about where the car is on the road, or if little steering corrections are necessary to keep it going in a straight line. Have your mechanic examine the suspension and make an estimate. Rubber bushings that come with the parts are not worth replacing by themselves. Others are available in repair kits and are easily replaced. When the cost to overhaul a part is the same or close to that of a new part, buy the new part. Either way, you pay for the removal and replacement labor.

Cracked Axle Boot

January/February 2003

My 1982 300D wagon has a cracked CV boot on the rear axle. Can I replace it myself, or should I leave it to a professional mechanic?

Replacing an axle boot requires two special tools, one to cut open the boot can, another to crimp the new can in place. These tools are expensive, and we've never seen them for rent. New axles aren't expensive in the aftermarket, and this repair is well covered in the service manual. We suggest replacing the axle itself. Boot kits cost about $100, and the labor time to remove and replace the axle is 1.5 hours and to replace the boot, 1.3 hours. If your shop charges $80 an hour, then it's $100 in parts and $100 in labor for the boot alone. Why not replace the axle for a little more?

Wheels

Alloy Wheel Repainting

September/October 1994

The alloy wheels on my 1978 300CD need repainting. One body shop says that they have had mixed success in repainting these wheels; they recommended sanding off the old finish, using an etching primer, then finishing with astral silver paint and a clear coat. Would you recommend this?

The *Mercedes-Benz Refinishing Manual* says that the original finish—an oven-baked, powder coat, metallic paint—cannot be reproduced in the field and recommends that the wheels be repainted using the same method as for body paintwork:

1. Thoroughly clean the wheel.

2. Sand bright or damaged spots to the extent that the oxide layer of the light-alloy is removed; roughen the webs with steel wool.

3. Paint with MB-2K primer filler. Air or oven dry and allow the wheel to cool.

4. Sand the entire surface to be painted with 400 (P600) grit wet, then finish with 600 (P1200) wet.

5. Spray with astral silver #9735 metallic base coat.

6. After 10–15 minutes flash-off time, apply MB-2K clear coat and dry.

Hubcap Color

July/August 1994

My 1976 450SL was painted #470 Colorado Beige with a hardtop in #424 Topaz Brown. Which color would have been original on the hubcaps?

Generally, when an SL has a hardtop color different from that of the body, the hubcaps are painted the hardtop color.

Lug Bolt Dimension Change

January/February 2004

If you've needed lug bolts in the past year, you may have been surprised at the bolts the parts man handed you. Looking for long bolts, you were given short ones instead. The threaded portion was the same length, but the extension to bring the bolt head out to the face of the wheel was missing. Mercedes-Benz has substituted the short bolt for most older longer bolts. Since many shops failed to properly torque the long bolts, many of them broke, and it is difficult to get the broken bolt out of the deep recess in the wheel. The new bolt is part 203 401 02 70. Superceded bolts include 124 400 00 70, 124 400 01 70, 124 400 04 70, 124 400 07 70, 201 400 00 70, and 126 400 00 70.

Always clean and lube a bolt's threads but not its spherical collar, which should be dry. Torque the bolts to the correct specification for your year and model.

Wheel Torques

May/June 1984

In response to recent questions, I checked the factory specifications regarding wheel lug bolt torque. *Service Information No. 40/45* of March 1983 gives the tightening torque for all models except the 600 as 110 Nm (81 ft-lb); the torque for the 600 is 170 Nm (110 ft-lb). These values are confirmed in the applicable microfiche and the *Model Introduction Book* for 1984. The earlier figure of 100 Nm (73 ft-lb) is superseded. These torques apply to all types of factory-supplied wheels: steel disc, light-alloy disc (same appearance as steel disc) and forged light-alloy.

In checking their torque, lug bolts should be loosened slightly, say one-eighth of a turn, then tightened with the torque wrench. Simply applying the required torque only insures that the bolt is at least as tight as required; it does not relax bolts that have been over-tightened.

If aftermarket wheels of any material or type are installed, the same torque values apply, since the governing factor in determining torque values is the clamping force that must be applied to the wheels without damaging hubs or other supporting elements.

C280 Wheel Bearings

May/June 2003

While rotating the tires on my 60,000-mile 1998 C280, I noticed that the left front wheel bearing has more play than the right front bearing when I move the wheels with my hands at the top and bottom of the wheel or at the left and right. Previously they had little play. How can I tell if the bearing is worn? Can the bearings be re packed, or are new bearings needed?

The only way to tell if wheel bearings are worn is to remove them, clean them, and inspect them. Look for discoloration, pitting, or galling of the bearing or race. You can repack the bearings and the hub. If the bearings are damaged, replacements are supplied complete with race and must be replaced together. If you think there is excessive free play, check it with a dial indicator. Wheel bearing clearance is set using a dial indicator, and clearance should be 0.01 to 0.02 mm (0.0004 to 0.0008 inch). Yes, that is ten-thousandths. Very few mechanics use a dial indicator to set bearing clearance, but that procedure is called for by Mercedes-Benz and bearing manufacturers. The procedure for removing, cleaning, repacking, resetting, and replacing wheel bearings is in the *Service Information*. Use only the correct Mercedes-Benz wheel bearing grease, available from any Mercedes-Benz parts counter. Do not mix Mercedes-Benz wheel bearing grease with any other grease. The grease quantities are 15 grams in the hub cap and 60 grams in the hub (including the bearings) on each side. Done correctly, according to the manual, wheel bearing service is a very satisfying do-it-yourself procedure.

Wheel Bearing Grease

January/February 1989

Can I use Valvoline grease to repack the front wheel bearings of my 1980 280CE? None of the approved brands are readily available. Valvoline makes three types—614 Val-Plex EP, 632 Special Moll EP and 733 DB Wheel Bearing Grease. Which can I use?

In 1982, DBAG adopted a new high temperature grease for front wheel bearings, part number 000 989 49 51. The replaced all previous types of grease, and it comes in small jars containing just the right amount for two front wheels. It is also sold in the U.S. as Shell Retinax AX, which will be tough to find.

If you wish to stick with Valvoline in the type of grease approved by DBAG before 1982, the 614 or 632 would work. Be sure that whatever you use is rated NLGI No. 2. The quantity specified is about 60 grams (about 2 oz) for each wheel; about 45 grams is used to fill the roller cages and smear the outside of the rollers, and 15 grams is put in the hub cap. The space between the bearings should not contain any appreciable amount of grease.

If you use the new Mercedes-Benz high temperature grease, avoid mixing it with the older type, as they are incompatible. See the September/October 1986 issue of *The Star* for more information.

280SL Rear Wheel Bearings

January/February 1989

The outer rear wheel bearings on my 200,000-mile 280SL started rumbling and were replaced, right and left. Although the car originally used a roller bearing on the right, and a grooved ball bearing on the left, my mechanic used the latter on both sides. He explained that based upon his 30 years' experience, this was the best course. What do you think?

We can't agree with your mechanic that the grooved ball bearing is the best choice for replacement of the old roller bearing in your car. The original left rear wheel bearing in your car was a grooved ball bearing, part number 183 981 00 25; the right side had a self-aligning roller bearing, part number 000 981 05 06. These bearings have the same inside and outside diameters, so they are physically interchangeable. In different combinations they are also used in 108-, 109-, 111- and 113-series cars, including the 280S/SE/SEL, the 300SEL's, the 280SE coupes and convertibles and the 280SL. Some versions of these models used another grooved ball bearing, part number 001 981 15 25.

Normal design practice is to select a ball bearing when rotational speed is more important than load and, conversely, a roller bearing when load is more important. For a given size of bearing, the ball type will tolerate greater speeds than the roller for a given load, but the roller bearing will tolerate higher loads for a given speed. Of course, there's a broad area in which either type is well within its capabilities in either load or speed.

The reasons for selection of bearing type may be because the rear axle of these cars is asymmetrical. The left axle tube is fastened to the differential housing, so the axle shaft is more rigidly located than the right axle shaft, which is in a tube with a sliding joint; the self-aligning bearing adjusts to any variation. On the lighter and lower-powered cars such as the 280S, both wheels have grooved ball bearings. The 280SL and the 280SE coupe and cabriolet have one self-aligning roller bearing. The 108- and 109-series cars with V8 engines (280SE 4.5, 300SEL 6.3, etc.) use roller bearings, part number 000 981 05 06, on both sides.

Rear wheel bearing replacement is one of the rarest of repairs. As attested by their 200,000-mile life on your car, selection was on the conservative side. Axle shaft speed never exceeds 2,000 rpm (at about 140 mph), a low speed for either ball or roller bearings in this size. We wouldn't bother changing the right bearing back to the roller type now, but if noise ever develops again, you'll know where to look. As to why self-aligning bearings aren't used on both sides, we expect that it was for cost reasons; a roller bearing is usually more expensive to manufacture than a ball bearing.

Wheel Bearing Service Intervals

January/February 1993

How often should the front and rear wheel bearings be repacked on my 190E 2.3-16?

Rear wheel bearings are factory lubricated for the life of the car, so there's no recommended service interval. Failure is extremely rare. There is also no set period for replacement of front wheel bearings or lubricant, but since front brake discs occasionally need replacement, wheel bearing inspection and service are included in that job. Otherwise, an interval of about 60,000 miles seems about right. Because of changes in bearings and lubricants, intervals set for older cars are no longer applicable.

Steel Wheels for W124 Cars

November/December 1988

Where can I buy steel wheels to mount snow tires on my 260E?

Steel wheels for 124 models are available from dealers as part number 124 400 12 02. These 6½ x15-inch wheels fit the 260E, 300D Turbo, 300TD Turbo, 300E and 300CE and accept 195/65-15 snow tires.

Tires

Flat Tires
May/June 2000

My 1979 450SL has covered only 33,000 miles, but after replacing the tires recently, it developed a front-end shimmy when first driven after being parked for several days. After I drive a few miles, the shimmy disappears. Most of the front end bushings have been replaced, and the tires have been rebalanced twice. Is this a steering problem?

The vibration is most likely due to the tires. As they cool after driving, flat spots form at the ground contact patch. After a few miles of driving, the tires warm up enough to become more flexible, so the flat spots are worked out, smoothing the ride. Low tire pressure can exacerbate the problem, so make sure the pressures are correct. The longer a tire sits with weight on it, the more likely it is to develop a flat spot. Some tires may also be susceptible to flat-spotting. If you can't live with it, you may have to buy a different tire.

Super Sticky Stoppers
March/April 1987

I recently fitted a set of Ronal R9 7 x 16 wheels and 205/55VR16 Goodyear VRS tires on my 1986 300E. The ABS now seems to require more pedal pressure before it engages. Why?

Because ABS only engages when one tire slips beyond a certain amount, and your stickier tires slip less and stop better at a given pedal pressure, your ABS now doesn't operate until a higher rate of deceleration (and higher pedal pressure). Theoretically, if your tires had perfect grip, the ABS would never operate, even if you stood on the brake pedal. Conversely, if you put on a set of narrow, smooth tires and drove on ice, the ABS would engage at a much lower level.

Radial Tire Rotation
September/October 1990

I understand that radial tires can be rotated criss-cross, but others tell me that they should only be rotated back to front. Who's right?

Mercedes-Benz AG and Pirelli both recommend that if radial tires are rotated, they must not be criss-crossed. The tires must be kept so that they always turn in the same direction. Both also recommend that tires be rotated only if the process is started and continued before the tires show any typical front-wheel or rear-wheel wear. Usually this would mean at intervals no longer than 5,000 miles. Practically speaking, radial tires are seldom rotated today; it seems just as well to leave them in their original positions.

Approved Tire Lists
July/August 2002

Our wheel and tire guide in the March/April issue mentioned a list of replacement tires approved by Mercedes-Benz, and several readers asked where this list could be found.

For 1986 through 1999 models, *Service Information P-SI-40.10/20 P*, September 2000, lists factory-approved summer, all-season, and winter tires as well as factory-approved summer tires for accessory wheels and steel wheels for winter tires. For 2000–2001 models, *Service Information P-SI-40.10/033* lists factory-approved summer, all-season, and winter tires. Earlier models are covered by a variety of *Service Information* publications. Such publications are available through Mercedes-Benz USA's Customer Assistance Center, 800/FORMERC; Mercedes-Benz dealers should have copies accessible to owners.

"Engineered Like No Other Car in the World ..."

September/October 1990

To demonstrate your creativity and wit, simply send us a funny caption for this photograph from the Mercedes-Benz archives of motoring humor. Besides winning undying fame in the annals of MBCA, the winner may also receive a fine, framed limited-edition print of this photograph with his or her winning caption inscribed below it. We can always use a good laugh!

January/February 1991

What a bunch of wise guys! We expected a good response to the Caption Contest in the September/October issue, and you came through. Almost all entries were funny. Some were even printable. We just hope DBAG's lawyers have a sense of humor, especially when they learn that more than a few wits coyly suggested the headline above.

Without further fanfare, the first place winner is Greg Franks, Nashville Section, for his caption:

"Not all of the planned options panned out for the 1963 models."

Greg will receive a framed original print of the photograph with his winning caption engraved on a fragment of genuine German imitation bakelite window trim. Here's a sampling of Honorable Mention entries, listed alphabetically by author:

"You've heard of a 220D. You've heard of a 220S. Well, here's a 220V2!"
Jay Baumler, Western Reserve

"The first 190D to successfully enter a California freeway."
Frank Blanchard, North Texas

"From little acorns—Peter Sauber's early efforts at turbocharging a Mercedes-Benz."
Jim Harper, Minute Man

"After a long night assembling the turbo kit without instructions, Fred was ready to fire her up."
Charles Houser, International Star

"Uh, Werner, are you sure this extension cord is supposed to be permanently attached to this new trap oxidizer?"
Mike Phillips, Sacramento

"Evel von Knievel prepares for his first attempt at jumping the Rhine River."
Fred Rose, Milwaukee

"Oh well, I guess a nuclear-powered catalytic converter was a lousy idea anyway."
Jack Sauerland, Southwest Florida

"Do you think they'll put us in the modified class?"
Denis Simmons, International Stars

"Sure it's fast on acceleration, but how long is that extension cord?"
Chuck Stewart, Western Michigan

"I know EPA requires these new catalytic converters on next year's models, but I sure hope Engineering can shrink the size before we go into production."
Paul Streckewald, Los Angeles

"Crash dummies were assigned driving positions in tests of DBAG's re-entry into space technology. A frustrated rocket scientist looks at one."
Bill Walters, Central Coast

"This prototype catalytic converter also proved useful in thwarting tailgaters."
Steve Wirtes, Houston

Chapter 7
Brakes

November/December 1991

September/October 1993

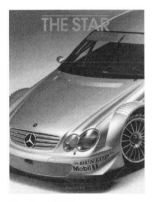

May/June 2002

Bleeding and Fluid

by Frank King,
Technical Editor

*November/December
1991*

This kind of bleeding isn't really bloody. It's a procedure for which the Germans have a better name, *Entlüftung*, meaning to rid of air. The term describes the process of causing a liquid to flow out of a container so that trapped or entrained air or gas is also removed. In our cars it is usually brake fluid, diesel fuel, or coolant that is bled. Here we'll talk only of bleeding brakes and brake fluid.

Bleeding is necessary when air gets into the brake system. Like any gas, air compresses readily and acts as a cushion in hydraulic fluid. The brake pedal feels spongy and may even be pressed to the floor without fully applying the brakes. Bleeding then becomes absolutely necessary.

Brake fluid is hygroscopic—it readily absorbs moisture from the air. Water (from condensation or contamination, etc.) dissolves in brake fluid and thus lowers the fluid's boiling point. Boiling produces vapor, which is compressible and can lead to brake failure, called "brake fade". Since brake calipers and pistons become hot in normal use, the boiling point of the fluid must be high enough to prevent boiling.

As a safety precaution, Mercedes-Benz long recommended that brake fluid be replaced annually. This interval was recently doubled to two years.

Replacing brake fluid requires bleeding until only fresh fluid is present throughout the system. Three methods of bleeding brakes force fluid to flow from the master cylinder and out of a bleed valve at each wheel. From the least recommended to the most, they are 1) the two-man method, 2) the vacuum method, and 3) the pressure method.

Two-Man Method

This method, the only system in the early days of hydraulic brakes, was described in Mercedes-Benz owner's manuals as late as 1959. When done correctly the steps were:

1. Keep the brake fluid reservoir full while bleeding.

2. At one wheel slip a bleeder hose over the nipple of the bleeding screw and put the other end of the hose in a glass jar. Put enough brake fluid in the jar so that the hose end is always covered by fluid.

3. Loosen the bleeder screw.

4. Push the brake pedal down and release it slowly, repeating until no more bubbles appear in the jar.

5. When pushing the pedal down for the last time, hold it down until the bleed screw has been tightened.

6. Do the same at the other wheels.

7. Replenish the fluid reservoir and close it.

This method is often modified by eliminating the bleed hose or allowing it to discharge without keeping the end under fluid. The man in the car pushes the pedal to the floor and holds it there while the man at the wheel closes the bleed valve before the pedal is released. The pedal is pushed again and the bleed valve opened to repeat the process until clean-looking fluid comes out.

This method eliminates air from the system if done carefully. In practice, air is often drawn back into the system if the bleed valve is not closed at the right time or if the pedal is released too soon. There is, however, a much more serious flaw in this method. Figure 1 is a master cylinder of mid-1950's vintage, for drum brakes; Figure 2 is a 1990's master cylinder, serving disc brakes via two separate circuits. In both, plastic cups or sleeves move with the pistons in tight, sealing contact with the cylinder walls.

In normal use the piston stroke always covers approximately the same section of the cylinder; the start of a stroke is dictated by the location of the filling and compensating bores. As brake pads or linings wear, the wheel pistons shift accordingly, but their increased distance from the master cylinder is taken up by additional brake fluid.

Back when the two-man method was in use, some service managers refused to replace brake fluid annually because they had so many complaints from customers who experienced leaking brake systems afterward. Leaks were caused by damage to the plastic cups and sleeves in the master cylinder. The section of the cylinder in which the piston normally moved was polished with use, but the area beyond it was rougher, with corrosion and deposits. When pistons were pushed into this corroded area during two-man bleeding, cups and sleeves were damaged, causing a leak.

The two-man method can be used successfully by careful and tedious work, keeping the outer end of the hose in fluid and taking only very short strokes with the brake pedal.

Vacuum Method

Vacuum bleeding eliminates the objections to the two-man method and is generally satisfactory as long as there are no stubborn air pockets. In the vacuum method the fluid reservoir is emptied of old fluid and filled with fresh. Then one end of a hose is connected to the bleed nipple, the other end to a vacuum pump. Either a hand pump or a pump powered by compressed air may be used, but it must have a receptacle between the bleed valve and the pump. The bleed valve is opened, and fluid is drawn through the system into the receptacle. When it is clean and no more bubbles come through, the valve is closed and the process repeated at the other wheels.

Because the master cylinder piston never moves, the vacuum method avoids damaging the cups and sleeves. Because the wheel cylinder is under

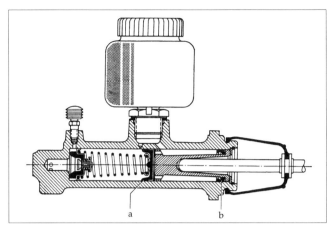

Figure 1. Old-style brake master cylinder has seals at a) primary cup and b) secondary cup.

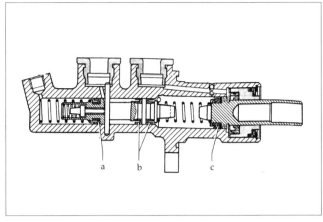

Figure 2. Newer master cylinders serve two brake circuits so have seals at a) primary sleeve, b) separating sleeve and c) another primary sleeve.

constant outside vacuum, there's no chance of air getting into it. This method requires only one man but is slow. Since the force expelling fluid and air is only a partial vacuum, probably no more than 0.5 bar (7 psi), trapped air is not moved very forcefully.

Pressure Method

Pressure bleeding employs a container holding fresh fluid which can be pressurized. The brake fluid reservoir on the master cylinder is removed, and a hose from the pressurized container is connected in its place. The container is usually pressurized to about one bar (15 psi). The bleed valve is then opened at one wheel after another, and the old fluid is simply caught for disposal. Brakes are usually bled in order—right rear, left rear, right front, left front—so that the longest line is bled first, thus minimizing the chance of an unbled section.

The pressure method has none of the other systems' defects. Still, on 1991 and later models with ASR (Acceleration Slip Control), a power bleeder that can be pressurized to 2 bar (29 psi) must be used. This is because there is more piping and the ABS/ASR hydraulic unit to be bled.

Brake Fluid

The fluid we've talked about so far is DOT 4 brake fluid, as supplied by Mercedes-Benz under part number 000 989 07 07 10. It has a dry boiling point of 510°F and a wet boiling point of 333°F. DOT 3 brake fluid has lower boiling points and isn't approved for use in Mercedes-Benz cars. DOT 5, silicone brake fluid, is not hygroscopic.

When silicone brake fluid first appeared on the market, the more venturesome rushed to install it. DOT 5 was favored by the U.S. Army for vehicles serviced in army depots, but manufacturers of automobiles for the public avoid it, for good reasons.

When moisture gets into DOT 3 or DOT 4 brake fluid, as it surely will in time, the boiling point of *the entire mixture* goes down slowly because the water mixes with the brake fluid, as it does in antifreeze. When moisture gets into DOT 5 fluid, and it will, it doesn't mix. It remains in discrete droplets or drops. The fluid's boiling point is unaffected, but the water drops will boil at 212°F and freeze at 32°F. A drop of water turned to steam will cause more trouble than an equal volume of air, and a frozen drop of water in a master cylinder valve could make at least one brake circuit ineffective. Free water in the brake system can also cause corrosion. In some models the brake light switch is particularly subject to such corrosion.

DOT 5 fluid is 2.4 times more compressible than DOT 4 or DOT 3 fluid. We tend to overlook the fact that liquids are compressible because the amount is usually insignificant. Brake lines are very long in relation to the volume of the fluid, and line

pressure can be several hundred psi, so fluid compression translates into linear motion at the pedal. Thus the more compressible silicone fluid provides a softer pedal feel than that of DOT 4 fluid.

Silicone brake fluid is not as good a lubricant between the sleeves and cylinder walls as DOT 4. Finally, the seals and sleeves are made of rubberlike plastic designed for use with DOT 3 or DOT 4.

Conclusion

Mercedes-Benz now recommends replacing brake fluid every two years, preferably in the spring. Many choose to stick with the older recommendation of annual replacement, particularly if the brakes are subject to hard use. Only DOT 4 brake fluid should be used. Mercedes-Benz brake fluid exceeds FMVSS (Federal Motor Vehicle Safety Standard) #116 requirements by a considerable margin. Incidentally, the Mercedes-Benz package calls the fluid "DOT 4 (DOT 3)" because it also meets DOT 3 standards. This labeling is also used on other (but not all) brands of DOT 4.

Brake fluid is based on glycerol, a broad group of chemicals which taste sweet but are poisonous to man and animals. In this respect it is similar to antifreeze, based on glycol. Brake fluid is very corrosive to paint. Always read all container warnings.

Fouled Brake System

**by Frank King,
Technical Editor**

*September/October
1993*

One fortunately rare potential disaster in automotive maintenance is the introduction into the braking system of any substance other than brake fluid. The brake fluid should be DOT 4, but DOT 3 will not contaminate the system—it just doesn't work as well and should be replaced with DOT 4. The calamity is the addition of such fluids as engine oil, transmission fluid, antifreeze, oil of any kind, or any other liquid.

We have had reports of such happenings, either through accidentally pouring the forbidden liquid into the brake reservoir or mistakenly using some such substance for cleaning up after repairs. At one time Mercedes-Benz did allow the use of denatured ethyl alcohol for cleaning, but this was firmly and strictly rescinded in *Service Bulletin 42/89* of January 1985.

So what do you do after discovering that someone has topped up the brake reservoir with engine oil, ATF, or some unknown fluid? If the mistake is noticed within seconds after the addition, the entire reservoir can be removed before the poison has had a chance to adulterate the previous contents of the reservoir or to permeate the system even slightly. However, if more than a few minutes have passed and the brakes have been used, a major operation is called for.

Simply flushing the system with brake fluid would be about as effective as applying a Band-Aid to the bite of a black mamba. Mineral oil is extremely lethal to the brake system's rubber or plastic components. Restoring the system to a safe and serviceable condition requires the following procedure.

All metal parts of the system must be removed and disassembled, discarding every rubber or plastic part including seals, o-rings, gaskets, brake light switches, and brake hoses. All metal parts must be thoroughly cleaned, including the brake lines. It is probably easier and less costly to simply replace the steel brake lines rather than attempting to clean them. They may be starting to rust anyway. Metal components must be washed with carbon tetrachloride or a dry cleaning fluid then with alcohol (preferably ethyl) and finally blown dry with compressed air.

Metal parts can then be reassembled using all new rubber and plastic seals and parts. In reassembling, use only brake fluid to moisten seals, o-rings, and gaskets for ease in fitting. Fill the system with DOT 4 brake fluid and bleed the entire system at least twice.

ABS News Release

January/February 1971

STUTTGART, West Germany—A new, advanced braking system that prevents lock-up during emergency stops has been announced and demonstrated here by the Daimler-Benz AG, the world's oldest auto maker.

The new electronic braking control carries the name of Anti-Bloc System (ABS for short), and has been under development since 1966. Officials said the system is adaptable to its Mercedes-Benz passenger cars, trucks and buses, and that it will be available on all passenger car models within the next few years.

The age-old problem of controlling a vehicle during panic stops, particularly on poor or slippery surfaces and in corners, has been practically eliminated with ABS. It is no longer possible to lock up the wheels, thanks to the electronic sensing unit.

Braking distances are also considerably shortened, particularly on wet roads, and braking in curves without losing control now becomes possible thanks to ABS.

A Mercedes-Benz sedan (all of which are equipped with four-wheel power disc brakes as standard) can be stopped from 60 mph in 160 feet on a dry surface. With ABS installed, the same sedan can be stopped in 138 feet—a reduction of 24 feet, or 16 percent.

More important than the distance, however, is the speed with which the deceleration is effected. In braking, deceleration increases toward the end of the total stopping distance. At the point where the vehicle equipped with ABS came to a stop (138 feet), the vehicle without ABS still has a speed of 25 mph.

With normal braking systems, when the wheels are locked the front ones are no longer capable of being steered, as they have lost their adhesion with the road surface. With ABS, since this does not occur, the front wheels can be steered at all times. This permits the driver to avoid an obstacle without taking his foot from the brake pedal.

The ABS braking control, developed by Daimler-Benz in conjunction with Teldix, a German electronic company, consists of sensors on all four wheels, an electronic device and a hydraulic control valve unit.

As soon as a wheel begins to lock as a result of excessive pressure on the brake pedal, the automatic system reduces the braking force to maximize the gripping capacity of the tire.

The sensor at the wheel transmits to the electronic unit the locked condition which causes the electronic unit to reduce the pressure of the brake fluid enough to stop the locking.

The cycle repeats itself in milliseconds until the car has stopped or until pressure on the brake pedal is removed.

In an emergency stop, the ABS keeps all wheels within the range just before the point of locking, which permits maximum adhesion.

Although Daimler-Benz financed approximately half the development costs of the Anti-Bloc System, it has signed an agreement with Teldix to make the system available to other automobile manufacturers in the interest of furthering automotive safety.

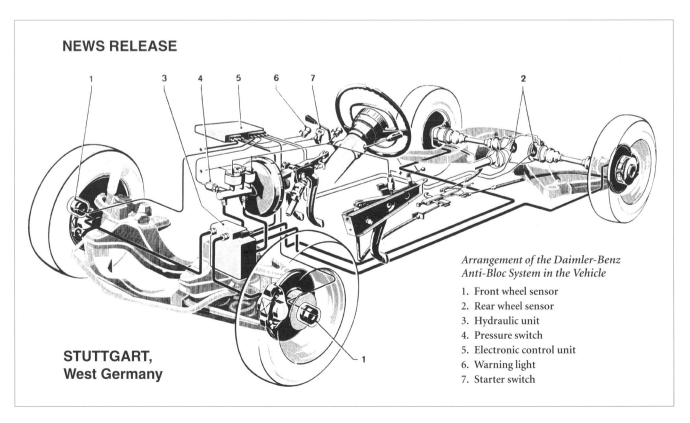

NEWS RELEASE

STUTTGART, West Germany

Arrangement of the Daimler-Benz Anti-Bloc System in the Vehicle

1. Front wheel sensor
2. Rear wheel sensor
3. Hydraulic unit
4. Pressure switch
5. Electronic control unit
6. Warning light
7. Starter switch

124-Chassis Brake Pad and Rotor Replacement

**by Stu Ritter,
Technical Editor**

*May/June
2002*

Photos in this article
by the author.

*How to service the brakes on your
1986–1995 E-Class car.*

While writing the maintenance chapter of our E-Class book (due out soon), we described the procedure for changing brake pads and replacing rotors, so we thought it would make a good how-to article for you. Before we start, let's discuss brake pads, rotors, technique, and safety.

Safety First

When working on brakes, safety is the first concern. The work isn't dangerous, but the black brake dust on the brakes and wheels is. Avoid inhaling this dust. Its particles are so fine that they settle deep into the bronchi, which the medical folks say is *verboten*.

Wear a respirator, not the thin paper masks used around hospitals and on Tokyo streets but a good fitting HEPA respirator. HEPA means very fine particulate filtration. A HEPA mask is really necessary when doing brake work. We have worn one since 1975, and all our mechanics have had one available. The shop has filters for doing brake work and organic vapor cartridges for working near toxic chemicals. Buy a good respirator and use it whenever you expose yourself to toxic dusts or vapors.

Please read the labels on the aerosol chemistry that you use. Most folks pay little attention to these warnings, which guide you in safe use of the product. It's foolish to ignore them. Your health, your life, and the happiness of your

family depend on your following the instructions. When the can's instructions say not to spray in an enclosed area, use it outside. "Avoid contact with skin" means avoid contact, period. If you want to live a normal healthy life, heed the warnings on chemical products. Most professionals wear respirators, rubber gloves, eye protection, and hearing protection. We treat health hazards seriously, and you should, too. Aerosol brake cleaning solvents are particularly hazardous.

Preparation

To reduce the amount of dust you have to deal with, wash off as much of it as possible. High-pressure car washes work well but only with cool brakes, as the water can quickly warp a brake rotor. Wear eye protection when using the sprayer; it's no fun to get the back-splash in the eye, and you have no time to blink.

Use rubber gloves to keep brake dirt from grinding into your fingers and getting under your fingernails. It's hard to scrub out, so the best defense is to prevent it from getting in. These days, disposable rubber gloves are standard wear in most repair shops. They save having to scrub up at the end of the day and are much gentler on your hands than using pumice soap or chemicals to clean them.

Follow the usual precautions about jacking and using safety stands. If you are unfamiliar with the correct techniques for lifting a car and placing it on stands, find a good automotive textbook in your local library, and read up. You should also have a copy of your car's repair manual, maintenance manual, or the Mercedes-Benz CD-ROM covering your chassis. Never attempt any repair on your car until you have read the manual and understand how the factory wants you to do the job.

Wheel Bearing Adjustment

For instance, most people don't know that wheel bearings must be set using a dial indicator. While many mechanics argue this point and won't do it, the factory manual calls for it, and all bearing manufacturers forbid any other method of setting bearing pre-load. The preload for Mercedes-Benz cars is only 0.01 to 0.02 mm, four to eight ten-thousandths of an inch. We have yet to meet a human being who could accurately determine that play. We had every mechanic who ever worked for us first set wheel bearing clearance by hand, as they always had done; then we hooked up a dial indicator to see how far out in left field they were. Cheap dial indicators, made in China, are available from machinist supply houses such as MSC (Machinist Supply Co., 800/645-7270). They cost about $10, with a decent magnetic base available for another $20. It is well worth the investment to have properly set wheel bearing pre-load. The procedure for using the dial indicator is in the manuals and should be adhered to.

Brake work requires only a few hand tools: a punch for the brake pad pins, a large screwdriver, a large pair of water pump or channel-lock pliers, a hammer and needlenose pliers. A brass brush is also handy.

Mercedes-Benz disk brake systems use two styles of brake calipers. Up until the 124 and 201 chassis, all brake calipers were fixed (except for certain 126 cars). From the start of the 124 and 201 models, floating calipers appeared. The method of changing pads is different between the two, so we'll describe both.

Fixed Brake Calipers

The subject car is our own 400E. In the photographs you may spot the stainless steel/teflon braided brake hoses and a little sheet metal added to the brake backing plate, which extends the backing plate back into the air stream, around the 8x16-in wheels on the car.

You'll need new brake pads, new brake pad wear sensor wires, and a packet of Mercedes-Benz brake pad paste (part 001 989 10 51). Brake pad wear sensor wires should be replaced every time brake pads are replaced, whether they show contact or not. These inexpensive sensors live in a harsh environment so should not be trusted a second time. Brake pad paste is a high-temperature lubricant that goes on the back of the brake pad backing plate and along the edges of the plate that contact the caliper guide rails. The small amount on our finger in **Photo 1** is all it takes, a little on the edges and the rest on the back of the pad. One little sixty-cent package of pad paste will do a couple of sets of pads. Use it sparingly; better too little than too much. Braking is about friction, not lubrication.

Photo 2: Once the wheel is removed, remove the brake pad wear indicator sensor wire from the plug connection on the brake caliper.

Remove the brake pad indicator sensor wire from both brake pads. Knock out the brake pad retaining pins. With ATE calipers, the pins are knocked out directly; on Girling/Bendix calipers, remove the securing clips, then knock out the pins.

Photo 3: Using the channel-lock or water pump pliers against the backing plate of the brake pad and the caliper, squeeze the brake pad back away from the brake disk.

Photo 4: Remove the brake pad; repeat for second brake pad.

Photo 5: Using a stiff wire brush, clean the guide tracks in the caliper, where the brake pad edges slide.

Photo 6: Using the water pump pliers or a large screwdriver, push the caliper pistons back until they are flush with the surface of the caliper. Check the

Photo 1

Photo 2

Photo 3

Photo 4

Photo 5

Photo 6

dust boots; if they are damaged, the caliper must be repaired.

Check the vent slots on the brake disk to be sure they are clear of obstructions to the flow of cooling air.

As shown in Photo 1, apply a little brake pad paste to the edges of the brake pad that contact the guide channels in the caliper and to the back of the backing plate. Install the new pads, then re-install the retaining spring and pad retaining pins. Insert the wear sensor into the pad and the connector on the caliper. Route the wires under the retaining clip.

To push the pistons against the new brake pads, pump the brake pedal. The first stroke will feel as if nobody is home as the pads move into place, but pump until pedal feel is normal. Adjust the brake fluid level to the maximum mark on the brake fluid reservoir.

Reinstall the wheels, then road test and bed-in the new brake pads by braking 8 to 10 times from 50 mph to 25 mph with light pedal pressure. Allow the brakes to cool between each application, and avoid hard braking during this process.

Floating Brake Calipers

The demonstrator car for the floating caliper is a 300E.

Photo 7: Using a small screwdriver, pry open the brake pad wear sensor channel cover. Avoid excessive force. Using needlenose pliers, remove the plug connection from the caliper.

Photo 8: Unscrew the lower holding bolt (13-mm wrench B) while using a counterhold (15-mm wrench A), and remove the bolt.

Photo 9: Swing the brake caliper upward and hold in position with a hook made from a welding rod or coat hanger. Don't let the caliper hang from the brake hose.

Photo 10: Remove the brake pads. Don't use the caliper to change the steering angle, or you will bend something. Check the dust boots; if they are damaged, the caliper must be repaired.

Photo 11: Using the water pump pliers, push the piston back until it is flush with the caliper bore; be careful to avoid damaging the dust seals.

Photo 12: Install the brake pad paste on the pads as described above. Insert the brake pad wear sensor wire (arrow) into the inner brake pad, then insert the pads into the pad carrier.

Unhook the brake caliper and rotate it into position; secure it with the new self-locking bolt that comes with the brake pad kit. As you tighten the bolt, apply an equal counterhold as shown during disassembly. Torque to 25 lb-ft. (35 Nm). Never re-use the self-locking bolt.

Insert the brake pad wear sensor wire into the plug on the brake caliper, and install it in the plastic channel; close the channel cover.

To push the pistons against the new pads, pump the brake pedal until it feels normal. Adjust the brake fluid level to the maximum mark on the fluid reservoir. Re-install the wheels, and road test and bed-in the new brake pads as described above.

Photo 7

Photo 9

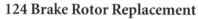

Photo 11

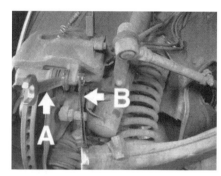

Photo 8

Photo 10

Photo 12

124 Brake Rotor Replacement

Let's discuss brake rotor replacement on the 124 chassis. On older cars this is more complex, requiring hub disassembly and the use of a dial indicator to reset wheel bearing clearance. Front rotors on 1984 and newer (201 and upward) models can be replaced quickly and easily. Book time for older models runs 2.8 to 3.2 hours for both front rotors, which includes wheel bearing service. Consult the correct shop manual for the procedure on older cars.

Before starting to replace the rotors, make a pair of hooks to support the weight of the brake caliper (about 20 lb). Brake calipers should never be allowed to hang by the brake hose, as that can damage the hose.

Both fixed and floating brake calipers are attached to the steering knuckle by two bolts; because they are coated with Loctite, they are hard to loosen. After removing the pads from the caliper, remove the two mounting bolts.

Photo 13: Remove the brake caliper.

Photo 14: Hang it out of the way on the hooks you made (arrow).

Photo 15: Remove the Allen-socket button head cap screw from the brake rotor.

Photo 16: Remove the brake rotor. While this is simple in dry climates, in areas with high humidity and road salt it can be difficult because the rotors can rust solidly onto the hubs. Sometimes they can be soaked with a high quality rust-buster—such as Kroil (Kano Laboratories, 615/833-4101) or PB Blaster—then hammered off. The professional technique is to heat the rotor with a propane or oxyacetylene torch to break the bond between the rust and the hub. If the hubs are heated with an oxyacetylene torch, check the wheel bearing grease afterward. As the rotors are re-installed, coat the hub/rotor contact surfaces with anti-seize compound to avoid this problem in the future.

Photo 17: Using a manual or motor-driven wire brush, clean all foreign materials off the hub mounting surface.

Remove any protective coating from the new brake rotors; lacquer thinner is a good solvent. Install the new rotor, and screw in the button head cap screw to a torque of 7 lb-ft. (10 Nm).

Photo 18: Reinstall the brake caliper, tightening the mounting bolts to 85 lb-ft (115 Nm). Clean the caliper bolt threads using Loctite Klean and Prime or Primer and use Loctite Blue Thread Locker on the threads, all according to the manufacturer's instructions.

Reinstall the brake pads and follow the bedding-in procedure above. New brake rotors offer less braking force with new pads than do old rotors and new pads, so be careful when first driving with this new combination.

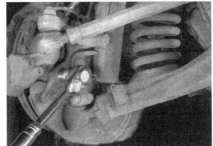

Photo 13

Photo 14

Photo 15

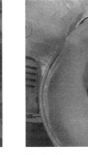

Photo 16

Photo 17

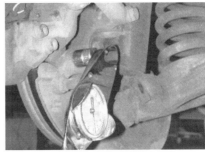

Photo 18

Technical and Restoration Forum

Technical and Restoration Forum

Drivability

Dragon Brakes
January/February 1996

Just after we bought our 1990 560SEC with 65,000 miles on it, the rear brake calipers and rotors had to be replaced. The rotors were blue from heat, and the mechanic said after he test-drove the car that it was OK. Now, a couple of thousand miles later, the rotors look normal, but the brakes feel soft, and there's three times as much brake dust on the rear wheels as on the fronts. What should we do?

Have the brakes checked, probably by another mechanic. Normally, the front brakes wear three times as fast as the rears, but yours seem to be doing just the opposite. The mushy pedal means that the brakes are overheating, so they won't work properly. The brakes are probably still dragging, and the fault may be in the hydraulic system. Next time you stop the car after a normal period of driving, feel the front and the rear wheels near the center. The rears should be much cooler than the fronts. If the rear brakes are warmer, they are probably dragging. No matter what, have them checked immediately by a Mercedes-Benz expert.

Mushy Brakes
January/February 1987

My 1980 300SD brake pedal feels spongy and goes too far down. With the car at rest, it can be pumped back up, where it stays until the car is driven. My mechanic has not been able to correct this, which he says is not hazardous. Could this be a fault of the master cylinder?

In 1983 MBNA issued a service instruction on spongy brake pedals, describing the most probable cause as improper bleeding.

When bleeding, the brake pedal must be fully depressed at least three times for each wheel, with the bleed screw open. At least 3 oz (80 cc) of fluid must be discharged, and bleeding should continue until the fluid is free of bubbles. When the pedal is pressed to the floor, it should be held there until the bleed screw is tightened, then released slowly so that fluid free of air is drawn from the expansion reservoir. Then as the brake pedal is depressed again, the bleed screw is opened again. The expansion reservoir must be kept full during bleeding.

To check the functioning of the master cylinder, actuate the brake pedal several times with the engine off; this exhausts the vacuum in the brake booster. Then depress the pedal with moderate pressure, holding it down for a full minute. The brake pedal travel should not change during this time.

With the engine running, the brake pedal will go down further as vacuum builds, which may create the impression that travel is excessive. All of the above assumes that your car's brake fluid is fresh. Most owners (and mechanics) forget that brake fluid should be changed annually.

Soft 280SL Brake Pedal

January/February 1992

Even after replacing the master cylinder, flex lines, and a leaky caliper, my 1971 280SL continues to have a soft brake pedal. Can you suggest another possibility?

A spongy pedal can be caused by air in the system, a master cylinder with an internal leak, or water in the fluid (if the brakes fade after hard use). If the fluid was replaced, and if the brakes were bled properly, and if there are no leaks at the other calipers or elsewhere, I'd suspect the master cylinder.

Check the master cylinder as follows. With the engine off, depress the brake pedal firmly six or seven times to exhaust the vacuum reservoir. Then press it down hard and hold it. If the pedal slowly drops farther while you hold the same force on it, the master cylinder is leaking internally (or externally, if you see brake fluid on the floor). Improper bleeding can damage a master cylinder. If the fluid wasn't changed regularly, corrosion in the brake cylinders may have worn the seals, allowing a slow leak that's tough to find.

Vacuum Loss Affects Brakes

July/August 1994

The brakes on my 1979 300D work great while moving, but while stopped, to keep the car from moving forward, I must press down much harder. Where should I look first?

Your vacuum system is faulty. A diesel produces no vacuum from the intake manifold, so vacuum needed for the brakes, transmission, door locks, engine turn-off, etc. is supplied by a vacuum pump on the front of the engine. Lack of vacuum may be caused by pump failure or by leaks from vacuum lines or the vacuum reservoir. Locating the trouble requires a vacuum pump and gauge to test the pump and each section of the system. The brake booster may be leaking vacuum. Any competent mechanic familiar with Mercedes-Benz diesels should be able to locate the trouble with little difficulty.

230SL Front Brakes

March/April 1985

After braking, the front brakes of my 230SL do not completely release, and as a result, they overheat severely. I have installed new factory calipers, but that didn't help. Very little brake pedal pressure is required, so the booster seems to be working. An acquaintance has the same problem with his 230SL, and we would appreciate your advice.

There are at least two possible causes. First, the caliper pistons may not have proper clearance, perhaps due to corrosion. This is unlikely with new calipers, but let's look at it anyway. When the brake pedal is free, brake fluid pressure should be zero and the pads should be barely in contact with the disc; actually, there will be a slight clearance. The wheel should turn freely.

When the brakes are applied, the pistons move slightly toward the disc and compress the seals between piston and caliper. When pressure is released, the seals relax and the piston moves back. All of these movements are barely perceptible, and checking them requires a special pressure gauge and a dial indicator and gauge block to measure movement at specified pressures. At 70 psi, movement should be 0.01–0.015 mm; at 1,320 psi, it should be 0.01–0.21 mm. If the observed values are higher or lower, the piston seals must be replaced. If you don't have access to a gauge, make sure the pistons and bores are free of dirt and corrosion; you should be able to press the piston back into the bore manually with a block of wood.

The second possible cause is a plugged compensating bore in the tandem master cylinder, which will require its reconditioning or replacement. In view of the age of your car, this seems most likely. You should also check for misalignment of the caliper and disc, worn wheel bearings and proper disc thickness.

Brake Master Cylinder Wear

May/June 1998

After a mechanic replaced the brake pads and brake fluid on my 1983 300TDT, the brake pedal went to the floor, and I had to have him replace the master cylinder. Do you think that the pressure applied while bleeding the brakes blew out the seals?

The factory-approved method of changing brake fluid involves a pressure bleeder, which should not exceed 15 psi (30 psi for cars with ABS). During the process, the piston in the master cylinder is in the normal released position. A 15-psi pressure should not damage the seals, which normally operate under far higher pressures. The problem was more likely caused by age, wear, and corrosion. No seals last forever, and moisture in the fluid causes corrosion in the bore of the master cylinder. When the pedal and piston travel beyond their normal range in that bore, as is often the case when replacing fluid, the seals wear on the corroded surface. Pressure bleeding reduces this problem, but it is still not unusual, especially when the old two-man "up-down" method is employed.

Ti-iime Is on My Side

September/October 2003

The FSS indicator on my 1998 E320 tells me to check the brake pads for wear. Is this message generated by wear, by miles, or by time?

The FSS monitor receives a signal from wear sensors in the front brake pads. Depending on your car's options (ESP, ASR, etc.), it may also have one or more sensors on the rear pads. The sensor wire is set into the brake pad at the point of maximum safe wear. As the pad wears down, the wire's insulation wears away, so the wire contacts the brake rotor, completing a ground for the monitor and closing the circuit.

It's an Emergency

January/February 2001

Is there an easy way to adjust a W126 emergency brake when the adjusting nut is frozen?

The emergency brake should be adjusted at the brake shoes first. Generally the cable adjuster above the driveshaft does not need to be touched. The star wheel which adjusts the emergency brake shoes is accessible through the lug-bolt holes in the rear brake rotor. Rotate it until the shoes grab the rotor, then back it off five teeth. Remove the rotor so you can see how it works. Adjust the cable adjustment only if after adjusting the shoes, the emergency brake pedal goes down more than five to seven clicks. When the pedal goes to the floor, the shoes have often deteriorated and the friction material is rolling around inside the rear rotors.

Brake Booster Failure

November/December 1997

When my 1963 220SE Convertible is first driven, the brake boost system doesn't work, but it improves after a few miles and several brake applications. Because of an earlier leaky automatic transmission diaphragm, transmission fluid got into the vacuum system; could this be causing the problem? A new factory brake boost unit costs $1,500, so I bought one from a wrecked 220. Can these units be rebuilt?

Evidently a vacuum leak is allowing loss of the vacuum which was accumulated in the vacuum reservoir. The transmission fluid sucked into the system is a possible cause, but it may be just normal deterioration of the booster due to age. With a properly functioning booster, I would expect brake boost to be normal even after the car has stood idle for at least a week; even then, vacuum should be produced quickly. This condition should be repaired at once. You may be left with no boost at all, so it's dangerous, and it will only get worse. The original booster can be tested in the car; if it is not leaking, the leak may be elsewhere and must be found.

Brake Pads

Brake Dust Shields

May/June 1985

Do brake dust shields affect brakes? I have heard that they are not recommended.

Because they may interfere with brake cooling, Mercedes-Benz disapproves of all the various dust shields sold to keep the front wheels free of brake dust. Last week a mechanic was telling me about a customer complaining about rapid brake pad wear. The mechanic reminded the customer that he had warned him when he installed dust shields that they could have a deleterious effect on the brakes. Regular washing is the safest alternative, or you could substitute harder brake pads.

Brake Dust Problems Cured by Elbow Grease

September/October 1988

Having read and listened to all the complaints about brake dust on alloy wheels, I delight in relating my solution. Waxing the wheels (at the same time as the car—every six months or so) makes them look better longer and makes it harder for dust to stick. Every couple of weeks I hose off the wheels, which removes about half the dust. The other half comes off easily with a soft rag and warm, soapy water. At 35,000 mi, my 1982 300SD's wheels look new.

Your solution has the fringe benefit of preserving the finish on your wheels, too.

300E Brake Pad Life

May/June 1987

At approximately 12,000 miles I had to replace the brake pads on my 300E. Other Mercedes-Benz cars I've had have gone over 30,000 miles before replacement; my present 190 has 28,000 miles, mostly city driven, without replacement. The service manager told me that 12,000 miles is common, but it's expensive maintenance. Why the difference?

I'd say that 12,000 miles is about average. I get around 10,000 on the stock pads on my 240D, and most owners experience similar pad wear. There is, however, a great variance involving personal driving habits, type of driving and pads used. One member in rural Indiana tells me he gets 60,000 miles; others get 5,000.

Replacement Brake Pads

January/February 2003

Has The Star *published any articles on brake pad replacement? I'm tired of all the brake dust on my 1992 500SL. Can you recommend the best replacement pads, Porterfield, Pagid, Teves, or Textar?*

I do not recommend aftermarket brake pads. With Mercedes-Benz, brake dust is just a fact of life. The factory prohibits brake dust shields and specifies the compound for brake pads. Aftermarket brake pad makers use only one compound for every brake pad for every car. The factory uses several compounds and manufacturers to obtain exactly the right braking feel for each model. Do yourself a favor, and stick with factory-recommended pads.

Breaking in Brakes

January/February 2004

What is the right way to break in new brake pads?

When backing out of the garage after a pad change, use care, as little braking effect is available. Before driving the car, pump the brake pedal several times to move the pads into contact with the rotors. The first 10 stops should be as gentle as possible, with time between each stop for the pad and rotor to cool. From 30 to 35 mph, come to a slow, smooth stop.

The machined surface of the brake pad has microscopic hills and valleys, and the surface of the rotor probably isn't exactly parallel to the brake pad. You must wear the pad down to the rotor surface and wear the pad surface smooth. When making your first stop or two, it is very important that the pads don't get hot. You are stopping only on the high points of the pad material, perhaps 10 percent of the pad's total surface, so those tiny high spots get hot. This hardens the pad material below the high spots, so the brakes never feel right. Gentle stops with cooling between them allow long brake pad life, and the brakes will feel the way they were engineered to feel. If the brake pedal pulsates, the only way to be sure which rotor is involved is to measure the rotors' run-out with a dial indicator. You can also jack up the car and turn the wheels. If you find one that has tight spots as a wheel rotates, it is probably the rotor to check first.

300E Brake Pad Rattle

May/June 1993

At about 30,000 miles the front brake pads of my 1991 300E began rattling in the calipers when driving on rough roads. We discovered this because the rattle stops when the brakes are applied. My mechanic suggested replacing the pads (only part worn), and this stopped the problem, but after another 8,000 miles, it's reappeared. What can I do besides replacing pads every 8,000 miles?

Either 1) the spring clips have insufficient tension or are incorrectly installed, or 2) the bolts on which the pads slide may be worn. The cure is to 1) bend the clips to increase tension or install them correctly, or 2) replace the sliding bolts. This problem, known since 1987, was dealt with in MBNA's *Diagnostic Directory*, microfiche 1, position 9E.

Front / Rear Brake Pad Wear

September/October 1992

A dragging rear brake on my 300D caused me to check the pads. I found the rears worn out while the fronts still had 50-percent depth. I expected the front pads to wear out first. Why didn't mine?

On most cars the brake proportion is around 75-percent front, 25-percent rear, so if everything is normal, the rear brake pads should outwear two or three sets of front pads. Your experience suggests that one or both rear brakes may have been dragging, i.e., not releasing properly. This could have been due to a defective brake hose or problems in the caliper. After a drive, feel each wheel at the hub to see if one of the rears is significantly hotter than the other—or hotter than a front brake. A dragging pad will cause one wheel to heat more than normal.

Brake Rotors

Brake Rotor Wear

January/February 2001

My 1985 380SL has been maintained well, but at 42,000 miles, the front brake rotors need replacement. The rotors have never been turned, and the mechanic says they just wear. Two other Mercedes-Benz cars and other makes have never had such short rotor life. Am I safe waiting until the red warning light comes on to get new rotors?

All brake rotors have a minimum thickness specification. During each normal brake application you lose some pad friction material and a smaller amount of rotor steel. Most Mercedes-Benz cars get two to three sets of pads to each set of rotors. I don't recommend turning rotors, since there's little difference between brand new and minimum thickness (usually about 2.5 mm). Cars from the 1960s and early 1970s didn't seem to use rotors as quickly, but they also didn't have brakes as powerful as those of later cars. Since much less braking is done by the rear brakes, rear pads and rotors last much longer than the fronts.

The sensor measures pad thickness, not rotor thickness, so it cannot warn you that the rotors are too thin. That determination requires physical measurement. When the front brake pads are worn to the rotors, a yellow light should come on, not a red one. It's safe to drive until the yellow light appears but when it does, be prepared to replace the rotors and pads, including packing the front wheel bearings. If a red brake light comes on either your emergency brake is on or the brake fluid level is low. Check your owner's manual and become familiar with various warning lights.

Turning Rotors *Verboten*

January/February 2004

I always understood that Mercedes-Benz brake rotors could not be turned. When I bought my 1984 300D, I took the rotors in for turning, and the lathe squealed like mad. It hated those rotors! Also, most Mercedes-Benz rotors are so inexpensive that turning them would appear to be false economy, no?

Right. Unless the rotor is a new, very thick, late-model part, there is insufficient material in the rotor to cut away much of it, and you usually can't get rid of a pulsing brake pedal that way.

Most importantly, rotors made by Mercedes-Benz are surface-ground on a Blanchard grinder to insure that the two braking surfaces are absolutely parallel. When you cut rotors on a brake lathe, there is no way to guarantee such alignment. When your 300D rotors were new, they were 12.6-mm thick. The wear limit is 10 mm, leaving you 2.6 mm to wear down. That's about a tenth of an inch total with half on each side, not much.

The rotor wear limit insures that the brake caliper's pistons do not travel too far out in their bores as the brake pads wear. When the pistons travel out too far, they wear the seal because the piston is canted sideways a bit as it travels out of the bore. The amount of material you must remove from the rotor to get it back to square and clean the surface usually takes it beyond the wear limit. It doesn't make sense to turn rotors when it's just as cheap to replace them and have new, true units.

Brake Lines

Blocked Brake Hoses

January/February 1996

The brakes on my new (to me) 1967 250SE Coupe pull to the left then to the right. I've bled them several times and replaced the front rotors, but it doesn't help. The right front caliper doesn't seem to let fluid flow as easily as the others.

This is a common problem with old cars. The brake hose lining can swell and deteriorate internally, blocking flow of fluid to or from individual calipers, causing the brakes to pull or to stick on and drag. Brake hoses are one of the most important yet neglected parts of any car. They should be checked for cracking regularly and replaced, depending on weather and driving conditions, about every 10 years. Unless service records indicate that your car's calipers have been rebuilt recently, it probably would be smart to do so, replacing all the o-rings and rubber seals.

Braided Lines

March/April 2004

After I replaced my flexible brake lines with stainless steel braided lines, the brakes respond quicker and feel firmer. Is this because under pressure the stainless steel lines don't expand as much as rubber lines?

The stainless steel braid is for abrasion resistance only. The Teflon hose inside it is what doesn't expand. The stainless steel braid can cut through all sorts of things, including steel, so be sure the lines are routed to avoid contact with other parts. Use wire tie-wraps to keep the stainless steel braid away from other components. Check the hose routing at every maintenance service and whenever you work on the brakes. The Teflon hose inside the stainless steel braid is very stiff and doesn't expand with pressure or temperature.

ABS

ABS Indicator Light Flicker

November/December 1992

Occasionally the ABS indicator light comes on briefly (other than when starting) then goes off. I cleaned the ABS wheel sensors, and my mechanic says nothing is wrong with the brake system, but the light still flashes sometimes. Any ideas?

The ABS warning light comes on if power in the electrical system drops below 10.5 volts, even momentarily. When voltage rises, the ABS is reactivated, and the light goes off. Because this may happen very quickly, it may appear as a flash. When the ABS is off, the brakes function normally (i.e., in the old-fashioned way), but have the electrical system checked for possible problems with the battery, the alternator, the wiring, or the voltage protection circuit.

Eight-Minute Abs

September/October 1996

The ABS on my 1990 300TE seems to actuate inappropriately. How do I clean the sensors?

Clean the teeth on the front brake rotors as follows. Buy two cans of disc brake cleaner. Jack up and block the front of the car so the wheels are off the ground. Remove the ABS sensor, and spray cleaner into the sensor hole while rotating the wheel. Put paper under the wheel, as lots of black stuff will come out; this brake pad dust gets into the teeth on the rotor. It can interfere with the signal to the ABS computer and cause it to pulse occasionally. After cleaning, replace the sensors.

On a deserted road, brake hard from 60 or 70 mph to a stop to exercise the brake calipers. Don't brake so hard that the wheels lock. Do this several times, and see if it solves erratic ABS pulsing. It worked for me.

Your ABS may show a symptom that can be traced to a bad sensor cable from one of the front brakes. Put a volt-ohmmeter across the inner and outer coax for the cable where it disconnects on top of the inner fender well. Set the VOM so that you can read voltage from the sensor when you spin the wheel. With the wheel spinning, wiggle the cable vigorously all along its length. If the reading jumps up and down rather than transitions smoothly, the cable is bad.

ABS Brake Bleeding

January/February 2003

I had a hard time bleeding my ABS brakes. I top up the reservoir, open the bleed screw at the caliper, and pump the brake pedal. Fluid runs out of the bleed screw for about five pedal strokes then stops. The reservoir fluid level stays the same, and the brake pedal feels soft, as if air is in the system. If I use a power bleeder on top of the reservoir and pump compressed air to push onto the fluid, air comes out of the open bleed screw, not fluid. The brake pedal stays soft, and there's no brake action on the caliper. What is wrong?

Your technique is incorrect. Don't pump the pedal with the bleed screw open, especially on an ABS-equipped car. Leaving the bleed screw open allows air to be sucked back into the lines each time you release the pedal. Hold the pedal down each time and close the bleed screw before releasing the pedal, so you only push out fluid and do not suck in air on the return stroke.

When pedal-bleeding a non-ABS car, avoid using the full stroke of the brake pedal; in other words, don't push the pedal to the floor. Under normal use the brake pedal never goes to the floor, so the master cylinder's piston doesn't normally travel through its full stroke. If you floor the pedal during bleeding, the piston sweeps a section of the master cylinder bore that hasn't been swept before, and a good chance exists that burrs and corrosion in that area will destroy the rubber cups on the master cylinder piston, causing fluid leakage and consequent brake failure.

Mercedes-Benz prohibits pedal-bleeding ABS-equipped cars; they require a pressure bleeder that develops two bars (about 30 psi) pressure. Cars with ABS and ASR have a further requirement to bleed the ASR portion of the ABS unit. This is done whenever the system is opened for work but is not required when changing brake fluid as routine maintenance.

Chapter 8

Heating,
Air-conditioning

March/April 1988

May/June 1997

September/October 2002

The Care and Feeding of Your Automatic Climate Control

by George Murphy, Smoky Mountain Section

March/April 1986

Photos in this article by Frank Barrett.

Problems with the automatic climate control system of 1976–1981 models are avoidable. This article provides you with a basic understanding of how the system, particularly the servo unit, works and what you can do to improve it and prolong its working life. In a future issue we'll show you how to repair a faulty servo unit.

Automatic climate control system problems usually involve the servo unit, which translates commands received from the driver to control the flow of coolant and air in the heating and air-conditioning systems. The servo was originally supplied to Chrysler, which discontinued its use in 1972. Mercedes-Benz cars first used the unit in the 1976 model year. Models/years with this servo are:

1976: 116 sedan series only

1977: 116 series plus 300D and 280E

1978: same as 1977, plus SL models

1979: same as 1978, plus all 123-series

An improved system replaced the servo for the 1981 model year except

Climate control servo has connections for vacuum (top), electrical and coolant (bottom) lines.

on the SL, which got the new system for 1982. If your car has the old servo, replacement can cost from $175 to $400, depending upon who does the work.

Servo Function

The desired interior air temperature is maintained as a result of various control signals provided by a sensor chain and amplifier shown in Figure 1. The sensor chain consists of four components connected in series (one after the other). The first is the servo assembly (1), containing a motor-driven feedback potentiometer, a water regulating valve, a blower speed switch and a vacuum distributor. The other

Side view of servo shows typical crack in center housing (white line).

three components in the chain are the temperature selector wheel (2), the in-car air temperature sensor (3) and the ambient (outside) air temperature sensor (4). The amplifier (5) contains a fixed resistance, against which the varying resistance of the sensor chain is constantly measured.

Let's look at the sensor chain components:

Servo Assembly (1): To maintain the selected air temperature, the servo assembly (see Figure 2) continually adjusts air and coolant flow. It contains an electric motor-driven gear train activated by signals from the amplifier. The servo adjusts air temperature through three functions:

Vacuum distributor (round); blower switch arm (dark, left) and contact plate (right).

Coolant valve fits into center housing, controls flow through lower housing (right).

a) Adjustment of an integral hot water valve to control hot water flow through the heater core. Coolant enters and leaves the servo through the four tubes in the lower housing.

b) Regulation of blower speed through a remotely-mounted resistor block. This resistor block is fed current by a switch arm in the sensor which moves over contacts as the servo shifts from one mode to another, thus varying blower speed.

c) Adjustment of an integral vacuum distributor valve which controls the combinations of air flap positions for outside air intake, foot well air, dash air and defroster air. These flaps are operated by vacuum distributed by the valve, which has several positions.

A cold engine lockout switch in the lower section of the servo unit prevents the blower from operating until the engine is warm enough to provide warm air for heating. This bi-metallic switch directs vacuum to the master blower switch (activating it) at temperatures above 104°F and disconnects vacuum at temperature below 68°F (disabling it). The cold engine lockout switch responds to both ambient air and engine coolant temperatures.

The servo also contains a feedback potentiometer, part of the sensor chain. This potentiometer increases in resistance as the servo enters the cooling mode and decreases in resistance as the servo enters the heating mode.

Temperature Selector Wheel Potentiometer (2):
This device changes resistance as you move the temperature selector wheel. When a higher temperature is selected, resistance increases; when a lower temperature is selected, resistance decreases. Since the potentiometer is in series with the other components in the sensor chain, the resistance of the entire chain is altered accordingly.

In-Car Temperature Sensor (3):
The in-car sensor is a temperature-sensitive resistor called a thermistor. Located in the car's interior, it can accurately measure air temperature. As

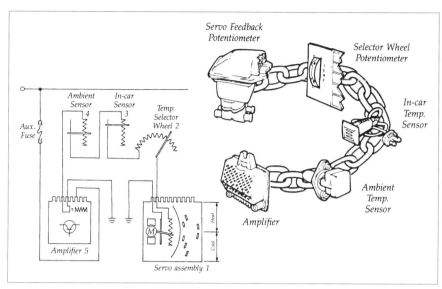

Figure 1. Automatic climate control sensor chain.

interior temperature rises, the sensor's resistance decreases; as temperature falls, resistance increases. Again, this affects the resistance of the entire sensor chain. To reduce response time and increase control accuracy, interior air is drawn over the in-car sensor when the blower is running. Air is conducted over the sensor via a tube connected to the suction side of the blower housing.

Ambient Temperature Sensor (4):
The ambient air sensor is also a thermistor and is in the outside air intake duct. Its operation is identical to that of the in-car sensor except that it measures the temperature of

incoming outside air. Outside air is drawn over the sensor when the blower is in operation.

Amplifier (5):
The amplifier measures the total resistance of the sensor chain (the selector wheel potentiometer, the in-car sensor, the ambient temperature sensor and the servo feedback potentiometer). This total resistance is compared with a fixed resistance within the amplifier. If the two are unequal, the amplifier actuates the servo motor until both resistances become equal. The in-car and ambient air temperature sensors allow for continuous adjustment of the servo via the amplifier. In this way,

Removing top cover shows lines entering vacuum distributor; electrical connections drop through top plate.

Motor, gears below top plate activate coolant valve, contact arm, vacuum distributor.

the selected temperature is maintained despite changing in-car and ambient air temperatures. The feedback potentiometer in the servo assembly also aids the amplifier in maintaining a selected air temperature by limiting the response of the servo, preventing over-control.

What Can Go Wrong?

The following failures have been noted in servos:

Coolant Leakage from Cracked Center Housing: The plastic center housing may crack due to stresses caused by assembly screws, which do not permit expansion of the center housing as it heats. When this center housing cracks, coolant may leak from the unit. If undetected or ignored, coolant loss can cause engine failure due to overheating, frequently meaning a complete engine rebuild or replacement.

There are two ways to repair the center section. First, Mercedes-Benz sells a replacement kit, described in the September/October 1983 issue of *The Star*. Besides a new plastic center section and various other parts, this kit contains spring washers to fit under the screw heads so that the center housing may expand, reducing the possibility of over-stressing and cracking the part. The other alternative is to use an aftermarket kit with an aluminum center section, more resistant to cracking than the original part.

Internal Leakage: An o-ring on the water valve shaft may fail, allowing engine coolant to reach the servo motor and gear train. This will eventually corrode the gears and cause the motor, which is quite powerful, to strip the primary gear in the gear train. The leaky o-ring is virtually impossible to replace, as it is held in place by a "one-way" assembly washer. Internal leakage is evidenced either by coolant leaking from any of the four drain holes just above the center housing or by moisture on the blower switch arm contacts (after the top cover is removed).

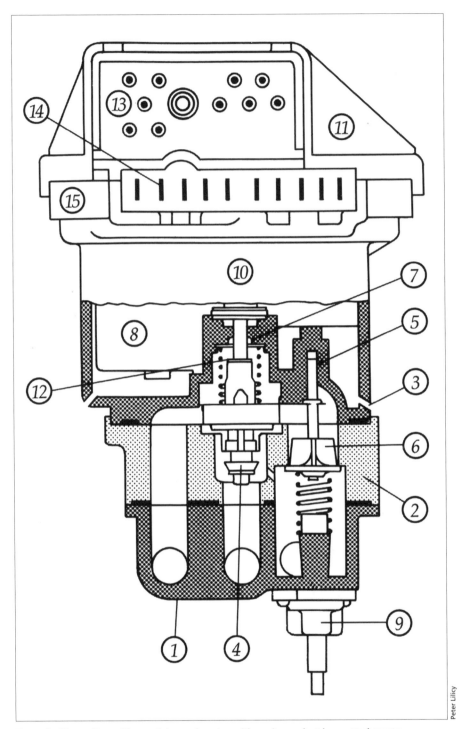

Peter Lilley

Figure 2. Climate Control Servo: 1, Lower housing with engine coolant hose attachments; **2,** center housing (can be replaced with factory or aftermarket unit); **3,** drain hole; **4,** coolant valve; **5,** poppet valve shaft; **6,** poppet valve; **7,** O-ring on coolant valve shaft; **8,** electric motor; **9,** cold engine lockout switch; **10,** gear train (hidden); **11,** top cover; **12,** valve connector clip; **13,** vacuum connections; **14,** electrical connections; **15,** top plate.

Water Valve Separated from Shaft:
Dirty engine coolant can foul the close tolerances in the water flow regulating valve. This results in more friction and thus more force being applied to the valve connector clip. When the clip fails, the water valve will separate from its shaft. The servo then appears to operate normally, but there is no change in air temperature (assuming that the air-conditioning system is OK). Blower speeds seem to change normally, and the air flaps operate, but the system delivers air at only one temperature (warm or cool, depending on the position of the valve at failure).

Open Servo Feedback Potentiometer:
This is a rare failure and hard to diagnose. On my car, in Auto Low or Auto High with the compressor switch on, the system would deliver ice cubes at the dash vents. Adjusting the temperature selector wheel had no effect. If the compressor was switched off, the wheel had to be turned above 80°F before any heating took place. The potentiometer is under the servo's top cover and is driven by the gear train.

Preventive Maintenance

You can help prevent o-ring failure and separation of the water valve shaft. First, run the system through a full heating and cooling cycle weekly in accordance with the owner's manual (good practice with any car). This moves the water valve through a full stroke to clean out deposits which may be accumulating in the valve chamber, creating friction and valve connector clip failure. Operate the automatic climate control in the Defrost mode for at least five minutes. Then select Auto High or Auto Low and dial in 65°F (full cold) for five minutes. Selecting DEF also operates the air-conditioning compressor if ambient air temperature is above 38°F, thus lubricating the compressor seals, which can dry out and leak.

The next preventive step is to thoroughly flush the servo with fresh water during your bi-annual anti-freeze change. DBAG recommends changing engine coolant every two years. If you follow this schedule, your servo will probably last longer—and so will your engine. Some servos that we have opened look as if the coolant has never been changed. The water passages were almost completely plugged, and the water valve was stuck, causing the motor drive gear to be stripped or the valve connector clip to fail.

Cracked center housings are hard to prevent. On rebuilding, use spring washers on the center housing screws to accommodate heat expansion. Or use the aluminum center housing mentioned above.

Useful Information

The servo assembly was made by Ranco in Mt. Vernon, Ohio, for use on some Chrysler cars of the early 1970's. Its Chrysler part number is 3441530. Cost is about $300 at Mercedes-Benz dealers and about $215 at Chrysler dealers, or the part can be ordered from some independent parts suppliers for about $175. The Mercedes-Benz plastic center section repair kit is part number 000 830 01 98 and costs about $40. Installation is covered by *MBNA Service Information 83/38.*

Repair of 1977–1981 Automatic Climate Control Servos

by George Murphy, Smoky Mountain Section

May/June 1986

Photos in this article by Frank Barrett.

Here's how to rebuild the automatic climate control (ACC) servos found on 1977–1981 models. Their design and operation was described in the March/April 1986 issue. With a few tools and some patience, you can do the work yourself.

The procedure is presented in parts, depending on what has failed in your servo. It helps to have one or two failed servos on hand for reference and spare parts. Your friendly mechanic or dealer usually junks failed units because it is uneconomical for him to repair them, so he may give you one from his junk pile.

Part I: Check Out

This procedure should be performed only if the servo does not have a cracked or leaking midchamber. If the midchamber is cracked, go to Part IV, Midchamber Replacement. You can check out the servo in the car or on the bench with vacuum and electrical connectors unplugged. See Fig. 1. The electrical connector pins are numbered 1 to 10 from left to right looking at the connector side of the servo.

Connect a digital volt-ohmmeter to pins 1 and 2 (feedback pot). Set it on a scale to read at least 2000 ohms. The meter should read 1400 ±100 ohms if the servo was in the Park position when disconnected. Next, connect +12 volts to pin 4, –12 volts to pin 5. The servo should run smoothly to the Hot position, then stop. Resistance of the feedback pot should decrease slowly and stop at 200–400 ohms.

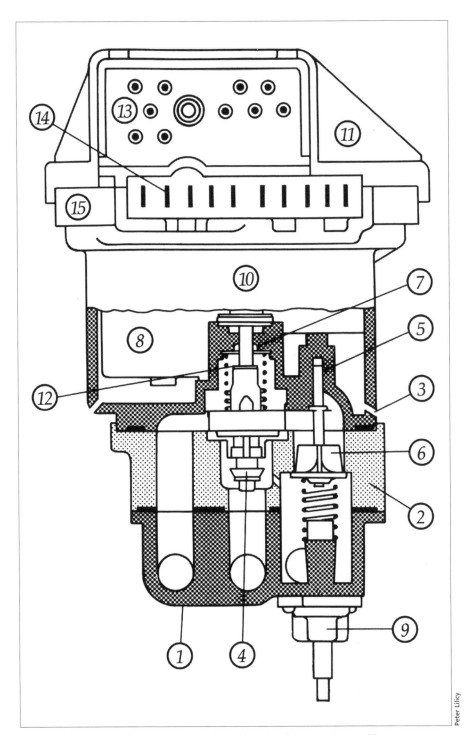

Figure. 1. Climate Control Servo: Lower housing with coolant hose attachments (1); midchamber (2) can be replaced with factory or aftermarket unit; drain hole (3); coolant valve (4); poppet valve shaft (5); poppet valve (6); o-ring on coolant valve shaft (7); electric motor (8); cold engine lockout switch (9); gear train (10), hidden; top cover (11); valve connector clip (12); vacuum connections (13); electrical connections (14), and top plate (15).

Peter Lilicy

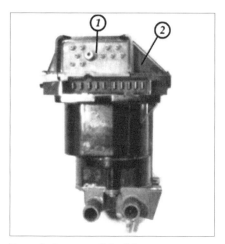

Figure 2. Connector Side of Servo: vacuum connections (1); top cover (2); electrical connections are numbered left to right, 1-10.

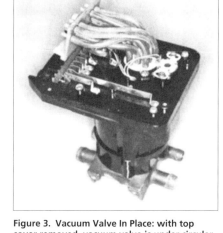

Figure 3. Vacuum Valve In Place: with top cover removed, vacuum valve is under circular plate where hoses enter vertically.

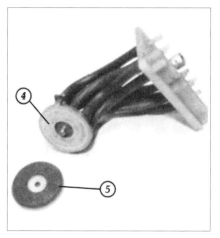

Figure 4. Vacuum Valve Detail: removed from servo, small holes can be seen in vacuum valve (4) and grooves in vacuum valve disk (5).

Check that the internal water valve is open by blowing or directing water through the small nozzle on the red lower section of the servo. There should be no restriction of flow. If there is little or no flow, the water valve may be separated from its drive shaft. Go to Part III, Water Valve Repair.

Reverse the power connections: +12 volts to pin 5, –12 volts to pin 4. The servo should run smoothly to the Cold position. Resistance of the feedback pot should increase slowly and stop at 1800–2000 ohms.

Now check that the internal water valve is closed by closing off the two larger nozzles opposite the small nozzle and blowing or directing water through the small nozzle on the lower section of the servo. There should be no flow. If the water valve is open, the drive connection may be damaged. Go to Part III, Water Valve Repair.

If all is OK to this point, connect +12 volts to pin 3, –12 volts to pin 5. The servo should move part way toward Hot and stop at the Park position. At this point feedback pot resistance should read 1400.

When the servo is running, it should run at a constant speed, with no slowing or binding. At no time should feedback pot resistance go to infinity, i.e., open. If so, a new feedback pot is needed; obtain one from a discarded unit and re-calibrate the servo per Part V.

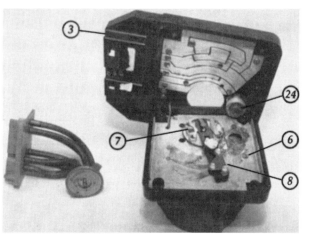

Figure 5. Blower Speed Switch: blower speed switch segments are in top plate (3); drive assembly (6); vacuum valve tension spring (7); blower speed switch arm (8); feedback pot (24).

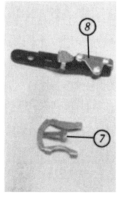

Figure 6. Blower Speed Switch Detail: vacuum valve tension spring (7) fits on vacuum valve drive with blower speed switch arm (8).

If the water valve appears to operate properly and the feedback pot has no open spots, the servo is probably OK. If problems still persist, check the amplifier with a known good replacement.

Part II: Upper Housing Inspection

Before you do anything else, check the servo to determine if the valve shaft o-ring has leaked. If there is evidence of leakage, discard the servo. The valve shaft o-ring is secured in the upper housing by a one-way assembly washer which cannot be removed to permit replacement of the o-ring.

Remove the sealant and screws securing the top cover. Hold the vacuum connector, (1) in Fig. 2, while removing the top cover (2). Remove the two screws securing the vacuum valve (4) in Fig. 4 to the top plate and remove the vacuum valve (Fig. 3). Leave all the short hoses attached. The vacuum valve disk (5) in Fig. 4 may come off with the valve; set it aside in a clean place.

Remove the four screws securing the top plate to the upper housing and raise the top plate for access to the drive assembly, (6) on Fig. 5. The red and black servo motor wires prevent complete separation of the top plate from the drive assembly. Carefully remove the vacuum valve tension spring (7) and blower speed switch arm (8) from the drive assembly (Fig. 6).

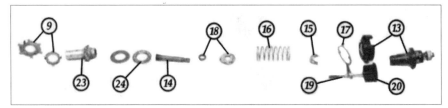

Figure 7. Water Valve: l. to r., two drive flanges (9); water valve drive nut (23); drive nut bearing (24); water valve shaft (14); o-ring and assembly washer (18); valve spring (16); water valve connector clip (15); poppet valve shaft (19); poppet valve lever (17); poppet valve (20); water valve (13).

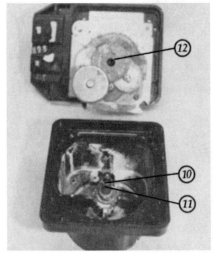

Figure 8. Gear Train Detail: Gear train (12) lies beneath top plate, above thrust button (10) and spring (11).

Figure 9. Valve Connector Clip: Actual width of clip is about 5/16 in; be sure it is shaped as shown.

Lift the top plate from the upper housing. As you lift out the drive assembly (Figs. 7 and 8), note the location of the two drive flanges (9), thrust button (10) and thrust button spring (11). The flanges, button and spring may stick to the grease on the main drive gear (12).

Inspect the gears for damaged or missing teeth. If the gear train is wet or corroded, or if there is any evidence of water on the inside of the upper housing, the valve shaft o-ring is bad, and so is the servo. Discard it and find one that is dry inside. If you have a clean dry upper housing, go to Part V, Reassembly and Calibration.

Part III: Water Valve Repair

If the water valve (13) is separated from its shaft (14) the cause is most likely dirty coolant which fouls the tight clearances in the valve passages. Fouling causes the water valve to bind,

causing high forces to be exerted on the water valve connector clip (15). When the connector clip fails, the water valve is normally left in the Cold position, preventing hot water from circulating through the heater. The servo may appear to operate, but no heat is evident in the car.

Clean the water valve parts. Inspect the water valve connector clip and make sure it is shaped as shown in Fig. 9. Use needlenose pliers to carefully re-shape the clip if needed.

Drive the servo to the Cold position by connecting +12 volts to pin 5 and −12 volts to pin 4. Caution: Hold the green water valve drive shaft (14) to prevent it from rotating while the servo is running. The shaft should travel outward and permit more clearance for assembling the water valve.

See Fig. 7. Inspect the water valve where it connects to the clip. The depressions on each side must not be

damaged or broken, otherwise the clip will not hold. The rectangular hole in the end of the valve mates with a corresponding drive boss on the end of the green water valve drive shaft.

Snap the water valve connector clip (15) into the groove on the green water valve drive shaft (14). Position the sides of the clip parallel to the long side of the rectangular shaft drive boss.

Place the valve spring (16) over the shaft and clip, then carefully lower the water valve with poppet valve lever (17) onto the spring. Push the valve down against spring tension until it engages the connector clip. The tiny ears on the clip should snap into the depressions on each side of the water valve. You'll know if it's secure because the spring force against the valve will test the clip connection. Give it a slight tug to ensure that the connection is solid. Look closely between the spring coils at the clip; the sides of the clip should be flush and tight against the water valve.

Install the poppet valve shaft (19) without the poppet valve (20) into the poppet valve lever (17). The lower plain end of the shaft fits into the guide hole in the center housing with the flange on the shaft under the poppet valve lever. The other end of the shaft looks like a nail head; this end is for the poppet valve (installed later).

Push down on the washer on the water valve (13) against spring tension and note that there are grooves on each side of the valve. One groove is longer than the other. Rotate the valve until the longer groove faces the corner of the upper housing nearest the number 1 electrical connector pin. This assures finer control over hot water flow through the valve. Assemble the midchamber to the servo as directed in Part IV below.

Part IV: Midchamber Replacement

The best solution for a cracked midchamber is to replace it with an aluminum one. Midchamber replacement will not solve a malfunctioning servo but will only solve cracking or leaking problems.

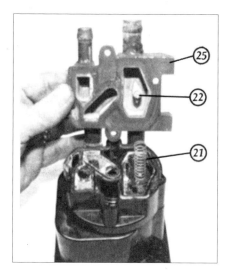

Figure 10. Lower Assembly: Bottom of servo includes poppet valve spring (21), knob (22), and lower section (25).

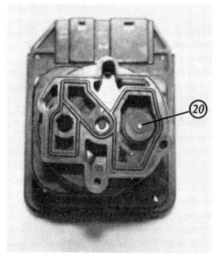

Figure 11. Bottom View of Midchamber: With lower section removed, poppet valve (20) is visible in midchamber.

This procedure may be used to supplement the instructions in the aluminum section kit.

Remove all hoses and brackets from the servo to permit easier handling. Remove the sealant and loosen the four screws securing the lower (red) section to the servo (Fig. 10). Carefully raise the lower section noting the position of the poppet valve spring (21). Remove spring, gasket and lower section. If the coolant passages are full of crud, you haven't been properly flushing your cooling system. See Part VI, Care of Your Servo.

Cut the poppet valve (20 in Fig. 11) in half with a razor blade or Exacto knife and remove it as shown in the midchamber replacement kit instructions. Lift off the cracked midchamber. Be careful not to rotate the water valve, as calibration can be disturbed. If the water valve is separated from its shaft, go to Part III, Water Valve Repair.

Clean the gasket surface and areas around the water valve. An old toothbrush and spray cleaner like Formula 409 work well here. Be sure the poppet valve shaft (19) and poppet valve lever (17) are not bent (Fig. 7). Place a new gasket in the upper housing groove and position the new aluminum midchamber on the unit. Make sure the poppet valve shaft (19) is in its mating guide hole in the upper housing (Fig. 7). The water valve should slide easily into the center hole of the midchamber.

Press the new poppet valve (20) onto its shaft (19) as shown in the instructions. Make sure the head of the shaft pops through the top of the poppet valve. The poppet valve must be free to move off its seat; don't force it down into the midchamber passage.

Carefully clean the gasket surface of the lower red section. Place the new gasket on the midchamber. Position the poppet valve spring (21) on the poppet valve so it will engage the knob (22) in the lower section as it is mated to the midchamber (Fig. 10). Mate the lower section to the midchamber. Insert the screws and tighten evenly in an alternating pattern. Don't overtighten; the upper housing is plastic and the threads strip easily.

Before reinstalling the servo in your car, flush the engine cooling system thoroughly to prevent further problems with your rebuilt servo. See Part VI, Care of Your Servo.

Part V: Reassembly and Calibration

The water valve and midchamber should now be properly installed and the unit ready for reassembly of the upper housing components. Grasp the water valve drive nut (23 in Fig. 7) and move the water valve up and down to assure that it moves freely. You should feel spring tension as the valve assembly is raised.

Apply white grease to the drive nut ball bearing (24) under the water valve drive nut (23). Carefully turn the drive nut clockwise until it bottoms out. The drive nut has now raised the water valve until the spring is fully compressed, stopping further rotation of the drive nut.

With the two drive flanges (9) removed, temporarily place the drive assembly (6) over the upper housing locating posts (shown in Fig. 5). Place the blower speed switch arm (8) on the drive and carefully place the top plate on the upper housing, making sure it seats properly. Don't force it down. Be sure the feedback pot gear (24 in Fig. 5) engages the drive gear through the hole in the metal drive assembly plate. Make sure the motor wires (red and black) lead properly through the access hole in the drive assembly plate.

Feedback Pot Calibration

Insert two screws in opposite corners to secure the top plate for the following steps. Connect the VOM to pins 1 and 2 (feedback pot). Set it on a scale to read at least 2000 ohms. The meter should read 1400 ±100 ohms if the servo was in the Park position when disconnected.

Connect +12 volts to pin 4, −12 volts to pin 5. The servo should run smoothly to the Hot position and stop. The resistance of the feedback pot should decrease slowly and stop at 200 to 400 ohms. Reverse the power connections: +12 volts to pin 5, −12 volts to pin 4. The servo should run smoothly to the Cold position and stop. Feedback pot resistance should increase slowly and stop at 1800–2000 ohms.

If all is OK, connect +12 volts to pin 3, −12 volts to pin 5. The servo should move part way toward Hot, stopping at the Park position. Feedback pot resistance should be 1400 ±100 ohms. If it isn't, loosen the pot adjusting screws and adjust the pot position until you get 1400 ±100 ohms.

Repeat the tests in the two previous paragraphs and, if necessary, adjust the pot until the feedback pot resistance always reads 1400 ±100 ohms when the servo stops at the Park position coming from the Cold position (1800–2000 ohms). Important: When the servo is running, at no time should the feedback pot resistance go to infinity, i.e., open. If so, a new feedback pot is needed; you may be able to salvage one from a discarded unit.

Assembly

Remove the top plate screws and carefully remove the top plate and drive assembly. Don t rotate the feedback pot or the gear drive—they are now set up for calibration with the water valve. Check that the water valve drive nut (23 in Fig. 7) is seated in the clockwise direction as above.

Grease the two drive flanges, then place the small shaft drive flange (9) on the drive nut (23) with the legs downward so as to engage the knobs on the drive nut. Place the large shaft drive flange (9) on the drive nut with legs downward. Rotate the drive nut 14 turns counterclockwise, which places the water valve at the Park position, matching the position of the gear drive and feedback pot set in the steps above.

Grease the thrust button (10 in Fig. 8) and its spring (11) and place them in the hole in the end of the water valve drive nut (23 in Fig. 7). Place the drive assembly on the upper housing, taking care to assure that the thrust button and spring fit into the hole in the main drive gear (12 in Fig. 8). Be sure the drive plate seats down over the locating posts at the four corners of the upper housing. It may rock slightly due to the points on the edges.

Use electrical contact cleaner to clean the blower speed switch arm contacts (8 in Fig. 5) and the switch segments beneath the top plate, then carefully lower the top plate onto the upper housing, again taking care that the feedback pot engages the drive gear through the hole in the drive assembly.

Secure the top plate with all four screws, making sure it seats solidly onto the upper housing. Place the vacuum valve tension spring (7) so that the four legs fit into corresponding holes on the vacuum valve drive (25 in Fig. 10). Clean the vacuum valve disk (5 in Fig. 4) and its mating valve face (4) and lightly spray with Armorall or equivalent.

Direct air through each vacuum hose to make sure that the tiny passages are clear. If your car is a diesel and there is black oil in the vacuum valve or its hoses, the engine vacuum pump diaphragm may be leaking.

Place the vacuum valve disk (5) over the tension spring and make sure the square drive pin engages the corresponding square hole in the vacuum valve drive. Place the vacuum valve against the valve disk and press the assembly down against the tension spring pressure as you engage the alignment notch in the side of the valve opening. Secure the valve in place with its two assembly screws. Be sure the valve is seated properly into the top plate opening; don't force it. It would now be prudent to repeat the feedback pot calibration, as described above.

Place the top cover on the unit, taking care that the vacuum connector slides into the grooves on the cover. Secure the cover with four assembly screws.

Part VI: Care of Your Servo

When your servo is ready for installation, flush it with clean water. If your car's cooling system has not been flushed in the last two years, do so. With the servo removed, you can direct a stream of water through the heat exchanger to flush out dirt and corrosion.

It may be easiest to attach some of the cooling hoses before installing the servo, particularly in the 300D. Check the water passages (red part) for obstructions before connecting hoses. With the servo in place, make sure the electrical and vacuum connections are clean, then connect the coolant hoses and tighten the clamps.

Refill the cooling system, but leave the radiator cap off. Start the engine and select DEF to drive the servo to full flow position (hot) to allow maximum coolant circulation. You may have to add more coolant as air vents from the system. When coolant is at the proper level, replace the radiator cap.

About once a week, cycle the servo full stroke by selecting DEF for about five minutes (or until very hot air is blowing from the defrost nozzles), then select AUTO HI or AUTO LO and dial in 65 degrees. Let the system cycle for about five minutes, then go back to the desired setting.

Whenever the cooling system is flushed, the servo must be removed to permit full flow through the heater coils and prevent debris from collecting in the servo's passages. Such debris is the prime cause of servo failure. Happy motoring!

Tools Required:

- digital volt-ohm meter (VOM)
- two test leads with alligator clips
- 12-volt DC power source
- needle-nose pliers
- straight screwdriver
- Phillips-head screwdriver
- razor blade or Exacto knife

1981–1985 Automatic Climate Control: How It Works and How to Fix It

by George Murphy, MBCA Technical Committee

November/December 1991

Photos in this article by the author.

An article in the May/June 1986 issue covered the pre-1981 automatic climate control (ACC) system. Here we'll tackle the 1981–1985 version, with a horizontal row of pushbuttons.

Gone is the multi-function servo valve. Heating water flow in these cars is controlled by a simpler device, a mono-valve. Blower speed changes and vacuum switching are controlled electronically. This newer system doesn't provide the infinite control of heating and cooling available in pre-1976 manual systems, but it is slightly more versatile and reliable than the 1977–1981 system.

The control unit (see photo below) in the center console comprises a temperature dial (3), a pushbutton switch unit (4), and a blower switch (5). The temperature dial provides stepless adjustment of in-car temperature between Min (no heat) and Max (full heat). At Max, full uncontrolled heating occurs; at Min, full uncontrolled cooling, both at blower speed 5 (high). Automatic temperature and blower speed selection works only for pushbuttons b, c, and d for uncontrolled heating

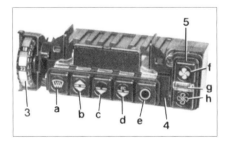

ACC control panel includes temperature wheel, pushbutton unit, and blower switch.

only, and with blower switch g on Automatic. The EC button provides no cooling below the temperature of outside air.

Pushbutton Functions

Blower Switch (5): The blower can operate in any of six speeds. In pushbutton mode b, c, or d, blower air volume is:

Switch	Air Volume	Blower Speed (s)
t (top)	maximum	6
g (center)	automatic	2, 3, 4 or 5
h (bottom)	minimum	1

Pushbutton e (Off): Cuts off air supply to the interior. The blower does not operate, and there is no heating or cooling.

Pushbutton d (Economy): In this position the air-conditioning compressor is off. Fresh air enters the car and is heated, if necessary, to maintain dialed-in temperature. If needed, warm air flows from the footwell and side nozzles with a little going to the defroster nozzles.

In vent mode, air is routed to the center and side instrument panel nozzles. Minimum in-car temperature depends on outside temperature and solar heat gain, which you know about if you own a black car! At low outside temperatures the blower and air supply stay off until engine coolant temperature reaches about 100°F. If blower Automatic is selected, the blower runs at speeds 3 to 5. You can conserve fuel by using the EC button for heating and ventilation as much as possible.

Pushbutton c (Normal): In this position the air-conditioning compressor is on when outside temperatures are above 35°F. Fresh air enters the car and is heated or cooled as necessary to maintain dialed-in temperature. During cooling, no air flows from the footwell nozzles.

During heating, warm air flows from the footwell and side nozzles with a little going to the defroster nozzles. The ranges can overlap, providing air from the center and the legroom nozzles at the same time. If the system shifts to cooling, the fresh/recirculating air flap closes down to about 80 percent recirculating air.

Pushbutton b (Bi-level): During heating, air is routed to the windshield, side vents, and footwell nozzles. During cooling, air goes to the center instrument panel nozzles, too. The refrigerant compressor operates at outside temperatures above 35°F.

Pushbutton a (Defrost): The blower operates in its highest speed (6) only. Maximum heated air is routed to the windshield for defrosting—the temperature dial has no effect. The refrigerant compressor operates if outside temperatures are above 35°F.

In-Car Temperature Sensor: This sensor is under a grille at the center of the instrument panel. The sensor measures in-car temperatures and transmits signals to the electronic amplifier, which compares them to the temperature dial setting, then adjusts blower speed and hot water flow through the heat exchanger via the monovalve. An air hose connects the sensor housing to the blower to draw inside air over the sensor for faster temperature response.

Heat Exchanger Temperature Sensor: This sensor measures air temperature in the heat exchanger plenum and sends a signal to the electronic amplifier for additional temperature control.

Mono-Valve: This valve controls the rate of flow of engine coolant through the heat exchanger. Magnetically actuated, the valve is opened and closed by signals from the electronic amplifier to admit more or less hot coolant to maintain the dialed-in temperature. A check valve in the bottom of the mono-valve housing

Mono-Valve: arrow indicates check valve, which prevents backflow of hot coolant into heat exchanger when heating is switched off.

Recirculating pump moves coolant through system at low engine speeds.

prevents hot coolant from entering the heat exchanger when the engine is not running (mono-valve open).

Recirculating Pump: A small electric pump in the engine compartment circulates a uniform flow of coolant through the heat exchanger at low engine speeds. The pump is switched on by the electronic control unit whenever the footwell nozzles are open (heat mode).

What Goes Wrong …

Mono-valve: These valves frequently fail to operate due to internal leakage. Generally, symptoms are no heat in Defrost mode or full heat in all modes. Usually the rubber diaphragm inside the valve cracks and leaks, which is easy to repair. You need Mercedes-Benz part number 000 835 06 44, valve insert, available at Mercedes-Benz dealers or from Performance Analysis Co., 1345 Oak Ridge Turnpike, Suite 258, Oak Ridge, TN 37830; 615/482-7260.

Before starting this repair, be sure the cooling system pressure is released; allow the engine to cool, then carefully open the radiator cap. Find the mono-valve in the engine compartment, on the firewall. Remove the two-wire electrical connector from the coil, and undo the four assembly screws securing the top of the valve. To make room to work on the valve, you may have to loosen its mounting bracket. Remove the coil (g) and shield (f) (see photo below). Grasp the valve insert (b), and gently pull it (with washers c, d, and e) straight up and out of the body (a).

Be sure the internal seat inside the body is clean; flush it with clean water if necessary. Put the new valve insert in the body, making sure the diaphragm seats in the recess in the valve body. Place the washers (c, d, and e) on the new valve insert in the order shown.

Replace the shield and coil with the notches between them aligned so that the coil seats properly. It may protrude slightly due to spring tension of the wavy washer (d). Replace the four assembly screws and tighten them evenly but not too tightly (the body is plastic, so the threads strip easily). Clean the contact pins and replace the electrical connector. Coil resistance can be checked with an ohmmeter; it should be 10–20 ohms. You can also test the assembled valve by momentarily connecting 12 volts to the electrical connector pins; it should make a clicking sound.

Refill the cooling system. Operate the ACC through all modes, and check for leaks and proper operation.

Pushbutton Panel

The second most common failure we've seen is in the climate control's pushbutton panel. Time, heat, and vibration combine to cause minute cracks in the soldered connections inside the unit. Many units sent here for repair have poorly soldered joints which have cracked after a few years.

The printed circuit board repair outlined below has worked in only about two-thirds of the cases encountered but is worth a try before replacing this expensive device (about $250 list price).

First, remove the pushbutton unit as follows. Pull off the radio knobs and remove the radio molding. Remove the screws holding the lower edge of the wooden panel, then carefully pry out the lower edge of the panel covering the pushbutton unit.

Remove the screws holding the top of the pushbutton panel. You may have to loosen (but not remove) the bolts in the slots of the housing. Slightly pull out the holder for the pushbutton unit at the top, and lift it out upward. Pull off the 12-point plugs at the left and right and the sockets for instrument lights. Remove the holder for the pushbutton unit from the unit itself.

> *Publisher's note -*
>
> *The mono-valve photo (left) has been modified by the publisher based on feedback from readers of this book. Washer c and washer e have been transposed to reflect the correct assembly order of the valve insert.*

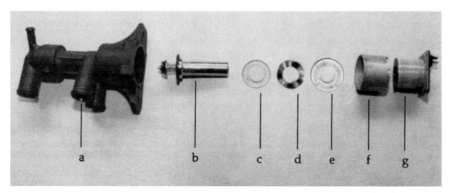

Mono-valve disassembled: body (a), valve insert (b), washers (c, d, e), shield (f), and coil (g).

Disassembly

Remove the temperature dial by squeezing the plastic spring clips together to allow the clip to release from the pushbutton unit; carefully pry the dial unit away from the main body.

Remove the five pushbuttons from the main unit and the three pushbuttons from the blower switch by pulling them straight outward. If you need to pry with a small screwdriver, insert it under the bottom of the button and apply counter-pressure against the top so that the button is forced out; it will snap outward off the shaft. Note which button goes where and how it is oriented (make a sketch). Remove the front plastic cover from the unit, held on by spring clips. Remove the blower switch from the unit in the same manner as the temperature dial. Note how the light diffusers mount to the main unit.

Remove the bottom cover from the unit, held in place by spring clips. Carefully pry the printed circuit board upward at the rear of the main unit so it clears the rear of the housing, and slide it upward and out to the rear. The side panels will probably fall off. Note how they are keyed to grooves in the main housing.

Circuit Board Repair

To repair the printed circuit boards, you need a pencil-type soldering iron of no more than 25 watts plus a small amount of fine resin core solder wire.

Pushbutton panel, showing internal relays and circuit board.

These can be obtained at Radio Shack for a few dollars.

Inspect the printed circuit boards for burned-through copper foil. The foil side is a confusing pattern of thin copper foil conductors soldered to the wire leads of parts on the opposite side. The control unit generally fails when soldered connections on the foil side loosen due to vibration or heat. If you're careful, it's possible to re-solder the connections and get the unit working again. For this you'll need a steady hand and the 25-watt soldering iron (and possibly a magnifying glass to inspect your work).

Position the printed circuit board solidly, foil side up, in a well-lit work area. Starting at one edge of the board, carefully apply heat with the tip of the soldering iron to each solder joint on the board. Apply only enough heat to cause solder around the connecting wire or lug to momentarily melt, then remove the soldering iron, and allow the soldered joint to "freeze". Make sure no solder flows to an adjacent connection, or you'll get a short circuit. If the joint appears to lack enough solder for a good connection, add a little. Solid state devices can't tolerate heat, so use care with the soldering iron.

After re-soldering each connection on the board, look closely for solder "bridges" between connections, which can cause a short circuit. The connections may appear slightly discolored from your re-soldering, but no harm should occur if you were careful with the heat. Be sure to re-solder the fillets between the side board and the bottom board; most cracked joints occur here.

Disassemble the blower switch and re-solder the connections inside. Note how the plastic rocker fits between the two switch halves.

Reassembly

Place the two black side panels on the printed circuit board assembly, and slide it into the main unit at an angle so that the side panels fit into the grooves in the main housing. The assembly will snap into place in the main housing.

Replace the bottom cover. Reattach the blower switch to the right side of the main housing, then position the light diffusers and attach the front cover. Press each pushbutton onto its respective post using your sketch. Reinstall the unit in the car.

To protect your circuit board from future blow-out, install a one-amp in-line fuse in the power supply wire to the auxiliary electric water pump. The pump is under the hood, usually on the right wheel well; on S-class cars, it is between the two firewalls. If the pump motor binds, this fuse will blow, preventing burnout of the printed circuit board.

Blower Motor

Another failure mode involves the heater blower motor. This system operates the blower continuously whenever any button except Off is pressed. After 80–90,000 miles, or 5–6 years, the blower motor brushes usually wear and no longer make good contact with the commutator. This is generally evidenced by a delay of several minutes before the system starts—or the blower may start when you hit it with your hand. A new blower can be expensive, so it's worthwhile to remove it and install new brushes.

The brushes are fairly soft and are hard to find. Don't use power tool brushes; they are too hard and will groove the commutator. If you can't find brushes to fit, call us (615/482-7260). We've found a manufacturer who custom makes the correct brushes to fit, and we have some available.

The assistance of Ed Wilson, Houston Section, is gratefully acknowledged.

How to Repair Solenoid-Type Automatic Climate Control Valves

by George Murphy, Smoky Mountain Section

July/August 1986

Photos in this article by the author.

Mercedes-Benz's 1981 and later models with automatic climate control (ACC) use a different temperature control method than earlier models (see The Star, March/April 1986*). The newer units are simpler, but unfortunately they also suffer failures. If yours isn't working properly, here's how to repair it.*

Automatic climate control failure in 1981 and later models usually involves coolant leakage or simply failure to operate. Symptoms include no heat on defrost mode (DEF) or full heat in all modes. The rubber diaphragm mounted on the ACC valve insert may also crack and leak. These valves are much easier to repair than the servos on pre-1981 models (for repair of those, see *The Star*, May/June 1986). To do the job on your 1981 or later car, you'll need a valve insert, part number 000 835 06 44, available at most Mercedes-Benz dealers or from Ragtops, Box 393, Frostburg, MD 21532; (301) 689-5123.

Repair Procedure

First, locate the solenoid in the engine compartment or between the double firewall, depending on your model. Remove the electrical connector from the coil and undo the four assembly screws securing the top of the coil. Remove the coil (g) and shield (f).

Grasp the valve insert (b) and gently pull it (along with washers c, d, and e) straight up and out of the body (a). Note the assembly order of the washers. Make sure the internal seat inside the body is clean. Flush it with clean water, if necessary.

Place the new valve insert in the body, making sure the diaphragm seats into the recess in the valve body.

Automatic climate control valve insert.

Then place washers c, d, and e on the new valve insert in the order shown. Reinstall the shield and coil, aligning the notches between them so the coil seats properly. It may protrude slightly due to spring tension of the wavy washer (d). Reinstall the four assembly screws and tighten them evenly but not too tightly. The body is plastic, so the threads are easily stripped.

Reinstall the electrical connector, then refill and vent the cooling system. Operate the ACC through all modes, and check for leaks and proper operation. Happy motoring!

> **Publisher's note -**
>
> *The mono-valve photo (bottom of page) has been modified by the publisher based on feedback from readers of this book. Washer* c *and washer* e *have been transposed to reflect the correct assembly of the valve insert. Changes to the text have been made to match the revised callout letters in the photo.*

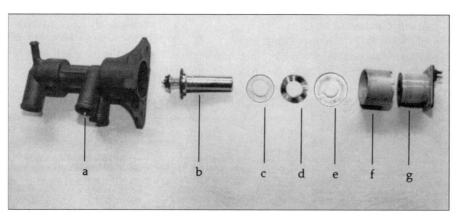

ACC solenoid coil (g), shield (f), washers (c, d, e), valve insert (b), solenoid body (a)

Heater Control Lever Replacement

Rusty Steele, Cornhusker Section

March/April 1988

Photos in this article by the author.

Tired of those broken heater/ fan/vent levers on your 1968–72 280/300SE/SEL 3.5/4.5/6.3 or SL? Here's how you can fix them quickly, easily and inexpensively.

When the plastic heater/fan/vent control levers on the good old 108-, 109- and 113-body cars break with age, heater/fan/vents are tough to control. When I bought my car, I drove merrily away from the seller's home, turned on the heat, and the end of the lever fell off in my hand! I laughed. Mr. Seller had cunningly glued the end of the broken lever back on so that it looked fine, but as soon as I touched it, the party was over!

Replacing the four levers with factory units means lots of time, effort and money—and stock replacements may eventually break, too. Stock lever replacement requires removing the dash, no small job, but you can replace them quickly with a stronger part without doing that.

Here's How

First, order a set of four Dura-Levers from one of the firms who advertise them in *The Star*. A set costs $107, not cheap but much less than doing it the factory way. The black, glass-filled plastic nylon levers come with clear instructions and a small Allen wrench.

Using your fingers or a pair of pliers, break off the old lever at each end where it attaches to the rotor plate inside the dash. If your old levers are as brittle as mine were, this'll be dead easy. Inside the lever slot you'll now see the black rotor plate with two notches in it. With the old lever gone,

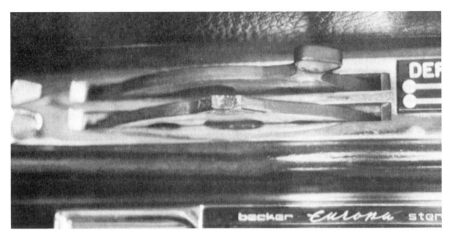

Above: Broken heater and fan control levers are common as old material becomes brittle.

Right: Two-piece replacement is fastened by screw.

Above: Two-pronged claw is inserted first, then handle part is added.

Right: Screw is tightened with Allen wrench provided.

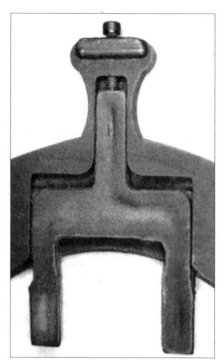

Claw and handle parts of replacement slide together easily.

you can rotate the control with a small screwdriver in these notches.

The replacement lever has two parts. One, a two-pronged claw, fits into the two notches; the other, the handle, slips over the claw. An Allen screw fastens the two parts together so that they clamp onto the rotor plate.

Installation

Put the claw into the two notches in the plate. For the top lever, the teeth go up; for the bottom lever, they go down. You'll feel the claws grip the back of the plate. Pull back on the claw to hold it in place, and slip the handle over it. Be careful that the claw doesn't lose its grip.

(This is the fiddly part; it may take a couple of tries, but you'll do it.) If the rotor plate doesn't line up with the slot, gently lever it into alignment with a small screwdriver at one end of the slot, then slip the claw and handle into place.

Screw the Allen screw into the handle, tightening it with the Allen wrench. This pulls the claw against the back of the rotor plate and pulls the handle against the front of the plate, clamping things into place. As you tighten the screw, the claw and the handle slide together. When they're snug, you'll feel the screw tighten. Give it another one-quarter turn, then resist the urge to tighten it further. This small screw won't take much torque to strip the threads. (Believe me, I know.)

The handle part has a lip that fits over the edge of the rotor plate. With everything in place, turn the lever each way and, using a flashlight, look into the slot to make sure that the lip fits properly against the plate. If not, back off the screw and move the handle into place with the screwdriver.

That's all there is to it. The new levers hold well, even if your heater cables are stiff. We replaced two levers, one above the other. Despite our car's stiff cables, the new levers work just fine. We understand that an experienced mechanic requires anywhere from six to eight hours to replace the stock levers, so the 20 minutes that this bumbling amateur spent on the job represent a considerable savings.

Heater Levers Revisited

January/February 2000

A heater control lever on my 1972 280SE 4.5 recently broke. A dealer quoted me an outrageous price to fix it, as they would have to tear apart most of the dash to gain access. I recall reading about a kit to replace the levers from the front. Is the kit still available, and does it work?

Your memory is correct. Dura-Lever replacement heater control levers are available from Performance Analysis. The levers can be installed easily without disassembling the dash. Members report that they work fine.

How to Replace Your W108 / 109 Heater Control Levers

by Randy Durrance, Milwaukee Section

November/December 2001

Photos in this article by the author.

Replacing the originals is not as tough as you've heard.

Because of their passenger-safety design, heating and ventilation control levers in U.S. 108- and 109-chassis cars (roughly 1968 through 1973 280 and 300 models) periodically need replacement. The hard rubber used for the exposed section of the levers deteriorates over time. Aftermarket replacement handles are available; they are easy to install but look different from the originals. If the inside colored plastic part of the original lever is damaged, it will not work (Photo 1). Used infrequently, the heater valves can become difficult to move, causing lever breakage from increased stress. In 20-odd years of working on Mercedes-Benz cars, I've done this replacement many times; though it requires a fair level of mechanical aptitude, the job is not as intimidating as it may seem.

Preparation

The most common mistake made when trying to replace broken levers is to try to do so with the assembly still in the car. I've replaced levers without removing the aluminum housing from the dash, but the easiest way to replace them is to remove the assembly. If you work on a bench, fewer pieces are damaged, and you can see where everything belongs. Allow a day for this job, put on some light music to keep yourself calm, and prepare.

Suggested Tools

- 1/4-in-drive ratchet (an articulated head is a plus)
- Regular 10-mm and deep-well 14-mm 1/4-in-drive socket
- Stubby or offset Phillips-head screwdriver (I prefer the roller-clutch offset)
- Regular #2 Phillips-head screwdriver
- Long flat-blade screwdriver
- Long needle-nose pliers
- Magnetic pick-up tool (you will drop something into the dash)
- Spare Bosch spark plug or long 4-mm screw (I'll explain why later)
- Several spare clips for the cable ends and cable housings. The only way to be sure you will lose none is to have spares. They are inexpensive yet can save hours if you happen to flip one into the dark recesses of the heater box
- Calm, quiet work area

Parts List

- One heater lever, upper left (blue) 000-835-17-40
- One heater lever, upper right (grey) 000-835-18-40
- One heater lever, lower left (red) 000-835-15-40
- One heater lever, lower right (red) 000-835-16-40
- Two heater valve seals, 000-835-12-58
- Two heater valve seals, 000-835-48-98
- Cable to housing clips, 000-833-00-81 (a couple of spares)
- Cable to lever clips, 000-994-99-41 (a couple of these, too)
- Six glove box retaining clips, 123-990-00-92

Getting Started

This job requires removing a fair portion of the dash panel. Everything right of the ignition switch and left of the passenger-side air vent will come out to give you room to work (Photo 2). Once you understand how the dash fits together, the process is not bad.

First, remove the glovebox door. Remove the two Phillips-head screws from the inside, and pull the glovebox door toward you from the hinges. Two clips may stay in the glovebox door; pull them out and save them. Remove the glovebox lamp by pulling down on the tab at its end; remove the latch

Photo 1. If inside plastic handle is broken (lower left), aftermarket replacement levers won't work.

Photo 2. Your first job is to make room to work.

plate (two more Phillips-head screws) inside the top of the glovebox.

Remove the grey retaining clips that hold the glovebox in place. The original retaining clips have a pin in the center that must be pushed through before they can be removed. You can usually recover most of the pins from within the dash and re-use the retainers. Still, it is a good idea to buy a few replacements to have on hand. Later retainers have a mushroom-shaped pin that is pried up to release them. Using a trim tool or a screwdriver, pry between the glovebox (plastic housing) and the metal dash structure, and remove the trim clips. Pull out the glovebox by squeezing the top and bottom of the box toward one another, and push the glovebox lamp cable through the lamp opening.

Next, remove the ashtray, ashtray housing, and cigar lighter. The housing is held in by three Phillips-head screws and by the switch for the glovebox lamp. Unscrew the plastic collar from the glovebox lamp switch, and remove the switch. To remove the lighter, disconnect the plug at the rear. The plug fits onto a stamped steel piece. Grasp the steel piece, turn it counterclockwise, and remove it and the spring washer under it from the lighter assembly. With a 14-mm deep-well socket, remove the retaining nut for the cigar lighter assembly. The bracket will come off the back, and the lighter assembly can be removed through the front of the dash (Photo 3).

Remove the radio, speaker grille, and speaker (if equipped) plus the under-dash panel at the transmission tunnel. If the car has no separate amplifier for the radio, you can leave the trim panel below the center of the dash in place, but removing it makes retrieving dropped items easier. If the heater valves need attention, it also lets you catch the coolant that leaks out.

The Real Work

Now that you have created some space, the real work can begin. At the right side of the lever assembly, carefully disconnect the electrical plug for the lamps. The plastic housing that the plug attaches to is easily broken, and some pieces are no longer available as spare parts, so *be careful*. Reach through the speaker opening in the dash pad, and disconnect the plug from the blower switch at the left rear of the lever assembly.

Remove the trim plate from the front of the heater lever assembly. The studs for the trim piece also secure the lever housing to the dash. To do this, move all of the levers toward the center of the trim plate. 10-mm nuts at the left and right side hold the plate in place. Using the ratchet, work through the opening where the ashtray was to remove the nut on the right; work through the radio opening to get the left one. The two washers under each nut—one flat, one "wavy"—are important. They prevent the assembly from vibrating loose.

Remove them from the studs on the trim plate with a small magnet. At this point the lever assembly can be moved slightly to get at the connections for the control cables.

The bottom of the lever assembly has four cables, two on each side. The outer cables control the heater valves; the center ones open and close an air door on either side of the heater box. The top cables are the main air inlet cable at the left and the defrost/floor cable at the right. Begin by disconnecting the lower cables, working through the radio opening. The cables mounted directly on the levers are held by a clamp screw (Photo 4) which is released by loosening the upper screw through an access hole in the aluminum plate of the lever assembly.

Using a regular Phillips-head screwdriver, and working through the speaker opening, loosen the screw a few turns until the cable can be released. Remove the retaining clip for the cable outer covering, and move the cable out of the way. Next, the other two cables at the center can be disconnected by carefully prying the "pressed-on" black clips from the looped ends of the cables.

The upper cables are held in place by similar pressed-on clips. With all of the cables and electrical connections removed, carefully guide the lever assembly through the glovebox opening. Now that the assembly is out of the car, look it over and get familiar with the relationship of the parts. The lever assembly is comprised of four plastic levers pivoting on two hollow plastic barrels. Notice the location of the

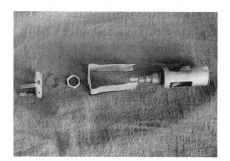

Photo 3. Cigar lighter assembly.

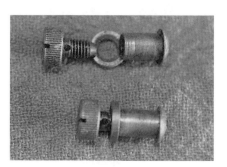

Photo 4. Heater control cable clamping screws.

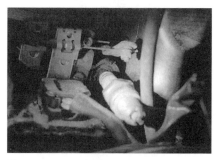

Photo 5. Use spark plug to remove heater valves.

plastic light guides on the right side. The upper one illuminates the cigarette lighter, and the lower one provides lighting for the ashtray.

Heater Valves and Cables

Take time to check the operation of the cables in the dash. Any stiffness or binding should be dealt with now. When a cable binds, the cause is usually not the cable itself but what the cable operates. Often the heater valves are tight, leaking, or seized from non-use. Since the valves are not available as a spare part without the heater core, take care to avoid damaging them. This is where the spark plug comes in. Unscrew the slot-head screw, and disconnect the lever that connects to the heater valve and the limit-stop from under it. Leave the cable connected to the small bracket, and just move out of the way. Screw the small end of the spark plug into the end of the heater valve (Photo 5). Now you have a handle to work with.

Push the heater valve inward slightly. Remove the snap-ring, and clean any residue from the opening. Once the opening is clean, the valve will slide out easily. Pay attention to the direction of the opening in the side of the heater valve in relation to the heater box. To indicate which end is up, scribe a small mark on the valve body, and make a note about the position of the mark. Even experienced mechanics err by failing to mark the valve or forgetting what the mark means. Do that, and you'll have to take

the valves apart again later, which is no fun when everything is in place. As the heater valves are removed, the system will lose 6 to 8 ounces of coolant, so use a small container or an old towel to keep it out of the interior.

The valves will fit into the heater core four ways, and three out of the four are wrong. To avoid confusion, remove only one valve at a time. Replace the seals, and clean the valve (Photo 6). Each heater valve has two seal rings, a large one on the outside and a smaller one where the valve shaft goes through the seal plate. Use o-ring lube or silicone grease (dielectric grease works fine) to lightly lubricate the o-rings on the valve before reinstalling it.

Lower Control Panel Disassembly and Re-Assembly

Begin disassembling the heater lever housing by removing the screws from the black plastic covers on the upper part of the cylinders (Photo 7). The covers are in two pieces that have to be taken apart to get them out. Work carefully with these; they are very fragile. The cylinders will now slide through the heater levers and out the bottom of the housing.

With everything apart, give it a good cleaning. If the levers have been replaced before, there may be lubricant on the housing and/or cylinders. Clean it off. There is no need for lubricant between the cylinders and the levers. In fact, sticky lubricant can attract dirt and debris, eventually making the levers harder to move.

Pay attention when removing the fresh air/blower (blue) control lever. The small, spring-loaded plunger (near the switch contacts) can be easily lost (Photo 8). To remove the lower (red) control levers, carefully pry the pressed-on clips from the pin in each lever.

Clean the housing; transfer the screws and pins from the old heater levers to the new ones. Put the spring-loaded detent in the blue lever before inserting it into the slide for the blower switch. Check that the upper (blue and grey) levers each have a pin for attaching the cable. Be sure to do this before putting the assembly back into the car. Nothing will make your day like having to take it out again to install the pins (I've done that...once). Likewise, make sure that the clamping screws are installed in the lower heater control levers. To allow room for the cable ends to enter the hole between the washer and the lower section, these clamping screws must be opened two turns.

Clean the trim plate. On the back of it, there should be some old masking tape at the edges where the plate touches the wood trim. While the trim plate is out, replace this tape. If the plate rests directly on the wood, besides damaging the wood, it can create annoying noises.

Putting It Back Together

Installation should start with the lower cables that pass through the clamping screws. These are the most difficult to align, but it helps to know that the hole for the cable is parallel to the slot in the

Photo 6. Heater valves; left side has retainer and o-rings removed.

Photo 7. Lever assembly, top view; outer barrel covers removed, showing lamps.

Photo 8. Blower control lever (blue) with detent plunger.

end of the screw and to have the clamp screw open *at least two turns* (Photo 9). I've seen mechanics spend an hour trying to connect the cables when all that was stopping them was that they didn't have the clamping screws open (one more time) at least two turns. The wire goes between the lower part of the screw and a concave washer. Before locking the cable housing to the lever assembly, wait until the wire portion of the cable is inserted through the clamp screws. The clips that hold the cables to the aluminum housing should be placed over the housing side first, then slipped into place around the cable. The clips have a small protrusion that lies against the cable to keep it tight (Photo 9). Installing them in the wrong direction makes the job much more difficult.

After connecting the lower cables, work through the speaker opening to connect the upper cables. Once those are connected, install the trim plate and the nuts to hold the assembly

in the dash. Connect the blower switch and the plug for the lamps. Here, installation is the reverse of removal, but take care to align one of the openings in the cigarette lighter housing with the light bar. Otherwise, it will not be lit. The other caveat involves the glovebox and glovebox door installation. Put the two clips over the hinges for the glovebox door. Be careful that the hinges are not caught behind the glovebox when installing it, and pay attention to the top of the box. The clip at the top for the latch screws can get pushed off and disappear into the dash. Slide the door back over the hinges (with the clips on them). Align the glovebox door and latch by leaving the screws a bit loose, aligning the door until the edges are even, then tightening the screws.

If all has gone as planned, you now have a set of functioning heater control levers that will need no attention for another 10 or 15 years. Well done! It really wasn't that hard to do it right.

Photo 9. Lever assembly, bottom view; heater air door cable in clamp screw (center, near barrel) and heater valve cable.

Fixing the 107 / 116 Heater Flap

by Dieter Arnold, International Stars Section

November/December 1988

A fellow member's 1975 450SL had a heater problem; the control levers stuck, making it impossible to turn off the heat. They sometimes stuck in the down position, making it impossible to turn on the heat. He was told that the only way to repair the controls was to replace the heater box, which is expensive, so for two summers he wired the heater valve in the off position. But there is an alternative.

The problem was that the foam hinges on the heat-mixer flaps were deteriorating with age, causing the flaps to jam in the heater box. New parts are not available individually, so replacing the entire heater box assembly is the normal way to guarantee lasting success. But there is a less expensive procedure that seems to work. This involves removing and modifying the heat-mixer flaps. If you do this yourself, get ready to spend a good 10 hours under the dash of your car. This is not a quick fix!

The modification works on any early-1970's 116 (450SE/SEL, etc.) or 107 (SL) models with manual heater controls (without automatic climate control). The only parts required are two 10-cent springs from your local hardware store. These should be about 1/4-in wide, 1-in long and not too strong (about the strength of a ballpoint-pen spring, only more elastic). Plan on doing both flaps according to these instructions:

Remove the center console assembly with radio, power window switches, etc. Remove the heater and A/C control lever assembly, including support brackets and cables. Remove the front carpets and rear heater ducts from the heater box. Remove the lower heater box tray, held in place by four clips that slide into place at the four corners.

With the tray removed, look up at the heater box, and you'll see the two heat-mixer flaps. Remove the C-clips and pins that connect the flaps to the control levers, and remove the flaps. Getting the flaps out may be difficult;

you'll have to lift and rotate the flaps while removing them. If the foam on both sides of the flaps is badly disintegrated at the edges, find some replacement foam. Otherwise, simply trim the foam to the edges of the flap so that none extends beyond the edges.

Find the opening in the center of the flap and carefully peel back the foam near the center line, where you will drill hole A (see Figure 1). Drill this

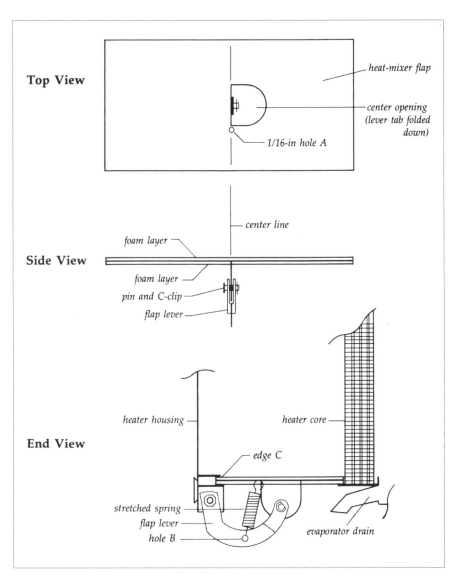

Figure 1. Heat-mixer flap.

new 1/16-in diam. hole 1/8-inch from the opening at the center line. Hook one end of the one-inch spring through hole A, glue the foam back over the opening or, if you are replacing the foam, scrape both sides clean and glue new foam into place. The foam should be the exact same size as the flap (you will not be including the foam hinge as with the original flap).

Reinstall the flap into the heater box, and reconnect the pin and clip to the flap lever. Now hook the other end of the spring through hole B in the flap lever (the existing hole). The spring should hold the flap edge C down into the box so that it can't jam, while still allowing the flap to move freely.

Reassemble everything in reverse order of removal. Reinstall the lower tray. Pay attention to the two square rubber drains from the evaporator housing. They are often plugged with dirt or may come loose while removing or reinstalling the tray.

Before installing the console, check the heater system with the engine running to make sure the controls work properly. Check that the heater valve (on the firewall) opens and closes. This valve is operated by a series of vacuum switchover valves and microswitches on the heater controls. If everything works, button it up and enjoy the heat—if and when you want it.

Converting Your R-12 Air-conditioning to R-134a

by Stu Ritter,
Technical Editor

*September/October
2002*

Photos in this article
by the author.

Considerable misinformation is floating around among do-it-yourselfers and professionals about converting 1992 or earlier Mercedes-Benz air-conditioning systems from Freon R-12 to the newer Freon R-134a or a so-called "drop-in" replacement refrigerant. Here is the most current information about this change.

Owners of air-conditioned pre-1993 models may eventually have to decide whether or not to convert from R-12 to R-134a refrigerant, which also involves changing the compressor and other hardware. As R-12 grows more expensive, converting to R-134a makes sense if and when your car's air-conditioning system needs major work. It makes no sense to convert to R-134a purely for ideological or ecological reasons such as "it's better for the planet." As long as R-12 is contained within a properly working system, it does no harm and works well to keep you cool. Only if your R-12 system must be opened for repair should you consider conversion.

Will R-134a cool your car as well as R-12 did? If the conversion is done correctly, you'll notice little difference between the two.

What will conversion cost? Assuming that the compressor is being replaced at the time of conversion, we estimate that a proper conversion will add $200 to $400 to the cost of the other work, depending on how it is engineered. Compressors and receiver/dryers for R-134a are standard parts these days. Hoses must be replaced and temperature and pressure switches changed.

Converting your car's air-conditioning from R-12 refrigerant to R-134a refrigerant involves federally mandated recycling procedures; the job is best done when the compressor has to be replaced.

This article covers cars with rotary or swashplate compressors. Earlier piston-type compressors do not convert well, so cars from the 1960s and early 1970s using York compressors are not candidates for R-134a conversion.

Legal Ramifications

Since 1992 the federal government has mandated control of refrigerant gases. Anyone who exchanges these gases must be licensed (under Section 609 of the Clean Air Act) and must use a gas recycling device called a recycler. A license allows the holder to purchase R-12 or R-134a Freon. Releasing chloro-fluorocarbons (CFC, aka Freon) into the atmosphere is against the law because it depletes the ozone layer of the earth's stratosphere. The CFC molecule is extremely stable and long-lasting, but the chlorine atoms do the damage. If you care about the survival of your descendants, you will not release CFCs into the atmosphere.

The stratospheric chemistry involved is known and documented by many sources, including the Environmental Protection Agency (EPA). Information is available on the EPA's Stratospheric Ozone hotline, 800/296-1996. Fines for venting CFCs reach $25,000 per day, and the EPA pays up to $10,000 to informers. So if Joe next door is working on his air-conditioning system and blowing refrigerant into the air, you may be able to boost your kids' college fund. De-pressurizing any air-conditioning system is a job for a qualified shop, not a do-it-yourself task.

Modern refrigerants such as R-134a are hydrocarbon fluorocarbons—HCFCs, not CFCs—and contain no ozone-depleting chlorine atoms, but they still add to the overall global warming trend of atmospheric organic compounds through the greenhouse effect. Hence air-conditioning repair requires that refrigerants be recycled to prevent stratospheric accumulation and exacerbation of global warming.

The formula for R-134a is 1,1,1,2-tetrafluoroethane CF_3CH_2F. Environmental concerns led to the phasing out of CFC R-12, which was last made in 1995. Converting an R-12 system to R-134a—or considering one of the so-called drop-in replacement gases—requires thought.

Drop-In Refrigerants

Part of your conversion decision may involve choosing a new refrigerant, and we strongly recommend the now-common R-134a. Alternative refrigerants exist, but we don't recommend them. According to Mercedes-Benz—and we agree—the only suitable replacement for R-12 is R-134a. While other EPA-approved replacement gases exist, they involve too many problems.

The mandated recycling requirement governs all conversions. Using a refrigerant other than R-12 and R-134a involves too much risk of contaminating the recycled Freon. Having multiple recyclers, each dedicated to one of several gases, is impractical for a repair shop. Cross-contamination is another serious problem for the professional because it not only ruins the recycled gas, it can also contaminate expensive recycling equipment. De-contaminating such equipment takes hours of time plus the cost of a new dryer and filters. Since the government mandates recycling requirements, the machine's condition is critical to avoiding problems and fines.

The old refrigerant must be recovered until the car's system pressure is below four inches of mercury, then the system must hold vacuum for five minutes at that level and for two minutes when re-checking. This ensures that all refrigerant is out of the system and that nothing is left to raise system pressure. Even junkyards use recyclers. A $2,500 gas identifier is beyond the means of most repair shops, so they refuse to work

on anything other than R-12 and R-134a systems. If you are considering a conversion, think about its impact on future serviceability.

What Is Changed

Converting from R-12 to R-134a involves changing at least the lubricating oil for the compressor, the seals (o-rings) throughout the system, the hoses that carry refrigerant around the system, and the receiver/dryer. The expansion valve in the evaporator should also be changed to the newer R-134a version. If you plan to use the existing compressor, evaporator, and condenser, then you can expect

Recycled R-12 Freon can be used to fill R-12 systems.

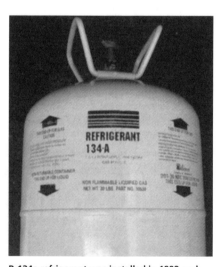

R-134a refrigerant was installed in 1993 and later Mercedes-Benz cars.

a reduction in system efficiency. Mercedes-Benz R-134a systems, in use since 1992, increased the size of these components to offset the slightly lower thermal efficiency of R-134a. Installing a bigger compressor is impractical due to manifold and mounting difficulties. When converting, all components must be R-134a rated, including the compressor.

Lubricating oils for the two systems are different. R-12 systems use mineral oil. Early R-134a systems use PAG (polyalkene glycols), and later R-134a systems use POE (polyol ester). Mineral oil is incompatible with PAG and POE oils, which are incompatible with each other. Even one-percent mineral oil remaining in an R-12 system will contaminate a POE-oiled system, so it is critical to clean all old oil out of the system. PAG oils have high-temperature problems and difficulties with aluminum bearings; POE oils have no such problems. POE oil requires a sterile system; PAC oil is more tolerant. Since the mid-1990s, POE oils have become the industry standard, replacing the PAG oils used when R-134a was first installed.

System Parts

To differentiate them from the old R-12 parts, o-rings meant for R-134a use are green, like the tags on R-134a-compatible expansion valves and receiver/dryers. All o-rings in the system must be changed when converting.

Because R-134a is a smaller molecule than R-12, it was once thought necessary to change all hoses. The R-134a barrier hose is much stiffer than the earlier R-12 hose. Recent research indicates that lubricating oil in a system converted to R-134a will soak into the older R-12 hose and stop molecular-level leakage. So if you want to use an R-12-style hose to keep your older car's engine compartment looking original, use that good old red Aeroquip 1540, usually −10 size. It will seal.

Don't try to convert without replacing the hose; the mineral oil soaked into an old hose will react with the new PAG or POE oil and contaminate the system. Almost any hydraulic shop that carries Aeroquip hose can convert your existing hoses to the correct R-134a barrier hose. Ask your local independent which hose shop he uses. Mercedes-Benz dealers usually install new hoses.

Water Contamination

Because both PAG and POE oils have a high affinity for water, it is important to avoid water contamination. Hoses should be stored sealed, and oil bottles should be tightly capped. Add oil only after the system has been evacuated to boil off residual moisture. When putting the system under vacuum to boil out moisture, use a heat lamp or hot-air blower to warm the components, which helps remove the moisture. It is easy to boil water out of the system under vacuum, but it is difficult to get water out of the lubricating oil.

Leaking Systems

Speaking of hoses and fittings, a misconception exists among repair folks that they cannot refill a leaking R-12 or R-134a system. No EPA rule prevents this, though some states have stricter rules. Check with local and state agencies, but ultimately your mechanic is responsible for minimizing leakage. To be certain that no major leaks exist, a responsible air-conditioning technician always tests a system before filling it.

Avoid testing a system by using vacuum. If a large leak exists, a vacuum pulls outside air and moisture into the system. Proper testing requires 50 psi of pressure and must be done with the appropriate refrigerant gas. Other gases will contaminate the system. Due to the explosive nature of mixing lubricating oils with oxygen and Freon, oxygen should never be used in an air-conditioning system.

Electronic sniffers or fluorescent dye are used to check for leaks. Because they are so sensitive—they can find leaks of less than one ounce per year—electronic sniffers require that engines be off when testing.

As air-conditioning systems age and hose connections loosen, minor leaks occur. Some leaks depend on the temperature of the system, some depend on engine vibration, some on system pressure. To find a leak, you need to replicate the operating condition causing it.

Cleaning the System

Before the Clean Air Act, several CFC-based cleaning solvents did a great job of cleaning a system. Use of CFCs or the old standby, methylchloroform, is now prohibited for system cleaning. When converting to R-134a, avoid chlorinated solvents, as chlorine molecules break down the R-134a refrigerant.

Flushing methods have also changed. If your system has had a compressor failure and metal debris exists throughout it, the system should be flushed in sections. Flushing through the service ports will not clean the system properly because the cleaning flush will short-circuit, taking the path of least resistance. Work in small sections of the system, with the cleaning apparatus in series with the system. After a compressor failure, an in-line filter should be installed to catch remaining contamination and prevent damage to the new compressor.

Most R-12 to R-134a conversions happen after the failure of a major component, usually the compressor. Failure of a Nippondenso compressor (used in W201 models onward—124, 129, 140, et al.) may leave the so-called "black death", a dark mixture of oil, metal, and Teflon caused by loss of lubricating oil and destruction of Teflon seals and aluminum pistons. Debris carried through the system leaves black crud everywhere. Then the system must be properly cleaned, with everything from the firewall forward being replaced. The evaporator passages are big enough to allow flushing, but the condenser cannot be flushed because of its tiny passages. The hoses, compressor, and receiver/dryer must be replaced, which is why compressor failure offers a prime opportunity to switch to R-134a. If

the compressor has blown up, a filter drier should be installed in front of the expansion valve.

Other Refrigerants

Besides the standard R-134a, several blended refrigerants are available, but we strongly advise using R-134a. Among blended gases, Freeze-R-12, made by Technical Chemical, mixes 80-percent R-134a and 20-percent HCFC-142b. Frigi-C, from Intermagnetics General, is 39-percent HCFC R-124, 59-percent R134a, and 2-percent butane. Each of these gases requires a separate, dedicated recycler. It makes no sense to use a blend when R-134a is the standard gas, available everywhere. If your air-conditioning ever needs professional service, almost any air-conditioning shop can help you. Each gas has unique fittings for the service ports, and if a shop sees anything other than R-134a fittings, they are unlikely to work on the system because of the risk of contaminating their recycled Freon supply.

In our opinion, some replacement gases are dangerous. OZ-R-12 and HC-R-12a are flammable; R-405A contains perfluorocarbon, which has an extremely high global warming potential; and R-176 contains R-12. Stick with the standard R-134a gas.

Working with refrigerants is not inherently hazardous, but several caveats exist. When working on air-conditioning systems, always wear eye protection. A shot of liquid refrigerant in your eye can cause permanent blindness. Keep refrigerant off bare skin; it causes frostbite. Work with adequate ventilation; prolonged breathing of vapors is dangerous and can cause death without warning. Use refrigerant cylinders for no purpose other than their original use.

The Conversion Process

So how does a shop actually convert from R-12 to R-134a? When a compressor fails, other parts must also be replaced, so this is an ideal time to convert. When compressors destruct internally, they send metal particles throughout the system, so sometimes refrigerant replacement is the only recourse.

First, the system is evacuated using a recycler for that specific gas, which in a Mercedes-Benz is Freon R-12. (Remember, de-pressurizing any air-conditioning system must be done by a qualified shop.) When all the old gas has been removed (compressor failure does not necessarily involve loss of Freon), the system is disassembled. As each component is removed, it is examined for contamination or damage. If no contamination exists, the conversion can continue. If contamination is present, the system must be properly cleaned with approved solvents, which may require the services of a professional air-conditioning shop or a Mercedes-Benz repair facility.

New parts are then installed. The Mercedes-Benz Technical Data Manual (TDM) lists oil capacities for replacing system components; adhere to them carefully. Once the system is closed—with its new receiver/dryer, new expansion valve, new hoses, new compressor and whatever else was needed—it is placed under deep vacuum for several hours using the technique described above to remove all residual moisture. After the system has been vacuumed, oil is added to the compressor. It is more difficult to add the oil after the compressor is mounted, but that is the best way to prevent oil/water contamination. The system should then be vacuumed and vacuum-tested again.

Charging a system with R-134a must be done by weighing the charge. Using the sight glass to determine refrigerant level causes overfilling because too much R-134a must be used to remove bubbles (unlike R-12 systems, bubbles appear in the sight glass of R-134a systems at engine idle). The R-134a charge is 90 percent of the R-12's weight, so a system that used 2.2 lbs (1 kg) of R-12 will use 1.98 lbs (0.9 kg) of R-134a.

Pressures and Results

A major difficulty in converting to R-134a involves the size of the existing condenser. Models with R-134a refrigerant as original equipment have larger-capacity compressors and condensers than the R-12 systems. The larger condenser allows greater heat transfer, which keeps the high-side pressures in check and cools you better.

Our shop's first R-134a conversions did not yield spectacularly low duct temperatures. We had difficulty keeping the air much below 45°F. The high-side pressures were around 350 psi, too high. After experimenting with temperature switches for the auxiliary fan, we found it best to have the fan run whenever the compressor was engaged, using the compressor signal to trigger the fan relay. This kept the high-side pressures around 250 psi—acceptable for the operating conditions—and lowered the duct temperature to 39°F, also acceptable. When this auxiliary fan modification was retrofitted to previously converted cars, our customers approved.

The bottom line: Consider converting to R-134a if and when your air-conditioning system needs major work. As long as your R-12 system is not leaking and works properly, leave it that way.

Cooling System and Air-conditioning Tune-Up

by John Lamb,
Minuteman
Section

*May/June
1997*

Photos in this article
by the author.

Warm weather can test your climate control system daily. This article will help you to maintain your car's cooling and air-conditioning systems via easy inspections and service with no special tools or knowledge.

You can prevent expensive repairs and gain a working knowledge of the two systems. All work described here was performed on a 1990 300D 2.5 Turbo, a 124 chassis with a 602 diesel engine.

Before beginning, observe safety precautions. Do not open hoses, radiator caps, or covers; do not open or tamper with air-conditioning hoses, connections, or service ports; both systems operate at high pressures. The radiator and air-conditioning condenser have sharp metal edges; use caution. Electric cooling fans can start unexpectedly with the engine off. It is illegal to release refrigerants into the atmosphere. Before working around the engine, let it cool, and make sure it is off. Wear protective gloves, safety glasses, and protective clothing to prevent burns. Read the instructions before beginning.

Inspection

1. Inspect belts and hoses; replace those showing wear, cracking, or distortion.

2. Check every coolant hose clamp for tightness.

3. With the engine cold, remove the radiator cooling system cap and look at the coolant. It should not be discolored, muddied, or creamy. If it has not been flushed within two years,

do so. Use only Mercedes-Benz coolant mixed 50/50 with water. Draining and replacing the coolant involves removing the radiator drain plug and the engine block drain plug. Recycle old coolant. When refilling the cooling system, the large upper radiator hose can be removed from the engine, and coolant can be poured directly into the engine, preventing trapped air and overheating.

4. Inspect the electric cooling fans, which should spin freely. If not, debris may be lodged in the fan housing (photo 1). Remove debris using a vacuum or a nozzle with shop air (photo 2).

Removing the Fan Shroud and Belt-Driven Fan

The fan shroud and fan are removed together. The fan is fastened to the coolant pump by one bolt, which

requires an 8-mm hex head socket to loosen it. The coolant pump hub must be held stationary by a special tool while the bolt is loosened (photo 3), Mercedes-Benz part number 603 589 00 40 00 or Snap-on tools part #YA9122 (fan clutch locking tool). You can make your own tool by bending a 3/16-in steel rod.

1. Using a screwdriver, remove the two clips attaching the fan shroud (photo 4).

2. Lift the fan shroud slightly to separate it from its lower mounting. The shroud is held at the bottom by two tabs which slide into slots. These tabs must be correctly installed during reassembly.

3. Insert the 8-mm socket into the bolt at the center of the fan (photo 5). While rotating the fan clockwise, feel for a hole about 1/4-inch in diameter

Photo 1. Spin both cooling fans by hand.

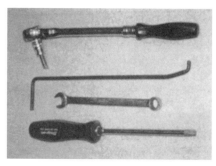

Photo 3. Tools needed: 8-mm hex head socket, ratchet, locking tool, 13-mm wrench, lever handle.

Photo 2. Remove debris using compressed air.

Photo 4. Fan shroud clips (arrows) to be removed.

Photo 5. Rotate fan using 8-mm hex head socket (arrow).

Photo 6. Locking tool ready to insert in hub hole.

Photo 7. Fan clutch locking tool (arrows) in position to prevent fan spinning.

Photo 8. Close-up of locking tool (arrow) in coolant pump hub.

Photo 9. Fan being removed with shroud.

Photo 10. Front of fan showing dirt buildup in hub.

Photo 11. Flush and blow out radiator and air conditioning condenser.

Photo 12. Poly V-belt correctly installed. Dirt or grease on belt can cause compressor to stop.

Photo 13. Remove nut with 13-mm wrench.

inside the coolant pump hub. Stop rotating when the hole is at about 12 o'clock (photo 6). If the socket does not bottom out in the bolt head because of dirt, remove the socket and clean the bolt head with an unbent paper clip.

4. Insert the fan clutch locking tool into the hole above, and rest the top of the tool to the right of the tensioner bolt area of the cylinder head (photo 7).

5. With the locking tool secure, remove the fan center bolt, then remove the locking tool. Photo 8 shows the tool installed.

6. Wiggle the fan assembly off its shaft and remove the fan and shroud (photo 9); wiggle the plastic tab on the shroud around the upper coolant hose. Always store the fan upright; if it is stored horizontally, fluid inside the hub will drain out.

7. Remove leaves and debris from the air-conditioner condenser and radiator. Clean the fan using detergent and water (photo 10). In hot months, debris prevents the condenser and radiator from cooling properly.

8. Using an air nozzle or water hose, flush remaining debris by forcing air or water both ways through the radiator

cooling fins (photo 11). Debris in the fins cuts cooling efficiency. Do not use a high pressure washer or hose down a hot radiator; do not bend or damage the fins.

9. Inspect the poly V-belt. Check its underside for cracks or splits. The belt should be tight on the pulleys. If necessary, replace the belt before reinstalling the fan and shroud.

10. Reassemble the fan and shroud. With the locking tool in the pump hub, install and tighten the fan center bolt to 45Nm (33 lb-ft). Remove the locking tool. I recommend putting a few drops of Loctite locking compound on the fan center bolt threads.

Photo 14. Release tension on bolt, move handle counter-clockwise.

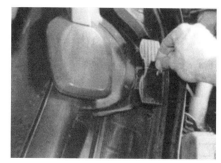

Photo 15. Remove center grill and check for leaves and debris.

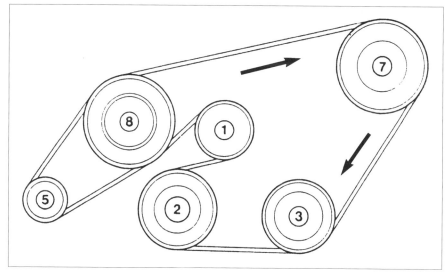

Figure 1. Belt layout for 602 diesel engines; belt rotates clockwise; 1) tensioner pulley; 2) crankshaft pulley; 3) A/C compressor; 5) alternator; 7) power steering; 8) coolant pump

the pulleys, the tensioner may have extended, pushing the tensioner pulley to its limit. Retract the tensioner by pushing down on the pulley with the heel of your hand. You will feel the pulley move slowly against hydraulic pressure. Once it bottoms out, quickly install the belt on the pulleys. The ribbed portion of the belt must contact the ribbed portion of all the pulleys. Do not crush or crease the belt.

7. Using the leverage tool, rotate the black plastic piece clockwise while pushing the bolt back through the hole so the nut can be installed. Install and tighten the nut.

8. Reinstall the fan and fan shroud as above. Start the engine and check for proper operation with the air-conditioner on and the steering wheel being turned.

Air-Conditioner Operation

For the climate control system to operate efficiently, the interior vents must be fully open, and the control knobs set to maximum cooling. Plenty of cool air must flow across the condenser (heat exchanger at front of car), belt tension on the compressor drive pulley must be correct, and the system must have a correct refrigerant charge.

Air-conditioning cannot cool the interior to comfortable levels quickly if the car has been in the sun all day. If you have a thermometer that goes to 150°F, leave it in the car exposed to direct sunlight. When you return, you'll be amazed at the temperature.

Checking the Air-conditioning

The tasks below can be done by the do-it-yourselfer observing safety precautions. Actual repairs should be left to a professional technician with correct service equipment.

1. Set all the temperature wheels to maximum cooling, recirculation on, with the vent fan on High. Start the engine, and while watching the compressor pulley, have the helper push the air-conditioning button

11. Drop the fan shroud lower tabs into the slots at the bottom while inserting the center tab at the top; reinstall the clips.

Removing and Installing the Poly V-belt

Installing a new belt takes about 20 minutes. The old belt (and the locking tool to remove the fan) can be kept in the trunk for emergencies. The tensioner automatically tensions the new belt, making adjustments unnecessary.

1. Remove the fan and fan shroud as above, then sketch the pulleys and the belt installation before removing the belt. See Figure 1 and photo 12. You might want to protect the radiator with a sheet of cardboard.

2. Remove the nut (photo 13), using a 13-mm wrench.

3. Insert a leverage tool in the black plastic hole and lever (rotate) the tool counter-clockwise to relieve tension (photo 14). Simultaneously, push the bolt back out of the tensioner hole toward the back of the engine. Do not remove the bolt.

4. Slowly release the tension on the tool, then remove the belt.

5. Inspect the tensioner parts. The tensioner pulley should spin freely by hand without making grinding noises or feeling rough. If not, replace it. If you have a degreaser, clean the front of the engine before installing the new belt.

6. Install the new belt with the writing facing you (photo 12). If you have trouble installing the belt on all

on. The pulley clutch should click and begin turning at belt speed. If not, the air-conditioning fuse, relay, dash control panel, or wiring to the compressor is faulty. Check the fuse (in the fuse panel) first. The air-conditioning pulley is behind the driver's side headlight at the bottom of the engine. If the air-conditioning does not operate, it is possible that refrigerant has leaked from the system, causing the system to stop itself. A professional technician needs to fix this problem.

2. Verify that the mechanical cooling fan is drawing air through the radiator by revving the engine. The electric fans may come on within seconds; if not, check their fuse. Inspecting the compressor and drive belts is easier if the fan shroud and fan are removed. Check the temperature gauge to prevent overheating while testing, and don't run the engine for more than two minutes this way. The electric cooling fans are turned on by a refrigerant pressure switch and by an engine coolant temperature switch.

3. Check the sight glass for liquid flow during air-conditioner operation using a flashlight; liquid should flow with few bubbles visible. The sight glass may have to be cleaned with a Q-tip and glass cleaner. See Figure 2. The

sight glass, which allows you to watch refrigerant flow, is in a metal filter /dryer can behind the driver's side headlight in the engine compartment.

4. Place a pocket temperature gauge in the center outlet vent. Run the engine at 2,000 rpm with the ACC on maximum cooling and the highest vent fan speed. The air temperature should be about 63°F (17°C), assuming outside temperature of 100°F (37.7°C) and relative humidity of 90 percent. On an 80°F (26°C) day with the same humidity, the temperature should be about 48°F (9°C). A pocket digital temperature gauge (part #temp1a) is available from Snap-on tools and elsewhere.

This test is only approximate and should not be done in direct sunlight or when the temperature and humidity are quite high. If the air does not cool adequately, a problem may exist in the ACC system.

Final Wrap-up

Inspect the ventilation duct inlets for blockage or debris. Remove the center grill and vacuum the duct areas at the windshield base (photo 15). If the car passes these tests and inspections, it's ready for summer. If not, have it professionally serviced now.

Figure 2. Sight glass (arrow) in refrigerant filter/dryer.

Technical and Restoration Forum

Technical and Restoration Forum

Air-conditioning

Aging Air-conditioner

May/June 1996

My 1980 300SD, with about 130,000 miles, was stored for about a year. The engine was run once every two weeks, but the air-conditioner was not cycled. Now the system leaks at the receiver-dryer. My local guru says the problem relates to internal decomposition of the system. Debris was getting into the expansion valve. Another mechanic says that when he has similar problems with U.S. cars, he flushes the system, but my guru says this hasn't worked with the Mercedes-Benzes that he's tried it on. Any advice?

Long periods of not running the air-conditioner on your 16-year old car have allowed its seals and hoses to deteriorate from insufficient lubrication. Debris from the inner lining of the hoses may be clogging the expansion valve.

Technical Advisor George Murphy suggests replacing all the hoses, then (to remove existing particles) backflushing and cleaning the system. Do this with the compressor bypassed and the expansion valve removed, then replace the expansion valve and the receiver/dryer. Once the system operates properly, exercise it weekly. Do so by running the engine to full operating temperature (it should have an 85-degree thermostat), then push the Defrost button. This operates the compressor and the servo. After five minutes of Defroster operation, select Auto Hi or Auto Lo (compressor on), and move the temperature dial to 65°F for maximum cooling. This will help to deter the effects of age and non-use.

450SEL Air-conditioning Icing

March/April 1988

My 1977 450SEL's air-conditioning has an icing problem. After an hour's use, the air-conditioning system drips water on the driver's side (next to the gas pedal) and on the passenger's side. The drain is clean and open. Could a faulty sensor cause an icing problem? Also, the system doesn't cool as well as I think it should.

If the sensor fails in your car, it could result in the evaporator icing up, which would become evident as a reduction of air flow into the car. When the sensor works properly, it turns off the compressor if the temperature of the air coming through the evaporator drops below about 35–37°F. Passengers then notice that there is no cooling, but cooling soon resumes as the evaporator warms up.

The dripping in your car can only come from condensation. The plastic tray intended to catch condensate dripping from the evaporator must either be warped or have a build-up of dirt so that the water can't get to the drains.

To check whether you have a real icing problem, start the car, and let it run with the air-conditioning on and set at minimum temperature. Stick a long-stemmed thermometer into the center cold air outlet. Close all other outlets as far as possible. When the temperature of the outlet air drops to 34°F (or possibly higher), the compressor should switch off and stay off until the evaporator warms up. If the compressor doesn't switch off, you have a defective evaporator temperature regulator (ETR) switch. In your car, this switch is on the upper side of the air-conditioner housing with a capillary tube running down between the fins of the evaporator. If ice forms, it will do so on the evaporator where condensation normally occurs, so drips will still fall into the tray.

Air-conditioner Controls

November/December 1988

After about an hour of operation, the air-conditioner in my 1982 380SL cycles off. It can only be cycled on again by turning the temperature wheel to the minimum setting. The wheel can then be adjusted to the desired temperature, and the unit operates until it cycles off, when I have to begin again. What's wrong?

By turning the wheel to "Min", you bypass the various temperature sensors (except the evaporator sensor). Check and re-solder the electrical connections to all sensors, to the connector for the temperature regulator (silver box) and to the push-button switch. Next, have someone test the system with test 126 589 03 21 00 if you can. If not, replace the temperature regulator.

Heat Sensor Location

November/December 1994

The automatic climate control on my 1985 300D turbo-diesel works fine, but when outside air temperature rises to about 80°F, the thermostat must be rolled to just before clicking onto the full Hot position to keep from freezing out the occupants and to reduce the fan speed. Is this normal?

I have the same experience with the climate control in my own 1985 300D. I believe that the cause of the high cooling power when the control is set to Hot is the location of the temperature sensor on the dash, where it gets radiant heat from the sun. For relief, push the low-speed fan button or switch temporarily to Economy mode, which supplies outside air with no cooling.

190D 2.5 Turbofans

November/December 1990

I've never seen the two electric cooling fans in front of the radiator of my 1987 190D 2.5 Turbo come on, even when idling with the air-conditioning on in 100-degree heat. Yet the engine has never come close to overheating. What turns these fans on, and when should they come on?

Your auxiliary fans are just that, and they operate in tandem. They are switched on simultaneously, in the lower of two speeds at a refrigerant pressure of 20 bar (about 290 psi), and in the higher speed at an engine coolant temperature of 221°F (105°C). You'd probably have to tow a trailer up a mountain with the air-conditioning on to get these fans to operate.

Top-Down A/C

November/December 1991

With the air vents open on my 1976 450SL, warmer than ambient air comes through them. Turning on the air-conditioning eliminates the problem, but I feel foolish driving a convertible on a nice evening with the top down and the air-conditioning on! I've been told that the airflow is picking up engine heat. Is there a way to stop this?

The problem is inherent with the design of the system, and newer systems have it, too. It's a matter of compromise between different ways of getting proper response from the system. When the controls are set to provide fresh air, it flows through passages which become hot from engine compartment heat. This is aggravated in your 1976 450SL because it has a catalytic converter in the engine compartment. Even though it has no catalytic converter, my 1985 300D has a similar problem. In warm weather I must run the air-conditioning because engine heat warms the ambient air even when no engine coolant goes through the heat exchanger.

Quick Cure Unsure

March/April 1998

When the air-conditioning in my 1983 300SD quit, I found that opening the fuse box and spraying the fuses with CRC quick-drying electronic cleaner made the system work fine, but I have to repeat this every few months. Is there any other way to make the air-conditioning work right?

Many air-conditioning problems come from bad soldered joints on the push-button circuit board rather than fuses. The traditional quick-and-dirty fix for an unblown but apparently non-conducting fuse is to simply rotate it to ensure good contact. Mercedes-Benz fuses have contacts of soft tin alloy so that the connection actually cuts in slightly for better contact. Other makes of fuses have harder contacts which may loosen and allow dirt or grease to spoil the contact. Be sure the fuse box cover fits tightly.

Wet Socks

November/December 1997

My 1987 560SL has a water leak that I've been unable to find. A few drips fall from above the gas pedal during sharp turns or on steep grades; while driving in the rain, the carpets get wet. The drain tubes in front of the dash have been cleaned, and I've spent a lot trying to find this leak without result.

One likely source of water is condensation from the air-conditioning system. This normally drips onto a tray which drains into a tube leading out under the car. The tray can fill up with dust, pollen, or other debris which blocks flow to the drain. The tray can then overflow inside the car, especially in sharp corners. The only fix is to remove the tray and clean it. The leak may appear to be caused by a rain leak because high humidity during rainstorms increases the amount of condensation.

Heating

Stiff Heater Levers

July/August 1992

My original heater levers are fine but operate stiffly. I don't want to break them, so how can I lubricate them or otherwise free up the cables?

The levers and cables are usually not the culprits, rather it's corrosion in the valves that control coolant flow to the heater cores in the engine compartment. These valves can be disassembled, the corrosion removed, and lubricated. Exercising them regularly helps.

300E Gurgle Kits

November/December 1992

Whenever the heat is on, my 1988 300CE has a loud gurgling noise behind the dash. A "gurgle kit" was installed and the system bled, but the noise persists.

The gurgling in 300-series cars was addressed in MBNA's *Service Information 83/33a* and *Diagnostic Directory, Topic 83-91011*. Two different treatments are prescribed, one for cars built from April 1988 (chassis end number A751393) to May 1990 (chassis end number B249838) and the other for cars produced either before or after this block.

The first group was to get the gurgle kit; the others were simply to get a precise bleeding procedure. One paragraph of the above Service Information says:

"Please be informed that on vehicles other than listed..., the heater core is of a different design. The cause of noise is presence of air in the coolant system, and the complaint can be corrected by proper bleeding (see *Diagnostic Directory 2 Microfiche, Topic 83-91011*). Installation of the 'Gurgle Kit' in those vehicles would not be beneficial, and in fact could cause other problems." The listing referred to is the 4/88 to 5/90 group. If your car is in that group, use of the gurgle kit is correct.

The bleeding procedure for cars before or after the group is: 1) fill the cooling system to the indicated mark on the expansion tank while the engine is cold; 2) remove the supply hose from the cylinder head to the heater core at its top end, fill it with coolant, and re-install; 3) switch the ACC system to Max heating and run the engine until the thermostat opens.

230SL Heat Control

January/February 1991

When driving my 1964 230SL with the fresh air vent open and the heater lever in the cold position, outside air coming through the vent is warmed, making the car uncomfortable. I've been told that early 230SL's had no way to block hot water flow through the heat exchanger with the cold air vent open, so the heat exchanger warms air entering the vent. My car has no access hole in the firewall like later 230/250/280SL's. This hole seems to lead to the linkage blocking hot water flow through the heat exchanger. How can I stop the warming of outside air?

The early 230SL heater controlled heat delivered by mixing hot and cold air, with no means of stopping coolant flow to the heat exchanger. As the air flaps deteriorate with age, more heat leaks through, even in hot weather. The best fix is to restore the heater flaps to original condition, since the heat exchanger provides additional radiator capacity (that's why it's common in 1960's cars to turn on the heater if the car runs too hot).

Shut-off valves were adopted in later 230SL's (and 250/280SL's), but it was normal for the valves to not close completely unless very carefully maintained. Then you got warm air in hot weather, even with the heater off. It wouldn't be difficult to modify your car to the later SL configuration by adding a valve in the line to the heat exchanger.

108 Heater / Defroster Motor Tip

September/October 1991

If you've ever had to drive a 108-bodied car in winter with a broken (and hard to reach) heater motor, here's a hint that will help until you can fix it. Turn your A/C fan on, and turn the modulator all the way to the left (essentially off). The A/C fan will circulate warm air from the heater core and keep all but your tootsies from frostbite. This technique is particularly effective at defrosting a windshield, partly because the A/C is probably kicking in (in all but the coldest weather) to help dehumidify the passenger compartment air. I ferried a 4.5 100 miles through terrible ice and fog and arrived with a clear windshield using this trick.

Uneven Heat

November/December 1988

The automatic climate control system in my 1979 300D produces uneven air temperatures on each side of the car in the heating mode. When the heat first comes on, there's plenty on each side, but when the interior temperature approaches the temperature set by the driver, and the fan speed drops, the driver's side air gets cold; the passenger's side air stays warm. The air-conditioning works fine except when the heat is on (to dry out de-misting air, for example). I've checked everything but can't find a cause.

Sometimes air gets trapped in the coolant in the upper part of the heater core on the driver's side. This problem was recognized around 1981, and DBAG produced a kit to correct it. Described in *MBNA Service Information Bulletin 83/1* of April 1981, the kit's part number is 923 835 00 99. It includes two parts—a switchover valve (part number 001 540 35 97) and a temperature switch for the auxiliary water pump (part number 002 821 18 51). Instructions come with the kit and are also in the *Service Information Bulletin*.

Blower

Chirping Sound
March/April 1998

My 1985 500SEL has a chirping sound from the passenger-side footwell. Since the problem goes away in the summer, I assume it is the heater blower. Is there a fix short of a new blower motor?

First, check to make sure the noise is coming from the blower motor. Disconnect the blower by turning off the system or removing the fuse. If the blower is the cause, it may need only new brushes, but it must be removed even for this work. Because most ACC blower motors run almost continuously, it's usually best to replace them while you have them out.

Funny Smell in 300D
May/June 1988

My 1985 300D has about 80,000 miles on it, and whenever I turn the climate control fan on High, a strange odor occurs. How can I eliminate the odor?

Odors from the air-conditioning or heating system usually come from dirt or debris that collects on the drainage tray beneath the evaporator unit. Mold can develop there and give off odors. The only sure cure is to take out the tray and clean it, a long and difficult job. You could try to spray a mixture of disinfectant into the fresh air intake, but you probably couldn't get enough into the system to do much good, and any strong chemical could damage some of the system's components.

Blower Blues
January/February 1990

The only time the heater/air-conditioner blower comes on in my 1978 450SL is when the air-conditioning or the defroster is on. When I set the climate control to any temperature setting, the blower won't come on.

The trouble could be a defective coolant temperature sensor/switch. For your blower to be on when the push-button switches are set to Auto Hi or Auto Lo, coolant temperature must be above 104°F (40°C), or the ambient temperature must be above 68°F (20°C), or both. With the switches set to Def, the blower works regardless of coolant temperature. The switch that I suspect is on the bottom of the A/C servo.

Another possibility is that leaks in your vacuum system are preventing proper operation of the vacuum-actuated switches. Because the cowling of the 450SL is very close to the engine, the compartment gets very hot, and rubber or plastic components dry out and crack. Replace the rubber tubing under the hood, and check the tightness of the vacuum system. You might also check with our climate control expert, George Murphy, 615/482-7260 (h).

Why spend $369 more for an Einspritzer?

First off, what *is* an Einspritzer?

(Outside of being the E in SE. As in Mercedes-Benz 220SE. Or 300SE.)

Spritzer means *sprayer. Ein*spritzer means *in*-sprayer.

Or, in simple American, a fuel injector. A fuel injector does just what a carburetor does. But it does it much better.

That's because with a conventional carburetion system, one carburetor provides the fuel-and-air mixture for up to eight cylinders. With Einspritzers, each cylinder gets its fair share from its own individual spritzer. Result: the engine "breathes" easier.

Mercedes developed the Einspritzer on the racing track. It helped make Mercedes cars

the undisputed kings of the *Grand Prix* circuit until they were retired from racing in 1955.

But Einspritzers cost far more to make than a conventional carburetor system. That's why the Mercedes 220SE, for instance, is $369 more than the 220S. Many Mercedes buyers can't see it. They point out that the 220S gives them all the speed and acceleration they'll ever want.

In fact, except for a few observant car buffs who look for things like whether it says 220S or SE on the back of your Mercedes, no one will know the difference anyway.

Until you pull up to a stop light. And the light turns green.

Spritz. *Swish-h-h-h-h!*

MERCEDES-BENZ

Going abroad? Your local Mercedes-Benz dealer can order your Mercedes for delivery to you anywhere in Europe—at lowest factory prices—with the American equipment you want. And he'll provide complete service when you return to the states. For particulars, see your dealer or write to Bob Stevens, Mercedes-Benz Sales, Inc., South Bend 27, Indiana.

Advertisement from January/February 1965 issue.

Chapter 9
Care and Preservation

January/February 1988

January/February 1996

July/August 1985

How to Wax Your Car Like the Pros

Dennis Adler, Contributing Editor

May/June 1994

Photos in this article by the author.

Get ready for the 1994 concours d'elegance season …

Maybe you think that washing your car is a simple matter of pouring some detergent into a bucket of water, splashing it over the car with a rag, then rinsing off the dirt with a garden hose. That $2.95 discount car wax is probably good enough, too. For many car owners it's as simple as that, but for professionals working on restored cars or excellent original examples, washing and waxing is serious business, and there is a method to the art of cleaning and detailing.

Everyone who's ever owned a collectible car has at one time or another spent the better part of a Saturday trying to get that show car shine. Those of us who attend local and national MBCA shows are sometimes in awe of the wax jobs we see. Those owners may have paid upwards of $200 to get it done. That's the average rate these days for a professional detailer. Well worth it, too. From start to finish, it takes five to seven hours to completely wash, polish, wax, and detail a car. Well, here's how to save that $200!

To show you how the pros do it, we're going through the step-by-step procedure with Robert Geco, of Concours Auto Care in Los Angeles. So grab your favorite wash bucket, your garden hose, and a note book....

The Wash

The first step is to get rid of surface dirt and grime. Start at the roof and wash downward to the rocker panels. The pros recommend using two separate towels or wash mitts, one for the upper body, the second for the lower rocker panels and wheels. This keeps heavy road grime from being

Park in a shaded area to keep the paint cool. Never wash or wax your car in direct sunlight.

Wash your car with a liquid designed especially for cars. Use either a washing mitt or terry towel; start at the top and work downward. To ensure that dirt from rocker panels and wheels is not carried back to the fenders, doors, deck lids or roof, use a separate mitt or towel for the lower body.

Wheels can be cleaned with a brush and hose. Use a cleaner properly formulated for your type of wheels.

brought up from the lower panels to the hood, fenders, and roof, where they can scratch paint or chrome. It's also important to frequently and thoroughly rinse your mitt in the wash bucket to remove dirt, grease, or grit.

Bob started with a washing product designed specifically for cars, in this case Meguiar's Hi-Tech Wash (No. 00), formulated to foam away dirt and grime without using harsh detergents. Home detergents may be good for dishes, laundry, and walls, but they are too caustic for automotive paint. Detergents can burn paint, strip away protective coats of wax, and leave streaks. Special washing mixtures developed just for automotive paint are completely different from household cleaners.

Gather a supply of 100-percent cotton terry towels—their bigger nap lets you soak up water without scratching the paint. Still, be careful. As the towel gets dirty, replace it with a fresh one. And with scratching in mind, remove your jewelry, your watch and your belt. If you have one, a painter's smock will prevent buttons and snaps from hitting the car. If you have an air compressor, blow out all residual water in seams, around crevices, and along the edges

of moldings and trim. Open the trunk, hood, and doors, and get all the water out of the jambs and along seams.

Cleaning the Surface

Didn't we just wash the car? Yes. Clean it? No. The next step is to remove surface degradation, scratches, and oxidation. For this, you need one of the many cleaners available. In the old days we called these "rubbing compounds"; they definitely remove paint, so stick with the mildest that will do the job on your car's paint.

Selecting the right cleaner depends upon paint condition. Meguiar's offers three grades—Mirror Glaze 1 Medium-Cut Cleaner, Mirror Glaze 2 Fine-Cut Cleaner, and Mirror Glaze 4 Heavy-Cut Cleaner. This 280SL has an extremely well maintained finish and just a few surface blemishes. Overall, the No. 2 Fine-Cut Cleaner worked on 90 percent of the car. It was coarse enough to take away light oxidation and surface scratches without cutting into the paint. An oxidized finish would require a medium-abrasive cleaner, and seriously chalked paint would need the heavy duty stuff.

Before applying the cleaner, remove minor trim and lights if you can. To prevent them being scuffed by the buffing pad, tape off the trim, badges, and emblems. There are two approaches to taping off before using an electric buffer. Tape off and protect all rubber parts. The abrasive can damage them, and residue from cleaner is difficult to remove from rubber. Give the same attention to chrome trim.

If they are easily removable, take off the windshield wipers; otherwise, wrap them in terry cloth. Another consideration is the masking tape you use. You don't want masking tape with a high adhesive content. Use either 3M masking tape or a special masking tape for auto detailing, available in auto supply stores. Be sure the car doesn't stand in the sun with masking tape on it; acid from the tape can cause other problems.

To prevent cleaning compounds or polishes from getting into the car's interior, mask off air intakes or cowl grilles. As a fail-safe to avoid over-buffing any hard edges with an electric buffer, mask the inner edge of the engine compartment around the hood line, where the hood opens. This applies to any hard edge on the body, where the paint is thinner. Always take extra care with a buffer in working around edges; if you're not an expert, work by hand.

If your grille can be removed easily, as on the 230/250/280SL, it should be removed, along with the secondary grille. Both pieces can be cleaned and set aside for reassembly after waxing.

Bob did most of the work by hand, but an electric buffer saves time and elbow grease. Again we stress that when using any electric buffer or polisher, you must avoid hard edges on the body because they have less paint. Do these later by hand.

Keep the buffer pad in flat contact with the body, and run the wheel at low rpm. Use a buffer, not a grinder with a buffer pad. Grinders can turn the pad at up to 7,000 rpm and damage the paint. Professional buffers such as the Black & Decker 6138 have adjustable speeds, usually from 1,500 to 3,000 rpm. Bob suggests staying under 1,750 rpm. Let the buffer work the compound into the paint at slow rpm, and you'll get a better result. Periodically lift the buffer and check your work. Never buff the finish dry. Always leave a little haze so that you have lubricity between the pad and the paint. The residue wipes off easily with a terry towel.

After cleaning, you may still need to remove some surface scratches. The key is to remove these flaws, not fill them. Go to a heavier-cut cleaner, and use a fresh polishing pad. Never mix compounds on the same pad.

Final Cleaning

Before this step, remove any masking tape on the painted surfaces, but leave the tape intact on trim and rubber. The third step in preparing the car is another cleaning process. We're going to use Zymöl HD Cleanse to remove residue on the surface and condition the paint. Another excellent product for this purpose is Meguiar's Sealer and Reseal Glaze. This step feeds back some of the lost oils and sets up the paint for the final wax. HD Cleanse should be applied with bare hands, allowing you to feel slight imperfections left in the

Protect plastic and rubber parts (as well as wipers, vents, and pinstriping) from cleaning compounds. Automotive masking tape will eliminate damage or extra cleanup. Tape should also be applied around the edges of the engine compartment. The air vent has been covered to prevent compound from spraying into the interior. To keep compound from getting onto the rubber wiper blades, wrap them in a towel.

paint surface. After this product sets, it can be gently rubbed out with another clean white terry towel, and you'll see the start of a great shine. Most of these non abrasive products will not harm rubber or plastic.

The Wax

Several products can be used as a final wax. In this case we used Zymöl Destiny; others prefer Meguiar's No. 26 Hi-Tech. Destiny, which is 57-percent white Brazilian carnauba, leaves a glass-like finish. A jar sells for $300 but will wax the average-size car approximately 15 times. Zymöl also makes a less expensive wax called Carbon at $40 a jar, but it doesn't have the white carnauba content. The difference between white and yellow carnauba is that white provides a deeper gloss and shine. The higher the content of white carnauba, the better the wax.

Still, your success depends more on the cleaning steps than on your choice of final wax. Many waxes have developed a devoted following, almost a mystique. We encourage you to try systems by different makers and find the one that's best for you. Expensive fad products are unnecessary.

Apply the wax by hand, using a portion about the size of a quarter. Rub it between the palms of your hands to heat the wax, then apply it. Do one section at a time—half the hood, a fender, a door, etc. After it dries to a haze (only a few minutes), rub it out with a clean white cotton towel.

Final Touches

Clean? Yes. But still not ready for show. Final detailing involves the fine-toothed comb approach. Here's what separates the winners from the also-rans.

In the engine compartment (assuming that you already have a show quality engine room and don't need to steam-clean it first), use a vacuum with a brush to remove dust. Wipe down all painted and polished surfaces in the engine compartment. Use a dressing on rubber parts to give

Oxidation or fine scratches in the paint can be polished away using a fine cleaner, just coarse enough to take away light oxidation and surface scratches without cutting paint thickness. To save time, we used a buffer to apply the cleaner, but it can be done more safely and just as well by hand, especially by most of us amateurs.

Use a clean terry towel to wipe away cleaning compound, leaving a smooth surface ready for the next cleaning step.

Zymöl HD Cleanse is applied by hand in small areas, then polished by hand.

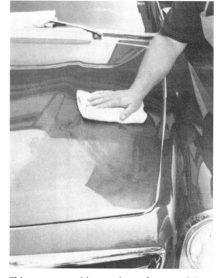

This removes residue on the surface, conditions paint by feeding back some oils that have been lost, and sets up the surface for the final wax application.

them a clean surface. Take care to get into the hood hinges, where sadistic judges love to look.

The trunk needs the same attention on carpet and rubber mats. Clean around the hinges and any crevices or cracks where judges might check. In the tool kit, make sure all tools are present and in like-new condition.

One of the last things you'll do is take a small detailing brush or an old toothbrush and go over crevices, around window moldings, headlight bezels, and trim to remove wax residue. Inside the wheel wells (again assuming that they are clean), detail the inner fender liners with furniture polish. Pledge works great, especially on the SL's textured painted surface.

Your car's interior needs equal attention. Carpeting, trim, door handles, hinges, controls, buttons, etc. all need to be cleaned, and again, crevices need to be brushed out. Use furniture polish for the wood and a good dressing for the leather and/or plastic. Make sure the door sills are clean and polished. Lastly, clean the windows, especially the corners, where haze and oxidation from leather and plastic accumulate.

The nth degree will take a little longer. That means getting under the car and cleaning the insides of the bumpers if they are accessible. The final step is to ensure that all lights and controls operate—emergency flashers, brake lights, turn signals, wipers, license plate lights, and horn. Carry spare fuses and bulbs to the show.

Touch-up paint should also be on hand in case you scratch the inner hood latch!

After going completely over your car from bumper to bumper, pay yourself $200 and take the rest of the day off!

Thanks to Robert and Sharon Geco and to John Linden for lending his 280SL and field experience.

Products

Washing Products
Meguiar's 00 Washing Solution for Automobiles

Zymöl Wash

Eagle One Wash

Cleaning Compounds
Meguiar's Hi-Tech 2

One Grand Auto Polish

Zymöl HD Cleanse

Final Wax
Zymöl Destiny

Eagle One Yellow Wax

Meguiar's 26 Hi-Tech Wax

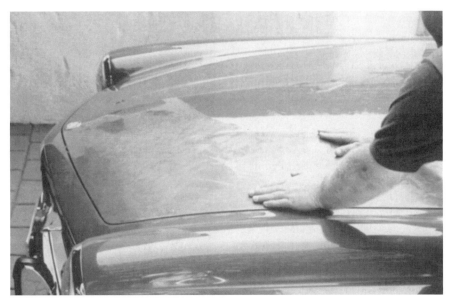

Wax is applied by hand and allowed to dry to a light haze. Wax should never be allowed to sit too long, as it becomes increasingly difficult to rub out.

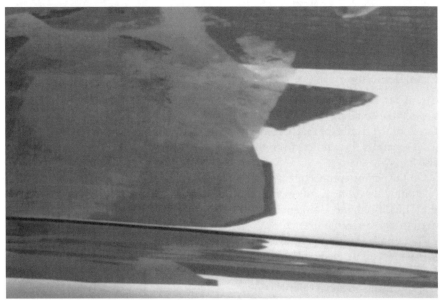

The deep, mirror like finish is evident compared to a section not yet rubbed out.

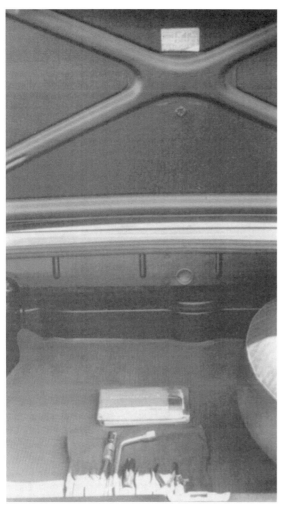

The trunk needs the same attention as the interior. Clean around hinges and in crevices or cracks where judges might check. In the tool kit, make sure all tools are present and in like-new condition.

Interior detailing is tedious, but every part down to the pedal rubbers must be perfect for an award.

How to Fix Paint Chips— The Right Way

by Scott Grundfor, Restoration Editor

January/February 1996

Photos in this article by the author.

With practice, you can make those ugly paint chips disappear.

Years ago, assembling a 300SL we'd restored as a show car, we accidentally put a few small chips in the new paint. After the car was completely assembled and finished, we repaired the chips by sanding the damaged area, applying primer, block-sanding it, and spot-painting a section of the panel, trying to keep the repair as small as possible. Matching the color might have required painting the whole panel, which was time-consuming and expensive.

A friend in the auto detailing business suggested a way to repair the chips quickly and economically. He proposed brush-touching the chips with a dab of paint. I thought the paint would look as if it had been brushed, but he described the process of building up the paint just above the original level then gently sanding it down. We tried it, and we could see that unless you knew exactly where the chip was, you could never see the repair. The process works best with solid colors; metallic colors may come out blotchy.

A Better Way

First, get the right touch-up paint for your car. For a recent model with original factory paint, a Mercedes-Benz dealer can sell you a small bottle of touch-up paint with an integral brush. If you don't know the name of the color, if it has faded, or if the car has been repainted, your local automotive paint store can match a paint sample and sell you a pint or so. Your car has a code used to determine the formula for mixing the color.

You'll need touch-up paint, a fine brush, a tiny sanding block, color sanding paper, mag polish, and wax.

Mix the touch-up paint thoroughly, making sure you get the pigment off the bottom of the can.

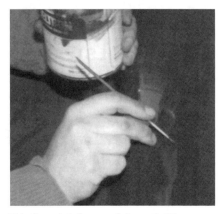

Thin the paint, then carefully apply it in miniscule amount directly into the chip; good lighting helps.

Clean the chipped area. Paint will not stick to a surface with wax, grease, or silicone on it. Dilute a liquid detergent, and use a sponge or soft rag to clean the area around the chip, especially the chip itself. Clean off any accumulated residue. Let it dry. If you see bare metal, dry it immediately to prevent rusting.

This works well for a small chip, perhaps caused by a rock, but a long scratch takes more skill and patience; it can be repaired, but rarely. Practice on a small, out of-the-way area so that if you make a mistake, it will be hidden. This process is not recommended for a car with a lot of chips. If that's the case, consider repainting the panel. For one or two chips, this alternative saves the

difficulty and expense of spot-painting a larger area or repainting an entire panel.

If you spot-paint an entire area and blend new into existing paint, you have two dissimilar paints, the new paint and the original underneath. When you spot-paint an area then finish it, you might get an exact color match then, but in time the two paints applied at different times age differently, and a ring or spot will appear.

Applying Paint

With the area clean and dry, you'll need a good brush with a very fine point. A large brush will slop paint over the edge of the chip. To keep the paint inside the chip, you need a very small brush with just a few bristles.

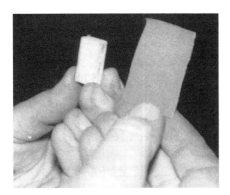

Make a miniature sanding block and wrap the ultra-fine sandpaper around it.

When the paint has dried a few weeks, mask off the area and lightly wet-sand the tiny hill down to the level of the surrounding old paint.

Polish out the fine scratches using mag wheel polish.

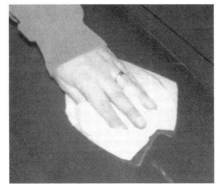

Finish off your invisible repair with a protective coat of wax.

Mix the paint thoroughly. Liquid paint settles as it stands, so mix in all the pigment at the bottom of the container, or the color will be off. If the paint is too thick to go on the brush and be applied in a light coat, it will need to be reduced to a thinner consistency. If you're using lacquer, you'll need lacquer thinner; if you are using acrylic enamel, use acrylic reducer. To get the desired consistency, paint should be thinned approximately one part thinner to one part paint, or one-half thinner to one part paint.

With the brush, build successive light layers of paint into the chip. Paint shrinks as it dries, so build the layers gradually. If you put one big glob of paint into the chip, it will continue to dry for months, shrinking as it does so. Even if you finish it flat, a few months later a crater will develop where the repair was made. Allow drying time of at least an hour or two between paint layers. The longer you wait, the better the finish you'll get, so let the paint

dry thoroughly. Two to four layers of paint will be needed to fill the crater. Because the paint will shrink, build the final layers a little above the crater surface. It should be fairly close but slightly above the surrounding paint. Let this dry for several weeks. In the meantime, your car won't look awful. It will look like you simply brush-touched that area, which will certainly look better than the chip. The key to this entire process is that the paint must dry thoroughly.

Finishing

Learning the skill of finishing is another key to success. You'll need a cube about an inch square that is perfectly flat on at least one side to use as a small wet sanding block. If you don't have something flat of this size, cut a block of hardwood. Before sanding, you might mask off the area by putting tape about an inch away all the way around. Then if you get a little

aggressive in your sanding, you won't sand and scuff the surrounding area.

Use 1,000-grit or 1,200 grit ultrafine wet sandpaper. You need very little; a sheet will cost about a dollar at an automotive paint store. Tear off a tiny square, enough to wrap around the block, then use a sponge to wet the area as you sand. Use the sandpaper and block to level the paint mound down to the surrounding original paint. Use the lightest possible pressure on the block, and gently wear down the little mound. Sand a little and very lightly—this can take mere seconds— then dry the area and inspect it. When you see that the mound has disappeared, you've gone far enough.

Avoid sanding too much. If the paint is old or thin, or if you sand too hard, you'll go right through the finish. If you very carefully let the block float with just the gentlest pressure over the little mound of paint built up over the chip, you'll wear off the top of the new surface without removing much if any of the surrounding paint. Ideally, you'll scuff it just a bit.

Next, use magnesium polish, Mother's or Blue Magic, available at most automotive stores. Magnesium is the finest abrasive I've found for compounding paint. Use a soft cloth in the area scuffed by the sandpaper, and rub until the scratches are gone. Rubbing in one direction works best. After polishing, wipe the area dry and inspect it. If you see deeper scratches, do a little more polishing with the mag polish.

Finally, wipe the surface clean and use wax or automotive polish (carnauba wax or similar), to finish the area around the chip. Done right, you've filled the chip and finished the top so that it blends in nicely. If you look very closely, you may see the spot. If you notice bubbles trapped in the paint (they produce white specks in the center of the chip) your paint was probably too dry, too thick. As you grow more skillful in applying wetter, thinner layers, the surface will not bubble.

This method can effectively repair a chip without painting an entire panel. I've used it on show cars, where it even holds up to the scrutiny of judges.

Leather Care

by Burt Mills, Contributing Editor

January/February 1988

Photos in this article by the author.

Whether you're ordering it in your new car or restoring it in your old car, leather upholstery is expensive. With even a modicum of care, though, it is one of the most durable of interior materials.

The leather interior of your Mercedes-Benz represents a considerable investment. In fact, you'll usually find that it will cost more to replace the leather than it cost new. So it makes sense to take the best possible care of leather upholstery.

Properly maintained leather will last for many years. It is common to find Mercedes-Benz cars of the 1920's and 1930's with the original leather seats still soft and supple.

Aside from cuts and punctures, the most common danger to leather upholstery is that it dries out. Once this happens, cracks appear as the skins lose their elasticity, become brittle and shrink. Once dry, they can split under pressure.

The most common drying culprit is sunshine. Sun, glaring through windows, heats up your car's interior.

This draws moisture from the leather, making it brittle and causing the dyes to fade. We've all seen once-red leather seats faded to orange in areas bleached by the sun.

Areas especially prone to sun damage include the sides and tops of cushions, the dash and the top of the rear seat, and the leading edge of the front seat. Convertibles suffer not only from sunlight but often from water, which hastens the drying process. Carried by the wind, dirt and grit lodge in pleats and seams, holding moisture, which can cause the threads to rot and fail.

Buttons, buckles, key rings and wallets in rear pockets rub against leather seats and may eventually cause dry leather to split. Lap and shoulder straps of seat belts can cause wear, too, as can children's safety seats, briefcases and sharp objects carried on seats.

How to Keep New Leather Looking New

Regular cleaning and conditioning of leather can make it last for many years. If you start when the leather is in good condition, this need not be a difficult chore.

If the lower seat cushion can be removed, do so. A stiff-bristled brush might scratch the leather or even break threads, so use a vacuum cleaner to pull out dirt from pleats and seams. A soft-bristled toothbrush might be handy, too.

There are several leather cleaners and conditioners available. Connolly Hide Food, Concours d'Elegance, Fiebing's, Lexol, Viscol and Color Plus's Softener are favorites. Mercedes-Benz also sells a leather cleaner, part number 000 986 05 71. Concours d'Elegance, Color Plus, Fiebing's and Lexol make separate cleaners and conditioners. Connolly combines the two into a soft, creamy paste. All work well.

Directions are on the container, but a few tips are in line. A soft-bristled nail brush dipped in leather cleaner

is good for scrubbing between pleats, along seams and in wrinkles and crevices. A small sponge holds the cleaning agent better than cloth. Use a modest amount of cleaner. Clean one panel or section at a time, rinse away excess cleaner, then wipe dry with a soft, clean cloth.

After the leather cleaner, use a conditioner, which is wiped on, allowed to stand for 10–15 minutes, then wiped dry with a clean, soft cloth.

Color Plus makes Flex-Fill Crack Eliminator, which should be used sparingly, only on thin crease and crack areas. It is only for use when re-dyeing leather; otherwise, the filler shows.

How to Remove Stains From Leather

Water-soluble stains can usually be removed from leather by cleaning with a sudsy, non-alkali soap/water solution. Start from the outer edges of the spot and work toward the center. Keep water to a minimum, and rinse, then dry with a soft cloth.

Non-water-soluble stains can usually be removed by light applications of leather cleaners such as Fiebing's or Lexol. Using a sponge

Good filler and colorant allow you to fill cracks, change colors and retain pliable feel.

soaked in the solution, work from the outside toward the middle of the spot. Rinse and dry after each application. It's better to use several light coats than fewer heavy coats. Wait 24 hours between applications.

The finishing coats, applied after drying, protect leather from absorbing most staining liquids. But if this has been worn away, and you're staring at un-dyed hide, oily stains can be absorbed in these areas. In these cases, re-dyeing will be necessary.

Never use abrasives or petroleum products to remove stains from leather. They won't remove the stains, and they can ruin the leather. If the upholstery is really dirty, use a cleaner first, as above.

Preventing Damage to Leather

Cleaning and conditioning leather twice yearly will usually keep leather upholstery pliable and prevent cracking. This doesn't take much time, and it also helps to preserve the color.

Unless the leather is covered by a cloth to protect it from the sun, don't leave your car in bright sunlight for long periods. The folding cardboard windshield shades not only keep the steering wheel and dash cooler but also help to protect the front seats.

Some cleaning solutions used on other parts of the car's interior may damage leather, so be sure to protect it from any product not specifically designed for use on leather. Some inferior sheepskin seatcovers may damage leather; if a strong chemical tanning agent was used, there may be a risk that residue from the agent may penetrate into leather seats, causing the leather to become over-tanned. A sheepskin cover that is too stiff may abrade the leather on your seats. High

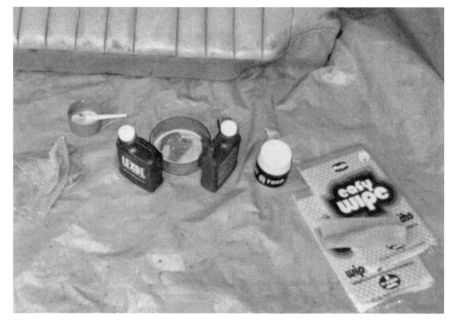

Cleaning and conditioning your leather requires little more than elbow grease.

quality sheepskins should not have these problems, though.

Re-Dyeing Leather

Sometimes re-dyeing leather is the most practical way to make old leather look presentable. Re-dyeing is neither difficult nor time-consuming.

Dirt, stains and the old finish must first be removed. Cleaning with a non-alkali soap/water solution is the first step, followed by an application of dye remover. Fiebing's and Color Plus make excellent products. Use them as directed on the can to remove old surface dyes and finishing coats. Beware of so-called miracle paints claimed to give satisfactory results on leather. These can crack, peel and damage the leather after a short time.

Buy leather dye from a leather dealer in a color as close as possible to

the original; Color Plus has a variety of dye colors available. It's difficult to re-dye from a dark color to a much lighter shade, but you can go a few shades darker. Don't use shoe repair store dyes. Apply the dye as directed, using even strokes with a dauber and being careful to avoid overlaps. Several light coats cover best. Be sure the dye reaches into seams, wrinkles and pleats.

Re-dyeing leather won't make it brittle, as the cleaning and pre-dyeing steps may soften it somewhat. Once re-dyeing is completed, regular applications of conditioner will help to keep the leather durable and supple and preserve the color.

Thanks to Andreas Reidemeister, John Grm, Jr., Lexol and Color Plus for their assistance in the preparation of this article.

How to Maintain Your Mercedes-Benz Wood

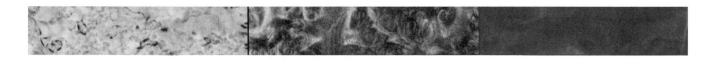

by Mark Wallach,
MBCA Technical
Committee

*July/August
1984*

Simple maintenance will keep your wood interior trim in like-new condition. In our May/June 1983 issue, well-known automotive wood authority Mark Wallach described the evolution of the use of wood in Mercedes-Benz cars. That article featured special color identification photos illustrating the different types of wood employed to beautify the interior of your car. In a July/August 1983 article, Mark took us on a visit to the wood shop at Daimler-Benz. This article tells you how to keep your car's wood in good condition.

Almost every Mercedes-Benz car ever built has decorative wood in it, the major exception being the 190SL. The amount of wood used in the cars is surprisingly high. The 220S/SE coupe/convertible had 15 pieces, the 6.9 sedan 20 pieces and the coachbuilt 600 sedan from 46 to 65 pieces, depending on the model. In the 1960's the Sindelfingen wood shop housed 600 men making parts, but now it is down to about 300 craftsmen.

All wood is made on production tooling, but each piece is custom fitted to the car, especially on low production models which could differ slightly from one car to the next. Serial numbers stamped or inked on wood parts do not match the car's serial number and sometimes do not match other parts on a given car, since they may have been scrambled on the assembly line or specially fitted.

Nitrocellulose and Polyester

Since 1928, only two wood finishes have been used; nitrocellulose lacquer and polyester. Nitrocellulose lacquer was discovered almost accidentally as a gunpowder by-product by DuPont. It was first used as an automotive body paint on Cadillacs in 1923. As an interior wood finish, it seems to date from 1928, when it was used in France. From 1928 to 1970–71, all Mercedes-Benz interior woodwork was finished in nitrocellulose lacquer polished to a bright, full finish. The term "full" means that the wood's surface grain is filled with enough coats of lacquer so that the surface is completely smooth. For instance, lacquer finish on buried wood has the clarity and depth of a still pool of cool water.

The Big Change…

During the 1970–71 model year, the factory introduced new body styles with less wood. The wood that remained was finished in a two-part plastic polyester, which reduced production costs and speeded up deliveries from the wood shop. Polyester is sprayed onto the bare wood over a primer (see page 38, May/ June 1983 issue) in two heavy coats applied about 20 minutes apart. The film coat fills the wood pores and builds to about 25 thousandths of an inch in thickness above the surface. After chemically hardening for three days, the polyester is machine sanded and polished to a bright smooth finish that has a slightly plastic look.

Some 280SE 3.5 coupes and convertibles of the 1970–71 period were finished in either lacquer or polyester as the factory phased in the new finish. There also seems to have been some experimental finishes in epoxy that show up once in a while. This epoxy is very tenacious, requiring over a week of stripping prior to refinishing.

How to Clean Your Wood

The secret of caring for your wood finish is to treat it as an exterior finish! If your pre-1970–71 car seems to have dull wood, consider it to be like an exterior finish that has not been polished for 20 or 30 years. Lacquer suffers from surface dirt, wax and normal oxidation, all of which dull its brightness.

Wax is removed with a household wax cleaner from your local supermarket. Just follow the printed instructions. Next, compound the surface with DuPont white polishing compound—about $3 for a round, flat can from any auto supply store. You may apply it either by hand or on a cloth, but I recommend using your bare hand. The heat of friction can dry out compound on a cloth, and the resulting dry grains can scratch the lacquer.

After the lacquer is cleaned and polished, use DuPont #7 liquid cleaner to remove the faint blue haze left on the surface by the compound.

Post-1971 polyester finishes can be cleaned with wax remover, which may alone be enough to brighten the finish.

If that won't do the job, try DuPont #7 to avoid the work of compounding the surface. If that doesn't work, it's back to Plan A, the three-step procedure described earlier.

What do you do after that? Absolutely nothing!

Magic Polishes

Magic spray polishes can accelerate the migration of solvents and complex polymers from the wood and reduce the life of the finish. Silicone, used in most of these polishes, goes right through the finish and contaminates the base wood. If you must put something on your wood, use something without silicone. Butcher's wax clouds the surface and reduces the brightness. Don't use Armorall on wood; its manufacturer doesn't recommend it. Mercedes-Benz polish (part number 000 986 05 61) does not contain silicone and is recommended.

If All Else Fails...

Once a wood surface has begun to crack or alligator, no secret chemical can restore it to new condition. I have tried chemicals that soften lacquer to enable the hairline cracks to seal together, but this is only useful for very light cracks in household furniture. The cracks are dark because water vapor has condensed in them, permanently staining the wood.

Don't try to sand the surface. The wood veneer is only 20 thousandths of an inch thick and very fragile, especially on curved surfaces, so sanding will only damage it. If the wood finish is cracked, nothing will help except refinishing.

Looking at the bleached, cracked wood in your car, you may wonder what its original color was. It's easy to see! Just open the glovebox door. That is the only place in the car that the wood has not faded. Surprise! The original color is that of a melted Hershey bar!

How to Restore Mercedes-Benz Woodwork

by Mark Wallach, MBCA Technical Committee

July/August 1985

If you took high school shop, you know how to finish wood. Stain it, then wipe on a coat or two of thinned varnish, and the wood shop project was ready to take home to Mom. Proper automotive wood refinishing, while far from that quality, is not unattainable to the dedicated restorer.

Daimler-Benz used a lacquer finish on its veneered interior wood from the late 1920's until 1970–71. Since then, their wood has been finished with a two-part polyester plastic. Restoring the lacquer-finished wood is eminently feasible, but repairing the two-part catalyzed plastic of newer cars is beyond the technical facility of the home restorer. If you have wood problems on your late-model car, which has a polyester finish, you are usually better off to simply buy replacement parts, used or new. Of course, replacement of the older, lacquer-finished wood parts is not so simple, so here's how to make those look like new again.

This article covers re-graining, actually repainting the grain on damaged pieces to match the surrounding grain. Re-veneering, on the other hand, is only necessary when all the wood in a car has been seriously damaged. As a guide to the number of wood parts, 220S coupes and convertibles have 15; 220SE, 280SE and 300SE coupes and convertibles have 12, 6.3 and 450 sedans 23, and 600 sedans from 46 to 53. The 230/250/280SL's have five parts, including the rear trim on the hardtop.

Refinishing lacquered woodwork requires several personal attributes:

patience, patience, patience and a good pair of hands, a phrase well used by surgeons, dentists and dice players. Let's list the steps, then we'll describe them in detail:

1. Strip old finish
2. Repair defects
3. Fill wood pores with paste filler
4. Stain base wood
5. Color/grain repairs
6. Ten coats of lacquer
7. Scuff with 400-grit sandpaper
8. Ten more coats of lacquer
9. Scuff with 500-grit sandpaper
10. Ten more coats of lacquer
11. Scuff with 600-grit sandpaper
12. Ten more coats of lacquer
13. Scuff with 1200-grit sandpaper
14. Polish
    a) white compound
    b) liquid compound
    c) DuPont #7

Stripping

Use a non-flammable marine stripper that does not require a water wash. Read the instructions and wear protective goggles because a splash in the eye can blind you. Provide plenty of ventilation because fumes can induce serious health problems. Using a plastic spatula, scrape with the wood's grain. When

the surface is clean, wash it with lacquer thinner, using a natural fiber fingernail brush to clean the pores of the wood. The gunk in the pores must be removed to be replaced later with a paste wood filler. If the veneer lifts in some areas, the glue bonding it to the base wood has aged and loosened. They can't be re-glued, so don't bother saving the bits and pieces of veneer. The radio speaker grille on SL and SE cars has 11 pieces, and the stripper will loosen them all. My best advice is to disassemble this grille completely, as it can be sanded and reassembled later.

Repairing Defects

Here's where it gets slightly difficult. If the veneer is loose, it is normal practice to slit the bubble on the loose part and inject glue beneath the veneer. Use a yellow wood glue, not white, for this repair. Clamp the part, but protect the wood's surfaces. Small sections of missing veneer can only be rebuilt by using a wood surfacing putty. Fill the area level and let it dry for two or three days to shrink, then refill it. Then sand the area flush with the surface of the surrounding veneer. Sanding the thin veneer requires a very subtle touch to allow you to see through the sandpaper with your fingertips to read the surface condition. We use 220- to 400-grit wet/dry sandpaper (used dry). This uses a lot of paper, but it's the only way. Sand with the grain for straight-grained wood or in a circular pattern with burled wood. After repairs and sanding, it is very important to vacuum the surface to clean the dust from the pores.

Paste Wood Filler

Over a three- to six-month period, lacquer shrinks slightly and reflects the smoothness of the surface beneath it. If the wood pores are not filled and if the surfaces are not level, the final finish will not be smooth. The usual furniture refinisher uses a heavy lacquer sanding sealer to fill the pores. While cheap and fast for furniture with open pores, it is not our cup of tea. Use a paste wood material that physically fills the pores. This has an advantage that improves the final product—the filler color is darker than the wood, so the darker color in the pores brings out the beauty of the wood's grain. Applying filler is one of the messiest jobs since mud pies in third grade. Again, read the instructions. We usually use brown mahogany filler, mixing it with a natural shade to dilute the base color. Use burlap to wipe the surface.

Inspect the pores with a magnifying glass. If they are not filled flush, repeat and check your wiping style. After drying the wood for several days, sand the surface lightly with 400-grit to remove surplus paste. Clean the back of each piece.

Staining

The wood tones cannot be seen in bare dry wood. Only by wetting the surface can the real color be seen. Lightly wipe the surface with benzene or alcohol. Do not use water, which will lift the grain and possibly loosen the paste filler. No water ever near wood! A super-light coat of lacquer on the surface will bring up the color to allow inspection. The wood has usually bleached to a light yellow, which some think is the real color. The genuine color is about the shade of a melted Hershey bar. Check the inside of the wooden glove box door or find a corner that has been covered by another part.

N.G.R. means non-grain-raising, designating a type of stain that will not lift the grain. This stain is highly concentrated, and since you can't bleach the wood to a weaker shade after application, the stain should be diluted. Veneers take stain differently from solid wood trim. To compensate for the various colors and materials, vary the concentration for each piece. When completed, all pieces should be the same shade. Spray another light coat of lacquer to hold the color, which will look a little different when dry. When the colors are matched to your satisfaction, the repairs can then be colored. You will actually be hand-graining the repaired area to match the grain of the surrounding veneer. This requires some artistic skill and a full palette for color blending. The technique is called faux bois, and libraries have books on it. Color-fast blending colors are available, but do not use furniture refinishers' aniline dyes. These are not light-fast and will fade to purple in sunlight. It is difficult to paint the right pattern and color, but when you get it right the sense of achievement is overwhelming!

After coloring the repairs, the detail areas are painted solid black, as factory original. These detail areas include the defroster outlets as seen through the windshield and the inside edge of window trim visible only from outside. For a before/after record and to reference these areas, take photographs before starting. Since fluorescent lamps emit a blue light, check the staining and repairs only in sunlight. Work done under normal fluorescent lights will not be correct in sunlight, where the car is usually seen. Special lamps are available but not justified for a one-time job.

Lacquering

Most auto body shop mechanics who can paint a car will say they can do a super job on woodwork too because lacquer is lacquer. Acrylic lacquer has every necessary attribute except one—it will not adhere to wood. It also has a gray tone and will break down in an alligator pattern. Furniture shops use household lacquers that have a narrow temperature durability range —from 55° to 95°F. While a 40° range is adequate for houses, car interior temperatures can range from -20° to 160°. Household lacquers are unable to comply with expansion of the base wood and will fatigue across the grain. Polyester finishes are also very hard and will likewise fatigue and crack. We use a flexible lacquer specially formulated for us to withstand automotive conditions (information on availability of this lacquer appears at the end of this article).

Polyurethane will lift the colors on the repairs, thus cannot be used. Imron is polyurethane, and spraying it without special equipment can be very hazardous to your health. Imron contains poisons that penetrate spray masks, are absorbed through the skin and built up in your body.

Lacquer can be used to work up colors, is a very forgiving material and can be sanded smooth. Scratches or other damage can be easily filled and sanded smooth, and lacquer's clarity and patina are superb. Most importantly, it is authentic.

Spray 10 coats of lacquer over a two-day period. Spraying usually requires a spray gun and either a booth or a clean open area, but there are alternatives. One is to brush on the lacquer with a badger brush, $25–$30 but worth it. Another is to find a half-pint aerosol-operated spray gun; these work but consume prodigious amounts of aerosol cans. To get the solvents out, let the parts dry for 72 hours.

The finish is sanded after each 10 coats, so the in-between coats do not have to be perfect. If the coats are thin, you might spray 20 coats before sanding. There has to be enough lacquer on the part to withstand sanding, which levels the surface until it is blemish-free. Sand dry, even if the paper is wet/dry. Water fills the surface blemishes, making them invisible.

Repeat the spraying and sanding until the surface is perfect. The idea of 40 to 60 coats of lacquer shocks the average person, but sanding removes most of it, so the average thickness of the finished coating is 12 to 15 mils (thousandths of an inch).

The final scuffing with 1200-grit leaves the surface dull, as expected. Doing the job at home means hand polishing, and because we did it that way for years before we perfected the right combination of machine wheels, compounds, speeds and skill, we can testify that this is hard work but worth it. You may be able to polish with an electric drill and a sewn wheel about eight inches in diameter. We use DuPont white polishing compound, available at any auto parts store for $2.95 a flat can. Smear it very lightly on the part, then rub it in with your fingertips and the heel of your palm. Don't use a polishing cloth because the heat of the friction dries out the polish in the cloth, causing the dried grains to scratch the finish.

The second polishing uses Turtle-brand liquid polishing compound, producing a bright surface with a blue haze. This haze is removed with a final polish with DuPont #7 Cleaner. Again, read the instructions. Turtle Wax and DuPont assure me there are no harmful chemicals in these compounds. The final cleaning with DuPont #7 takes off all surface debris.

Installation includes felt on the bottom of certain parts, new screws and washers. Don't tighten the screws too much, as that can stretch the wood; the newly finished parts need time to settle into place.

When it's all over, and you sit behind the wheel admiring your handiwork, the sense of pride and accomplishment make it all worthwhile. Bon chance!

Sources of Supply

A complete catalog of wood finishing supplies is available from Albert Constantine & Sons in New York.

Plastic Windows

**by Frank King,
Technical Editor**

*March/April
1988*

It's an unfortunate fact that the part of a Mercedes-Benz most susceptible to damage and the ravages of time and weather is the soft top of a convertible. This subject was covered at StarTech 1987 and reported in the July/August 1987 issue. Not dealt with there were the plastic windows in the soft top. These are made of an acrylic material chemically similar to the car's paint and subject to the same kinds of damage: scratches, water spots and aggressive airborne contaminants. The effect of these is intensified when the top is folded in the storage compartment. Owner's manuals instruct that the plastic window should be cleaned only by wiping with a cloth soaked with detergent, then wiped dry. We assume that the detergent is to be diluted with water, as for washing the car.

While researching on waxes and polishes, we noticed that Meguiar's catalog of professional car care products included a cleaner and a polish for plastic windows. On the telephone Meguiar's assured us that these products were effective and approved by plastics manufacturers. Samples of their Mirror Glaze 17 Professional Plastic Cleaner and Mirror Glaze 10 Professional Plastic Polish were furnished to us by Meguiar's. MBNA sent us a window that had been removed from a soft top because of extensive damage of the type mentioned above.

To be sure that we weren't trying to restore something that could be fixed by careful washing, we washed the window in lukewarm water and Ivory dishwashing detergent in the bathtub, using a soft cotton wash cloth, rinsing in clean water and drying with a soft towel. The window was now clean, but damage to the outside surface was not only clearly visible but could be felt with the fingertips. Mirror Glaze 17 Cleaner was then applied according to directions to an area about eight inches square in the upper center of the window. About an hour and a half was spent cleaning, wiping off and checking, repeating as needed. All the really gross spotting was removed, and the general appearance and transparency were greatly improved.

The stubborn spots and marks were examined with a jeweler's loupe. The cloudy marks, particularly the stripe down the center, were found to consist of very fine scratches. Some of the stubborn spots were slightly colored and appeared to have penetrated into the plastic material. When felt with the fingertips, the smoothness of the cleaned area was in sharp contrast to the damaged area. More work with the cleaner would have removed practically all of the spots and scratches, the exceptions being deep scratches and infiltrated discolorations.

The cleaned area was then treated with Mirror Glaze 10 Polish, designed to restore clarity and provide a measure of scratch resistance. We concluded that the use of these products would help to keep the plastic windows in good condition and delay the usual deterioration in appearance and transparency. A reliable source informs us that there is a plastic cleaner called Novus that also does a good job. It is sold in motorcycle shops and marinas, where other good cleaners may also be available.

Technical and Restoration Forum

Technical and Restoration Forum

Metallic Paint Cracking

September/October 1986

My 1979 300D's metallic silver paint is just beginning to show signs of "spider web" deterioration. What can I do?

The clear coat on top of the metallic paint is cracking, mainly due to weather (ultraviolet radiation, humidity, temperature fluctuations, etc.). This usually affects horizontal surfaces such as roofs, hoods and trunk lids first. If you catch it in time, before the metallic paint beneath it is damaged, you may be able to buff off the clear coat and replace it. Otherwise, it's time to repaint the car. Proper care can help to preserve metallic paints, which have improved over the years. See the July/August 1983 issue of *The Star* for an article on washing and care of all finishes.

Dash Cracks

March/April 1988

What can I do to prevent my vinyl dash from cracking on cold winter nights?

We've never seen a simple solution to this widespread problem. There seem to be two causes: loss of some of the compounds that keep the material flexible through slow evaporation, and expansion and contraction of the vinyl at a different rate than that of the metal beneath it. Exposure to hot sunlight does the most damage, so the most effective prevention is to keep sun off the dash. Plenty of covers are sold to protect the dash. Some liquid spray-on vinyl treatments claim to retard cracking by preventing the vinyl from drying out. Nobody seems to have sufficient long-term experience

to judge their effectiveness, so about all you can do is to check the labels until you find one that claims to help prevent cracking.

If your dash is already cracked, you could replace it with a factory unit, repair it (with a vinyl repair kit, a local vinyl repair service or an auto upholstery shop) or install a dash overlay. These obviously vary widely in effectiveness, cost, appearance and longevity, so the choice is yours.

Sticky Windshield Question

September/October 2001

If I replace the windshield on my 560SL, a show car, can the three stickers be removed from the old glass and be put on the new windshield? The stickers are a blue Mercedes-Benz VPC Quality Control decal, the rectangular white "Daimler-Benz product" signature sticker, and the collector vehicle registration sticker. If the two factory stickers must be replaced, where can I get them?

The "Daimler-Benz product" sticker can be purchased through any Mercedes-Benz dealer; the sticker even has a small part number printed on it. For the VPC sticker, check with the best parts man at your dealership, and he may be able to research it. Windshield replacement businesses are used to changing registration stickers, so I wouldn't worry about that. If they ruin it, you'll get a new one in a year anyway.

Engine Cleaning

January/February 2004

Cars built from August 1994 onward have a clear anti-corrosion coating applied in the engine compartment that looks like a clear coat of paint. The only approved method of cleaning these engine compartments is with steam cleaners. Cold water solvents, such as Gunk Engine Bright, should not be used, as they attack protective coatings installed at the factory. Cars built from December 1989 through July 1994 had protective wax installed at the time of manufacture. If engine compartments on these cars are cleaned with solvents, protective wax (000 986 33 70/10 for 400-ml spray, 000 986 33 70 for 1-liter can) must be reinstalled. When reinstalling the protective anti-corrosion wax, several caveats must be followed; see *Service Information 98/48*, March 1995. Don't clean a hot engine; the engine should be cold or warm to the touch. Don't apply protective wax until everything in the engine compartment is dry. Don't apply wax to the exhaust system, belts, or pulleys.

Convertible Top Maintenance

January/February 2004

Here's how to clean a convertible top:

1. Remove bird droppings immediately.

2. When removing ice or snow, do not use scrapers with sharp edges.

3. Do not clean soft tops or rear windows with gasoline, thinners, tar removers, spot removers, or other organic solvents.

4. Periodic cleaning by spraying with a garden hose and rinsing with clean water is sufficient. A thorough washing should be done only when the top is very dirty.

5. Clean the soft top with a soft brush, always brushing in the same direction, from front to rear.

When washing the top:

1. First clean with a soft brush while the top is dry.

2. Use ample lukewarm water with a neutral detergent. Clean the top using a soft brush or sponge.

3. Heavily soiled areas can be cleaned with a concentrated detergent.

4. Rinse thoroughly with clean water.

5. Allow the top to dry.

Waterproofing:

1. Completely clean the top.

2. Cover all surrounding paint and window areas, including plastic windows.

3. Spray the top with Mercedes-Benz waterproofing spray 001 986 31 71. Spray lightly and evenly from a distance of approximately 12-in, and don't let any area get too damp.

4. Let dry for about two minutes, then spray again.

5. If the seams leak, seal them with Mercedes-Benz seam protection compound 000 989 40 20 on the inner part of the top.

Cleaning rear plastic windows:

Pre-wash the rear and side windows with clean water and dry them. With a lint-free cloth, apply Mercedes-Benz plastic glass cleaner 001 986 30 71, then clean again using a dry cloth.

Mercedes-Benz waterproofing spray contains silicone, so do not spray it on car paint. Remove overspray using Mercedes-Benz silicone remover 000 986 71 11 repeatedly until the area is completely clean.

Chassis and Engine Numbers

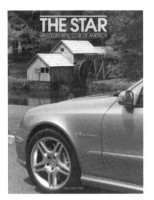

July/August 2003

November/December 1997

January/February 1988

A Guide to Daimler-Benz Chassis and Motor Numbers

by W. Robert Nitske,
Contributing
Editor

*January/February
1988*

*Quick, what's the difference
between a W123 and an OM602?
Read this, and you'll know.*

Besides the model numbers on the trunk lid of every Mercedes-Benz, which represent a tale unto themselves, DBAG has an internal numbering system for its chassis and motor designs. These W (chassis) and M (motor) numbers bear absolutely no resemblance to the numbers on the trunk lid, so there's more than a bit of a mystery about them.

Some material in this article was printed in our March/April 1983 issue. A multitude of new Mercedes-Benz models has since appeared. All, including 1988 models, are included in this updated tabulation. (Years shown in the accompanying chart are years of production, not model years.)

Throughout the history of Mercedes-Benz, consistency in model designations has evidently never carried a strong priority, so the problem of identifying body styles and engines is an ever-challenging experience. To compound the problem (and to come up with some interesting models), DBAG has put nearly every one of their powerplants into nearly every one of their contemporary chassis.

At times the basic W numbers have additional letters and numbers to indicate the production designation and identify the precise model. The current 124 coupes, for example, are sometimes designated C124; station wagons may have a number preceded by S, and long-wheelbase sedans may have numbers preceded by V. The 123 body, for instance, generally referred to as the W123, had 26 variations.

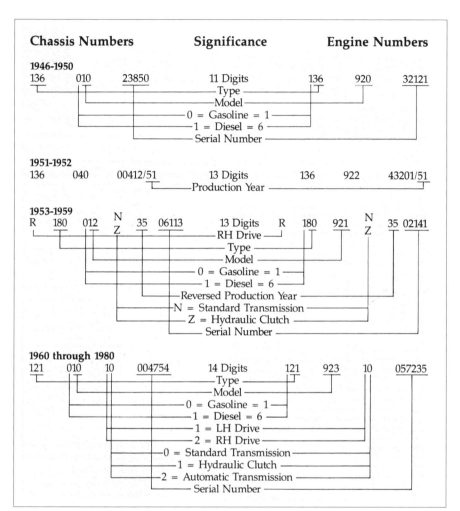

Chart from: *The Numbers Game: Chassis and Engine Numbers*
September/October 1986

Engine numbers also have more than just three numbers indicating variations on a basic design. The 116 V-8 had 27 different specifications. Only Heinz—and Baskin-Robbins— have more varieties.

The Early Days

W numbers, for *Wagennummer* or car number (chassis number), were, in less complicated times, the same as that of the engines in them. Even then, engine numbers were not always simple. In the larger cars of the middle 1920's, engine numbers were longer than they are now. In the large K models

of 1927–1933, the body was W98456, and the engine was M98456 (M for Motor). This method was used for supercharged models until the S and SS cars. For instance, the 710 SS was number 06; W06 for the chassis and M06 for the 27/170/225-hp motor. That 06 number, incidentally, was used for all further developments of these models and even the enlarged 720 SSKL. In between were the 06S, 06III, S06 and 06RS. To confuse the issue, all 700SS, 710SS, 720SSK and 720SSKL cars had an engine of 7,056-cc displacement but not the same horsepower output.

The other K models (500K, 540K, etc.) and the 380 generally had matching chassis and engine numbers, as in W22 and M22, or W24 and M24, but not in the further developed line. Later the W24 chassis came with the M24/I or M24/II, and the later W29 carried the M24/II engine. (The W22 chassis was the 380; the W24 and W29 were the 500K and 540K.) And then there was the 580K at the 1939 Berlin Auto Show with the W129/II chassis and the M124 engine of 5,800-cc displacement. But that is definitely another story.

Obviously we were detoured there by the mysticism of the legendary supercharged models, so let's discuss the more sober 170 line as a pre-World War II example. The six-cylinder 170 model of 1931–1936 was the 15 type; chassis W15, engine M15. Quite simple. When the four-cylinder models came on the scene, the 170V got the W136 body with the M136 engine. The rear-engined 170H was the 28: W28 and M28, but from then on, things got a bit mixed up. The 170SV was a W136S and M149; slight alterations had taken place. With only the three exceptions above, the 170 models were basically W136 chassis with M136 engines.

The 1950s and Later

In later years the basic body styles received a number which was adhered to throughout the entire production run of all closely related models. For instance, the 230/250/280SL cars all had the W113 body with a suffix added to indicate a slight alteration: A for the 250SL and E28 for the 280SL—the 28 evidently related to the 2.8-liter displacement. Their engines were the M127, M129 and M130. The 300SL coupe was the W198I, the Roadster 198II, both with M198 engines. The 450SL, first built in 1970 as the 350SL, had the new 107 body, and so did all subsequent models, the 450SL, 450SLC, 380SL, 380SLC, 500SL, 560SL, etc. The 4.5-liter engines were all M117.

The 450SE S-Class models introduced in 1972 had the 116 body. The 280S sedans were the W116 V28, the 350SE was the W116 E35 and so on. Even the 450SEL 6.9 had that same body style and was the W116 E69. The 2.8 engine was M110, the 3.5 was the M116 and the 6.9 was M100, the same number as the engine that powered the 300SEL 6.3 and the 600.

All of the mid-1970's middle class models shared the 115 body. These

included the intermediate 200 and 220 sedans, 250 coupes and the larger engined (M130) 280 line, along with the 3-liter diesel 240D 3.0 or 300D. Although considerably improved, their basic engine numbers remained. But the new 5-cylinder, 3-liter diesel engine had the OM617 designation (OM meaning "*Oel Motor*", oil motor) with the later turbo version known as OM617A.

Introduced in 1979, the new S-Class (*Sonderklasse*, special class) had the new W126 body, still with us in the 560 sedan/coupe series. Again these bodies shared a wide variety of engines and trim levels—the 280S/SE/SEL, 380SE/SEL, 500SE/SEL, 300SD, 420SE/SEL, etc. Even the later 420SEC and 560SEC shared the same basic body but not engine numbers: W126E42 and W126E56 but M116 and M117.

The most prolific of recent body styles has been the W124-series mid-range cars first introduced in 1984. Beginning with the European 200 sedans, 230E, 260E and 300E models and their corresponding diesel versions, then diversifying into the station wagons (200T, 200TD, 300T, 300TD, and 300TE), this series now includes the new coupes, the 230CE (124E23) and the 300CE (124E30).

The compact 190 (W201) models were also built in a wide range but only in sedan variants. From the plain 190 2.2 to the 2.3-liter 16-valve gasoline version and the 2.5-liter turbo-diesel, all had versions of the M102 gasoline engine or the OM601 and OM602 diesels, the same powerplants as the diesel variants of the larger W124-bodied cars. The OM601 is a four-cylinder diesel; the OM602 is a five-cylinder, and the OM603 is the new six-cylinder diesel. The recent M102 gasoline engine is a four, and the newer M103 is a six.

The list beginning on page 379 includes models from 1946–1987, both European and U.S. Years are those of manufacture rather than model years. No, there will be no quiz.

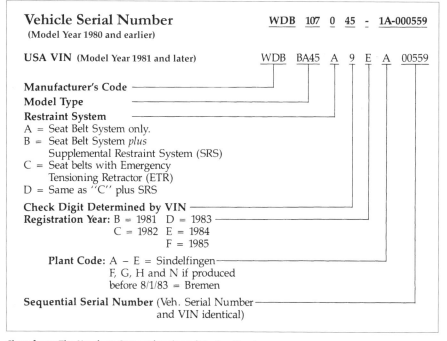

| Vehicle Serial Number (Model Year 1980 and earlier) | WDB 107 0 45 - 1A-000559 |
| USA VIN (Model Year 1981 and later) | WDB BA45 A 9 E A 00559 |

Manufacturer's Code
Model Type
Restraint System
A = Seat Belt System only.
B = Seat Belt System *plus* Supplemental Restraint System (SRS)
C = Seat belts with Emergency Tensioning Retractor (ETR)
D = Same as "C" plus SRS
Check Digit Determined by VIN
Registration Year: B = 1981 D = 1983
    C = 1982 E = 1984
    F = 1985
Plant Code: A – E = Sindelfingen
    F, G, H and N if produced before 8/1/83 = Bremen
Sequential Serial Number (Veh. Serial Number and VIN identical)

Chart from: *The Numbers Game: Chassis and Engine Numbers*
September/October 1986

Chassis and Engine Type Numbers

by W. Robert Nitske, Contributing Editor

November/December 1997

Quick, what's the difference between a 124D25 chassis and a 208? Read this, and you'll know.

The list of chassis and engine designations for models introduced 1988–1997 (beginning on page 379) is a continuation of the 1946–1987 list published in our January/February 1988 issue and reproduced in *Technical Reprint No. 2.* The detailed explanation accompanying that list explained the often complicated and perplexing system employed to designate the chassis and the engines in Mercedes-Benz cars sold in Europe and the U.S. It remains valid.

Recently the factory's model numbering system underwent a significant change. On official documents the former *W* (for *Wagennummer,* chassis number) disappeared, and only numbers were used. Also, special model prefixes and suffixes—such as C for coupe, E for fuel injection, L for long wheelbase, and T for station wagon—were left off the trunk lid of the cars. Only the displacement designation—190, 300, 560—was used, but diesel-powered models had the words Diesel or Turbodiesel on the right side of the trunk. Of course, there were exceptions! From model year 1994 onward, the classes were C (Compact), E (Executive), S (Special), and SL (Sports Light).

The recently introduced sports car was badged SLK, while the CLK is the coupe combining C-Class and E-Class components. A new class was created when the All-Activity Vehicle appeared as the M-Class, being badged ML320 as a V-6 and (yet to come) ML430 as a V-8. Another newcomer, the V-Class, for Van, is luxurious enough to be considered a family car here. The small A-Class is also included but not the even smaller smart city car. Built by Micro Compact Car, it may have no family designation since it is not officially badged as a Mercedes-Benz.

Since 1994 at least 11 models have been introduced, a striking diversion from past DBAG policy whereby model changes and new models were few and far between. Production runs lasted as long as 17 years for a popular model, but today's buyers demand fresh faces more often. This list also includes interesting models not offered in North America, for instance the C230 Turbo, which puts our SLK230's supercharged four into a C-Class sedan. Several other European models shown were never imported to the U.S.

The three digits in the listing for chassis and engine numbers are

Daimler-Benz AG

only the principal numbers. They are followed by a period and another three digits for the specific chassis and engine of a particular model. There is absolutely no assurance that these designations are permanent. The coupe version of the former S (earlier SEC) is now a CL, obviously capitalizing on the description of the successful CLK. The years on the list are those of manufacture, not model years.

While many anxiously seek logic in Mercedes-Benz model designations, others are content to accept them as they are, with all the peculiarities that make them so interesting.

Chassis and Engine Numbers: 1946–1997
(Based on worldwide sales)

Sales Designation	Years Built	Chassis (W) No.	Engine (M) No.
170V	1946–53	W136I-V	M136
170S	1949–52	W136IV	M136
170Sb	1952–53	W191	M136
170S-V	1953–55	W136VIII	M136
170D	1949–53	W136I-VI	OM636
170Ds	1952–53	W191	OM636
170S-D	1953–55	W136VIII	OM636
220	1951–53	W187	M180
220a	1954–56	W180	M180
300	1951–56	W186II-IV	M186
300d	1958–62	W189	M189
300S	1951–58	W188I, II	M188
180	1953–57	W120I	M136
180a, b, c	1957–62	W120II-IV	M121
180D, 180Db	1953–61	W120I, II	OM636
180Dc	1961–62	W120III	OM621
300SL	1954–63	W198I, II	M198
190SL	1955–63	W121II	M121
190, 190b	1956–61	W121II, III	M121
190c	1961–65	W110	M121
219	1956–59	W105	M180
220S	1956–59	W180II	M180
220SE	1958–60	W128	M127
190D, 190b	1958–61	W121I, II	OM621
190Dc	1961–65	W110	OM621
220	1959–65	W111/1	M180
220S	1959–65	W111/2	M180
220SE	1959–65	W111/3	M127
300SE	1961–67	W112/3	M189
230SL	1963–67	W113	M127
250SL	1966–68	W113A	M129
280SL	1967–71	W113E28	M130
600	1963–81	W100	M100
200	1965–68	W110	M121
200D	1965–68	W110	OM621
230	1965–68	W110	M180
230S	1965–68	W111/1A	M180
250S	1965–69	W108II	M108
250SE	1965–68	W108III	M129
250SE coupe	1965–67	W111III	M129
300SE & SEL	1965–67	W108IV	M189
300SE coupe	1965–67	W109III	M189
300SEL 6.3	1968–72	W109E63	M100
200	1967–76	W115V20	M115
200D	1967–76	W115D20	OM615
220	1967–73	W115V22	M115
220D	1967–76	W115D22	OM615
230	1967–76	W114V23	M180
250	1967–72	W114V25	M114
280S	1967–72	W108V28	M130
280SE & SEL	1967–72	W108E28	M130
280SE coupe	1967–71	W111E28	M130
300SEL	1967–70	W109E28	M189
250C & 250CE	1968–72	W114V25	M114

Sales Designation	Years Built	Chassis (W) No.	Engine (M) No.
280C	1969–76	W114V28	M130
280SE 3.5	1969–71	W111E35/I	M116
300SEL 3.5	1969–72	W109E35/I	M116
280	1970–76	W114V28	M130
280SE & 280SEL 3.5	1970–72	W108E35	M116
350SL & 350SLC	1970–80	W107E35	M116
280 & 280C	1971–76	W114V28	M110
280E & 280CE	1971–76	W114E28	M110
280S	1972–80	W116V28	M110
280SE	1972–80	W116V28	M110
350SE & 350SEL	1972–80	W116E35	M116
230/4	1972–76	W115V23	M115
240D	1973–76	W115D24	OM616
280SEL	1973–76	W116E28	M110
240D & 300D	1974–76	W115D30	OM617
280SL & 280SLC	1974–85	W107E28	M110
200	1975–80	W123V20	M115
200	1980–85	W123V20	M102
200D	1975–85	W123D20	OM615
220D	1975–79	W123D22	OM615
230	1975–81	W123V23	M115
230E	1979–85	W123E23	M102
240D	1975–85	W123D24	OM616
250	1975–85	W123V25	M123
280	1975–81	W123V28	M110
280E	1975–85	W123E28	M110
300D	1975–85	W123D30	OM617
300D Turbo	1975–85	W123D30A	OM617A
240DT	1978–86	W123D24	OM616
300DT	1977–86	W123D30	OM617
230T	1978–80	W123V23	M115
230TE	1979–86	W123E23	M102
250T	1977–82	W123V25	M123
280TE	1977–86	W123E28	M110
450SL & 450SLC	1971–80	W107E45	M117
450SLC 5.0	1977–81	W107E50	M117
300SD	1977–80	W116D30A	OM617A
230C	1976–80	W123V23	M115
230CE	1980–85	W123E23	M102
280C	1976–80	W123V28	M110
280CE	1976–85	W123E28	M110
300CD	1977–81	W123D30	OM617
300CD Turbo	1981–85	W123D30A	OM617A
300TD Turbo	1979–86	W123D30A	OM617A
280S	1979–85	W126V28	M110
280SE & 280SEL	1979–85	W126E28	M110
380SE & 380SEL	1979–85	W126E38	M116
500SE & 500SEL	1979–91	W126E50	M117
200T	1980–86	W123V20	M102
380SL & 380SLC	1980–85	W107E38	M116
500SL & 500SLC	1980–89	W107E50	M117
300SD	1979–85	W126D30A	OM617A
300SDL	1986–87	W126D30A	OM603A
380SEC	1980–85	W126E38	M116
500SEC	1980–91	W126E50	M117

(continued on next page)

Chassis and Engine Numbers: 1946–1997
(continued)

Sales Designation	Years Built	Chassis (W) No.	Engine (M) No.
190	1984–91	W201V20	M102
190E	1982–93	W201E20	M102
190E 2.3	1983–85	W201E23	M102
190E 2.3-16	1983–87	W201E23/2	M102
190D	1983–93	W201D20	OM601
190D 2.2	1983–85	W201D22	OM601
200	1984–92	W124V20	M102
230E	1984–92	W124E23	M102
260E	1984–90	W124E26	M103
300E	1984–93	W124E30	M103
200D	1984–94	W124D20	OM601
250D	1984–93	W124D25	OM602
300D	1984–93	W124D30	OM603
300D Turbo	1984–87	W124D30A	OM603A
190D 2.5	1984–93	W201D25	OM602
190D 2.5 Turbo	1986–93	W201D25A	OM602A
200TD	1985–91	W124D20	OM601
250TD	1985–94	W124D25	OM602
300TD	1985–93	W124D30	OM603
200T	1985–90	W124V20	M102
230TE	1985–92	W124E23	M102
300TE	1985–92	W124E30	M103
190E 2.3	1985–93	W201E26	M102
260SE	1985–92	W126E26	M103
300SE & 300SEL	1985–91	W126E30	M103
420SE & 420SEL	1985–91	W126E42	M116
560SEL	1985–92	W126E56	M117
300SL	1985–89	W107E30	M103
420SL	1985–89	W107E42	M116
420SEC	1985–91	W126E42	M116
560SEC	1985–91	W126E56	M117
560SL	1985–89	W107E56	M117
230CE	1987–91	W124E23	M102
300CE	1987–93	W124E30	M103
190E 2.5-16	1988–93	W201E25	M102
300E 2.6	1990–92	W124E30	M103
E250D	1992–94	W124D25	OM602
E250 Turbo	1988–95	W124D25	OM602
E300D Turbo	1989–95	W124D30A	OM603A
E300DT	1992–95	W124D30A	OM603A
200TE	1988–92	W124E20	M102
220TE	1992–93	W124V20	M102
190E 1.8	1990–93	W201E18	M102
560SE	1988–91	W126E56	M117
200CE	1990–93	C124	M102
220CE	1992–94	C124	M102
320CE	1992–94	C124	M103
300SL	1988–93	R129	M103
300SL-24	1988–93	R129	M104
500SL	1988–92	R129	M119
600SL	1991–93	R129	M120
300D 2.5	1989–91	124D25	OM602
350SDL	1989–91	126D35A	OM603
400E	1991–93	124	M119
500E	1991–93	124	M119
350SD	1990–91	140	OM603

Sales Designation	Years Built	Chassis (W) No.	Engine (M) No.
300SE/SEL	1990–92	140	M104
400SE/SEL	1990–92	140	M119
500SE/SEL	1990–92	140	M119
600SE/SEL	1990–92	140	M120
500SEC	1992	126	M119
600SEC	1992	126	M120
200E	1985–92	124	M102
220E	1992–93	124	M111
280E	1992–93	124	M104
320E	1992–93	124	M104
280TE	1992–93	124	M104
320TE	1992–93	124	M104
SL280	1993–98	R129	M104
SL320	1993–98	R129	M104
300SE 2.8	1992	140	M104
C36 AMG	1994–97	202	M104
C180	1992–2000	202	M111
C200	1994–2000	202	M111
C220	1993–96	202	M111
C280	1993–97	202	M104
C200D	1993–95	202	OM601
C220D	1993–97	202	OM604
C250D	1993–2000	202	OM605
E200	1993–95	124	M111
E220	1993–95	124	M111
E320	1992–95	124	M104
C200	1994–2000	202	M111
S350D	1994–95	140	OM603
S280	1994–98	140	M104
S320	1994–99	140	M104
S420	1994–99	140	M119
S500	1994–99	140	M119
S600	1994–99	140	M120
C250D	1993–96	202	OM605
C230	1996–97	202	M111
E200	1995–99	210	M111
E230	1995–98	210	M111
E320	1995–2002	210	M104
E300D	1995–99	210	OM606
SL280	1995–98	129	M104
SL320	1995–97	129	M104
E280	1995–97	210	M104
E420	1996–97	210	M119
E50 AMG	1996–97	210	M119
E220D	1995–99	210	OM604
E290D Turbo	1996–99	210	OM602
E250D	1996–99	210	OM605
S300D Turbo	1996–98	140	OM606
SLK200	1996–2000	170	M111
SLK230	1996–2000	170	M111
SLK320	1997–2004	170	M104
V230D	1996–99	638	OM601
V200	1996–99	638	M111
V230	1996–99	638	M111
CLK320	1997–99	208	M112
ML320	1997–2003	163	M112
ML430	1998–2001	163	M113
A160	1997–2001	168	M166
A140	1997–2001	168	M166

Chassis and Engine Numbers: 1998–2007

(Based on USA and Canada sales)　　　compiled by Stuart Dickstein

Sales Designation	Model Year(s)	Chassis No.	Engine No.
C230	1998	202.023	111.974
C230 Kompressor	1999–2000	202.024	111.975
C230	2006–	203.052	272.920
C230 Kompressor	2004–2005	203.040	271.948
C230 Kompressor Coupe	2002	203.747	111.981
C230 Kompressor Coupe	2003–2005	203.740	271.948
C240	2001–2005	203.061	112.912
C240 Sport Wagon	2003–2005	203.261	112.912
C240 4Matic	2003–2005	203.081	112.916
C240 4Matic Wagon	2003–2005	203.281	112.916
C280	2006–	203.054	272.940
C280 4Matic	2006–	203.092	272.941
C320	2001–2005	203.064	112.946
C320 4Matic	2003–2005	203.084	112.946
C320 Wagon	2002–2005	203.264	112.946
C320 4Matic Wagon	2002–2005	203.284	112.953
C320 Sport Coupe	2004–2005	203.764	112.946
C350	2006–	203.056	272.960
C350 4Matic	2006–	203.087	272.970
C32 AMG	2002–2004	203.065	112.961
C43 AMG	1998–2000	202.033	113.944
C55 AMG	2005–	203.076	113.988
CL55 AMG	2001–2002	215.373	113.982
CL55 AMG	2003	215.373	113.982
CL55 AMG	2003–	215.374	113.991
CL500	1998–1999	140.070	119.980
CL500	2000–2006	215.375	113.960
CL550	2007	216.371	273.961
CL600	1998–1999	140.076	120.982
CL600	2001–2003	215.378	137.970
CL600 Bi Turbo	2003–2005	215.376	275.950
CL600 Bi Turbo	2006	215.376	275.960
CL600 Bi-Turbo	2007	216.376	275.953
CL65 AMG	2005–2006	215.379	275.980
CLK320	2003–2005	209.365	112.955
CLK320 Cabriolet	1998–2003	208.465	112.940
CLK320 Cabriolet	2004–2005	209.465	112.955
CLK350	2006–	209.356	272.960
CLK350 Cabriolet	2006–	209.456	272.960
CLK430	1998–2002	208.370	113.943
CLK430 Cabriolet	2001–2003	208.470	113.943
CLK500	2003–2006	209.375	113.968
CLK550	2007	209.372	273.967
CLK500 Cabriolet	2004–2006	209.475	113.968
CLK550 Cabriolet	2007	209.472	273.967
CLK55 AMG	2002	208.374	113.984
CLK55 AMG	2003–2006	209.376	113.987
CLK55 AMG Cabriolet	2002	208.474	113.984
CLK55 AMG Cabriolet	2004–2006	209.476	113.987
CLK63 AMG Cabriolet	2007	209.477	156.982
CLS500	2006–	219.375	113.967
CLS550	2007	219.372	273.960
CLS55 AMG	2006–	219.376	113.990
CLS63 AMG	2007	219.377	156.983
E320	2003–2005	211.065	112.949
E320 CDI	2005–2006	211.026	648.961
E320-4Matic	1998-2002	210.082	112.941
E320 4Matic	2004–2005	211.082	112.954
E320 Wagon	1998–2003	210.265	112.941
E320 Wagon	2004–2005	211.265	112.949
E320 4Matic Wagon	1998–2003	210.282	112.941
E320 4Matic Wagon	2004–2005	211.282	112.954
E320 BLUETEC	2007	211.022	642.920
E350	2006–	211.056	272.964
E350 4Matic	2006–	211.087	272.972
E350 Wagon	2006–	211.256	272.964
E350 4Matic Wagon	2006–	211.287	272.972
E430	1998–2002	210.070	113.940
E430 4Matic	2001–2002	210.083	113.940
E500	2003–2006	211.070	113.967
E500 4Matic	2004–2006	211.083	113.969
E500 Wagon	2005–2006	211.270	113.967
E500 4Matic Wagon	2004–2006	211.283	113.969
E550	2007	211.072	273.960
E550 4Matic	2007	211.090	273.962
E55 AMG	1999–2002	210.074	113.980
E55 AMG Kompressor	2006	211.076	113.990
E55 AMG Wagon	2006	211.276	113.990
E63 AMG	2007	211.077	156.983
E63 AMG Wagon	2007	211.277	156.983
G500	2002–2006	463.249	113.962
G55 AMG	2002–2004	463.246	113.982
G55 AMG Kompressor	2005–2006	463.271	113.993
GL320 CDI	2007	164.822	642.940
GL450	2006–	164.871	273.923
ML320	1997–2003	163.154	112.942
ML320 CDI	2007	164.122	642.940
ML350	2003–2005	163.157	112.970
ML350	2006–	164.186	272.967
ML430	1999–2001	163.172	113.942
ML500	2002–2005	163.175	113.964
ML500	2006–	164.175	113.964
ML55 AMG	2000–2003	163.174	113.981
ML63 AMG	2007	164.177	156.980
R350	2006–	251.165	272.967
R500	2006–	251.175	113.971
R320 CDI	2007	251.122	642.950
R63 AMG	2007	251.177	156.980
S350	2006	220.067	112.972
S430	2000–2006	220.170	113.941
S430 4Matic	2003–2006	220.183	113.948
S500	2000–2006	220.175	113.960
S500 4Matic	2003–2006	220.184	113.966
S550	2007	221.171	273.961
S550 4Matic	2007	221.186	273.968
S55 AMG	2001–2002	220.173	113.986
S55 AMG	2003–2006	220.174	113.991
S600	2001–2002	220.178	137.970
S600 Bi Turbo	2003	220.176	275.950
S600 Bi Turbo	2004–2006	220.176	275.960
S600 Bi Turbo	2007	221.176	275.953
S65 AMG	2006	220.179	275.981
S65 AMG	2007	221.179	275.982
SL500	1994–1997	129.067	119.982
SL500	1998–2002	129.068	113.961
SL500	2003–2006	230.475	113.963
SL550	2007	230.471	273.965
SL55 AMG Kompressor	2003–2006	230.474	113.992
SL600 Bi Turbo	2007	230.477	275.954
SL600	1994–2002	129.076	120.983
SL600 Bi Turbo	2004–2006	230.476	275.960
SL55 AMG	2007	230.472	113.995
SL65 AMG	2005–	230.479	275.981
SLK230	2001–2004	170.449	111.983
SLK280	2006–	171.454	272.942
SLK350	2005–	171.456	272.963
SLK32 AMG	2002–2004	170.466	112.960
SLK55 AMG	2005–	171.473	113.989
SLR McLaren	2005–	199.376	155.980

Appendix 2
WIS on the Web

by Stu Ritter,
Technical Editor

*July/August
2003*

*Mercedes-Benz technical information
is now available via the Web.*

WIS on the WEB

We're talking information with a capital "I" here. "WIS" is the Workshop Information System, produced by Mercedes-Benz USA for mechanics. As mentioned in our previous issue, MBUSA is now putting it all on the Web. All of the technical service information that you can absorb in one sitting, and more, is available at www.startekinfo.com. This site takes you to the heart of the information system developed and operated by MBUSA to satisfy EPA requirements regarding availability of service information for owners and independent repair shops.

Initially, while designing the site, MBUSA intended to make information available in a 10-tiered system. Do-it-yourselfers would access down to tier two or three at no charge, while independent repair shops could purchase access down to tier seven or so, while tiers eight through ten would have been internal material for Mercedes-Benz dealers. In meetings with other auto importers and manufacturers, MBUSA decided that it was best to simply make everything available to everyone. The only material held back is internal data used between Mercedes-Benz dealers and DaimlerChrysler.

Exploring the Site

So that we could report to you, the members, we have had the opportunity to navigate the site, and it's amazing!

It's all there. Having worked as a professional Mercedes-Benz technician for 30 years, we can tell you that we would have killed to have this level of information available for current models. The site covers current production cars in detail and prior models in bits and pieces, depending upon their age. It presents useable information for every model from the W124 E-Class forward and complete information for the W140 S-Class.

Everything you would ever want to know is presented in an interactive manner that makes using the material fairly user-friendly. Considering the huge amount of information on this complex site, MBUSA has done a tremendous amount of work to make access possible. The same system used by dealership technicians, it even includes training materials.

Let's roam the site, see what's up and how it works, and find out how you gain access and use it.

Signing-On

On the sign-on page, you provide your user ID and password. Access is on a subscription basis. You can buy 24 hours (one contiguous 24-hr period) of access for $20. Independent repair shops and others who will make constant use of the site can subscribe for $300 a month or $2,500 a year. For the Mercedes-Benz-only independent shop, this might seem expensive, but actually it isn't. A repair shop could easily spend that much each year to stay current with paper and microfiche materials. Previously, the computer-based WIS alone cost $2,500 per year, and this new site goes far beyond its contents. All-makes, all-models shops can enter the site each time they need it for the $20 fee, which is much cheaper than purchasing the information elsewhere.

The left column of the start page contains several useful links for your first go-through. Read them. Before

you even subscribe to the system, you can download and read any existing recalls applicable to your car.

First-time users must go to the home page, www.startekinfo.com, and click the About Site button at the top. Then, in the left column, you will find Technical Requirements. Before going further, read this to insure that your computer is up to par. The minimum processor required is a Pentium II at 450 MHz with 128 Mb of RAM. Our old desktop unit, with a 450 MHz Pentium III with 196 Mb of RAM, worked very well. Because the downloads can be large, a broadband Internet connection is suggested.

Using the site requires three software downloads. You must have a current version of Adobe Acrobat Reader, available on the Technical Requirements page, which links you to Adobe. You must also download and install Autodesk WHISK and Java Web Start. Going through this process using the startekinfo.com site was easy. While you have the About Site button pushed, go through all the left column links to see what is going on. Notice that under the Links button, MBCA is listed!

Complete instructions are provided via the left-column link Installation Instructions. Read these before trying to download the required software so you won't make mistakes. The site is complex, and it helps to follow instructions to the letter. Print out the instructions so you have a copy as you do the installation.

You must also use Internet Explorer, version 5.5, or Netscape, version 7.x or higher. When we tried to use the site with Netscape 4.79, it wouldn't work. The site works well with Opera, Crazy Browser, Mozilla, and many other modern web browsers. If your browser takes you through the sign-up pages, it will function with the rest of the site. The wiring diagrams will not work with Netscape browsers, and you must have Java enabled and accept cookies.

Read the Instructions

The most important piece of information under About Site is the User's Guide, which presents screen shots and navigation aids in a 23-page document that is required reading. As we will mention later, read the help files whenever they appear. If you are not intimately familiar with current MBUSA information systems, the help files allow you to use the system properly. Attempting to blunder around will be very frustrating.

The FAQ (Frequently Asked Questions) section is currently small but will grow with user feedback. The How To button downloads PDF documents explaining how various categories of information can be read

and navigated. The clear explanations here minimize the time you spend becoming familiar with the Mercedes-Benz information system. The explanations cover using the STAR wiring, bulletins, diagnoses, and WIS while on-line. File these four How To's for reference. If you find problems in the system after reading the applicable documentation, you can use the Contact Us button to get in touch with MBUSA.

That takes care of the pages available before you decide to subscribe. Once you have paid your subscription fee (on-line, easy to do) you can begin navigating the depths of the site.

Which models are covered, you ask? The answer depends upon the

information system you are querying. The most important system is the WIS. The Infobox, the main WIS navigation tool, goes back to the W123 chassis (1977–85) and includes gasoline and diesel models. The coverage is not complete, and we found quite a few holes. The 1981–91 W126 S-Class is covered in detail. Both the 1984–93 W201 190E and the 1986–95 W124 E-Class are covered in much more detail, and everything newer has complete coverage. Invest $20 to spend a day in this pool of service information, and you can dig around to your heart's content to determine if there is enough there to draw you back in again. Late-model owners beware; you will be inundated.

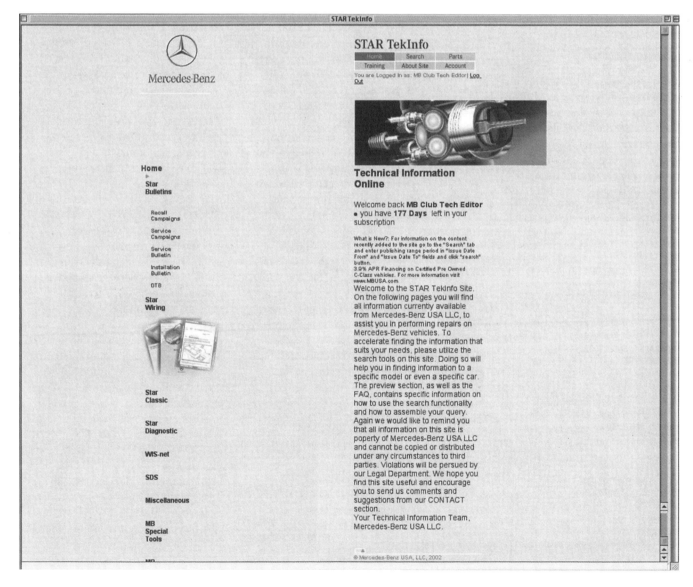

Getting Started

The subscriber home page offers left-column navigation buttons covering the entire information system. Each button takes you to a unique page that branches out into a particular information system: Bulletins, Wiring, Intro, Operator, Classic, Diagnose, WIS, and SDS.

A quick search under all bulletins for our 1993 400E yielded 443 PDF documents. Many just glance over the 400E, but some contain in-depth information that we will get around to reading later. Under the Star Bulletins heading are recall campaigns, service campaigns, service bulletins, installation bulletins, and diagnostic trouble bulletins (DTB's). Again, a quick search brought up 334 service bulletins. We have a lot of reading ahead of us!

Next stop on the info express is Wiring. Get ready for some large downloads; an ISDN, DSL, or cable connection pays off. These wiring diagrams are the same as MBUSA provides to dealership technicians. Each wiring diagram (also known as the Electrical Troubleshooting Manual, or ETM) is completely interactive. Specify the chassis, hit the search button at the top of the page, and the system lists all available wiring diagram pages. For the W210 chassis, it brought up 169 possibilities.

It takes time to become familiar with the information delivery system and how it works, but it is worth reading all the tabbed buttons such as legend, diagnostics, connectors, and abbreviations. The abbreviations button, which gives you a complete list of acronyms used, is conveniently located so that you can use it without disturbing a wiring diagram download. A tabbed browser, such as Crazy Browser, helps here, allowing instant simultaneous access to several pages without waiting for a "refresh."

Using a tool provided, you can draw a rectangle within a wiring diagram and enlarge just that portion to read the detail. You can right click on the mouse for a large menu of options, everything from zooming to panning and delving into layers plus sending information to the printer and going forward or backward in your search. Zooming in and out is also possible by holding down the left mouse button and moving the mouse upward for zoom-in and downward for zoom-out. The system can print up to five consecutive pages of wiring.

Wiring is color-coded with the correct color against a black background, so the diagrams are easy to read. With the pan tool (the little hand that you grab things with) you can grab the wiring diagram and move it around on the open black background. Connector views and pin-out charts are included. We can't emphasize enough the need to push all Help buttons, whenever and wherever you see them, as the help sections are full of information about navigating within the system. Read all of the information about button functions. The more help sections you read, the more comfortable you will be finding your way around and using the many features built into this system. All in all, it's very impressive.

The ETM system starts with the 1992 W140 S-Class chassis and contains all cars built after that model year.

The wiring section can print out a wiring diagram shown on the screen. The diagram is printed in black and white, but the wiring is color-coded as in older wiring diagrams, with letter combinations for the wire's base color and its traces. Setting your printer on landscape mode—to print the diagrams that way—yields a neat print-out. The diagram just about fills the width of the paper. With these very satisfactory diagrams, you should have no problem following current flow.

More Guides

Star Finder, located with the ETM, is one of the nicest features. Click on Star Finder, and you get a photographic component locator. Once you know a part's name (from the wiring diagram), you can bring up a photograph of its location on the car. An outline of the car uses a red dot and text to show the general location of the component, and a photograph shows the specific location. In the photograph, if disassembly is required to get to the component, it has been done. A description under the photograph indicates the correct name of the component.

Star Intro is the next link on the left navigation column. Offerings are currently limited to the newest vehicles; the 2001, 2002, and 2003 model year Introduction to Service manuals are shown. We assume that as time passes and more information is installed, earlier Introduction to Service volumes may be included. It is important to have the "intro's" because they contain information unavailable elsewhere. As a working mechanic, we always referred to the intro's and kept a complete collection on the shelf.

Next up is Star Operator. This is a collection of the books that come with the car when it is delivered: owner's manuals, maintenance booklets, telephone and voice recognition system manuals, and audio system manuals, among others. Coverage here is limited to 2001 and later models.

Star Classic, the next title in the navigation column, is a short list of available CD-ROMs, covering every model built since World War II. The near future will bring a new series of CD-ROMs, superior to the original product. Instead of using scans of existing paper manuals, the new CD's will be made electronically from the WIS and the Service Microfiche system. The new CD's, exact copies of information on the web site, will include the ETM's and all Introduction to Service volumes applicable to a particular chassis. Service bulletins and fast-moving part numbers will also be included in a manner linking everything together. The CD's will be much more interactive than previous versions. Prices will also be lower, and the CD's will have a completely new user interface. The new CD's are being supplied in the order of chassis being phased out of production, with current plans for the 140, 202, 129, then the 210. Stay tuned for availability dates.

Diagnostic Codes

Now we come to the real meat of the site, Star Diagnostic. Download the help materials at the beginning and read them, then save them for future reference. Under the general heading is DTC (Diagnostic Trouble Codes). To quote the site, "DTC covers all emission-related codes and trouble-shooting guides as of MY 1994 to present." When the DTC page opens, click on Models to find everything from the E-Class W124 (1994 and later) onward. There are lists of all engine trouble codes and the diagnostic trees used to fix problems—very involved, very complete. The diagnostic tree is interactive with the problem; mousing over the remedy brings up another page of tests, showing test instructions, the expected results, and the remedy.

Also in the left navigation column on the DTC page are Engines, Diesel Engines, Transmissions, and Electronic Selector Lever. Diesel Engines covers the 1996–99 OM606 engine and refers you to the Diagnostic Manuals for information. The help notes under diesel engines refer you to the WIS, which we'll get to shortly. Access to the trouble code system will greatly assist independent repair shops.

Next stop under the diagnostic page is the Diagnostic Manuals. The left-hand navigation column lists Body & Accessories, Chassis & Drivetrain, Engines, Diesel Engines, Information/ Communications, and Climate Control. For example, we clicked on Information/Communications and chose model 129, instrument clusters. This brought up Diagnosis, consisting of function testing and a complaint-related diagnostic chart. In addition, the electrical testing program instructs you how to prepare and actually test. Clicking on "preparation for testing" brings up the WIS pages, showing tools, connections, and test procedures. This interactivity will help do-it-yourselfers unfamiliar with the information system.

The third navigation entry under Diagnostics is Protocol Data, listing 17 fuel injection schemes and break-outs of how control modules are coded. We doubt that many of us will use this section much. Some downloads here are quite large, and even with a DSL connection they can take some time.

Use the Help Section

Now we come to the heart of the repair information for amateur mechanics. The first time you start WIS, read the on-line help. We counted 88 pages of help notes explaining the system and how to use it. This is not an intuitive program. You must read and follow the instructions, or you will become frustrated trying to move around within the system's depth. Read the instructions. The first instructions on the help pages cover searching for answers. Here is a quote:

"WIS-Online enables fast and effective access to the Mercedes-Benz workshop literature, e.g. for repairs, maintenance, etc. Literature can be searched in WIS-Online using a number of search variants. To this end, the search context must be defined according to the starting situation. The search context contains information used to search the literature. The search context includes the vehicle data in the form of type (model)/engine/unit (major assembly) models, the groups, sorted by functional groups and functional subgroups, the info-types, the chosen search mode, e.g. Standard search, Changes new, Extended search, Directory, Document no."

Thousands upon thousands of documents are stored within the WIS system, so you must get a grip on how the system stores information to best utilize your time. Before you plunge in, spend time reading. For a quick start, enter your chassis number (preceded by WDB) in the correct box, and hit the directory button. This brings up the WIS table of contents for your particular model and its chassis series. You could probably spend 24 hours reading the information brought up through just this button. Everything from oil capacities to approved oil specifics, or perhaps Service Informations. If you choose to read the Service Informations about your car, WIS will access all of them, broken down by part number groups. A search button lets you search within the results obtained from your initial inquiry. It goes on and on and on. Read the instructions. Please, read the instructions!

Repair Procedures

Every repair procedure for every car from the W124 chassis onward is included within WIS. The index goes back to the 1977 W123 chassis cars, but that information is not complete. The R107 is covered in detail, considering its long model run. The W201 (190E) is also covered in detail. For folks with later cars, this is the only source of information. For those of you who have bemoaned the lack of repair or maintenance information for your C-Class or W140 S-Class cars, it's all here—everything you ever wanted to know and 100 times more!

Type in your chassis number, then go to the bottom of the page and hit the documentation button, and you will be brought to the main group index. This index is completely expandable. Click on the "+" next to the main group heading, and you open the entire group. You will start to recognize some numbering, as it is the same as the usual part number sequences. Once the group is expanded and you find the specific subgroup you want to visit, you can specify the type of information you wish to retrieve on the right side of the page. Most of the time, we clicked on the star button, which illuminated all check boxes. Thus we could see what is available and skip what we don't want to read, but we stumbled onto lots of information that we never knew existed.

You can also search within results by symptoms of problems and under what conditions the symptoms appear. This searches relevant documentation to see if the symptoms have been previously reported and if they are attached to any repair information.

With our 400E chassis number installed, we went to group 99, Printed Matter, and checked all info-types. WIS returned 58 documents relevant to our car. You can spend a very long time reading. Once you find the document you need, you can toggle the document to occupy the whole page then toggle back to the index. The system uses a horizontally-split screen, so it's hard to read the document until you toggle it to full screen.

While many other functions of startekinfo.com can be saved to your hard drive as html documents for later use and reference, information within WIS can only be sent to your printer. Because WIS opens within its own Java Web Start window, there is no easy way to save information to your computer other than sending it to the printer. Under FILE options, there is no save function, only exit. Have lots of paper ready in your printer!

System Test

We tested the WIS to see how difficult it was to use to obtain maintenance information. Assuming we didn't have the W124-chassis CD-ROM, we opened WIS, went down the list, highlighted our model, and clicked on documentation in the lower right-hand corner. That's two clicks. We then clicked to open the Overall Vehicle sub-heading and clicked on Maintenance. That's four clicks. We also clicked once for all headings under info-types. That's five clicks. Moving the cursor down the list in the document window, as it passed over each sub-heading, you could see the applicability in the "Valid" box and the document name in the "Title" box, making it easy to determine whether or not the document was applicable.

We stopped scanning when we ran over the maintenance sub-heading applicable to our 1993 400E. At this point it requires a double click, or you can go to the top of the page and click on an eye button to see the document. That's seven clicks. That brought up the maintenance chart for our car with links connecting to the actual jobs. The links were not highlighted in red, as the interactive links are, so we could not use the WIS for maintenance in this instance. Perhaps the links will be made live later, as the WIS is filled in. For cars later than 1994, most links are active.

Going back to the document title window, we clicked on upkeep service (every 15,000 miles). This brought up the W124 maintenance chart with several pages available via tabs at the top of the document window, showing the maintenance procedures, highlighted so we could get to the actual jobs for any W124 built after July 1, 1993, though a lot of information also applies to earlier versions. The appropriate maintenance system check sheet appears in the document window, so we printed it. This gave us the handy check sheet that all good Mercedes-Benz shops use to make sure that every job is done during a service.

Since our car is used mainly for city driving, we decided to check the maintenance schedule for taxicabs. Besides having the heavy-duty check sheet available, many of the links were live for the 124 chassis, so we were able to examine the jobs themselves. This WIS sure has a lot of information!

Keeping Current

The final button on the left-hand column activates the SDS or Star Diagnostic System, which explains how to purchase the system on a diagnostic laptop and keep it up to date. This is interesting reading, showing you what an independent repair shop must buy to work on new cars and stay current. Independent shops can no longer survive with just an ohmmeter. They must invest in Mercedes-Benz-specific diagnostic equipment. Read the information on this page, then download the order form and check the pricing.

In the 30 years we spent as an active Mercedes-Benz mechanic, we always lusted after complete factory information. We bought every manual the factory published, so as the years went on, our paper manual shelf grew longer and longer. During the 1990's the amount of information grew exponentially. Just the Electrical Troubleshooting Manuals for all chassis would have cost thousands of dollars. Microfiche was expensive, too.

All the literature was expensive. Now it is all available in one place for a fee that is reasonable considering the amount of information you can access. We congratulate MBUSA for supplying us with a superior, information-laden web site.

Special thanks to Mike Kunz, Darek Okoniewski, and Maryalice Ritzmann from MBUSA for their assistance.

Technical Information Resources

The information compiled in this book was current at the time of original publication in *The Star*. Some has since been superseded in the factory-authorized service regimen due to improvements in techniques and materials, or in response to government mandates or other reasons. In particular, many specified lubricants and other service products have been replaced by one or more generations of improvement. Similarly, service procedures and techniques are often updated in factory-authorized technical literature.

Before undertaking any of the service or repair procedures detailed in the articles in this book, take the time to research currently approved service products and information to ensure proper care and service of your Mercedes-Benz. MBCA members are welcome to contact the club's technical advisors, listed in each issue of *The Star*. Having your model information and Vehicle Identification Number (VIN) at hand will help dealer, MBUSA and MBCA representatives respond to your needs.

For Mercedes-Benz models less than 20 years old, your Mercedes-Benz dealer's parts department is the most immediate source for current factory-approved service products and technical literature. The Mercedes-Benz Customer Assistance Center at 800-FOR-MERC will also be able to provide information and products.

Complete, up-to-the-minute information on current and recent models is available in read/print electronic form on the Internet from Mercedes-Benz USA's Star TekInfo service information site. The article beginning on page 382, "WIS on the Web" by Stu Ritter, details how to use this online system.

For Mercedes-Benz models more than 20 years old, the Mercedes-Benz Classic Center USA is the authorized source for updated service product knowledge, technical service literature and genuine replacement parts.

Authorized Mercedes-Benz Information

- **Mercedes-Benz USA Customer Assistance Center**
  website: mbusa.com
  telephone: 800-FOR-MERC
  (800-367-6372)

- **Mercedes-Benz Classic Center USA**
  website: mbusa.com/classic
  telephone: 866-MBCLASSIC
  (866-622-5277)

- **Mercedes-Benz Star TekInfo**
  website: startekinfo.com

Mercedes-Benz Club

- **Mercedes-Benz Club of America**
  website: mbca.org
  telephone: 800-637-2360

  The MBCA website has many links to model-specific groups.

Index

Contributors' Index

Dennis Adler

Award winning author, photographer and historian Dennis Adler is the Editor-in-Chief of *Car Collector* magazine and recognized as one of the leading automotive photojournalists in the world. During his 30-year career he has written over 25 books and had more than 5,000 articles and photographs published. Mr. Adler's most recent books include *The Art of the Automobile—The 100 Greatest Cars* and *The Art of the Sports Car—The Greatest Designs of the 20th Century*, published by HarperCollins; *Porsche —The Road From Zuffenhausen*, published by Random House; and *Duesenberg*, published in 2004 by Krause Publications.

See page 356.

Dieter Arnold

See pages 237, 339.

Frank Barrett

Having emigrated from England to America with his family in 1952, Frank graduated from the University of Pennsylvania in 1965 and became an engineer, writing about and photographing German cars as a hobby. In 1982 he turned this avocation into a vocation when MBCA named him editor/publisher of *The Star*, a position he still enjoys. Having since published more than 10,000 pages, he can always find fresh Mercedes-Benz material. His book, *The Illustrated Mercedes-Benz Buyers Guide*, is now in its fourth edition. Besides owning Toad Hall Motorbooks, which imports and sells Mercedes-Benz and Porsche titles, Frank also maintains extensive automotive archives and serves as a director of The Colorado Grand, a charity event for old sports cars.

See pages 150, 254.

Ken Chipps

Ken has been a car enthusiast since he was a teenager. His first car was a 1963 Alfa Romeo 1300 Giulietta and he still owns a 1973 Alfa Romeo 2000 Spider Veloce. Over the years he and his wife have owned several Mercedes-Benz automobiles, the most recent being a 2002 S430. After spending 28 years working for the State of Texas, he is now an Associate Professor of Network and Communications Management at DeVry University-Dallas.

See pages 6, 8.

Randy Durrance

Randy was a master of custom electronic ignition modifications to 1950s and 1960s Mercedes-Benz, including the 300SL. Among many vehicles, he owned an extensively modified 1969 300SEL 6.3, which could do a 14.6-second ¼ mile. He competed with it at many MBCA Starfests, as well as SCCA autocross events. He founded and owned W.R. Durrance Engineering in Appleton, Wisconsin, and was a Mercedes-Benz- and ASE-certified Master Technician. He died in 2003.

See page 335.

Michael Egan

Michael Egan has owned Mercedes-Benz vehicles for 40 years, his first being a 190SL during his undergraduate years in the mid-60s. He grew up in the 50s and 60s as part of the sports car generation in New England, known as the land of the foreign cars. His earlier cars during this period included an Austin-Healey 100/6, MG TD and Porsche 356 SC Cabriolet. For the past 19 years he's owned a 280SL (W113), the classic among his current new sedans. He is a Senior Foreign Affairs Officer with the State Department, Washington, D.C., and retired USAF colonel.

See page 234.

Harry J. Goos

Harry bought his first Mercedes, a 230SL in 1967, and has owned Mercedes-Benz cars ever since. His wife Ruth owned her first Mercedes when she and Harry met, and they've been enthusiasts together ever since. They joined MBCA in 1976. Harry was elected president and newsletter editor of the newly formed Northeastern Pennsylvania section in 1981.

See page 190.

Scott Grundfor

Scott graduated from UCLA in 1970 and founded Scott Restorations in Arroyo Grande, California. His restorations have received many national honors and have been featured at the Museum of Contemporary Art and the Museum of Natural History in Los Angeles. He has specialized in the history and restoration of vintage Mercedes-Benz vehicles, especially the legendary 300SL. He is the Restoration Editor of *The Star* and has judged at Pebble Beach Concours d'Elegance.

See page 362.

Charles Herrmann

See page 254.

Brian Imdieke

Brian Imdieke has served as V.P. of operations for American Sheetmetal, Inc. since formation of the business in 1983. Before he founded the business, Brian was trained in the art of precision metal fabrication at DMF, Inc. in Tempe, Arizona, and subsequently employed as a tool and precision metal fabricator at McDonnell Douglas Aircraft Corporation in Mesa, AZ. Brian has been a Mercedes-Benz enthusiast since 1979 and enjoys working on these fine machines for relaxation in his spare time.

See page 41.

Edward Jahns

See page 38.

Matt Joseph

Matt is an automotive writer and restorer. He writes regularly for several magazines and for a newspaper chain. He also appears on TV and is heard on radio on automotive topics. Matt owns and operates MATTCO, a small restoration shop that specializes in pre-1940 Lincolns and early postwar Aston-Martins. Matt is currently working on a revised edition of his book, *The Standard Guide to Automotive Restoration*. It is scheduled for publication in mid-2005.

See page 257.

Frank King

Joining MBCA in 1971, Frank became its national technical director and technical editor of *The Star* in 1977. He contributed extensively to more than 140 issues, and even at the age of 94 was still writing incisively on a wide variety of Mercedes-Benz technical and historical topics. Educated as a civil engineer, Frank retired from Curtiss-Wright in 1978 and devoted full time to the club as a volunteer. Over more than 20 years he personally and patiently answered thousands of letters and telephone calls from MBCA members seeking good technical advice. In 1992 he became the inspiration for and the first recipient of Daimler-Benz AG's highest honor for club members, the Silver Star Award, recognizing a lifetime of accomplishment. A quiet gentleman but always a fan of interesting cars, he passed away in 1999.

See pages 10, 20, 22, 36, 98, 101, 124, 126, 134, 137, 152, 157, 189, 191, 204, 220, 260, 264, 271, 278, 289, 292, 304, 306, 371.

John Lamb

John has been in the automotive field for more than 16 years. He has authored several books on automotive technology and is on the editorial board for two trade and enthusiast magazines. He has presented on automotive technology around the world and currently is an automotive instructor with a major German manufacturer. He holds a BSEE degree from Worcester Polytechnic Institute.

See pages 5, 12, 15, 18, 24, 28, 34, 68, 70, 154, 156, 178, 196, 345.

Jim Mahaffey

Jim has a BS in Physics, and an MS and a PhD in Nuclear Engineering. He worked for 25 years as a Senior Research Scientist at the Georgia Tech Research Institute, researching topics from cold fusion to mathematics. He also taught electronics in the Georgia Tech School of Physics. He is currently the Director of Technology at Air2 LLC, where he is working in microwave vibrometry. Jim has owned Mercedes-Benz automobiles continuously since 1967 and has lost count of the number of VDO clocks he has repaired.

See pages 32, 140, 176, 179, 208, 221, 224, 228, 231, 266.

Mike Mate

See drawings on pages 6, 124, 127, 158, 160, 260, 286.

Paul S. Meyer

Paul owns a 1983 240D that has been a one-family car since delivery in December 1982. He prizes his 240D because maintenance and many repairs can be owner performed. He likes low-powered cars because tires, brakes and batteries last longer and fuel goes further, all better for the environment. Paul's other car is a 1966 VW Beetle. Paul has been editor of newsletters, guest editor and consulting editor for professional (boarded) journals, occasionally writes book reviews and has sold printing.

See page 97.

Burt Mills

See pages 37, 364.

George Murphy

George serves as the National Technical Director of MBCA and a contributing editor to *The Star* and other publications, in which he has authored numerous articles about care and repair of Mercedes-Benz automobiles. George has always performed the majority of maintenance and mechanical work on his own cars and has lots of hands-on experience with many Mercedes-Benz models. He is the owner of Performance Analysis Company, manufacturer of all-aluminum climate control servos and rebuilder of Mercedes-Benz climate and cruise control components. He operates the MBCA engine oil analysis program and performs appraisals on Mercedes-Benzes.

See pages 66, 79, 81, 218, 250, 252, 277, 320, 324, 329, 332.

W. Robert Nitske

Born in Germany, Bob Nitske devoted his life to preserving Mercedes-Benz history. In 1927 he watched the first race at the then-new Nürburgring, and a few years later he emigrated to the U.S. His books include *The Complete Mercedes Story, Mercedes-Benz, A History, Mercedes-Benz 300SL, Mercedes-Benz Diesel Automobiles,* and his ever-popular *Mercedes-Benz Production Models.* Bob's contributions to *The Star* began in 1956, when he drove his new 300SL through Europe reporting on Grand Prix races. Having helped establish MBCA in the 1950s, he served as its national president in 1998–1999. In 2000 he was awarded the Mercedes-Benz Silver Star. He wrote for *The Star* until his death in 2003.

See pages 376, 378.

Stu Ritter

Stu began working on Mercedes-Benz vehicles in 1970 and continued in dealerships until 1975 when he opened his own shop in Denver. He ran his shop from 1975–2000 and then sold it to his shop foreman. He is currently technical editor of *The Star* and also writes feature articles. He authored the *Mercedes-Benz E-Class Owner's Bible* with Bentley Publishers and is currently involved with product implementation for DST Inc., an IBM business partner providing Web-based parts ordering for GM AC Delco and Ford Motorcraft independent warehouses.

See pages 2, 46, 76, 84, 87, 90, 93, 130, 145, 238, 283, 308, 341, 382.

Mike Roth

Mike has been in the MBCA since 1978. He was the President of the Los Angeles section from 1980–1982 and is currently on the Cincinnati section board. He is a specialist in the field of business revenue improvement and has helped hundreds of individuals and companies like IBM and P&G grow profits and select sales winners. Mike's company is the most experienced and successful franchise of the Sandler Sales Institute in southwest Ohio.

See page 201.

Max Scheinwerfer

See page 197.

Raymond Schlicht

Raymond is a licensed professional mechanical engineer for an electric power generating station and lives in Arlington, Virginia. He has been actively involved in the old car hobby for better than 30 years, personally restoring several cars from the ground up. These include several British sports cars and a straight-eight Packard. His current project is a complete nut-and-bolt restoration of a 1967 Mercedes-Benz 250SL "California Coupe" that he and his wife have owned and enjoyed since 1985.

See page 234.

Rusty Steele

See page 333.

Fred Vetter

Fred began flying open cockpit trainers before World War II and retired in 1970 as a Brigadier General and commander of the 436th Military Airlift Wing at Dover Air Force Base, Delaware. He then spent 30 years as a public servant and community activist, championing projects such as renovations to the Dover police station. He enjoyed chatting old cars with Dover Litho founder George Frebert while the two turned wrenches on Fred's 1967 250SE Coupe, which won many awards. He died in 2002.

USAF photo, courtesy of the Air Mobility Command Museum.

See page 268.

Mark Wallach

Mark was born in St. Louis, served in the U.S. Air Force from 1943–1946 and graduated from UCLA and the University of Texas. At Le Mans, he was team manager for a 1957 Porsche 550A, 1958 Ferrari 250 TR, 1959 Porsche RSK and 1960 Ferrari SWB. He has been a contributor to *Motor Trend*, *Hot Rod* and *Popular Science*, and a wood expert for MBCA and Rolls Royce Owners Clubs. He currently makes and restores wood rim steering wheels for Ferrari, Maserati, Cunningham and Jaguar Cars.

See pages 366, 368.

Farrell Wiser

Farrell is retired from IBM. He has driven about 2 million miles in the 44 years he serviced hardware and software in Utah. During that time he did all the repair/maintenance of the cars he drove (as well as 2 tractors, and 10 custom built cars), and the cars his 7 children have owned and driven. He has owned and maintained about 35 Mercedes-Benz, including 1978 300D, 1981 300D, 1982 300D, 1982 500SE Euro, 1985 300D, 1987 560SEL and 1994 S320. The last four in the list are still in the family and running fine.

See page 186.

Selected Books and Repair Information From Bentley Publishers

Mercedes-Benz

Mercedes-Benz
E-Class Owner's
Bible™
1986–1995

Bentley Publishers
ISBN 0-8376-0230-0

Driving

Alex Zanardi: My Sweetest Victory
Alex Zanardi with Ginaluca Gasparini
ISBN 0-8376-1249-7

The Unfair Advantage
Mark Donohue
ISBN 0-8376-0073-1(hc); 0-8376-0069-3(pb)

**Going Faster! Mastering the Art of Race
Driving** *The Skip Barber Racing School*
ISBN 0-8376-0227-0

**A French Kiss With Death: Steve
McQueen and the Making of** *Le Mans*
Michael Keyser ISBN 0-8376-0234-3

Sports Car and Competition Driving
Paul Frère with foreword by Phil Hill
ISBN 0-8376-0202-5

**Driving Forces: The Grand Prix Racing
World Caught in the Maelstrom of the
Third Reich** *Peter Stevenson*
ISBN 0-8376-0217-3

The Technique of Motor Racing
Piero Taruffi ISBN 0-8376-0228-9

Engineering/Reference

**Supercharged! Design, Testing, and
Installation of Supercharger Systems**
Corky Bell ISBN 0-8376-0168-1

**Maximum Boost: Designing, Testing,
and Installing Turbocharger Systems**
Corky Bell ISBN 0-8376-0160-6

**Bosch Fuel Injection and Engine
Management** *Charles O. Probst, SAE*
ISBN 0-8376-0300-5

Race Car Aerodynamics *Joseph Katz*
ISBN 0-8376-0142-8

**Scientific Design of Exhaust and
Intake Systems** *Philip H. Smith and
John C. Morrison* ISBN 0-8376-0309-9

**Road & Track Illustrated Automotive
Dictionary** *John Dinkel*
ISBN 0-8376-0143-6

Bosch

**Bosch Automotive Handbook,
6th Edition**
Robert Bosch GmbH ISBN 0-8376-1243-8

**Bosch Handbook for Gasoline Engine
Management, Updated 3rd Edition**
Robert Bosch GmbH ISBN 0-8376-1390-6

**Bosch Handbook for Safety, Comfort
and Convenience Systems**
Robert Bosch GmbH ISBN 0-8376-1391-4

Alfa Romeo

**Alfa Romeo All-Alloy Twin Cam
Companion 1954–1994**
Pat Braden ISBN 0-8376-0275-0

Alfa Romeo Owner's Bible™
Pat Braden ISBN 0-8376-0707-8

Audi

**Audi A4 Service Manual: 1996–2001, 1.8L
turbo, 2.8L, including Avant and quattro**
Bentley Publishers ISBN 0-8376-1675-9

**Audi A4, A4 Avant 2002–2005,
A4 Cabriolet 2003–2005, S4, S4 Avant,
S4 Cabriolet 2004–2005: Repair Manual
on CD-ROM**
Audi of America ISBN 978-0-8376-1256-0

**Audi TT Service Manual: 2000–2006,
1.8L turbo, 3.2L including Roadster and
quattro** *Bentley Publishers*
ISBN 0-8376-1500-3

**Audi A6 (C5 platform) Service Manual:
1998–2004, including A6, allroad quattro,
S6, RS6** *Bentley Publishers*
ISBN 0-8376-1499-6

**Audi TT Coupe 2000–2005,
TT Roadster 2001–2005: Official
Factory Repair Manual on CD-ROM**
Audi of America ISBN 978-0-8376-1261-4

BMW

BMW Enthusiast's Companion™
BMW Car Club of America
ISBN 0-8376-0321-8

**BMW 3 Series Enthusiast's
Companion™** *Jeremy Walton*
ISBN 0-8376-0220-3

**BMW 6 Series Enthusiast's
Companion™** *Jeremy Walton*
ISBN 0-8376-0193-2

**BMW 3 Series (E46) Service Manual:
1999–2005, M3, 323i, 325i, 325xi, 328i, 330i,
330xi, Sedan, Coupe, Convertible, Sport
Wagon** *Bentley Publishers* ISBN 0-8376-1277-2

**BMW 5 Series Service Manual: 1997–2002,
525i, 528i, 530i, 540i, Sedan, Sport Wagon**
Bentley Publishers ISBN 0-8376-0317-X

**BMW 7 Series Service Manual:
1988–1994, 735i, 735iL, 740i, 740iL, 750iL**
Bentley Publishers ISBN 0-8376-0328-5

**BMW Z3 Roadster Service Manual:
1996–2002, including Z3 Coupe,
M Coupe, M Roadster**
Bentley Publishers ISBN 0-8376-1250-0

Jeep

Jeep Owner's Bible, Third Edition™
Moses Ludel ISBN 0-8376-1117-2

Jeep CJ Rebuilder's Manual: 1972–1986
Moses Ludel ISBN 0-8376-0151-7

MINI Cooper

**MINI Cooper Service Manual: 2002–
2004, including MINI Cooper, MINI
Cooper S** *Bentley Publishers* 0-8376-1068-0

Porsche

Porsche: Excellence Was Expected
Karl Ludvigsen ISBN 0-8376-0235-1

**Porsche 911 (964) Enthusiast's
Companion: Carrera 2, Carrera 4
and Turbo, 1989–1994**
Adrian Streather ISBN 0-8376-0293-9

**Porsche 911 Carrera Service Manual:
1984–1989** *Bentley Publishers*
ISBN 0-8376-0291-2

**Porsche 911 SC Service Manual:
1978–1983** *Bentley Publishers*
ISBN 0-8376-0290-4

**Porsche Carrera 964 and 965, 1989–1994
Technician's Handbook: Without
Guesswork™** *Bentley Publishers*
ISBN 0-8376-0292-0

Volkswagen

**Volkswagen Jetta Service Manual: 2005–
2006, 1.9L TDI PD diesel, 2.0L turbo FSI
gasoline, 2.5L gasoline** *Bentley Publishers*
ISBN 0-8376-1364-7

**Jetta, Golf, GTI, Service Manual:
1999–2005, 1.8L turbo, 1.9L TDI diesel,
PD diesel, 2.0L gasoline, 2.8L VR6**
Bentley Publishers
ISBN 0-8376-1678-0

**Golf, GTI, Jetta 1999–2005, Jetta
Wagon 2001–2005: Official Factory
Repair Manual on CD-ROM**
Volkswagen of America
ISBN 978-0-8376-1264-5

**Volkswagen Touareg 2004–2007: Repair
Manual on DVD-ROM** *Volkswagen of
America* ISBN 978-0-8376-1269-1

**Jetta, Golf, GTI 1993–1995, Cabrio
1995–2002: Service Manual, 1.9L TDI,
2.0L, 2.8L VR6**
Bentley Publishers ISBN 0-8376-0366-8

**Passat, Passat Wagon 1998–2005:
Repair Manual on CD-ROM**
Volkswagen of America
ISBN 978-0-8376-1267-6

**Volkswagen Passat Service Manual:
1998-2005, 1.8L turbo, 2.8L V6, 4.0L W8
including wagon and 4Motion**
Bentley Publishers ISBN 0-8376-1483-X

**Super Beetle, Beetle and Karmann Ghia
Official Service Manual: Type 1,
1970–1979** *Volkswagen of America*
ISBN 0-8376-0096-0